READINGS IN ABNORMAL PSYCHOLOGY AND MENTAL HYGIENE

READINGS IN ABNORMAL PSYCHOLOGY AND MENTAL HYGIENE

EDITED BY

W. S. TAYLOR
PROFESSOR OF PSYCHOLOGY IN SMITH COLLEGE

WITH AN INTRODUCTION BY

JOSEPH JASTROW
PROFESSOR OF PSYCHOLOGY IN THE
UNIVERSITY OF WISCONSIN

D. APPLETON–CENTURY COMPANY
INCORPORATED

NEW YORK   LONDON

130
T21r

326

15679

TO

P. T.

PREFACE

The selections to be found in this volume have been chosen for their usefulness as so many sections of a textbook for students. To that end, writings of primarily historical or controversial interest, or authors' points of view as such, have been disregarded in favor of what seemed to be contributions to understanding phenomena.

Of the material so included, it may be said that, on the whole, acquaintance with elementary psychology is presupposed; only brief mention is made of feeble-mindedness, as occupying principally a neighboring field; no more psychiatry is touched upon than the student of abnormal psychology needs to be familiar with; and the problems of delinquency and crime, mediumship, mysticism, "the racial unconscious," etc., are not brought in, because for those subjects the general principles of abnormal psychology would seem to require first consideration.

The especial emphasis in this book is upon "functional" phenomena—processes which may be regarded as the core of abnormal psychology, as well as most illuminating for students of general psychology, of medicine, of sociology, and of education. The language employed here is taken for the most part to express the stimulus-response point of view.

It is assumed that instructors may wish to develop a number of topics differently, drawing more adequately upon original authors, many of whom are suggested in these pages; and that for further perspective, references, and definitions of terms, Professor James Winfred Bridges' *Outline of Abnormal Psychology* (Adams) will often be of use.

The initial inspiration for this undertaking came from Professor Joseph Jastrow, who suggested the need for some such volume. To him I am indebted further for exceedingly valuable suggestions as to procedure.

I wish to express appreciation, also, to authors and publishers, for the privilege of citing from their works; to those students of abnormal mental conditions who, at Professor Jastrow's invitation, sent valued materials and suggestions (as summarized by Miss Theresa M. Jackson: cf. Bibliography); to Mr. R. L. Walkley,

viii PREFACE

Librarian of the University of Maine, and his assistants, for aid in many ways; to Mr. Harold E. Pressey, Mr. Theodore W. Munroe, Miss Theresa M. Jackson, and Miss Alberta Getchell, for help in various phases of the preparation of the manuscript; to Mrs. Robert R. White, Jr., for reading the proofs; to Miss Maude G. Leadbetter, for preparing the index; and, more than all, to my wife, for constant coöperation.

W. S. T.

CONTENTS

CHAPTER III

CAUSES OF NERVOUS AND MENTAL DISEASE

CHAPTER IV

HISTORICAL SKETCH OF TREATMENT AND THEORY OF THE FUNCTIONAL NEUROSES

CONTENTS

CHAPTER V

SOME BASIC PSYCHOLOGICAL CONCEPTIONS

ADJUSTMENTAL ORGANIZATION

SOME FUNDAMENTAL ACTIVITIES

CHAPTER VI

THE PRINCIPLE OF DISSOCIATION

CHAPTER VII

MEMORY IN RELATION TO ABNORMAL PSYCHOLOGY

CONTENTS

CHAPTER VIII

MEANING AND ITS SIGNIFICANCE

CHAPTER IX

SYMBOLISM

CHAPTER X

WISHES, SENTIMENTS, COMPLEXES, SYSTEMS

CHAPTER XI

CONFLICT AND SOME OF ITS MANIFESTATIONS

CONTENTS

CHAPTER XVIII

THE NATURE OF SUGGESTION

CHAPTER XIX

HYPNOTIC CONDITIONS

CHAPTER XX

ILLUSIONS AND HALLUCINATIONS

CHAPTER XXI

DREAMS

CHAPTER XXII

HIGHER PROCESSES IN THE LIGHT OF ABNORMAL PSYCHOLOGY

CHAPTER XXIII

PROBLEMS OF PERSONALITY AND CHARACTER

CHAPTER XXIV

GENERAL CONCEPTIONS OF FUNCTIONAL DISORDERS

CHAPTER XXV

PSYCHOTHERAPY

CHAPTER XXVI

SOME GENERAL ILLUSTRATIONS

CHAPTER XXVII

MENTAL HYGIENE

Contents

INTRODUCTION

I

In the reconstruction of psychology which began a half-century ago but went forward with a markedly accelerated advance in the present century, no discipline has contributed more importantly and more significantly than the study of the abnormal phases of mental behavior. Abnormal psychology has enriched and given an added meaning to many of the concepts of "historical" psychology, has conferred a new insight into the sources and development and meaning of mind and the incidents and conditions of the mental life. This applies to principles, theories, outlook, as well as to the detailed study of motives and expression, to a detection of the grosser and finer mechanisms of conduct, and to the understanding and control of the mental development. It has given to the study of psychology an impetus and a direction which is distinctive and far-reaching. In this influence no other phase of psychology rivals it unless it be the genetic, with which it affiliates congenially and indispensably.

It has thus come about that a knowledge of the leading facts and principles of abnormal psychology forms an integral part of the psychologist's training, even if it is carried no further than the college curriculum of "majors" and "minors" in any of the group of the humanized sciences—psychology, education, sociology, philosophy, most centrally. Its appeal carries to other students and to many groups of serious readers. It has a vital message for the practical-minded humanitarian, now conveniently known as a "social worker," in whose field devotion and high purpose require the support of authentic information and critical insight. The abnormal touches upon so many of the phases of human interest and behavior—in the anthropological retrospect, in the versatile application of the active life of desire and motive, in the interpretation of types of personality, in formulating the sources of temperament and character—that it enters into the equipment of the well-informed reader with responsible participation in the world in which we have our psychological as well as our practical being. More specifically, the note of *mens sana* in the demands and

obligations of the modern life is so dominant, the risks and temptations that beset the maturing of modern adult interests and
adjustments are so complex and insidious, that "mental hygiene"
has expanded its meaning, has penetrated in unexpected applications into the fiber of our thinking and the spirit of our practice;
it has come to replace the casual old-time "guide, philosopher, and
friend" in the varied guidance by which the more expert, more
experienced, more mature minister to human welfare. Abnormal
psychology has already achieved the position of a basic science to
those professions that require an understanding and direction of
human behavior in its normal as well as its wayward manifestations. This circumstance increases the demand for a helpful body
of source material.

Logically considered, "abnormal psychology" is the proper name
for the entire body of doctrine, the system of interpretation, the
development of concepts, under which the mental expert of to-day
proceeds, whatever his direct or indirect purpose. This position
of dominance may be questioned by the psychiatrist—literally the
physician of the psyche—and the historical evidence favors his
claim. Logically, however, psychiatry is an application—in its
comprehensive modernized practice, the most important one—of
the body of doctrine that abnormal psychology expounds from a
yet more comprehensive outlook. The stress of practice and experience is ever insistent, and each generation must minister to it
with such insight, fortified by principle and theory, as it commands.
The mentally disturbed and defective, the victims of brain disorder
and irregular disposition, must receive aid and direction; as a
(medical) specialty psychiatry occupies a far better established
field (though a more limited one) than does abnormal psychology;
but in the logical ordering of the mental sciences, abnormal
psychology takes the directive position.

If we inquire why the experience of the psychiatrist remained so
long out of range of the domain of the psychologist, since to our
insight its bearings are so direct and significant for his pursuit,
we come upon many reasons for this circumstance; the chief one
will suffice: that the concept of mind and its functions (faculties
in the older sense) that dominated until recent days was hopelessly
handicapped by assumptions derived from a philosophic approach,
somewhat dogmatic rather than scientific in temper, and directed
by a moralizing bias. The psychologist as we recognize him had
not appeared; there were philosophers with strong and often shrewd
psychological interests. Such a term, current half a century ago,
as "psychological medicine" sought an *approachment* that would

have been more effective had there been a larger clientele to sponsor it. But the historical delay in the recognition of abnormal psychology has a larger justification. Other advances had to appear and make their notable contributions before the psychologist and the psychiatrist could offer mutual recognition to one another and establish their places in the sciences. Foremost, the evolutionary view of man and his structure and functions had to penetrate to every phase of biological thinking; man's mental or psychic nature had to be viewed under the same approach, as subject to like conditioning, as his bodily nature; the physiology of the nervous system had to be developed to an understanding of its complex detail of structure and function, so commanding that it may well be called the neurological insight; within its own province psychology had to attain that objective view of its data that is best characterized as behavioristic in the broadest meaning of the term. In brief, psychologists had to learn to think biologically, neurologically, behavioristically before they were ready for the reconstruction of their science which would bring the abnormal into the focus of their interest.

All this has been sufficiently advanced in recent years that the accomplishment may be pointed to as one of the significant achievements of modern science. This reconstruction has proceeded upon an incorporation and technical development of the *experimental* method; the researches of the psychological laboratory embody its results and add a vast mass of data—organized, accurate, objective —that justify the close affiliation of the psychologist with technical experts in other sciences. In further extension and similarly directed is the *clinical* study of mental behavior, likewise developing a technique, which keeps the psychologist's thinking within the orbit of common experience, and turns him to that total behavior in all its complicated setting of original constitution and environmental conditioning, which vitalizes as well as humanizes his science. And in this combined change of emphasis and expansion of outlook he comes again to the evolutionary view, which looks upon mental life as a growth and a direction, and makes of him a geneticist. The native reactions of childhood, of infancy most specifically, acquire a richer and indeed a momentous consequence, carrying over to the abnormal issues. In view of these "historical" considerations, it is intelligible why abnormal psychology has come late to its proper recognition, why the present generation is the first to include in its interpretation of life that complex aspect of behavior to which this volume is devoted.

II

The most helpful way to indicate the leading concepts that direct abnormal psychology in its present channels of interest and investigation will be to survey in terms of a selected group of principles the mode of interpretation and application that confers understanding of the abnormal in mental life.

1. *The Psychogenetic Principle.*—Foremost in the group is what may be generalized as the psychogenetic principle. Though long recognized in the modern phases of psychology, it represents in its recent version the development of a concept in directions possible only to the mental science of to-day. The underlying idea may be traced in the older psychological usage as the converse of "the influence of the body on the mind" (which may be called the principle of physiological psychology) by demonstration of the "influence of the mind on the body." This in its enriched and differently centered reference becomes the principle of psychogenesis. It came to the fore in the truly original discovery of Freud, that certain symptoms in hysterical cases were induced by a "psychic" mechanism—more specifically that a paralysis or a blindness or an anæsthesia may be the bodily expression of a fear or an incapacity or a surrender as a mode of escape from an emotionally distressing situation. The "unreality" of hysterical phenomena had been made clear, but under the Freudian interest "hysterical" acquired a more precise meaning and an unexpected extension. The Freudian aspect of the psychogenetic principle has come to dominate the literature. Previous to this contribution similar phenomena were well recognized in the varied action of suggestion; clinically the fact that both ailments and cures may arise through suggestion (whether the treatment involves a special technique or proceeds by the religious route of faith in shrine or relic or exorcism) proves the psychogenetic origin as well as removal of the disorder.

Just how far the psychogenetic principle carries in the present-day explanation and treatment of the neuroses is by no means clear. The ardent Freudian is inclined to interpret many types of mental disorder as of psychogenetic origin, or as conditioned by psychogenetic factors. The most convincing and establishing application is to the *functional nervous disorders* as they are commonly called, particularly and most of all to hysteria. The Freudian interpretation has added many subsidiary principles related to the commanding position which psychogenesis assumes in abnormal psychology. The hypnotic state, historically important, assumes a new significance in the light of recent investigation. At one time explained mystically (animal magnetism), then neurologically (cataplexy), then psychologically (suggestion), it now finds its clue psychogenetically in dissociation. The recognition of this factor appeared independently of the Freudian contributions; its historical antecedents may be traced in the varieties of trances, now described as lapses, fugues, amnesias, in dual personalities, as well as in dreaming and in the slighter instances of absent-mindedness—all forms of dissociation.

The principle of dissociation attempts to explain the *mechanism* by which the psychogenetic principle operates. One aspect of it, dominant in Freudian doctrine, becomes the principle of the subconscious. Psychogenesis, alike in neurotic manifestations and within the normal field, works in the subconscious domain. Much of the mental life lives and moves at subconscious levels. Just how far these subconscious tendencies may be organized is again differently interpreted by psychologists of one school or another; the amazing records of "multiple personality" indicate its most elaborate manifestations. Further points of emphasis in the Freudian interpretations are the importance of day-dreaming (phantasy) in the genesis of the conditions which we have come to speak of as the complexes; the conflict which they engender is referred to some form of suppression which the conscious "censor" imposes upon the instinctive urges to psychic expression. At this point the study of mechanisms passes over to the study of motives, which in part is more pertinent to later considerations.

The limitations of the psychogenetic principle, as already indicated, are by no means established. That many forms of mental abnormalities have a physiological, that is, a neurological, origin, and therefore illustrate the very converse of the psychogenetic principle, is equally a contribution of recent investigations. Most distinctive is the glandular psychology which accounts for many forms of abnormalities through overaction, or underaction, or lack of balance among the several complex contributors to the integrity and welfare of the psychic apparatus, the knowledge of which comes from the new science of endocrinology. The functions of the internal secretions have assumed a no less significant rôle than that of psychogenesis. The physiological contribution is equally indispensable. In the development of abnormal psychology the enthusiastic recognition of the psychogenetic principle must not obscure the field of physiological conditioning. The importance of the physiological approach is convincing as the distinctive place of the *autonomic nervous system* in the vital economy has been disclosed by remarkable investigation. Unquestionably the clue to many forms of nervous trouble as well as to temperamental liabilities lies in the operation of the autonomic system, which biologically is far older in the history of the race and serves more fundamental and vital functions than the later central nervous system with which we associate the more elaborate mental mechanisms. The manner in which one set of data, one approach, corrects and supplements another is itself a guiding principle of abnormal psychology. Not only is there danger on the part of those who have to interpret neurotic symptoms and to minister to neurotic patients, to attribute to the "higher" mechanisms what belongs to the "lower"; but in the direction and interpretation of normal conduct the correct division of influence from "above" and "below" is a difficult art and forms an engaging field of modern inquiry.

One phase of the controversy as to the scope of operation of the psychogenetic mechanisms centered about the procedure of *psychoanalysis*. It is unfortunate that the many-sided bearings of the Freudian principles were so long hostilely received through the emphasis which overzealous practitioners placed upon psychoanalysis, the value of which as a practical expedient must be judged by clinical evidence. Not only may one remain in every true sense a Freudian and yet question the complete validity of the motives and specific mechanisms as set forth by Freud and his early followers; but one may appraise the value of the psycho-analytic procedure critically and even assign it a modest place while recognizing the high value for abnormal psychology of the system of principles of which psycho-analysis is but a therapeutic application. To continue the discussion would require more detailed survey of the factors of the Freudian system than is here possible. The scope of such further exposition may be suggested by mentioning the part which the motive of sex plays in the Freudian psychology, and by indicating how differently the master urges (including sex) are interpreted by those who follow yet divergently along the line of Freudian development, such as Jung, or Adler, or Rivers. Still more controversial is the validity of the specific plot of the "family romance" as Freud has developed it, which finds in the possible (distorted) relations of parent and child the clue not only to certain of the neuroses (such as the "Œdipus complex"), but a leading principle of interpretation of other forms of maladjustment.

Indeed, the ramifications of the psychogenetic principle are endless. Taken retrospectively the same order of thinking leads to the interpretation of early human history (anthropologically) as examples of similar Freudian products; totems, taboos, myths, social regulations appear as (abnormal) complexes, akin to those that characterize the neuroses. It leads to the interpretation of dreams, not only as aids to the psycho-analytic revelations, but as variously illustrative of the urges, motives, symbolisms, compensations, projections, and other mechanisms that figure in the Freudian psychology. Followed in another direction, it emphasizes the instincts, the emotions, the forms of behavior distinctive of early childhood, the significance of the great reconstruction that we call adolescence—all of which considerations may as appropriately be included in the portions of this summary that follow.

It is true of the psychogenetic principle that it is a product dominantly though not exclusively of the general line of inquiry that has established abnormal psychology. Its position of preeminence yet leaves room for a similar comprehensive formulation of the converse physiological or neurological principles that indicate the possible sources within the nervous system of the mechanisms of behavior. Both have contributed notably to the development of abnormal psychology.

2. *The Dominance of the Emotions.*—While not so intimately connected with the line of development that gave rise to abnormal psychology (since it belongs to other provinces and indeed to general psychology as well), the significance of the emotional life in human behavior is a characteristic principle that directs inquiry in the field covered by this volume. It is one of the merits of the Freudian approach that it recognizes the directive emotional factor in its study of the mainsprings of conduct; in so far it serves to correct the intellectualist psychology—with its too exclusive focusing on the products of intelligence and the mechanisms of the mind as an instrument of problem-solving, and congenially reënforces the behavioristic interpretation. The most general terms convenient to this reference are *temperament,* as emphasizing the inherent hereditary disposition, and *character,* as the product of the shaping of response under stress of the environment. The temperamental factor rests upon the deepest instincts as the motive sources of behavior, the clues to development, and the origins of abnormalities. It assigns a place of leadership in all these respects to the great trunk-line emotions—anger, fear, sympathy— and follows their integration into all the complicated emotions of self-assertion, the vast ego, assertions with their development into sentiments, and their varied expression in the struggle for pleasure, for power, for a place for the self.

It is in the course of this expression that the Freudian conflict arises, since the individual, by nature a thorough egoist, comes in conflict with the similar strivings of others and with the organized social pressure. That self-assertion is intimately bound up with sex-assertion and early acquires and ever retains a sex quality and differentiation, is a position common to all varieties of Freudians (and non-Freudians) though with different emphasis and bearing. It is indeed the different placement of the several urges centering about the ego-assertion and the will to prevail that serves as the clue to the position of Jung and of Adler, leading to the preference of the term "individual psychology" for their contributions. The rôle of conflict appears likewise in the Freudian distinction between the "pleasure" principle and the "reality" principle. In the realm of mind, with its strong and varied urge for self-assertion, there arises the world of the imagination-phantasy, romance, day-dreaming, and ever with the flavor of wish (the Freudian wish) ; opposed to it is the insistent pressure of things as they are and the required adjustment to the stern realities of the established social system, which restricts behavior, moulds character, clashes with temperament, and directs each and all of the master emotions, regulating our angers, our fears, our sympathies, as well as our pleasures. So much of the emotional life is socialized, though arising upon the individualistic trends, that abnormal psychology shares with social psychology the direction of conduct and its interpretation; it is the emotional maturing of the individual that becomes the joint concern of these two great divisions of modern psychology. In this view civilization becomes a system for the control of the emotional life as comprehensively, and in nature's scheme more originally, than it is an enterprise of intellectual control of the resources of the environment and the skillful direction of the occupations of men in satisfaction of their needs. The emotions dominate; at first simple pleasures, then desire for notice, then ambition, rivalry, and finally the great socialized struggles of individuals and groups, tribes and nations and the varied castes and classes of the social order. Yet the adjustment to the intimate group, the family, the playmate, the rival, remains the most active of the control factors for the checking of angers, the discipline of fears, the ordering of sympathies, the acquisition of prides and shames; and in this more intimate field the Freudian psychology finds its major conditioning and the sources of the abnormal likewise. Social institutions appear as so many devices for the further manifestation, exercise, and enhancement of the satisfaction of needs first appearing in the closer circle. The dominance of the emotions is thus characteristic of the modern trends in social as well as in abnormal psychology, and furthermore in the educational direction of human behavior under the principle of growth or maturing. It occupies a position of vantage in the common boundary where the several provinces of psychological thought and practice meet, and makes the practical problem of education so largely a wise expression and control of the emotional life.

3. *The Abnormal in the Normal Mind.*—A fertile principle of abnormal psychology is that all the distinctive abnormal tendencies, many of which may be viewed as temperamental issues or liabilities, appear in the normal mind in restrained form, active on a smaller scale, a counterpart in miniature. The interpretation of normal behavior through the concepts that arise from the study of the abnormal may be variously illustrated. We may take first the close relation of the functional neuroses as above defined to traits of temperament and character. The terms *hysterical* and *neurasthenic* offer the most comprehensive and convincing instances. An adequate knowledge of hysteria has come to be indispensable to the interpretation of ordinary character traits. Hysteria in the medical or clinical sense is a definite though extremely variable neurosis; yet equally the term hysterical is applicable to a type of temperament and to a considerable range of traits that are congenial to it. Just what are the distinctive traits of hysteria, the several foci of radiation of the typical orders of hysterical manifestations, and what is their relation to one another, is still a puzzling problem. But in its solution our understanding has gone far enough to serve as an important clue in the interpretation of normal behavior through all the seven ages and countless relations of men. In the formulation of one writer, the human race is by nature hysterical, all primitive peoples are hysterical, children are notably hysterical, and the steadiest of us likely to become so under severe stress; so that the problem of civilization is to reduce the native hysteria of the human race. Under the same approach it appears that some of the manifestations in pronounced hysteria are resolved into reversions or regressions on the part of adults, back to outgrown forms of response natural and pardonable in children. It is indeed a difficult task to become fully adult; the essential aim of a normal education is to subdue or direct to desirable issues (sublimation in the Freudian terminology) the native hysterical trends, thus once more emphasizing the dominance of the emotions and the genetic principle. Imperfect maturing and regression result in childish behavior; the appeal to reason finds its rationale as the only available control to offset the native emotionalism; education for emotional stability and control is the

goal idea. Such social menaces as fanaticism appear likewise as hysterical excesses, interpretable as abnormal phenomena; and the difficulty in establishing rational conduct lies in the stronghold of the same order of liabilities as lead to hysteria.

Under a similar approach we come upon the problem of types. The hysterical type may appear in fully developed clinical stature, but more commonly as a temperamental trend to which a more generic name is more fitting. Best known among the normal types but open to abnormal expression is the distinction made by Jung in elaborate detail between the *extrovert* and the *introvert*, which has about the same orbit of application as the more popular distinction of James between the tender-minded and the tough-minded. Underlying this and all other true types is a (conjectural) mode of organization of the central nervous system. Individuals are simple or complex, in large measure doubtless through the influence of the forces of the environment to which they are required to make adjustment, but no less so through the inherent and original differences of temperament, properly designated as types. It is in this reference that the most profitable discussion of sex is likely to be developed; for the differences of interests and zests and occupations and the composite of traits characteristic of the male and the female have a temperamental origin. They are as significant in their normal as in their abnormal varieties and appear in the different liabilities to neuroses which men and women present. The early view of hysteria as a feminine liability is at once a recognition and a misinterpretation of a true distinction. Quite similarly is neurasthenia more common and marked in the male. For the moment the essential point is that forms of response developing upon a marked temperamental disposition (and in so far a neural conditioning) and in turn some of them more congenial to the feminine and others to the masculine psychology—though present in both—find their clue in the clinical forms of functional neuroses such as hysteria and neurasthenia. An hysterical trait accordingly means one that is akin to the typical symptoms of hysteria, yet the kinship must be to some one symptom which belongs to a cluster or group or complex composed of ramifications and derivatives from one dominating trait, such as over-emotionalism in hysteria, or a tendency to narrow and lapsed consciousness, or in neurasthenia a susceptibility to fatigue and an obsession with fears and a tendency to feel pain acutely (hyperæsthesia and hyperalgesia), the psychic pains or depressions particularly. Similarly a neurasthenic trait is one that is of the same order as the typical symptoms of that distressing malady. Traits common to all, frequent in normal individuals, yet show a marked variation of higher frequency or intenser development among those with favoring dispositions. In this illumination, susceptibility to hypnosis is congenial to the hysterical temperament, as Charcot a half-century ago both discovered and in a measure misinterpreted; so are trances and multiple personalities, so are high-strung, excitable, over-emotional enthusiasms; while hypochondria and the complete prostration and lack of power to direct thought and conduct, commonly called nervous breakdown, or any tendency to lose the zest of activity, is neurasthenic. The abnormal issues become the most convenient and helpful clues to the classification of traits present in moderate degree in the normal, but particularly in the normal of the predisposed type; and sex or race may be a similar predisposition.

4. *Constitutional and Environmental Factors.*—Abnormal psychology has a strong interest in the principle or the problem belonging to general psychology that attempts to determine what phases of behavior may be attributed to original temperament or constitution, and how far what men do and enjoy and what belief attitudes they are likely to accept, is to be regarded as the issue of environmental influences. The problem clearly overlaps that of types, of sex, and mainly that of the deviates or divergents from normality toward the abnormal. It is familiar in the recognition of the psychopathic individual by constitution and in the traits of behavior formerly too readily considered as faults of character or vicious rebellion—in brief the problem of crime and the criminal tendencies. The modern insight has made the study of the defective and delinquent part of the practical social problem of dealing with the subnormal. It serves as an instructive instance of the composite emotional and intellectual factors that determine deviation. The feeble-minded, the retarded, the low mentality that may be expressed quantitatively in the subnormal intelligence-quotient, stands for the intellectual defect; while the readiness to yield to temptation, the feeble inhibition of impulses, the uncontrollable passions, the morbid delight in cruelty, the insensibility to the ordinary sympathetic reactions, represent the feeling aspect of the low-grade individual.

The problems of genius and the gifted child, the distribution of special facilities—the limited virtuosities in precocious musical prodigies, the performances of lightning calculators, chess geniuses —no less propose the issue of native capacity and training. The existence of the occasional superior psychopathic individual still further complicates the issue. It is in these concrete instances that the interest of the abnormal in constitution and environment appears. It is continued in the studies of heredity, alike of the decadent and the genius, and leads to the proposals of eugenics and the measures of euthenics. Thus variously and intimately does abnormal psychology make contacts with the practical regulation of social institutions in educational and other public care, in selection and stimulation of the constitutionally desirable, in protection from the menace of the undesirable. These topics belong to the survey here presented, though their consideration follows the perspective of principle and understanding rather than that of the clinical problems of control of abnormal behavior.

5. *The Genetic Principle.*—The principle of interpretation of the mental life as a growth and maturing and decline, though belonging to the great division of genetic psychology, receives a special illumination from the abnormal side, notably in the Freudian system. The supreme importance of the earliest phases of child life is set forth by Freud as responsible in some instances for or symptomatic of liability to neuroses in maturer years, that hark back to an upsetting experience in childhood. The "abnormal" application does not stop there. It directs renewed attention to the typical symptoms of the neuroses of the several stages of development. Forms of abnormal behavior in infancy and childhood are now recognizable as foreshadowing the assets and liabilities of later periods. There has appeared a new view of undesirable child-habits as a neurological problem. Most of all has the emphasis been placed upon the significance of adolescence as the great emotional reconstruction and upon the emancipation of the child from the dominance of the parent as the essential problem of maturing. The dangers of over-indulgence as well as over-suppression shape the educational policy. In Freud's hands there develops the concept of parent fixation—specifically as directed to the parent of opposite sex—and the delineation of the psychic development in terms of the "family romance." This need not be accepted as of general application, any more than one need accept the diffuse sexuality of the child, while yet recognizing that it has an authentic bearing upon the genetic process. It plays a part in the mental hygiene of youth.

That the mental life is a growth appears in the recognition of the several typical neuroses and psychoses as characteristic of the distinctive ages of man. The story of dementia præcox alone indicates how significant is development in the diagnosis and prognosis of mental disorder. There appear in turn the major psychoses of mature life and their conditioning, and finally those of old age, the dementias of the terminal stages of the psychic cycle. The relation of the periods of maximum sexual vigor to the psychoses, as well as those of sexual loss, is but another phase of the recognition of the genetic principle. The genetic cycle as considered in every phase of the neuroses and abnormalities of adjustment, influences the interpretation of every chapter in abnormal psychology of to-day.

6. *Sanity and Mental Hygiene.*—From the practical side there is no more comprehensive product of the set of ideas that have brought into being the science of abnormal psychology than that which bears the name of mental hygiene. Our views of sanity have been deepened and broadened. The implications of a safe and sane civilization have been set forth in terms of the psychology of the human race and of the individual. The social-anthropological regulations appear as attempts to safeguard and minister to the psychic needs of the socialized individual. The collective social abnormalities thus arising, from prejudice and fads to mob action and psychic epidemics, give evidence that the same forces leading to individual neuroses may give rise to neuroses of tribes and groups and nations. At every stage and in every phase of mental development the hygienist is prepared to direct and control, to approve and discourage, to stimulate and check trends and activities according to the system of value that inspires his efforts. He develops or profits by the clinical view of life and its products; his interests run parallel to those of the abnormal psychologist; his is most specifically the art and practice of which abnormal psychology is the science and theory. The responsibilities of leadership require a most comprehensive outlook, including a "neurological" insight. No more convincing evidence of the scope of abnormal psychology and its influence in modern thought could be presented than that of the prompt acceptance and remarkable development of mental hygiene.

III

With these suggestions of the origin, animus, and mode of procedure of abnormal psychology, it remains only to indicate that in so rapidly growing and recent a development, a source-book seems to offer the most suitable means of making available authoritative presentations from a large and varied field. Eventually one psychologist and another will prepare a more systematic text properly entitled "Principles of Abnormal Psychology." Such a volume would well supplement in more systematic fashion the data here assembled; but "Readings" have the advantage of flexibility and brevity of reference as well as of reflecting the varied and mutually supporting views of many writers.

While a handbook of "Readings" considers rather directly its use as a text or a constant basis of reference in a teaching course, it has no less in mind the needs of the independent student and professionally interested reader; this volume may be used in any order of topics or any selection that meets the interests of the reader or the plan of the course. The order and prominence and emphasis of topics and particularly the specific selection of extracts from the literature, together constitute a position and approach which the author regards as warranted. Advantages and disadvantages of one order or arrangement must be balanced against those of another. After a preliminary orientation that places the "abnormal" in modern psychology, Professor Taylor uses the clinical approach as the most direct introduction to the fundamental data, making the primary contact with the forms of abnormal phenomena as they occur clinically in cases of mental disorder. Thus concretely oriented, the student becomes familiar with the fact material, the dominant concepts, the mode of consideration, the technique, in brief, that has become established in practice and current in the literature, the great bulk of which is the product of the interest of the psychiatrist. This section is projected on a sufficient scale to serve as a summary of the "neuroses" and presents that gateway to the abnormal in its realistic clinical setting. By including treatment it leads to such procedures as *hypnosis*, which in turn makes room for mental therapeutics in their historical development, as well as to psychoanalysis, which stands as the most familiar phase of the Freudian system; this in its several ramifications occupies an extensive area of the "Readings."

But the major portion of the volume is devoted to the central problems of abnormal psychology and the points of view as well as the data that have been developed in their pursuit. The principles that have been selected for emphasis may serve to indicate its scope, though the compendium goes beyond this range in that it includes a considerable body of case material illustrative of the findings upon which interpretation rests. The proper balance between data and interpretations has been admirably maintained, the needs of science and practice equally considered.

In planning his volume some three years ago, it was my intention to "edit" the enterprise and coöperate in the selection of the "readings" and in the integration of the whole into a consistent and comprehensive guide to the study of abnormal psychology. At an early stage I was compelled by personal circumstances to abandon this plan and transfer the work to Professor Taylor. I had already made the proposal of collaboration to him and was promptly impressed with his professional competence for the task. The volume thus properly appears under his name as sole author. My part has been limited to that of consultant in matters of selection; at several stages I have reviewed the manuscript and offered suggestions and references. The credit of the work belongs to Professor Taylor. I record my appreciation of his ability and devotion in carrying through a difficult compilation. He has made the book a valuable compendium, reflecting his grasp of a complex field.

JOSEPH JASTROW.

READINGS IN ABNORMAL PSYCHOLOGY AND MENTAL HYGIENE

CHAPTER I

THE FIELD AND ITS IMPORTANCE

A Present-Day Conception of Mental Disorders

CHARLES MACFIE CAMPBELL, *A Present-Day Conception of Mental Disorders*, 25-27, 47, 49-50, 53 (Harvard, 1924)

The sort of material which is before us when we try to frame a general conception of mental disorders . . . is a motley group. It includes respectable bankers peevish with their wives; scrupulous housewives with immaculate and uncomfortable homes; children with night-terrors and all sorts of wayward reactions; earnest reformers, intellectuals, æsthetes; delicate and refined invalids, evasive and tyrannical, with manifold symptoms and transitory dramatic episodes; patients delirious with fever, or reduced by a great variety of organic diseases; patients frozen with melancholy or indulging in an orgy of exuberant activity; patients living in a fantastic world with morbid visions and communications and uncanny influences, in whose universe one sees no coherence or logical structure; patients keenly logical and argumentative, embittered, and seeing around them a hostile world with which they refuse to compromise.

Now how can we bring order into this chaos, how can we find a path through this jungle? The answer is very simple. We have merely to discard our mediæval attitude toward these sick or handicapped people, and to study the problem which they present as a problem of human nature working under difficulties. We have to study the disordered behavior of the total organism in the same way in which we study the disordered behavior of a single organ, such as the heart.

1

In studying the behavior of the heart we observe its action, not only as the patient lies in bed, but also in its response to the demands made upon it on exercise. We review the history of the heart, note whether there has been some original fault in its equipment, and study the experiences through which it has passed, such as episodes of undue physical strain or exposure to the poisons of infectious disease; we study the other systems of the body, to see if they are exerting a detrimental influence on the action of the heart.

With these data before us we are able to judge the nature and severity of the actual disorder of the heart, and to outline treatment either by directly regulating its function or by clearly formulating the conditions and the restrictions within which it may best carry on its work. . . .

[To return to our topic of mental disorders,] it is very difficult to know in the individual case the rôle played by each of the complex forces . . . , the rôle played by the disordered chemistry of the system, by underlying weakness of other organs, by the influence of poor physical hygiene of various types. It is not easy to appreciate the stress of the life situation, the influence of early training and experiences, of early blunders and groping. It is not easy to trace the exact origin of the behavior and to demonstrate the source of distorted beliefs in the early ideas of the child or the more primitive conceptions of early man.

Ignorance of these matters we must admit, but we may claim to have banished mystery from this branch of medicine. There is to everyone, who has not lost the faculty of imagination, mystery when we get down to the fundamentals of any science; but that is the only sense in which we can admit that there is mystery in relation to mental disorders. Mental disorders can be explained in the light of the same general principles which explain the working of our bodily organs, the evolution of the instincts, the origin of human culture, and the early phases of individual development in infancy and childhood. . . .

It may not be true that we are all a little insane; it is certainly true that we all have to face the same fundamental problems of life, and the problems before which the nervous or mental patient has broken down are only different in degree from those which each cultivated man has to face.

Significance of the Abnormal as Compared with the Morbid

JOSEPH JASTROW, *The Subconscious*, 164-166 (Houghton Mifflin, 1906) ; used by permission of and by special arrangement with the publishers

The term "abnormal" should be liberally interpreted. It does not intrinsically carry with it the imputation of disease; for that the word "morbid" is more precise. Its underlying connotation is that of pronounced or significant variation from rather well-defined, fairly accepted norms. With waking regarded as the normal condition, sleep becomes abnormal; with sensibility to pain and to the ordinary stimuli of sight and hearing as the normal state, anæsthesia and intense absorption become abnormal; in deviation from the normally elastic emotional temperament, responding readily to the natural excitements of grief and joy, the persistently depressed tone of the melancholic is abnormal; in comparison with the slowly developing and limited capacity for the manipulation of number-relations or of musical expression, with which most children are endowed, the performances of an arithmetical prodigy or of a precocious musical genius are abnormal; in contrast with the recognized inability of the average man to rescue from the subconscious the vague associations of lapsed memories, the devices of those who are able to perform this sleight-of-mind are likewise abnormal. The mere uncommonness of a phenomenon has little relation to its significance as an abnormal variation; the abnormal is not the monstrous. Dreaming is extremely common, but presents a profoundly significant variation from the normal flow of thought. Lightning calculators are uncommon; but, however readily their marvelous performances excite popular curiosity, they arouse psychological interest in so far as they serve to impart some insight into the processes by which such results are obtained. The hypnotic state is rather easily induced, and in some form has for ages excited observation and astonishment; but it began to be profitably studied when pertinent analysis indicated the significance of what curiosity had merely confused. It is not the mere fact of difference, but of a difference that yields in analysis a knowledge of its nature, that gives to the abnormal its true significance. It is because the abnormal presents an instructive variation from the usual relations of things, that its study illuminates and enlarges our conceptions of the complexity and marvel of the normal. It acts not only as a microscope, bringing minute features within the field of vision, but in addition, like the differential staining of the histological specimen, it presents in contrasted outline the delicate tracery of tissue that to the unaided eye must ever remain invisible.

Abnormal Psychology and Experimental Psychology

FRANK WATTS, *Abnormal Psychology and Education*, 9-11 (Appleton, 1924)

It may be interesting and helpful at this stage to attempt a brief comparison between Abnormal Psychology and another vigorous offspring of the same parent, Experimental Psychology, accepting them in the ordinary but of course erroneous sense as distinct sciences. Experimental Psychology follows generally the method of the older physical sciences, and depends largely upon the artificial isolation under suitable and pre-arranged conditions of those factors which it intends quantitatively or qualitatively to study, relying upon repetition and variation of the conditions of the experiment to provide adequate means for the exhaustive study of the problems which may arise. In the province of Abnormal Psychology, nature has already, by the intensification of certain psychic factors, practically isolated, under the most favorable conditions, interesting material for study. . . . As time progresses, however, the scope of the two branches of general psychology must inevitably and to a very great extent overlap. Up to the present, the effect of experimental psychology upon the methods of abnormal psychology may be seen in the growing desire for artificial variation of the data of study with a view to the more thorough scrutiny of the theories which have been formulated—in many cases only too lightly—about the nature of the abnormalities involved, while the influence of the latter branch of psychology upon the former may be seen in the increasing transference of the interest of the experimenter from the investigation of matters of sensory discrimination, which have been proved to have very little—if any—value as indicating the general trend and efficiency of the mind, to the investigation of the facts of the intellectual, emotional, and æsthetic life of man.

From what has already been said, it may be gathered by the reader that the normal may easily be separated off from the abnormal in practical work: this is not so. The delimitation of the one from the other follows purely arbitrary lines, and these have only been laid down with any attempt at scientific precision during the past few decades. A graphical representation of men's mental "efficiency," based on the examination of large random groups of examples, would show us probably the characteristic bell-shaped frequency curve, with a huge number of cases representing the normal heaped about the dome and upper slopes of the curve, and a lesser number of doubtful interpretation shading off on each side by imperceptible gradations into the comparatively few cases of the definitely abnormal.

Abnormal Psychology and the Study of the Subnormal Mind

[HENRY H. GODDARD]; adapted from "The Sub-Normal Mind versus the Abnormal," *Jour. Abn. Psychol.*, 16: 47-50, 54 (1921)

The terms abnormal and subnormal are two words with a clear distinction, which can be of great usefulness in clarifying our discussions if we can agree upon what we wish to connote by each one.

Almost the first use of the Binet-Simon Scale in this country was made by Dr. Huey in testing out the entire population of the Lincoln Institution for the Feeble-Minded and by the writer in testing the population of the Vineland Training School. Since none of these inmates was found to have an intelligence above 12 years, it was inferred that this was the upper limit of feeble-mindedness and the lower limit of normality. It was further inferred that all persons who were old enough to have a higher intelligence but who had the rating of 12 years or less were feeble-minded or subnormal. Samplings were made in other institutions for the feeble-minded with the same result. On the basis of these results, the American Association for the Study of the Feeble-Minded at its annual meeting at Lincoln, Ill., in 1910, tentatively adopted a classification of the feeble-minded which has become universally accepted, namely, those with a mentality of 2 years or less were to be designated as idiots, those of from 3 to 7 inclusive imbeciles, and from 8 to 12 morons.

The view that everybody who tested 12 years or less was feeble-minded prevailed until the results of the mental tests in the army reduced this to an absurdity. The army findings that 10 per cent. of the soldiers had a mentality of 10 years or less and another 15 per cent. a mentality of 11, and 20 per cent. a mentality of 12, giving as a result that 45 per cent. of the army had a mentality of 12 years or less, threw an entirely new light upon the problem of subnormality and feeble-mindedness. It is obviously not true that 45 per cent. of the population is defective and not everybody who is even 10 years old mentally is feeble-minded.

We have evidently been guilty of bad logic. In the early history of mental tests several students finding that various groups of farmers, housemaids and even some legislators who were obviously *normal* in the popular acceptation of that term, tested under 12 years, drew the hasty conclusion that the tests were unreliable.

It is now clear that the only thing at fault was the concept of who is feeble-minded. Had these investigators pointed out to us that there were great groups of people of 10, 11, and 12 year mentality who could not possibly be called feeble-minded they would have made a distinct contribution.

To replace ourselves on the right track we must call to mind the definition of feeble-mindedness. This has always included not only the mental level but the inability to get along in the world, "manage their own affairs with ordinary prudence and compete with their normal fellows." The error lies in the wrong inference that all who test 12 years or less are incapable of maintaining themselves.

The next problem can now be considered: Why are some 10 year olds feeble-minded and others not? If we accept provisionally the 13 year mind as the lower limit of normality, then we have the condition that some people with mentality of from 8 to 12 are subnormal but not feeble-minded. This, as a matter of fact, we know to be true. What, then, is the distinction between subnormal and feeble-minded in these cases? According to the definition of feeble-mindedness the difference is in their ability to take care of themselves. In other words, a person of mentality from 8 to 12 is generally able to manage his affairs and compete in the struggle for existence unless in addition to his low mentality he is handicapped by other disadvantageous traits, such as, for example, high temper. A certain man of 10 year mentality could earn enough money to support himself if it was not for his violent temper whereby he continually loses his jobs.

One writer has suggested that in view of these new discoveries we must re-define moron. This is not necessary unless we wish to make the term stand for *all persons* with mentality 8 to 12. According to the classification adopted by the American Association for the Study of the Feeble-Minded the term moron was to include that group of the *feeble-minded* who have a mentality from 8 to 12, not all persons from 8 to 12. The term moron is improperly used when it is applied to any person who is not feeble-minded, no matter what his mentality.

The term subnormal would therefore seem to be applicable to the feeble-minded and to such other persons as have a mentality below whatever age may be agreed upon as the lower limit of normality.

It has been customary to speak of the various grades of intelligence as being ranged along an upward trending curve. On such a line, all below a certain established point could probably be designated subnormal. They comprise the group that has not developed to the required level. This is in line with the long established custom of describing the feeble-minded as cases of arrested mental development. The organism is normal and functions normally as far as it goes but its development has stopped too soon.

By etymology the abnormal person is the one that deviates from the normal line. To include all such deviates our upward curved line as a diagram of developing intelligence must be extended laterally to become a band or ribbon which can be divided lengthwise by a line separating the normal from the abnormal. Precisely where that dividing line is to be drawn it is not yet possible to say. So far as adults of normal level are concerned this is the old question of who is insane and who is not.

The new contribution to this problem is the discovery that children and persons of low mental level are as often abnormal as subnormal. In other words, our band or ribbon is divided lengthwise into the normal and abnormal and horizontally into the normal and subnormal. The lower part of our ribbon is subnormal and a section of that is both subnormal and abnormal. It is important to note that abnormality in this subnormal level may be the result of the deterioration of a mind originally normal, as well as of disease in a naturally subnormal mind. It is perhaps of some use to think of this division on the basis of structure and function as it seems to be largely such a matter. The subnormal person is one of incomplete structure; the abnormal is one of imperfect function.

If this view is accepted we should refer to the person whose mind is found to be *functioning* badly as abnormal. He might be either below, at or above the normal level.[1]

---

[1] Many former studies are worthless and the literature must always be carefully scrutinized before we can accept and apply the conclusions that may have been drawn from data that were assumed to be homogeneous but were not.

In the future, cases should be carefully examined for functional peculiarities before one can be sure that one is working with a homogeneous group.

Abnormal Psychology and Problems of Conduct

FLORENCE MATEER, *The Unstable Child*, 44, 50-54, 234 (Appleton, 1924)

So far, the whole tendency of clinical psychology has been to emphasize the spectacular problems which it has met. The lesser problems of the children in whom conditions have not gotten to a point where the abnormal tendencies completely overshadow the normal traits receive but little attention. It is these very cases on whom a brief period of helping means the most for recovery, and they are proportionately so numerous that their correction is important as being a definite benefit to the community. . . . A bright normal child is, if allowed natural development, a joy and pleasure. There is a definite group of children, however, who . . . develop peculiar ideas, monomanias, specialized fears, queer solitary habits, moody habits of introspection and analysis. For instance, a child of three and a half who could read Eugene Field and enjoy him, who wrote and spelled correctly any word he had ever seen, and who tested over six mentally, centered all his energy for months on the fear that the world supply of paper would give out before he grew up. Another child of five, testing nine, expressed all of his lack of desire to live, his cynical attitude, his depression, in chants such as,

> Life is a dark hole,
> Life is a dark hole.

In such cases, the multiplicity of symptoms of abnormal ways of thinking are often so great that there seems no possible hope for normal adult life. In the case of the three-and-a-half-year-old mentioned above a diagnosis of infantile insanity was made by a prominent alienist. No hope of recovery was given. To-day, at eleven and a half, the boy is to all practical purposes a boy like other boys, with his own maturity and widely-ranged interests unharmed and generalized past that baby stage where intelligence, unpropped by experience, threatened his normality and had actually stunted his body into extreme frailty.

How the one grew out of the other was a matter of psychological aid and specialized education. The diagnosis in itself would have misled. It was the concentration upon possible alleviation of the condition that solved the problem. . . .

A far more common problem, however, is the child who tests "at age," but who, nevertheless, cannot learn, cannot get on in school

and who often develops behavior difficulties about the same time
as his other inabilities are discovered. Such children have given
indications of the complexity of the problem from the very first
time a group of normal children were reëxamined on the Binet
Scale. . . . The child who now tests "at age" may have reached
the limit of his mental development. Next year may find him one
year retarded, the next two years, the next three years. He has run
true to what we know of the normal pattern for intelligence growth,
so far as he goes. In these children any diagnosis is absolutely a
matter of clinical refinement. "Potentially feeble-minded" is really
not a diagnosis only, but diagnosis (he is not inferior enough to
be called feeble-minded now) and prognosis (other findings indicate inability to progress much further). The very need for, and
formulation of, this term is sufficient proof of the inadequacy of
mental age as a diagnostic method and of the need for every possible
refinement in our testing methodology.

The writer can but reiterate an earlier conclusion:[1] . . .

.·. . At two an idiot, an imbecile, a moron, and a normal may all
seem practically the same. Then the idiot drops out of the race, stays
at that level. Somewhere, in the next four or five years the imbecile
falls behind, but the moron may be even ten or eleven before he
evidences any real deficiency on our present systems of tests. Yet
the difference has been there all along. The moron was as feeble-
minded, potentially, at the age of two, as at twelve. The normal
child was as surely normal. There is an innate difference hard to
describe but all who know defective and normal children often recognize this qualitative difference before any quantitative test has demonstrated its presence. It seems as though with some the evolutionary
nisus has spent itself with the effort necessary to bring into being,
with others there is no energy there to meet the demand for speech,
with others concrete stimuli can evoke satisfactory responses but
there is not enough motive power to meet the demand for response
to the faint stimulations made by abstract ideas, theories, principles,
etc. But the normal child is entirely different. He lives only as an
incarnation of activity. He is activity, innate, flooding, spilling with
every new stimulus, responding with growth to every new demand
made upon him.

But the mental-age relation to the diagnosis does not bear only
this single aspect of deviation. There is also the child who tests
below and who is nevertheless up to grade in school work. Nor

---

[1] Florence Mateer, "The Diagnostic Fallibility of Intelligence Ratios,"
Ped. Sem., Dec., 1918, 391.

does that end the problem. It is no uncommon thing to find a child who tests two, three, or more years below and who makes up part or even all of this retardation in a spectacular fashion when the cause for his retardation is even partially eliminated. How is one to tell when a child who is retarded needs the opportunity and will use it in recovery and when he has reached his ultimate intelligence height and is going to stay there? . . .

Closely related to this is the problem of the child whose mental age decreases. Clinic observation of this as an actual fact is a recent development. . . . A child may test two years now and one year in six months from now, or ten years now, when he is nine, ten when he is ten, and nine or eight or seven by the time another year or two have passed. Of course, such cases are rare, but they *do* occur and even if we found only one such instance it would be enough to upset any secure clinical applicability of mental-age findings in evolving prognoses. . . .

And then another problem confronts us, so-called child hysteria. Just how much variability the quims and quirks of a definite hysteria may cause in test findings, only research will enable us to state. It is highly probable that most of the children who test low but who seem comparatively normal in other ways may belong in this group. Is the hysteriac differentiated by mental age? Emphatically, no. Can he be distinguished by other psychological methods? Most certainly, yes.

Just what do all these problems mean for the future of clinical psychology, itself? . . .

We shall always have delinquency, delinquents, the necessity of handling them. The question is: Are we going to handle them as a logical result of our civilization and its imperfections, or are we going to lay the blame upon them, already the unfortunate ones? They are waste material. Have we not seen enough of the utilization of waste material in industrial fields to spur us on to the analysis and utilization of this most expensive of all waste material —human beings?

["No one of our findings is so important as the general discovery that the study of mental conflicts is a scientific method of approaching certain problems of misconduct, and that in this method lies the possibility of rendering great human service."—William Healy, *Mental Conflicts and Misconduct,* 325 (copyright, 1917, by Little, Brown & Co.).]

The Relation of Abnormal Psychology to Social Psychology

Editorial Announcement, *Jour. Abn. Psychol.*, 16: 1-4 (1921)

Interest in the subject of social psychology is rapidly growing, and there are many courses given in it in colleges throughout the country. It is doubtful whether this stage of interest and importance would have been attained but for the contemporary development of a sister science, abnormal psychology. . . .

In a broad sense the personality of the individual as one of the radiant points of social action offers a field for practical and theoretical investigation. . . . Our knowledge of the subject has been immeasurably broadened by contributions from abnormal psychology. The fears and obsessions, the unconscious mental processes, the disassociations, the persistence of infantile traits repressed or expressed, passivity and activity, relation to reality, balance and compensation in the emotional sphere, all make their appearance and play their part in normal human personality and the adjustments between the personality and the social order.

If we enter the sphere of more permanent social relations, the many adjustments of the human being to his social environment require an understanding of socio-psychological laws. The adjustments of husband and wife as well as those between parents and children bring us into close touch with contributions from the abnormal psychology of the Freudian school. In the social adjustments of deviating personalities abnormal concepts are also of great value. . . .

We may consider also larger and more permanent groups such as the caste, the professional society, the nation, and the race. To the study of such bodies sociology has heretofore given considerable attention. It is important however to have a psychological statement of nationality and "the national mind." The rôle of nations in peace and war, and the problems of a society or league of nations call for aid from the psychological student of these large units.[1] Biology and comparative methods are also brought to

---

[1] ["The world is only large enough to support a sane, productive population. (Alfred Korzybski, *Manhood of Humanity*, Dutton, 1921.)

"Man is a strange as well as an interesting animal; his behavior is a bundle of amazing paradoxes, a mixture of constructive and destructive tendencies. Extraordinarily boastful of possessing a more complicated and highly organized brain than any other animal, he is exceedingly reluctant to make intelligent efforts to learn how to use this superior organ. that is,

bear with social psychology in considering the differentiation, development, and improvement of racial stocks. We are led further in this direction to primitive society and the intricate relations of social and abnormal psychology to folk-lore, tradition, myth, and custom.

The Social and Economic Importance of Mental Diseases

JAMES V. MAY, *Mental Diseases*, 30-33, 188 (Badger, 1922)

Although the incidence of mental as compared with other diseases prevalent in the community cannot be established with absolute accuracy, sufficient evidence has been presented to warrant the statement that from the standpoint of the public health we are dealing with no other problem of equal importance today. The state care of mental defects, epilepsy, tuberculosis and the deaf, dumb and blind is, for various reasons, of much less consequence to the community than the hospital treatment of mental diseases. The defective, delinquent, criminal and dependent classes combined do not equal in number the population housed in our state hospitals for mental diseases. Nor does the number of cases cared for in the general hospitals of the state, county or municipal type compare in any way with the mental cases coming under state or federal supervision. It can, I think, be said without any fear of contradiction that no other disease or group of diseases is of equal importance from a social or economic point of view. Perhaps nothing emphasizes this fact more strongly than the report recently issued from the Surgeon General's office relative to the second examination of the first million recruits drafted in 1917. Twelve per cent of

---

to think and to act sanely. Quick to admit, when evidence is presented, that reasoning is a more complex process than is generally believed, he does not readily bestir himself to secure more definite information about the emotional and mental habits essential for reasoned living. Forced by the exigencies of war to realize that military efficiency and morale were seriously impaired by sending soldiers with poorly balanced brains and nervous systems to the front, he still ignores the unpleasant fact that unsoundness of mind in times of peace, the inability to reason correctly and to act intelligently in the presence of emergencies, is perhaps the greatest menace to an organized society. . . . Visions and plans for leagues to establish and maintain peace will not be as effective in preventing war as the dissemination of the right kind of knowledge in regard to the development and cultivation of sane and peaceful, as distinguished from insane and belligerent, attitudes of mind. . . ."—Stewart Paton, *Signs of Sanity*, 3-4, 6 (Scribner, 1922).]

these were rejected on account of nervous or mental diseases. The number disqualified for service finally reached a total of over sixty-seven thousand.[1]

Mental integrity is now looked upon as a military necessity and is insisted upon as one of the important requirements of the soldier. It has been demonstrated conclusively that only men of the most stable mental equilibrium can withstand the stress and strain of modern methods of warfare. Nor are peacetime requirements any less exacting. In commercial competition the law of the survival of the fittest is practically absolute. The feeble-minded often inherit wealth, but they rarely acquire it. Vaccination for the prevention of smallpox is compulsory and the isolation of communicable diseases dangerous to the public welfare is rigidly enforced. At the same time we allow many paranoiacs the freedom of the country and they occasionally assassinate a President. Psychopaths are not infrequently elected to public office and epileptics are not disqualified from driving high-powered and dangerous motor vehicles. The engineers of our fastest trains must not be color blind, but they occasionally are victims of the most fatal of all mental diseases,—general paresis. The navigating officer of a transatlantic liner, responsible for the lives of hundreds of passengers, must pass an examination for a license, but he may be dominated by delusions which escape observation because they are not looked for. Important trials, where human lives were at stake, have been presided over by insane judges. Army officers in command of troops in time of war have been influenced by imaginary voices. Insurance companies issue large policies to individuals suffering from incipient mental diseases which could be detected by even a superficial psychiatric examination.

Serious consideration should be given to the advisability of subjecting to a careful mental examination such persons, at least, as are to be charged with an entire responsibility for the lives of others. It is a question as to whether this procedure is not indicated in the case of other important public trusts where the interest of the community should be safeguarded.

The correlation of psychiatry and psychology as scientific aids

---

[1] ["Of all causes for rejections from the army up to February 1, 1919, according to Bailey, . . . mental and nervous diseases ranked fourth numerically. The 'neuropsychiatric' causes were:—psychoses, eleven per cent; neuroses, fifteen per cent; epilepsy, nine per cent; organic nervous diseases or injuries, eighteen per cent; mental defects, thirty-two per cent, and constitutional psychopathic states, nine per cent; a total of 67,417 cases."—*Ibid.*, 188.]

to industrial efficiency promises to open up entirely new and important sociological fields of research which have only recently attracted attention.[2] This is a subject of far reaching importance. The extent to which the industrial classes of the country are affected is shown by the following analysis of the occupations represented by 104,013 admissions to New York state hospitals: 1. Professional—(clergy, military and naval officers, physicians, lawyers, architects, artists, authors, civil engineers, surveyors, etc.) 1,926 or 1.8 per cent; 2. Commercial—(bankers, merchants, accountants, clerks, salesmen, shopkeepers, shopmen, stenographers, typewriters, etc.) 7,572 or 7.2 per cent; 3. Agricultural—(farmers, gardeners, etc.) 5,942 or 5.7 per cent; 4. Mechanics—at Outdoor Vocations—(blacksmiths, carpenters, enginefitters, sawyers, painters, etc.) 8,564 or 8.2 per cent; 5. Mechanics at Sedentary Vocations—(bootmakers, bookbinders, compositors, tailors, weavers, bakers, etc.) 7,501 or 7.2 per cent; 6. Domestic Service—(waiters, cooks, servants, etc.) 21,037 or 20.2 per cent; 7. Educational and Higher Domestic Duties—(governesses, teachers, students, housekeepers, nurses, etc.) 21,861 or 21 per cent; 8. Commercial—(shopkeepers, saleswomen, stenographers, typewriters, etc.) 1,140 or 1.09 per cent; 9. Employed at Sedentary Occupations—(tailoresses, seamstresses, bookbinders, factory workers, etc.) 4,310 or 4.1 per cent; 10. Miners, Seamen, etc., 581 or .56 per cent; 11. Prostitutes, 81 or .08 per cent; 12. Laborers, 12,962 or 12.4 per cent; No occupation, 7,820 or 7.5 per cent; Unascertained, 2,715 or 2.6 per cent.[3] This certainly indicates an enormous economic loss to the community.

The intimate relation between mental diseases, alcoholism, ignorance, poverty, prostitution, criminality, mental defects, etc., suggests social and economic problems of far reaching importance, each one meriting separate and special consideration. These problems, while perhaps essentially sociological in origin, have at the same time an important educational bearing, invade the realm of psychology and depend largely, if not entirely, upon psychiatry for a solution.

---

[2] Ball, Jau Don: The Correlation of Neurology, Psychiatry, Psychology and General Medicine as Scientific Aids to Industrial Efficiency. *Am. Jour. of Insan.*, April, 1919.

[3] Nineteenth Annual Report of the State Commission in Lunacy, N. Y., 1908.

The Cost of Insanity

E. STANLEY ABBOT; adapted from "Preventable Forms of Mental Disease and How to Prevent Them," *Boston Med. & Surg. Jour.*, 174: 555 (1916): with, however, later figures taken from bulletin of Nat. Com. Ment. Hyg., "Patients with Mental Diseases, etc., in Institutions in the United States," Jan. 1, 1920; and *Mental Hyg. Bull.*, June, 1925

Insanity is widespread. At the time of the last national census (1920) there were about the same number of insane in hospitals as there were students in the colleges and universities of the country.

The cost of caring for them was $75,000,000 a year. The economic loss due to their being unable to work was estimated at more than $300,000,000 annually. The sum of these would reach over $375,000,000.

In the United States in 1920 there were 232,680 insane persons in public or private hospitals. There must be some thousands of milder cases taken care of at home. About 75,000 cases are now admitted to hospitals annually.

These figures do not include the feeble-minded, of whom it is estimated that there were 40,519 in the United States in 1920. Nor do they include the inebriates and epileptics.

The Need for Mental Hygiene

AUSTEN FOX RIGGS, "The Psychoneuroses: Their Nature and Treatment," *Am. Jour. Psychiat.*, 108-109 (July, 1923)

When one realizes that at present [1923] in the United States there are *more* hospital beds occupied by diseases and disorders of the central nervous system than by all other diseases combined; and when one holds up this crying need, this tremendous financial and social wastage, to the great possibility of preventing, through the timely application of knowledge, a great majority of all of these diseases and disorders, one cannot fail to get at least a preliminary realization of the practicability of the principles of mental hygiene and the enormous importance of broadcasting its knowledge. Mental hygiene societies are springing up in many states, and this year what promises to be a nation-wide educational movement of immense importance and value has begun. As citizens as well as physicians we owe this crusade against ignorance and prejudice our best support, and as physicians we should be the very first group to become educated. To those of us particularly interested in the Psychoneuroses mental hygiene holds out the highest hope; for early recognition in childhood of the elements making for nervousness is fully possible and when parents are educated to recognize these elements and adopt the proper methods of training the neurotic liabilities of these children, I believe then future breakdowns will be avoided. This, however, is only *one* of the great educational possibilities of mental hygiene.

Interesting in connection with this chapter is Professor Donald A. Laird's study of laymen's conceptions and misconceptions of phenomena of abnormal psychology, as described in "The Duty of the Psychopathologist to the Man on the Street" (*cf.* Bibliography).

CHAPTER II

NOMENCLATURE, CLASSIFICATION, AND DIAGNOSIS

General Symptomatology

[William A. White]

When we come to survey the aberrations of mental processes, we find distortions of all the functions of receiving impressions, recalling them, elaborating upon them, and responding in any of the ways of emotion, affection, or overt action. In Dr. William A. White's *Outlines of Psychiatry*, e. g., we find a presentation of the following topics: *Sensory anomalies* (anesthesia, hyperesthesia, paresthesia); *disorders of attention* (aprosexia or enfeeblement of the power of voluntary attention, and hyperprosexia in "which the attention of the patient is completely absorbed by some thoughts"); *disorders of perception,* including illusions, hallucinations of various types (pseudo-, hypnagogic, auditory, visual, kinesthetic, etc.), clouding of consciousness ("in any degree, from a scarcely noticeable departure from clear consciousness to actual coma"), dream states, and disorientation; *disorders of memory* (amnesia, hypermnesia, and paramnesia); *disorders of the content of thought,* including delusions (fixed, changeable, systematized, unsystematized, endogenous, and exogenous), fixed ideas, obsessions, and autochthonous ideas; *complexes; dreams; disorders of the train of thought* (flight of ideas, circumstantiality, retardation, and paralysis of thought); *Ganser's symptom,* "or, as it has been called, the symptom of approximate answers" to, for example, simple arithmetical questions; *disorders of feeling and emotion* (exaltation, depression, emotional deterioration, morbid anger); *disorders of action,*—decreased psychomotor activity, increased psychomotor activity, impulsions (including "the so-called manias, such as kleptomania or morbid impulse to steal, pyromania or morbid impulse to set things on fire, dipsomania or impulse to drink, etc."), compulsions, stereotypies (of attitude, movement, and speech), negativism, motor suggestibility, and psychomotor inhibition; and *disorders of personality* (transformation of the personality, depersonalization, and multiple personality). These topics are also given fairly detailed treatment in Dr. Aaron J. Rosanoff's *Manual of Psychiatry* [1] and in similar works. A most convenient marshalling of descriptive definitions of the phenomena is provided by Prof. J. W. Bridges in his *Outline of Abnormal Psychology*.

The Problem of Classification

[WILLIAM A. WHITE; C. B. BURR]

When the question of the *classification* of the different psychoses is approached, as Dr. White remarks,[2]

a condition of affairs is found which leaves much to be desired. . . .

It is true that the symptoms of mental disorder tend to arrange themselves into groups, but the constancy of these groups is a very variable factor, and like the epileptologist who no longer speaks of epilepsy as a concrete entity but speaks rather of the epilepsies, so we are getting away from the idea of distinct, definite psychoses and are using such terms as the dementia paralytica group, the manic-depressive group, the hysteria group, etc.

These groups, the so-called types, are not clean-cut entities but are only groups of symptoms which either seem to occur more frequently in combination or else have been more definitely and clearly seen because of the nature of that combination. In fact classical types as such may be said to be in the minority. The mass of cases seen are combinations more or less intermediate in character. The conception of types in order to be accurate must be from a broad biological viewpoint. Types are like species. They have innumerable transition and intermediate forms. It is as if overlooking a vast though young forest. Here and there are certain trees which because of their size or prominent location stand out distinct from the others. These would at once be picked out by

[1] 19-75.
[2] William A. White, *Outlines of Psychiatry*, 8th ed., 24-26 (Nervous & Mental Diseases Publishing Co., 1921).

the observer of types, yet the forest as a whole is not composed of these but of the immense number of smaller trees among which these few stand out definitely, and a more detailed study of the majority of the trees of approximately the same size would reveal minor differences of structure; for example, in the form of leaf, thickness of bark, inclination of branches, color of flowers, etc., many of which might only serve to distinguish the individuals, while others would be of sufficient importance to constitute varieties, or even species. . . .

As a matter of fact our knowledge of the psychoses is altogether too limited at present to justify the expectation that the problem of classification can be solved. Any attempt at grouping mental disorders under separate heads must now, as always, be but tentative and incomplete. Classifications grow with changing concepts. . . .

Dr. C. B. Burr remarks [1] that

the names commonly employed in the classification of mental disease chiefly stand for groups of *symptoms: Mania* being a Greek word, meaning furor; *Dementia* being derived from two Latin words: *de,* without, and *mens,* the mind; *Paranoia,* from Greek words *para,* defective, and *nous,* understanding. One notable exception is in the name *Melancholia,* which comes from two Greek words meaning "black bile," it being supposed by the ancients that this affection was incident to disorder of the liver.

The classification of insanity and the study of insane conditions have undergone modifications almost revolutionary in very recent years. The former division of insane conditions into *States of Mental Elation, States of Mental Depression,* and *Structural Brain Disease with Prominent Mental Manifestations,* is generally regarded as inadequate for clinical study. The so-called states of mental elation and states of mental depression are now considered under the head of manic-depressive insanity, the terms mania, hypomania, delirious mania, etc., being employed to indicate the symptoms in existence during the excited periods; "depressive states" and "apathetic states" being used to designate the condition in depressed periods heretofore described as melancholia, and the term melancholia limited in its application to mental depression occurring in the senile or presenile (involutional) period of life. Terminal dementia and dementia following acute forms heretofore

---

[1] *Practical Psychology and Psychiatry,* 5th ed., 74-76 (Davis, 1921).

designated as chronic dementia, dementia after mania, and dementia after melancholia are no longer admitted as entities in classification, those cases of insanity heretofore studied under the latter heads being relegated to other groups. This reformation in classification has been due to the recognition of a state underlying the morbid nervous processes of which so-called mania, melancholia and dementia are the expression, namely, the neuropathic organization. Under the old classification embarrassment was frequently encountered in clinical study because of the mixed manifestations in the so-called acute forms of disease, the maniacal patient being rarely consistently maniacal and showing an exalted state of the emotions, the depressed patient displaying from time to time fluctuations in the emotional states to an extent incompatible with the grouping of symptoms under states of emotional depression. Further, the so-called recurrent mania (*folie circulaire*) presented the picture of alternating states of elation and depression with or without intervals of lucidity, the pendulum at one time swinging over to lowered emotional tone, then to the other extreme. These clinical facts led to the study of the manic-depressive insanities under the one head, and the essential unity of so-called mania and melancholia is now generally recognized. Simultaneously with the disappearance of these forms of disease as clinical entities, there was brought forth a name under which is included certain conditions of psychical degeneration displaying by turns the symptoms of mania and melancholia, of stupor and of dementia. Its existence is regarded as marking psychical degeneration from the beginning. It is the so-called dementia præcox. . . .

Classification and Descriptions of Mental Diseases

American Psychiatric Association, "Statistical Manual for the Use of Hospitals for Mental Diseases," 3rd ed., 3-4, 16-37

This is the official classification as adopted and amended by the American Psychiatric Association.[1] Explanatory notes of the various clinical groups and types follow the classification.

---

[1] [As the "Foreword" to the "Statistical Manual" explains:

"The American Medico-Psychological Association (now the American Psychiatric Association) at its annual meeting in New York, in May, 1917, adopted the report of its Committee on Statistics, which outlined a uniform classification of mental diseases and a system of statistics for hospitals for mental diseases. A standing Committee on Statistics was appointed by the Association to promote the introduction of the system

1. *Traumatic psychoses*
2. *Senile psychoses*
3. *Psychoses with cerebral arteriosclerosis*
4. *General paralysis*
5. *Psychoses with cerebral syphilis*
6. *Psychoses with Huntington's chorea*
7. *Psychoses with brain tumor*
8. *Psychoses with other brain or nervous diseases*

    (a) Cerebral embolism
    (b) Paralysis agitans
    (c) Meningitis, tubercular or other forms (to be specified)
    (d) Multiple sclerosis
    (e) Tabes dorsalis
    (f) Acute chorea
    (g) Encephalitis lethargica
    (h) Other diseases (to be specified)

9. *Alcoholic psychoses*

    (a) Delirium tremens
    (b) Korsakow's psychosis
    (c) Acute hallucinosis
    (d) Other types, acute or chronic

---

throughout the country. This committee met in New York City on February 7, 1918, and in cooperation with the National Committee for Mental Hygiene outlined a plan of procedure. As close relationships have always existed between the Association and the National Committee for Mental Hygiene, it was thought wise for the Committee on Statistics to become an advisory committee to the Bureau of Statistics of the National Committee, and to have the work of introducing the new system and of collecting statistics from the hospitals carried out by the Bureau.

"Since that time the classification has been submitted to all of the state hospitals and to other public and private institutions for mental diseases, and two editions of this manual and the eighteen standard tabular forms adopted by the Association have been prepared and distributed. In response to requests received from many superintendents, the series of schedule cards outlined in this pamphlet (pages 9-13) were printed and have been furnished at cost to institutions desiring them. The funds to carry on this work have been provided by a special appropriation from the Rockefeller Foundation.

"The classification and the uniform statistical system have met with general approval and have been adopted by nearly all of the state hospitals and by many other public and private hospitals. The demand for the manual has been so great that a third edition has now become necessary. This revision is essentially the same as the second edition, but the instructions have been slightly modified to correspond with changes in the clas-

10. *Psychoses due to drugs and other exogenous toxins*

  (a) Opium (and derivatives), cocaine, bromides, chloral, etc., alone or combined (to be specified)
  (b) Metals, as lead, arsenic, etc. (to be specified)
  (c) Gases (to be specified)
  (d) Other exogenous toxins (to be specified)

11. *Psychoses with pellagra*

12. *Psychoses with other somatic diseases*

  (a) Delirium with infectious diseases
  (b) Post-infectious psychosis
  (c) Exhaustion delirium
  (d) Delirium of unknown origin
  (e) Cardio-renal diseases
  (f) Diseases of the ductless glands
  (g) Other diseases or conditions (to be specified)

13. *Manic-depressive psychoses*

  (a) Manic type
  (b) Depressive type
  (c) Other types

---

sification. Although such changes do not affect the principal clinical groups, some of the controverted types have been omitted.

"The Committee wishes to renew its former recommendations that much care should be exercised in compiling statistics in the several hospitals and that the suggestions in this manual should be closely followed. In this way accurate, nation-wide information concerning mental diseases and the operations of hospitals for their treatment can be made available to supervisory boards, managers and superintendents and to other persons interested in hospital management and in the scientific study of mental disorders.

JAMES V. MAY, *Chairman*
E. STANLEY ABBOT
ALBERT M. BARRETT
C. MACFIE CAMPBELL
OWEN COPP
GEORGE H. KIRBY
SAMUEL T. ORTON
FRANKWOOD E. WILLIAMS
  Committee on Statistics, American Psychiatric Association

THOMAS W. SALMON
EDITH M. FURBUSH
HORATIO M. POLLOCK
  For *The National Committee for Mental Hygiene*"]

14. *Involution melancholia*

15. *Dementia præcox (schizophrenia)*

16. *Paranoia or paranoid conditions*

17. *Epileptic psychoses*

18. *Psychoneuroses and neuroses*

    (a) Hysterical type
    (b) Psychasthenic type (anxiety and obsessive forms)
    (c) Neurasthenic type
    (d) Other types

19. *Psychoses with psychopathic personality*

20. *Psychoses with mental deficiency*

21. *Undiagnosed psychoses*

22. *Without psychosis*

    (a) Epilepsy without psychosis
    (b) Alcoholism without psychosis
    (c) Drug addiction without psychosis
    (d) Psychopathic personality without psychosis
    (e) Mental deficiency without psychosis
    (f) Others (to be specified)

DEFINITIONS AND EXPLANATORY NOTES

The following explanatory notes and definitions of the various clinical groups [1] were prepared for the Committee by Dr. George H. Kirby, Director, Psychiatric Institute, Ward's Island, New York City.

1. *Traumatic psychoses*

The diagnosis should be restricted to mental disorders arising as a direct or obvious consequence of a brain (or head) injury producing psychotic symptoms of a fairly characteristic kind. The amount of damage to the brain may vary from an extensive destruction of tissue to simple concussion or physical shock with or without fracture of the skull.

Manic-depressive psychoses, general paralysis, dementia præcox,

---

[1] [For historical discussions of these concepts, with statistics, *cf.* James V. May, *Mental Diseases*, 273-536.]

and other mental disorders in which trauma may act as a contributory or precipitating cause, should not be included in this group.

The following are the most common clinical types of traumatic psychosis and may be specified in the diagnostic grouping.

Traumatic delirium: This may take the form of an acute delirium (concussion delirium), or a more protracted delirium resembling the Korsakow mental complex.

Traumatic constitution: Characterized by a gradual post-traumatic change in disposition with vasomotor instability, headaches, fatigability, irritability or explosive emotional reactions; usually hyper-sensitiveness to alcohol, and in some cases development of paranoid, hysteroid, or epileptoid symptoms.

Post-traumatic mental enfeeblement (dementia): Varying degrees of mental reduction with or without aphasic symptoms, epileptiform attacks or development of a cerebral arteriosclerosis.

2. *Senile psychoses*

A well defined type of psychosis which as a rule develops gradually and is characterized by the following symptoms: Impairment of retention (forgetfulness) and general failure of memory more marked for recent experiences; defects in orientation and a general reduction of mental capacity; the attention, concentration and thinking processes are interfered with; there is self-centering of interests, often irritability and stubborn opposition; a tendency to reminiscences and fabrications. Accompanying this deterioration there may occur paranoid trends, depressions, confused states, etc. The following clinical types may be recognized, but these often overlap.

Simple deterioration: Retention and memory defects, reduction in intellectual capacity and narrowing of interests; usually also suspiciousness, irritability and restlessness, the latter particularly at night.

Presbyophrenic type: Severe memory and retention defects with complete disorientation; but at the same time preservation of mental alertness and attentiveness with ability to grasp immediate impressions and conversation quite well. Forgetfulness leads to absurd contradictions and repetitions; suggestibility and free fabrication are prominent symptoms. (The general picture resembles the Korsakow mental complex.)

Delirious and confused types: Often in the early stages of the psychosis and for a long period the picture is one of deep confusion or of a delirious condition.

Depressed and agitated types: In addition to the underlying deterioration there may be a pronounced depression and persistent agitation.

Paranoid types: Well marked delusional trends, chiefly persecutory or expansive ideas, often accompany the deterioration and in the early stages may make the diagnosis difficult if the defect symptoms are mild.

Pre-senile type: This so-called "Alzheimer's disease" is an early senile deterioration which usually leads rapidly to a deep dementia. It is reported to occur as early as the fortieth year. Most cases show an irritable or anxious depressive mood with aphasic or apractic symptoms. There is apt to be general resistiveness and sometimes spasticity.

3. *Psychoses with cerebral arteriosclerosis*

The clinical symptoms, both mental and physical, are varied depending in the first place on the distribution and severity of the vascular cerebral disease and probably to some extent on the mental make-up of the person.

Cerebral physical symptoms, headaches, dizziness, fainting attacks, etc., are nearly always present, and usually signs of focal brain disease appear sooner or later (aphasia, paralysis, etc.).

The most important mental symptoms (particularly if the arteriosclerotic disease is diffuse) are impairment of mental tension, i.e., interference with the capacity to think quickly and accurately, to concentrate and to fix the attention; fatigability and lack of emotional control (alternate weeping and laughing), often a tendency to irritability is marked; the retention is impaired and with it there is more or less general defect of memory, especially in the advanced stages of the disease, or after some large destructive lesion occurs.

Pronounced psychotic symptoms may appear in the form of depression (often of the anxious type), suspicions or paranoid ideas, or episodes of marked confusion.

To be included in this group are the psychoses following cerebral softening or hemorrhage, if due to arterial disease. (Autopsies in state hospitals show that in arteriosclerotic cases softening is relatively much more frequent than hemorrhage.)

Differentiation from senile psychosis is sometimes difficult, particularly if the arteriosclerotic disease manifests itself in the senile period. The two conditions may be associated; when this happens preference should be given in the statistical report to the arteriosclerotic disorder.

High blood pressure, although usually present, is not essential for the diagnosis of cerebral arteriosclerosis.

4. General paralysis

The range of symptoms encountered in general paralysis is too great to be reviewed here in detail. As to mental symptoms, most stress should be laid on the early changes in disposition and character, judgment defects, difficulty about time relations and discrepancies in statements, forgetfulness and later on a diffuse memory impairment. Cases with marked grandiose trends are less likely to be overlooked than cases with depressions, paranoid ideas, alcoholic-like episodes, etc.

Mistakes of diagnosis are most apt to be made in those cases having in the early stages pronounced psychotic symptoms and relatively slight defect symptoms, or in cases with few definite physical signs. Lumbar puncture should always be made if there is any doubt about the diagnosis. A Wassermann examination of the blood alone is not sufficient, as this does not tell us whether or not the central nervous system is involved.

5. Psychoses with cerebral syphilis

Since general paralysis itself is now known to be a parenchymatous form of brain syphilis, the differentiation of the cerebral syphilis cases might on theoretical grounds be regarded as less important than formerly. Practically, however, the separation of the non-parenchymatous forms is very important because the symptoms, the course and therapeutic outlook in most of these cases are different from those of general paralysis.

According to the predominant pathological characteristics, three types of cerebral syphilis may be distinguished, viz.: (a) meningitic, (b) endarteritic, and (c) gummatous. The lines of demarcation between these types are not, however, sharp ones. We practically always find in the endarteritic and gummatous types a certain amount of meningitis.

The acute meningitic form is the most frequent type of cerebral syphilis and gives little trouble in diagnosis; many of these cases do not reach state hospitals. In most cases after prodromal symptoms (headache, dizziness, etc.) there is a rapid development of physical signs, usually cranial nerve involvement, and a mental picture of dullness or confusion with few psychotic symptoms except those related to a delirious or organic reaction.

In the rarer chronic meningitic forms which are apt to occur a long time after the syphilitic infection, usually in the period in which we might expect general paralysis, the diagnostic difficulties may be considerable.

In the endarteritic forms the most characteristic symptoms are those resulting from focal vascular lesions.

In the gummatous forms the slowly developing focal and pressure symptoms are most significant.

In all forms of cerebral syphilis the psychotic manifestations are less prominent than in general paralysis and the personality is much better preserved as shown by the social reactions, ethical sense, judgment and general behavior. The grandiose ideas and absurd trends of the general paralytic are rarely encountered in these cases.

6. *Psychoses with Huntington's chorea*

Mental symptoms are a constant accompaniment of this form of chorea and as a rule become more marked as the disease advances. Although the disease is regarded as being hereditary in nature, a diagnosis can be made on the clinical picture in the absence of a family history.

The chief mental symptoms are those of mental inertia and an emotional change, either apathy and silliness or a depressive irritable reaction with a tendency to passionate outbursts. As the disease progresses the memory is affected to some extent, but the patient's ability to recall past events is often found to be surprisingly well preserved, when the disinclination to cooperate and give information can be overcome. Likewise the orientation is well retained even when the patient appears very apathetic and listless. Suspicions and paranoid ideas are prominent in some cases.

7. *Psychoses with brain tumor*

A large majority of brain tumor cases show definite mental symptoms. Most frequent are mental dullness, somnolence, hebetude, slowness in thinking, memory failure, irritability and depression, although a tendency to facetiousness is sometimes observed. Episodes of confusion with hallucinations are common; some cases express suspicions and paranoid ideas.

The diagnosis must rest in most cases on the neurological symptoms, and these will depend on the location, size and rate of growth of the tumor. Certain general physical symptoms due to an increased intra-cranial pressure are present in most cases, viz.: headache, dizziness, vomiting, slowing of the pulse, choked disc and interlacing of the color fields.

8. *Psychoses with other brain or nervous diseases*

This division provides a place for grouping a variety of less common mental disorders associated with organic disease of the nervous system and not included in the preceding larger groups. On the card the special type of brain or nervous diseases should be mentioned after the group name. The following are the diseases most frequently met with:

(a) Cerebral embolism (if an incident in cerebral arteriosclerosis it should be placed in group 3)

(b) Paralysis agitans

(c) Meningitis, tubercular or other forms (to be specified)

(d) Multiple sclerosis

(e) Tabes dorsalis (paresis to be carefully excluded)

(f) Acute chorea (Sydenham's type). Hysterical chorea to be excluded

(g) Encephalitis lethargica

(h) Other diseases (to be specified).

9. *Alcoholic psychoses*

The diagnosis of alcoholic psychosis should be restricted to those mental disorders arising, with few exceptions, in connection with *chronic* drinking and presenting fairly well defined symptom-pictures. One must guard against making the alcoholic group too inclusive. Over-indulgence in alcohol is often found to be merely a symptom of another psychosis, or at any rate may be incidental to another psychosis, such as general paralysis, manic-depressive insanity, dementia præcox, epilepsy, etc. The cases to be regarded as alcoholic psychoses which do not result from chronic drinking are the episodic attacks in some psychopathic personalities, the dipsomanias (the true periodic drinkers) and pathological intoxication, any one of which may develop as the result of a single imbibition or a relatively short spree.

The following alcoholic reactions usually present symptoms distinctive enough to allow of clinical differentiation and should be specified in the statistical report.

(a) *Delirium tremens:* An hallucinatory delirium with marked general tremor and toxic symptoms.

(b) *Korsakow's psychosis:* This occurs with or without polyneuritis. The delirious type is not readily differentiated in the early stages from severe delirium tremens, but is more protracted. The non-delirious type presents a characteristic retention defect with disorientation, fabrication, suggestibility and tendency to misidentify persons. Hallucinations are infrequent after the acute phase.

(c) *Acute hallucinosis:* This is chiefly an auditory hallucinosis of rapid development with clearness of the sensorium, marked fears, and a more or less systematized persecutory trend.

(d) *Other types, acute or chronic* (to be specified).

10. *Psychoses due to drugs and other exogenous toxins*

The clinical pictures produced by drugs and other exogenous poisons are principally deliria or states of confusion; although sometimes hallucinatory and paranoid reactions are met with. Certain poisons and gases apparently produce special symptoms, e. g., cocaine, lead, illuminating gas, etc. Grouped according to the toxic etiological factors the following are to be differentiated:

(a) Opium (and derivatives), cocaine, bromides, chloral, etc., alone or combined (to be specified)

(b) Metals, as arsenic, lead, etc. (to be specified)

(c) Gases (to be specified)

(d) Other exogenous toxins (to be specified).

11. *Psychoses with pellagra*

The relation which various mental disturbances bear to the disease pellagra is not yet settled. Cases of pellagra occurring during the course of a well established mental disease such as dementia præcox, manic-depressive insanity, senile dementia, etc., should not be included in this group. The mental disturbances which are apparently most intimately connected with pellagra are certain delirious or confused states (toxic-organic-like reactions) arising during the course of a severe pellagra. These are the cases which for the present should be placed in the group of psychoses with pellagra.

12. *Psychoses with other somatic diseases*

Under this heading are brought together those mental disorders which appear to depend directly upon some physical disturbance or somatic disease not already provided for in the foregoing groups. In the types designated below under (a) to (e) inclusive, we have essentially deliria or states of confusion arising during the course of an infectious disease or in association with a condition of exhaustion or a toxæmia. The mental disturbance is apparently the result of interference with brain nutrition or the unfavorable action of certain deleterious substances, poisons or toxins, on the central nervous system. The clinical pictures met with are extremely varied. The delirium may be marked by severe motor excitement and incoherence of utterance, or by multiform hallucinations with deep confusion or a dazed, bewildered condition; epileptiform attacks, catatonic-like symptoms, stupor, etc., may occur. In classifying these psychoses a difficult problem arises in many cases if attempts are made to distinguish between infection and exhaustion as etiological factors. For statistical reports the following differentiations should be made:

Under (a) "Delirium with infectious diseases" place the *initial deliria* which develop during the prodromal or incubation period or before the febrile stage as in some cases of typhoid, small-pox, malaria, etc.; the *febrile deliria* which seem to bear a definite relation to the rise in temperature; the *post-febrile deliria* of the period of defervescence including the so-called "collapse delirium."

Under (b) "Post-infectious psychoses" are to be grouped deliria, the mild forms of mental confusion, or the depressive, irritable, suspicious reactions which occur during the period of convalescence from infectious diseases. Physical asthenia and prostration are undoubtedly important factors in these conditions and differentiation from "exhaustion deliria" must depend chiefly on the history and obvious close relationship to the preceding infectious disease. (Some cases which fail to recover show a peculiar mental enfeeblement.) In this group should be classed the "cerebropathica psychica toxæmica" or the non-alcoholic polyneuritic psychoses following an infectious disease as typhoid, influenza, septicæmia, etc.

Under (c) "Exhaustion deliria" are to be classed psychoses in which physical exhaustion, not associated with or the result of an infectious disease, is the chief precipitating cause of the mental disorder, e. g., hemorrhage, severe physical over-exertion, deprivation of food, prolonged insomnia, debility from wasting disease, etc.

Of the psychoses which occur with diseases of the ductless glands, the best known are the thyroigenous mental disorders. Disturbance of the pituitary or of the adrenal function is often associated with mental symptoms.

According to the etiology and symptoms the following types should therefore be specified under "Psychoses with Other Somatic Diseases":

(a) Delirium with infectious disease (to be specified)
(b) Post-infectious psychosis (to be specified)
(c) Exhaustion delirium
(d) Delirium of unknown origin
(e) Cardio-renal disease

(f) Diseases of the ductless glands (to be specified)

(g) Other diseases or conditions (to be specified).

13. *Manic-depressive psychoses*

This group comprises the essentially benign affective psychoses, mental disorders which fundamentally are marked by emotional oscillations and a tendency to recurrence. Various psychotic trends, delusions, illusions and hallucinations, clouded states, stupor, etc., may be added. To be distinguished are:

The *manic* reaction with its feeling of well-being (or irascibility), flight of ideas and over-activity.

The *depressive* reaction with its feeling of mental and physical insufficiency, a despondent, sad or hopeless mood, and in severe depressions, retardation and inhibition; in some cases the mood is one of uneasiness and anxiety, accompanied by restlessness.

The *mixed* reaction, a combination of manic and depressive symptoms.

The *stupor* reaction with its marked reduction in activity, depression, ideas of death, and often dream-like hallucinations; sometimes mutism, drooling and muscular symptoms suggestive of the catatonic manifestations of dementia præcox, from which, however, these manic-depressive stupors are to be differentiated.

An attack is called *circular* when, as is often the case, one phase is followed immediately by another phase, e. g., a manic reaction passes over into a depressive reaction or vice versa.

Cases formerly classed as allied to manic-depressive should be placed here rather than in the undiagnosed group.

In the statistical reports the following should be specified:

(a) Manic type

(b) Depressive type

(c) Other types.

14. *Involution melancholia*

These depressions are probably related to the manic-depressive group; nevertheless the symptoms and the course of the involution cases are sufficiently characteristic to justify us in keeping them apart as special forms of emotional reaction.

To be included here are the slowly developing depressions of *middle life and later years* which come on with worry, insomnia, uneasiness, anxiety and agitation, showing usually the unreality and sensory complex, but little or no evidence of any difficulty in thinking. The tendency is for the course to be a prolonged one. Arteriosclerotic depressions should be excluded.

When agitated depressions of the involution period are clearly superimposed on a manic-depressive foundation with previous attacks (depression or excitement), they should for statistical purposes be classed in the manic-depressive group.

15. *Dementia præcox (schizophrenia)*

This group cannot be satisfactorily defined at the present time as there are still too many points at issue as to what constitute the essential clinical features of dementia præcox. A large majority of the cases which should go into this group may, however, be recognized without special difficulty, although there is an important smaller group of doubtful, atypical, allied or transitional cases which from the standpoint of symptoms or prognosis occupy an uncertain clinical position.

Cases formerly classed as allied to dementia præcox should be placed here rather than in the undiagnosed group. The term "schizophrenia" is now used by many writers instead of dementia præcox.

The following mentioned features are sufficiently well established to be considered most characteristic of the dementia præcox type of reaction:

A seclusive type of personality or one showing other evidences of abnormality in the development of the instincts and feelings.

Appearance of defects of interest and discrepancies between thought on the one hand and the behavior-emotional reactions on the other.

A gradual blunting of the emotions, indifference or silliness with serious defects of judgment and often hypochondriacal complaints, suspicions or ideas of reference.

Development of peculiar trends, often fantastic ideas, with odd, impulsive or negativistic conduct not accounted for by any acute emotional disturbance or impairment of the sensorium.

Appearance of autistic thinking and dream-like ideas, peculiar feelings of being forced, of interference with the mind, of physical or mystical influences, but with retention of clearness in other fields (orientation, memory, etc.).

According to the prominence of certain symptoms in individual cases the following four clinical forms of dementia præcox are usually differentiated, but it should be borne in mind that these are only relative distinctions and that transitions from one clinical form to another are so common that satisfactory statistics can hardly be collected regarding these clinical types.

Paranoid type: Cases characterized by a prominence of delu sions, particularly ideas of persecution or grandeur, often connectedly elaborated, and hallucinations in various fields.

Catatonic type: Cases in which there is a prominence of negativistic reactions or various peculiarities of conduct with phases of stupor or excitement, the latter characterized by impulsive, queer or stereotyped behavior and usually hallucinations.

Hebephrenic type: Cases showing prominently a tendency to silliness, smiling, laughter, grimacing, mannerisms in speech and action, and numerous peculiar ideas usually absurd, grotesque and changeable in form.

Simple type: Cases characterized by defects of interest, gradual development of an apathetic state, often with peculiar behavior, but without expression of delusions or hallucinations.

16. *Paranoia or paranoid conditions*

From this group should be excluded the deteriorating paranoid states and paranoid states symptomatic of other mental disorders or of some damaging factor such as alcohol, organic brain disease, etc.

The group comprises cases which show clinically fixed suspicions, persecutory delusions, dominant ideas or grandiose trends logically elaborated and with due regard for reality after once a false interpretation or premise has been accepted. Further characteristics are formally correct conduct, adequate emotional reactions, clearness and coherence of the train of thought.

17. *Epileptic psychoses*

In addition to the epileptic deterioration, transitory psychoses may occur which are usually characterized by a clouded mental state followed by an amnesia for external occurrences during the attack. (The hallucinatory and dream-like experiences of the patient during the attack may be vividly recalled.) Various automatic and secondary states of consciousness may occur.

According to the most prominent clinical features the epileptic mental disorders may therefore be specified as follows:

Epileptic deterioration: A gradual development of mental dullness, slowness of association and thinking, impairment of memory, irritability or apathy.

Epileptic clouded states: Usually in the form of dazed reactions with deep confusion, bewilderment and anxiety or excitements with hallucinations, fears and violent outbreaks; instead of fear there may be ecstatic moods with religious exaltation.

Other epileptic types.

18. *Psychoneuroses and neuroses*

The psychoneurosis group includes those disorders in which mental forces or ideas of which the subject is either aware (conscious) or unaware (unconscious) bring about various mental and physical symptoms; in other words, these disorders are essentially psychogenic in nature.

The term neurosis is now generally used synonymously with psychoneurosis, although it has been applied to certain disorders in which, while the symptoms are both mental and physical, the primary cause is thought to be essentially physical. In most instances, however, both psychogenic and physical causes are operative and we can assign only a relative weight to the one or the other.

The following types are sufficiently well defined clinically to be specified in the statistical report.

(*a*) *Hysterical type:* Episodic mental attacks in the form of delirium, stupor or dream states during which repressed wishes, mental conflicts or emotional experiences detached from ordinary consciousness break through and temporarily dominate the mind. The attack is followed by partial or complete amnesia. Various physical disturbances (sensory and motor) occur in hysteria, and these represent a conversion of the affect of the repressed disturbing complexes into bodily symptoms or, according to another formulation, there is a dissociation of consciousness relating to some physical function.

(*b*) *Psychasthenic type:* This includes the anxiety and obsessional neuroses of some writers. The main clinical characteristics are morbid fears or phobias, obsessions, doubts and impulsions, feelings of insufficiency, nervous tension and anxiety. Episodes of marked depression and agitation may occur. There is no disturbance of consciousness or amnesia as in hysteria.

(*c*) *Neurasthenic type:* This should designate the fatigue neuroses in which physical as well as mental causes evidently figure; characterized essentially by mental and motor fatigability and irritability; also various hyperæsthesias and paræsthesias; hypochondriasis and varying degrees of depression.

(*d*) *Other types.*

19. *Psychoses with psychopathic personality*

Under the designation of psychopathic personality is brought together a large group of pathological personalities whose abnormality of make-up is expressed mainly in the character and intensity of their emotional and volitional reactions. To meet the demands of current usage, the term for this group has been short-ened from the older one "psychoses with constitutional psychopathic inferiority" with which it is synonymous. Individuals with an intellectual defect (feeblemindedness) are not to be included in this group.

Several of the preceding groups, in fact all of the so-called con-stitutional psychoses, manic-depressive, dementia præcox, paranoia, psychoneuroses, etc., may be considered as arising on a basis of, psychopathic inferiority or constitution, because the previous men-tal make-up in these conditions shows more or less clearly abnor-malities in the emotional and volitional spheres. These reactions are apparently related to special forms of psychopathic make-up now fairly well differentiated, and the associated psychoses also have their own distinctive features.

There remain, however, various other less well differentiated types of psychopathic personalities, and in these the psychotic re-actions (psychoses) also differ from those already specified in the preceding groups.

It is these less well differentiated types of emotional and voli-tional deviations which are to be designated, at least for statistical purposes, as psychopathic personality. The type of behavior dis-order, the social reactions, the trends of interests, etc., which psychopathic personalities may show, give special features to many cases, e. g., criminal traits, moral deficiency, tramp life, sexual perversions and various temperamental peculiarities.

The pronounced mental disturbances or psychoses which develop in psychopathic personalities and bring about their commitment are varied in their clinical form and are usually of an episodic character. Most frequent are attacks of irritability, excitement, depression, paranoid episodes, transient confused states, etc. True prison psychoses belong in this group.

In accordance with the standpoint developed above, a psycho-pathic personality with a manic-depressive attack should be classed in the manic-depressive group, and likewise a psychopathic person-ality with a schizophrenic psychosis should go in the dementia præcox group.

Psychopathic personalities without an episodic mental attack or any psychotic symptoms should be placed in the *without psychosis* group under the appropriate subheading.

20. *Psychoses with mental deficiency*

This group includes the psychoses with various types of intel-lectual deficiency or feeblemindedness. The degree of mental deficiency should be determined by the history and the use of standard psychometric tests. The intellectual level may be denoted in the statistics by specifying borderline, moron, imbecile, idiot.

Acute, usually transient psychoses of various forms occur in mentally deficient persons and commitment to a hospital for mental diseases may be necessary. The most common mental disturbances are episodes of excitement or irritability, depressions, paranoid trends, hallucinatory attacks, etc.

Mentally deficient persons may suffer from manic-depressive attacks or from dementia præcox. When this occurs the diagnostic grouping should be manic-depressive or dementia præcox as the case may be.

Mental deficiency cases without psychotic disturbances should go into the *without psychosis* group under the appropriate subheading.

21. *Undiagnosed psychoses*

In this group should be placed the cases in which a satisfactory diagnosis cannot be made and the psychosis must therefore be regarded as an unclassified one. The difficulty may be due to lack of information or inaccessibility of the patient; or the clinical picture may be obscure, the etiology unknown, or the symptoms unusual. Cases placed in this group during the year should be again reviewed before the annual diagnostic tables are completed.

Cases of the type formerly placed in one of the allied groups should not be put in the undiagnosed group except for some special reason. Most of the cases hitherto called allied should be placed in the main group to which they seem most closely related.

22. *Without psychosis*

This group should receive the occasional case which after investigation and observation gives no evidence of having had a psychosis. The only difficulty likely to be encountered in the statistical reports will arise in the grouping of patients who have recovered from a psychosis prior to admission. In such cases, if the history, the commitment papers or the patient's retrospective account shows that a psychosis actually existed immediately before admission, that is, at the time of commitment, then the case should be considered as having suffered from a mental disorder, and classification under the appropriate heading should be made.

If it is determined that no psychosis existed, then the condition which led to admission should be specified. The following come most frequently into consideration:

(a) Epilepsy without psychosis
(b) Alcoholism without psychosis
(c) Drug addiction without psychosis
(d) Psychopathic personality without psychosis
(e) Mental deficiency without psychosis
(f) Other conditions (to be specified).

STATISTICAL TABLES RECOMMENDED

A series of eighteen statistical tables is recommended for the use of all hospitals for mental diseases. These provide for the systematic presentation of the data that should be annually compiled by every such institution and that should be available for use by everyone interested in psychiatry or the treatment of mental diseases. These tables are:

Table 1. General information.
Table 2. Financial statement.
Table 3. Movement of patients.
Table 4. Nativity and parentage of first admissions.
Table 5. Citizenship of first admissions.
Table 6. Psychoses of first admissions, types as well as principal psychoses to be designated.
Table 7. Race of first admissions classified with reference to principal psychoses.
Table 8. Age of first admissions classified with reference to principal psychoses.
Table 9. Degree of education of first admissions classified with reference to principal psychoses.
Table 10. Environment of first admissions classified with reference to principal psychoses.
Table 11. Economic condition of first admissions classified with reference to principal psychoses.
Table 12. Use of alcohol by first admissions classified with reference to principal psychoses.
Table 13. Marital condition of first admissions classified with reference to principal psychoses.
Table 14. Psychoses of readmissions.
Table 15. Discharges of patients classified with reference to principal psychoses and condition on discharge.
Table 16. Causes of death of patients classified with reference to principal psychoses.
Table 17. Age of patients at time of death classified with reference to principal psychoses.
Table 18. Duration of hospital life of patients dying in hospital, classified with reference to principal psychoses.

The National Committee for Mental Hygiene has printed a series of forms to be used in preparing the foregoing tables and is furnishing them without charge to every institution requesting them or that signifies its willingness to coöperate in the general movement for uniform statistics. The forms are numbered to correspond with the tables. In order to secure uniformity in the compilation of these tables . . . explanations and definitions are submitted [in the "Statistical Manual," pp 37 ff].

Many of the phenomena found in the foregoing accounts will be discussed in later pages of the present volume. But no attempt is made to represent every mental disorder.[1] On the contrary, mechanisms which underlie the more "mental"— "functional" as contrasted with "organic" or "structural" [2] —disorders will receive most attention. For immediate illustration, however, there follow a few selections from the literature on symptomatology and classification. The numbers under which the cases are presented refer to the headings on the classification above.

---

[1] For detailed descriptions, cf. J. W. Bridges, *Outline of Abnormal Psychology;* or, with illustrative cases, such works as William A. White, *Outlines of Psychiatry;* Aaron J. Rosanoff, *Manual of Psychiatry;* James V. May, *Mental Diseases;* Irving J. Sands and Phyllis Blanchard, *Abnormal Behavior;* and E. E. Southard and Mary C. Jarrett, *The Kingdom of Evils.* Prof. Abraham Myerson discusses Symptoms, Groups of the Mental Diseases, the Psychoneuroses, Epilepsy, Dementia Praecox, Manic-Depressive Insanity, Paranoid Psychoses, Involution Diseases, and Senile Dementia, briefly, but in a manner that is highly critical, in his volume, *The Inheritance of Mental Diseases.*

[2] "To say that a disease is functional is to say that changes in the mode of its functioning may cure it and that the organic lesion that always exists is such that it can be cured by the transformation of the mode of functioning. To say that a disease is organic is to affirm, on the contrary, that the lesion of the organ will not be influenced by changes in the mode of functioning, and that consequently all psychotherapy is useless. This is the first psychotherapeutic diagnosis."—Pierre Janet, *Principles of Psychotherapy,* 256 (copyright, 1924, by The Macmillan Company; reprinted by permission).

General Paralysis [4]

A

WALTER S. HUNTER, *General Psychology*, rev. ed., 79-81 (Univ. of Chicago Press, 1923)

Paresis, or *progressive general paralysis,* is a nervous and mental disease correlated with a certain type of cerebral syphilis. On the physical side there is not so much a paralysis as there is a general weakness. On the mental side progression is made in various typical ways to a final *dementia,* or loss of mentality. This gradual change may extend over a period of from one to five years. It is practically uniformly fatal. Apparent recoveries or remissions are usual, only however to be followed by a relapse and a fatal termination. Most frequently the disease appears in middle life, although juvenile paresis is also found. . . .

Quotation may be made from Church and Peterson (1908) in description of the early symptoms: [1]

General paresis is one of the most insidious forms of insanity as regards its gradual, almost unnoticeable onset. Very often this early stage presents symptoms which lead to its being mistaken for neurasthenia. Indeed, the earliest symptoms may be neurasthenic in character, or even a combination of hysteria with neurasthenia. Sleeplessness, tremor, irritability of mood, hypochondriacal depression, dull headache, ophthalmic migraine, pains in various parts of the body, general malaise, loss of appetite, and digestive disorders— these are the manifestations which may be readily misinterpreted as purely of functional nature. It is only when other symptoms in addition to these are presented that a suspicion of a more serious malady may be entertained or the diagnosis actually established. These symptoms are, on the mental side: little faults of memory; errors in speech or writing; the misuse of words; the leaving out of letters, syllables, or words, or their reduplication in writing; growing indifference to the higher sentiments; loss of the critical faculty; small lapses in the proprieties, and failure of interest in the more important affairs of life. As these mental features become more and more pronounced, the patient loses and mislays things, makes mistakes in money matters, errs in appointments, confuses persons and objects, forgets his way, becomes easily angered, markedly offends

---

[1] A. Church and F. Peterson. *Nervous and Mental Diseases,* 832 (Saunders, 1908).

the proprieties, shows extravagance in the use of money, evinces distinct loss of ethical feelings, exhibits proclivities to sexual and alcoholic excess, and becomes negligent of his dress.

After this initial, or *prodromal,* period the above symptoms increase in intensity. Amnesias (memory losses) become greater. Grandiose or depressed delusions become more striking; excesses more frequent and serious. On the bodily side many disturbances appear of which the following are typical: muscle tremors, particularly in the tongue and face; speech defects leading to a "drunken speech"; failure of the pupils of the eyes to contract to an increase in light intensity (Argyl-Robertson pupils); epileptiform or apoplectiform convulsions; and disorders of the hair, skin, and bone (trophic disorders). In the final stages the dementia becomes more and more profound, physical helplessness is usually complete, and death follows.

B

E. E. SOUTHARD and MARY C. JARRETT, *The Kingdom of Evils,* 215 (copyright, 1922, by The Macmillan Company); reprinted by permission

The degree to which general paralysis or paresis may mimic other disorders, such as dementia præcox and paranoia, is suggested in the following:

Carl Spindler came from a public health hospital with the diagnosis of dementia præcox. His case was found to be one of general paresis requiring commitment. He was incoherent, and very talkative, to the effect that he was going to Washington to take the President's place, that the girls were all crazy about him, and that he had plenty of money. He was a well-built man of thirty-three of German descent. He had worked in packing houses until he enlisted in the army. He had seen service in France, where he had got a number of shrapnel wounds and had been gassed. He was transferred to a state hospital for prolonged care.

The "structural" or "organic" character of the disease thus illustrated by Southard and Jarrett is apparent from the recent development of a very promising treatment for these cases, namely, the drug tryparsamide.[1]

---

[1] *Cf.* Robert Percival Parsons, "Tryparsamide and Sulpharsphenamine in the Treatment of Neurosyphilis"; W. F. Lorenz, A. S. Loevenhart, W. J. Bleckwenn, and F. J. Hodges, article on tryparsamide (Bibliography).

Manic-Depressive Psychoses [13]

IRVING J. SANDS and PHYLLIS BLANCHARD, *Abnormal Behavior*, 186-187 (Moffat, Yard, 1923)

In the Manic-Depressive Psychoses there are as yet no definitely proven pathological changes found in post-mortem examination, nor are there as yet any definitely established pathological findings from other sources which bear an undisputed relationship to this disorder. We must bear in mind, however, that there is an extensive group of scientifically inclined medical workers, who are utilizing every modern method of diagnostic procedure in their endeavor to solve the causes underlying these disorders. However, while we are anticipating results that may prove a boon to humanity, yet in the present state of our knowledge no data are available that could explain the mechanisms involved in these cases other than psychogenic ones. We therefore must regard this group also as a type of reaction to a situation on the part of individuals possessing a distinct mental make-up. Individuals of such make-up were described in the previous chapter as either the manic or the depressive type of personality; the former manifesting it by being overactive, vivacious, high-strung and enthusiastic, inclined to overdo things, participating in many fields of endeavor, but finishing few of their undertakings, and the latter by displaying a tendency to worry over insignificant matters, brooding over trifles, being subject to frequent blue spells, rather slow and deliberate in their physical activities, and hardly ever happy, but rather fault-finding and discouraging. Whenever any situation arises which requires considerable tact, judgment, and increased capacity for adjustment, an attack of psychosis may result. Such demands for unusual adjustment may be physiological in nature, occurring in such crises as puberty, adolescence, puerperal state (child-bearing), menopause (change of life), etc. Diminished physical endurance following illness, business troubles, unhappy family incidents and at times an unexpected happy occurrence, may precipitate an attack.[1]

---

[1] [*Cf.* Charles Macfie Campbell, "On the Mechanism of Some Cases of Manic-Depressive Excitement" (Bibliography).]

Manic-Depressive Psychoses, Manic Type [13(a)]

AARON J. ROSANOFF, *Manual of Psychiatry*, 5th ed., 273-275 (John Wiley & Sons); reprinted by permission of the publishers

The following case is a good example of delusional mania:

Gabrielle L., fifty-two years old, housewife. Family history unknown. The patient has always been impressionable and lively; intelligence normal. She had five previous attacks of mania, the first at the age of nineteen; all terminated in recovery.

The present attack began with rambling speech, assaults upon others, and tendency to alcoholic excesses; the patient, though usually temperate, began to drink to intoxication. She was taken to the Clermont Asylum, where Dr. Boîteaux issued the following certificate of lunacy: "Condition of acute mania with extreme disorder of ideation, speech, and conduct. Illusions of the senses. Obscene actions. Ideas of grandeur: owns millions, heavens and earth. Excited, difficult to control."

On February 25, 1904, one month after the patient's admission to the asylum, examination was as follows: Medium stature, strong constitution, slight obesity, skin flushed, voice loud, gestures lively, clothing disarranged, hair down over the shoulders. From the beginning the patient showed extreme familiarity. She offered her arm to the physician, whom she took to be the husband of the head nurse, and laughingly asked the latter if she was not jealous. She was well oriented as to place; she knew that she was in the Insane Asylum at Clermont where she had already been five times before. Her orientation of time was somewhat inaccurate: she said the year was 1904, that it was the spring of the year, and gave the date as March 25 (actual date February 25, 1904); on being asked to think a while and make sure of the date, she said: "Why, of course it is March, a few days ago we had a holiday, that was Mid-Lent." (She was evidently referring to Shrove Tuesday.) Later other ideas appeared and it became impossible to prevail upon the patient to reflect properly before speaking. She had a certain realization of her condition: she said she felt odd, "at times driven to play all sorts of silly pranks." She was very obedient, and always started out with remarkable eagerness to carry out any order that might be given her. But her extremely mobile attention caused her to be each instant distracted from the object to be attained. She was asked to write a letter: "Why, certainly! To whom?" "To whomever you wish." "Very well, to the President of the Republic? To the Minister of War? No, I shall write to my husband." Then she began to write: *To Mr. L., Gardener in C. . . .* Then turning again to the physician: "Because, you know, we have been living in C. . . . for the past eighteen years. I have a house there. The hospital at C. . . . belongs to me. I know Sister Antoinette there. They wanted me to disguise myself as a Sister, but my husband wouldn't have it. He adores me, my husband does!" She was again asked to write, which she did, jabbering all the time and reading aloud everything she wrote. Every moment her attention kept being distracted by the conversation of the persons in the room, although they spoke in a low voice and upon matters which did not concern the patient. They spoke, in fact, about another patient who helped the nurses with the service in the dining-room. "Good gracious!" exclaimed the patient, interrupting her writing and bursting out with laughter, "that woman is pretty stingy with her bread! One would think she was paying for it! It was I that gave her the money to buy it with!" When asked again to continue her letter she willingly resumed her writing. A minute later they spoke about another patient, and someone made the remark, "She does not sleep." This started the patient again: "Who, I? I don't sleep? Why, I sleep like a dormouse!" It is to be noted that she wrote slowly, seeking for words. Having had but little schooling, writing in her case did not develop into an automatic function. She threw down her pen after having written a few disconnected lines. She was then given a paper and asked to read aloud one of the news items. Her attention was at once attracted by a picture below the news item and she exclaimed, pointing to it: "Here is a pretty woman! She resembles Mrs. P." She was again urged to read. She read the first line with difficulty, owing to her poor vision, and continued to read on the same level in the next column. Again the above news item was pointed out to her. It was about some poor old man. The patient at once stopped her reading. "This is a jolly story! The poor old man! and the veterans! I visited them once, also the building for arts and for commerce." With a good deal of urging she was finally induced to read the entire news item; but it made very little impression on her mind; a quarter of an hour later she was unable to tell even briefly what she had read, declaring simply that it was something about an old man. "It is very sad," she added, "sad and humiliating. Thinking of death always distresses me, but I am very fond of flowers. My husband is a gardener in C. . . . He buys his seeds from Vilmorin, also his tobacco."

Numerous unsystematized *grandiose delusions:* she is a midwife, she studied for forty years; she is a millionairess, owns mansions; her husband has invented perpetual motion, made the model with nothing but his knife; he has also invented a method for making cheese boxes out of the stalks of rye, which he will sell for ten cents apiece. He is related to the King of Italy and is of noble descent. In her delusions the patient showed marked suggestibility: she was asked, "Have you ever been on the stage?" "Why, yes, I played in *The Chimes of Normandy.*" Here she began to sing: "Will you look this way, will you look that way?" Her children are also actors. She played with them at the Castle Theatre, also with Sarah Bernhardt. Here her eye fell upon the word "Minister" printed in large letters in the paper; she said: "My husband has not yet been made Minister, but with his ability he will not have to wait long." She has no hallucinations, but numerous *illusions,* especially those of vision. She thinks she knows all those about her. One nurse is her cousin, another is her neighbor living across the street. Her *motor excitement* is very marked. The patient tries to do every kind of work; she makes a few sweeps with the broom, then suddenly rushes to assist a nurse carrying a pail of water, then leaves the nurse with her pail of water to go and make peace between two quarreling patients. Without any intention of malice, she has frequent altercations with other patients who are annoyed by her screams, her songs, and her wild pranks. She picks up all sorts of objects and accumulates them in her clothes: scraps of paper, bits of glass, wood, and metal, pieces of bread and cheese. She herself laughs when an inventory is taken of all this rubbish, and makes no objection to its being taken away from her.

No noteworthy disorders in her general condition. She eats at all times, abundantly and gluttonously. Sleep somewhat disturbed: she passes part of the night wandering about the dormitory, singing and jabbering.

Manic-Depressive Psychoses, Depressive Type [13(b)]

IRVING J. SANDS and PHYLLIS BLANCHARD, *Abnormal Behavior,* 198 (Moffat, Yard, 1923)

A man (33 years of age) was brought from the New York City Prison being charged with "unlawful possession of firearm." The patient was apprehended in a city park after drawing his revolver in an attempt at suicide.

Physically, the patient was a well developed and well nourished individual. His heart and lungs were normal; there were no neurological disorders. There were no evidences of any blood disease.

Patient said:

"I wanted to kill myself. I tell you there is no use in living. People don't like me; they don't want me. Everybody seems to avoid me. They shun my company—what is there for me to live for?"

Mentally the patient was very sad; definitely depressed; he spoke in a very slow, retarded manner. Showed moderate difficulty in concentration. He would sit for hours in the same place, and expressed ideas of insufficiency. He had no insight into his condition. His memory was good. His attention was somewhat defective. Orientation was intact. He was committed to the state hospital for treatment, diagnosis being Depressed Phase, Manic Depressive Insanity.

Manic-Depressive Psychoses, Other Types [13(c)]

IRVING J. SANDS and PHYLLIS BLANCHARD, *Abnormal Behavior*, 198-200 (Moffat, Yard, 1923)

A young female (25 years of age) was brought into the psychopathic ward in a state of excitement, after having thrown two of her nieces out of the window, killing one and seriously injuring the other. The history showed that she was born in Russia; had but little schooling, and was considered generally bright and attractive, having many friends, and being quite popular with everybody with whom she came into contact. During the late war, she had undergone many privations, and had witnessed many acts of cruelty, for she lived near the fighting zone. She had to spend many days in cellars and was forced to go without food for long periods. After the peace treaty was signed, the family emigrated to America, but they experienced unusual hardships in getting here and on one occasion while waiting in line to have her passport viséed, a riot broke out and many people standing near her were killed. On reaching this country, she found her brothers (who had emigrated to America before the war) in very good financial condition, and she received a very cordial welcome. For a few months she appeared quite content and happy. Then she became somewhat dissatisfied with conditions. She had secured employment in a clothing factory, but she could not keep at it. She also had trouble with her teeth and had several of them drawn. While in the dentist's chair she suddenly became ugly, insulted the dentist, and returned to her home appearing quite excited. She could give no account of her actions. She went to the bedroom where the children were playing and threw them out of the window.

On the observation ward she was very impulsive and excited. Spoke incoherently and incessantly; bit one of the nurses; expectorated on anyone coming near her; tore her linen and bit her own fingers. She would cry a good deal and appeared to be very depressed. She was finally committed to a state hospital where for a period of four months she was very excited, assaultive, had to be placed in restraint, and was kept in the ward for the violent patients. At the end of that time she gradually became quieter. Gained insight into her condition; spoke relevantly and gained considerable weight. She discussed her difficulties very freely, and apparently made a complete recovery from her psychosis at the end of ten months. She was diagnosed as a case of Manic Depressive Psychosis, Mixed Phase.

From these typical cases it may be realized that the abnormal behavior of the Manic Depressive embraces almost every conceivable form, ranging from mild eccentricities to the most serious antisocial conduct.

Dementia Præcox (Schizophrenia) [15]

E. E. Southard and Mary C. Jarrett, *The Kingdom of Evils*, 473-475 (copyright, 1922, by The Macmillan Company); reprinted by permission

The schizophrenic cases—dementia praecox . . . form a large and important group in the field of psychiatry. Beginning most frequently during adolescence or early adult life and having a very grave prognosis, schizophrenia affords many distressing social situations. This psychosis has two main characteristics: (a) a splitting of the personality (schizophrenia) and (b) a tendency to deterioration. "Splitting" means that there is no longer a congruity between the three psychological elements that form the personality; namely, the intellect, the affective reactions, and the will. The result is emotional apathy, loss of interest in one's family, lack of normal activity, inability to carry out one's purpose. The majority of persons afflicted with this form of disease develop ideas of persecution, believe they are being followed, interfered with, not given a square deal, and the like. Hallucinations are apt to be prominent. These disorders associated with a general psychic decrepitude may necessitate commitment in an institution for the insane. When the disease remains chronic, the patient may continue in an institution for the remainder of his life. The social procedures in the chronic committed cases are relatively simple. It is not, however, correct to assume that no case recovers. Many patients with dementia praecox make fair recoveries and are able to live in the community. Often the defect resulting from the disease is mild in degree. Even so, these patients need guidance and aid, and most of them require some form of social assistance.

The schizophrenic group is brought to the attention of the social worker chiefly, during the early or incipient period of the disease. For months and often for years before a patient has the outstanding symptoms of a psychosis, mental peculiarities, character anomalies, unusual actions, and maladjustments lead to observation by social agencies. Unless an astute psychiatrist sees the patient in this early state, the person is likely to be considered as stubborn, unreliable, delinquent, obtuse, peculiar, or lazy, rather than ill and a proper subject for understanding, sympathy, and help. Many are the difficulties, delinquencies, and misfortunes due to early symptoms of the disease.

Despite the relative impossibility of effecting cures in the disease with our present knowledge, it is surprising how much may often be accomplished to improve the social reactions of these patients by proper social adjustments. Unfortunately much useless effort is expended by social workers in attempts to aid such persons before their disease has been diagnosed.

The symptoms which may be manifested by schizophrenia patients are numerous and varied. In fact, Kraepelin, in his latest classifications, considers seven varieties of dementia praecox and the closely allied paraphrenias. It is obviously not desirable to present the medical points of this complex disease except in a medical treatise. It may be noted that the symptoms result in peculiarities in the patients that lead to a lack of "empathy."

Medical science has not solved the major problems of schizophrenia, i.e., etiology and pathology. As a corollary no specific treatment is known. Every case must be carefully considered, however, from the purely medical side for evidences of endocrine disorder, organic disease, and metabolic disorder, as well as for psychological factors in the life of the patient. Life experience and environmental conditions play an important rôle in the development of the psychosis. So the social worker may have a function in prevention and treatment as well as in social adjustment.

It is important to place schizophrenic patients under care at the earliest possible moment; as it is with any person developing a disease, acute or chronic. Many schizophrenics show character anomalies from early childhood that are suggestive. Among these traits may be mentioned "shut in" personality, inability to make friends and take part in communal activities with zest, supersensitiveness, over-conscientiousness, egocentricity, metaphysical ruminations, obstinacy, phantasy-formation, or day-dreaming. *These characteristics cause such persons to be considered peculiar, eccentric, exceptional, or difficult; whereas they should indicate a careful psychiatric examination.*

Dementia Præcox, Paranoid Type [15]

IRVING J. SANDS and PHYLLIS BLANCHARD, *Abnormal Behavior,* 182-184
(Moffat, Yard, 1923)

A young man (25 years of age) was brought from the City Prison being charged with "unlawful possession of firearms." This history of this patient revealed that he had been born in Italy and was brought here by his parents when he was a boy five years of age. He had gone through school and had reached the last grade at 14 years of age. He was then taken from school in order to help support the family, and he was always rather suspicious, somewhat stubborn and difficult to manage. He had complained of the neighboring people because they "were interfering with him" and on one occasion he had struck one of his friends because the latter was forcing women to look at the patient in a peculiar way. He was discharged from the army because of some mental trouble.

At the hospital the patient showed a very well-preserved physical condition. There was no evidence of any disease of the central nervous system.

A psychometric examination was performed, but the result was unsatisfactory as he showed a suspicious, rebellious attitude stating that the examiner was trying to influence his mind. He said that the reason for his possessing a revolver was that people were persecuting him and following him; that wherever he went they looked at him in a very peculiar way. The reason for their action was that he was very much liked by his officers in the army and since then they were all jealous of him. Lately the lady with whom he was boarding was in the habit of looking at him in a peculiar manner. He thought she probably had sexual designs on him but that it was an immoral thing to do; therefore she was trying to poison him. He believed she had influenced all the other men of the neighborhood so that nobody would now look at him. Furthermore, they were preventing him from securing any decent employment. They were making threats and were going to harm him; his food was now being tampered with and electricity was being put into his body. He therefore bought a revolver, in order to protect himself. He took a trip from New Jersey to New York and on the ferryboat people were making disparaging remarks about him, and had some secret code as evidenced by the whistling of the boats in the river, all of which was with the intention of doing away with him. He therefore took the revolver and flashed it before the other passengers, "to frighten them" and prevent them from possibly harming him. His condition was diagnosed as that of Dementia Praecox, Paranoid Type, and he was sent to the hospital for observation and treatment.

Dementia Præcox, Catatonic Type [15]

AARON J. ROSANOFF, *Manual of Psychiatry*, 5th ed., 239-242 (John Wiley & Sons); reprinted by permission

Adrienne P., patient at the St. Anne Asylum, corset maker, twenty-five years old at the onset of her illness. Heredity: paternal grandfather died at the age of sixty years of senile dementia; father is an alcoholic, has been committed twice; paternal aunt committed suicide. The patient began to walk and speak very late in childhood; menstruation appeared at the age of seventeen, has been regular but painful. She showed no abnormality in intelligence or disposition. At nineteen, pleurisy. At twenty-four, during a sojourn in London, a severe attack of scarlet fever with pronounced albuminuria; patient was sick three and a half months; convalescence lasted two months. Since then (fall of 1897), the relatives noticed a change in the mental condition of the patient from the letters which she wrote home. On her return to France Adrienne was gloomy, irritable, apathetic. She refused to work and often even to rise in the morning. Complete loss of appetite, headache. Much worried about her health, she consulted several physicians but with no appreciable result.

On October 20, 1898, acute symptoms set in in the form of disorders of perception. The people are "droll," the dishes served in the restaurant are "droll," life is "droll" and "absurd." At the same time hallucinations of vision appeared: the patient saw men following her, also ghosts and stars. On October 26 she started out to go to her sister who lived in the suburbs of Paris; failing to find her she walked at random and wandered around the country for two days and two nights. She was found walking along a railroad track, her hair undone, her clothes in disorder; they arrested her and took her to the Corbeil Hospital where she remained eight days in complete mutism. On her return to her mother her mutism disappeared, but she gave no explanation of what she did, telling simply that she had seen things which frightened her: terrible men and animals. For some time she remained relatively quiet, but depressed and intractable. She refused to see a physician, though her mother begged her to do so. On the night of November 24 she suddenly became greatly excited, cried, gesticulated, and uttered incoherent remarks some of which were suggestive of hallucinations: she spoke of men following her and of saints whom she saw. She tried to throw herself out of the window.

On being brought to the clinic on November 28 she was in almost complete mutism. To all questions put to her she responded by outlandish gestures and grimaces bearing no reference to the questions. On being asked to write she tore the piece of paper which was offered her.

On December 1, at the occasion of a visit from her mother, Adrienne came out of her mutism but her remarks were incoherent. "She cannot see, she can see very clearly. . . . It is Alfred, it is Martin speaking to her. . . . They are not saying anything." It was very difficult to tell whether she really had hallucinations.

Toward the evening she became totally estranged from the external world. She no longer responded to any question.

Spells of excitement and of stupor have since then followed each other without any regularity, presenting respectively the characteristic features of catatonic excitement and of catatonic stupor.

The excitement is purely automatic. The same movements are constantly repeated monotonously and aimlessly. For hours at a time the patient goes through peculiar and incomprehensible gestures, striking the floor alternately with the right foot and with the left foot, and extending her arms and clinching her fists in a threatening manner but never striking anyone. She stands up in her bed in a dramatic attitude, draped with the blanket, and frozen, so to speak, in that position, uncomfortable as it is. In her attacks of excitement she displays considerable physical strength. On May 25, 1900, she made a steady persistent attempt to leave her bed and get out of the dormitory; her eyes were shut, her expression apathetic, and she uttered not a word or a cry. Several nurses held her back with difficulty.

Her utterances show either incoherence or verbigeration. On January 15, 1900, she stood up in her bed and sang for several hours: "The baker's wife has money," etc. On May 23, of the same year, she kept repeating during several hours without interruption "Hail Mary," etc.

She shows marked negativism. When spoken to she will give no response, showing absolute mutism; she resists systematically all attempts at passive movement: to open her mouth, to flex an extended limb, or *vice versa*. The command to open her eyes results immediately in a spasm of the orbicularis muscle. Refusal of food is at times complete, and then the patient has to be tubefed; at other times it is partial, the patient taking only liquid food which is poured into her mouth by means of a feeding cup and which she then swallows readily. On November 4, without any apparent reason, she ate spontaneously a piece of bread which she took from the table. For two days she thus took bread, cheese, and chocolate, but persistently refused everything else. Later she relapsed into the former state and now takes none but liquid food which has to be poured into her mouth. Her sensibility appears to be normal, but all reaction is annihilated. Painful pricking with a pin causes slight trembling, but no cry, nor any movement of defense.

In the stuporous phases the patient lies in her bed, completely immobile. Generally this immobility is dominated by negativism which is manifested by the same traits as those observed in her excited phases. On several occasions, however, she has shown very marked suggestibility. Thus once she submitted readily, though passively, to being dressed and taken to the office of the ward physician. When standing she remains motionless, yet she will walk mechanically as soon as she is pushed. When invited to sit down, the patient slightly flexes her legs and makes a movement as though starting to sit down, showing that the command is understood; yet she will go no further, but remains standing. When taken by the shoulder and slightly pushed she sits down without trouble. Her limbs are flaccid and present no resistance to any passive movement. Negativism persists only in the muscles of the mouth and eyelids, which remain closed and resist being opened. Cataleptoid attitudes are rare. One was, however, observed on October 30, 1900. The right arm was held for ten minutes in complete extension. On the following day this symptom disappeared.

The patient soils and wets her bed frequently, though not constantly, both during periods of excitement and during those of stupor.

The general nutrition is profoundly affected; the skin is discolored, the hair is falling out, and there is considerable emaciation: from December, 1898, until May, 1899, the patient's weight fell from 94 to 77 pounds.

In March, 1901, the patient, considered as being completely incurable, was transferred to another institution.

Dementia Præcox, Hebephrenic Type [15]

IRVING J. SANDS and PHYLLIS BLANCHARD, *Abnormal Behavior*, 174-177
(Moffat, Yard, 1923)

A young female (29 years of age) was sent by a city magistrate to the hospital for observation. A long record from the Domestic Relations Court showed that this patient had frequently appealed for help as a destitute person. The patient strongly objected to being taken to the hospital. Said she was in good physical and mental condition; thought there was nothing wrong with her in any way; that it was the duty of her husband to provide for her and that she was perfectly justified in applying to the Court for means of securing sustenance from her husband. Her father, in describing the patient, said that she was rather studious as a child; would read until late hours of the night; and instead of going out with the other girls she preferred to remain at home and read books, most of them, however, being of a strong sex color. She was always quite stubborn and obstinate, had to have her own way, and insisted upon having things done the way she wanted. She would spend hours before the mirror, and would take great pains in the care of her person.

Three years ago she met a man and married him after a courtship of only two days. She did not tell her parents of this man until after the wedding ceremony. One week after her marriage she became rather excited, came to her people and complained of her husband's refusal to support her. She stated that her husband was trying to do her physical harm; that he was tampering with her food; and he was causing peculiar feelings to creep through her body. At that time she was rather shabbily dressed; her hair was dishevelled and she showed peculiar twitchings of the face. She objected to her father looking at her, saying that it made her very uneasy and fearful. She left her father's home without announcing her departure and evidently returned to live with her husband. Two years ago she applied to the Domestic Relations Court for support from her husband. The social service worker attached to the court investigated home conditions and was told by the land-lady that the patient was definitely "peculiar." She would sit for hours smiling in a silly manner; she would often pour water out of the window at passers-by. She would often go to a corner of her room and talk away for hours; would stuff her ears with cotton. The patient would deny these allegations and it was impossible to get her to come for examination at the mental clinic. Six months ago she was finally brought to the mental clinic on the pretext of having her heart examined. It was impossible to interview the patient at that time, as she immediately became very abusive, say-ing that she was brought there for immoral purposes. She ran out of the clinic, and finally it was deemed advisable to have her sent to the observation ward by a city magistrate.

Physically the patient was very well developed; rather an at-tractive individual; very well nourished. Heart and lungs were negative. There was no evidence of any neurological disorder.

Mentally, the patient was very suspicious; was not coöperative; was very evasive. For a period of six days it was impossible to get her to admit any of her peculiar ideas. When eating, she would cautiously taste the food before eating it, refusing most of the dishes offered to her. When these acts were brought to her atten-tion she would refuse to discuss them, or denied them. Finally one of the nurses succeeded in gaining her confidence and to her she admitted her ideas of strong sexual nature and her hallucina-tory experiences. She informed this nurse that she was being fol-lowed by men on the street, who desired to have immoral relations with her. She believed her food was being tampered with and that a plot was on foot to have her poisoned. She said, "I went into a restaurant and ordered some coffee and apple pie; that made me sick. There was a soapy taste to it. Wherever I go now that same taste is present in all the food. Here, too, there is that taste. I must not sleep nights, because men come here and abuse me. Can you blame me for being careful? etc."

This patient was diagnosed as a case of Dementia Praecox, Hebe-phrenic Form, and was finally committed to a state hospital. She represents the type of person who so often is a source of trouble not only to her immediate family, but also to those with whom she comes into contact, as well as the social service worker, the court and the physician who might be called upon to help her solve her difficulties. It is quite obvious that such a person cannot pos-sibly live a normal marital life.

Dementia Præcox, Simple Type [15]

A

Irving J. Sands and Phyllis Blanchard, *Abnormal Behavior*, 180-181
(Moffat, Yard, 1923)

A young male (32 years old) was sent by his parents to the Red Cross, asking that he be taken care of in a hospital as there was something wrong with his mind. He spoke about big things but was unable to take care of himself. This boy was born in New York City, had a public school education and following his graduation from school he worked as an office boy. He showed no conduct disorder of any type until his discharge from the army was insisted upon by his people. He was drafted in 1917 and was put in the medical corps as an orderly. It was noticed then that this orderly was rather officious, disobeyed military rules and discipline, paid no attention to warnings of his superiors, and disregarded any advice given him. He was therefore transferred to another post but there, too, he interfered with the other men's duties, complained of the treatment he was receiving, was careless about his personal appearance and about the condition of his clothing. He finally was put in a military hospital for observation and there his condition was diagnosed as Dementia Praecox, Simple Form, and he was discharged on a surgeon's certificate of disability.

Following his return to civil life, he could not secure employment although at that time there were many vacancies in various fields of occupation, for an interview with any of the managers of the place would result in a conviction that the applicant was not in full possession of his faculties, and he would not be employed.

He spent his time on street corners discussing with anyone willing to listen to him all current historical topics; boasting of his own participancy in the war and blaming his superiors for not securing any promotion. His clothes were shabby and his personal appearance was quite uncleanly. At home he was rather meek though at times excitable and would fly into fits of temper whenever crossed by his parents. He was referred to the War Veterans' Bureau where vocational training was recommended. Several types of vocational guidance were suggested for him but he had no particular choice. He was placed at tailoring, but he showed no interest in the work; later he was transferred to carpentry, but there too he failed to show any interest. His attitude and manner drew the attention of the man in charge and it was finally recommended that he give up training and be placed under psychiatric observation. It was quite obvious that this man was suffering from a Dementia Praecox, Simple Type. His dull, listless attitude and manner; his mood indifference; his impulsive traits; the emotional inadequacy and his inability to secure any employment or to maintain any interest in his vocational training were definite symptoms of his disordered mind. It was therefore recommended that he be committed to a psychiatric hospital maintained by the Veterans' Bureau.

B

E. E. SOUTHARD and MARY C. JARRETT, *The Kingdom of Evils*, 284-287 (copyright, 1922, by The Macmillan Company); reprinted by permission

There is a form of schizophrenia (dementia praecox) to which the adjective *simplex* is added. In this form of the disease there is a certain deterioration and dulling of the emotional life which fails to be accompanied by the various so-called catatonic (formerly termed cataleptic) symptoms or by the delusions which are so frequent in most cases of schizophrenia. Moreover, in these so-called simplex cases the emotional deterioration may itself be slight, and it is commonly thought by psychiatrists that a great number of these cases of dementia simplex are found in the community at large, perhaps self-supporting or nearly self-supporting, with a history of having sustained a slight regression in their mental capacity insufficient to warrant or to suggest their internment in any hospital for the insane. It is, perhaps, a little difficult for the layman and even for some of the old-time physicians to think of cases of schizophrenia (dementia praecox) as "not insane." Until the concept of *mental disease that is not* (medico-legal) *insanity* becomes deeply imbedded in the lay mind, as well as in the minds of medical men and social workers, we shall not come through with a proper program of community mental hygiene.

Dana Scott, an unmarried man of thirty-seven, was brought to the Psychopathic Hospital for observation. The woman with whom he boarded told of violent fits of temper on Scott's part, during which clothing was torn and furniture knocked to pieces. As a matter of fact, the landlady greatly overdrew the story about Scott, as investigation failed to substantiate any destructive tendencies, nor was the landlady herself a good sort of person to live with. Nevertheless, with all the smoke there was some fire. It was generally agreed that Scott lacked ambition and initiative and might perhaps be the victim of some sort of mental defect. Had it not been for the landlady's character (an angel from heaven, it was said, could not live peaceably with her), Scott might have remained in the community even to this day without being noted by any expert to be psychopathic. He had been a rather queer child. It was told of him that he took books to the attic and stayed all day with them, omitting meals. The country neighbors who saw him daily did not consider him at all harmful. A nurse who brought him to the hospital said that he was one of the most willing and obedient patients she had ever had.

Here then was a man who was plainly in some sense a psychopath. Perhaps by straining a point he could have been committed to an institution. He was in charge of a guardian and had some little property, so that board could be paid for him. A place in the country was found in the family of a widow and her daughter. Here Scott could help with chores and might perhaps obtain some work in the neighborhood. Shortly letters were received from Scott telling how much he liked his new home. The family were well satisfied with him and pleased at having a permanent boarder who was so helpful.

It may be permissible to point out that with the old system, under which the public or private charitable institution "borrowed no trouble," the hospital work might have ceased with the diagnosis. In point of fact the social service was at first merely requested to secure a history. Yet, when such history was secured, perfectly obvious and valuable social-service measures stood revealed as the proper procedure. In institutions where psychiatric social work is carried out effectually this is no infrequent event, namely, that the social worker, sent out to secure a few facts, comes back with a series of rational measures.

Victims of the so-called simplex form of schizophrenia are often looked upon, even by physicians, as feeble-minded, nor is it at all possible in routine examinations always to determine medically with which condition one is dealing. The psychometric tests, executed by a properly grounded mental examiner, are sometimes of service; for instance, in the case of Scott, the Binet record stood at $12\frac{1}{5}$ years, and he was set down as beyond question not feeble-minded. His deterioration was not intellectual. The mental impairment was, as it characteristically is in all cases of schizophrenia, in the field of the emotions. There was a marked dulling of them. He was, from some points of view, not at all unintellectual; was, for example, a great reader of books on science and art, and conversed very fairly on current topics. Although psychopathic in this particular way, he had no savor of feeble-mindedness and would have been quite above the level of the majority of the teachings, which are so skillfully carried out for the feeble-minded in the schools appropriate for that group of defectives. There can be no doubt that his life with the widow and her daughter upon a farm was exactly the right fate for him. As with the psychological examination, so the physical and mental examination by psychiatrists at the hospital failed to show any striking deviations from normal, and the psychiatric impression of the case, based upon the medical and social history, was accordingly left at the diagnosis schizophrenia (dementia praecox) of the simplex form.

Of course many cases of schizophrenia, particularly of the catatonic group above mentioned, are not unlikely to become suddenly excited or violent; nor can it be absolutely excluded from the range of possibility that Scott may turn catatonic through some sudden access of the structural or functional disease which underlies his symptoms.

The layman, as well as the physician, must have forced upon his attention a certain sexuality in the symptoms of the majority of cases of schizophrenia (dementia praecox); but it would be an injustice to many examples of the disease to think of the sexuality as socially dangerous. Whatever bad habits in the sexual field and whatever bad table manners and other impolitenesses Scott might have been guilty of, probably all of these matters may never fall within the social danger zone. No doubt many of these psychopathically bad manners and customs can be, to a great degree, trained out of patients of this order by proper methods. Just as it is possible to train or tame certain animals without the employment of the methods open to a Socrates or a Plato, so it is possible to get sundry effects sometimes termed *reëducative* in cases of the schizophrenic group. Whether the training is in all cases a genuine rationalization with the Socratic or Platonic echo may be doubted. However this may be, the well-managed hospital for the chronic insane, harboring as it does so many victims of this disease, shortly becomes a very effective *school for schizophrenics*. In some governmental units, colonies for such schizophrenics have been developed, whose star patients are not those who, like Scott, are very easy to deal with from the outset, but patients who have passed through most violent and dangerous phases or phases of extreme apathy and utter economic worthlessness, only in the end to be schooled into a very fair efficiency. With respect to Dana Scott, then, we may perhaps regard the non-angelic landlady as really something of an angel in disguise.

Difficulty in Differentiating Dementia Præcox [15]

E. E. SOUTHARD and MARY C. JARRETT, *The Kingdom of Evils*, 295-299
(copyright, 1922, by The Macmillan Company) ; reprinted by permission

It is an open secret that it is not an easy psychiatric distinction
to draw in every case between schizophrenia (dementia praecox)
and cyclothymia (manic-depressive psychosis). The two diseases
are paired in the psychiatrist's mind as sister diseases, the former
rather more frequent than the latter, both in the number of first
cases developing and in the number remaining in state hospitals
under observation. When the diagnosis lies between schizophrenia
and cyclothymia, apparently the psychiatrist is statistically somewhat more likely to be right if he decides upon schizophrenia. It
should be insisted that psychiatrists chiefly familiar with the
chronic institutional material are somewhat more likely to take
a pessimistic view of the prognosis of mental disease in general
than are the consulting neurologists of out-patient departments or
of special practice or the specialists in charge of sanatoriums. In
the ten-day period of observation which the law tends to procure
for the majority of cases at the Psychopathic Hospital in Boston,
there will, perhaps, be an error in diagnosis between these two diseases of something like fifteen or twenty per cent; sometimes the
error will be upon one side, sometimes upon the other.

The present case of Paul Ernst is not the first in this book
in which doubt has reigned concerning the diagnosis schizophrenia
as against some other form of mental disease. At least three diagnoses, psychiatrically speaking, have been offered for Paul Ernst;
namely, alcoholic hallucinosis, dementia praecox, and manic-
depressive psychosis.

Ernst has been a patient twice at the Psychopathic Hospital,
once in 1913 and again in 1914-15. At the first admission there
seemed no doubt at all of the diagnosis of dementia praecox. He
had run about his house nude, broken up furniture, and attacked
members of the household. He refused to talk and became very
sullen and obstinate. Just before this he had begun to worry over
business matters and had grown morbidly depressed when an advance in salary was refused. One Saturday night he had been
quite broken up and discouraged and unable to sleep. Sunday ne
had been normal, but Monday grew wildly excited. His excitement had lasted twenty-four hours.

In the hospital he became very violent, at times requiring seven or eight attendants to put him in the wet pack. He shouted, screamed, swore, and cried out, talking either sarcastically or very angrily about his treatment. During inactive periods he assumed a disagreeably sullen manner. He remained for the most part quiet, inaccessible to the examiners, but evincing some flight of ideas in his talk.

He was committed to the Boston State Hospital where he remained a month but was discharged with the diagnosis manic-depressive psychosis. He became entirely clear in his mind before discharge. He now went back to his work as a salesman of a special kind of goods. He had never been alcoholic, so that the initial suggestion of alcoholic hallucinosis was unfounded.

After a time he began again to worry about finances. One day at the department store where he worked, he began to act peculiarly and left for home. There he smashed windows and brought down a chandelier. He was again brought to the Psychopathic Hospital and was there acutely maniacal for some three days, but after this interval a physical examination became possible, and he was found to be practically negative in all respects. Mentally he was suspicious, rather facetious, and non-coöperative upon admission but obviously perfectly oriented for time and place. He tore blankets and night shirt, was profane, obscene, and noisy and was treated by the prolonged baths and by packs. He either was not, or assumed not to be, interested in his surroundings, kept his eyes staring wide open, and winked constantly. He lay in bed in a rather strained position. For a while on the first day he stood in front of a window, talking, but there was a large question whether the behavior was in response to hallucinations. The psychiatric reader will note how difficult a diagnosis must be with such phenomena between schizophrenia and cyclothymia.

On about the seventh day there was a change of phase: he now appeared confused, was quiet but restive, and threw himself from the bed a number of times. He would burst into noises now and then, but was at other times apparently quite rational. Things going on about him he took in quickly and was rather mischievous in his remarks and actions. He began to speak of his wife and family and talked about wanting to go home. At the end of three weeks from his admission, it was possible to send him home in a clear state of mind. He thought that he really had heard false voices just after admission, but conceived that they might possibly be the talking of the attendants misinterpreted by him. He had however once thought that his brother was there talking. He tried to read *The Three Guardsmen,* but could not keep his mind on the book. He was discharged with the diagnosis dementia praecox, unimproved, despite the fact that his general status was for the moment markedly improved.

The social service now took charge of him, and for a period of some two years there is a running record which gives no sign of deterioration whatever. To be sure his former employers refused to take him back, though he had been formerly six years employed by the firm in a rather difficult job. He now had to take temporary jobs as salesman, acting from time to time as an extra. Amongst the measures of the social service were help to the family in the matter of clothes, more or less continuous reassurance of the wife as to the nature of her husband's situation and prognosis, advice concerning work on his part and the securing of vacations for the children.

Then came the death of the wife, upon learning which it was thought best to reopen the case from the social service point of view. However, despite the strain of the situation the family succeeded in adjusting itself, with the oldest daughter, a capable girl of seventeen, keeping the house. Meantime Ernst had remained steady, was working regularly, did not drink and showed no sign of deterioration. The success of the family adjustment is the more remarkable when it is considered that there are nine children (one of whom is choreic).

Is or is not this a case of schizophrenia? Perhaps the shrewd psychiatrist might say that time only would tell. Others might say that it was a case of dementia praecox that had gotten well or had made a compensation practically equivalent to recovery. Others might insist that the case was one of cyclothymia. For our part we may content ourselves with insisting that, whichever of these diagnoses is rendered, there is a certain statistical likelihood of error in diagnosis with our present knowledge (especially perhaps in the war group of cases). There may be noticed many instances of cases looking even more like schizophrenia than the present case of Ernst and yet turning out to be curable or capable of decided remission. Also it is worth while stressing the fact that the term "dementia" in the phrase dementia praecox should not be allowed to dominate anybody's conception of the disease schizophrenia. The so-called "dementia" is from the standpoint of all clear-cut cases a matter of deterioration *of the emotions* and not at all necessarily or characteristically of the intellect. The layman, social worker, or psychiatrist makes a grave error who carries over any ideas that he may possess concerning dementia and dements of the old-age group into the so-called dementia of dementia praecox.

Perhaps no more unfortunate term than dementia praecox has yet been devised for an important group of psychopathic patients.

Paranoia [16]

A

WALTER S. HUNTER, *General Psychology, rev. ed.*, 81-82 (Univ. of Chicago Press, 1923)

No changes can be found in the nervous system with which to correlate paranoia. It is therefore a functional disease. The heredity of paranoid patients shows marked neuropathic (abnormal nervous) tendencies. The disease itself may be characterized as one of chronic systematized delusions. . . . Many "cranks" and "peculiar" people that one constantly meets either are suffering from paranoia or are what may be termed *paranoid characters.* People who have had a single fixed idea largely elaborated, who have regarded themselves as persecuted and as set apart from their fellows in ability and character, are paranoiacs. In this group can be found many leaders who have won distinction in war, politics, and religion.

There seems to be good reason to believe that the systematized delusions of paranoia are defense mechanisms. Here, e.g., is a person who drifts from one job to another, failing at first from inability. Rather than admit his own inferiority, he begins to note seemingly suspicious behavior among his associates. They are spying upon him. They are carrying tales. They tamper with his work. Perhaps he reports the matter to his employer. Finally he is dismissed, and then he repeats the behavior in other situations. People soon begin to notice his peculiar actions, and their attention increases his persecutory delusions. Because his pains are many, he must have many enemies. Indeed, he is pursued by organized bands and groups. He may now hit upon the suggestion that the persecution results from his own great superiority—his associates are jealous of his skill. He is a Messiah, or the world's greatest soldier, or inventor, or what not. His manly characteristics are such that he is passionately loved by a beautiful lady whom his enemies prevent from coming to him—endless indeed is the list of delusions the paranoiac may have.

B

WILLIAM A. WHITE, *Outlines of Psychiatry*, 8th ed., 113-116 (Nervous & Mental Diseases Publishing Co., 1921)

The following is an example of the egocentric variety of this psychosis. The patient belongs to the querulous or litigant type of KRAFFT-EBING. He is an old negro man, a veteran of the Civil War.

He enlisted in the fall of 1863 in the 29th Illinois Colored Infantry in Chicago. Three days later he was sent on to Quincy, Ill., 160 miles south of Chicago. They went into camp and he remained there until May, 1864. At that time the soldiers were mustered from the State to Federal service. The patient was the captain of Company F, which consisted of colored soldiers, and he arranged his men in line for mustering. It was the custom for the captain to take the oath before the men did. One of the Federal officers asked the patient to take the oath of allegiance to the United States, renouncing his allegiance to all other countries, including Canada, where the patient had been born. The patient said that at that time he preferred to remain a subject of Britain and did not think that he should be forced to give up his allegiance, in that he had not enlisted under any such terms. Thereupon the officer refused to muster the company in but allowed the patient to remain at the head of Company F, taking charge of the post at Quincy, Illinois. The patient at once put the city under martial law. July 18, 1864, the company was sent to Chicago and was then requested to come to Washington, D. C., to be mustered in. Here again the patient refused to take the oath as was demanded of him and as a consequence they arrested him, took him from the company and sent him to prison at City Point, Va. After being confined there for a short time he was released, allowed to again take charge of the company, was promised pay at $100 a month for his services and in addition was not required to take the oath of allegiance. He says that he never received any pay for his services. The patient let the matter rest until 1880, thinking that rectification would be made in due course of time when the War Department would discover the injustice that had been done him.

In 1880, under Garfield's administration, patient wrote a letter to Robert T. Lincoln, then Secretary of War. He called the attention of the Secretary to his (the patient's) case. Mr. Lincoln gave the letter to John Sherman, then Secretary of the Treasury, asking the latter to look into the facts in the case. Sherman later wrote the patient that he acknowledged his services during the late rebellion but that he had lost all rights for the payment of services on the ground of desertion. . . . The patient says that he thinks that Sherman was trying to beat him out of the money so that he could keep it for himself and that this was one of the main charges which resulted in the removal of Sherman from his position as Secretary of the Treasury. The patient says that he had demanded of Sherman $500,000 for his eleven months of service, the kidnapping and false arrest and for his having been put back into the service without being regularly mustered into the service of the United States. The patient says that a clerk from the War Department came to him with a message from President Garfield and that $275,000 was offered to him. He accepted the same and was told to wait until they sent for him. He waited until May 20, 1884, and then sent to the War Department again to look after the case. Representative McKinley (later President) took the matter up, showed that there were 83,000 other men on similar false charge of desertion and by Act of Congress exonerated them all, with the patient at the head of the list. President Arthur then ordered Secretary of War, Lincoln, to give the patient a certificate of exoneration and to pay over to him the sum of $500,000. The patient does not know whether Congress had passed a bill to that effect or not. He says that Lincoln tried to put up a job on him. He arranged to meet the patient at the Second Precinct on U St. between Ninth and Tenth, saying that he wished to settle the matter with him privately. He was told that he was to be sent to the Government boarding house for a few days while negotiations were going on, but to his surprise he was sent to this institution March 14, 1885. He remained here until October 6, 1886. The patient states that Dr. Lyons of this institution, who at that time was First Assistant to Superintendent Dr. Godding, tried to poison him by putting drugs into his food—some of the drugs were croton oil, arsenic, henbane, etc. The patient considers it all a plot of Lincoln's to keep the money from him and to take it himself. According to the patient, Dr. Godding helped him to get a writ of habeas corpus and the patient was discharged in the District Court by Judge Cox. The patient conducted the case himself and Dr. Godding testified to his sanity. In 1886 he had the case brought up once more before Judge Montgomery. His lawyer, Walker, would not undertake to argue the case and the patient thinks that he also was in conspiracy against him. Judge Montgomery took the case from the jury and decided it himself, giving as his opinion that the patient's claims were not supported and deciding against the patient.

The patient again had the case brought up before the Senate and he says as a result, the judge was removed from the Bench. The patient claims that the Judge also was bought off by Lincoln, who was then no longer Secretary of War. The patient is sure that Lincoln got much of the money that he himself was entitled to. He says that he learned of this from the papers, that $250,000 was missing from the Treasury Department, that this was one half of his own money and that it was appropriated by Lincoln. The other $250,000 is still in the Treasury for him. Mr. Lincoln is now the President of the Pullman Car Company. The patient now desires to get the other $250,000. He promised to give Mr. Harbough and Dr. Glueck and the examiner a goodly portion of what he gets. Patient says that Cleveland tried to have him get his money but was held off by friends until the expiration of his administration; that President McKinley had practically decided to see that he got his money when he was assassinated; that Roosevelt had the matter up and had it all settled on the eve of his going out of office and that the case was also settled by Mr. Taft but that the money is being held up by both the political parties. Patient says that President Taft in his inaugural address spoke particularly of his own case and promised to see that he got the money. The patient claims that all the big men, not only in the United States but in every nation, know about him and his case; that it was the cause of the war with Spain, that Mr. Hilles, who last week resigned from ambassadorship to Germany, was asked to resign because he was one of the conspirators in the case and that he knows of several prominent men, including former Secretary of the Treasury Shaw and the present Secretary of War, Mr. Dickinson, who have their foot in the plot. He claims that he has been poisoned every once in a while for many years. Even things that he bought in the different grocery stores contained some drug or other. He says that Dr. Lyons, of New York, who was interested in the case on his first admission, has conspirators in this institution at the present moment. He is not sure whether or not he is being drugged at the present time. He says he would go to work if released but thinks he would soon be sent for to settle the case with the Government. Patient says he won't trouble them but he will not be out a day before their consciences will burn them so that they will come to him. He will then see that various officials in this institution will receive their just share of the money that he obtains.

From such extreme cases as the one Dr. White has described, we can gather the significance of paranoid tendencies in cranks,

fanatics, and "psychopathic personalities." *Cf.* Leonardo
Bianchi's *Text Book of Psychiatry.*

Epileptic Psychoses [17]

E. E. SOUTHARD and MARY C. JARRETT, *The Kingdom of Evils*, 469-470
(copyright, 1922, by The Macmillan Company); reprinted by permission

Epilepsy . . . is ordinarily a disease with at least (*a*) unconsciousness and (*b*) convulsions. An attack of unconsciousness
alone does not constitute epilepsy and does not in itself prove the
existence of epilepsy. Neither would a single convulsion, even
though it were very characteristic in its appearance, prove the existence of epilepsy. If, however, the diagnosis of epilepsy is once
established through medical observation of several attacks of unconsciousness with convulsions, then it becomes possible for the
physician to identify certain *minor attacks* and disorders of consciousness with little or no evidence of convulsions, as epileptic.
Accordingly when fainting spells, abstraction, blank feelings, and
episodes of loss of memory occur, the physician is very apt to think
of the possibility of epilepsy.

Modern work seems to have shown that there is an *epileptic
temperament* or personality in which self-consciousness (egocentricity) and inharmony and irritability are found. The epileptic mind seems, on the whole, a little childlike, even when there
is little proof of feeble-mindedness. Modern study of *epilepsy* has
shown that it is much *more exact to speak of epilepsies than of
epilepsy.*

The major or so-called *grand mal* attack of epilepsy consists in
a fall with unconsciousness and spasm. The spasm is at first a
steady tonic spasm, but there shortly appear interrupted or clonic
spasms. Automatic movements follow these clonic spasms. The
patient then either wakes up or passes into a deep sleep. On
waking the victim feels lame and weak in the convulsed muscles,
and his head may ache. There is often absolutely no warning of
these attacks though very striking warnings or so-called *aurae*
(such as flashes of light, sounds, or smells) may occur and as a
rule always in exactly the same form. The muscles are apt to be
affected, always in the same order, and the convulsion is then said
to "march" in a characteristic way. Tongue-biting and frothing
at the mouth are observed, and the patient may involuntarily urinate. It can readily be seen that the social worker who secures the

history of tongue-biting or urination in an attack of epilepsy may be contributing most important evidence for medical diagnosis.

It seems to have been proved that the epileptic attack of the nature above described may sometimes be represented by an acute mental attack without convulsion and even without evident loss of consciousness. Such an attack without characteristic features of epilepsy is termed an epileptiform equivalent. The patient may fall into a state of automatism or into a dream-state in which violent and destructive or criminal acts get done, of which the patient will have no remembrance. The crimes of violence committed by epileptics may be of the greatest brutality. . . . Alcohol is clinically known to bring out epileptic attacks.

Psychoneuroses and Neuroses, Hysterical Type [18(a)]

A

ABRAHAM MYERSON, *The Nervous Housewife,* 18 (copyright, 1920, by Little, Brown & Co.)

Physicians use the term psychoneuroses to include a group of nervous disorders of so-called functional nature. That is to say, there is no alteration that can be found in the brain, the spinal cord, or any part of the nervous system. In this, these conditions differ from such diseases as locomotor ataxia, tumor of the brain, cerebral hemorrhage, etc., because there are marked changes in the structure in the latter troubles. One might compare the psychoneuroses to a watch which needed oiling or cleaning, or merely a winding up,—as against one in which a vital part was broken. . . .

Of all the . . . psychoneuroses, hysteria is probably the one having its source mainly in the character of the patient. That is to say, outward happenings play a part which is secondary to the personality defect. Hysteria is one of the oldest of diseases and has probably played a very important rôle in the history of man. Unquestionably many of the religions have depended upon hysteria, for it is in this field that "miracle cures" occur. All founders of religions have based part of their claim on the belief of others in their healing power. Nothing is so spectacular as when the hysterical blind see, the hysterical dumb talk, the hysterical cripple throws away his crutches and walks. In every age and in every country, in every faith, there have been the equivalents of Lourdes and St. Anne de Beaupré.

In hysteria four important groups of symptoms occur in the housewife as well as in her single sisters and brothers.

There is first of all an emotional instability, with a tendency to prolonged and freakish manifestations,—the well-known hysterics with laughing, crying, etc. Fundamental in the personality of the hysterics is this instability, this emotionality, which is however secondary to an egotistic, easily wounded nature, craving sympathy and respect and often unable legitimately to earn them.

A group of symptoms that seem hard to explain are the so-called paralyses. These paralyses may affect almost any part, may come in a moment and go as suddenly, or last for years. They may concern arm, leg, face, hands, feet, speech, etc. They seem very severe, but are due to worry, to misdirected ideas and emotions and not at all to injury to the nervous system. They are manifestations of what the neurologists call "dissociations of the personality." That is, conflicts of emotions, ideas, and purposes of the type previously described have occurred, and a paralysis has resulted. These paralyses yield remarkably to any energizing influence like good fortune, the compelling personality of a physician or clergyman or healer (the miracle cure), or a serious danger. The latter is exemplified in the cases now and then reported of people who have not been out of bed for years, but are aroused by threat of some danger, like a fire, reach safety, and thereafter are well.

Similar in type to the paralyses are losses of sensation in various parts of the body,—losses so complete that one may thrust a needle deep into the flesh without pain to the patient. In the days of witch-hunting the witch-hunters would test the women suspected with a pin, and if they found places where pain was not felt, considered they had proof of witchcraft or diabolic possession, so that many a hysteric was hanged or drowned. The history of man is full of psychopathic characters and happenings; insane men have changed the course of human events by their ideas and delusions, and on the other hand society has continually mistaken the insane and the nervously afflicted for criminals or wretches deserving severest punishment.

Especially striking in hysteria are the curious changes in consciousness that take place. These range from what seem to be fainting spells to long trances lasting perhaps for months, in which animation is apparently suspended and the body seems on the brink of death. In olden days the Delphian oracles were people who had the power voluntarily of throwing themselves into these hysteric states and their vague statements were taken to be heaven-inspired. To-day, their descendants in hysteria are the crystal gazers, the mediums, the automatic writers that by a mixture of hysteria and faking deceive the simple and credulous.

B

PIERRE JANET, *The Major Symptoms of Hysteria*, 51-53 (copyright, 1920, by The Macmillan Company); reprinted by permission

Further important changes in consciousness are the somnambulisms, and the fugues, or extended wanderings in a state of consciousness which is out of continuity with—failing to remember and to be remembered by—the subject's ordinary waking mental life.   A good example of such a fugue is Janet's patient "Rou.":

The subject is a boy of seventeen, Rou., son of a neuropathic mother, rather nervous himself, who already had, when he was ten years old, tics and contractures in the neck, of which we shall speak in one of our following lectures [omitted].   At thirteen he often went to a small public house, visited by old sailors.   They would urge him to drink, and, when he was somewhat flustered, they would fill his imagination with beautiful tales in which deserts, palm trees, lions, camels, and negroes were pictured in a most wonderful and alluring way.   The young boy was very much struck by those pictures, particularly as he was half tipsy.   However, when his drunkenness was over, the stories seemed to be quite forgotten; he never spoke of travels, and, on the contrary, led a very sedentary life for he had chosen the placid occupation of a grocer's boy, and he only sought to rise in that honourable career.

Now there come on quite unforeseen accidents [symptoms], almost always on the occasion of some fatigue or a fit of drunkenness. He then felt transformed, forgot to return home, and thought no more of his family.   He would leave Paris, walking straight ahead, and go to a more or less great distance through the forest of St. Germain, or as far as the department of the Orne.   Sometimes he walked alone; at other times he rambled with some tramps, begging along the roads; he had but one idea left in his head; namely, to get to the sea, enlist in a ship and sail away towards those enchanting countries of Africa.   His journeys ended rather badly; he would awake suddenly, drenched, half starving, either on the highroad or in an asylum, without ever being able to understand what had happened, without any memory of his journey, and with the most ardent wish to go back to his family and his grocery.

I will dwell on only one of his fugues, which is particularly amusing, and was of extraordinary duration, for it lasted three months. He had left Paris about the fifteenth of May, and had walked to the neighbourhood of Melun. This time he was thinking about the means of succeeding in his scheme and of getting safely to the Mediterranean. Until then he had failed, owing to fatigue and misery: the question was to find means of living as he went along. A bright idea had occurred to him; not far from Melun, at Moret, there are canals that go more or less straight to the south of France, and in those canals there are ships laden with goods. He succeeded in being accepted as a servant on a ship laden with coal. His work was terrible; now he had to shovel the coal, now to haul the rope in company with a donkey called Cadet, his only friend. He was badly fed, often beaten, exhausted with fatigue, but, though you would scarcely believe it, he was radiant with happiness. He thought only of one thing,—of the joy of drawing nearer to the sea. Unhappily, in Auvergne, the boat stopped, and he was forced to leave it and continue his journey on foot, which was more difficult. In order not to be resourceless, he hired himself as a helper to an old china mender. They went slowly along, working on the road.

Then, one evening, an unlooked-for event took place again. The day's work had been a success; the two companions had earned seven francs. The old china mender stopped and said to R., "My boy, we deserve a good supper; and we will keep to-day's feast; it is the fifteenth of August." On hearing this, the boy heedlessly said: "The fifteenth of August? Why, it is the feast of the Virgin Mary, the anniversary of my mother's name-day." He had scarcely uttered these words when he appeared to be quite changed. He looked all around him with astonishment, and turning to his companion, said, "But who are you, and what am I doing here with you?" The poor man was amazed, and was quite unable to make the boy understand the situation; the latter still believed himself in Paris, and had lost all memory of the preceding months. They had to go to the village mayor's, where, with great difficulty, the matter was made more or less clear. The mayor telegraphed to Paris, and the prodigal child was sent back home. Is not that name, which suddenly evoked the memory of his mother and awakened him likewise, a pretty conclusion of a fugue?

C

PIERRE JANET, *The Major Symptoms of Hysteria*, 29-32 (copyright, 1920, by The Macmillan Company) ; reprinted by permission

Another clear type of hysteria is presented by Janet as follows:

We come back to the common story of a young girl twenty years old, called Irène, whom despair, caused by her mother's death, has made ill. We must remember that this woman's death has been very moving and dramatic. The poor woman, who had reached the last stage of consumption, lived alone with her daughter in a poor garret. Death came slowly, with suffocation, blood-vomiting, and all its frightful procession of symptoms. The girl struggled hopelessly against the impossible. She watched her mother during sixty nights, working at her sewing-machine to earn a few pennies necessary to sustain their lives. After the mother's death she tried to revive the corpse, to call the breath back again; then, as she put the limbs upright, the body fell to the floor, and it took infinite exertion to lift it again into the bed. You may picture to yourself all that frightful scene. Some time after the funeral, curious and impressive symptoms began. It was one of the most splendid cases of somnambulism I ever saw.

The crises last for hours, and they show a splendid dramatic performance, for no actress could rehearse those lugubrious scenes with such perfection. The young girl has the singular habit of acting again all the events that took place at her mother's death, without forgetting the least detail. Sometimes she only speaks, relating all that happened with great volubility, putting questions and answers in turn, or asking questions only, and seeming to listen for the answer; sometimes she only sees the sight, looking with frightened face and staring on the various scenes, and acting according to what she sees. At other times, she combines all hallucinations, words, and acts, and seems to play a very singular drama. When, in her drama, death has taken place, she carries on the same idea, and makes everything ready for her own suicide. She discusses it aloud, seems to speak with her mother, to receive advice from her; she fancies she will try to be run over by a locomotive. That detail is also a recollection of a real event of her life. She fancies she is on the way, and stretches herself out on the floor of the room, waiting for death, with mingled dread and impatience. She poses, and wears on her face expressions really worthy of admiration, which remain fixed during several minutes. The train arrives before her staring eyes, she utters a terrible shriek, and falls back motionless, as if she were dead. She soon gets up and begins acting over again one of the preceding scenes. In fact, one of the characteristics of these somnambulisms is that they repeat themselves indefinitely. Not only the different attacks are always exactly alike, repeating the same movements, expressions, and words, but in the course of the same attack, when it has lasted a certain time, the same scene may be repeated again exactly in the same way five or ten times. At last, the agitation seems to wear out, the dream grows less clear, and, gradually or suddenly, according to the cases, the patient comes back to her normal consciousness, takes up her ordinary business, quite undisturbed by what has happened.

I could tell you many more of these examples, for all the events of life may be reflected in one of these scenes. This patient acts over again a scene wherein he has been bitten by a dog; that one reproduces in his dream the emotion he had when he was wounded by the falling of the lift. This little girl fancies a scene of her school life, in which she was severely punished; that young girl reflects a scene of ravishment; a young boy repeats a quarrel in the street; another man lives through a chapter he has read in a novel, where thieves get through a latticed window and bind him tightly to his bed. This kind of delirium may vary over and over again in a thousand different ways. It is, however, very characteristic, and in all mental pathology you will not find another delirium that may be compared with it.

D

Pierre Janet, *The Major Symptoms of Hysteria*, 11-13 (copyright, 1920, by The Macmillan Company); reprinted by permission

However, we should not underrate the importance of the wealth of "physical" anomalies that so often appear in hystericals, as Janet says:

One of the greatest difficulties in the medical art and one of the greatest misfortunes of patients is that hysterical diseases are . . . uncommonly similar to all kinds of medical or surgical affections, for which they are easily mistaken. Contractures, paralyses, anesthesias, various pains, especially when they are seated in the viscera, may simulate anything; and then you have the legion of false tuberculoses of the lungs, of false tumours of the stomach, of false intestinal obstructions, and above all, of false uterine and ovarian

tumours. What happens as to the viscera also exists as to the limbs
and the organs of the senses. Some hysterical disturbances are
mistaken for lesions of the bones, of the rachis, for muscular or
tendinous lesions. Then the physician interposes, frightens the
family, agitates the patient to the utmost, and prescribes extraordinary diets, perturbing the life and exhausting the strength of
the sick person. Finally, the surgeon is called in. Do not try to
count the number of arms cut off, of muscles of the neck incised
for cricks, of bones broken for mere cramps, of bellies cut open for
phantom tumours, and especially of women made barren for pretended ovarian tumours. Humanity ought indeed to do homage to
Charcot for having prevented a greater depopulation. These things
no doubt have decreased, but they are still done every day. Not
long ago I saw a patient who had had an eye excised and the optic
nerve cut out for mere neuropathic pains. If I could only, by calling your attention and interest to the knowledge of this disease,
contribute to diminish the number of these medical crimes, I
should already have attained a very important result.[1]

Psychoneuroses and Neuroses, Psychasthenic Type (Anxiety and Obsessive Forms) [18(b)]

A

ABRAHAM MYERSON, *The Nervous Housewife*, 31-33 (copyright, 1920, by
Little, Brown & Co.)

By the term psychasthenia is understood a group of conditions in
which the bodily symptoms, such as fatigue, sleeplessness, loss of
appetite, etc., are either not so marked as in neurasthenia,[2] or
else are overshadowed by other, more distinctly mental symptoms.

These mental symptoms are of three main types. There is a
tendency to recurring fears,—fears of open places, fears of closed
places, fear of leaving home, of being alone, fear of eating or
sleeping, fear of dirt, so that the victim is impelled continually to
wash the hands, fear of disease—especially such as syphilis—and
a host of other fears, all of which are recognized as unreasonable,

---

[1] [Hysterical phenomena are taken up again in later chapters of the
present volume. Further descriptions, along with very Freudian interpretation, may be found in Charles Daniel Fox, *The Psychopathology of
Hysteria*. *Cf.* also Donald Elms Core, *Functional Nervous Disorders*.]

[2] [*Infra*, p. 83 ff.]

against which the victim struggles but vainly. Sometimes the fear is nameless, vague, undifferentiated, and comes on like a cloud with rapid heartbeat, faint feelings, and a sense of impending death. Sometimes the fear is related to something that has actually happened, as, fear of anything hot after a sunstroke; or fear of any vehicle after an automobile accident.[1]

---

[1] ["There is hardly anything about which a fear may not be developed. There are those who have fears of open spaces and are quite unable to cross a vacant lot, or even a street, without a tremendous and exhausting effort. Others fear closed spaces and are thrown into a panic in a crowd, or in a small room or a closet. Still others fear certain harmless animals such as cats, rats, chickens, dogs, horses; or they fear the dark, and certain noises, such as the wind. Then there is the fear of swallowing certain foods, or even of nearly all foods; fear of dirt, fear of water, fear of poverty, fear of old age, fear of loss of position, fear of certain people, fear of saying or doing improper things, fear of sin, fear of future punishment, fear of bodily functions, fear of attracting attention, fear of lying, fear of marriage, fear of child-birth, fear of nearly all new undertakings and situations, and a great host of fears associated with doubts and indecisions. In fact, there is probably nothing that some one has not had a fear about. Yet, most people afflicted with such fears are not insane, although some, of course, may be; and the fear is then only one of the symptoms of their insanity. . . .

"As an example of fear of high places, a veteran federal officer, bearing the scars of bandits' bullets which are surely mute badges of courage, had driven his car up into a mountain resort for his vacation. The last three miles of the mountain road approaching the camp were cut out from the side of the embankment so that in many places there was an almost sheer drop of several hundred feet at one side. Yet the road was an excellent one, wide enough for two cars to pass at many points, and with turnouts arranged at convenient places. It was a stage and tourists' road where scores of cars passed and repassed every day,—in short, a good mountain road.

"Now, this officer was accustomed to mountain driving and was an expert at the wheel. But it so happened that on the journey toward the camp the steep drop from the road was on his left, with the embankment on the right, so that in making the turns to pass other cars, his car was always in the inside toward the embankment. On the journey out, however, this condition would be reversed so that in making the turnouts when meeting other cars he would be on the outside at the verge of the precipitous road. Yet all this was of such little consequence, and there was so little actual danger, that the government which controlled the road had never thought it necessary to make it a 'one way' road. Nevertheless, the thought of having to make the return drive along this road to reach home so preyed on the officer's mind for the two weeks that it literally spoiled his vacation. He was really obsessed by two fears—the fear of the actual drive, and the still greater fear of ridicule from his associates should they discover that he was afraid—a fear of confessing a fear, if you please.

"In the end he did drive his car out without difficulty, even though it

There is also a tendency to obsessive ideas and doubts; that is, ideas and doubts that persist in coming against the will of the patient, such as the obscene word or phrase that continually ob-

---

happened that he encountered the very thing he had most dreaded—a car coming from the opposite direction which he was obliged to pass at one of the most difficult places in the entire road. But having accomplished this without mishap, all his apprehensions left him; even the very worst thing that could happen on the road—the thing he had been dreading so—was of comparatively trivial importance after all! And if he had been able to visualize this in advance he would have saved himself the two weeks of mental misery.

"In another case which came to our attention a man had succeeded in climbing the rather steep trail to Mount Wilson; but when he thought of the return he became paralyzed with fear. So great was this fear that in spite of all his efforts to overcome it, it at last became necessary not only to blindfold him, but actually place him under an anesthetic and carry him down the mountain in an army stretcher. Yet this trail was used daily by many people, was not dangerous, or in any manner unusual, nor was this man in most respects more timid, peculiar, or less successful than his neighbors. Such cases need sympathetic understanding, but also scientific treatment, for the defect is a real one requiring for its removal something more than argument. It is in just such instances that uncovering the origin of the fear complex and treating it with suggestion, whether under the name of Coué, or plain common sense, results in cures.

"These two experiences should, of course, suggest their own remedies. In actuality very few of our apprehensions of approaching dangers are ever realized. Imagination always exaggerates what reason should correct. Thus, a little common-sense reasoning about the situation would have cleared up matters for the apprehensive officer. He should have taken himself in hand somewhat as follows: 'Here is a road that has been in use for years and there has never been a bad accident. Thousands of people have driven over it without mishap, most of them far less skilful drivers than I. Wherefore, there can not be any very great danger either in coming in or going out.' And he might have added, had he been of a somewhat more philosophical turn of mind: 'And if it comes to the worst and I do drop over the cliff, it is almost certain and sudden death. And death is inevitable in the end, anyhow. So why should I spoil my holiday with fruitless worries?'

"Now, it is almost certain that in ordinary circumstances the officer would have reasoned in some such manner. But it so happened that this new hazard came upon him at a time when he was tired and nervously overwrought,—when his 'fighting glands' were less active than usual, and the centers of apprehension abnormally assertive. Complete rest would have quickly established normality. But worry is a sure preventive of this; and the 'glands of worry' seem to be accelerated in their action by use. *The more one worries, the more one tends to worry.*

"The really interesting thing about these cases of intense fears over trivial matters in normally courageous persons is the fact itself—the fact that even the most courageous individuals may have intense fears about things that other people practically disregard. And the encouraging thing

trudes itself on a chaste woman, or the doubt whether one has shut the door or properly turned off the gas. Of course, everybody has such obsessions and doubts occasionally, but to be psychasthepic about it is to have them continually and to have them obtrude themselves into every action. In extreme psychasthenia the difficulty of "making up the mind," of deciding, becomes so great that a person may suffer agonies of internal debate about crossing the street, putting on his clothes, eating his meals, doing his work, about every detail of his coming, going, doing, and thinking. A restless anxiety results, a fear of insanity, an inefficiency, and an incapacity for sustained effort that results in the name that is often applied,—"anxiety neurosis."

Third, there is a group of impulsions and habits.[1] Citing a few

---

is that most of these fears may be overcome by the simple process of common-sense reasoning after their origins have once been uncovered and explained. . . .

"*One should not confuse superstitious or morbid fears with what may be termed natural and normal fears.* Thus, the fear of accidental injury, or death, from one of a thousand different sources is natural and normal in so far as it serves as protection and to elicit caution and insure self-preservation. A person steps aside from the path of a swiftly moving automobile and escapes death by the margin of an inch without giving the matter a second thought. At most there is only a momentary startling which is entirely transient in the normal individual. He does not dwell long on the narrowness of his escape, nor brood over the possibility that to-morrow a passing motor-car will run him down. It is one of the natural daily hazards of existence.

"This is true also about a host of other ever-menacing dangers. We know that impending death or disaster lurks everywhere and always about us—storms, earthquakes, fires, automobile accidents, shipwrecks, disease, stalk our paths incessantly. But the normal individual takes these things as a matter of course and does not dwell morbidly upon them—does not worry over, or 'take them to bed with him.' When he does so, he is transforming natural fears or caution into morbid ones; his normal caution or indifference to unavoidable dangers from without has become a morbid fear of things from within himself. His attitude is no longer normal. It is not the actual danger of the thing itself that haunts him, but the morbid fear of that danger created within himself."—Edward Huntington Williams and Ernest Bryant Hoag, *Our Fear Complexes,* 30-36, 48-49 (Bobbs-Merrill, 1923).]

[1] ["It is not always possible to say just where useful habit merges into obsession. A certain individual, we will say, invariably puts on the left shoe before the right. This is a useful habit, fixed by constant repetition, useful because it relieves the brain of conscious effort. But suppose he decides some morning to put on the right shoe before the left; this new order so offends his sense of the fitness of things that he finds it hard to proceed; if he perseveres, his feet feel wrong to him; the discomfort grows until finally he is impelled to remove the shoes and replace them in the

absurd impulsions: A person feels compelled to step over every crack, to touch the posts along his journey, to take the stairs three steps at a time. The habits range from the queer desire to bite

---

usual order. In this case an act which started as a useful habit has been replaced by an obsession.

"Suppose, again, a person obsessed by the fear of poison is prevented from washing his hands before eating. He sits down, perhaps, fully intending to proceed as if nothing had happened, but the thought occurs to him that he may have touched something poisonous, though his reason tells him this is most improbable. He reviews the events of the day and can find no suggestion of poison; still the thought of poison obtrudes itself, and he finds it impossible to put anything which he touches into his mouth. He next wonders if he has not already put something into his mouth. This thought produces a mental panic, the blood mounts to his head, he becomes incapable of coherent thought or speech, and the task of finishing his dinner would now be beyond his power even if he had not lost all taste for it.

"Such illustrations of obsession in daily life, by no means rare, could be multiplied indefinitely, and may be perhaps better appreciated than the text-book illustration of the man who neglected to flick off with his whip a certain stone from the top of a wall, and who could not sleep until he had returned to the spot and performed the act.

"Suppose a man has always worn high boots and is accustomed to a feeling of warmth about the ankles. The desire for warm ankles may finally so dominate him that he not only cannot wear low shoes in mid-summer, but he cannot wear slippers, even in a warm room; and finally, perhaps, finds that he must wear woollen socks to bed. By this time the desire for a certain sensation is in a fair way to become an obsession. When you assure him that many wear low shoes throughout the winter, he asks if their ankles really feel warm. That is not the question. The question is, can one accustom himself to the ankles feeling cool, just as he accustoms himself to his face feeling cool. If he can, he has conquered a sensory obsession, and has made a step toward fitting himself to meet more serious vicissitudes with equanimity. . . .

"Few children are quite free from obsession. Some must step on stones; others must walk on, or avoid, cracks; some must ascend the stairs with the right foot first; many must kick posts or touch objects a certain number of times. Some must count the windows, pictures, and figures on the wall-paper; some must bite the nails or pull the eye-winkers. Consider the nail-biter. It cannot be said that he toils not, but to what end? Merely to gratify an obsession. He nibbles a little here and a little there, he frowns, elevates his elbow, and inverts his finger to reach an otherwise inaccessible corner. Does he enjoy it? No, not exactly; but he would be miserable if he discontinued. . . .

"It is during childhood that we form most of the automatic habits which are to save time and thought in later life, and it is not surprising that some foolish habits creep in. As a rule, children drop these tendencies at need, just as they drop the rôles assumed in play, though they are sometimes so absorbing as to cause inconvenience. An interesting instance was that of the boy who had to touch every one wearing anything red. On

one's nails to the quick that is so common in children and which persists in the psychasthenic adult, to the odd grimaces and facial contortions, blinking eyes and cracking joints of the inveterate

---

one occasion his whole family lost their train because of the prevalence of this color among those waiting in the station.

"The longer these tendencies are retained in adult life, the greater the danger of their becoming coercive; and so far as the well-established case is concerned the obsessive act must be performed, though the business, social, and political world should come to a stand-still. Among the stories told in illustration of compulsive tendency in the great, may be instanced the touching of posts, and the placing of a certain foot first, in the case of Dr. Johnson, who, it appears, would actually retrace his steps and repeat the act which failed to satisfy his requirements, with the air of one with something off his mind.

"A child who must kick posts is father to the man who cannot eat an egg which has been boiled either more or less than four minutes; who cannot work without absolute silence; who cannot sleep if steam-pipes crackle; and who must straighten out all the tangles of his life, past, present, and future, before he can close his eyes in slumber or take a vacation. The boy Carlyle, proud, shy, sensitive, and pugnacious, was father to the man who made war upon the neighbor's poultry, and had a room, proof against sound, specially constructed for his literary labors.

"The passive obsessions are peculiarly provocative of worry. Such are extreme aversions to certain animals, foods, smells, sounds, and sights, or insistent discomfort if affairs are not ordered to our liking. A gentleman once told me that at the concert he did not mind if his neighbor followed the score, but when he consulted his programme during the performance it distressed him greatly.

"Such instances illustrate the fact that when our obsessions rule us it is not the noise or the sight, but our idea of the fitness of things, that determines the degree of our annoyance. A person who cannot endure the crackling of the steam-pipe can listen with pleasure to the crackling of an open fire or the noise of a running brook.

"It is said that the sensitive and emotional Erasmus had so delicate a digestion that he could neither eat fish nor endure the smell of it; but we are led to suspect that obsession played a part in his troubles when we further learn that he could not bear an iron stove in the room in which he worked, but had to have either a porcelain stove or an open fire.

"If we can trust the sources from which Charles Reade drew his deductions regarding the character of the parental stock, Erasmus came fairly by his sensitive disposition. In 'The Cloister and the Hearth' we find the father of Erasmus, fleeing from his native land, in fear of his life on account of a crime he thought he had committed, frozen, famished and exhausted, unable to enter the door of a friendly inn on account of his aversion to the issuing odors. Forced by his sufferings at last to enter the inn, he visits each corner in turn, analyzing its peculiar smell and choosing finally the one which seems to him the least obnoxious.

"I have heard somewhere, but cannot place, the story of a prominent writer who was so disturbed by the mechanical lawn-mower of his

ticquer. Against some of these habit spasms, comparable to severe stammering, all measures are in vain, for there seems to be a queer pleasure in these acts against which the will of the patient is powerless.

B

ROBERT PERCIVAL PARSONS and W. S. TAYLOR, prepared for this volume

A CASE OF OBSESSIVE PHANTASYING

An American white, 31 years old, is awaiting military trial for sleeping on his post of duty. Day after day he sits around with his head on his hands, looking very dejected, though when he looks up and speaks to anyone his manner is courteous and pleasant. At other times he stands looking out the window for long periods, or paces back and forth gazing at the floor. The only peculiarity about his facial expression is a slightly worried look.

Upon being questioned, he confesses that he is worried about being a prisoner, about his habits of day-dreaming, his spermatorrhea, his flight of ideas, and the egocentricity of his thoughts.

He has tried to study many things, but never gets anywhere of late years. He thinks he suffers much from forgetfulness. It is impossible for him to concentrate upon one thing for any length of time, either because of the obsessions about to be described, or because of some tune which may run through his head for hours at a stretch. Thus, in reading a book well within the range of his intelligence, he finds that he has lost the connection by the time he has reached the middle of a paragraph, so must reread every paragraph.

He also complains of great nervousness. When an officer speaks to him he is so scared that he answers the first thing that comes into his head. Thus, when asked the date of his birth, he answered simply "1891," when in reality he knows it to have been in 1888. When it comes to being transferred he remembers what he has to

---

neighbor that he insisted upon the privilege of defraying the expense of its replacement by the scythe.

"Peculiar sensitiveness to sights, sounds, and smells seems to be a common attribute of genius. This sort of sensitiveness has even been credited with being the main-spring of genius, but it is improbable that the curbing of such aversions would in any way endanger it. However this may be, such supersensitiveness ill becomes the rest of us, and these extreme aversions surely clog, rather than accelerate, our efforts."—George Lincoln Walton, *Why Worry?*, 69-72, 59-60, 61-66 (Lippincott, 1920).]

get together, but gets so worked up as the time approaches that he is liable to leave half of his stuff. When in "chow" line he fails to get a knife or a fork or something, although these are arranged in order along his route to the dining hall. If he is asked to help the attendants in any way he is ready to do so, but the task is performed in a nervous, jerky manner, as though he will do it since someone must.

His orientation seems normal, as he answers all questions intelligently and realizes the abnormality of his own feelings and the bizarre character of his day-dreams. Thus, in describing the magic force he has imagined to make his phantasies seem more possible, he says: "Of course this is a foolish notion, but you asked me to tell you what I think about, so I'm telling you."

His dreams are of the ideal, with himself at the center of things. The magic force which, in the dreams, makes all things possible, is what he calls "liquid electricity," a pink fluid which comes highly concentrated in metal tubes. A tube the size of a cigar will run an automobile for a week. This force could be used to accomplish many reforms.

The first thing would be to move the capital of the nation to the middle of the country where it should have been built in the first place. The new "Washington D. C." would be laid out on an improved plan, however. Liquid electricity would be used to bore tunnels from various parts of the country to the site of the new Washington, which would be placed in an arid portion of the West. Each tunnel would be made by a man walking along with a cylinder of liquid electricity with a small hole in the end of the cylinder so that a fine stream of the energy would strike the earth ahead of him, causing it to retreat to the sides of the spray. If he wanted the tunnel larger he would simply increase the rate of flow of the liquid electricity.

Washington D. C. would be built in layers, four of which would be beneath the surface of the ground. On the first story below the surface, the streets would accommodate vehicles going north and south; on the next level below this the vehicles would be going east and west; next below this would be the north and south bound railways, beneath which are tunnels, all bored by liquid electricity, for trains going east and west. There would be several stations for each railway, to avoid congestion of traffic. Escalators would carry passengers from the stations to the surface. Below these railways are tunnels for the through express trains from New York to "St. Petrograd," in "Rooshia," run by the same electric power. Underneath the surface of the city, also, would be a complete system of water supply bringing the purest of water for drinking and for irrigation purposes from the Mackenzie River "of Alaska." This would be brought underground all the way from the North, with no openings into the tunnel except to allow some of the water to go out in places to irrigate dry territory.

All the buildings of the city would be built of "silver metal," which is the product of the action of liquid electricity upon cement. There would be many parks and public buildings, and no slums, as all the dependent and immoral characters would be gathered upon various farms in the country.

In a most pleasant part of the new Washington we should find the Schools of York, built with a view to educating every child in America whose parents could not afford to give it the training best fitted for it. These children would be brought to the city at Government expense over the railways which connect with all parts of the country. Every home in America would know of the opportunity to send children to the Schools of York. (When asked why the schools were called this, subject remarked that it was just a name for them.)

Religion in the city would be encouraged and all creeds allowed, but without any sectarian hindrances upon marriage, such as now exist between Catholics and Protestants and between Jews and Gentiles.

In the White House the subject would live as President, giving personal supervision to reforms throughout the nation. He would be unmarried, as (in this ideal state!) it would be a crime to pass his form of nervousness down to a new generation.

Subject said he had many other day-dreams. As an illustration of a different kind he told of a trip through the planets on a ship with frictionless walls, stored with food and condensed oxygen, and propelled by liquid electricity. Calling at the planet Mars, he would exchange ideas on political science, etc., and would bring back improved tools, animals, and plants. For example, he might find varieties of pumpkins which would produce the vegetables as big as barns.

Subject spends most of his time thinking about these things, even when working. He sleeps fairly well at night, but dreams a good deal. Off-hand, he does not remember anything unusual about his night dreams.

C

BERNARD EWER, *Applied Psychology*, 364-368 (copyright, 1923, by The Macmillan Company) ; reprinted by permission

Many psychasthenic ideas are of a very specialized character, sometimes accompanied by painful emotion, sometimes mere uncomfortable intruders into the mental life. Ideas of horrible dangers, ridiculous misfortunes, disgusting and repulsive objects may obsess the mind, defying every resolve not to think of them, and interfering seriously with business and happiness. They usually succumb, however, to a methodical countersuggestion, which substitutes other and harmless ideas for them, or develops them into a less disagreeable form. A few illustrations will suffice.

Münsterberg mentions the case of a man who suffered from a vivid tactual hallucination that his wrists were being cut. It gave way in a few days to the simple treatment of gazing steadily at his wrists for ten minutes at a time, until the visual sensations inhibited the hallucinatory tactual ones. In this instance the counteracting agency was perceptual. Frequently it is imaginative, as in the case of a young woman who, whenever she rose with the congregation in church, was beset by the idea that she could not sit down again, but would have to remain standing, to the amusement of all. Though the misfortune never occurred, and she was too sensible to be greatly distressed by it, she nevertheless found it in its own small way a nuisance. Instead of combating it directly she sidetracked it by imagining herself walking serenely out of church, whereupon it ceased to trouble her. Similarly, a man was repeatedly annoyed by the thought of catching his foot in a railroad switch while an oncoming train rushed upon him. The recurrent imagery probably arose from having heard or read of some such tragedy, and it always brought an organic thrill of painful fear. It yielded to a deliberate autosuggestion of extricating his foot by a peculiar twist. So, too, the milder forms of auditory hallucination, such as persistent ringing in the ears, may sometimes be removed or at least rendered less irritable, by being methodically associated with pleasant topics of reflection. The general principle in any case is that of constructing a definite channel for the release and transformation of the psychasthenic energy.

Turning to the class of psychasthenic impulses, we find such illustrations as habitual talking to oneself, needless counting and repetition of little actions, avoidance of persons on the street, inclination to petty and useless theft, profanity and indecent speech, wrong sex impulses, and the like. Since their motor character implies that they are in some measure ingrained in the psychophysical organism, they usually call for reëducational treatment with the same features of preliminary attitude of opposition, specific countersuggestion, antagonistic or side-tracking habit, which we have noted as applicable to other difficulties. Thus persons who persistently talk to themselves about their troubles overcome the impulse simply by choosing happier topics of conversation, a diversion of energy which soon puts an end to the habit. The unwillingness to meet acquaintances face to face, that strange shrinking which leads the victim to cross the street or turn a corner out of his way rather than undergo the experience, may sometimes be frustrated by assuming a positive attitude of courteous or even eager greeting, and formulating actively a cheerful salutation. When we grasp the principle of constructing artificially an attitude or idea which will touch off an opposing or divergent tendency, we find that the objectionable one lies within our power of control.

In settled cases a varied and protracted application of this principle is necessary. A young man who found that his impulse to profanity threatened to assume psychasthenic proportions sought to free himself altogether from the habit. He set about it by putting down in writing all the good reasons he could think of why he ought not to use profane speech, and reading them over daily. Further, he formulated a carefully worded pledge which he regularly repeated to himself night and morning. He also fined himself for infractions and periodically reported his progress to a friend. The latter factor proved especially efficacious. The unwillingness to make a bad report produced a subconscious mental set in the right direction, so that he eventually expurgated his vocabulary.

An interesting example of psychical reëducation is that of a girl who had been troubled from early childhood by a fear of noise. She was healthy and naturally cheerful, but suffered keenly from thunderstorms, explosive fireworks, roaring trains, and the like. A slamming door made her cringe, and the starter's pistol at a track contest served to keep her away from the field. "Some of my friends wonder why I tear up every paper bag I find," she said with a smile. She overcame the fear by a prolonged effort in which there were several graduated factors. It began with the deliberate imagination of noise, accompanied by persistent relaxation of the tense muscles, which automatically stiffened at the mere thought. From this she advanced to actual experience of noise, increasing degrees of which were provided in varied and ingenious ways by obliging friends, who participated in the treatment with the utmost cheerfulness. The process continued for several weeks with the general character of a protracted joke, and a steady elimination of the unpleasant reaction. The outcome was a comparative freedom from the fear, and a normal enjoyment of much that had previously been painful.

The difficulties under discussion in the foregoing paragraphs are not as a rule very serious; in fact they are so slight as hardly to deserve the designation of "psychasthenia." They are removed only by degrees from the graver psychasthenic afflictions, however, and it is worth while to learn how to deal with them intelligently along psychotherapeutic lines. In this way one may not only avoid their discomfort, but may also prevent them from developing into a more troublesome form.

Psychoneuroses and Neuroses, Neurasthenic Type [18(c)]

A

ABRAHAM MYERSON, *The Nervous Housewife*, 20-26 (copyright, 1920, by Little, Brown, & Co.)

The keynote of neurasthenia is *increased liability to fatigue.* The tired feeling that comes on with a minimum of exertion, worse on arising than on going to bed, is its distinguishing mark. Sleep, which should remove the fatigue of the day, does not; the victim takes half of his day to get going; and at night, when he should have the delicious drowsiness of bedtime, he is wide-awake and disinclined to go to bed or sleep. This fatigue enters into all functions of the mind and body. Fatigue of mind brings about lack of concentration, an inattention; and this brings about an inefficiency that worries the patient beyond words as portending a mental breakdown. Fatigue of purpose brings a listlessness of effort, a shirking of the strenuous, the more distressing because the victim is often enough an idealist with over-lofty purposes. Fatigue of mood is marked by depression of a mild kind, a liability to worry, an unenthusiasm for those one loves or for the things formerly held dearest. And finally the fatigue is often marked by a lack of control over the emotional expression, so that anger blazes forth more easily over trifles, and the tears come upon even a slight vexation. *To be neurasthenic is to magnify the pins and pricks of life into calamities, and to be the victim of an abnormal state that is neither health nor disease.*

The most purely physical symptoms constitute almost every-thing imaginable.

Pains and aches of all kinds stand out prominently; headache, backache, pains in the shoulders and arms, pains in the feet and legs, pains that flit here and there, dull weary pains, disagreeable feelings rather than true pains. These pains are frequently related to disagreeable experiences and thoughts, but it is probable that fatigue plays the principal part in evoking them.

Changes in the appetite, in the condition of the stomach and bowels, are prominent. Loss of appetite is complained of, or more often a capricious appetite, vanishing quickly, or else too easily satisfied. The capriciousness of appetite is undoubtedly emotional, for disagreeable emotions, such as worry, fear, vexation, have long been known as the chief enemies of appetite. . . .

Fundamental in the symptoms of neurasthenia is fear. This fear takes two main forms. First, the worry over the life situation in general, that is to say, fear concerning business; fear concerning the health and prosperity of the household; fear that magnifies anything that has even the faintest possibility of being direful into something that is almost sure to happen and be disastrous. This constant worry over the possibilities of the future is both a cause of neurasthenia and a symptom, in that once a neurasthenic state is established, the liability to worry becomes greatly increased.

Second, there is a special form of worry called by the old authors hypochondriacism, which essentially is fear about one's own health. The hypochondriac magnifies every flutter of his heart into heart disease, every stitch in his side into pleurisy, every cough into tuberculosis, every pain in the abdomen into cancer of the stomach, every headache into the possibility of brain tumor or insanity. He turns his gaze inward upon himself, and by so doing becomes aware of a host of sensations that otherwise stream along unno-ticed. Our vision was meant for the environment, for the world in which we live, since the bodily processes go on best unnoticed. The little fugitive pains and aches; the little changes in respiration; the rumblings and movements of the gastro-intestinal tract have no essential meaning in the majority of cases, but once they are watched with apprehension and anxiety, they multiply extraor-dinarily in number and intensity. One of the cardinal groups of symptoms in a neurasthenic is this fear of serious bodily disease for which he seeks examination and advice constantly. Naturally enough, he becomes the choicest prey for the charlatan, the faker, or perhaps ranks second to the victim of venereal or sexual disease. The faker usually assures him that he has the disorders he fears and then proceeds to cure him by his own expensive and marvelous course of treatment.

What has been sketched here is merely the outside of neurasthenia. Back of it as causative are matters we shall deal with in detail later on . . . matters like innate temperament, bad training, liability to worry, wounded pride, failure, desire for sympathy, monotony of life, boredom, unhappiness, pessimism of outlook, over-æsthetic tastes, unfulfilled and thwarted desires, secret jealousy, passions and longings, fear of death, sex problems and difficulties and doubt; matters like recent illness, childbirth, poverty, overwork, wrong sex habits, lack of fresh air, etc.

Fundamentally neurasthenia is a deënergization. By this is meant that either there is an actual reduction in the energy of the body (as after a sickness, pregnancy, etc.) or else something impedes the discharge of energy. This latter is usually an emotional matter, or arises from some thought, some life situation of a depressing kind.[1]

B

BERNARD EWER, *Applied Psychology*, 353 (copyright, 1923, by The Macmillan Company); reprinted by permission

Many a famous character in history has shown neurasthenic symptoms, and we may regard these as but the dark side of the traits which produced greatness. Sensitiveness and quick play of emotion have their peculiar value. The victim of neurasthenia often possesses a potency of intelligent sympathy which is a source of extraordinary power. Sympathetic intuition combined with cheerfulness and wisdom constitute a personal charm which not only wins loyalty, but also affords helpfulness of the highest order. A person of neurasthenic disposition ought frankly to face the alternative, "Shall I allow myself to become a slave to my nervous system, or make it my efficient servant in aiding others?"

---

[1] [*Cf.* Dr. Myerson's little volume, *When Life Loses Its Zest.*]

Psychoneuroses and Neuroses, Other Types [18(d)]

WALTER S. HUNTER. *General Psychology,* rev. ed., 83-87 (Univ. of Chicago Press, 1923)

Multiple Personality. The study of *multiple personality* offers another example of functional psychoses. . . . The average individual regards himself as a unitary being. He remembers the major portion of the things he encounters and of the actions that he performs. He has organized his behavior to such an extent that no feeling of strangeness attaches to the fact that his actions on the baseball-field are governed by different standards from those which control his conduct in business or in the home. Yet in a very true sense it can be said . . . that even though this individual's experiences are the possession of a single person, just as truly they may be regarded as belonging to three persons—a baseball self, a business self, and a home self. This view is justified by the fact of the three different standards of conduct which are used and by the fact of the very different interests of each self. It sometimes happens that the separation between the selves becomes so great that when one self is dominant no memory of the other selves exists; or even if the others are remembered, they are recognized as so different from the one dominant at the time that no question is raised in the mind of the individual whether or not there is really more than one self involved. Stevenson's story of Dr. Jekyll and Mr. Hyde is a well-known instance. A few people are met in daily life who approximate this condition, and the annals of science contain many demonstrated cases.

Multiple personality, as we have said, *is a functional mental disease.* It is closely related to hysteria, and is regarded by the eminent French psychologist Pierre Janet as identical with that psychosis. Like paranoia these mental disorders are striking reminders of salient features in everyday normal life. An American psychologist, Dr. Morton Prince, has written (1905) a very fascinating account of a Miss Beauchamp,[1] who came under his care and who finally proved to be a composite of four different personalities. All four of these selves, of course, used the same body, but each must be regarded as employing a different organization of units within the brain. In the following quotations we shall present some of the chief characteristics of this most interesting case.

---

[1] Morton Prince, *The Dissociation of a Personality.*

It was said in the beginning that, in addition to her normal self, and the hypnotic state known as B II, Miss Beauchamp may be any one of three different persons, who are known respectively as B I, B III, and B IV. . . . The numbers were affixed to the personalities as they were chronologically discovered. That is to say, when Miss Beauchamp first came under observation she was known of course by her own name. Later, when she was hypnotized, her mental state in hypnosis was known as the hypnotic self. Everything was then simple enough, for we had to do only with a person awake and hypnotized, and no extended nomenclature was required. Later, when another mental state was discovered, it became necessary to have distinguishing terms; so Miss Beauchamp was called B I, the hypnotic state B II, and the third state (at first thought to be a second hypnotic state, but later proved to be a personality) was named B III. Still later, a fourth state developed and was termed B IV.

B I was known as Miss Beauchamp.

B III was known as "Chris," in distinction from "Christine," the Christian name of Miss Beauchamp. Later, Chris took the name of Sally.

B IV had no other name, although Sally dubbed her "the Idiot." Now these three personalities had very sharply defined traits which gave a very distinctive individuality to each. One might say that each represented certain characteristic elements of human nature, and that the three might serve as an allegorical picture of the tendencies of man. If this were not a serious psychological study, I might feel tempted to entitle this volume "The Saint, the Woman, and the Devil." The Saint, the typical saint of literature, is B I. Her character may fairly be said without exaggeration to personify those traits which expounders of various religions, whether Christian, Buddhist, Shinto, or Confucian, have held up as the ideals to be attained by human nature. To her mind selfishness, impatience, rudeness, uncharitableness, a failure to tell the truth or a suppression of half the truth were literally sins, and their manifestation wickedness, to be cast out by fasting, vigils, and prayer. She frequently makes allusion to such sins in her letters. B IV is the Woman, personifying the frailties of temper, self-concentration, ambition, and self-interest, which ordinarily are the dominating factors of the average human being. Her idea in life is to accomplish her own ends, regardless of the consequences to others, and of the means employed. Sally is the Devil, not an immoral devil, to be sure, but rather a mischievous imp, one of that kind which we might imagine would take pleasure in thwarting the aspirations of humanity. To her pranks were largely due the moral suffering which B I endured, the social difficulties which befell B IV, and the trials and tribulations which were the lot of both.

Not the least interesting of the curious nervous phenomena manifested, are the different degrees of health enjoyed by the different personalities. One would imagine that if ill health were always based on physical alterations, each personality must have the same ailments: but such is not the case. The person known as B I has the poorest health; B IV is more robust, and is capable of mental and physical exertion without ill effects, which would be beyond the powers of B I; while B III is a stranger to an ache or pain. She does not know what illness means.

This personality, Sally, like the others at times is an alternating personality. But, besides this, at other times it is a group of dissociated conscious states, which, existing simultaneously with the primary self, whether B I or B IV, is technically termed a subconsciousness—a subconscious personality. This subconscious personality and the waking personality together represent a doubling of the mind. But this doubling exists because certain mental states have been dissociated from the main stream of consciousness and have acquired a more or less independent existence, and form an *extra* mind. As a result of long years of experience, the acquisition of long chains of memories, this second stream has acquired a wide field of mental life. Nothing of this life is known to the main stream of consciousness.[2]

These four selves had a curious relationship one to the other. B I knew only herself. B II knew herself and also B I, i.e., in reality knew the actual thoughts of B I without being told. B III knew herself and each of the first two. B IV knew only herself and was only known to B III through her actions. When we speak of B I's not knowing the other selves, we are pointing out remarkable instances of amnesia, or forgetting. All of these selves exist in the same body, but when B I, for example, is uppermost the other selves are forgotten and are absent. From the standpoint of consciousness they are non-existent. They persist only in a physical sense as changes of the brain. B III, however, knows what she herself thinks and can remember the thoughts and actions of B I. Without making quotations one can readily understand how at a loss and even how embarrassed B I might be by the situations into which B III might lead her. Particularly must this be the case since B III is the mischievous imp that she is.

We have not space to follow the history of this case through its many windings to the final discovery by Dr. Prince of who the *real* Miss Beauchamp was. We must be content with the final outcome. B II was the real girl, only asleep (hypnotized). B I and B IV were the disintegrations of B II. Sally (B III) was an alternating

---

[2] Morton Prince, *op. cit.*, 15-18.

personality to the real Miss Beauchamp. With the latter's final constant existence Sally disappeared. A description of B II can be given best in the words of Dr. Prince:

B II was a person so different from B I and B IV, so natural and self-contained, and so free from every sign of abnormality that there could be no doubt that I had again the Real Miss Beauchamp. There was none of the suffering, depression, and submissive idealism of B I; none of the ill-temper, stubbornness, and reticent antagonism of B IV. Nor was there any "rattling" of the mind, hallucinations, amnesia, bewilderment, or ignorance of events, as had been the case in the earlier experiments. She knew me and her surroundings and everything belonging to the lives of B I and B IV. She had the memories of both.[3]

Psychoses with Psychopathic Personality [19]

ROBERT PERCIVAL PARSONS and W. S. TAYLOR; prepared for this volume

PE attended a western university several years. He is now (1917) a minister, thirty-two years old, and although awaiting trial for military desertion, has the bearing of a gentleman.

His father was a common laborer who moved often and suddenly, without giving subject's mother much warning lest she get nervous. He died insane. The father seems to have been crude in every way, having no appreciation for education.

PE's maternal grandfather was a minister of fine character and rather wide influence. His (or his wife's) sister was insane. Our subject's mother is extremely sensitive, taking offense at merest trifles. She is described as being an inconsistent housekeeper: "While she would get up in the night to take a cover off her own bed and put it on one of the children, in the day the cooking would be of the plainest or poorest quality"; and if one of the children ventured to ask that she cook some little delicacy, she would fly into a tantrum at the "ingratitude" shown. She was never intimate with her children, and they never confided in her. She used to get into "regular fights" with her second daughter, pulling hair, using brooms, etc.

This heterogeneity of ancestry is manifest in the children. Our subject is, as already remarked, a minister; one brother drives a grocer's wagon; another brother is a college professor. One sister married a worthy man, but separated from him. She is admittedly

---

[3] Morton Prince, *op. cit.*, 519-520.

"queer." A second sister was dismissed from school as too dull to learn, is very nervous, and is known to be immoral. A third sister is well married, but is a lazy housekeeper, indifferent to her child, and peculiar—so bashful that she cannot tell what she wants to a clerk she has not purchased from often.

PE himself is "of an emotional disposition." As a boy he was a great reader, and made fine progress in school. He was converted by an evangelist when seventeen years of age, and resolved to enter the ministry. At college he failed in mathematics but did good work in historical and literary subjects. All went well until in a course called Old Testament Prophecy "higher criticism" got him "side-tracked on the matter of religion"; then a course on comparative religions led him to think that perhaps all theological speculation led to nothing. He was so upset by these problems that he dropped everything and joined a military organization to get away from it all.

In thirteen months' time, however, he secured a release and returned to school with a new conviction of the importance of the essentials of religion, purposing to study to preach. He supplied several small parishes while carrying on his studies. Soon his course was interrupted by his meeting a girl who "seemed to be the right one"; so he married her, and worked as a florist to obtain support. Then the war occurred, so he enlisted in that branch in which he "could render the best service."

His military record is clear for over a year. Quarrels with a non-commissioned officer decided him to change his location without permission, however, so he started from an eastern city for the Pacific Coast, on the theory that the West where he enlisted would be kinder to him than the East. He got as far as a place in Colorado, where he met a fellow who invited him to go camping in the mountains. He camped a few weeks, and finding himself short of funds, decided to surrender, so "bummed" his way to the nearest rendezvous and reported in.

This man seems to appreciate the seriousness of his offense, remarking that "it was a very foolish thing to do."

Adolescent "Psychoses" [1]

AUGUSTA F. BRONNER, "Effect of Adolescent Instability on Conduct," *Psychol. Clinic,* 8: 250-252 (1915)

It is true that in almost no cases of delinquency is there one cause that can be cited as the one and only factor which determines the behavior of the individual and which therefore is alone responsible for his offense. . . .

On the other hand, it may occur that the boy or girl becomes definitely delinquent for the first time at just the age of adolescence. Up to then he has shown no signs of waywardness; he has appeared a normal child, not difficult to control and exhibiting no unusual tendencies. Perhaps his previous record has been unusually good, his school reports have been satisfactory, he has been considered trustworthy and reliable. Suddenly his behavior changes, it becomes contrary to the tenor of his earlier life; he becomes unstable, unreliable, performing acts that are unusual, at least for him, foolish and erratic. Sometimes this erraticism is so extreme as to verge on an actual psychosis. All this occurs without any marked change in the external conditions under which he lives; though environmental circumstances remain the same, the individual alters noticeably.

The specific deeds actually performed vary from one person to another as does the length of time that they persist. . . .

Delinquent acts committed at this period cannot be judged in and of themselves. If adolescence as a factor is not taken into account, the judgment made is most likely to be erroneous. This does not mean that nothing definite should be done, that one must wait helplessly until adolescence has passed. On the contrary, constructive measures of all kinds are never more urgently necessary than at just the adolescent period.

[In order to illustrate these points, certain cases studied in the Psychopathic Institute of the Juvenile Court of Chicago are presented by Dr. Bronner further in her paper (omitted).]

---

[1] Not listed in the "Statistical Manual" of the American Psychiatric Association.

"Moral Imbecility" or "Moral Insanity": Is There Such an Entity? [1]

WILLIAM HEALY, *The Individual Delinquent*, 783-784 (copyright, 1920, by Little, Brown & Co.)

A "moral sense" seems to have appeared first in philosophical psychology with Locke, Shaftesbury and Hutcheson in the 17th and 18th centuries. In the last two generations of philosophical thought there has been a decided falling away from this conception. It is now clearly perceived that our notions of right and wrong are inextricably mixed up with social judgments, and with the evolution of social relationships. Not only do learning and experience in these matters come into play, but also native intelligence as well. One could almost say that the person who failed to appreciate his moral duties was the person who had not intelligence enough to realize what was best for even himself as a social being. Indeed, such definitely was the trend of Aristotelian thought.[2]

The results of our experience, and our main conclusion in this whole matter would better at once be set forth; discussion may then follow. When we began our work there was no point on which we expected more positive data than on moral imbecility. But our findings have turned out to be negative. We have been constantly on the look-out for a moral imbecile, that is, a person not subnormal and otherwise intact in mental powers, who shows himself devoid of moral feeling. We have not found one. Many cases have been brought to us as moral imbeciles, but they have always turned out somehow mentally defective or aberrational; or to be the victims of environmental conditions or mental conflict, and not at all devoid of moral feeling. Superficially the individual frequently has seemed to be mentally normal, as in the cases where there was great development of language ability,[3] but in every single instance a well-rounded investigation has shown distinct abnormality in some other field than the moral sense, or, in a few cases of children,[4]

---

[1] Not listed in the "Statistical Manual" of the American Psychiatric Association.

[2] For a clear-cut discussion of the problem of the "moral sense" consult John Dewey and James H. Tufts, *Text Book of Ethics*, 317-322 (Holt, 1908).

[3] William Healy, *op. cit.*, 473-490, 501-514.

[4] In these otherwise unexplained cases of children, I think it highly probable that had we done better work, psychogenetic or experiential elements back of the morbid behavior would have been discovered, as they were in many other instances.

further growth has carried the individual past a stage of anti-social conduct.

The Term "Insanity"

ABRAHAM MYERSON, *The Inheritance of Mental Diseases*, 14-16 (Williams & Wilkins, 1925)

Insanity is a term which has its roots in that period when men thought that the insane were possessed by devils, or when the moon was thought to cause mental changes, and it has the same kind of value that the words "lunacy" and "lunatics" have. At a later date the law stepped in to define insanity because property rights and the safety of the insane and the safety of others had to be conserved. Since the treatment of the insane is in part custodial and since such custody is essentially the deprivation of liberty and freedom in their most intimate and precious meaning, the law had to be invoked in this sphere of medicine as in no other. But the law is conservative, based on the conclusions and procedures of yore, is not interested in clinical distinctions and differences, and wants only to know "Does this man know the difference between right and wrong" (who does?), "does he know the distribution of his property or properties," "is he dangerous to himself or others?" The law is not interested in mental diseases, it cares not whether a man has dementia præcox or dementia paralytica and yet these two diseases are very far apart both in cause, pathology, treatment and hereditary importance. In other words though *biologically* and medically the mental diseases belong in separate categories, *legally and in the common mind* they are fused together in "insanity."

It is this relationship of law and common thought to the word insanity, and to any substitute word, which makes it useless and pernicious to psychiatry and to the discussion of heredity. For we have split up the fused mass of the insane, as the untrained mind and the past time saw it, into diseases of varying cause, pathology and course. To use the term insanity as if there were an entity corresponding to it is as if we thought all diseases of respiration were the same, and had a term, let us say, dyspnœa, for the general state of lung trouble. But we know that pneumonia, bronchitis, asthma, pulmonary tuberculosis, lung abscess, and hypostatic pneumonia are separate entities, having little or no relationship to one another, save as they have some symptoms in common. We have made progress in medicine not so much through *unifying* diseases and disease phenomena as by *isolating* them, by discovering that syphilis and gonorrhœa are *not* the same disease, though the great John Hunter declared they were; by discarding the term scrofula and demonstrating that many diseases from tuberculosis to anæmia were fused under the term; by isolating the enteric fever of our ancestors into typhoid and paratyphoid; by laboratory specific-reactions for various diseases as the Wassermann reaction for syphilis, the Pirquet test for tuberculosis, the Widal test for typhoid and the Schick reaction for diphtheria.

Moreover the idea of insanity [1] is not at all parallel to the idea of mental diseases. A man may have general paresis, which is one of the most common of the mental diseases, and yet not be "insane." By indisputable medical criteria he may be a victim of this disease, yet legally he may not be at all sick, since he may have no noticeable defect of judgment or disorder of conduct. Similarly with dementia præcox, manic-depressive insanity and paranoia—there may be years of the mental disease but no insanity in that the patient can pass muster as a sane man by the legal standards. Though in the case of the above mentioned diseases the majority of patients finally reach the status of insanity, there are other mental diseases where the great majority of patients and their physicians would fiercely resent the idea of mental disease at all and where insanity is only occasionally declared to exist. These diseases are known medically as the functional neuroses: neurasthenia, psychasthenia, and hysteria; and yet nothing is so purely mental as the fixed ideas, the fears, the paralyses, impulsions, and anæsthesiae of these conditions. Because we associate the term mental diseases with insanity we are loath to call things by their right names, and so fall into vicious mental habits.

The great Spencerian formula of evolution applies with remarkable pertinence to the evolution of our psychiatry. Formidably expressed the formula is in reality simple, and points out that an ill-defined homogeneity changes gradually into well-defined heterogeneities. So in psychiatry—we have started with an ill-defined, obscure, mystical homogeneity; insanity. As our subject has approached a science and we have thrown off the traditions which hampered, the ill-defined homogeneity has become broken up into well-defined mental diseases. While it is well to seek for underlying unities it is wise to remember that progress, at least for a long time, will lie in the direction of splitting up "unities" into clinical units.

---

[1] For a fascinating discussion of the subject of insanity as here presented see Southard and Jarrett, *The Kingdom of Evils*.

The Problem of Diagnosis

E. E. SOUTHARD and MARY C. JARRETT, *The Kingdom of Evils*, 451-452 (copyright, 1922, by The Macmillan Company); reprinted by permission

Now and then from a general social worker comes a request for lists of symptoms by which, supposedly, the different mental diseases may be recognized. Social workers who have dipped into works upon psychiatry can follow us when we say it is not at all impossible to match the symptoms of any disease which we may confront with the symptoms of several diseases as described in the medical books. In fact, the more thorough and accurate the psychiatric textbook, the more likely would be the facts in the particular case to match with the facts in the books as presented under a great variety of headings. It is not alone the tyro, but also the expert, who is amazed to find that all the symptoms in his case can be found, let us say, under the different headings of syphilis, dementia præcox, manic-depressive psychosis, etc. To use the language of medical logic, we can briefly put the situation by saying that in the field of mental diseases, there are few or no indicator symptoms. Any symptom, *e.g.,* mania, depression, persecutory ideas, grandiosity, hallucinations, and so on through the list, may be found alone or even in multiple combination with other symptoms of the list in virtually any one of the great groups of mental diseases.

A good many persons believe that a disease is composed of symptoms, but nothing is more erroneous. The symptom indicates the disease. The disease is an infinite mass of processes and of arrangements. It is a mistake to think that because it can be shown that general paresis has a certain kind of pupillary disorder and a certain kind of speech disorder, and a certain mental state characterized by feelings of grandeur, these three things, disorder of pupils, disorder of speech, delusions of grandeur, in any sense constitute the disease. No symptom constitutes the disease. No group of symptoms constitutes a disease. One rather comforting fact about mental disease is that, after all, there are so few symptoms to a given disease. The most complicated disease that runs through the entire make-up of the person, influences every move of his entire future, goes back to his entire past, will be found to have but one symptom, or two or three, rarely more than ten or a dozen symptoms. These must be, in the nature of things, mere indicators of the situation.

In short there are no indicator symptoms, or what are called in the books pathognomonic symptoms. In medicine there are certain pathognomonic symptoms; thus in smallpox, the pock of smallpox is pathognomonic; it does not occur in any other disease, and you get it when you have that disease. Of course there are some doubtful cases where you cannot make out whether you have got a pock or not of this characteristic sort. The pock of smallpox is so characteristic that we regard it as pathognomonic. The tubercle bacillus in tuberculosis is pathognomonic,—it does not occur except in tuberculosis. But in mental disease we have not any such pathognomonic symptoms that point to any certain disease.

There are a few combinations of symptoms or signs that indicate certain diseases. However, these combinations are probably beyond the range of a person not trained in medicine to use. There may be one or two small exceptions to this in the whole of medicine. A nurse, a layman, anyone can learn to diagnosticate smallpox from the pock just as well and perhaps better than a physician. Just as a man without knowing a thing about engineering says about his automobile "the engine is skipping." The man may not know what to do about it, or he may, without knowing anything about engineering, be able to fix it; so that people can make certain diagnoses which are merely recognitions of things, of data. But when it comes to mental disease this is not so. There are not any simple points by which to recognize it, and its complicated ways are not too easy for the medical mind or for any other mind.[1]

---

[1] ["We need to remember, too, that the underlying condition does not give rise to the symptoms of the disease directly, but usually only through a chain of mechanisms. It is for this reason that we have to make our series of inferences, many of the terms of which are themselves inferences or judgments instead of facts.

"It is not *that* the patient has this or that symptom, as mutism or resistiveness, but *why* he has it that is important. It will be for different reasons in different cases.

"We may find he is mute because of delusions, because of perplexity, or because of pure negativism, and we still must inquire why he has the delusions, the perplexity, the negativism; we must seek not only their psychogenetic origins but the physical origins as well."—E. Stanley Abbot, "The Principles of Diagnosis in Psychiatry," *Am. Jour. Insan.*, 74: 378 (1918).]

General Procedure in Diagnosis

IRVING J. SANDS and PHYLLIS BLANCHARD, *Abnormal Behavior*, 459-461
(Moffat, Yard, 1923)

Physical and mental diseases, intellectual inferiority, emotional conflicts, personality defects both native and acquired, bad environmental influences, and many other factors enter into the causation of conduct disorders. To determine the nature of any particular case, therefore, requires psychiatric, psychological and sociological study, as has been suggested in enumerating the personnel of the clinic.

The psychiatric study demands a thorough physical and medical as well as a complete mental examination. In addition to the ordinary medical examination, which means the heart, lungs, etc., the various neurological tests are made and clinical signs of glandular imbalance are taken into account. A serological examination is also indispensable. This means simply that a blood Wassermann test must be performed (and if necessary a spinal fluid examination made) to rule out the possibility of syphilitic infection as a cause of abnormal conduct. Metabolism studies (in cases which show signs of glandular disturbance), X-rays, and other laboratory aids to medical diagnosis are called into assistance whenever the superficial physical examination indicates the desirability for such procedure.

The mental examination consists of the usual psychiatric observation for hallucinations, delusions, disorientation for time or place, and other symptoms of mental disorder. It also includes a study of the mental life, with more or less utilization of psychoanalytic principles, with a view to revealing any possible emotional conflicts, obsessive ideation, etc.

The psychological study of the aberrant person is equally thorough in nature. It includes examinations for the determination of the general level of intelligence (such as the Stanford-Binet or the Army Alpha), and all sorts of tests for the establishment of the existence of special abilities or disabilities which may be utilized in vocational guidance. The data of the psychological study should offer not only an estimate of the individual's intelligence, which may be a contributory factor in the production of his misconduct, but also a picture of his potentialities for achievement, since the sublimation [redirection] of energies once used along anti-social lines into vocational or other socially approved activities is often an important step in the adjustment of the individual's behavior and the correction of his difficulties.

The sociological study should give an account of the hereditary and environmental influences which have been brought to bear on the personality development of the individual. The family history must be obtained in detail, with especial inquiry as to the existence of neurotic or psychotic taint, intellectual impairment, syphilitic or epileptic members, etc. The physical condition of the home, the economic status of the family, the attitude of the parents toward the individual as a child and his reactions to the father and mother, his early companions, his school and vocational career, his developmental history through infancy and childhood, must all be described as fully as possible. This social history gives us innumerable sidelights on the personality, and often reveals definite causes of abnormal reactions.[1]

Some Psychological Methods in Diagnosis

SHEPHERD IVORY FRANZ, "Experimental Psychopathology," *Psychol. Bull.*,
9: 145-146, 148-150 (1912)

A practical distinction which may be made and held to is that when an investigator is concerned chiefly with the general course of a disease and its treatment his interests are in psychiatry, but when his chief concern is the investigation of the development or interrelations of mental symptoms his interests are in psychology, and the emphasis, either on the psychological or the pathological aspect, makes his work either pathopsychological or psychopathological. This distinction is well brought out in the work of Gregor.[2]

Largely on account of the value association tests have for diagnosis, the number of researches on the association of ideas in the insane is more than on any other topic. . . . Of the greatest value is that of Kent and Rosanoff.[3] These investigators obtained 100 free associations [for words presented as stimuli] from each of 1,000 normal subjects and have carefully tabulated the results according to their frequency values, so that the results of any ab-

---

[1] For details regarding history-taking and clinical examination, *cf.* James V. May, *Mental Diseases*, 84-95.

[2] Gregor, A., *Leitfaden der experimentellen Psychopathologie*, 222 (Berlin: S. Karger, 1910).

[3] Kent, G. H., and Rosanoff, A. J., "A Study of Association in Insanity," *Am. Jour. Insan.*, 67: 37-96, 317-390 (1910).

normal subject may be directly compared with those of the 1,000 normal subjects. The grouping of the normal reactions resulted in the formulation of a table, or tables, of actual facts without the extended consideration of the logical characters of the reactions, as has been done by many previous investigators. . . . The results of 108 cases of dementia praecox showed a larger number of "individual" reactions than the normal or than any other form of insanity studied; of 33 cases of paranoiac conditions, a heterogeneous group, many showed no departure from the normal, and only a few cases closely allied to the dementia praecox group gave evidence of great abnormality; 24 cases of epilepsy showed many repetitions and many particles of speech as association reactions, and it is worthy of note that these cases were mostly in a state of advanced dementia; 32 cases of paresis gave varying reactions, those "presenting no considerable dementia or confusion and cases in a state of remission" gave practically normal reactions, and those showing mental deterioration showed many repetitions, associations to previous reactions, etc.; 32 cases of manic-depressive insanity showed slight variations from the normal, although there was a number of "sound reactions, word complements, and particles"; in 8 cases of involutional melancholia no evident abnormality was observed; 6 cases of alcoholic dementia showed no evidence of abnormality; and only one of the 4 cases of senile dementia showed more than the usual number of individual reactions.

In this connection the works of Klepper,[1] of Kilian,[2] and of Nathan [3] deserve mention. Klepper investigated the associations of epileptics and katatonics, which types of cases sometimes have a somewhat similar symptomatology and which are, therefore, difficult to differentiate. The characters of the associations differ in the two types which were investigated. Without going into the enumeration of the logical differences in the types of reactions it is evident that there are sufficiently well marked differences, and these are so great that the author concludes that he is able to differentiate one type from the other by the association tests alone, without having any history or case record. Kilian tested the associations

---

[1] Klepper, G., "Die Unterscheidung von epileptischen und katatonischen Zuständen, speziell aus den Assoziationen," *Klinik f. psychische u. nervöse Krankh.*, 6: 1-27 (1911).

[2] Kilian, K., "Zur Untersuchung der Assoziationen bei Maniakalischen," *Klinik f. psychische u. nervöse Krankh.*, 6: 28-32 (1911).

[3] Nathan, E. W., "Ueber die sogenannten sinnlosen Reaktionen beim Assoziationsversuch," *Klinik f. psychische u. nervöse Krankh.*, 5: 76-82 (1910).

of a case of manic-depressive insanity over a period of five months, during which there was a return to the normal condition. He found a gradual decrease in the number of klang and non-understandable reactions, a decrease in a number of perseverations of the associations, but there was a greater tendency to repetition of the stimulus words. Nathan worked on a case of imbecility, investigating principally the so-called senseless reactions, and found that many of these are due to sense impressions obtained or received immediately before or during the course of the experiments, others were due to ideas present in the mind of the subject, which were more or less stable and apparently personal, and some others were reactions to stimulus words given in previous tests. This study is of great psychological interest on account of its analysis of the senseless reactions, for these are more frequent than is commonly believed, and, as the writer has pointed out in another place, they can not be considered to be senseless for the subject, but senseless only as far as the logical beliefs of the experimenter are concerned.

CHAPTER III

CAUSES OF NERVOUS AND MENTAL DISEASE

As origins of functional disorders will be considered throughout later chapters, especially in connection with Problems of Personality and Character (*cf.* Chapter XXIII), the present chapter will consist of brief discussions of heredity, after the following general statement:

General Causes of Nervous and Mental Disease

WALTER S. HUNTER, *General Psychology*, rev. ed., 78-79 (Univ. of Chicago Press, 1923)

The causes of nervous and mental diseases are legion. Whatever interferes with the normal functioning of the nervous system produces nervous disease or defect and may also produce disturbances in consciousness. In such a list one may place: accidents, e.g., falls and wounds; hereditary or congenital defects; infectious diseases, e.g., scarlet fever, diphtheria, tuberculosis, and particularly syphilis; alcoholism; poisonings incident to certain occupations, e.g., lead and mercury poisonings; moral shocks, etc. Individuals vary greatly in their resistance to these disturbing factors. What will produce delirium, hallucinations, paranoia, or dementia in one person may leave another unaffected. The strain of nursing a parent during a fatal illness may produce hysteria in one person and only temporary exhaustion and distress in another. Syphilitic infection in one person may result in tabes, paresis, or other defect and in another may never manifest itself in the realm of nervous and mental disease. This lack of resistance may be termed an instability of nervous organization and is inherited.

The importance of heredity as a determining factor in any given case of disease can hardly be overestimated. We have had this brought to our attention already in the case of the Kallikak family. . . . This inheritance rests upon variations in the germ plasm of the individual, and is not a social inheritance in the sense that customs and traditions are. The social conditions surrounding the individual will determine largely the detailed content of his psychosis (abnormal mental state), e.g., they will determine the objects of his morbid fears; but they will not be the fundamental conditions of the disorder.

Heredity of Mental Abnormalities

A

A. J. ROSANOFF and FLORENCE I. ORR, "A Study of Heredity in Insanity in the Light of the Mendelian Theory," Eugenics Record Office, Cold Spring Harbor, N. Y., Bulletin No. 5 (Oct., 1911), 221-222, 225-228; quoted also by James Ford, *Social Problems and Social Policy*, 428-433 (Ginn, 1923)

From the earliest times physicians have recorded observations of the transmission of nervous diseases by heredity.

In modern times the accumulation of large amounts of material in the shape of clinical statistics published by hospitals has established beyond question the fact that heredity plays an essential part in the etiology of certain neuropathic conditions. Table I shows some statistical figures selected at random.

TABLE I

	Total Number of Cases with Known Histories	Cases Showing Heredity	
		Number	Per cent
Report of New York State Commission in Lunacy for the year ending September 30, 1909	2467	1259	51.0
Report of Michigan Asylum for the Insane at Kalamazoo for the years 1859-1908........	8531	4800	56.3
Report of Rhode Island State Hospital for the Insane for the year ending December 31, 1910	250	137	54.8

Figures such as these are for all forms of insanity, including those which occur on a basis of exogenous causes; yet even as they are, their significance becomes quite apparent when they are compared with figures representing the frequency of a neuropathic family history among normal subjects: 3 per cent according to Jost, 7.5 per cent according to Näcke.[1]

Aside from statistical data, studies of individual cases have revealed, on the one hand, the facts of atavistic and collateral heredity, and on the other hand, the fact of the frequent failure of transmission of neuropathic traits. In other words, there seemed to be no regularity in the working of heredity, and the generally accepted conclusion on the subject has been well voiced by Kraepelin: "We must therefore regard the statistics of heredity in insanity merely as facts of experience without finding in them the expression of a 'law' which should hold in every case." [2]

In recent years, however, it has been shown that human heredity, at least as far as certain traits are concerned, is subject to general biological laws. Special mention may be made of color of eyes,[3] color of hair,[4] form of hair,[5] brachydactyly,[6] some forms of cataract,[7] and retinitis pigmentosa,[8] as human traits which have been shown to be transmitted from generation to generation in accordance with the Mendelian theory.

As regards insanity and allied neuropathic conditions, the facts to which we have already referred, namely, the facts of atavistic and collateral heredity, direct heredity, and the frequent failure of transmission seem to point plainly to alternative inheritance. This suggests the likelihood of a mechanism of inheritance according with the Mendelian theory, and the present study has been undertaken with a view to determining whether indeed the neuropathic constitution is transmitted in the manner of a Mendelian trait. . . .

The total amount of psychiatric material which is available at this hospital [9] is very large. We found, however, that for various reasons, to be spoken of presently, the greater part of the material could not be utilized in our study.

In selecting cases our aim has been to exclude all those forms of insanity in the causation of which exogenous factors, such as traumata, alcoholism, and syphilis, are known to play an essential

---

[1] Cited by Kraepelin, *Psychiatrie* (7th ed.), I, 116.

[2] Kraepelin, *Psychiatrie* (7th ed.), I, 116.

[3] Davenport, *Science* (N. S.), Vol. XXVI, November 1, 1907; **Hurst,** *Proceedings of the Royal Society,* Vol. LXXX B, 1908.

[4] Davenport, *The American Naturalist,* Vol. XLIII, April, 1909.

[5] *Ibid.,* Vol. XLII, May, 1908.

[6] Farabee, *Papers of Peabody Museum,* Vol. III, 1905.

[7] Nettleship, *Report of the Royal London Ophthalmic Hospital,* Vol. XVI, 1905.

[8] *Ibid.,* Vol. XVII, Parts I-III.

[9] Kings Park State Hospital, Kings Park, New York.

part; and we have also systematically excluded psychoses which occur upon a basis of organic cerebral affections, such as tumors, arteriosclerosis, apoplexy, and the like. We are not inclined to dispute the possible influence of heredity in these conditions; we have excluded them merely for the purpose of simplifying our problem by avoiding the necessity of dealing with a complicating factor in the shape of an essential exogenous cause. Moreover there seemed to be reason to believe that the so-called functional psychoses and neuroses are more closely related to each other than to the conditions which we have sought to exclude; and since our material had to be largely massed together for statistical treatment it was important that it should be as homogeneous as possible.

More than half the patients at this hospital are either themselves foreign born or the children of foreign-born parents; and among those who were born in this country of American parents there are many whose homes are in distant states; thus but a small proportion remained whose families had for two or three generations resided in this country and were accessible to investigation.

Other difficulties in obtaining our data were due to the ignorance of some of our informants or to their reluctance or refusal to coöperate in the investigation; and in many cases the investigation had to be discontinued and the data already collected had to be discarded owing to incompleteness.

In the actual analysis of the data collected in the course of our investigation the problem in each case was to distinguish, on the basis of the information obtained by questioning the relatives, neuropathic states from the normal state and in the case of a neuropathic state to identify, if possible, the special variety. Such diagnosis often enough presents great difficulty when there is opportunity for direct observation, but when it has to be based upon observations of untrained informants related from memory the difficulty is, of course, greatly increased and with it the chance of error. We have endeavored to reduce the amount of error from this source by interviewing personally as many as possible of the nearest relatives of the patients whose pedigrees were being investigated, and by the practice of tracing almost all the families not farther than to the generation of grandparents, for the farther back our inquiries extended the more scant and more vague was the information which we were able to obtain.

To the difficulty of diagnosis is added the further difficulty which results from the impossibility in the present state of psychiatry of precisely delimiting the conception of the neuropathic constitution. To this matter we shall have occasion to revert in subsequent sections.

In the analysis of data it was often necessary in the case of a normal subject to determine whether the case was one of duplex or of simplex inheritance, it having appeared early in the course of our study that the normal condition was dominant over the neuropathic condition. The fact of simplex inheritance we were able in some cases to establish on the basis of the existence of neuropathic manifestations in the ancestors or collateral relatives of the subject; in other cases this evidence was lacking as our information did not extend to the more remote generations, so that it was necessary to assume the fact of simplex inheritance on the basis of the existence of neuropathic offspring: the two types of material have been treated separately. On the other hand, the fact of duplex inheritance was in every case based upon the absence of neuropathic manifestations in ancestors and collateral relatives, as far as known, as well as in the offspring; but inasmuch as in scarcely any case was the family history traced farther back than the third generation it is clear that the possibility of simplex inheritance was in no case positively excluded; we have here, therefore, another source of error which, fortunately, is slight, and affects the least important part of our material, namely, the cases of matings from which no neuropathic offspring have resulted.

On the whole, no pretension is made here of total elimination of error; but we believe that whatever errors remain they are not sufficient to invalidate the material as a basis for our study.

STATISTICAL ANALYSIS OF MATERIAL

In the Preliminary Report, *Bulletin No. 3,* Eugenics Record Office, which was based upon an analysis of the pedigrees of twelve families, it was shown that the neuropathic constitution is transmitted by heredity probably in the manner of a trait which is, in the Mendelian sense, recessive to the normal condition.

Sixty other families have since been investigated; the entire material now includes the pedigrees of seventy-two families, representing 206 different matings, with a total of 1097 offspring. In Table II this mass of data has been arranged so as to show the proportions of normal and neuropathic offspring which resulted from the various types of mating alongside of figures representing theoretical expectation according to the Mendelian theory.

Some of the data represented in the table require special explanation.

Among the offspring which resulted from matings of the first type, RR x RR, ten are recorded as being normal, although theo-

TABLE II

Types of Mating	Number of Matings	Total Number of Offspring	Died in Childhood	Data Unascertained	Neuropathic Offspring		Normal Offspring	
					Actual Findings	Theoretical Expectation	Actual Findings	Theoretical Expectation
a. RR × RR ∞ RR	17	75	11	0	54	64	10	0
b. DR × RR ∞ DR + RR	37	216	46	1	84	84½	85	84½
b₁. DR × RR ∞ DR + RR	56	284	20	4	106	130	154	130
c. DD × RR ∞ DR	14	61	13	3	0	0	45	45
d. DR × DR ∞ DD + 2DR + RR	7	34	5	0	8	7¼	21	21¾
d₁. DR × DR ∞ DD + 2DR + RR	55	335	39	3	99	73¼	194	219¾
e. DD × DR ∞ DD + DR	20	92	12	3	0	0	77	77
f. DD × DD ∞ DD	0	0	0	0	0	0	0	0
Totals	206	1097	146	14	351	359	586	578

retically all should be neuropathic. Of these ten one died at the age of thirty-eight years in an accident, during life suffered from asthma, had a son who died in convulsions; another is described as being easy going, is somewhat odd and possibly abnormal in make-up, is twenty-nine years of age; the rest are from eight to twenty-two years of age. In other words, in two of the ten subjects the neuropathic constitution is not positively excluded and the remaining eight have not reached the age of incidence.

The matings of the second and fourth types, DR x RR and DR x DR respectively, have been divided into two groups each, as already explained in the preceding section: thus groups b and d in the chart include the matings in which the simplex condition of either or both mates, as the case may be, is definitely ascertained, the existence of neuropathic manifestations either in ancestors or collateral relatives of the subjects appearing in the pedigrees; groups b_1 and d_1, on the other hand, include the matings in which the simplex condition of either or both mates is assumed to exist on the basis of the character of the offspring. It is perhaps not surprising that groups b_1 and d_1 are larger than b and d respectively when we consider the great likelihood of neuropathic taint, derived from an ancestor of a remote generation, being transmitted many times in the shape of a simplex condition, and at the same time the fact that our investigations extended in almost all cases no farther back than the generation of grandparents.

As is shown in the table the correspondence between theoretical expectation and actual findings is in some cases exact and in all cases remarkably close. It would seem, then, that the fact of the hereditary transmission of the neuropathic constitution as a recessive trait, in accordance with the Mendelian theory, may be regarded as definitely established.

B

ABRAHAM MYERSON, *The Inheritance of Mental Diseases*, 222-223, 319-320 (Williams & Wilkins, 1925). *Cf.* also the Bibliography of that work

In contrast to the foregoing point of view, it is not uncommon in psychotherapy to meet with such a policy as the following, as expressed by Dr. William A. White: [1]

". . . It is true that many students of heredity believe that all sorts of mental qualities may be traced directly from the ancestors. Those physicians, however, who deal with the problems of mental illness see, on the contrary, these peculiarities passed on because, as a part of the child's environment, they are impressed upon it during its developmental period. This view has been emphasized because it has been found possible to largely modify so many personal mental traits. Heredity as an explanation is therefore looked upon somewhat askance because it serves to block efforts at improvement. If a certain trait is hereditary, why! that's the end of it. There is nothing to be done. So frequently, however, something can be done that this explanation is being more and more put aside as inadequate."

To others, it is not clear that mental disorders are inherited in a perfectly simple fashion, so far at least as present categories go. With regard to their manifestations in subsequent generations, the following conclusions have recently been proposed:

1. That the paranoid diseases tend to paranoid states, perhaps finally to dementia praecox states.

2. That the manic-melancholic [manic-depressive] diseases are in the main followed by manic-melancholic diseases, but in a certain number, especially of doubtful cases by dementia praecox.

This brings up the important point that in several of the cases presented in this book [*op. cit.*] patients have gone through repeated attacks of what appear to be manic-depressive insanity to

---

[1] *The Mental Hygiene of Childhood*, viii-ix (copyright, 1919, by Little, Brown & Co.).

wind up with what appears to be dementia praecox. Of late years many have pointed out that catatonic states occur in manic-depressive insanity. It seems to me very probable on the basis of individual cases and the history of family mental disease that catatonic states are an intermediary form of mental disease, bridging the gap between manic-depressive insanity and dementia praecox.

3. That the involutional and senile state if paranoid, trend towards paranoid states and dementia praecox.

4. That the manic-depressive states of involution and senium trend towards manic-depressive and dementia praecox, especially the latter.

5. That dementia praecox in an ancestor trends towards dementia praecox in the descendants with a certain scattering incidence of imbecility. This imbecility seems to me to be in part at least of the Kraepelinian congenital or very early dementia praecox.

6. Neither for organic disease nor alcoholic disease can anything definite be said. Wherever good histories are obtained other and more definite psychopathic factors are found.

"It will thus be seen that all roads seem to lead to dementia praecox and from thence to imbecility." Quoting from my own publications [1] I find it over-emphasizes the drift of things from generation to generation. Paranoid characters remain very persistent, and so do manic-depressive characters even though a certain number of cases follow this drift. This may be stated, that when the disease gets worse from generation to generation it ends in dementia praecox, but this is not always the case and there must be a huge number of mild cases of mental disease in the descendants of the insane, who represent an upward trend, a recovery trend. Rare indeed is that mingling of stocks whereby a mental disease persists unaltered for more than two generations. As has been pointed out in a previous chapter the earlier onset of the disease and its worsening preclude propagation, for while the feeble-minded *may* have many illegitimate children dementia praecox patients do have less children than the normal population and as their marriage rate is low there finally comes a point in the history of many, perhaps of most psychiatric families when the stock dies out. . . .

In other words, a study of those environmental forces which alter character and the general trends of the physical and psychical life of individuals must be linked up to a study of those environmental forces which alter these sets of qualities in a family group or the

---

[1] A. Myerson, "Psychiatric Family Studies, Paper No. 1," *Am. Jour. Insan.*, 73. vol. 3: 355 (1917).

race. That long and arduous studies await us before we can even prepare to understand the problem of family mental disease needs no argument, but that is only another reason why they must be made. And especially they must be made before we leap into legislatures with demands that this or that measure be carried out, before we call for the wholesale sterilization of the feeble-minded, the insane, the epileptic, and the criminal as blithely as if we knew all about the inheritance of mental disease when indeed we know remarkably little. We have a right, I think, to pass laws that no one shall conceal the fact of mental disease when entering upon marriage and that the concealment of such disease shall be a cause for annulment, whether or not the individual was insane at the time of marriage. We have a right to ask for the sterilization of those types of feeble-mindedness which we know to run in families. Wherever mental disease exists in a family group for more than one generation, it would be wise for society to sterilize those of the second generation who go to institutions. I do not believe that we can ask much more than that in the present state of our knowledge and we cannot afford to be unduly dogmatic. The common sense and stolidity of legislatures, what seems to be stupidity, is often enough justified by the dogmatic attitudes of science, a dogmatism hard to understand by one who knows the history of the theories of science.

CHAPTER IV

HISTORICAL SKETCH OF TREATMENT AND THEORY OF THE FUNCTIONAL NEUROSES [1]

The Rise of Hypnotism

[JOSEPH JASTROW]; adapted by Theresa M. Jackson from (principally) his *Fact and Fable in Psychology*, 174-235 (Houghton Mifflin, 1900), the selections from which are used by permission of and by special arrangement with the publishers

Our knowledge of insanity, hysteria, and trance-conditions, of the nature of illusion and hallucination, of prepossession and suggestion shed a strong light upon religious ecstasy,[2] upon demon-possession, and upon cures by shrines and relics. Our historical survey might accordingly include an account of the states of insensibility and of the potent power of suggestion, which occurred in connection with the religious observances in the practices of ancient civilizations, and have always formed, as they still form, a characteristic cult among primitive peoples. But in the interests of unity and brevity it will be best to limit attention to those ancestors of hypnotism, of whose methods and practices we have fairly definite information.

In 1665 Valentine Greatrakes came from Ireland to England at Lord Conway's invitation to cure "that excellent lady of his, the pains of whose *head* . . . have not made her more known . . . than her other endowments." Though in this case the healer failed, he seems to have practiced widely and to have been generally successful with nervous complaints. He made a sharp distinction between diseases of organic and functional nature, making no pretense to cure "wherein there is a decay of Nature." Stubbe, his biographer and a physician, suggests that Mr. Greatrakes' body emanated some particular "Ferments" which would restore debilitated parts. There

---

[1] For details regarding the history of psychotherapy, *cf.* J. J. Walsh, *Psychotherapy;* Albert Moll, *Hypnotism;* and James V. May, *Mental Diseases,* 217-233.

[2] *Cf.* James H. Leuba, *The Psychology of Religious Mysticism.*

is nothing recorded that definitely suggests the production of the hypnotic state; but direct suggestion, reinforced by manipulations, obviously had much to do with the cures.

Next in importance chronologically is Friedrich Anton Mesmer, who graduated from the University of Vienna in 1776. He tried to revive astrological ideas [3] from a medical point of view and claimed to have evidence that the stars influenced us markedly. He defined the "quality of animal bodies, rendering them susceptible to the influence of heaven and earth," as "animal magnetism." The methods he employed in practical treatments were varied at different stages of his career but were always fantastic and emotionally appealing. After a series of controversies with learned Parisian societies, a commission to investigate Mesmer's work was appointed by the throne in 1784. After careful and ingenious tests, the report was unfavorable, being summed up as follows:

The commissioners concluded that the effects witnessed were due to an overstimulated imagination, to an anticipation of the result, to excitement and contagion. It may certainly be held that they underestimated the significance of what they saw. However, their verdict not only destroyed Mesmer's pretensions, but held out a rational, though in our present lights an inadequate, interpretation of the [really hypnotic] phenomena, then so sensationally presented to an excited and distraction-loving public.

It is not possible to enumerate here all the men who have contributed [4] more or less to the development and understanding of the phenomenon of hypnotism, but mention should be made of Puységur, a pupil of Mesmer, to whom the credit belongs for the first appreciation of the hypnotic condition and its importance.

In 1837 another of Mesmer's pupils, Dr. Oudet, a member of the Academy of Medicine, performed the painless extraction of a tooth, the patient being in a hypnotic condition. This operation attracted considerable attention.

---

[3] Such as those of Paracelsus, for example. Griffith remarks that "Paracelsus, a Swiss physician of the fifteenth century, is responsible, apparently, for the first definite expression, in modern times, of the facts which were later to fall under the term 'hypnosis.' He developed . . . a system of medical treatment based upon the assumption that stars and certain other bodies, including magnets, possessed a peculiar fluid or emanation which, when directed toward the human body, had a powerful influence upon it."—Coleman R. Griffith, *General Introduction to Psychology*, 330 (copyright, 1923, by the Macmillan Company); reprinted by permission.

[4] *Cf. Ency. Brit.*

About 1843 James Braid, an English surgeon, became interested in Mesmerism, and it was he who gave to the Mesmeric trance the name of "Hypnotism." At first Braid explained the results as being due to physical fatigue, but he later appreciated the importance of the psychological elements in hypnotism. Though Braid, by elimination of fantastic practices and theories, paved the way for a true science of hypnotism, his work was soon forgotten.

Among those who came to believe in the use of hypnosis in surgery was Elliotson, who was dismissed from a hospital staff through the skepticism of the other physicians.[5] Dr. Esdaile, also, reported in 1846 painless operations performed upon natives in India who were put into hypnotic states.

The period of modern hypnotism may be said to begin with Dr. A. A. Liébault, about 1866, who rediscovered the power of suggestion. His work attracted no attention and might have been forgotten as Braid's had been but for the interest of Bernheim, whose influence at Nancy, together with that of Charcot, 1878, (and Janet,) at Paris, established the recognized doctrines of modern hypnotism. The Paris school regards hypnosis as an artificial mental disease. By fixation of the eyes or other long-continued stimulation of the senses, they believe that the subject is reduced to "unconscious automatism." The Nancy school on the other hand regards hypnosis as a normal state. The school of Nancy today enjoys the most extensive following; and may be said to represent the dominant trend of present study. With the complete realization of the psychological significance of the hypnotic state, the fierce and adventurous struggle for existence of hypnotism may be said to terminate in its undisturbed adaptation to a scientific environment.[6]

The Freudian Movement

J. W. Bridges, "Psychoanalysis, a Contribution to the New Psychology," *Public Health Journal*, June, 1923, 1-7

A distinct movement in this field is that which is associated primarily with the work of Freud. The most common name for this general school is "Psychoanalysis." A sketch of the movement follows.

---

[5] *Ency. Brit.*

[6] Further references: J. Milne Bramwell, *Hypnotism: Its History, Practice and Theory;* George Barton Cutten, *Three Thousand Years of Mental Healing;* James Joseph Walsh, *Cures: The Story of the Cures that Fail.*

Psychoanalysis is sometimes spoken of as the New Psychology. The latter term has, however, a broader meaning. A quarter of a century ago treatises were being written on the New Psychology. These dealt chiefly with methods and results of laboratory experiments. On the other hand the term New Psychology might be applied to a movement in psychology even more recent than psychoanalysis, namely, Behaviorism. According to this school psychology deals only with behavior—with various kinds of responses to stimulations, and not at all with mind or consciousness.

The term New Psychology should properly be used to designate the modern views and methods of psychology as distinguished from the ancient and mediæval. The old psychology was a science of the nature and destiny of the soul. It began with unverifiable assumptions regarding a soul or mind and by a process of deductive reasoning arrived at equally unverifiable conclusions. The system thus built up was pure speculation, and psychology was at that time quite rightly regarded as a branch of philosophy. This view of the science, although given up by present psychologists, is still widely prevalent among the laity, and results in the equally prevalent view that the subject is mysterious and impractical.

The New Psychology is over half a century old. The first laboratory for the study of psychology was founded at Leipzig in 1870. Henceforth psychology like the other natural sciences was to begin with observed facts, and from these its conclusions were to be arrived at inductively. This empirical method in psychology separated it from philosophy as an independent science and led directly to its practical application. This is the final goal and ultimate justification of all science. A science that can contribute nothing in the service of mankind has in the writer's opinion no right to exist. Applied psychology is of course still in its infancy, but enough has already been done to justify its existence.

Psychoanalysis is merely one important contribution to the new psychology. It has in common with the whole modern standpoint an empirical starting point and a practical aim. The first contribution to this important phase of psychology was made by Sigmund Freud of Vienna in 1895.[1] Freud had studied under Charcot, the

---

[1] [It would be interesting to know all the origins of the Freudian Theory. As various authors have observed, there were many anticipations of the views of Freud. Thus Dr. W. L. Northridge, in his *Modern Theories of the Unconscious*, sketches relevant aspects of the doctrines of Plato, Leibniz, Schopenhauer, Herbart, Hartmann, Hamilton, J. S. Mill, Carpenter, MacNish, Abercrombie, and the French schools, as forerunners of psychoanalytic theory. A. W. van Renterghem, in *Jour. Abn. Psychol.*,

great French neurologist, and had imbibed the French conception of psychology as the study of human nature especially as it manifests itself in behavior; and his psychological views therefore fall into the same general category as those of Janet, Ribot and Wm. James. Freud arrived at his views as a result of his study of neurotic patients. He found that if the patient took his symptoms or his dreams as starting points, he could, through the process of free association, bring into consciousness more and more forgotten experiences from early childhood. Freud found that this course led inevitably to the revelation of childhood sexual material, and resulted finally in the removal of the patient's symptoms. This method he called psychoanalysis. Psychoanalysis is thus primarily empirical and practical. It is a form of psychotherapy; but it leads inductively to a psychological theory. . . .

Freud divides the mind into three parts: the *conscious,* the *foreconscious* and the *unconscious.* The conscious is that portion of the mind of which we are immediately aware. The fore-conscious is outside immediate awareness but can be very readily brought into consciousness. The unconscious consists of those experiences and desires which cannot be brought into consciousness by any ordinary means. Psychoanalysis is the method by which the unconscious is made conscious, by which forgotten childhood experiences are brought again to memory.

The unconscious originates out of *mental conflict.* According to Freud this is primarily a conflict between the perverse sexual wishes of childhood and the conventional morality which the individual is obliged to acquire. As a result of this conflict the original sexual wishes are *repressed* and a resistance is built up to prevent them from re-entering consciousness. This defence is frequently greatly over-developed, so that in consciousness there appears the opposite

---

9: 369 ff. and 10: 46-51, sketches the historical relation of Breuer, Freud, Jung, etc., to Charcot and others. An account of Freud's early studies in collaboration with Dr. Joseph Breuer of Vienna is given by Prof. Freud in his Clark University Lecture, "The Origin and Development of Psychoanalysis." Of the older writers, again, and quite apart from bearing upon any particular school, we note that Spinoza's *Ethics* abounds in psychotherapeutic insights; and Kant made important observations. (Illustrative quotations from Herbart are found in Prof. H. L. Hollingworth's *The Psychology of Functional Neuroses,* 4-6, and in Boris Sidis' volume, *The Foundations of Normal and Abnormal Psychology,* 200; from Schopenhauer, in Boris Sidis' *Symptomatology, Psychognosis and Diagnosis of Psychopathic Diseases,* xi-xii; from Hartmann in the latter's *Philosophy of the Unconscious;* and from Kant in Dr. Morton Prince's volume, *The Unconscious,* 251n.)]

of the repressed trend. It is the task of psychoanalysis to break down this resistance and reveal the original wishes.[2]

---

[2] ["Some years before the publication of Janet's first work a Viennese physician, Joseph Breuer, who later had as a colleague Sigmund Freud, hit upon a novel plan of dealing with hysteria. In a patient whom he was treating by hypnotism he found that some of the symptoms were permanently relieved whenever certain forgotten episodes in her life were recalled during hypnosis and free expression given to the emotions which were attached to them. These episodes were occurrences after which the symptoms had first appeared, and it was found that on all of these occasions the patient had had to repress some strong emotional excitement instead of giving vent to it by appropriate words and deeds. Some psychical shock or trauma was received and the accompanying emotions were repressed. Thus, for example, this patient suddenly became unable to drink, and as it was a very hot summer she suffered much from thirst. She would take a glass of water in her hand, but as soon as it touched her lips, she would push it away as if she were suffering from hydrophobia. In hypnosis, one day, she was talking of her English governess, whom she disliked, and finally told, with every sign of disgust, how she had come into the room of the governess and how that lady's little dog, which the patient abhorred, had drunk out of a glass. Out of respect for the conventions she had remained silent. Now, after giving energetic expression to her restrained anger, she asked for water and drank a large quantity without trouble. She awoke from hypnosis with the glass at her lips, and the symptom thereupon vanished permanently.

"The patient herself described this new mode of treatment as the 'talking cure,' and jokingly referred to it as 'chimney sweeping.' Breuer called it the 'cathartic method.' The giving vent to the emotion he termed 'abreaction.'

"These pathogenic memories, revealed in hypnosis, were unknown to the patient in the waking state. They were, as Janet would say, dissociated memories. But in hypnosis memory was widened and their recall was possible.

"When Freud, some years later, took up again, by himself, the researches which he had begun in collaboration with Breuer, he very soon found that not all the patients whom he wanted to cure could be hypnotized. He was, therefore, faced with the problem of how he could recover, from the patient, memories which the patient himself had forgotten. Here Freud recalled to mind what he had seen in Bernheim's hypnotic clinic at Nancy. He had seen Bernheim bring back to the waking consciousness the events of deep hypnosis by persistently assuring the patient that he could and would remember. Freud therefore applied the same method to his neurotic patients in the waking state. When he came to a point at which the patient could apparently remember no more he assured him that he could remember and that the correct memory would emerge at the moment when he pressed his hand on the patient's forehead. True, the right thought did not always come at once, but he found that the recollections so induced led surely if slowly towards the forgotten memories which underlay the symptom.

The nature of the unconscious is according to Freud *dynamic*. It consists of repressed childhood wishes which are ever striving to express themselves.[3] It is also, as intimated above, *sexual*. The

---

"But he found this 'pressure method' to be very exhausting. It was as if the memories were all there ready to come up, but were prevented from doing so by some force against which he had to struggle. The presence of such a force was shown by the resistance of the patient, and this resistance had to be overcome before he could be cured. Therefore, Freud thought, this force which now caused the resistance to the emergence of the forgotten memories must be the force which had originally caused the forgetting. Thus arose in Freud's mind his great conception of *repression* as the dynamic cause of dissociation and amnesia.

"His next problem was to find the nature of the force which had caused the repression and led to the forgetting. On reviewing the cases he had treated in this way he found that all the forgotten memories were of the sort that one does not care to remember and prefers to forget. They were memories of events or of thoughts whose recurrence to the mind was painful, and he came to the conclusion that repression is a defence reaction of the mind against ideas that are unbearable. Moreover, he found that in all those experiences which had acted as mental shocks and had led to hysteria, some wish had been aroused which was incompatible with the moral or cultural standards of the patient. There had been a short conflict in the mind, and the struggle was brought to an end by the repression of the unbearable wish. As an example we may take the case of a young girl analysed by Freud about this time. When her sister married, this girl developed a great attachment to her new brother-in-law. She looked upon it as mere family tenderness, but her love was far greater than she knew. While she and her mother were away from home, the sister fell seriously ill, and they were hastily sent for; but before they arrived home the sister died. While she stood by her sister's death-bed there flashed through her mind the thought, 'Now he is free and can marry me.' This thought, which for a moment revealed to her the intensity of her love for her brother-in-law, revolted her, and it was immediately repressed. She forgot that such a thought had ever occurred to her, but she fell ill with severe hysterical symptoms. During her treatment by Freud this wish again became conscious and its revival was accompanied by intense emotional excitement. As a result she was cured of her hysteria."—T. W. Mitchell, *The Psychology of Medicine*, 42-45 (Methuen, 1921); reprinted by permission.]

[3] [Interesting is the fact that these perverse childhood wishes are not necessarily assumed to have been in consciousness. As Freud says in his *Introductory Lectures on Psycho-Analysis:*

"I will expound to you those theoretical conceptions which alone have proved useful in giving greater definiteness to the term *repression*. For this purpose it is first necessary that we should proceed from the purely descriptive meaning of the word 'unconscious' to its systematic meaning; that is, we resolve to think of the consciousness or unconsciousness of a mental process as merely one of its qualities and not necessarily definite. Suppose that a process of this kind has remained unconscious, its being withheld from consciousness may be merely a sign of the fate it has undergone, not necessarily the fate itself. Let us suppose, in order to

energy that strives for expression is sexual energy. Freud calls it *libido*. The sexuality of the unconscious is, however, a perverse sexuality. It consists of sexual cravings of childhood which cannot be lived out in adult life in a civilized or conventionalized society. Among the most important of these are: autosexual craving or self love, homosexual craving or love of other persons of the same sex, incestuous craving or love of persons of the opposite sex within the same family, sadistic and masochistic craving or love of sexual cruelty and pain, and exhibitionistic craving or love of sexual display.

These repressed impulses manifest themselves in various indirect ways, for they cannot be completely annihilated. They express themselves symbolically in dreams. Dreams are thus wishes that cannot be fulfilled in real life. They reveal themselves in mannerisms and slips of the tongue. They are converted or transferred into neurotic symptoms. It is the aim of psychoanalysis to remove the symptoms by laying bare the underlying cause and directing the repressed libido into other harmless channels. This re-direction of the libido into higher, that is socially more desirable, channels, is called *sublimation*.[4]

---

gain a more concrete notion of this fate, that every mental process—there is one exception, which I will go into later—first exists in an unconscious state or phase, and only develops out of this into a conscious phase, much as a photograph is first a negative and then becomes a picture through the printing of the positive. But not every negative is made into a positive, and it is just as little necessary that every unconscious mental process should convert itself into a conscious one. It may be best expressed as follows: Each single process belongs in the first place to the unconscious psychical system; from this system it can under certain conditions proceed further into the conscious system. . . .

"*Repression* . . . is the process by which a mental act capable of becoming conscious (that is, one which belongs to the preconscious system) is made unconscious and forced back into the unconscious system. And we also call it *repression* when the unconscious mental act is not permitted to enter the adjacent preconscious system at all, but is turned back upon the threshold by the censorship."—*Introductory Lectures on Psycho-Analysis*, 248-249, 287 (George Allen & Unwin, Ltd., 1922.)]

[4] ["To the biologist perhaps the most striking characteristic of the work of this school is its complete acceptance of what one may call the human point of view. It seems to be satisfied that no useful contribution to psychology is to be obtained outside the limits of human feeling and behaviour, and to feel no impatience to expand its inquiries into a still larger field. It is not that the school has failed to show an extremely vigorous movement of expansion. Beginning as a mere province of medicine, and while its foothold there was still far from general recognition, it invaded the regions of general psychology, of æsthetics, ethnology, the

Carl Jung of Zurich studied psychoanalysis under Freud, but later departed from the master in the following way: Freud's conception of the libido, or sexual energy, is broadened to mean the urge, push, or energy of life which is manifested in other activities

---

study of folklore and myth, and indeed of all matters in which it could find its essential material—the records of human feeling and conduct. Beyond the human species it has shown remarkably little of this aggressive spirit, and it seems to feel no need of bringing its principles into relation with what little is known of the mental activities of the non-human animals.

"The absence of any strong pressure in the direction of establishing a correlation of all mental phenomena, whether human or not, is not a matter of merely theoretical interest. The actual practical success to be obtained to-day in such an attempt might possibly be insignificant and yet of great value in moulding the whole attitude of mind of the investigator towards lying wholly within the sphere of human psychology. However much one may be impressed by the greatness of the edifice which Freud has built up and by the soundness of his architecture, one can scarcely fail, on coming into it from the bracing atmosphere of the biological sciences, to be oppressed by the odour of humanity with which it is pervaded. One finds everywhere a tendency to the acceptance of human standards and even sometimes of human pretensions which cannot fail to produce a certain uneasiness as to the validity, if not of his doctrines, at any rate of the forms in which they are expounded. The quality I am trying to describe is extremely difficult to express in concrete terms without exaggeration or distortion. To those who have approached Freud's work solely by the path of medicine the idea that it can give any one the feeling of a certain conventionality of standard and outlook and of a certain over-estimation of the objectivity of man's moral values will seem perhaps merely absurd. That this is an impression which I have not been able altogether to escape I record with a good deal of hesitation and diffidence and without any wish to lay stress upon it.

"Psychoanalytic psychology has grown up under conditions which may very well have encouraged the persistence of the human point of view. Originally its whole activity was concentrated upon the investigation and treatment of disease. Many of its early disciples were those who had received proof of its value in their own persons, those, that is to say, who had been sufferers from their very susceptibility to the influence of human standards. The objective standard of validity by which the system was judged was necessarily that of the physician, namely the capacity to restore the abnormal mind to the 'normal.' Normal in this sense is of course no more than a statistical expression implying the condition of the average man. It could scarcely fail, however, to acquire the significance of 'healthy.' If once the statistically normal mind is accepted as being synonymous with the psychologically healthy mind (that is, the mind in which the full capacities are available for use), a standard is set up which has a most fallacious appearance of objectivity. The statistically normal mind can be regarded only as a mind which has responded in the usual way to the moulding and deforming influence of its environment—that is, to human standards of discipline, taste, and

as well as the sexual. This libido has two opposing trends: progression, the striving forward towards differentiation and the overcoming of intervening obstacles; and regression, a pull backwards toward the uniformity and irresponsibility of infantile and prenatal life. This regressive tendency is substituted for the incestuous love which Freud believed dominated the neurotic patient and enchained him to the past. *Mental conflict is fundamentally a conflict between these progressive and regressive trends.* A neurotic patient is one who instead of overcoming the obstacles in his path, has regressed to an infantile form of expression of the libido.[5]

---

morality. If it is to be looked upon as typically healthy also, the current human standards of whose influence it is a product must necessarily be accepted as qualified to call forth the best in the developing mind they mould. Writers of the psychoanalytic school seem in general to make some such assumption as this."—W. Trotter, *Instincts of the Herd in Peace and War,* 77-79 (copyright, 1916, by The Macmillan Company); reprinted by permission.

For more full exposition of the Freudian theory, *cf.* H. W. Frink's *Morbid Fears and Compulsions,* the writings of Ernest Jones, A. A. Brill, and, especially, of Freud.]

[5] [For the present purpose, it may be noted further that Jung introduced the word-association method of detecting what he called "complexes." A list of words is presented to the patient, who is instructed to respond to each with the first word that comes into his mind. Variations in the response are watched for as indicative of repressed emotional complexes. "The following are some of these 'complex indicators.'

(*a*) Delayed reaction to a stimulus word, or to the one following it.
(*b*) Unusual reactions, egocentric or predicate reactions.
(*c*) Repetition of the stimulus word, giving it with minor changes, or translating it into a foreign language.
(*d*) Perseveration, response to a word previously given.
(*e*) Superficial associations, naming object in sight, or rhyming.
(*f*) No response.
(*g*) Failure to reproduce the same response on repeating the experiment.
(*h*) Emotional and other responses, such as clearing the throat, gesture, stammering, sighing, weeping, laughing, surprise, etc."—J. W. Bridges, *Outline of Abnormal Psychology,* 54-55 (Adams, 1925). For a quantitative experimental study of this method, *cf.* Clark L. Hull and L. S. Lugoff, "Complex Signs in Diagnostic Free Association," *Jour. Exper. Psychol.,* 4: 111-136 (1921).

"Also, in this setting, may be mentioned Jung's differing conception of the unconscious. Below an unconscious system of memories and impulses derived from the individual's own experience, Jung "postulates another . . . stratum or form of the unconscious which is not the product of acquisitions during the individual life, but is inherited or innate. It contains the psychic potentialities which are common to every individual, such as the instincts and the congenital conditions of intuition—the 'archetypes of apprehension,' as he calls them. The sum of these inherited psychic potentialities he calls the 'Collective Unconscious,' because

Alfred Adler of Vienna also studied under Freud, but later developed his own system of individual psychology. Adler puts the main emphasis on the ego instincts instead of the sex instinct. The dominating impulse in life is not the sex instinct, but the wish for power and the wish for security. The desire for superiority is a compensation for a feeling of inferiority that is based upon an actual or supposed defect. Neurotic symptoms represent a protest against a constitutional inferiority or an inferior position in life. Thus, hysteria in women is frequently a protest against the supposed inferior position of women in general. Degeneracy, genius, and neurosis are, according to Adler, related in the following way: the degenerate succumbs to his inferiority—the compensation is unsuccessful. The genius completely compensates for his inferiority by remoulding himself or reality to suit his purpose. The neurotic

---

they are common to all men and not unique individual contents like those which form the personal unconscious.

"The collective unconscious is the part or form of the unconscious on which Jung now lays most stress. Here are to be found the instincts which we all have in common—the true determinants of our conscious actions. Here also are those primordial forms of thought and feeling which determine the uniformity of our apprehension of the world. These primordial thought-feelings—for they are feeling as much as thought— form the basis of intuition. Just as the instincts enter into or influence our conscious activities which we believe to be rationally motivated, so these primordial thought-feelings, which represent primeval man's way of apprehending the world, enter into or influence our conscious rational thinking. They are the source of all the myths and legends and religions of humanity, whose similarity amongst all peoples and in all ages is accounted for by their common origin in the collective unconscious of the race. In normal life they come to light in more or less disguised forms in dreams; in the neuroses they press obtrusively on the conscious personality, making difficult that adaptation to reality which is man's chief task; in the insanities they break through the accretions of ages of culture and civilization and manifest in their primordial forms."—T. W. Mitchell, *The Psychology of Medicine*, 74-75 (Methuen, 1921); reprinted by permission. For a criticism of this theory, *cf.* W. L. Northridge, *Modern Theories of the Unconscious*, 150*ff.* Jung's classification of personality types is discussed below (p. 656). See also the topic "Regression" in the present volume. Jung states his relation to Freud, in *The Psychology of Dementia Precox*, xix-xx; also in *Collected Papers*, vii-x (now published under title *Analytical Psychology*). His differences from Freud on the idea of sexuality, and on "the etiological significance of the actual present" (through failure to adjust), while emphasizing also the occasional etiological rôle of phantasy, are found in his *Theory of Psychoanalysis*, 81, 83*ff.*, 93, 88, 94, etc. Dr. Trigant Burrow gives an account of Jung's doctrine in *Jour. Abn. Psychol.*, 12: 161*ff.* (1917). A full account, of course, is provided in the publications of Jung himself.]

compensates by a fantastic creation. He negates reality and seeks refuge in fantasy. He compensates in day dreams or in behavior that does not adjust him properly to his environment. He attains power through sickness.[6]

As far as the technique of psychoanalysis is concerned, Jung and Adler are in practical agreement with Freud; but, while Freud explores the unconscious in order to reveal repressed sexual desires, Jung seeks to recall earlier forms of libido activity and to detach the subject from the past, and Adler attempts to show his patient that his symptom is really an indirect and unsuccessful expression of the wish for power. Some English and American psychoanalysts have developed a method and a point of view that embrace the best results of these three masters.

In the writer's opinion the psychoanalysts have contributed a great deal to psychology; and he will endeavor to state as concisely as possible this contribution as he sees it. Three points must be emphasized in the beginning. In the first place psychoanalysis is by no means co-extensive with psychology. It is a part of psychology, and many psychologists still regard it as controversial or of only minor importance. Secondly, psychoanalysis has been given a philosophical and speculative turn by Jung and others. Jung's reasoning is interesting and almost seductive, but it lacks the empirical foundation that Freud so greatly emphasized. Thirdly, the psychoanalysts often express themselves in an antiquated terminology that savors of mysticism and leads to confusion. It is difficult to separate fact from theory or to change an established

---

[6] [The concept of defense mechanisms owes much to Adler, who has shown the intimate connection between 'organ inferiority' and the mental life. The child or adult person who feels himself neglected, or ugly, or unloved, and consequently inferior, builds up a psychic compensation. He seeks refuge possibly by constructing an ideal world where he is not neglected or ugly, or he may remind himself of his own intellectual superiority or of the goodness of his deeds. Likewise, one whose vision is defective compensates for the fact by an acquired delicacy of touch or hearing. One who fears his lungs are weak may develop many mental peculiarities growing out of a solicitous attitude toward his respiratory apparatus, and he may, indeed, in combating his inferiority, develop a powerful physique."—Walter S. Hunter, *General Psychology*, 76-77 (Univ. of Chicago Press, 1923).

Adler's theory, emphasizing "the manly protest," is developed in his publications, *A Study of Organ Inferiority and Its Psychical Compensation, The Neurotic Constitution* and *Individual Psychology*. Dr. William A. White discusses Adler in *Jour. Abn. Psychol.*, 12: 168ff. Critical illustration with some restatement of Adler's general contribution is provided by Prof. English Bagby, in *Jour. Abn. Psychol.*, 18: 269-273.]

terminology, and no claim is made that the following exposition has completely attained either of these aims.

The fundamental contentions of psychoanalysis may, in the writer's opinion, be summed up in a single paragraph. Man is a product of inheritance and environment, of nature and nurture. The former often comes into conflict with the latter. The so-called mental conflict is chiefly a conflict between original nature and cultural morality, but diverse original impulses may also come into conflict with one another. This conflict may persist; or the outcome may be (a) domination of original nature, or (b) domination of habit, that is to say repression of original nature, with various indirect manifestations, or (c) modification of original nature to suit the social demands. . . .

The Autosuggestion Movement

Edward Huntington Williams and Ernest Bryant Hoag, *Our Fear Complexes*, 147-148 (copyright, 1923, by the Bobbs-Merrill Co.); reprinted by permission

A recent psychotherapeutic development to attract popular attention is that associated with the names of Coué and Baudouin:

It is Coué's belief that success depends upon training the imagination rather than in trying to re-educate the will. And from his experience he reaches the following conclusion which he sums up as laws:

1. When the will and the imagination are antagonistic, it is always the imagination which wins, *without any exception.*[1]

2. In the conflict between the will and the imagination, the force of the imagination is in *direct ratio to the square of the will.*

---

[1] [This involves what Baudouin speaks of as "the law of reversed effort," the formulation of which he attributes to Coué. "The frequency of spontaneous suggestions," he says, "above all, of bad ones, shows us that the first task of reflective suggestion must be to neutralize these noxious suggestions, to struggle against suggestions that are already in operation. Yet, now when we concentrate voluntary attention upon the good idea which we are to substitute for the bad idea, when we devote all our energies to the substitution, what will happen? A reversal of effort, nothing more. The harder we try to think the good idea, the more violent will be the assaults of the bad idea."—Frederick Pierce, *Our Unconscious Mind*, 109-110 (Dutton, 1922).]

3. When the will and the imagination are in agreement, one does not add to the other, but one is multiplied by the other.

4. The imagination can be directed.

"After what has just been said it would seem that nobody ought to be ill. That is quite true. Every illness, whatever it may be *can* yield to *autosuggestion,* daring and unlikely as my statement may seem; I do not say *does always yield,* but *can yield,* which is a different thing."

In Coué's own estimation, however, there are two classes of persons who are not amenable to autosuggestion: First, the mentally incompetent who are not capable of understanding what you say to them; and, second, those who are unwilling to understand. He does not say, but implies, there is a third class of patients that can not be cured by his method. These are the ones afflicted with organic diseases, such as cancer, malaria, syphilis, and many others —incurable, at least, by mental healing alone. . . .[2]

---

[2] ["Should any one doubt that Couéism is simply another form of hypnotism, or semi-hypnotism, he has but to recall the public demonstrations of hypnotists which almost every reader has witnessed. First of all Coué puts his patients through a preliminary course of treatment to make them more receptive to suggestion—just as the hypnotist prepares his subjects by a few simple experiments. 'Be careful always to keep your eyes fixed on the root of the subject's nose,' instructs M. Coué, 'and do not allow him to turn his eyes from yours for a single moment. . . . Always use a tone of command which suffers no disobedience. I do not mean that it is necessary to raise your voice; on the contrary it is preferable to employ the ordinary pitch, but stress every word in a dry and imperative tone.' This is the instruction of Mesmer, the method of every successful hypnotist. And Coué continues, 'When these experiments have been successful, all the others succeed which equally well can be easily obtained by carrying out to the letter the instructions given above.' And he makes the trite observation that some subjects are very sensitive and easily placed under control, while others require more treatment to get into their full confidence.

"In one of his experiments he says to the patient: 'Shut your eyes. Now you can not open them.' And *of course* the patient can not open them, for he is hypnotised. Every one who has witnessed public demonstrations of hypnotism will remember that this is one of the classic methods of beginning a hypnotic seance. The patient is first told that he can or can not do this or that thing when he has 'assimilated' the suggestion so that he must obey it, then he is ready for further suggestions, and ultimately for complete control in the hands of the hypnotist.

" 'And now,' proceeds M. Coué, 'when the subject has passed through the preceding experiment it is understood then that he is ripe for curative suggestion. He is like a cultivated field in which the seed can germinate and develop, whereas before it was but barren earth in which it would have perished.' "—Williams and Hoag, *op. cit.,* 153-155.

"[Then] the first thing to do is to give up striving, and allow the body

More Modern Developments

W. S. TAYLOR; prepared for this volume

In addition to attempts in various quarters to synthesize the best of the psychoanalytic contributions, we find efforts by Dr. Edward J. Kempf and others to base psychoanalytic conceptions upon physiological processes.[1] Here the autonomic nervous system and the ductless glands are emphasized especially. The data taken for support, however, and the inferences made in behalf of these views,

and mind to attain that state of complete relaxation which we have described as the pre-requisite for free association. Then just as the mind is beginning to drift away, as it were, into dreamland, then the desired end is allowed to come before the mind as vividly as possible, as something that is bound to happen, or something we are bound to do, because we cannot help doing it. If the state of relaxation has been properly attained the opposing tendencies which have previously inhibited the fulfilment of these desired ends will be in abeyance, and opposition removed. If the suggestion is reinforced by a strong emotion then its fulfilment is further assisted. There are really three stages in the process we have described. The first is the state of relaxation which has been sufficiently elucidated, the second is what we have called the state of mental drift when the diverse interests awakened by contact with the outer world begin to fade away, and interest begins to converge, as it were, of itself, upon some more or less vaguely realized goal. To this stage has been given the technical name of 'collection.' The third stage is called 'contention' when the direction of the drift is determined by the introduction of the desired end. The more vividly this end is imaged the more likely are the chances of its realization. But all through there must be no sense of striving or strain. Particularly good times for the practice are night and morning, just as you are gradually dropping off to sleep, or gradually returning to full waking consciousness.

"Another most interesting discovery that Coué made . . . was, that there is no necessity to repeat this process time after time in connection with each separate item in respect of which improvement is desired. But every night and morning *without fail*, betwixt sleeping and waking, the suggestion should be made, slowly, but as vividly as possible, 'Day by day, in all respects, I get better and better.' 'In all respects,' should be emphasized and underlined. Occasionally the details of the desired improvement should be dwelt on, such as, 'I am getting stronger, every organ in my body is functioning better and more regularly; I am facing my life with a more reasonable independence and confidence, my difficulties are diminishing before my increased capacity,' etc."—R. H. Hingley, *Psycho-Analysis*, 115-116 (Methuen & Co. and Dodd, Mead, 1922); reprinted by permission.]

[1] *Cf.* Edward J. Kempf, *The Autonomic Functions and the Personality*, and *Psychopathology*.

are distinctly open to question in many important respects.[2] Yet this biologizing tendency is expressive of a growing desire for solid physiological foundations for psychopathology.

In the meantime, there are available clear efforts to conceive at least the functional neuroses in general neurological terms. In this connection Dr. Morton Prince's volume, *The Unconscious,* is an outstanding work. Dr. John B. Watson, Professors H. L. Hollingworth, Max Meyer, Walter S. Hunter, Robert S. Woodworth, Howard C. Warren, and many others have expressed this point of view.[3] As such a position is presented somewhat fully in the selections which follow, it is unnecessary to develop it further at this point.

In closing our historical sketch, brief as it is, mention should be made of the great development resulting from the war experience. This has given rise to an abundant literature.[4]

---

[2] Dr. Frederic Lyman Wells has critically reviewed Kempf's later volume, *Psychopathology,* in *Jour. Abn. Psychol.,* 16: 392-400 (1921-1922).

[3] *Cf.* John B. Watson, "Behavior and the Concept of Mental Disease," and *Psychology from the Standpoint of a Behaviorist,* 412*ff;* H. L. Hollingworth, *The Psychology of Functional Neuroses;* Max Meyer, *The Psychology of the Other-One;* Walter S. Hunter, *General Psychology,* 78; Robert S. Woodworth, *Psychology,* 562 etc.; and Howard C. Warren, "The Subconscious." *Cf.* references provided in the writer's article, "Behavior under Hypnoanalysis," *infra* (Chapter xxiii).

[4] An example is Dr. Frederick W. Mott's *War Neurosis and Shell Shock.* Dr. Elmer E. Southard's *Shell-Shock and Other Neuropsychiatric Problems Presented in 589 Cases from the War Literature,* with its comprehensive bibliography, was reviewed by Southard in *Psychol. Bull.,* 16: 187-199. Dr. James V. May's chapter, "The Psychiatry of the War," in his volume, *Mental Diseases,* 185-201, with its references, is of interest here.

CHAPTER V

SOME BASIC PSYCHOLOGICAL CONCEPTIONS

ADJUSTMENTAL ORGANIZATION

The Conception of Stimulus and Response

HARVEY A. CARR, *Psychology*, 68-72 (Longmans, 1925)

The Reflex Arc Concept. The nervous system is usually regarded as a conductor. It is a medium for the transmission of energy from sense organs to muscles and glands, a device for translating sensory stimuli into movements of an adaptive character. Three general principles may be deduced from this conception.

All sensory stimuli must exert some effect upon the activity of the organism. Any stimulating condition that affects a sense organ necessarily releases energy, and the only outlet for this energy is the muscles and glands. The validity of this proposition can be tested by experimental means. A subject is requested to remain quiescent, and a number of his involuntary movements are graphically registered by mechanical devices. He is then subjected to various stimuli,—odors, sounds, contacts, etc. Almost without exception, stimulations of this sort produce some noticeable effect upon the character of the involuntary activities in some part of the body. . . .

All activity, ideational as well as motor, is initiated by sensory stimuli. The sensory-neuro-muscular mechanisms accumulate and store energy, and this energy can be released only by the incidence of extraneous forces upon the sensitive parts. In other words, neural impulses are not spontaneously aroused. This proposition must be regarded as an assumption, for its validity in the very nature of the case can never be submitted to a decisive experimental test.

Every movement resulting from a sensory situation inevitably modifies that situation, and this change or modification of the sensory situation constitutes a new sensory stimulus which in turn modifies the act that produced it. There is thus a continuous process of interaction between sensory stimuli and motor responses.

A stimulus arouses a movement, this response alters the sensory situation, this alteration of sensory conditions constitutes a stimulus that modifies the act, and this new response in turn arouses a stimulus that produces some effect upon the organism's subsequent behavior. . . .

The doctrine that all sensory stimuli exert some effect upon conduct does not mean that these effects can be readily observed. The inruption of a new stimulus may merely accelerate, retard, or slightly alter the character of the activities in which the organism is engaged at the moment. The effect may be limited to a slight disturbance of breathing or circulation, or the stimulus may merely alter the muscular tensions in certain parts of the body. Not every stimulus arouses a distinctive overt response.

The doctrine that all activity is initiated by sensory stimuli does not mean that the objective environment determines the character of an organism's behavior. In the first place, the energy of the response may be wholly disproportionate to the strength of the physical stimulus. For example, a weak sound may elicit a more vigorous response than a loud one. The nature of the act that is elicited by a stimulus is largely determined by intraorganic conditions,—by the structure and physiological disposition of the organism. No two organisms ever react to a stimulus in exactly the same manner. Neither is an organism wholly dependent upon the external environment for the initiation of its responses, for its activity may be initiated by intraorganic stimuli. For example, hunger, thirst, and internal pains are very powerful stimuli that largely determine the nature of the organism's reactions.

Integration

A

A. G. TANSLEY, *The New Psychology,* 38-40 (Dodd, Mead, 1924)

Professor Holt, in *The Freudian Wish,* points out that the behavior of an organism adapted to its surroundings is related rather to the objects and situations of those surroundings than to physical or chemical stimuli as such, and he holds that this takes place by the *integration* (i. e. the putting together to make a new whole) of simple motor responses to form complex ones. Thus the specific responses of an organism may be regarded as "functions" (in the mathematical sense) of the objects and situations of its environment; and the history of the evolution of response to environment,

i. e. of behavior, and of mind itself is, as Professor Holt most convincingly shows, the history of successive integrations of these "functions" to higher and higher (i. e. to more and more complex) purposes, accompanied by what he calls "recession" in consciousness of the primitive stimuli and the progressive subordination of the less complex functions.

The consideration of any consecutive set of actions that we perform will make clear this conception of integration.   For instance, if I go into a shop to buy something, all my actions in the shop—walking across the floor, asking for what I want, examining the things I am shown, saying which I will have, taking money out of my pocket and putting it on the counter, receiving my change, picking up the things and walking out of the shop—are integrated (i. e. put together into a whole) to form the main action of the purchase of the article.   Each of the single actions mentioned will be unconsciously performed if my consciousness is wholly occupied by the act of purchase as a whole. . . . The process of integration consists in their combination and subordination to a larger action, and when so combined the individual actions tend more and more to be performed unconsciously, to sink to the level of reflex action in which the psychical elements are lost.   But by attention these can at once be brought into consciousness again.

In the same way the "main action" we have taken as an instance —the purchase of the article—may be part of a more extended action, into which the purchase in question and many other acts are integrated, e.g., the furnishing of a house; and this again may be part of a still more extended action such as embarking on a career in a fresh place.   Actions of more than a certain degree of complexity cannot be performed entirely unconsciously, but when they are subordinated to a more extended action their specific effects are often notably diminished and tend to share in the effect of the extended action of which they are a part, a sign of the integration which has taken place.   Thus, for instance, actions which are unpleasant in themselves lose some of their unpleasantness when they form parts of an extended action whose end is strongly desired and whose effect is therefore highly pleasurable. A slackening of attention to the more extended action always tends to lead to its concentration on the subordinate ones and to bring them more vividly into consciousness.

This process of combination and integration of minor into major responses is the key process of the evolution of behavior—in animals of reflex actions into instincts, in man of simpler into more complicated and extended conscious actions.

We find, then, that specific responses to particular features of the environment are absolutely characteristic of all organisms, even the simplest. They are, in fact, the great distinguishing mark of the organism, as contrasted with inorganic matter, so far as its relations with the external world are concerned. In general, though not universally, these specific responses are "purposive" or "adaptive" in the sense that the response is appropriate to the stimulus in reference to the well-being of the organism or of the species.

B

WILLIAM H. BURNHAM, *The Normal Mind*, 31-33 (Appleton, 1924)

The Acme of Integration. The highest form of integration is found in the master tissues of the human organism, the nervous system, composed of billions of neurones. This is made up of the central nervous system and the autonomic nervous system. According to some students, notably Kempf,[1] the autonomic nervous system was the primitive original system, far older than the central nervous system, and the latter was developed after this. Possibly this may be true; but whatever the genetic sequence, to-day the evidence indicates that the central nervous system is the controlling system, and its special function is that of coördination and integration. No one has shown this so well as Sherrington, and this is the burden of his great book *The Integrative Action of the Nervous System.*[2]

The Term Integration. Perhaps a word should be said about this term integration. The derivation of the word is familiar. An integer is a unit; we are familiar with it in the study of integral numbers. An integer has not been broken up into fractions. And again we speak of a man of integrity, that is one with no break in his character, whose reputation is unsullied. Sherrington uses this word integration instead of the usual word coördination, thus putting emphasis on the unity, the wholeness of the organism under the control of the integrative action of the nervous system. Coördination puts emphasis on the parts united, integration on the whole which results from the integration of the parts.

Integration the Function of the Nervous System. One or two paragraphs from Sherrington's writings express the essential facts briefly and clearly.[3]

---

[1] E. J. Kempf, *The Autonomic Functions and the Personality*, Nervous and Mental Disease Monograph, No. 28 (1918).

[2] *Cf.* Bibliography.

[3] "Some Aspects of Animal Mechanism," *Science*, 56: 352-353 (1922).

The nervous system is that bodily system the special office of which, from its earliest appearance onward throughout evolutionary history, has been more and more to weld together the body's component parts into one consolidated mechanism reacting as a unity to the changeful world about it.   More than any other system it has constructed out of a collection of organs an individual of unified act and experience.   It represents the acme of accomplishment of the integration of the animal organism.

The portion in this system to which mind transcendently attaches is exactly that where are carried to their highest pitch the nerve-actions which manage the individual as a whole, especially in his reactions to the external world.   There, in the brain, the integrating nervous centers are themselves further compounded, interconnected, and recombined for unitary functions.

As he points out, the animal's great integrating system is there still further integrated in the brain cortex; "and this supreme integrator is the seat of all that is most clearly inferable as the animal's mind."

Thus integration is the essential characteristic of the normal body.   The study of the nervous system suggests clearly that integration is the essential characteristic of a normal mind as well.

The Interaction of Stimulus-Response Mechanisms

STEVENSON SMITH and EDWIN R. GUTHRIE, *General Psychology*, 43-47
(Appleton, 1923)

As no animal is ever acted upon by just one stimulus at a time, but at any given moment is exposed to a great *complexity of stimuli*, its resulting behavior is the interplay of many responses.   The action of any stimulus depends on the other stimuli that occur along with it.   A loud sound heard on the city streets causes a response different from that given to the same sound when the hearer is alone in the woods.

The combination of all the stimuli to which an animal responds at any moment is called a *situation*, and a combination of responses is called an act.[1]

If the situation that confronts the animal tends to arouse simultaneously two stimulus-response mechanisms there may occur one of two results.   One of the mechanisms, though not itself respond-

---

[1] These definitions are proposed by Watson, *Psychology from the Standpoint of a Behaviorist*, 10.

ing, may increase the tendency of the other to respond; or one may interfere with the action of the other.

The first of these results, where one system is an aid to the other, is called *facilitation*. This aid or reenforcement produces a more lively response in the system that is facilitated. Suppose a man, seeing a bear in the woods, responds by a dignified retreat. The bear now moves in the man's direction and he, previously walking, breaks into a run. Pigs eat more greedily when other pigs are sharing the meal, and almost any animal will partake more rapidly of the food that we threaten to remove. A toothache ends our delay in visiting the dentist, and a good appetite makes us respond promptly when summoned to dinner.

An increased tendency to act is to be expected when two stimuli lead to the same response, but this increased tendency may also occur in cases where the responses produced by the two stimuli are not the same.

The difference between facilitation and the summation of stimuli lies in this, that the stimuli combined in summation are all subliminal and occur serially, whereas the stimuli combined in facilitation may or may not be subliminal and if subliminal must occur simultaneously.

Contrasted with facilitation is the case of interference between two stimulus-response mechanisms. As a result of interference three things may happen; either both reponses are given with lessened energy, or one response is given with lessened energy and the other is not given, or neither response occurs. The hampering effect that one system has upon another is called *distraction*. The preventing effect which one system has upon another is called *inhibition*. If a trap is baited and an animal is led by the odor of the bait to approach the trap, and if there is no odor of man about the trap, the animal will seize the bait and be caught. If, however, the body odor of the trapper adheres to the trap, the animal will either take the bait less readily or will entirely disregard it. If the bait is taken reluctantly, the body odor is a distracting stimulus; and if it is not taken at all, the body odor is an inhibiting stimulus.

The reason one response prevails over the other is either that there is more resistance in the conduction path of one system than in that of the other, or that the relative strength of the two stimuli in terms of their thresholds is different.[1]

---

[1] For a discussion of the neural basis of interference see Sherrington, *The Integrative Action of the Nervous System*, 55, 115-149, 223 (Yale, 1906).

When interference so raises the threshold of both responses that neither is given, we have *mutual inhibition*. In this case a third stimulus may bring about a response that removes the animal from the first two stimuli, and the interference disappears. This may be seen in the case of a man who is addressed by someone while he is reading. He pauses in his reading and it is now doubtful whether he will answer the questioner or resume his book. One of these responses will eventually be given unless a third stimulus, such as the ringing of the telephone, causes him to disregard both book and questioner. Ordinarily man is acted upon not by two but by a multiplicity of stimuli, and his responses are determined by facilitating stimuli, inhibiting stimuli, distracting stimuli, and by the stimuli that primarily elicit the response.

When a spinal dog is simultaneously stimulated at a point on the shoulder and at a point several inches farther back, he scratches a spot somewhere between the two. His response is in the nature of a compromise. Man, as well, when stimulated to two distinct responses, often acts in a way that is a resultant of the two response tendencies. When playing ball with a stone we tend to throw it as if it were a ball to the person who is about to catch it, and we tend to refrain from throwing it because we are in the habit of not stoning our friends. The resultant act consists in throwing the rock gently.

Compromise in emotional responses is the rule rather than the exception. If a child's mischief annoys us, we respond to him both as to a child to be treated kindly and as to a nuisance to be abated. The resultant response is remonstrance with sad good humor. When a puppy is scolded his behavior is a compromise between affection and fear, and is somewhat suggestive of the politeness of human beings in the presence of strangers.

Professors Smith and Guthrie thus point out processes fundamental to the complexity of human behavior. Like the humble Coelenterate, *Carmarina,* whose manubrium may be halted midway between two equally stimulated points on its discoid subumbrella, we ourselves contain tendencies toward crude compromises between opposing stimuli. Fortunate it is, therefore, since our muscular organizations as well as environment so often require *alternatives* instead of compromises, that as Sherrington observes, the very complexity of the nervous system in vertebrates makes exact balancing of any two reflexes most unlikely.[1] There is "reciprocal innervation of antagonistic muscles"; and, between large systems of action, there definitely seems to be what Professor McDougall calls "inhibition by drainage":[2] of two opposed systems, if all is working well, one tends to *completely* inhibit the other, while going its own way unhindered, apparently through draining into itself the energy which would otherwise go into the rival channel. *This* sort of inhibition is the ideally normal sort, does not fill up any "unconscious" with "repressions," and is integral to integration.

In connection with this topic of inhibition, too, we may note what appears as the great general difference between all types of inhibition,[3] on the one hand, and every form of dissociation, on the other: Dissociation means *lack of influence* of one neural element upon another; they go their ways independently. Inhibition, on the contrary, denotes that the functioning of one neural element in some way is *actually hindered* by the activity of such other neural element or elements as are effecting the inhibition referred to.

The Mechanism of Inhibition

LEONARDO BIANCHI, *The Mechanism of the Brain*, 318-324 (Wood, 1922)

The development of inhibitory power in the psychic domain coincides with the appearance of the frontal lobes. It represents in the psychic field what resistance is in the physiological field. We know from the researches of physiologists, especially of C. Richet,[4] that the time taken by a nervous current to reach a central point and produce a reflex is in proportion to the length of the nerve or nerves involved. In other words, the length of time required is in direct ratio to the distance or the resistance, and this corresponds with the universal law that velocity is in inverse ratio to resistance. To the time required for transmission along the nerves there falls to be added a latent time occupied in the centre (in the

---

[1] Charles S. Sherrington, *The Integrative Action of the Nervous System*, 117-118.
[2] *Outline of Psychology*, 179n, 280.
[3] *Cf.* Raymond Dodge, "The Problem of Inhibition."
[4] *Rev. scientifique*, 1906.

cell of the spinal medulla, in the case of spinal reflexes), for the metabolism or transformation of the sensory nervous waves into motor or centrifugal waves. To-day, our knowledge of the histology of the nerve-cell has been so enlarged by the researches of Golgi, Ramon y Cajal, V. Gehuchten, Donaggio, Lugaro, Fragnito, and numerous other investigators, that we can find a ready explanation of the long loss of time in the nervous centre (group of cells). We can understand it to be due to the enormous resistance offered by the great twisting of endocellular and extra- or peri-cellular neuro-fibrils in a more or less extensive field of cells before the current assumes its centrifugal character in the motor paths.

As we cannot imagine inhibition to be a watchful, regulative power which is exercised from a distance, and much less think of it as an occult force, it is necessary to trace the phenomenon to its objective physical mechanism. There is no other way of understanding it.

It will help us to comprehend the phenomenon if we start out with the obvious fact that all the nervous organs together constitute a circulatory system for nerve-waves, which is much more complicated than that concerned with the circulation of the blood. No observer can have failed to be impressed by the fact that the circulation of the nerve-waves is regulated by the same laws as those pertaining to liquids in enclosed tubes and to the circulation of electric currents in conducting wires. This hypothesis has been confirmed by psycho-physical researches. We know that in the process of evolution of the nervous system new organs are developed and close anatomical relations are established between these and the pre-existing organs—in other words, the field of circulation of the nerve-waves becomes more extensive, and consequently a higher potential is required in order to overcome the increased resistances of the new paths, proportionately to the extent of the new field.[1]

One can readily understand that if, for any reason whatsoever (artificial irritation, morbid processes, excessive functioning, etc.), one area receives an addition to its nervous charge, this is to the detriment of the other areas, in which the charge will be diminished by just so much as it is increased in the excited part of the nervous system. The former are inhibited through the hyper-functioning of the latter. In accordance with this view, any central nervous organ may inhibit or be itself inhibited as circumstances occur.

---

[1] [In *Jour. Abn. Psychol.*, 1: 12-17 (1905), Prof. Pierre Janet explains some obsessive conditions as being due to an insufficiency of "psychic tension."]

We get disturbance of the equilibrium of the nervous circulation and increase of the charge in certain parts of the nervous system, when any field of propagation in the brain becomes suppressed or cut off from the other organs, owing to interruption of the paths of communication between them.

Given the free circulation of the nervous currents through all the central areas of the system which are connected with the peripheral areas by means of centripetal paths (the conducting wires), we get a greater charge of nervous force in the lower cerebral organs when these are separated from the higher, and this gives rise in turn to an increased excitability which resolves itself into augmented reflex action. Exaggeration of the reflexes and diminution of the time of reaction are due to the simple physical facts that the field of propagation is diminished and that consequently the nerve-waves become concentrated in a more restricted field of distribution. The tonic contraction of certain groups of muscles (on the opposite side) that follows immediately on removal of one cerebral hemisphere or of both cerebral hemispheres (contractions on both sides), such as observed by Sherrington,[1] is likewise an effect of suppression of an extensive field of propagation of the nerve-waves which are constantly being aroused by external stimuli and transmitted in a centripetal direction. These, finding their paths obstructed, over-run the lower centres, augmenting their potential, which, in turn, becomes discharged along the motor paths, thus giving rise to tonic contraction of the muscles in the first instance and to exaggeration of the reflexes in the next. We know that in the cerebral mantle there exist distinct areas for groups of muscles which contract, and for their antagonists which relax. We also know that on exciting the area belonging to the first group the corresponding muscles enter into a state of contraction, whilst at the same time their antagonists become relaxed. In the writer's view this is due to the fact that the potential in the area belonging to the antagonistic group of muscles becomes diminished during excitation of the other area.

That is the most likely interpretation that can be offered of the experiments of Sherrington, of Herring and Sherrington,[2] Topolanski,[3] Libertini, Oddi, and Fano.[4] The last-named physiologist

---

[1] Sherrington, "Decerebrate Rigidity," *Jour. of Physiol.* (Cambridge and London, 1898).

[2] Herring and Sherrington, *Arch. f. die Gesels. Physiologie,* and *Journ. of Physiology* (1898).

[3] Topolanski, *Arch. f. Ophthalm.* (Leipzig, 1898).

[4] Fano, *Archives italiennes de Biologie* (1895).

found that removal of the whole frontal lobe, including the sigmoid gyrus, led to shortening of the reaction-time, whilst electric stimulation of the frontal lobes lengthened it.

This lengthening of the time of reaction we call inhibition, but it is clear that it is nothing else than the physiological effect of an experimental physical condition—viz., an increase of the quantity of nervous waves in the frontal lobes owing to the influx that takes place under the action of the electric stimulus, and a consequent diminution of the charge of nervous force in the remaining parts of the cerebro-spinal axis. So far as this question is concerned, it is very doubtful what value is to be attached to researches made with the object of demonstrating that the frontal lobes are a centre of inhibition. All points of the cerebral mantle may either be inhibitory organs or may themselves be inhibited, according as they are stimulated or as other neighbouring or distant areas with which they have functional relations are stimulated.

The inhibitory power is greater or less according to the degree of functional dignity of the cerebral area concerned and, one might add, according to the number of associative relations which it has with other parts of the central nervous system. As the frontal lobe does not send any fibres directly to the spinal medulla, nor receive any from it (vide Chapter VII [1]), its inhibitory power over the spinal medulla can only be exercised through an indirect path. It is sufficient to see the number of associative fibres that run between the frontal lobe and the Rolandic area to be convinced, without stretch of imagination, that any stimulation of the frontal lobes must induce such a flow of nerve-waves, especially from the Rolandic area, that the nervous charge becomes lowered in all the rest of the cerebro-spinal axis which therefore finds itself in a hypo-functional condition. Vice versa when the frontal lobes are removed, the nerve-waves which were destined to pass to the frontal lobes, whose field is now destroyed or obstructed, accumulate in other centres and this explains their greater excitability.

Soundness of Organization

STEWART PATON, Signs of Sanity, 38-39, 67. 77-79, 94-95 (Scribner, 1922)

Soundness of body causes the strong man to rejoice in running a race, but it also often makes a man rejoice in an opportunity to think.

---

[1] [Leonardo Bianchi, op. cit.]

If we were called upon to pick out two of the most striking characteristics of this "soundness," we should point out first that the reaction is graded to the stimulus, and then that these reactions are appropriate to the occasion. The efforts made by a person possessing a sound body to overcome some obstacle are well adapted; that is to say, the movements accomplish their purpose promptly and effectively with no unnecessary loss of power. A person with a sound body does the right thing at the right time with minimum expenditure of energy. The precision and ease with which the really well-trained athlete does his work is a good example of physical soundness. Another illustration of soundness is the person without large muscular development, who succeeds admirably in directing his or her constructive impulses in productive work, and in checking destructive tendencies.

Any living organism if it responds to stimulation by well-graded and appropriate reactions exhibits the fundamental organization of the sound body that forms the necessary basis for the unified, harmonious, sound mind. . . . The embryo or very young animal is not prepared to grade its reactions to the occasion. It puts all its energy into every response, thus rapidly using up the energy available. When the organization of the nervous system becomes complex there is a proportion established between the strength of the stimulus and the subsequent reaction; and only when this stage is reached is the organism really prepared to respond so as to conserve and not dissipate energy. . . .

The body's efficiency in meeting and overcoming difficulties depends not only upon the movement of muscles, but upon the coordinated, properly adjusted responses of a great many organs—heart, lungs, endocrine glands, etc. Imperfect coördination spells inefficiency and waste of energy. Defective muscular responses may throw a very complicated system, including nervous and muscular systems as well as the glands of internal secretion, out of gear.[1] Probably one of the most instructive illustrations of the marvellous efficiency of organization required for the automatic control of energy which enables the animal to regulate its behavior to the best advantage, is in connection with the apparatus for regulating the supply of sugar, which represents a large part of the fuel supply for the human engine. Since it is so necessary as a defensive measure that energy, both mental and physical, should be quickly available and readily dispensed in an economic fashion, the stores

---

[1] Bainbridge, F. A., *The Physiology of Muscular Exercise* (Cambridge, 1919).

of blood-sugar are carefully protected; and in diabetes they are not so protected. When the animal is called upon to make an unusual effort, the sugar supply is quickly mobilized and the energy thus obtained is directed towards securing protection or aid either in flight or by some other form of reaction. The entire control of this substance is under the endocrine system (glands of internal secretion). Any interference with this system is apt to result in wasting of the sugar supply as, for instance, in diabetes. Emotional instability is very possibly associated with some disturbance in the storing up and release of the sugar supply. . . .

In the sound body, even if there is a momentary conflict of impulses, the energy accumulated is quickly redistributed and the proper balance between all the various functions is restored. Under all ordinary circumstances, an automatic selection of the impulses best adapted to the occasion is made, and then the harmony of the physical organization is preserved. We shall see . . . what an important bearing this harmony has upon the preservation of our sanity. If there is imperfect coördination of the various inherited and acquired tendencies to action, we cannot expect an effective organization of the mind in the struggle to adjust life. The adaptive processes represented in the rational control of our lives depend primarily upon the successful adaptation of the instinctive life; and these adaptations are the chief indications of soundness of body. The soundness of body that is essential for the successful adjustment of our lives to a very large extent depends upon the coördinating and organizing capacity of the brain and nervous system. The brain is the chief center of control for the remarkable organization necessary for soundness of both body and mind.

Organization through Dominance of the Later Nerve Structures

W. H. R. RIVERS, *Instinct and the Unconscious*, 22-23, 27-29 (Cambridge, 1922)

Observations on the sensory changes which accompany the regeneration of a divided and reunited nerve have led Head and his colleagues to distinguish two different kinds of mechanism on the afferent side of the nervous system.[1] Prolonged observations after

---

[1] H. Head, W. H. R. Rivers, and J. Sherren, *Brain*, 28: 99 (1905); H. Head and J. Sherren, *ibid.*, 28: 116 (1905); W. H. R. Rivers and H. Head, *ibid.*, 31: 323 (1908).

the division of nerves in Head's own arm brought out clearly the existence of two definite stages in the return of sensibility. In one of these, the protopathic stage, the sensations are vague and crude in character, with absence of any exactness in discrimination or localisation and with a pronounced feeling-tone, usually on the unpleasant side, tending to lead explosively, as if reflexly, to such movements as would withdraw the stimulated part from contact with any object to which the sensory changes are due. At this stage of the healing of the reunited nerve there are present none of those characters of sensation by which we recognise the nature of an object in contact with the body. The sensations are such as would enable one to know that something is there and that it is pleasant or unpleasant. It is also possible to distinguish between mere contact or pressure and stimulation by heat or cold, but within each of these modes of sensation there is no power of distinguishing differences in intensity nor of telling with any exactness the spot where the processes underlying the sensory changes are in action.

The second stage of the process of regeneration is characterised by the return of those features of normal cutaneous sensibility, such as exact discrimination and localisation, by means of which it becomes possible to perceive the nature of an object in contact with the skin and adjust behaviour according to this perception. The modes of reaction which make this exactness of discrimination and power of external projection possible are grouped together under the heading of epicritic sensibility. . . .

There is reason to believe that the two forms of cutaneous sensibility, which I have described, represent two different stages in the evolution of the nervous system with their associated varieties of consciousness. The facts seem best to fit with the hypothesis that the manifestations of protopathic sensibility which are suppressed belong to a crude form of nervous system which has been superseded by a later and more efficient mechanism. If now we pass to the central end of the nervous path by which the impulses subserving cutaneous sensibility reach the brain, Head working in conjunction with Holmes [2] has discovered a relation between the cerebral cortex and the optic thalamus very similar to that existing between protopathic and epicritic sensibility. In this case the special modes of activity they have studied are associated with structures which belong to widely separated stages of the development of the nervous system. The optic thalamus represents the dominant part of the brain of lower vertebrates, while the cerebral

---

[2] H. Head and Gordon Holmes, *Brain*, 34: 102 (1911-12).

cortex or neo-pallium developed far later. When by injury, disease, or operative procedure, the cortex cerebri has been put out of action, stimulation of the skin produces sensations characterised by a peculiar quality such as would be produced by over-weight of the affective aspect of sensation, very similar to that shown by proto-pathic sensibility. Moreover, there is an absence of objective character very similar to that of this form of sensibility. When the cortex is in action the affective over-response of the thalamus is largely suppressed under ordinary conditions, but the process of suppression does not come out so strongly as in the case of the peripheral nervous system because some of the primitive features which most need suppression have already suffered this fate. Thus, removal of cortical activity does not produce radiation and refer-ence of localisation because the suppression of these characters is still being maintained at the periphery.

Similar examples of suppression have been observed in the re-flexes. In reflex action a movement takes place in response to stimulation which depends on a highly-organised and strictly-determined physiological mechanism. The whole process is imme-diate and incapable of modification. With a given stimulus and an intact nervous system, the effect follows the cause with a simplicity and definiteness far more obvious than in the case of activity which is accompanied by consciousness. In the normal state most of the reflexes, at any rate those in which the limbs and exterior of the body are concerned, are of a kind which, were they accompanied by consciousness, would imply accuracy of localisation and other forms of discrimination.

Experiments on animals, in which there has been interference with the integrity of the nervous system, have shown the exaggera-tion of certain forms of reflex action, pointing to the existence of some degree of suppression, but it has been reserved for injury of the nervous system in Man to show this process in its most char-acteristic forms.

Head and Riddoch [3] have observed a number of patients in whom the spinal cord has been completely divided, and in these cases have been able to study the functions of the lower end of the spinal cord when isolated from the rest of the nervous system. In such cases they find a peculiar form of reflex with characters un-known when the nervous system is intact. The reflex shows itself in movements, chiefly of flexion, involving mainly the stimulated side of the body, but far more widespread than is the case with the

---

[3] H. Head and G. Riddoch, *Brain*, 60: 188 (1918) ; G. Riddoch, *ibid.*, 264.

reflexes of health. The reflex can be produced by stimulating almost any part of the limbs or trunk below the site of the injury. The nature and extent of the movements does not vary with the locality of the stimulus as in normal reflexes, but is of much the same nature whatever the stimulated part. Moreover, the movements of the limbs and trunk muscles are accompanied by sweating and contraction of the bladder. This form of reflex has been called by Head and Riddoch the "mass-reflex." They note that such a mass-reflex would form an excellent answer to noxious stimuli in the lower animals. Owing to the necessary conditions of their observations the movements are limited to part of the body, but similar movements of the whole body would tend to remove an animal from noxious stimulation. They point out that this kind of reflex would be useless for the purpose of discrimination. The "mass-reflex" has a generalised character and shows an absence of discrimination and localisation which reminds us at once of the characters of protopathic sensibility. The special feature of interest from our present point of view is that this diffused and generalised reflex is wholly suppressed in the normal human being, the suppression having taken place in favour of reflexes delicately regulated according to the locality and, to some extent, according to the nature of the stimulus. Here, as in the case of protopathic sensibility, the suppression has been so complete that the presence of the mass-reflex is only revealed by disease or injury. It has been so successful that it needed the vast scale on which injuries of the central nervous system have been produced during the war to enable Head and Riddoch to discover the presence in Man of these old and long-suppressed processes.

SOME FUNDAMENTAL ACTIVITIES

The Conception of Instinct in Man

A

WESLEY RAYMOND WELLS, "The Anti-Instinct Fallacy," *Psychol. Rev.*, 30: 228-232 (1923)

The fundamental error in the instinct theory, according to many recent deniers of instinct, is the failure to observe that all action-patterns, or at least all socially significant ones, are *acquired,* either after birth, or at least after the fertilized ovum has begun its development. Therefore, these critics assert, all socially significant action-patterns should be looked upon as habits, not instincts, since the term "instinct," through scientific usage, properly refers only to inherited forms of response. There is assumed, at least implicitly, in this position of the deniers of instinct the view that whatever is inherited must be due wholly to germinal factors, and cannot be acquired, that is, cannot be subject to a developmental history under environmental influences. It is this assumption which constitutes the fundamental fallacy in the writings of the majority of the anti-instinct psychologists at the present time.

The tendency that I refer to may be sufficiently indicated merely by reference to such names as those of Messrs. Bernard, Allport, Kuo, Kantor, and Ayres, to mention no others, and I will quote brief typical statements from only two of them. One of them asserts: "Human instincts . . . in the adult individual are completely absent." "It is axiomatic that all our reactions, no matter how basic or widespread, must have a history in the actual behavior life of the person. No capacity or potentiality can be anything but an acquired reaction system." [1]   And another says similarly: "In the present paper we attempt to deny not only the classification of instincts, but their very existence." "The so-called instincts are in the last analysis acquired trends rather than inherited tendencies." [2]   Not all of those whom I have called the anti-instinct psychologists, to be sure, deny the existence of instincts *in toto,* as Mr. Kuo does. Some of them accept what *they* call instincts; but what some of them call instincts are only simple action-patterns that are more properly called mere reflexes. And, even though they do not all deny completely what *they* regard as instincts, they do deny the instinct theory as it is believed in by those who attempt to make use of it as a fundamental hypothesis in social and abnormal psychology. . . .

A partial reconciliation of opposing views may conceivably be effected through an examination of the precise meaning of 'inherited' and 'acquired.' In calling attention to the fact (which should have been obvious, but which seems to have been generally overlooked) that all action-patterns do have a developmental history under environmental influences in each individual, these writers have done a valuable service; but they err in supposing that

---

[1] Kantor, *Psychol. Rev.,* 27: 52 (1920); 28: 330 (1921).
[2] Kuo, *Jour. of Phil.,* 18: 648 (1921). Further references to writings of anti-instinct psychologists may be found in my [Wells'] article in the *Jour. of Abn. Psych.,* 16: 336 (1921-1922).

structures having a developmental history may not at the time be inherited, in the only proper meaning of the term. Such an error arises from accepting uncritically the false popular contrast between 'inherited' and 'acquired,' which would make them mutually exclusive.

Even if the question at issue were one merely of verbal usage, it would be important, for it is of the utmost importance in scientific discussion to have a precise terminology. But, as will be seen, the question is much more than merely verbal, for there are involved facts which have an important bearing on the instinct theory. Sir E. Ray Lankester as long ago as 1894 called attention to some of these facts,[3] and Professor E. S. Goodrich a year ago in his presidential address at Edinburgh before the Zoölogy Section of the British Association for the Advancement of Science gave an excellent review of the topic.[4]

'Inherited' in its strict sense means 'acquired in individual development as a result of germinal factors, or determiners, plus *normal* environmental influences.' Non-inherited structures are those acquired under the influence of abnormal [5] environmental conditions, and without direct germinal sources. . . .

It is true, obviously, that all habits are acquired action-patterns, and that the formation of habits can be traced in the developmental history of the individual. The converse of this, however, that all action-patterns the development of which can be traced must be habits, does not follow. All men are mortal, but not all mortal creatures are men. The simple fact is that inherited structures, whether of fur and feathers, bone and muscle, physical stature and eye coloration, or nervous tissue (including synaptical connections), while conditioned in part by germinal determiners, are not transmitted *as such* in the germ-plasm. A normal environment must be presupposed from the moment of fertilization. A child that grew up without a surface, such as the floor or ground, upon which first to lie and sit, would never creep, stand, and walk, but such an

---

[3] "Acquired Characters," *Nature*, 51: 102, 103 (1894-1895).

[4] "Some Problems in Evolution," *Science*, 54: 529-38 (1921).

[5] The term 'abnormal' as here used does not denote anything pathological, but rather the biologically unusual. The terms 'constant' and 'variable' might be substituted for 'normal' and 'abnormal,' if misconstruction of these words could be avoided. In the biological literature, however, the terms 'normal' and 'abnormal' when applied to environmental conditions do not have the connotation that they have in psychological literature when applied to types of behavior; and I have had in mind the biological usage, since this paper has dealt largely with a biological problem.

environment would not be normal, or even possible. No gregarious instinct of any sort could be inherited in an individual reared from birth in complete isolation, for such would not be an environment biologically normal or possible.

It has been shown experimentally in the case of easily observed inherited structures that the substitution of an unusual or abnormal environment will cause the development of structures unlike those normally inherited in the species. A striking experiment is that of Professor Stockard,[6] first performed in 1907, by which the fish *Fundulus* developed a single, median eye when the amount of magnesium chloride was increased above the normal in the sea-water in which the eggs were developing. Yet paired eyes are properly regarded as hereditary in the fish *Fundulus*. Other experiments might be cited but this one is enough to illustrate the point at issue.

The normally *inherited* paired eyes of the fish *Fundulus* are *acquired* in the sense of developing under *normal* environmental influences, without which they would not come into existence. The fact that they are acquired in this sense does not take them from the list of heritable characters; it simply illustrates a situation of universal extent, namely, that 'inherited' means 'determined by germinal factors plus normal environmental conditions.'

B

ROBERT S. WOODWORTH, *Psychology*, 109-116, 137-138 (Holt, 1921)

We would propose . . . to consider an instinct as an inner adjustment, or tendency to reaction. It is this, rather than just a reaction. When a stimulus promptly arouses a reaction, and that ends the matter, we speak of reflex action—provided, of course, the connection between stimulus and response is native. But when a stimulus sets up a tendency to a reaction that cannot be immediately executed, or towards an end-result which cannot immediately be reached, and when the tendency so aroused persists for a time in activity, and gives rise to preparatory reactions, then we speak of instinct. . . .

The instincts of mammals are rather loosely organized. Mammals are more plastic, more adaptable, and at the same time less sure; and this is notably true of man. It would be a mistake to

---

[6] C. R. Stockard, "The Development of Artificially Produced Cyclopean Fish—'The Magnesium Embryo'," in the *J. of Exper. Zool.*, 6:285-337 (1909).

suppose that man has few instinctive tendencies; perhaps he has more than any other creature. But his instinctive behavior has not the hard-and-fast, ready-made character that we see in the insects. . . . Instinct does not lead him straight to his goal, but makes him seek this way and that till he finds it. His powers of observation, memory and thought are drawn into the game, and thus instinct in man is complicated and partly concealed by learning and reasoning. . . .

A fully organized instinct is one where the necessary preparatory reactions are linked up closely with the main reaction-tendency, so that, once the main tendency is aroused to activity, the preparatory reactions follow with great sureness. The main team of neurones is closely connected with the subordinate teams that give the preparatory reactions; and these connections do not have to be acquired by experience and training, but are well formed by native growth. Just the right preparatory reactions are linked to the main tendency, so that the whole series of acts is run off with great regularity.

In a loosely organized instinct, the main tendency is not firmly linked with any specific preparatory reactions, but is loosely linked with a great many preparatory reactions, and so gives quite variable behavior, which, however, leads on the whole towards the main goal.

While a creature under the spell of a fully organized instinct is busy, one driven by a loosely organized instinct may be better described as restless. He tries this thing and that, and goes through the kind of behavior that is called "trial and error." A closely knit instinct, then, gives a perfectly definite series of preparatory reactions, while a loosely organized instinct gives trial and error behavior. . . .

You will hear it stated, by some, that there are just two instincts, and that all instinctive behavior belongs under the head of one or the other of these two. The one is the instinct to preserve one's individual life, and the other is the instinct to propagate the species. Mating, nesting, and care of the young come under the reproductive instinct, while feeding, flight from danger, and shunning extreme heat or cold are modes of self-preservation. This seems logical enough, but it is very bad psychology. It amounts to a classification of native reactions from an external point of view, without any consideration of the way the individual is organized. . . .

Neither of these two big "instincts" is a behavior unit in any sense. Take the "instinct of self-preservation," for example. It would certainly have to include both feeding and escape from danger. But feeding and flight from danger do not belong in a single series of acts; they are two distinct series, and represent two distinct tendencies. . . . If the danger-avoiding tendency is aroused, the whole feeding and digestive activity is checked for the time being. The two instincts are antagonistic, in their actual operation; throw one into action, and you throw the other out. It is only from an external point of view that the two can be classed together; in the organization of the individual they are entirely separate.

Not much different is the "instinct of reproduction." In birds, to be sure, there is a fairly continuous series of reactions, that begins with mating, continues with nesting, laying eggs and incubating them, and ends in the care of the young birds. But in mammals there is no such continuous series of reproductive acts, but mating comes to a close and an interval elapses in which there is no behavior going on that has anything to do with reproduction. . . .

A complete account of an instinct would cover the following points: the stimulus that naturally arouses it, the end-result at which it is aimed, the preparatory reactions that occur, external and internal; and also, from the introspective side, the conscious impulse, the peculiar emotional state (if any), and the special sort of satisfaction that comes when the end-result is reached. Further, we should know what modifications or disguises the instinct takes on in the course of experience—what new stimuli acquire the power of arousing it, what learned reactions are substituted for the native preparatory and final reactions, and what combinations occur between the instinct in question and other reaction-tendencies.

Besides all this, it would be very desirable to present convincing evidence that each instinct listed is a genuine instinct, a part of the native equipment, and not something built up by experience and training.

The Presence of Fundamental Urges

J. A. HADFIELD, *Psychology and Morals*, 13 (Methuen & Co. and Robert M. McBride, 1923); reprinted by permission.

Every one, except the mentally deficient, has *all* the instincts. It is often said of someone: "He is without fear"; of another, "She has no sexual instincts." It may be true so far that their instincts do not manifest themselves as such in conscious life, and may, therefore, escape recognition, but all the instincts are nevertheless present and operative in every normal life. Their influence may be detected in conduct in disguised forms, as when a man by his excessive bravado demonstrates the fear he represses, or when a woman betrays her sexual curiosity by her prudery.[1]

Reflexes Involved in Fundamental Activities

FLOYD HENRY ALLPORT, *Social Psychology*, pp. 49-50, 56, 79-80 (Houghton Mifflin, 1924) ; used by permission of and by special arrangement with the publishers

Reflexes involved in Fundamental Activities.   The behavior repertory of the newborn infant seems at first acquaintance a random, poorly coördinated, and unadapted affair.   Yet under careful observation there will be recognized certain adaptive responses of profound significance in directing future development.   In order to appreciate these reactions we may recall the experiments of Professor Sherrington upon the 'spinal dog,' an animal whose nervous mechanism had been reduced to spinal reflexes by severing the cord at the base of the brain.[2]   To a pin-prick upon the bottom of the foot this simple nervous system responded by jerking the foot upward away from the stimulus.   This adaptive reaction, moreover, prevailed when other stimuli were competing with the injury to the foot for the determination of the final common path.   Both the scratch reflex, elicited ordinarily by tickling the shoulder, and the reflexes maintaining the posture of the limbs, were inhibited in favor of the withdrawing response.   Nocuous, or harmful objects, therefore, coming into contact with the receptors ('nociceptive' or pain end organs) of the body, evoke reflexes which are imperative in their action, protective or adaptive in their effect, and prepotent in their ascendance over other stimuli in controlling the final common path.   There are also prepotent reflexes, such as sex responses, which are accompanied by conscious pleasure rather than pain.   In the male frog during the breeding season the response of clasping the female is so powerful that the transection of his spinal cord above and below the shoulders fails to loosen his embrace.

---

[1] ["Notwithstanding the frequency with which asexuality is met with in women, I am strongly inclined to the opinion that the sexual instinct in the sex is never really absent, excepting, of course, in late life and in organic disease.   No woman is born without it.   When apparently absent it is only inhibited or dissociated by the subtle influences of the environment, education, conflicting sentiments, etc."—Morton Prince, *The Unconscious*, 467 (copyright, 1921, by The Macmillan Company) ; reprinted by permission.]

[2] *The Integrative Action of the Nervous System*, 226-234.

The human being has inherited a number of prepotent reflexes which are fundamental not only in their original potency, but in the control which they exert over habit formation throughout life. Ultimately, as well as genetically, they are prepotent. Most of these reflexes are functional at birth; one, the sensitive zone reflex, appears in early infancy; while the sex activities alone require a considerable period for the development of the structures concerned. We may recognize six important classes of human prepotent reflexes:

> Starting and Withdrawing
> Rejecting
> Struggling
> Hunger Reactions
> Sensitive Zone Reactions
> Sex Reactions

It should be emphasized that each of these activities comprises, not a single reflex, but a large group of effector movements occurring upon the application of the appropriate stimulus. In the following discussion the singular form will be used solely for convenience. The reflexes of any prepotent group include responses in the visceral as well as the somatic, or skeletal, effectors. . . . *The prepotent reflexes are subject to modification by synaptic changes in their central portions. The effects of such changes are (1) to extend the range and complexity of the stimuli capable of exciting the response, and (2) to refine and specialize the response itself. The first effect, which may be called an afferent modification, is brought about by the principle of the conditioned response; the second, resulting in an efferent modification, is due to the selection and fixation of successful random movements in the processes of habit formation and thought.* . . .

Sensitive Zone Reactions and Sex Reactions

FLOYD HENRY ALLPORT, *Social Psychology*, 67-76 (Houghton Mifflin, 1924); used by permission of and by special arrangement with the publishers

SENSITIVE ZONE REACTIONS. *Response of the Infant to Tickling.* At about the age of six weeks a light stroking of the baby's lips or pressure upon the cheek will evoke a smile. Soon other regions of the body, such as the orbits, neck, axillæ, lower ribs, thigh (just above the knee), and soles of the feet, become sensitive to pressure or light touch. The responses elicited are mild squirming movements, 'pseudo-withdrawing' in type, arching of the back, thrashing of arms and legs, giggling, and finally laughing. Why these zones are sensitive, and why their cutaneous receptors should be connected with the spasmodic responses of ticklishness, we can only conjecture. Little is known of their physiological or biological significance. The affective state under mild sensitive zone stimulation is pleasant. The random tossing and squirming responses become refined with motor development into movements which bring about a continuance of the agreeable attack and a surrender to it. Witness a child holding up its foot to be tickled again. For this reason we may classify these reactions with those of hunger under approaching responses, in spite of the fact that the stimulus seems to be external rather than visceral.

Relation of the Sensitive Zones to Hunger and Sex. There is an early association of the sensitive zone reactions with those of hunger in that the mouth is concerned in both. Nursing combines the stimulation of this region and the consummation of the hunger cycle in one series of acts.[1] Freudian psychology, on the other hand, assumes that the sensitive zones of the child have a sexual significance, and applies to them the term 'erogenous zones.'[2]

---

[1] In pigeons there is a curious combining of these two mechanisms. In billing the sensitive zones of the beak are involved in a series of amorous activities. It is, however, by similar movements that the young thrust their beaks into the parent's mouth in order to obtain food. The latter action has, in fact, been observed under certain conditions to evoke in the parent the characteristic sexual response. (C. O. Whitman, *The Behavior of Pigeons*, 64, 65-67, 107-08.)

[Of interest in this connection is Prof. James L. Mursell's article, "The Sucking Reaction as a Determiner of Food and Drug Habits." This article is Part II of a series, "Contributions to the Psychology of Nutrition," of which Part I appeared under the title, "Hunger and Appetite."]

[2] ["That repressed sexuality plays an important part in the conflicts of the ego is well known to all who are acquainted with analytical psychology. According to Freud, the sexual impulse dates from earliest childhood and is an essential element in every stage of self-appreciation. A summary of the process by which the infantile ego develops to maturity is as follows: The child is by nature 'polymorphous perverse'—that is, both physically and psychically he possesses elements which in the mature individual would be considered perversions. Physiologically, what are known as 'erogenous zones'—tissue which is capable of what in mature life is sexual excitation—are diffused through the organism. As the child passes through the 'latent period' of later childhood and adolescence, these 'erogenous zones' are concentrated as it were in the organs which are to serve the purpose of reproduction. If for any reason this process of

While this interpretation cannot be fully credited, there are certain significant resemblances between ticklishness and sex reactions. (1) Both give rise to approaching responses having the effect of en-

concentration is checked, and remains in later life incomplete, the mature individual will be afflicted with certain tendencies to sex perversion.

"Similarly the psychosexual passes through a metamorphosis in normal development. The erotic interest of the child, at first quite without any object at all, is soon attached to one or the other of the parents, then, in the 'narcissus period' is centered upon the individual himself, after which, normally, but not without some storm and stress, it becomes detached and capable of 'object love'—that is, love of a person of the opposite sex. This psychic process is by no means a smooth and easy matter. It is attended at every stage with such dangers that a very large number of people never achieve it entire. Various kinds of 'shock' and wrong educational influence, or overindulgence on the part of the parents, may cause the psychosexual interest of the ego—or 'libido'—to remain 'fixed' at some point in its course. It may retain vestiges of its early undifferentiated stage, appearing then in the perverted forms of 'masochism'—sexual enjoyment. of self-torture—or 'sadism'—sexual pleasure in torturing others. Or the libido may remain fixed upon the parent, rendering the individual in some degree incapable of a normal mature love life. He has never quite succeeded in severing his infantile attachment to his mother and transferring his interest to the world of social relations and mature experiences. If he meets with a piece of misfortune, he is likely to seek imaginary security and compensation by a 'regression' of the libido and a revival of childlike affection for the mother image. As this return is, in maturity, unconsciously resisted by the horror of incest, a conflict results. The individual then develops certain mechanisms or 'complex formations' in defense of his ego against this painful situation. The withdrawal of the libido from the ordinary affairs of life renders the latter valueless. Thoughts of death and like compulsory mechanisms ensue. The patient has become a neurotic.

"Psychoanalysts make much of this latter situation. They term it the 'Œdipus complex.' They assert that in its severer forms it is a common feature of psychoneurosis, while in less marked form, according to Jung, it underlies, and is the real explanation of the 'birth of tragedy,' being also the meaning of much religious symbolism, including the Divine Drama of Christian tradition. It is not, therefore, only the psychoneurotic whose unconscious takes the form of the 'Œdipus complex.' Under certain conditions it is manifest in normal people. . . .

"Again the growing libido may become fixed in the 'narcissus stage.' Between the period of love of parents and object love, the adolescent youth passes through a period when he is 'in love with himself.' The fact that many people remain in some measure fixed in this period of their development is not surprising when we remember that self-feeling occupies a central place in the unconscious at all times. Many of the world's greatest men have doubtless been characters in which there was a slightly more than average fixation at this point. Inordinate ambition is, I should say, an evidence of such a fixation. If one possesses great natural ability he may under such circumstances be able to forge ahead to his goal, overcoming

hancing the tactual stimulation.   (2) Both are pleasurable in the affective quality of their sensations, and there is a strong introspective resemblance between the experiences of itch, tickle, and lust.

the conflicts which such a fixation always raises, and show no greater evidence of pathology in his career than is seen in the usual saying that 'genius is always a little queer.' The typical crowd-leader would, on analysis, I think, show something of this 'narcissus complex,' as would doubtless the great run of fanatics, bigots, and doctrinaires, 'hundred per cent' crowd-men all.

"According to Brill, these 'auto erotic' persons are always homosexual, their homosexuality manifesting itself in various ways. The overt manifestations of this tendency are known as perversions. Certain persons who have suppressed or sublimated these tendencies, by means of certain defense mechanisms, or 'fictions,' as Adler would call them, get along very well so long as the defense mechanism functions. There are cases when this unconsciously constructed defense breaks down. An inner conflict is then precipitated, a marked form of which is the common type of insanity, 'paranoia.' "—Everett Dean Martin, *The Behavior of Crowds*, 63-67 (Harper, 1920).]

The foregoing point of view has by no means met with a unanimous reception, however. Dr. Frederic Lyman Wells states the case as follows:

"Perhaps most important are the issues involved in the psychoanalytic conception of sexuality. Few phases of these doctrines can have done more harm to their own cause or to the cause of truth. Where the function of science should be to delimit our concepts and give them clearer meanings, psychoanalysis has reduced this term to the level of an affective expression, deprived of every connotation that gives a distinctive place in the language of realistic thinking.

"We are all familiar with the protests that arise against psychoanalysts assigning a sexual significance to so many human activities, and we are equally familiar with the answer—that we do not understand Freud's conception of sexuality, and, anyway, we are simply making an exhibit of our cultivated resistances to a proper recognition of this factor. Now we have no objection to calling a spade a spade when it is impossible to call it a lily; but it is very perplexing when our colleagues employ the term to designate clubs, hearts, diamonds and no trumps. Anaxagoras said that snow was black, challenging any one to disprove his assertion; and by quite similar process do you assert that the *Wonnesaugen* of the month-old infant is a 'sexual' reaction. Assuredly it is true that the numerous elementary activities which you have characterized in this way are determined by a unitary guiding principle; but is it on that or any account wise and just to call that principle sexual? . . .

"What seems to have actually happened in the minds of those responsible for the dilution to infinity of the sexual concept, is that the word has become identified with and displaced the broader concept of the hedonic. Organisms tend, in the most multiform ways, to all sorts of activities that result in pleasure. These activities usually, but not necessarily, run parallel to those resulting in the objective advancement of the organism or its species; among human beings the conflict is particularly marked. We do not clearly know the rôle of the hedonic factor in determining

(3) In the mating of adults the stimulation of both (sensitive and sexual zones) are combined in a series of love-making events culminating in copulation. On such occasions—for example, in the

---

the reaction, but natural selection would, of course, tend to the survival of those organisms in which the hedonic and beneficial factors were best combined. The essential thing for us is the fundamental organic property of preserving those reactions which bring pleasure, and giving up those which do not. This is properly formulated in psychoanalysis as the *Lustprinzip*, or pleasure principle. To some extent, this principle doubtless determines reaction-trends constitutionally, as we know that coördinated series of responses may be inherited; to some extent it is, doubtless, also a process of trial and error adjustment. Human beings are physiologically so constituted that the great part of the elementary pleasures are derived through the stimulation and activity of various but rather definite areas, different portions of mucous surface, the alimentary canal, and the like. It is a great anticipatory misnomer to call these the 'erogenous zones' in childhood; the erotic function of such as develop one at all, is quite subsequent and secondary. Only from our knowledge that in the life history of the individual certain of these trends do later take on a sexual character, do we regressively irradiate this adjective over all of them, and because the child reacts upon the various pleasure areas rather unselectively, characterize a doubtfully sexual disposition with the unhappy cacophemism of *polymorph pervers*. I should sooner apply the term to Freud's conception of sexuality. What we have to start with are a number of possibilities for pleasurable reaction, between which a developmental selection takes place, and for the best of evolutionary reasons, those are the most likely to survive and flourish, which are involved with the reproductive instinct. But, of course, the underlying *Lusttrieb* of the organism may develop in various ways, without relation even to the genital areas, not to mention sexuality. . . .

"The principal word of constructive criticism in psychoanalysis is then, Look to your formulations! Let no one elude this issue with the idea that it is unimportant as a mere matter of words. No phase of psychoanalysis is unimportant that is an essential factor for its judgment and appreciation as a department of science, and is, to-day, responsible for much of the negativistic attitude in those quarters from which the first encouragement should have come. Examine these theories of mental function squarely, and with the same freedom of resistance as is urged upon those who look to you for help. Has due care been exercised to keep the interpretation of your splendid body of observational data within the limits of what they really showed, or is it often subordinated to impressiveness of statement, with just a tinge of what we clinically know as the 'desire to astonish'? Have you never said 'Freud has discovered,' where he only surmised? The same looseness of formulation that, perhaps, facilitated their applicability to data of clinical observation, has unquestionably retarded their assimilation with the more rigid standards of experimental proof. In the correction of these conditions lies the best hope of mutually supportive progress."—Frederic Lyman Wells, "On Formulation in Psychoanalysis," *Jour. Abn. Psychol.*, Oct.-Nov., 1913.

As Dr. C. Macfie Campbell observes, "In one child unequivocal sexual

embrace of lovers—the sensitive zones become particularly potent in producing responses. These regions may be said to represent the infantile stage of development in a complex system which, in the adult, includes the sex zones proper. Their chief interest for social psychology lies in their importance in the problems of adjustment within the family.

Pleasurable Habits based upon the Sensitive Zone Reflexes. The caressing which children commonly receive and solicit is intimately associated with sensitive zone stimulation. Their cuddling of dolls and toys, and expressions of love toward these objects, have their root in the same source. There are many afferent modifications of the reflexes arising from the stimulation of these zones. The earliest is the transfer of the stimulus from the tickling itself to the person who does it. After a few such titillations the baby will laugh in a most 'tickled' fashion upon the mere approach or sudden movement of the parent. It is not improbable that the effort to obtain praise and the avoidance of censure (sometimes spoken of as social instincts) are partially derived in a similar manner. Words and tones of approval are connected with caresses, playful behavior, and other stimulations of sensitive zones by the parent; and they come to evoke the same responses as the latter, namely, actions inducing their continuance and repetition. This process is the basis not only of a large amount of filial childhood affection, but

---

manifestations appear at a very early age, the child seems early sensitized to stimuli of this order and soon begins to accumulate experiences which load its later character; in another child the same stimuli may cause little response, and the sexual life only manifests itself much later and in less disturbing fashion. We are not entitled to take the more sensitive and precocious child as the type and to assume that in the other child there has been the same evolution, repressed and disguised. Affection and emotional dependence on relatives and friends are attitudes much too complex to be expressed in simple sexual terms, they contain important factors which are not necessarily disguised or modified expressions of sexual forces. In different individuals the hedonic and the energic aspects of the sex life vary considerably; it is not only a question of plus or minus, of repression or expression, of sublimation or vicarious indulgence.

"The mode in which the individual meets the tests of life, deals with the endogenous demands of his cravings, with the situations which occur during puberty, adolescence and adult life, whether celibate or married, is a function not merely of one single system, but of the total personality. There is perhaps no better test of the general stability of the individual than the demands associated with the sex life; in analyzing the successes and failures in regard to this adaptation there is a danger of abstraction and simplification, and of over-emphasis on what is merely one component in the complex forces which make up the total personality."—C. Macfie Campbell, "The Sex Instinct," *Jour. Abn. Psychol.*, 16: 247-248 (1921).]

also of the susceptibility of the individual to control and development through social influences.

SEX REACTIONS. *The Original Sexual Reflexes.* During the age of puberty there occurs in both sexes a rapid development of the receptors and effectors employed in sex behavior. Hormone secretions from the cells of Leydig stimulate the growth of the secondary sexual characteristics, the genital organs mature, the erogenous zones upon contact yield pleasurable sensations, while the secretions of the reproductive, and possibly other glands afford an internal stimulation for sexual activities. There is meanwhile the familiar adolescent awakening of tender feeling and the various forms of love.

The original stimulus for sex responses is not, as is popularly supposed, an individual of the opposite sex. It is rather an internal excitant. In the male it is the gradual distention of the seminal vesicles, a condition requiring a fairly periodic discharge of their contents. The distention produces an increase of tonicity in the wall of the vesicle, and this internal activity, combined, no doubt, with similar glandular effects in other parts of the pelvic viscera, stimulates the interoceptive end organs in these parts. In the female the excitatory visceral changes are probably caused, not by distention, but by some hormonic (glandular) process occurring about the time of menstruation. The response which follows this stimulus consists of random and restless activity quite analogous to that in the case of hunger. The tumescence of the sex organs sets up further stimulations in these parts, which provide allied afferent processes having the same outlet (that is, through random seeking movements) as the visceral stimulus. The movements are sufficiently directed to bring the erogenous areas already yielding lust sensations into contact with some object, thereby adding external tactual stimulations to the original and purely internal stimulus. In the human species (and in some animals) stimulations from the contact of the sensitive as well as erogenous zones are added to the excitations during the sexual embrace. In the male copulation thus raises the tonic contraction of the muscle of the genital apparatus to such a pitch that it breaks over into the phasic contractions by which the accumulated sexual secretions are discharged. The complete sexual reaction, therefore, involves a chain of prepotent reflexes. It begins with an internal stimulus caused by glandular activity and distention, followed by crudely directed reflex responses which bring the highly sensitized and tumescing organs into contact with some object in the environment. Contact with this object contributes sufficient stimulation to evoke a second group of reflexes, those of emptying the contents of glands and vesicles whose distention was the original cause of the activities described. After sexual satisfaction, therefore, as after the satisfaction of hunger, the organism lapses for a time into quiescence.[1]

The internal character of the original sex stimulus is clearly shown in those animals which have well-marked breeding seasons. Such seasons depend directly upon the periodic activities of the sexual glands and smooth muscle. A pigeon which is not 'in season' will evade or repel any approach made by the opposite sex. On the other hand, a male bird in the period of sex excitement will begin the usual courtship antics at once, and, in the absence of the female, will make advances to individuals of its own sex.[2] Among human beings, although the relations of the sexes are greatly complicated by recognition, imagination, and other cortical processes, the original sexual stimulus is also unquestionably internal in its location. Stimulation from the physiological activities of the internal sex organs, rather than the sight of a member of the opposite sex, is the drive to action. The normal sex life of adults, while it is not so clearly cyclical as that of lower animals, is nevertheless timed according to the occurrence of a true organic need.

The Afferent Modification of Sexual Reflexes. Sex Attraction. The long period of childhood and youth preceding sexual maturity affords an extensive opportunity for training, through social tradition and example, in the lore of sex and the significance of male and female. The boy and girl know about family life and, in a general way at least, the procreative function of marriage. They learn from their elders the part played in life by courtship and love-making, as well as the habits and attitudes of chivalry, modesty in regard to one's person, and reticence upon sex topics. Habits which must inevitably control and modify the prepotent reflexes of sex are thus established *well before the appearance of the reflexes themselves.* When the first awakening of the internal sexual urge is felt, the boy, if he has been properly instructed, knows that the female is the proper object of his searching movements. He is further aided in this new adjustment and in understanding the contact which it involves by the experience of the sensitive zone stimulations. These he has known from infancy, and they have already given a meaning, as yet non-sexual, however, to caresses and other expressions of affection. The realization that a member of the

---

[1] For certain portions of this account the writer is indebted to a theory of sex reactions (as yet unpublished) developed by Mr. F. T. Hunter.

[2] Whitman: *loc. cit.*

opposite sex is the most satisfactory object of the sex desire thus represents a stimulus transfer, or allied conditioned response, by which the sight of a possible mate augments, or of itself directly evokes, the seeking responses which originally were produced only by the organic stimulus. As in the afferent modification of other prepotent reflexes which we have studied, language and other social influences are of the highest value in the conditioning process.

A striking instance of the afferent modification of the sex reaction by social agencies among pigeons has been recorded by Whitman.[1] If a male ring dove is reared from infancy among carrier pigeons, and then placed at maturity among birds of his own species, he cannot be induced to mate with them. The breeding activities, however, speedily commence as soon as he is brought into the presence of a *carrier* female. The sexual drive—that is, the internal stimulating secretions—and the random activities to which they lead, are truly innate and hereditarily determined. The act of pairing between male and female, however, seems to be the result not of instinct but of learning.

To the average adult the opposite sex appears so obviously fitted for the mating process that he is likely to assume the apprehension of this fact to be instinctive. He has forgotten, however, that turbulent adolescent period before his sexual adjustment was perfected. Children pass through various stages in the comprehension and use of sex objects. In the absence either of enlightenment or of opportunity for coition the adolescent youth associates his sex feelings with those fortuitous objects or situations (for example, pressure of clothes, climbing trees, etc.) which afford contacts with the genitals during random movements, thus providing pleasurable erotic experiences. Masturbation, homosexuality, and other ready means for attaining the same end follow more or less inevitably. In the mature individual sex gratifications of this sort are termed *perversions,* because they indicate the persistence of a false or inadequate training in these matters. In childhood, however, they are only to be expected, in the absence of social control and direction, as natural stages in the process of learning by trial and error. Here again learning, rather than instinct, must be the guide in the search which is finally to end with mating in the normal heterosexual manner. Many perverts and neurotic adults are now known to be persons who have never advanced beyond the childhood stage in the education of the prepotent reflexes of sex.

The Problem of Sex Training. The moral of the preceding dis-

[1] *Loc. cit.*, 68.

cussion is not far to seek. It is as pernicious to withhold information necessary for the development of the prepotent sexual responses as it would be to allow the child to grow up in ignorance of the objects upon which he should condition his reactions of avoidance, rejection, and food-seeking. If direction through social agencies is neglected, the youth must fall a victim to the more crude and often disastrous mistakes of trial and error in the process of learning sex behavior. To wait for puberty to arrive before beginning sex instruction is not only to throw away the priceless years of childhood which should be used in building up the proper attitudes for sexual maturity, but also to run the risk of allowing habits to be formed which are antagonistic to the normal sex reactions of the adult. One important caution, however, must be borne in mind. The mere informing of the child in sexual matters, if not combined with the formation of attitudes, principles, and habits proper to persons possessing such knowledge, is as likely to produce harmful as it is beneficial results. The mere desire to "tell the child the truth" is in itself no adequate justification for imparting the physiological facts. The aim should be not merely sex enlightenment, but sex training.[1]

The efferent side of the sexual reflexes is as much in need of modification through learning and social guidance as is the afferent. Breeders of animals are fully aware of the crudity and clumsiness of random movements made in efforts for sexual union. In the human race the untaught youth is equally devoid of the knowledge and skill necessary for conjugal love-making and a wholesome sex life. A large proportion of marital discord and unhappiness results from the lack of knowledge and training whereby the random movements arising from the sex stimulations may be developed into responses nicely adjusted to the needs of both husband and wife. As for the broader aspects, such as the wise choice of a mate, the regulation of the reproductive function, and the application of the laws of heredity, we are but on the threshold of progress.

---

[1] Reports of social workers reveal the importance of the pre-adolescent years for establishing wholesome attitudes toward sex adjustments. A psychologist in charge of work with delinquent girls divided her prostitute cases into two classes: those who were reformable, and those for whom nothing could be done. The latter class consisted almost entirely of girls who had been brought up in immoral home surroundings or who had been the victim of an assault (usually by a male relative) before the age of puberty. (E. R. Wembridge, "Work with Socially Maladjusted Girls," Jour. Abn. Psychol., 1922, 17: 79-87.) The sex drive is so powerful that, if the proper inhibitions have not been established before adolescence, the chances of building them up after that period are very slight.

Sex and Sensitive Zone Reactions in Familial Behavior. There is a general agreement among psychologists that the family responses, such as parental and filial behavior and feeling, are intimately connected with the sex reactions. Among both human and sub-human creatures the birth and rearing of offspring is an intrinsic part of a cycle which begins with courtship and selection of a mate. There extend throughout this cycle a continual internal excitation and a series of reactions to stimulations of the sensitive and erogenous zones. The incubation of eggs by birds and the suckling by mammals (including man) fall within this class of pleasurable and approaching reactions. Parental as well as conjugal behavior is largely conditioned by internal stimulation. The distention of the crop in certain birds and the rapid secretion of milk in mammals are the immediate stimuli for feeding the young.[1]

The love life of a human being is lived through contact, not only with the spouse, but also with the children. For most adults, to see a baby is to desire to fondle it in a very lover-like fashion. The love reactions toward children are similar to those which the child manifests toward its parents or other relatives. That is, they are responses mainly to stimulations of the sensitive zones, and are productive of caressing and fondling movements. The stimulation of sexual zones and true responses of sex are forbidden by custom and social standards. It seems probable, however, when we recall the fusion of sensitive zones and sexual reactions in the adult, that the internal sex drive allies its stimulation with that of the sensitive zones to bring about the reaction of fondling (final common path). Periods of sex excitement, moreover, are associated both in man and the lower animals with periods of unusual fondness for offspring.

The law of conditioned response is also operative. If a woman loves her husband and her home, her lover-like responses will be extended to a new stimulus, the child, which through its origin as well as through its immediate presence is closely connected with the beloved objects. The reverse side of the picture is sometimes seen in hospitals where illegitimate children are born whose mothers are in the throes of shame and fear, and perhaps of hatred of the men who caused their maternity. The absence of the usual mater-

---

[1] Absence of abnormalities of this internal excitement probably account for such parental anomalies as defective cycles, abandoning of nests, and devouring of litters of young. See Whitman, *loc. cit.* For some valuable observations on the physiology of the 'maternal instinct,' consult Rabaud, E., "L'Instinct Maternal chez les mammifères," *Jour. de. Psychol.*, 1921, 18: 487-95.

nal feelings is often conspicuous in such cases.[1]   Social standards and early training are likewise very important in determining the attitude which the parents adopt toward their offspring.   Another evidence that parental love depends upon contact and experience is the fact that it grows with the child.   Parental and maternal pride develop, and attractive plans are laid for the child's future. The fondling, nursing, protecting, and planning grow into definite *maternal and paternal habits*.   These habits, sometimes loosely spoken of as instincts, rest upon the instinctive prepotent reactions of sensitive zones and sex; but their real development is brought about by the interplay between these innate mechanisms and the environment of the family.

The Sex Reactions and Learning.   Considered in this broad manner the sex reactions are close rivals of hunger as drives in the learning process.   In order to obtain access to the female the male dog or cat, through the trial-and-chance success method, will rapidly learn the use of the release mechanism of a puzzle box.   The struggles of a mother bird in similar experiments to gain access to her nest and young result in effective learning by the same method. In human society the efferent modifications by which custom requires that the sex reactions shall be consummated lead into many productive fields.   The lover must conform to the standards set for courtship, desirability of character, and economic standing.   He must give up the irresponsible vagaries of youth for the sober achievement of the man.   A vocation must be learned if he is to support the wife and children which are necessary to his love-life.   Here, as in the case of the other instinctive bases of learning, we find that the social inheritance through schools and elders, and the use of language and thought processes, are of paramount importance.   The nature of the vocation chosen in many cases depends upon fundamental individual interests or abilities; but the zeal with which it is studied and practiced is directly proportional to the inciting effect of the combined stimulations of hunger, sex, and the sensitive zones—in short, to the demands of economic and domestic life.

'Sublimation.'   A great deal of speculative writing has been done on the so-called process of 'sex sublimation.'   It is believed by some that the sexual drive represents a kind of free-floating energy which can be transformed by suppression and redirection

---

[1] See J. B. Watson, *Psychology from the Standpoint of a Behaviorist,* 257-58.   Also Ruth Reed, "Changing Conceptions of the Maternal Instinct," *Jour. Abn. Psychol.,* 1923, 18: 78-87.

into some 'nobler' pursuit, such as science, art, religion, or charity. In the present writer's opinion, it is nearer to the truth to say that the intellectual and cultural achievements of man represent things done *in the interest* of sex, and as a means to a more satisfactory adjustment of the sexual life, than to assume them to be a substitution for or transformation of the sex drive. Many a young man whose passions led him into devious and profligate ways has been converted through marriage into an efficient producer. Sex is the spur which keeps native ability and talent always at their maximum effort. The operation of the sex drive under the stabilizing influence of family life is a factor of progress second to none in human society. One of the most serious problems of our higher and professional education is the restlessness and distracting influence produced by enforced celibacy long after the sexual maturity of the student. Much time and energy is diverted from study into seeking such sex excitements as chance and a conflict with the sense of propriety may allow. If this sexual effort could be allied with the goal of scholastic and professional attainment, as it might be in some cases by early marriages with child-bearing deferred, instead of being allowed to detract from serious study, the gain both in work and happiness would be enormous.[1]

Egoistic Tendencies

BERNARD GLUECK, "The Ego Instinct," *Jour. Abn. Psychol.*, 16: 226, 228, 229-231 (1921)

While there is no usually accepted classification of native tendencies, the same general patterns in average persons can be recognized though under various names. Mr. A. G. Tansley, e.g., can be understood when he speaks of those tendencies which collectively make for the preservation of the individual, securing "self-realization," as "the ego-complex." [2] There is convincing evidence that the general "drive" so indicated is fundamental to a wide variety of psychopathic phenomena, including both the more obvious sorts and the subtler kinds that permeate daily life:

What renders the ego-instincts, or better still, the ego-complex,

---

[1] [On 'sublimation,' *cf.* also G. V. Hamilton, *Objective Psychopathology* 328-329.]

[2] *The New Psychology*, 209 *circa.*

in the sense of Tansley, pathological, and what are the manifestations of such a pathological state? It would be, to my mind, pure speculation to start with, to endeavor to determine what the situation may be here congenitally. In spite of the fact that we are apt to see in certain states of maldevelopment of personality, such for instance, as in epilepsy, feeble-mindedness, and in certain types of constitutionally inferior individuals, indications of a pathological ego-equipment it is not very safe to assume absolutely that the ego-instincts may be affected congenitally. Certainly, it would seem altogether too speculative an enterprise to endeavor to be in any way precise and specific concerning possible congenital modifications of the ego. What is true of the wider field of psychopathology is coming to be recognized more and more as being true also of those states which we were in the habit of stigmatizing as defects, namely, that the life experiences, in the broadest sense of this term, with which the individual has come in contact are the real determinants of personality and character, and that we are on much safer ground when studying these more tangible and concrete facts in their possible influence upon the personality than is offered by the speculations concerning heredity and congenitalism. . . .

The emotions associated with the ego-complex in which we are particularly interested are those which are coupled with the twin instincts of self-assertion and self-abasement, namely, the positive and negative self-feeling of McDougall, or the feeling of elation and depression, since upon the condition of these twin instincts probably depends the habitual state of the morale of the individual. And is it not some sort of problem in self-respect, or feeling of adequacy, or of morale that we most often encounter in psychopathological reactions? . . .

Since a normal state of the ego probably depends in the main upon a proper balancing of the instincts of self-assertion and self-abasement, it would be well to consider primarily the conditioning influences upon these two instincts. Among these conditioning influences those which have to do with various inferiorities are commonly met with in psychopathology. The inferiority to start with may be relative or actual and may depend upon some structural or functional defect or upon a mere feeling of inferiority induced psychologically as a result of any possible variety of life experience.

The subject of the inferiority feeling or inferiority complex has been dealt with adequately by many authors and requires no treatment here. Indeed, it forms the basis of Adler's psychological scheme. What must be emphasized over and over again is that the manifestations of a pathological exaggeration of the ego, or of the obverse state is much more often something in the nature of a re-active compensatory manifestation than an inherited, fixed and unchangeable anomaly of character and make-up. Of considerable practical importance is the growing belief that it is distinctly within the realm of a practical mental hygiene to prevent the occurrence of these pathological reactive phenomena of the ego-variety. It is one of the most pressing problems of the day in the field of educa-tion, since a proper recognition of the rôle of success and failure in the shaping of the ego, and of the perniciousness entailed in the growing tendency on the part of the modern parent to wish to re-live his own life, only in a more elaborated and maximated degree through the lives of his children, should do much to prevent many a frustrated career. It is this pernicious tendency which is largely responsible for the maladjustments resulting from a too great dis-crepancy between aspiration and endowment. The family tragedies at the basis of a pathological need for self-maximation on the part of one or both parents is almost inevitably reflected in the person-ality and make-up of the children, either in the form of an actual crushing of the self with a persistent state of timidity and lack of morale, or in a frantic need for a compensatory exaggerated egoism. These reactive phenomena of the ego may manifest themselves, as they frequently do in overt behavior reactions of a selfish, anti-social nature, especially when the behavior is the result of a reflective rationalisation, as in the case of habitual offenders against the law, of certain "captains of industry," or prophets of a new order. Or, the manifestations may be more or less symbolic, and by that token, are apt to be more strictly pathological as in the case of various delusional and hallucinatory elaborations of the intimidated hebe-phrenic or aggressive paranoiac.

Especially deserving of further study are those pathological elaborations of an ego-ideal, the roots and instigators of which have become definitely repressed into the unconscious. Since here any possibility of constructive adjustment is ruled out from the start, the patient is not even conscious of the main objective of his frantic drive for self-maximation and the goal persists in eluding him. In the meantime, the pathological need and drive for compensa-tion, the roots of which remain out of reach of the individual's awareness lead to persistent behavior reactions which are distinctly pathological in their ego-manifestations. . . .

Those who have had to deal in civil life with situations which resemble to some extent the exigencies of warfare have been fa-miliar with the pathological reactions which have received so much attention in connection with the world war. I am referring to pathological reactions observed in connection with imprisonment, especially under exceptionally rigid conditions of deprivation and balking of the ego, and occasionally, in connection with the imminent threat to life in those condemned to execution. We have had occasion to observe repeatedly these reactions in all the various forms which were manifested at the front, and some years ago published case studies which showed clearly the situational character of those neuroses and psychoses and their essential recoverability when only the ego-instincts were involved.

An Illustrative Topic: "Exhibitionism"

STEVENSON SMITH and EDWIN R. GUTHRIE, "Exhibitionism," *Jour. Abn. Psychol.*, 17: 206-209 (1922)

According to Freudian theory, original human nature includes an instinctive tendency to exhibitionism which, in its primary form, displays itself in acts of immodest exposure, and which has various derivative forms, such as demanding attention in the presence of others, being noisy and silly when strangers are about, and showing excitement when under observation. The original stimulus for this instinctive removal of clothing and unadorned parading is not described, but the implication is that it is the sight of other people.

An examination of this thesis, that all ways of making one's self conspicuous are modifications of an instinctive tendency to sexually immodest acts, will show two points of serious weakness. In the first place, it is only necessary to examine the development of any exhibitionary act to discover that it is learned. In the second place, it seems possible to demonstrate that many forms of exhibitionism are for the most part the result of non-sexual mechanisms. If these propositions can be demonstrated, exhibitionism is shown to be neither instinctive nor necessarily derived from sex behavior.

Our present knowledge of the acquiring of habits by infants makes it possible to explain how exhibitionism may be developed through learning. Even emotional reactions to visual stimuli are possible only as conditioned responses, and are never the instinctive result of what the baby sees. Watson has shown how a baby develops a conditioned fear response. Fear may be produced by the sight of an animal, provided the baby has first been frightened by a sound stimulus while looking at the animal.

It is probable that any emotional response may come to be conditioned in the same way upon visual stimuli. The preference of children for noisy toys is attributable to the fact that noise arouses emotion and secures attention. For the same reason children pay more attention to human beings than to inanimate objects. Human beings, because they move about, converse, and interfere with the baby, are more likely to stimulate the baby's emotions. Hampering the baby's movements is an original stimulus to rage, and such a stimulus usually occurs when human beings are present and are looking at the baby. Thus excitement becomes conditioned on the situation of *being looked at*. Sex excitement is aroused by the stimulation of erogenous zones, and the baby usually receives this stimulation at the hands of others, and usually when without clothing. Thus the sight of others, or the removal of clothing, may become the substituted stimulus for sex excitement. Children are excited in the presence of others because the sight of people is the most frequent accompaniment of those original stimuli that produce emotion. This excitement reinforces learning, so that responses aroused by and directed toward people come to have very low thresholds.

When a habit is firmly established and an occasion arises when the successive stimuli upon which its performance depends are not all present, there is a marked emotional disturbance. Most habitual responses of children to other people depend upon being looked at, spoken to, and played with. When the attention of others is withdrawn, the child's habits are disrupted and he is emotionally wrought up, just as a man fumbles with his hat, increases his pace, and behaves queerly when his greeting to an acquaintance goes unnoticed. The boisterous or silly acts of the unnoticed child are compromise responses. The adult who is present, but not attentive, starts habits going in the child which can not be completed without the adult's coöperation. Under these circumstances children perform many acts that might be called random, but that are in the nature of compromise responses depending upon the unusual array of stimuli and upon the emotion resulting from the blocking of habitual modes of behavior. Finally the children do something annoying, amusing, embarrassing, or otherwise striking, and the people present give attention.

Many of these attention-securing acts of children are what we call exhibitionism, and these acts become fixed as habitual responses to people who are not paying attention, just as the successful responses of the cat in the puzzle-box become attached to the stimulus of the door-opening device. By trial and error every child hits upon the acts that secure him attention. Swearing is such an attention-securing act, and for this reason swearing is readily learned by

children. No word is called profane that does not shock the hearer.
If Freud had been less interested in sex, the prevalence of blas-
phemy might well have led him to enumerate it among the instincts,
notwithstanding its diverse expression in many languages. This
would be hardly less absurd than to regard the particular forms of
immodesty determined by various folkways as an instinctive mechanism. . . .

Exhibitionism is probably then not an instinct. Neither is it
always derived from sex behavior. Anger is as likely as love to be
its emotional reinforcement. Exhibitionary acts are learned through
trial and error responses to the situations in which children are
placed and the striking likenesses in the exhibitionism of children
the world over have as their cause similarities in culture and the
commonality of human nature. Their equally striking differences
are due to differences in culture and to the idiosyncrasies of situation confronting every one.

Aspects of Gregariousness

SANGER BROWN II, "The Herd Instinct," *Jour. Abn. Psychol.*, 16: 232-237
(1921)

In enumerating trends important in abnormal psychology,
frequent mention is made of those reactions which, in the average adult individual at least, express his sensitiveness to the
life of the other members of the group. These reactions, usually
very influential in the individual mental life, and affecting
directly the great trends already discussed, are often labeled
simply "the herd instinct."

Dr. Sanger Brown has discussed this topic partly as follows:

A study of the development of the mind, and of its normal and
abnormal processes, has been carried on, until recently, through
studying man chiefly as an isolated individual. But within the
past few years it has been indicated from a number of sources, that
such a study is incomplete unless, at the same time, man is considered in relation to others in his group. Man does not live alone,
and in isolation. He is gregarious, and his life is inseparable from
the lives of others. So to learn of his mental development, he
should not be studied solely as an individual, as such, but also as
his life brings him into association with others.

These facts have always been appreciated to some extent by a few; but Trotter, probably more than any one else, has emphasized their importance and their significance.[1]

Today, we think of man as being highly individualistic, of his thinking and acting, for the most part, independently, at least within reasonable limits. But if we look into this more closely, we realize that man is less individualistic than he appears to be. At least the majority of men do not live in complete intellectual isolation, as regards their thoughts and opinions.[2] . . .

Herd influence with savages called for great conformity, even in their everyday affairs of life. There were endless prohibitions, taboos, rituals and ceremonies, which governed the way everything was done. These methods became customs and laws, closely bound up with the life of the people, so that eventually morals, religion, tribal customs, craftsmanship, and indeed nearly all matters of life and death, were governed by prescribed forms laid down from time immemorial. The carefree savage, as we might be inclined to think of him, was in reality to a very great extent a slave. . . .

---

[1] W. Trotter, *Instincts of the Herd in Peace and War.*

[2] ["Direct observation of man reveals at once the fact that a very considerable proportion of his beliefs are non-rational to a degree which is immediately obvious without any special examination, and with no special resources other than common knowledge. If we examine the mental furniture of the average man, we shall find it made up of a vast number of judgments of a very precise kind upon subjects of very great variety, complexity, and difficulty. He will have fairly settled views upon the origin and nature of the universe, and upon what he will probably call its meaning; he will have conclusions as to what is to happen to him at death and after, as to what is and what should be the basis of conduct. He will know how the country should be governed, and why it is going to the dogs, why this piece of legislation is good and that bad. He will have strong views upon military and naval strategy, the principles of taxation, the use of alcohol and vaccination, the treatment of influenza, the prevention of hydrophobia, upon municipal trading, the teaching of Greek, upon what is permissible in art, satisfactory in literature, and hopeful in science.

"The bulk of such opinions must necessarily be without rational basis, since many of them are concerned with problems admitted by the expert to be still unsolved, while as to the rest it is clear that the training and experience of no average man can qualify him to have any opinion upon them at all. The rational method adequately used would have told him that on the majority of these questions there could be for him but one attitude—that of suspended judgment. . . .

"It should be observed that the mind rarely leaves uncriticized assumptions which are forced on it by herd suggestion, the tendency being for it to find more or less elaborately rationalized justification of them."—W. Trotter, *Instincts of the Herd in Peace and War,* 35-37 (copyright, 1916, by The Macmillan Company); reprinted by permission.]

However, man of today, while still gregarious and social, has developed very strong individualistic characteristics. Herein we have a significant situation. On the one hand, we still have herd influence, although in a somewhat altered form, and on the other, we have this strong individualistic tendency. The existence of the two makes for conflicting purposes. . . .

A brief illustration will suffice. A man of good intelligence and education struggled along in a law office for fifteen years, at a profession for which he was temperamentally unfitted. When the war came, he had a respite for three years, and these were the happiest years of his life. Then he went back to the office, but the life which had been barely endurable before, was now no longer endurable at all. He became more and more oppressed with it all, and in the course of time he, who had formerly been discontented and 'a failure only, became, in addition, a patient.

If this youth had not been reared under the tradition of following the profession of law, at which his father and his grandfather gained eminence, he might have chosen a career for which he was temperamentally fitted. Had social opinion, in his case, made it possible for the son of a prominent man to quit his profession, when he found he was unfitted for it, results might have been different. Had he possessed the strength and courage to have overcome, unassisted, this pressure of opinion, and to have made a change regardless of it, his case would doubtless have been otherwise. But while it appears that all of these things should have been possible, one can appreciate circumstances in which they are not.

Of the many people in the world who find themselves in quite similar situations, probably only a few become patients. They are failures, or at best incomplete successes, and they contribute to the sum total of discontent.

Perhaps the most important class of all, who come under this category, are those who for various reasons, cannot conform to the opinions or traditions of any established group whatsoever. There are some people who do not fit in anywhere. Some of them have intellectual limitations or handicaps, but as a whole they are the nonconformists who seem to be swimming against the stream. They are not necessarily patients from the beginning, but they furnish the group from which the patients of psychopathologists are drawn. . . . Because of their somewhat unusual personalities, they encounter exceptionally difficult problems in life, in a world fashioned for people constituted otherwise than themselves. . . .

A just criticism of the narrower Freudian psychology of the past has been that the treatment has dealt almost exclusively with the individual regardless of his social environment. It is also probable that we will wish in the future to place greater emphasis upon what have been recently termed "the situation types" of neuroses and psychoneuroses. In such types conflicts in which herd instinct plays a part are very evident, and we should supplement our study of the individual in such cases by a more thorough study of environmental influences. This is particularly true of such conditions arising in the early years of life.

Fear Behavior

BORIS SIDIS, *Nervous Ills*, 27-28, 29-30 (Badger, 1922)

The neuroses of the war called much attention to those tendencies frequently called "the fear instinct." Sidis' analysis of the degrees of functioning of this general pattern follows:

The fear instinct . . . passes through three stages:

    I.   The Stimulating Stage
   II.   The Arrestive, or Inhibitory Stage
  III.   The Paralyzing Stage.

In its milder forms when the fear instinct is but nascent, it serves as a sort of trigger to the activities of the organism. The animal may for a moment stop whatever activities and pursuits in which it happens to be engaged, and have its interest turn in the direction of the particular new stimulus, whether it be of an auditory, visual, or olfactory character. The fear instinct is just strong enough to suspend present interests, and direct its activities to the new source of the unknown stimulus.

When the source is unfamiliar, the animal becomes prepared for action. The energies are aroused for attack, or for hiding, freezing, or running, according to the mode of defense to which the animal has been adapted in its adjustments to the stimulations of its environment. . . .

..*The fear instinct in its initial stages is perfectly normal, and is as indispensable to life as hunger and thirst.* It is only in the more advanced and extreme stages that the fear instinct becomes pathological, and is apt to give rise to psychopathic states. . . .

If this stage of fear instinct does not become intensified, the organism recovers its control,—many of the disturbances pass away, and the following reaction may come with a greater release of energy, developing a greater output of activity than under normal conditions. In short, the fear instinct may still serve as a stimulation to greater effort, but the chances of such a result are far smaller than in the first stage, which is essentially of a stimulating, useful, and healthful character.

The second stage of the fear instinct is the possibility of a pathological state, and, if persistent, leads directly to the third stage with consequent paralysis and danger of destruction. The first stage of fear is fully normal, helpful, and self-defensive. The second stage is harmful, but with the possibility of recovery and restitution of normal function. The third stage leads to destruction and death.

In the third stage there is paralysis of function of most of the muscular, secretory, excretory, circulatory, intestinal, and nervous systems. The animal is petrified with fear, and falls into a state of paralysis, rigidity, cataplexy, or in a state simulating death. This last stage of the effects of the fear instinct is pathological, and instead of conducing to the good of the individual, really leads to his destruction and death. The fear instinct in its extreme cases is not a help to the organism, but is distinctly a hindrance, and is felt as such by the organism which experiences it.[1]

Feeling and Emotion

FLOYD HENRY ALLPORT, *Social Psychology*, 84-98 (Houghton Mifflin, 1924) ; used by permission of and by special arrangement with the publishers

The Nature of Emotion. Let us imagine a man crossing a busy thoroughfare with the consciousness of moderate safety, when, from an unexpected quarter, an automobile horn sounds loudly at his elbow. He dodges in a reflex manner away from the source of danger, and makes for a place of safety. This is the outward, or somatic, portion of the response, belonging to the class of prepotent reflexes discussed in the preceding chapter, and brought about by

---

[1] [Sidis' psychopathological views contrast sharply with those of Freud, since for Sidis "the fear instinct" is the fundamental factor. As he says (*op. cit.*, p. 32) : "The fear instinct is intimately related to the innermost principle, characteristic of all life, namely, the impulse of self-preservation." Again (p. 43) : "I may assert without hesitation that in all my cases of functional psychosis, I find the presence of the fear instinct to be the sole cause of the malady. *Take away the fear and the psychosis or neurosis disappears.*"]

the cerebrospinal nervous system. There is another component, however, a visceral, or internal, response produced by efferent impulses through the autonomic system tó the smooth muscle of the internal organs. Referring to the small figure, we may illustrate

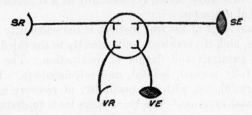

SCHEME TO SUGGEST THE INTERRELATIONS OF THE CEREBRO-SPINAL AND AUTONOMIC SYSTEMS

SR, somatic receptor; *SE*, somatic effector; *VR*, visceral receptor; *VE*, visceral effector. The circle indicates the brain or spinal cord. *SR* may be connected with either *SE* or *VE*. *VR* may be connected with either *SE* or *VE*. [This figure, from Professor Allport's *Social Psychology*, p. 36, is used by permission of, and by special arrangement with, Houghton Mifflin Company.]

this component by connecting the afferent neuron from *SR* with the efferent *VE*. The visceral response includes changes in rate of the heartbeat, stopping of digestive activities, and liberation into the blood of energizing products of ductless glands. There may also be effects of the sympathetic nervous system on the outer surface of the body, such as pallor and erection of the hairs. The face likewise assumes an expression of alarm, a response innervated, perhaps, by the cerebrospinal and the autonomic fibers together.

A diffuse pattern of response, invading both the somatic and the visceral regions of the body, is thus the immediate result of a sudden, unexpected, prepotent stimulus. But this is only half the story. We are equipped with receptors which are capable of being stimulated by these movements of the body and by changes within the body. . . . Afferent neurons carry these excitations to the appropriate sensory areas of the cortex, a process accompanied by sensory awareness of the bodily movements and changes involved. There enter consciousness: (1) kinæsthetic sensations from the movements of the arms, legs, and trunk; (2) kinæsthetic sensations from the movements of facial expression; (3) organic sensations from the visceral responses; and (4) cutaneous sensations from thè effects of sympathetic control in the blood vessels and other structures of the skin. These sensory qualities fuse into a mass of vaguely discriminated organic and bodily experiences, which, having its focus in the interior of the body, seems to spread out and pervade our whole being. This fused complex of sensory experience is what we call an *emotion*. In the illustration used it is the emotion of fear.

The emotion does not come directly upon the perception of the danger signal, nor with the realization of its meaning. It is connected rather with the response (visceral and somatic) to the signal, and is not felt until the response is made. The emotion of fear is the way the body *feels* upon reacting to a terrifying situation. It depends upon this reaction, but it in no way initiates or directs it. This statement of the case is called the *James-Lange theory*. Theory it is, to be sure; but it contains so much truth that it has been able to hold its ground against eminent critics. Its main defect is one of omission, in that it fails to differentiate the patterns of visceral and somatic response giving rise to the different emotions of common experience. It does not distinguish, for example, between the patterns of response capable of arousing the consciously distinct emotions of anger and fear. We shall presently suggest a theory which will remedy this defect. First, however, it will be necessary to ascertain what distinct types of emotion exist, and then take account of the physiological mechanisms at their service.

The Classification of Emotions. Introspection upon emotional consciousness reveals two characteristic facts: (1) Every emotion has an *affective element;* that is, it may be classed as either pleasant or unpleasant. (2) Every emotion has some distinctive quality by which it may be recognized apart from its affective aspect. Disgust and rage, for example, are both unpleasantly toned states; but they can be clearly distinguished in consciousness. There is, in other words, some *differentiating factor* which serves to distinguish between emotions which are alike in respect to the affective component. The principal emotions having an *unpleasant* feeling element are disgust, fear, rage, grief, and the somewhat emotional quality of intense bodily pain. Pain and disgust are relatively simple conditions, involving little specialized somatic activity. The chief emotions characterized by *pleasant* affectivity are elation, mirth, and love both of the conjugal and consanguineal sort. The unpleasantly toned emotions, such as fear and rage, represent the return afferent impulses from prepotent activities of the avoiding type; while the pleasant states attend the preparatory or consummatory phases of the approaching activities.

The Physiology of Feeling and Emotion. If we search for some physiological mechanism suitably correlated with the antagonistic poles of pleasantness and unpleasantness, upon which our emotional classification is based, we shall find it in the autonomic nervous system and the viscera. The physiological antagonism between the cranio-sacral and the sympathetic portions of the autonomic is admirably suited to be the correlate of this antithesis of affective quality. It [has been shown] . . . that these two divisions innervate the same organs, and produce in them exactly opposite types of reactions. It may now be further stated that it is the *sympathetic* portion which functions during the intense and *unpleasant* emotional excitements of anger, fear, and bodily pain. During the *pleasantly* toned activities of digestion and sex behavior, it is the *cranio-sacral* division which holds sway. It is worth while to describe these antagonistic visceral effects somewhat more in detail. They are summarized diagrammatically in [the figure from Cannon]. . . .

During the process of digestion a state of tonus is maintained in the smooth muscle which facilitates the movements required for this work. Fibers from the cranial nerves bear to the viscera the nervous impulses which produce this tonicity. The salivary and gastric glandular secretions necessary for eating and digesting are also augmented by the cranial division. Suppose now the individual sees a mortal enemy, or is faced with the fear of imminent destruction. The visual stimulus will arouse impulses which, entering the central nervous system, will be discharged through the efferent sympathetic fibers to the smooth visceral muscle. These impulses are inhibitory in character. They reduce the muscle tone of the digestive organs and bring their processes to an end. A similar inhibitory effect is produced upon the salivary and digestive glands. The parched condition of the mouth in fear, which results from the suppression of the salivary secretions, is well known.[1]

---

[1] ["The remarkable researches of Pawlow (*The Work of the Digestive Glands* (English Translation), London, 1902), and his co-workers in Russia on the *work of the digestive glands*, and those of Cannon (for a summary of Cannon's work, see his article, 'Recent Advances in the Physiology of the Digestive Organs Bearing on Medicine and Surgery,' *Jour. Med. Sc.*, 1906, New Series, Vol. CXXXI, pp. 563-578) in America on the *movements of the stomach and intestines* have revealed that these functions are influenced in an astonishing degree by psychical factors.

"Although it has long been known that the sight of food under certain conditions would call forth a secretion of gastric juice in a hungry dog (Bidder and Smith, 1852), and common observation has told us that emotion strongly affects the gastrointestinal functions, increasing or diminishing the secretions of saliva and gastric juice, and even producing dyspeptic disturbances and diarrhœa, it has remained for Pawlow and his

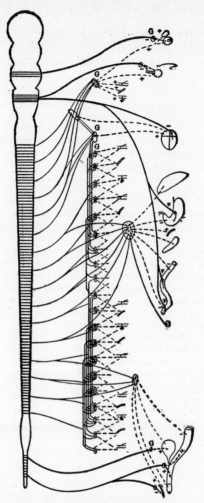

DIAGRAM OF THE MORE IMPORTANT DISTRIBUTIONS OF THE AUTONOMIC
NERVOUS SYSTEM

The brain and spinal cord are represented at the left. The nerves to
skeletal muscles are not represented. The preganglionic fibres of the
autonomic system are in solid lines, the postganglionic in dash-lines. The
nerves of cranial and sacral divisions are distinguished from those of the
thoracico-lumbar or "sympathetic" division by broader lines. A + mark
indicates an augmenting effect on the activity of the organ; a — mark, a
depressive or inhibitory effect. For further description see the text of
Dr. Walter B. Cannon's volume, *Bodily Changes in Pain, Hunger, Fear,
and Rage* (Appleton, 1915), from which this figure was taken by permission.

The cranio-sacral division dilates the muscular walls of the blood vessels, thus facilitating the absorption of food materials, or allowing the external genital organs to be engorged with blood in the

---

co-workers to demonstrate the important part which the 'appetite,' as a psychical state, plays in the process of digestion. In hungry dogs a large quantity of gastric juice, rich in ferment, is poured out when food is swallowed, and even at the sight of food, and it was proved that this outpouring was due to psychical influences. Simply teasing and tempting the animal with food cause secretions, and food associations in the environment may have the same effect. 'If the dog has not eaten for a long time every movement, the going out of the room, the appearance of the attendant who ordinarily feeds the animal—in a word, every triviality—may give rise to excitation of the gastric glands.' (Pawlow, *op. cit.*, 73.) This first secreted juice is called 'appetite juice,' and is an important factor in the complicated process of digestion. 'The appetite is the first and mightiest exciter of the secretory nerves of the stomach.' (*Id.*, 75.) Pawlow's results have been confirmed in man by Hornborg, Umber, Bickel, and Cade and Latarjet. The mere chewing of appetizing food, for instance, is followed by a copious discharge of gastric juice, while chewing of rubber and distasteful substances has a negative result. Depressing emotions inhibit the secretion of juice (Bickel). More than this, Cannon (*Am. Jour. Med. Sc.*, 1906, p. 566. See also 'The Influence of Emotional States on the Functions of the Alimentary Canal,' by the same writer (*ibid.*, April, 1909) for an interesting résumé of the subject) in his very remarkable experiments on the movements of the stomach and intestines, found that in animals (cat, rabbit, dog, etc.), gastric peristalsis is stopped whenever the animal manifests signs of rage, distress, or even anxiety. 'Any signs of emotional disturbance, even the restlessness and continual mewing which may be taken to indicate uneasiness and discomfort, were accompanied in the cat by total cessation of the segmentation movements of the small intestines, and of antiperistalsis in the proximal colon.' Bickel and Sasaki have confirmed in dogs these emotional effects obtained by Pawlow and Cannon.

"The effect of the emotions on the digestive processes is so important from the standpoint of clinical medicine that I quote the following summary of published observations from Cannon: 'Hornborg found that when the boy whom he studied chewed agreeable food a more or less active secretion of the gastric juice was started, whereas the chewing of indifferent material was without influence.

" 'Not only is it true that normal secretion is favored by pleasurable sensations during mastication, but also that unpleasant feelings, such as vexation and some of the major emotions, are accompanied by a failure of secretion. Thus Hornborg was unable to confirm in his patient the observation of Pawlow that mere sight of food to a hungry subject causes the flow of gastric juice. Hornborg explains the difference between his and Pawlow's results by the difference in the reaction of the subjects to the situation. When food was shown, but withheld, Pawlow's hungry dogs were all eagerness to secure it, and the juice at once began to flow. Hornborg's little boy, on the contrary, became vexed when he could not eat at once, and began to cry; then no secretion appeared. Bogen also reports that his patient, a child, aged three and a half years, sometimes

erectile condition necessary for copulation. In fear, anger, and acute pain, on the other hand, the sympathetic impulses dominate and drive the cranio-sacral responses from the field. The blood

---

fell into such a passion in consequence of vain hoping for food, that the giving of the food, after calming the child, was not followed by any secretion of the gastric juice.

" 'The observations of Bickel and Sasaki confirm and define more precisely the inhibitory effects of violent emotion on *gastric secretion.* They studied these effects on a dog with an œsophageal fistula, and with a side pouch of the stomach which, according to Pawlow's method, opened only to the exterior. If the animal was permitted to eat while the œsophageal fistula was open the food passed out through the fistula and did not go to the stomach. Bickel and Sasaki confirmed the observation of Pawlow that this sham feeding is attended by a copious flow of gastric juice, a true 'psychic secretion,' resulting from the pleasurable taste of the food. In a typical instance the sham feeding lasted five minutes, and the secretion continued for twenty minutes, during which time 66.7 c. c. of pure gastric juice was produced.

" 'On another day a cat was brought into the presence of the dog, whereupon the dog flew into a great fury. The cat was soon removed, and the dog pacified. Now the dog was again given the sham feeding for five minutes. In spite of the fact that the animal was hungry and ate eagerly, there was no secretion worthy of mention. During a period of twenty minutes, corresponding to the previous observation, only 9 c. c. of acid fluid was produced, and this was rich in mucus. It is evident that in the dog, as in the boy observed by Bogen, strong emotions can so profoundly disarrange the mechanisms of secretion that the natural nervous excitation accompanying the taking of food cannot cause the normal flow.

" 'On another occasion Bickel and Sasaki started gastric secretion in the dog by sham feeding, and when the flow of gastric juice had reached a certain height the dog was infuriated for five minutes by the presence of the cat. During the next fifteen minutes there appeared only a few drops of a very mucous secretion. Evidently in this instance a physiological process, started as an accompaniment of a psychic state quietly pleasurable in character, was almost entirely stopped by another psychic state violent in character.

" 'It is noteworthy that in both the positive and negative results of the emotional excitement illustrated in Bickel and Sasaki's dog the effects persisted long after the removal of the exciting condition. This fact Bickel was able to confirm in a girl with œsophageal and gastric fistulas; the gastric secretion long outlasted the period of eating, although no food entered the stomach. The importance of these observations to personal economics is too obvious to require elaboration.

" 'Not only are the secretory activities of the stomach unfavorably affected by strong emotions; the movements of the stomach as well, and, indeed, the movements of almost the entire alimentary canal, are wholly stopped during excitement.' (*Am. Jour. Med. Sc.,* April, 1909.)

"So you see that the proverb, 'Better a dinner of herbs where love is than a stalled ox and hatred therewith,' has a physiological as well as a moral basis.

vessels are constricted, and the blood is driven from the interior of the body to the limbs where it is needed for violent exertion. It is commonly known that fear (for example, fear of the consequences or fear of impotence) prevents the free flow of blood to the sex organs, and thus inhibits the tumescence necessary for the sex act.

"Nearly any sensory or psychical stimulus can be artificially made to excite the *secretion of saliva* as determined by experimentation on animals by Pawlow.

"It is probable that all the *ductless glands* (thyroid, suprarenal, etc.), are likewise under the influence of the emotions. The suprarenal glands secrete a substance which in almost infinitesimal doses has a powerful effect upon the heart and blood vessels, increasing the force of the former and contracting the peripheral arterioles. The recent observations of Cannon and de la Paz have demonstrated in the cat that under the influence of fear or anger an increase of this substance is poured into the circulation (Cannon and de la Paz: *Am. Jour. Physiol.*, April 1, 1911). Cannon, Shohl and Wright have also demonstrated that the glycosuria which was known to occur in animals experimented upon in the laboratory is due (in cats) to the influence of the emotions, very probably discharging through the sympathetic system on the adrenal glands and increasing their secretion (Cannon, Shohl, and Wright, *Ibid.*, December 1, 1911). The glycosuria is undoubtedly due to an increase of sugar in the blood. It is interesting to note, in this connection, that there is considerable clinical evidence that indicates that some cases of diabetes and glycosuria have an emotional origin. The same is true of disease of the thyroid gland (exophthalmic goiter).

"Most of the viscera are innervated by the sympathetic system, and the visceral manifestations of emotion indicate the dominance of sympathetic impulses. 'When, for example, a cat becoms frightened, the pupils dilate, the stomach and intestines are inhibited, the heart beats rapidly, the hairs of the back and tail stand erect—all signs of nervous discharge along sympathetic paths' (Cannon). Cannon and his co-workers have further made the acute suggestion that, as adrenalin itself is capable of working the effects evoked by sympathetic stimulation, 'the persistence of the emotional state, after the exciting object has disappeared, can be explained' by the persistence of the adrenalin in the blood. There is reason to believe that some of the adrenal secretion set free by nervous stimulation returning in the blood stream to the glands stimulates them to further activity, and this would tend to continue the emotional effect after the emotion has subsided. 'Indeed it was the lasting effect of excitement in digestive processes which suggested' to Cannon his investigations. (These effects of adrenalin suggest that the secretion may take some part in pathological anxiety states.)

"According to Féré (*Pathologie des Emotions*, 1892), the *pupils* may dilate under the influence of asthenic emotions and contract with sthenic emotions. However that may be, the dilatation of the pupils during states of fear may be demonstrated in animals."—Morton Prince, *The Unconscious*, 426-433 (copyright, 1921, by The Macmillan Company); reprinted by permission.]

Fear has likewise an inhibitory effect upon micturition, a process normally brought about by the sacral efferent fibers. Constriction of the blood vessels is accompanied by increase in blood pressure. By the use of an instrument for reading these fluctuations of blood pressure, one can often detect in a witness the presence of a fear emotion, otherwise concealed, a state usually indicative of guilty knowledge which the subject is afraid of disclosing.

The heart is retarded by the vagus nerve (cranial), and accelerated by the sympathetic, the latter effect forcing a liberal supply of blood to the arms and limbs where it is needed in the bodily struggles likely to be involved in conditions of violent emotion. The sympathetic fibers also convey impulses to the liver, releasing stored sugar so that it can be distributed by the blood to the peripheral organs engaged in combat or flight.[2] One of the most important effects of the sympathetic impulses is the exciting of the adrenal glands, small bodies lying near the kidneys, causing them to pour their secretion, adrenin, into the blood stream. Professor Cannon found that adrenin acts directly upon the heart, arteries, digestive organs, and other tissues, in precisely the same manner as the impulses of the sympathetic fibers. It serves, therefore, in the strong unpleasant emotions as an aid to the sympathetic by augmenting and prolonging its effects. It helps to maintain the body "upon a war footing."

A Theory of Feeling and Emotion. It is evident that the two antagonistic mechanisms which we have been considering, the cranio-sacral and sympathetic divisions, are allied with two groups of emotions having opposed qualities of feeling, pleasant and unpleasant respectively. The unpleasant group, exemplified by pain, fear, and rage, results from bodily changes which serve the ends of withdrawing and defense, and which are brought about by the sympathetic division. There is no difficulty theoretically in concluding that all conscious states tinged with unpleasant feeling derive that feeling from the invasion of the various bodily organs by impulses from the sympathetic.

The chief pleasures of mankind, on the other hand, center about the cranio-sacral functions of nutrition and sex. The digestive operations induced by the cranial division are probably the reactions whose return afferent impulses convey much of the feeling of pleasure in eating. Salivary and other digestive reactions come by conditioned reflex to be attached to stimuli which accompany the taste of the food, such as the *sight* of the food or surrounding

---

[2] These functions have already been described in [*op. cit.*] pp. 32-35.

objects. The pleasure reaction is therefore transferred to these attendant stimuli, and our preparatory as well as our consummatory approaching reactions become fraught with pleasant feeling. The same extension applies to the pleasures of the sex life, controlled by the sacral division. The facilitating sacral discharge into the pelvic organs becomes conditioned by the *sight* of the loved one, or even by a token or remembrance, so that the pleasure reaction is habitually experienced as the affective core of the emotion of love. It is not improbable that consanguineal as well as true sexual love derives its pleasantness component in a similar fashion.

A certain exception must be made to the statement that craniosacral impulses underlie pleasant emotional states generally. There are several sources of pleasant affectivity, such as bodily exercise and habit, excitement of games, elation, and mirth, which possess no discoverable relation to the cranio-sacral functions, nor (with the exception of excitement and mirth) to autonomic activities of any sort. These pleasant states appear to be due to afferent impulses from reactions carried out by unimpeded *cerebrospinal* impulses. They are somatic rather than visceral in origin.

To recapitulate: Emotions are fundamentally distinguishable as pleasant and unpleasant. The first part of our theory undertakes to explain this affective basis. Finding a certain physiological process to be present in the entire group of unpleasant emotions, and an antagonistic process common to pleasant emotions, we infer that these processes form the basis of conscious unpleasantness and pleasantness respectively. *The cranio-sacral division of the autonomic, supplemented under certain conditions by the cerebrospinal system, innervates those responses whose return afferent impulses are associated with the conscious quality of pleasantness. The sympathetic division produces visceral responses which are represented in consciousness as unpleasantness.* Before proceeding to the second portion of the theory, we shall review a few additional lines of evidence confirming the hypothesis just stated.

Evidence from Introspection and Latent Period. In conscious experience unpleasantness is usually a more definite, identifiable, and imperative quality than pleasantness. The unpleasant emotions are more numerous and characteristically emotional than the pleasant. We shall observe later that they are also represented by a far greater variety of facial expressions than are pleasant states. On the physiological side there are analogous conditions. The sympathetic motor impulses are necessarily stronger than the cranio-sacral, and are prepotent over the latter. They are more widely diffused through the viscera, and they reinforce somatic motor activities of a more violent, varied, and characteristic sort.

The length of time required for arousal (latent period) is another point in the evidence. We should expect, according to the theory, that unpleasantness would be slower of arousal than pleasantness. The synapses of the sympathetic ganglia have a higher resistance than those of the cranio-sacral division. If this were not so, our digestive and other vital functions would be subject to continual interruption through minor emotional excitements. Dr. Cannon regards the sympathetic ganglia as protective barriers, which can be crossed by invading impulses only in case of unusual need for defense or escape. They are thus a protection against harmful excess of emotion. There are also longer stretches of unmedullated post-ganglionic fibers (see figure) in the sympathetic than in the cranio-sacral division; and conduction is slower in non-medullated than in medullated neurons. These conditions—namely, greater synaptic resistance and slower rate of transmission—both indicate that the effects produced by the sympathetic fibers must be slower to appear than those of the cranio-sacral.

Common experience justifies this inference. Compare, for example, the latency of unpleasant feelings with the quick thrill of pleasure derived from pleasant tastes or erotic sensations. The case of stumbling on the stairs is a good example. In the writer's experience there is a sudden reflex recovery of balance; and then, *when several steps have been descended,* there wells up gradually a mass of unpleasant organic sensations. Annoyance and anger also have a long latent time. A characteristic non-emotive 'foreperiod' has been found in extensive collections of introspection upon anger.[3] In babies a good anger cry may take as long as a half-minute, or longer, to develop. The laughter response to the pleasant stimulus of tickling is, on the other hand, immediate.

The sharp antagonism which exists between the two divisions of the autonomic, when considered in connection with the introspective oppositeness of pleasantness and unpleasantness, offers further support for the theory we are discussing. Fear inhibits pleasant emotions. And on the pleasant side the drive of sexual love is one of the strongest agencies in dispelling the unpleasant anger in family quarrels.

To sum up, we find the first part of our theory supported from both the introspective and behavioristic viewpoints by definiteness,

---

[3] Richardson, R. F., "The Psychology and Pedagogy of Anger," *Educational Monographs,* No. 19.

imperativeness, latent period, and antagonistic character of the emotional responses.

How are the Emotional Reactions further Differentiated? There remains to be explained the *differentiating factor,* through which the emotions within a single affective class—for example, fear and anger—may be physiologically distinguished. Since the autonomic functions for all the unpleasant emotions are of the same type, we must look elsewhere for our distinguishing mechanism. *We propose that the differentiating factor arises from the stimulation of the proprioceptors in the muscles, tendons, and joints of the somatic part of the organism; and that afferent impulses from these somatic patterns of response add to the autonomic core of affectivity the characteristic sensory complexes by which one emotion is distinguished from another of the same affective class.* Somatic postures and attitudes are generally taken, or overt responses made, in nearly all emotional situations. Different, and somewhat antagonistic, somatic effector groups are brought into play according to whether the individual attacks or flees. The facial expressions as well as bodily movements are strongly differential.[4] Return afferent impulses from these responses add in consciousness the distinguishing qualities which serve to differentiate the emotion of anger from that of fear. Without these impulses the two states would be simply unpleasant, and indistinguishable. As to the pleasant emotions, we may ascribe the differentiating factors—for example, in the various types of love—to the habits of adjustment toward the loved object. To love a baby is to fondle it, or at least to assume the attitude of fondling it, in a lover-like fashion. This is an abridgment of the complete set of responses which affords the full emotion of sexual love. In friendship the somatic component may be reduced to a touch of the hand or a half-embrace. Some facilitation of the sacral and allied mechanisms probably forms the pleasant affective core of all these experiences.

The temporal relations of the two components in the proposed theory offer some corroboration. When the objective situation arousing anger or embarrassment has been removed, the visceral component, being more sluggish than the somatic, outlasts the latter in the form of a purely unpleasant affective (not emotional) state which delays the recovery of composure. In the case of stumbling on the stair, the starting (somatic) response was completed before the sympathetic affective component was felt. The

---

[4] [See Professor Allport's pp. 200-232, which treat of "Facial and Bodily Expression."]

emotion, therefore, was not true fear, but simply an intense unpleasantness. When an animal or a child is pursued and brought to bay, the shift from intense fear (in flight) to intense rage (in attack) is too sudden to admit of a complete change in the visceral pattern. We may plausibly attribute it to the quicker change in the response pattern of the striped muscle, superimposed upon the constant visceral undercurrent of unpleasant affectivity. Bodily pain and grief also pass quickly into anger through a change in the nature of the somatic responses.

Evidence from Genetic Development. The emotional states of the newborn baby appear to be undifferentiated. Judging from behavior alone, they have no further character than pure unpleasant affectivity. The first prepotent stimuli which act upon the infant are usually those for which the somatic responses are diffuse and undifferentiated. Internal pains of hunger and colic, and unfavorable temperatures, are among such stimulations. The somatic responses, crying, kicking, etc., are the same for all of them. At the beginning, therefore, of the life of feeling there is little to differentiate the emotional states beyond the mere qualities of pleasantness and unpleasantness. The child has feelings of unpleasantness, but not yet definite unpleasant emotions. We may call this simple, unpleasant experience of the newborn the 'protopathic' state. The *affective* component, then, is not only the fundamental basis of classification, but also the most primitive ingredient of human emotion. Before long (probably as soon as the appropriate stimuli are brought to bear) the child brings into play the various prepotent somatic responses, such as struggling, rejecting, and withdrawing. Thus the differentiating factors are added to the sympathetic pattern, and anger and fear emerge as distinct emotions.

Conditions Favoring the Arousal of Unpleasant Emotions. A fuller comprehension of the subject may be obtained by stating the neural conditions necessary for the arousal of the unpleasant emotions. . . . The conditions referred to are those which help in breaking through the high resistance of the sympathetic synapses and sending inhibitory impulses to the smooth muscle. (1) The first condition is that of the intensity of the stimulus. Almost any sensation becomes unpleasant if it is made sufficiently intense for the energy of the impulse to cross the sympathetic threshold. The peal of thunder continues to arouse fear throughout adult life. Our theory at this point offers a good basis for distinguishing physiologically between pains which are unpleasant and those which are not. It is well known that light pains on the skin are far from unpleasant. Unpleasant pains are severe ones: their efferent impulses are powerful enough to break through into the sympathetic. The same consideration explains the pseudo-emotional quality often ascribed to intense bodily pain. (2) Repetition or insistence, such as repeatedly touching on a 'sore point,' or the neural summation of petty annoyances in producing anger, is another condition favoring the arousal of unpleasant emotion. (3) Suddenness of the stimulus, or lack of proper somatic adjustment of the cerebrospinal system, often causes the impulse to be discharged through the sympathetic efferents. The fear aroused by the strange, the uncanny, or the extraordinarily large (that is, objects toward which we have no developed habits of response) belongs in this class. (4) Blocking of the usual somatic responses to the powerful drives, such as those of food and sex, usually through social agencies, is a potent factor in bringing about an invasion of the sympathetic. Thwarting of the vital needs, as in industrial conflicts, evokes not only overt struggle reactions, but also violent emotions of fear and anger. Grief results from blocked, or thwarted, love reactions in situations where overt responses, such as attacking others, would do no good. (5) Finally, the state of visceral tonus or preparation may be an important factor in lowering the sympathetic threshold and increasing unpleasant emotionality. Irritability, and other emotional attitudes indicate a permanent lowering of the resistance. Transitory effects, or moods, also increase susceptibility to fear or anger. When feeling fine, a baby will enjoy a vigorous roughing which at another time would throw him into a fit of rage. Petitions for money are tactfully withheld from the *pater familias* until the close of a good dinner.[5]

---

[5] ["It is possible that in certain cases a check to the overt response might be followed by a check or decrease to the emotion as well. It is not *necessary* that the nervous energy saved by the check must be drained into the autonomic apparatus. It might be used up in *other* skeletal responses or in intellectual activity; and the energy already flowing into the autonomic apparatus might change and follow the same course. If, for example, there is a check to mating behavior, the accompanying emotion is just as likely to be diminished. The totality of the energy released by the situation may be used up in excessive physical activity or intellectual pursuits. On the other hand a progressive attainment of the love-object or realization of the love behavior is likely to be accompanied by an actual intensification of the correlated emotion, because the emotion-producing stimulus is progressively intensified. . . .

"The view here expounded has certain implications for medical psychology, which can only be mentioned without elaboration. Whenever a situation demands overt response such as escape, fighting, or mating, and the required response is checked or inhibited, the visceral and glandular

Complex Emotional States in Social Behavior. The foregoing account has dealt with the physiology of the more elementary emotional reactions. Our subjective lives, however, would be of a primitive sort if we were limited to these few basic types. There are many *nuances* of feeling which comprise a large number of combinations of the elementary emotions under varying conditions. There are, moreover, states in which both pleasant and unpleasant elements may be identified. A simple object or situation acting upon a limited area of smooth muscle can, of course, produce but one type of affective response, either pleasant or unpleasant. If the control is assumed by the cranio-sacral, the antagonistic sympathetic effects are inhibited, and *vice versa*. If, however, the situation is complex, that is, if we are apt to respond with varying reactions to different aspects of it, we may expect that certain regions of the viscera may be under the control of the cranio-sacral, while other regions will have been invaded by the sympathetic impulses. The result will be a mixed emotion, containing representatives of both the pleasant and unpleasant divisions of our classification. Grief is an example of such an emotion. It contains (1) the pleasant feeling-tone of the love reaction, and (2) the unpleasant thwarted feeling of sadness because it is impossible for the habitual love response to be fully carried out. This explanation of 'mixed' emotional states is, of course, purely tentative. Since it affords a possible manner in which to conceive the physiological factors, it may be useful in our present lack of more precise knowledge.

There are many complex emotional states which are familiar in daily life. Varying degrees of the affective qualities combine with

response may as we have shown, be intensified and prolonged. This places an undue and somewhat unnatural strain upon the autonomic apparatus. Such a strain if long continued may result in marked physical disturbances, gastrointestinal and others. These disturbances are at first of the so-called functional variety, such as nervous indigestion; but it is well known that these functional disorders may ultimately terminate in organic changes, such as gastritis and gastric or intestinal ulcer. Another result of this tension in the autonomic system is a fatigue and weakening of the whole apparatus. The writer feels convinced that various forms of visceroptosis have sometimes a so-called psychological origin. Such a consequence is of course more likely to occur in the case of those persons who by original nature or training have a pronounced tendency to inhibit overt expression in an instinct-emotion producing situation. He who expresses little may really feel most keenly, while he who expresses himself readily may feel less keenly and escape some of the unfortunate consequences of too intense emotion."—J. W. Bridges, "A Reconciliation of Current Theories of Emotion," *Jour. Abn. Psychol.*, 19: 339-340 (1925).]

the major emotions of fear, anger, and love, and also with somatic attitudes for all possible reactions toward self and others. The main attitudes in which *fear* seems to be important are awe, reverence, bashfulness, surprise, wonder, suspicion, loathing, and anxiety. *Anger* is recognizable in resentment, remorse, jealousy, envy, reproach, scorn, and hatred. *Love* plays a part in gratitude, grief, pity, sorrow, fascination, and perhaps humility. A number of bodily attitudes, other than attacking, fleeing, and caressing, combine with pleasantness and unpleasantness to produce special emotional reactions. These states are represented by numerous varieties of approach and avoidance, as well as by joy, elation, pride, conceit, shame, domination, submission, and feelings of inferiority.[6]

The range of human feelings is indeed extensive. There are probably hundreds of *nuances* of emotional attitude which contribute to the richness as well as the delicacy of social intercourse. Modern fiction is primarily a play upon these attitudes. They are of interest for social psychology because they indicate the complexity of inter-individual adjustments in society. Almost every emotional *nuance* represents an attitude not only to feel but to react in a highly specific fashion toward some other human being.

The Social Conditioning of Emotional Response. A certain college professor relates a story of an unaccountable liking which he took for a man in whom he could discover no qualities to merit such affection. Upon analyzing this feeling, he fancied that it was chiefly the peculiar chuckle of the man that attracted him. This clue led to the recall of a former roommate of college days with whom the professor had spent many a pleasant hour. The roommate had possessed a chuckle almost identical with that of the new acquaintance. We find here the mechanism of the conditioned response in the emotional sphere. The pleasure responses experienced with the roommate had been attached (transferred) to a particular social stimulus which was present at the time, namely, the sound of the chuckle. This conditioned emotional reaction persisted for years and formed the basis of a new friendship upon purely emotional grounds. Many, if not most, of our likes and dislikes in first im-

---

[6] For a more complete subjective analysis of the complex emotions the reader should consult Professor McDougall's *Social Psychology*, chs. 5 and 6. It is interesting also to try to analyze the components of these complex states in the corresponding facial expressions (*cf.* Chapter IX [Allport, *op. cit.*]).

[Relative to Professor McDougall's analysis, just mentioned, the student may wish to see the diagram in Henry Herbert Goddard's volume, *Psychology of the Normal and Subnormal*, opp. 142.]

pressions are due to similar transfers of feeling through identical elements of social stimulation. Our pleasure at seeing old classmates is like that which we experience in revisiting the haunts and byways of childhood. We are led back through the present stimulus to the old, but not obliterated, habits of emotional response.

Fetishes and other tokens operate upon human feelings by the same principle of conditioning. The savage attaches to an effigy all the awe and mystery which he feels for the spirit it is supposed to embody. To a lover a lock of hair is sacred because it calls forth a wave of tender feeling of the same kind as that evoked by the entire person of the beloved. For the same reason wedding gowns are treasured, and attics are filled with trunks lined with keepsakes and similar hoarded treasures.

Sentiments are another important class of conditioned emotions and attitudes. The political orator has only to mention the 'orphan children' or the 'rights of the people' to reduce his audience to a state of tender compassion or righteous indignation. The names of national heroes, the standard of colors, slogans such as 'Liberty' and 'Equality,' and reiterated lofty ideals are great rallying points for the popular emotions. The spoken word is here used to evoke all the feeling associated with it through ages of tradition and custom. As a means of social control, whether for good or for ill, this arousing of sentiment through language stimuli is a process of inestimable significance.

The Control and Direction of Emotion as a Social Problem. Professor Cannon has pointed out the energizing effects of emotion, if not too extreme, upon the bodily activity which the situation demands. Through the sympathetic impulses, and especially through adrenin, the effects of fatigue are removed, metabolism increased, and the whole body energized to a degree unknown in calmer moods. These 'unknown reservoirs of power' are, however, more of an asset to primitive than to civilized man. They are Nature's provision for strength in the violent emotions attending pursuit and flight and mortal combat. The needs of civilized society are of another order: physical struggles and the violent emotions which accompany them are a menace rather than a benefit to modern man. The anger emotion cannot be used to support overt violence, because we must repress this form of reaction in favor of a more socialized 'competition.' We cannot even yield ourselves to fear and precipitate flight regardless of the consequences to others. On every hand we find that the needs of society have set up barriers to those exertions in which the visceral components of emotion raise the body to its highest level of attainment. It is only in such abnor-

186   READINGS IN ABNORMAL PSYCHOLOGY

mal and destructive phenomena as wars and racial and industrial riots that the primitive fury of the emotional energy can fully expend itself. While endowed, therefore, with a capacity for highest efficiency in war, civilized man is normally committed to a régime of peace. How can we reconcile these opposed requirements and utilize the emotional reservoirs of energy for constructive purposes? This is one of the greatest social problems.

It is not only for the acquisition of power, the superman ideal, that the emotional problem is a socially important one. At many points the social pressure is so great as to threaten *all* activity through which the emotion may find its release. If somatic responses are totally inhibited, the visceral energizing effects can be discharged only inwardly. There is produced an extended, intensified, and lasting state of unpleasant internal feeling. If social and familial ties are too strong, there will result a complete blocking of overt anger release, leading to the development of an introverted, moody, and ineffective personality. Love emotions are often iniquitously repressed by austere social influences. In this case autoeroticism, erotic day-dreaming, and symptoms of neurotic dissociation may appear. How shall we steer successfully between the evils of anti-social violence and libertinism on the one hand, and the suppression of the life processes of the individual on the other? This is a second great problem in the field of social adjustments.

REFERENCES

Cannon, W. B., *Bodily Changes in Pain, Hunger, Fear, and Rage.*
Ribot, Th., *The Psychology of the Emotions,* part I, chs. 6-9; part II, chs. 2-4, 8.
James, Wm., *Principles of Psychology,* vol. II, ch. 25.
Woodworth, R. S., *Psychology, a Study of Mental Life,* chs. 7, 9.
Warren, H. C., *Human Psychology,* ch. 14 (secs. 1, 2), 17.
Hunter, W. S., *General Psychology,* part II, chs. 4, 5.
McDougall, Wm., *An Introduction to Social Psychology,* chs. 5, 6.
Watson, J. B., *Psychology from the Standpoint of a Behaviorist,* chs. 6, 7 (249-52).
Watson, J. B., and Rayner, R., "Conditioned Emotional Reactions," *Jour. of Exp. Psychol.,* 1920, 3: 1-14.
Allport, F. H., "A Physiological-Genetic Theory of Feeling and Emotion," *Psychol. Rev.,* 1922, 29: 132-39.
Kempf, E, J., *The Autonomic Functions and the Personality,* 17-90.
Crile, G. W., *The Origin and Nature of the Emotions,* 55-90.
[Robinson, E. S., and Richardson-Robinson, Florence, *Readings in General Psychology,* 452-488 (Univ. of Chicago Press, 1923)].

Emotion as Aid to New Adjustments

GEORGE M. STRATTON, "An Experience during Danger and the Wider Functions of Emotion," *Problems of Personality* (C. Macfie Campbell and others, eds.), 61-62 (Harcourt, Brace, 1925)

Emotions in their sthenic phase, it would seem to me, are not mere energisers but are also diversifiers, leading to a fresh or less usual organisation. Emotions are awakeners of dormant functions; and when awakened, these sleeping powers are given a special direction and objective. But emotions are also repressive; and, while some functions are awakened, others are rendered dormant or are forced into a dissociated action.

In all this it is clear, I believe, that the function of emotion is not confined to the motor region; it extends far beyond this, into the cognitive field. And in this cognitive field the emotions serve likewise both as energisers and as reorganisers. As energisers; for where a function properly connected with the emotional impulses is already active or becomes active, it becomes more vigorously active because of the emotion. But also as reorganisers; for, in the cognitive awakening which emotion brings, there is an increased intellectual fertility, with varied and novel ideas put at the disposal of the vague impulses. There is, however, no mere miscellany of ideas rising up, and in confusion. There is, rather, a rise especially of such as promise some use in the present crisis. And among them there is a rapid selection and rejection, an organisation of some of them about the focus of present action, while others are dissociated and either vanish or become grouped about some other centre.

A wide service is thus rendered by [sthenic [1]] emotion. For when so stirred, the individual finds himself at a new level of behaviour both in body and in mind, being enabled to meet his crisis with a more complete array and organisation of his powers, and these not of his muscles only, but of his entire psycho-physical constitution.

---

[1] [Note, in contrast, the disintegrating effect of extreme fear, "blind rage," and the like.]

CHAPTER VI

THE PRINCIPLE OF DISSOCIATION

Where Dissociation Is Possible

Boris Sidis and Simon P. Goodhart; adapted from *Multiple Personality*, 27-32 (Appleton, 1919)

A psychological analysis reveals to us the fact that psychic elements constituting the sensory compounds are of such a stable character in the nature of· their combinations that dissociation is well-nigh impossible. The union of sensory elements with other sensory presentative groups and compounds is not free in its character. The psychic elements in these elementary psychic compounds are indissolubly bound. Sensory presentative elements enter into what may be figuratively termed chemical union, the elements being so intimately interrelated and interconnected as to give rise to a psychic tissue in which they are structurally integrated, forming a continuous organic unity. The psychic elements of the sensory presentative compound are, so to say, grown into one organic whole, and no dissociation can possibly be effected without injuring the constituent ingredients of the organic psychic compound. A sensation of red, of sweet, or of pain, is in reality a compound of many psychic elements, but their combination is so stable, firm, and indissoluble that the elements cannot be freed from their union.

In passing to perceptual systems in which the sensory compounds enter as constituents, we find that the component elementary sensory groups can be experienced separately under different conditions and circumstances. We can close our eyes and walk up to the object of perception, say the chair, and thus experience the free muscular sensations of distance. One thing, however, is clear, that the sensory groups appear in different compounds, and though never entirely free, may still be regarded as capable of relative isolation by forming constituents of different compounds. The groups of the percept are *bound* in the total aggregate, but, unlike the elements in the sensory group, they are *not fixed* in an indissoluble union.

Turning now to representation, we find that the constituent elements are *free* in their interrelations. The relation is of such a nature as to be highly unstable and easily dissociated as soon as association is formed. In representation the constituent elements, though forming an association, still stand out clear and distinct as independent elements.

The elements and relations in perception are fixed. Not so is it in representation. In representation the horse may have its mane on the back and tail in front, the ass may preach or prophesy, the chair and table may have tongues and carry on conversations. What cannot be done in representation? The very foundation of the universe may be removed and another world with new relations may be created.

Dissociation

CHARLES HUBBARD JUDD, *Psychology*, 279-294, 296-297 (Ginn, 1917)

Sleep, the influence of drugs, hypnosis, and insanity as forms of disorganization. We may examine three distinct cases of dissociation in order to make clear in detail what is meant by mental disorganization. First, there is in sleep a form of normal suspension of central nervous activity which has been provided by nature for the purpose of recuperating the individual. This nervous condition is accompanied by a temporary interruption of normal conscious processes. Second, there are certain forms of dissociation and partial reconstruction which are very similar in character to sleep, but do not serve the purposes of recuperation as does normal sleep. The conditions here referred to may be induced by the use of drugs or by certain other devices, conspicuous among which are the methods of inducing hypnosis. Finally, the dissociations and partial reconstructions, which are temporary in hypnosis and after the use of certain drugs, may appear in a great variety of relatively permanent forms in the different types of insanity. One or two of these typical forms of insanity will be referred to later, in order to exemplify the conditions which result from permanent disorganization.

The physiological conditions of sleep. The physiological conditions which present themselves in the nervous system during sleep are not fully understood, but their general character can be described with sufficient clearness for our purposes. In the first place, the condition of fatigue in the nerve cell has been found to be a condition of somewhat depleted tissue in the cell body. There are also certain chemical changes resulting from fatigue. These are demonstrated by the different degrees to which fatigued and normal cells respectively take on the coloring substances which are used in staining microscopic sections of the tissue. . . . Sleep must be a condition in which these cells are supplied with nutrition and return to their normal state of energy and activity. During the period of sleep, each cell seems to be capable of insulating itself from the neighboring parts of the nervous system. There are some extreme conditions, probably pathological in character, in which the dendrites of the nerve cells curl up and form, instead of extending branches, little knotty balls across which stimulations cannot easily pass. This curling up of the dendrites is probably a very much more radical change than occurs under the ordinary conditions of sleep. The synapses, or interlacing of fibers, which connect a cell with other cells or incoming fibers, are interrupted in most cases, not by any gross movement of the dendrites but rather by some chemical change in the tissue which makes it difficult for the stimulation to pass across from one cell to another. There are known chemical substances which affect primarily the synapses and prevent stimulations from being transmitted from cell to cell. All of these indications go to show that the nerve cell, when it enters on the process of recuperation, tends to give up its normal transmitting function, and devotes itself for the time being to the processes of building up tissue.

The closing of avenues of stimulation in sleep. The external characteristics of a sleeping individual are clearly intelligible in terms of the physiological changes which have been described. In the first place, the individual becomes less and less susceptible to stimulations from the outside world. This means that when any form of external energy acts on the nervous system, it finds the nervous system relatively inert. The receiving organs are closed and their cells are probably in a chemical condition unfavorable to any vigorous activity. Even when stimulations are received at the periphery and are transmitted to the central nervous system, they make headway through the tissues with the greatest difficulty. They do not follow the well-defined paths which are used in normal life, but are diffused throughout the whole organ.

Various degrees of dissociation. The condition of the individual need not be a condition of complete sleep in order to show this inertness of the nervous system. There are many conditions of fatigue in which the nervous system shows, before sleep sets in, more or less of a tendency to resist external stimulation. Furthermore, the different stages of sleep are by no means equal in their degree of dissociation. This has been shown by experiments in which the amount of noise necessary to arouse a sleeping individual has been made the measure of the intensity of sleep. The result of such experiments is to show that a person goes to sleep rapidly and profoundly during the early part of the night, and from this time on gradually comes back to a condition of susceptibility to stimulation. . . . The curve rises rapidly, indicating, as stated, that the amount of stimulation necessary to arouse the nervous system increases rapidly in the early hours of sleep; it falls off gradually toward the end, indicating a gradual waking of the subject.

Dissociation in the central processes. Not only are the cells of the sleeper's nervous system impervious to external stimulation, but they are uncoupled in such a way that the stimulations which succeed in entering the nervous system do not follow the ordinary paths of discharge. This uncoupling of the central nerve cells does not take place in equal degree in all parts of the nervous system. The large cells of the spinal cord are able to resist the effects of fatigue, and the spinal cord may be said never to sleep under normal conditions. For this reason, stimulations which reach the spinal cord from the surface of the body are always transformed into reflex impulses and sent to the muscles of the trunk and limbs. The spinal cord is in this case uncoupled, not within itself, but only with reference to the higher centers. The reflexes are very much simpler in form and more likely to appear under these conditions than when the stimulus has an open path to the higher centers. Thus a cold or uncomfortable hand will always be moved reflexly in sleep. The medulla, like the cord, seems to be able to resist, to a great extent, the tendencies toward fatigue, for many of the organic processes, such as circulation and respiration, are maintained through the nerve centers in the medulla, while the rest of the nervous system is closed to external stimulation and to any well-ordered activities.

Dreams as dissociated groups of ideas. One effect of the uncoupling of the various nerve tracts in the organs of the central nervous system above the medulla is that any processes which take place in these higher organs because of strong stimulations, or because of some abnormal excitability in the nervous system, are fleeting and irregular. The higher centers probably do not all of them sink into the same degree of inactivity even in a normal individual, and the slightest abnormality may result in a heightened activity in certain parts. The facts of consciousness which correspond to these irregular, detached activities in the central nervous system during sleep are easily understood when it is recognized that the nervous system is acting not as a single organized system but as a disorganized group of centers. To put the matter in terms of experience, one may say that an idea which presents itself during sleep is not related to the general body of ideas by which the experiences of ordinary life are checked and held under criticism. If, in ordinary life, the idea suggests itself to some individual that he has enormous possessions, he is immediately reminded by the evidences of his senses and by the familiar surroundings and limitations of his sphere of action that the idea is merely a subjective imagination. If, on the other hand, one should have this idea in his dreams, under conditions which would remove it from all restricting relations, it would obviously be compelling in its force and would be accepted by consciousness as an unqualified and unlimited truth. It would be dissociated from the other ideas which fill normal consciousness, and this dissociation would determine its character in such a way as to make it distinctly different from the processes of coherent thought built up in normal life.

Dreams impressive only because they are uncriticized. It will be seen from such considerations as these that a mature individual is brought in his sleep into a condition somewhat similar to that exhibited in the irregular and unrestrained imaginings of children. The young child constructs imaginations and is quite unable to criticize them because of his lack of experience and because of the lack of organization within his experience. The lines of organization are not laid down in the child; in the dreaming adult, though systems of ideas have been built up, they are for the time being interrupted, and the processes of mental life lapse into unsystematic and uncritical forms. There is, for this reason, a certain freedom from all kinds of restraint, which accounts for the highly erratic character of dreams.

Motor processes suspended by dissociations in sleep. The third characteristic of sleep follows naturally from these which we have been discussing. Muscular movements are almost completely suspended in normal sleep. The muscles relax more than they do in any condition of waking life, just because the nervous system sends only very much reduced stimulations to the muscles, and, as we have repeatedly seen, the muscles are quite unable to perform their work when they are not stimulated by the nerves. The few straggling stimulations which succeed in getting through the nervous system to the muscles are lower reflexes or they are irregular and without coördination. The movements which appear are, therefore, often more incoherent than the fleeting dream experiences which accompany the activities in the central nervous organs. Indeed, in most cases, any intense movements of the muscles during sleep indicate a distinctly abnormal condition and are closely related in character to the irregular coördinations which appear in certain forms of drug poisoning.

Narcotic drugs dissociative in their effects. The discussion of the phenomena which attend the use of drugs will aid in the understanding of what has been said about sleep. It is a familiar fact that certain narcotics produce a condition very closely related to sleep. The narcotic drug closes the avenues of sensory reception, reduces central activity or renders its processes irregular and incoherent, and suspends muscular contraction. If the drug is taken in a relatively small dose, so that its effect upon the nervous system is slight, these various effects may be produced in slight degree only. The effect in this case will be most marked in the irregularity of ideas and in the incoördination of the movements.

Effect of alcohol on the nervous system. A familiar effect of a drug is the intoxication which is produced by alcohol. The chemical condition of nerve cells and consequently the relations between them are in some way affected by alcohol, and the stimulations are interrupted or become irregular in their transmission through the tissues. The fact that a man under the influence of alcohol sees things moving irregularly, or sees them double, depends upon the incoördination of the muscles of the eyes. The fact that he is unable to walk steadily shows the incoördination of the muscles of the legs. There is a corresponding irregularity in the flow of his ideas; and his credulousness for the ideas which suggest themselves to him is analogous to the ordinary credulousness of a dreaming sleeper. The imperviousness of such an individual to the stimulations of the outside world is also a well-known fact.

Overexcitation is also dissociative. In the case of any one of the drugs which produces dissociative conditions in the nervous system, the condition may be overcome by the ordinary processes of recuperation by which the organism throws out the drug. In some cases the effort of the organism to restore the normal condition leads to a reaction which is abnormally intense. We may then have for a time, as a result of reaction to the drug, a state of hypersensitivity and a more vigorous activity within the central nervous system and in the muscles. The dissociating effects of such intense activity in the nervous system may be, so far as consciousness and muscular coördination are concerned, quite as abnormal as the depressing effects of fatigue or complete suspension of nervous activity. Thus, if the stimulations coming to the central nervous system are much increased in their intensity because the nervous tissue has been thrown into a condition of heightened activity, there may be an irregularity in the central nervous processes due to the abnormally strong currents of excitation and to the impossibility of restraining these currents of stimulation within the ordinary channels of connection and discharge. The disorganization here is like the disorganized behavior of a stream that overflows its banks.

Toxic effects of certain diseases. There are certain conditions produced in nature which are quite analogous to those which are produced by drugs. Such conditions appear in fevers when the organism is under the influence of certain toxic substances produced by the organism itself or by bacteria lodged in the body; under such conditions the nervous system is rendered hypersensitive through the chemical action of these foreign substances on the tissues. The delirium of the fever patient presents clearly the picture of too intense activity in the central nervous system, and the muscular activity of such an individual is directly related to his irregular and excessive central processes. Such a person may also be excessively sensitive to slight sounds or other irritations of the organs of sense.

These negative cases as evidences of the relation between normal consciousness and organization. These different cases show the relation between nervous organization and mental organization, and by their negative characteristics confirm the discussions of the preceding chapters, in which it has been maintained that normal mental life is a continuous process of integration and organization.

Hypnosis a form of dissociation closely allied to sleep. The condition known as hypnosis has long been the source of superstitious wonder, and much has been said and written in regard to it which would tend to increase the mystery which attaches to it. In many respects it is a condition closely related to normal sleep. On the other hand, it has certain peculiar characteristics which differentiate it from ordinary sleep. These peculiarities can, however, be fully understood under the formula adopted in explanation of normal sleep, provided that formula is slightly modified to include certain specialized forms of dissociation.

Hypnosis as partial dissociation. While normal sleep involves the uncoupling or dissociation of the nervous elements, especially of the type which suspends activity in the higher centers, hypnosis involves a dissociation which is partial and leaves a part of the higher centers in action. To put the matter in simple terms, we may say that in normal sleep the cerebrum is dissociated from the lower centers, and all the centers in the cerebrum are dissociated from each other; whereas, in hypnosis only a part of the cerebrum is dissociated from the lower centers. The remaining part of the cerebrum continues to carry on its activities and, indeed, profits by the cessation of activity in the dormant portion, for the active part of the nervous system is, in such a case as this, supplied with an unusually large amount of blood, and its activity may reach a much higher level of intensity, because of this superior nutritive supply and because of the concentration of all of the nervous activity in one region. Such a crude statement as this is undoubtedly too simple in its terms, and yet it represents the situation in principle.

Methods of inducing hypnosis. The way in which the condition of partial or hypnotic dissociation is produced in the nervous system differs with the practice of different hypnotizers. One of the characteristic methods of producing hypnosis is to require the subject to gaze at some bright object until a kind of partial stupor comes over him. He may then be aroused to activity through the sense of hearing. The ideas which he receives and the activities which he performs have, under these conditions, many of the characteristics of dissociation. Another way of producing hypnosis is to soothe the subject into a sleeplike condition. Stroking the forehead or the face is very commonly practiced by hypnotizers. Here again, the appeal to the subject, after the dormant condition has set in, is through the sense of hearing or even through the sense of vision.

Hypnosis more readily induced after it has once been established in a subject. When a subject has been frequently hypnotized, it is possible to reproduce the hypnotic condition without elaborate preliminaries. The subject acquires what may be called a habit of dissociation. A simple order from the hypnotizer is enough to throw the subject into the condition. Sometimes the habit is carried to such an extent that the subject is able to throw himself into the hypnotic condition. Such self-induced hypnosis is known as auto-hypnosis. The ability to produce the hypnotic state in the subject does not depend upon any peculiar powers on the part of the hypnotizer; it depends rather upon his ability so to influence his subject that the condition of partial sleep described shall be induced. The essential condition with which the subject himself must comply, in order to come under the influence of a hypnotizer, is that he concentrate his attention. The only persons who cannot be hypnotized are young children, idiots, and insane persons, all of whom are unable to concentrate attention. This statement effectually disposes of the popular belief that only weak-minded persons can be hypnotized. The most effective method of avoiding hypnosis is to scatter attention as much as possible over a great variety of objects.

Concentration of attention is always favorable to hypnosis and allied conditions. The audience which gives close attention to a speaker or performer is susceptible to a species of hypnosis; while, on the other hand, there is no danger of hypnosis in a distracted audience. The methods of inducing hypnosis have been accidentally discovered from time to time by performers who are then able to give striking exhibitions of their discovery. Many oriental jugglers begin their performance, the success of which undoubtedly depends upon their hypnotic influence over their audiences, with a dance in which the body of the performer is moved with a gradually increasing speed, which inevitably induces a gradually increased concentration of attention on the part of the observer. When this dance grows more and more rapid and more and more engaging to the attention, the observer is completely mastered and the main performance may be undertaken. The hypnotic influence of such a dance is very frequently augmented by the burning of incense, which has more or less of a narcotic effect upon the observers. In like manner, certain animals are probably drawn into a hypnotic state by the movement of snakes. This has frequently been reported in the case of birds and monkeys.

Various characteristics of the hypnotized subject. When the hypnotic state has been produced, the phenomena exhibited are of two distinct types. First, there is a suspension of certain activities, and, second, there is an abnormal heightening of other activities. This may be seen with reference to the reception of sensory stimulations. Certain stimulations are no longer received by the hypnotized subject. For this reason the condition has sometimes been used by savage tribes for surgical purposes, exactly as in modern life we use drugs which will produce a dissociation of the nervous system and thus prevent pain from excessive external stimulation. On the other hand, certain other senses may be opened to stimulation. A hypnotized subject may be wholly anæsthetic in his skin, while still retaining the ability to receive impressions through certain of his other senses. Indeed, the concentration of nervous activity in certain particular senses results in such a heightening of their ability to receive impressions that the subject may perform most astonishing feats of sensory receptivity. He may hear very faint sounds or he may see remote visual objects. It is to be noted that this hyperæsthesia of the senses is not so extraordinary as it would at first sight seem to be. We all become hyperæsthetic when we concentrate attention in any direction. If one is listening for an important signal or watching for some object which is of great importance to him, he will be using his nervous energy in the emphasized direction and will be correspondingly impervious to impressions from other sources. The conditions in hypnosis are merely exaggerations of those which appear in ordinary life.

Ideas not subjected to criticism in hypnosis. Turning from the sensory processes to the central processes, we find again that certain activities are entirely in abeyance, while others are much intensified. If, for example, it is suggested to a hypnotized subject that he is an animal instead of a human being, the suggested idea may take such large possession of him as to command his whole attention and guide his activity. If a normal individual is told that he is an animal, he immediately brings to bear upon the suggested idea a great variety of incompatible experiences, which make it clear that the statement is false and unacceptable. In the case of the hypnotized subject, very much as in the case of the dreamer, the corrective ideas, which constitute the fabric of normal life, are absent, so that the single idea takes full possession of the mind and commands belief as the accepted content of consciousness. This credulousness of the hypnotic consciousness is described by saying that the subject is very open to suggestion. Anything that is said to him will be accepted, and any form of interpretation of experience which is offered to him will be taken up without serious question and without any effort on his part to criticize the ideas which have been given him by the hypnotizer. Suggestibility has very frequently been emphasized to the exclusion of the converse fact that the hypnotized subject is quite incapable of subjecting any ideas to critical comparison. So also the positive increase in sensitivity has been the impressive fact; the diminution of sensibility has often been overlooked. The negative considerations are, however, essential to a complete understanding of the case, just as the negative considerations are of importance if we would understand the credulousness exhibited in dreams.

Dual personalities in hypnosis. The central nervous conditions which are induced in hypnosis are sometimes sufficiently unstable to produce the most complex phenomena. It is sometimes found that the dissociated parts of the cerebrum are not only dissociated from each other, but they are also, to a certain extent, capable of independent action. Thus, while one part of the cerebrum seems to be dealing with impressions received through the sense of hearing, another part may be engaged in responding to tactual impressions. Or, the case may be rendered even more complicated by the fact that the impressions coming from one ear seem to serve as stimulations for certain activities, while auditory impressions received on the opposite side of the body are effective in producing an entirely different set of experiences and responses. There result in such cases what are known as dual and multiple personalities. By personality, as the term is used in such cases, is meant any organized group or system of ideas and activities. The various groups of systematized activities and ideas which exist side by side in a hypnotized subject owe their separation to nervous and mental dissociation; each personality is, therefore, a relatively less complex system than that which exists when the whole cerebrum is acting as a single organ. The division of an individual into a number of systems of organization appears in other states than the hypnotic state, and it may result in certain permanent or certain temporary disruptions of personality, which have been noted in such stories as that of Dr. Jekyll and Mr. Hyde.

Dual personalities in other than hypnotic conditions. From time to time one reads of a case of lapse in memory which amounts to a dissociation of personality. A man forgets who he is or what business he has been following. He is sufficiently normal in his general organization to respond to a great variety of impressions in a regular fashion, but the complex structure of mental life breaks down and the man is only partly reconstructed in the second self. Tertiary and quaternary personalities may appear in all possible combinations. The secondary or tertiary personality may know its fellows, but may be itself quite forgotten. Several cases have been described in which personality *B* knows not only its own acts and emotions but also the acts and emotions of the other personality *A*. Sometimes *B* not only knows but heartily dislikes *A*. Sometimes two personalities exist simultaneously within the same body and seem to have separate lives and characters. The writer knew of a case of a young man who was the object of superstitious wonder in the village in which he lived, because he had two personalities. These two personalities knew each other and held long discussions with each other. Often, when they came to a turn in the road, they disagreed with each other as to the direction in which their body should move, and the passer-by could see the abnormal man mumbling an argument between his two selves.

Dual and multiple personalities analogous to the various selves of normal life. The details of such cases are baffling in the extreme, but nothing can be clearer from our earlier studies than the general formula of dissociation, with the added fact of partial organization around different centers. The matter becomes more intelligible if we remember that even in ordinary life there is a subdivision of experience into different systems. We distinguish, even in common parlance, between the business self, the social self, and so on. Each one of these selves is only partially related to the other systems of experience and forms of behavior. The man who is buried in the details of a business transaction is just as oblivious to considerations of a literary sort as the hypnotized subject is oblivious to a certain group of possible experiences. We do not call the ordinary absorption of the self in business a case of multiple personality, because the neglected personality in the case of the business man is not so remote but that it can be immediately called out, if he turns his attention to some literary considerations. The normal individual is capable of transferring his attention and interest from center to center according as the external environment demands, while the hypnotized subject or abnormal person is, through dissociation, quite incapable of a rapid transfer of attention or of correlating the different phases of his experience.

Hypnosis a transient condition, insanity permanent. We shall return to the discussion of multiple personality under the general head of insanity, for the fundamental distinction between insanity and hypnosis is to be found in the degree of permanency which is attained in the former state, as contrasted with the more transient character of the hypnotic condition.

Movements sometimes normal in hypnosis, because the lower centers are not dissociated. In the meantime, it is necessary to add a few comments on the motor activities of hypnotized subjects. These motor activities frequently exhibit little or no departure from the ordinary coördinations of normal life. The hypnotized subject is capable of walking, often of writing or producing certain other complex forms of movement. Such continuation of the bodily co-ordinations is explicable on the ground that the lower centers of the nervous system are not dissociated by the changes that take place in the higher centers. Whenever the higher centers are able to send stimulations to the lower centers, these lower centers are capable of responding with their usual degree of coördination. The lack of organization is exhibited rather in the inability to maintain a normal balance between the various centers which call the lower centers into play. It is to be noted, however, that the movements of hypnotized subjects sometimes indicate by their clumsiness and lack of precision that the disintegrating force has affected certain of the motor channels as well as the central organizations. This is especially true when the attempted act involves a complicated coördination.

Insanity a permanent form of disorganization, introduced in many cases by dissociation and settling into an abnormal reorganization. As has been indicated in the earlier paragraphs, insanity is a form of relatively permanent dissociation. Certain forms of delirium, which have been referred to before, furnish the best introduction to the study of insanity. In delirium the subject is so highly excitable that the normal avenues of stimulation and discharge are for the time being completely disrupted, and the currents of nervous activity and the corresponding facts of experience are dissociated. As delirium disappears and gives place to the usual intensity of nervous activity the individual may return to the earlier normal condition or, on the other hand, there may be left behind a permanent abnormal state, because the earlier forms of organization are not fully restored. One of the most characteristic symptoms of all forms of insanity is found to be the existence of certain hallucinations or fundamental abnormalities in the subject's world of ideas. The insane person believes himself to be Julius Cæsar or some Biblical character, or even some divinity. There is no difficulty in recognizing the fact that the idea of transferred identity may come into the mind of any normal individual. It is, however, in the case of a normal individual immediately criticized and abandoned, because of its incompatibility with the person's general knowledge of the world and his place in it. When the compact organization which has been built up in normal experiences has once given way, and the idea that one is Julius Cæsar or some other character has presented itself as a center of reconstruction in the midst of the resulting chaos, there is a possibility of an abnormal reorganization of experience. The individual is no longer restrained by that system of ideas which has been laboriously built up through contact with the world; the result is that the whole later ideational life of the individual loses its adaptation to the real world. The characteristic fact in certain cases of insanity is, accordingly, not describable in simple terms of dissociation; it is rather to be defined in terms of dissociation with an abnormal association or integration following upon the breaking down of the normal system. In other cases, disintegration is the more obvious fact. The individual simply loses control of his ideas, and his mind seems to be flooded with an incoherent mass of experience. His words reflect this incoherency of ideas, and his behavior indicates an absence of self-control. Such disintegrated forms of consciousness and behavior commonly appear in the last stages of almost every kind of insanity, even where there has been for a time reorganization about an abnormal center.

Types of Dissociation

FREDERIC LYMAN WELLS, *Mental Adjustments*, 156-157 (Appleton, 1922)

Every one who is to speak of dissociated mental functions must posit something from which the dissociation takes place. What is the dissociated function dissociated from? A simple kind of dissociation occurs in hysteria, where the patient does not feel a touch upon some particular portion of the body. That portion is said to be anesthetic. We call it so because "he," the patient, does not feel it. Sensation is present, because there is some involuntary reaction to the touch, but "he" does not feel it; it is dissociated from "him," not integrated with "him." The sum of all memories that this word "him" implies in this case, is the mental system from which dissociation, as we shall here discuss it, takes place. A convenient name for this system is, the *main personality*.[1] In the writings of Janet and Prince, one finds *personal consciousness*. The two are used interchangeably; either form is used that seems the clearer for the purpose in hand.

This chapter describes the dissociation of mental processes from the main personality, with some other phenomena not strictly of this class, but obviously related to it. These dissociations are of several kinds. We have . . . a possible example of the first kind, in a breakdown of the digestive system. Here a process is dissociated not only from the personal consciousness (as it is normally), but also from the main tendency to survival. We shall meet a few other examples. In such cases, the distinguishing feature is the dissociation of some involuntary or unconscious function of the organism. Second, the ability to move one side of the body, or the lower half of the body, or to make the movements of speaking, may be lost. It is like a paralysis of the muscles that make these movements. Certain movements of these muscles are lost to the control of the main personality. They are dissociated from it. Third, a patient whose retina is unaffected may be unable to see objects outside the direct line of vision. Though his skin is healthy, he may be unable to feel a touch at some special spot. When this happens, it is a form of sensation, instead of a movement, that is dissociated from the main personality. Fourth, *ideas* may manifest themselves in a great variety of ways, without the main personality's being aware of the ideas. Prince's patient of the bell-towers gave a fair example of

---

[1] Introduced in this sense by August Hoch.

this, when her hand wrote automatically something not in the awareness of the then dominating personality. Fifth, the main personality may lose control of the organism, which is then dominated by a system of ideas split off from it. (Somnambulisms, fugues, multiple personality.) Sixth, the main personality may be aware of the occurrence of a mental process, but not recognize the existence of the process as a part of the main personality. (Externalization, projection.) For example, a patient complains that the "voices" hurl insults at him. Of course, the voices come from nobody but himself; but he does not recognize the voices as coming from himself.

CHAPTER VII

MEMORY IN RELATION TO ABNORMAL PSYCHOLOGY

Memory, as fundamental to all branches of psychology, is touched upon so frequently throughout this volume, that neither its general aspects nor its abnormalities will have extended treatment in the present chapter.[1] There are a few features, however, of the processes of impression or learning, of retention or conservation, and of reproduction or revival, that require attention at this point.

An Understanding of Memory

MORTON PRINCE, *The Unconscious*, 1-3, 52, 134-135, 131-132, 230, 238-239 (copyright, 1921, by The Macmillan Company); reprinted by permission

If we consider memory as a *process,* and not as specific phases of consciousness, we shall find that it is an essential factor in the mechanisms underlying a large variety of phenomena of normal and abnormal life. These phenomena include those of both mind and body of a kind not ordinarily conceived of as manifestations of memory. . . . What we ordinarily and conventionally have in mind when we speak of memory is the conscious thought of some past mental experience. But when we conceive of memory as a process we have in mind the whole mechanism through the working of which this past experience is *registered, conserved,* and *reproduced,* whether such reproduction be in consciousness or below the surface of consciousness.

Memory is usually looked upon as something that pertains solely to consciousness. Such a conception is defensible if the meaning of the term is restricted to those facts alone which come within our conscious experience. But when we consider the mechanism by which a particular empirical fact of this kind is introduced into consciousness we find that this conception is inadequate. We find

---

[1] A most comprehensive single reference on the abnormalities of memory is Pierre Janet, *The Mental State of Hystericals,* 75-116.

203

then that we are obliged to regard conscious memory as only the end result of a process and, in order to account for this end result, to assume other stages in the process which are not phases of consciousness. Though the end result is a reproduction of the ideas which constituted the previous conscious experience, this reproduction is not the whole process.

More than this, the conscious experience is not the only experience that may be reproduced by the process, nor is the end result always and necessarily a state of consciousness. *Conscious memory is only a particular type of memory.* The same process may terminate in purely unconscious or physiological effects, or what may be called physiological memory to distinguish it from conscious memory. Along with the revived ideas and their feeling tones there may be a revival of the physiological experiences, or processes, which originally accompanied them; such as secretion of sweat, saliva and gastric juice, the contraction and dilatation of the blood vessels, the inhibition or excitation of the heart, lungs and other viscera, the contraction of muscles, etc. These visceral mechanisms, being originally elements in a complex process and accompaniments of the idea, may be reproduced along with the conscious memory, and even without conscious memory. As this physiological complex is an acquired experience it is entitled to be regarded as memory so far as its reproduction is the end result of the same kind of process or mechanism as that which reproduces ideas.

Then, again, investigations into the subconscious have shown that the original experience may be reproduced subconsciously without rising into awareness. . . . It is not difficult to show that perceptions of the environment which *never even entered the fringe of the personal consciousness, i. e., of which the individual was never even dimly aware,* may be conserved. Indeed, the demonstration of their conservation is one of the important pieces of evidence for the occurrence of coconscious perception and, therefore, of the splitting of consciousness. . . .

From this you will easily understand that while, as you have seen from concrete observations, we can have conservation of experiences without memory (reproduction) we cannot have memory without conservation. Three factors are essential for memory, and memory may fail from the failure of any one of them. Unless an experience is registered in some form there will be nothing to preserve, and memory will fail because of lack of registration. If the experience has been registered, memory may fail, owing to the registration having faded out, so to speak, either with time or from some other reason; that is, nothing having been conserved, nothing

can be reproduced. Finally, though an experience has been registered and conserved, memory may still fail, owing to failure of reproduction. The neurographic records must be made active once
more, stimulated into an active process, in order that the original
experience may be recalled, i. e., reproduced. Thus what we call
conscious memory is the final result of a process involving the three
factors, registration, conservation, and reproduction. . . .

Neurograms. Whatever may be the exact nature of the theoretical alterations left in the brain by life's experiences they have received various generic terms; more commonly "brain residua," and
"brain dispositions." I have been in the habit of using the term
neurograms to characterize these brain records. Just as telegram,
Marconigram, and phonogram precisely characterize the form in
which the physical phenomena which correspond to our (verbally or
scripturally expressed) thoughts, are recorded and conserved, so
neurogram precisely characterizes my conception of the form in
which a system of brain processes corresponding to thoughts and
other mental experiences is recorded and conserved.[1] . . .

There is every reason to believe that intrinsically *there is no
essential difference between those physiological dispositions and
activities of the lower nervous centers* (*subcortical ganglia and
spinal cord*), *which condition and determine unconscious behavior,
and those dispositions and activities of the higher centers—the cortex—which condition and determine both conscious and unconscious
behavior.* The former are undoubtedly innate in that they are primarily conditioned by inherited anatomical and physiological pre-
arrangements of neurons and the latter are preëminently acquired
through experience although probably not wholly so. . . .

---

[1] Of course it must not be overlooked that such neurograms are pure
theoretical conceptions, and have never been demonstrated by objective
methods of physical research. They stand in exactly the same position as
the atoms and molecules and ions and electrons of physics and chemistry,
and the "antibodies" and complements" of bacteriology. No one has seen
any of these postulates of science. They are only inferred. All are theoretical concepts; but they are necessary concepts if the phenomena of
physical, chemical, and bacteriological science are to be intelligible. The
same may be said for brain changes if the phenomena of brain and mind
are to be intelligible.—*Ibid.,* 132.

Richard Semon (Die Mneme, 1908) has adopted the term Engramm with
much the same signification that I have given to Neurogram, excepting
that Engramm has a much wider meaning and connotation. It is not
limited to nervous tissue, but includes the residual changes held by some
to be left in all irritable living substances after stimulation. All such
substances are therefore capable of memory in a wide sense (Mneme).—
Ibid., 131 n.

That the subcortical centers are capable of memory seems to have been shown for the first time by Rothmann's dog. This mindless animal proved to be capable of a certain amount of education. It learned to avoid hitting against objects, and to do certain tricks —jumping over a hurdle and following on its hind legs a stool upon which its fore feet were placed as the stool was dragged forward. "In the perfection of all these performances the influence of practice was easily recognized." This means, if the interpretation given is correct, that new dispositions and new connections may be acquired within the lower centers *without the intervention of the integrating influence of the cortex* or conscious intelligence.[2] This is an important contribution for apparently the attempt to educate brainless animals had not been previously made, and their capability for education demonstrated. [Of course Rothmann's experiment needs to be confirmed. M. P.]

The important bearing which this fact has upon this discussion is that it shows that unconscious processes are capable of memory, that is physiological memory.

Conditions of the Memorial Functions

MADISON BENTLEY, *The Field of Psychology*, 258-259 (Appleton, 1924)

Our experimental knowledge of many of the conditions of memory (*e.g.,* the amount perceived, the organization of the primary incorporation, the perceptual constellation and train; sensory clearness, context, intent to remember, practice, fatigue and so on) is still imperfect; but it is certain that all these matters do affect both the fidelity of memory and the rate and amount of true memorial recall. We know quite definitely that time affects the memory both by way of transformation and by way of decay and disintegration. The experiments of Philippe have demonstrated the tendency for the specific memory to be transformed in the direction of a stock type, *i.e.,* of some neutral and undated acquisition which, because of its fixity, is more useful than the particularized memory. A similar change in memories is commonly induced by verbal description. When an acquaintance strikes us as "tall" or as "homely" or as "awkward," our declining memories of him are likely to be changed to conform to the stock "tall" or "homely" or

---

[2] Dr. Morgan in his work, "Instinct and Experience," 1912, published before Rothmann's observations, remarks that this "is not inherently improbable" although it had not as yet been demonstrated.

"awkward" man. A part of our surprise upon noting that a long absent acquaintance is not exactly as we had remembered him is due to the application of these verbal epithets which are apt to fit too loosely the individual case. Again, there is some evidence that our simpler memories at least (as to colors and of grays) suffer modification through similar perceptual experiences subsequent to their "registration." If that is true, then a remembered medium gray surface would tend to grow lighter when the memory-interval was filled with light-gray perceptions and darker when filled with dark-gray perceptions. The wonder is that the bodily residues of perception, being various and multitudinous, do not constantly cross and commingle and so cancel all possibility of the dated and individualized memory.

Finally, the appearance of any memorial function is dependent upon appropriate conditions at the time of recall. Some men have maintained that there are spontaneous memories; that memories come of their own initiative without waiting for favorable conditions. Herbart believed that ideas were forces which tended to thrust themselves into existence and were only barred from "consciousness" by counter and inhibiting forces keeping them down. Fouillée, the French moralist, later wrote a psychology of *idées forces*,[1] and this doctrine has recently been revived in a modified form as "perseveration," a term which stands for a periodic strengthening of cerebral or mental residues, called "perseverative tendencies." These tendencies have been supposed to bring imaginal processes spontaneously into existence, and so, under favorable circumstances, to lead to memory. No one of these forms of spontaneous memories is sufficiently supported by empirical evidence to be credible. It is likely that the initiation of the memorial functions always needs a push; always needs some favoring circumstance within the central nervous system to set it going.

Emotional Memories

A

MORTON PRINCE, *The Unconscious*, 103-106, 414-415, 418 (copyright, 1921, by The Macmillan Company); reprinted by permission

There is an analogous class of phenomena which ought to be mentioned among the possible data bearing upon the theory of memory, although too much weight cannot be placed upon them

---

[1] A. Fouillée, *La psychologie des idées forces* (1893), 2 vols.

as their interpretation is not wholly clear. I will discuss them in detail later in connection with the phenomena of the emotions. They are certain *emotional phenomena* which are attributed by some writers to ideas in a state of conservation. It has been demonstrated that ideas to which strong feeling tones are attached are accompanied by such physiological effects as disturbance of respiration, of the heart's action, of the vaso-motor system, of the secretions, etc., and also by certain *galvanic phenomena* which are due to the diminution of the electrical resistance of the body, probably caused by increased secretion of sweat.[1]

Now the point is that such phenomena are sometimes experimentally obtained in connection with certain test words [2] spoken to the subject experimented upon, although he has no recollection of any incident in his life which could have given an emotional tone to the word and, therefore, can give no explanation of the physical reaction. By various technical methods, however, memories of a forgotten emotional experience in which the idea (represented by the word) plays a part and through which it derived its emotional tone are resurrected. I have been able to obtain such reactions from test words which investigation showed referred to the incidents of terrifying dreams which were *completely forgotten* in the waking state. When the test word was given, the subject might, for instance, exhibit a respiratory disturbance—a sudden gasp—without conscious knowledge of its significance, and the galvanometer, with which the subject was in circuit, would show a wide deflection. Recovery of the dream in hypnosis would explain the meaning of the emotional disturbance excited by the word. The interpretation which has been put upon such phenomena is that the residua of the forgotten experience are "struck" by the test word. As the forgotten experience originally included the emotion and its physiological reaction, so the residua are linked by association to the emotional mechanism and when stimulated function as a subconscious process and excite the reaction. If this interpretation, strongly held by some, be correct, the phenomena are important for the support they give to the theory of conservation. They would indicate that conscious experiences must be conserved in a

---

[1] According to recent researches of Sïdis in conjunction with Kalmus, and later with Nelson ("The Nature and Causation of the Galvanic Phenomenon," *Psychol. Rev.*, March, 1910) similar galvanic phenomena under similar conditions may be caused by the *generation* of an electric current within the body.

[2] The test word (e. g., boat, stone, hat, etc.) of course represents an idea which may have various associations in the mind of the subject.

very specific subconscious form, one that is capable, without becoming conscious memory, of exciting the physiological apparatus of the emotions in a manner identical with that of conscious emotional ideas. They are open, however, to a simpler explanation, whether more probable or not: namely, that it is not the residua of the forgotten experience which unconsciously excite the physiological reaction, but the auditory symbol, the test word itself. The symbol having been once associated with the emotional reaction, it afterwards of itself, through a short circuit so to speak, suffices to induce the reaction, though the origin of the association has been forgotten and, therefore, the subject is in entire ignorance of the reason for the strong feeling manifestation. On the other hand, in some instances test words associated with emotional experiences which *originally* were entirely coconscious and *had never entered conscious awareness at all* give the reactions in question.[3] As coconscious memories of such experiences can be demonstrated it would seem at first sight as if under such conditions the word-reactions must come from a true subconscious process—the subconscious memory. And yet even here it is difficult to eliminate absolutely the possibility of the second interpretation. There are, however, a large number of emotional phenomena occurring in pathological conditions which can only be intelligibly interpreted as being due to the residua of previously conscious experiences functioning as a subconscious process. These phenomena we shall have occasion to review in succeeding lectures. They are too complex to enter upon at this stage.

Aside, then, from these word-reactions we have a sufficient number of other phenomena, such as I have cited, which indicate that conscious experiences when conserved must persist in a form capable of exciting purely physiological reactions without the experiences themselves rising into consciousness again as memory. The form must also be one which permits of their functioning as intelligent processes although not within the conscious field of awareness of the moment. . . .

We ought not, however, to be too sweeping in our generalizations and go further than the facts warrant. We are not justified in concluding that the linking of an affect to an idea always includes a subconscious mechanism. On the contrary, as I have previously said, probably in the great majority of such experiences, aside from obsessions, no such mechanism is required to explain the facts. . . .

---

[3] Morton Prince and Frederick Peterson: "Experiments in Psycho-Galvanic Reactions from Coconscious (Subconscious) Ideas in a Case of Multiple Personality," *Jour. Abn. Psychol.*, April-May, 1908.

It is quite possible, if not extremely probable, that in the simpler types, at least, of the emotional complexes, the association between the idea and affect becomes so firmly established that the conscious idea alone, without the coöperation of a subconscious process, is sufficient to awake the emotion; just as in Pawlow's dogs the artificially formed association between a tactile stimulus and the salivary glands is sufficient to excite the glands to activity, or as in human beings the idea of a ship by pure association may determine fear and nausea, the sound of running water by the force of association may excite the bladder reflex, or an ocular stimulus the so-called hay fever complex. So in word-association reactions, when a word is accompanied by an affect-reaction the word itself may be sufficient to excite the reaction without assuming that an "unconscious complex has been struck." The total mechanism of the process we are investigating must be determined in each case for itself.

B

H. L. HOLLINGWORTH, *The Psychology of Functional Neuroses*, 44-45 (Appleton, 1920)

[A] case is described by Haberman as follows: "A neurotic patient was brought to me because of persistent vomiting spells, at first but occasional, later very frequent. She had been 'pumped,' lavaged, dieted, physicked, and treated with innumerable drugs. Nothing had helped. My analysis brought out the fact that the parents of the girl had wished her to marry a certain man who was physically offensive to her. The girl objected and the parents persisted. There were arguments, quarrels, scenes. The man was disgusting to her. One night he called and the girl felt nauseated. After he left she vomited. Expecting him the following evening, she vomited before he came. Thereafter she had vomiting spells every time the man was expected or called. Even thinking about him brought on the attacks. . . ."

An adult patient is described as having attended the opera on one occasion after a bilious attack. "On looking over the balcony he became so dizzy that he presently had to leave. The week after, this time not bilious, he attended the opera again, and, looking over the balcony suddenly became dizzy again, and felt so uncomfortable that he could not sit through the performance. This state of affairs became so permanent that he finally had to give up the very desirable seat in the balcony" (Haberman, "Probing the Mind," *Med. Rec.*, Dec. 1, 1917). The case is adequately described by saying that the single detail (sitting in the balcony) reinstated the total reaction that had previously been made to the more complex situation of being bilious, upset, sitting in the front seat at the opera, in the balcony, and peering over the railing. In a still more exaggerated form simply "going to the opera" or "hearing an opera air on the phonograph" might reinstate the same complete symptom picture.

CHAPTER VIII

MEANING AND ITS SIGNIFICANCE

The Nature of Meaning

A

A. WOHLGEMUTH, *A Critical Examination of Psycho-Analysis*, 22 (London: George Allen & Unwin, Ltd., 1923)

Suppose a man sees an orange for the first time in his life. It is for him at first only a coloured spherical body. He learns its name, and on handling the object he becomes aware of its temperature, of the relative smoothness of its surface, of its elasticity, and its characteristic smell. He learns that it is a fruit, on peeling it notices its structure, and finally he discovers its taste. Seeing an orange on some subsequent occasion all these details, then, having once been conscious processes, may come back, or can be brought back to consciousness, i. e. the visual experience of an orange will occasion conscious processes similar to previous ones, the tactile, thermal, olfactory, gustatory, and other experiences may be "recalled," "revived," or "remembered." On a later occasion the name "orange" need not bring back all these details in their entirety, but the word has "acquired a meaning," it simply means an orange.

How are we now to represent to ourselves the neural correlates of this *Meaning?* I conceive it in this way. To all those manifold psychic experiences that occur on those occasions when new facts about the orange were learnt there correspond physiological processes in numbers of neurone-groups, and connections between these groups were established; with the cessation of the physiological and corresponding psychical processes the neurone-groups and their connections remained modified, and *dispositions* to be more easily excited together were established; associations were formed, as the psychologist would say. When, then, on this future occasion the word orange is seen or heard, all these groups of neurones are, owing to the said formed associations, set, more or less, in an

212

incipient state of excitation, and to them there exist, then, corresponding psychic processes of small intensity, clearness, etc., which constitute the acquired meaning of the word orange.

B

ROBERT CHENAULT GIVLER, *The Ethics of Hercules*, 22-24, 20-21 (Knopf, 1924)

Certain it is, at least, that the more meaningful or significant any word is, the more does it stir up latent tendencies to action throughout our whole organism. Political and religious slogans are telling examples of this. "Great is Diana of the Ephesians!" "Remember the Maine!" "For God, for Country, and for Yale!" have been for some persons phrases of the maximal philosophic content. Moreover, the same word may arouse different meanings (or action-patterns) in different people, depending not only on how the word is spoken, but also on the mood of the auditor. It is a matter of common observation that the shout of "Fire!" calls forth by no means the same responses from an insured landlord as it evokes from an uninsured tenant, while the mention of *water* will stimulate one sort of reflex action in a thirsty man, and quite another sort in a man who has just been rescued from drowning.

It is plain, then, that if physiological science has achieved the least light upon the problems of psychology, the meaning which any word or phrase possesses is not something that the sound of the word or its written symbol is endowed with, or something that filters through from any Platonic realm of ideas, but the meaning of any word is given to it by the person who speaks or hears it. Moreover, this endowment of meaning is implicit in the arousal of action tendencies [1] at the time when the word is spoken or heard. In the example recently cited, the word "fire" had a different meaning for the insured landlord from what it had for the uninsured tenant

---

[1] Dr. George W. Crile has coined the appropriate phrase "action-pattern" to describe the mechanism involved in cases just cited. Crile's "action-pattern" is, indeed, practically identical with Holt's "specific response," and with Titchener's "motor set," of which phrases the latter two are to-day familiar to most students of psychology. Briefly, this action-pattern is simply a more or less fixed way in which some part of the body produces a movement. It depends principally upon the physical structure of the part, as well as upon its muscle and nerve supply, and secondly upon the habits of movement which external stimuli have repeatedly produced in it.

because the habits of precaution which the former had acquired established a different motor attitude toward fire than did the procrastination of the latter. Consequently, the shouting and the conflagration were stimuli in the presence of which the landlord could be calm, while the tenant could not.

The application of this principle of the dependence of meaning upon action-patterns extends, however, to other situations than those in which emotional riots are observable. Indeed, we undertake to say that even such plain, concrete words as *basket, horse,* and *river* have a meaning because they arouse us to motor activities of one sort or another. It may well be, of course, that we start to think of a basket in terms of its color, or shape, or its cost; and of a horse in like terms; while we think of a river only in connection with its height during seasons of drought or flood: but eventually the basket will, by implying *receptacle,* lead in our imagination to the acts of filling and emptying; while the horse will be finally pulling our loads or carrying our weight on his back; and the river will be either waded or swum by us, or become related to our necessities or pastimes (our habits) in some other manner. And when we thus develop a specific action-pattern toward such an object, we are said to know what it *means.*

C

MORTON PRINCE, *The Unconscious,* 321-326, 328 (copyright, 1921, by The Macmillan Company); reprinted by permission

As a result of previous experiences various associations have been organized with ideas and these complexes form the setting or the "context" (Titchener) which gives ideas meaning. As the secondary images give meaning to sensations to form ideas (or perceptions), so these associated complexes as settings give meaning to ideas. This setting in more general terms may be regarded as the attitude of mind, point of view, interest, etc. Just as the context in a printed sentence gives meaning to a given word, and determines which of two or more ideas it is meant to be the sign of, so in the process of all perceptions the associated ideas give meaning to the perception. Indeed it is probable that the context as a process determines what images shall become incorporated with sensations to form the nucleus of the perception. . . .

The idea horse [1] as the content of consciousness includes more

---

[1] I intentionally do not here say idea *of* a horse because the use of the preposition (while, of course, correctly used to distinguish horse as an

than the primary and secondary sensory images which constitute a perception of an animal with four legs distinguished anatomically from other animals: The idea includes the meaning of a particular kind of animal possessing certain functions, useful for particular purposes and occupying a particular place in civilization, etc. We are distinctly conscious of this meaning; and although we may abstract more or less successfully the visual image of the animal from the meaning, and attend to the former alone, the result is an artifact. Likewise we may as an artifice abstract, to a large degree, the meaning from the image, keeping the latter in the background, and attend to the meaning.

That meaning—just as much as the sensory image of an object—is part of the conscious content of an idea becomes apparent at once, the moment the setting becomes altered and an object is collocated with a new set of experiences (knowledge regarding it). X, for example, has been known to the world as a pious, god-fearing, moral man, a teacher of the Christian religion. My perception of him, so far as made up of images, is, properly speaking, that which distinguishes him anatomically from other men of my acquaintance, that by which I recognize him as X and not as Y. But my perception also has a distinctly conscious meaning, that of a Christian man. This meaning also distinguishes him in his qualities from other men. Now it transpires to every one's astonishment that X is a foul, cruel, murderer of women—a Jack-the-Ripper. My perception of him is the same but it has acquired an entirely different meaning. A bestial, villainous meaning has replaced the Christian meaning. So almost all objects have different meanings in different persons' minds, or at different times in the same person's mind, according to the settings (experiences) with which they are col-

---

idea from a material horse, or the former as a particular idea among ideas in general) has led, as it seems to me, insidiously to specious reasoning. Thus Mr. Hoernlé (Image, Idea and Meaning, *Mind*, January, 1907) argues that every idea has a meaning because every idea is an idea *of* some thing. Although this is true in a descriptive sense, psychologically idea-of-a-horse is a compound term and an imagined horse. The idea itself is horse. The speciousness of the reasoning appears when we substitute horse for idea; then the phrase would read, a "horse is always a horse of something." I agree, of course, that every idea has a meaning, but not to this particular reasoning by which the conclusion is reached, as when, for example, Mr. Hoernlé when traversing James' theory cites "image *of* the breakfast table" to denote that the breakfast table is the meaning of the image. The image *is* the (imagined) breakfast table. They are not different things as are leg and chair in the phrase, "leg of the chair," where chair plainly gives the meaning to leg.

located.   My perception of A has the meaning of physician, while one of his family perceives him as father or husband.   My perception of a snake, it may be, has the meaning of a loathsome, venomous animal, while a naturalist's perception may be that of a vertebrate representing a certain stage of evolution, and a psychologist holding certain theories may perceive it with a meaning given by those theories, viz.: as a sexual symbol.

This fact of meaning becomes still more obvious when we reflect that the meaning of a perception, as of A's personality as a physician or father, may occupy the focus of attention while the images of his face, voice, etc., may sink into the background.

Every one is agreed then that every idea or combination of ideas has "meaning" of some sort.   Even nonsense syllables have in a psychological sense some meaning, which may be an alliteration of sound, or a symbolism of nonsense (e. g., "fol-de-rol-di-rol-dol-day") or as suitable tests for psychological experiments.   I am speaking now, of course, of meaning as dealt with by psychology as a content of consciousness, and not as dealt with by logic.   Every one also will probably agree that the content of an idea is a composite of sensory elements (images) and meaning—I would like to say of perception and meaning; but the use of two abstract terms is likely to lead to a juggling with words by turning attention away from the concrete facts for which the terms stand, and by connoting a sharp distinction between perception and meaning which, as I observe the facts, does not hold.   Indeed the common though useful habit of psychologists of treating meaning as an abstract symbol without specific reference to those elements of the content of consciousness for which it stands has, it seems to me, led to considerable confusion of thought. . . . If meaning is a part of the content of consciousness it must be analyzable into specific conscious elements (images, thoughts, words, feelings or what not) representing to some extent and in some way past experiences. . . .

The difference between that which we call perception and that which we call meaning is one of complexity.   The less complex we call perception, the more complex, meaning.   Both are determined by past experiences the residua of which are the settings.

Meaning, Setting, and the Fringe of Consciousness

MORTON PRINCE, *The Unconscious*, 338-342, 344-350, 174-175, 350-351 (copyright, 1921, by The Macmillan Company) ; reprinted by permission

The content of the fringe of consciousness considered as a subconscious zone. It is obvious that all the past experiences which originate the meaning of an idea cannot be in consciousness at a given moment. If I carefully introspect my imaginal perception or idea of an object, say of a politician, I do not find in my consciousness all the elements which have given me my viewpoint or attitude of mind toward him—the meaning of my idea of him as a great statesman or a demagogue, whichever it be—and yet it may not be difficult, by referring to my memory, to find the past experiences which have furnished the setting which gives this viewpoint. Very little of all these past experiences can be in the content of consciousness, and much less in the focus of attention, at any given moment, nevertheless I cannot doubt that these experiences really determined the meaning of my idea, for if challenged I proceed to recite this conserved knowledge. And so it is with everyone who defends the validity of the meaning of his ideas.

The question at once comes to mind in the case of any given perception, how much of past experience (associated ideas) is in consciousness at any given moment as the setting which provides the meaning?

That the meaning must be in consciousness is obvious; else the term "meaning" would have no meaning—it would be sheer nonsense to talk of ideas having meaning. As I have said, the meaning may be in the focus of attention or it may be in the fringe or background according to the point of interest. If in the focus of attention, meaning plainly may, synchronously or successively, include ideas of quite a large number of past experiences, but if in the background it may be another matter. In this case it may be held, and probably in many instances quite rightly, that meaning is a short summary of past experiences, or summing up in the form of a symbol, and that this summary or symbol is in the focus of attention or in the fringe of awareness, i. e., is clearly or dimly conscious. . . .

When speaking colloquially of the content of consciousness we have in mind those ideas or components of ideas—elements of thought—which are in the focus of attention, and therefore that of which we are more or less vividly aware. If you were asked to state what was in your mind at a given moment it is the vivid elements, upon which your attention was focused, that you would describe. But, as everyone knows, these do not constitute the whole field of consciousness at any given moment. Besides these there is in the background of the mind, outside the focus, *a conscious margin or fringe* of varying extent (*consisting of sensations, perceptions, and even thoughts*) *of which you are only dimly aware.* It is a sort of twilight zone in which the contents are so slightly illuminated by awareness as to be scarcely recognizable. The contents of this zone are readily forgotten owing to their having been outside the focus of attention; but much can be recalled if an effort to do so (retrospection) is made immediately after any given moment's experience. Much can only be recalled by the use of special technical methods of investigation. I believe that the more thoroughly this wonderful region is explored the richer it will be found to be in conscious elements.

It must not be thought that because we are only dimly aware of the contents of this twilight zone therefore the individual elements lack definiteness and positive reality. To do so is to confuse the awareness of a certain something with that something itself. To so think would be like thinking that, because we do not distinctly recognize objects in the darkness, therefore they are but shadowy forms without substance. When, in states of abstraction or hypnosis, the ideas of this fringe of attention are recalled, as often is easily done, they are remembered as *very definite, real, conscious elements,* and the memory of them is as vivid as that of most thoughts. That these marginal ideas are not "vivid" at the time of their occurrence means simply that they are not in such dynamic relations with the whole content of consciousness as to be the focus of awareness or attention. What sort of relations are requisite for "awareness" is an unsolved problem. It seems to be a matter not only of synthesis but of dynamic relations within the synthesis. . . .

Amnesia develops very rapidly for the contents of the twilight region, as I have already stated, and this renders their recognition difficult.[1]

In favorable subjects memory of that portion of the content of consciousness which is commonly called the fringe can be recovered in abstraction and hypnosis. In these states valuable information can be obtained regarding the content of consciousness at any given

[1] The development of amnesia seems to be inversely proportionate to the degree of awareness, provided there are no other dissociating factors, such as an emotional complex.

previous moment,[2] and this information reveals that there were present in the fringe conscious states of which the subject was never aware, or of which he is later ignorant owing to amnesia. I have studied the fringe of consciousness by this method in a number of subjects. A number of years ago *a systematic study* of the field of the content of consciousness outside the focus of awareness, including not only the fringe but what may be called the ultra-marginal (subconscious) zone, was made in a very favorable subject (Miss B.), and the general results were given in an address on the "Problems of Abnormal Psychology" [3] at the Congress of Arts and Sciences held in St. Louis (1904). I may be permitted to quote that summary here. The term "secondary consciousness" is used in this passage to designate the fringe and ultra-marginal (subconscious) zone.

"A systematic examination was made of the personal consciousness in hypnosis regarding the perceptions and content of the secondary consciousness during definite moments, of which the events were prearranged or otherwise known, the subject not being in absent-mindedness. It is not within the scope of an address of this sort to give the details of these observations, but in this connection I may state briefly a summary of the evidence, reserving the complete observation for future publication. It was found that—

"1. A large number of perceptions—visual, auditory, tactile, and thermal images, and sometimes emotional states—occurred outside of the personal consciousness and, therefore, the subject was not conscious of them when awake. The visual images were particularly those of peripheral vision, such as the extra-conscious [marginal or ultra-marginal] perception of a person in the street who was not recognized by the personal waking consciousness; and the perception of objects intentionally placed in the field of peripheral vision and not perceived by the subject, whose attention was held in conversation. Auditory images of passing carriages, of voices, footsteps, etc., thermal images of heat and cold from the body were similarly found to exist extra-consciously, and to be entirely unknown to the personal waking consciousness.

"2. As to the content of the concomitant (dissociated) ideas, it appeared, by the testimony of the hypnotic self, that as compared with those of the waking consciousness the secondary ideas were

---

[2] This is due to the well-known fact (demonstrated in a large variety of phenomena) that ideas dissociated from the personal consciousness awake may become synthesized as memories with this same consciousness in hypnosis.

[3] See *Proceedings*, also *Psychol. Rev.*, March-May, 1905.

quite limited. They were, as is always the experience of the subject, made up for the most part of emotions (e. g., annoyances), and sensations (visual, auditory, and tactile images of a room, of particular persons, people's voices, etc.). They were not combined into a logical proposition, though in using words to describe them it is necessary to so combine them and therefore give them a rather artificial character as 'thoughts.' It is questionable whether the word 'thoughts' may be used to describe mental states of this kind, and the word was used by the hypnotic self subject to this qualification. Commonly, I should infer, a succession of such 'thoughts' may arise, but each is for the most part limited to isolated emotions and sensorial images and lacks the complexity and synthesis of the waking mentation.

"3. The memories, emotions, and perceptions of which the subject is not conscious when awake are remembered in hypnosis and described. The thoughts of which the subject is conscious when awake are those which are concentrated on what she is doing. The others, of which she is not conscious, are a sort of side-thoughts. These are not logically connected among themselves, are weak, and have little influence on the personal (chief) train of thought. Now, although when awake the subject is conscious of some thoughts and not of others, both kinds keep running into one another and therefore the conscious and the subconscious are constantly uniting, disuniting, and interchanging. *There is no hard and fast line between the conscious and the subconscious, for at times what belongs to one passes into the other, and vice versa.* The waking self is varying the grouping of its thoughts all the time in such a way as to be continually including and excluding the subconscious thoughts. The personal pronoun 'I,' or, when spoken to, 'you,' applied equally to her waking self and to her hypnotic self, *but these terms were not applicable to her subconscious thoughts, which were not self-conscious.* For convenience of terminology it was agreed to arbitrarily call the thoughts of which the subject is conscious when awake the *waking consciousness,* and the thoughts of which when awake she is not conscious the *secondary consciousness.* In making this division the hypnotic self insisted most positively on one distinction, namely that the secondary consciousness was in no sense a *personality.* The pronoun *I* could not be applied to it. In speaking of the thoughts of this second group of mental states alone, she could not say 'I felt this,' 'I saw that.' These thoughts were better described as, for the most part, unconnected, discrete sensations, impressions, and emotions, and were not synthesized into a personality. They were not, therefore, self-conscious. When the waking self was hypnotized, the resulting hypnotic self acquired the subconscious perceptions of the second consciousness; she then could say 'I,' and the hypnotic 'I' included what were formerly 'subconscious' perceptions. In speaking of the secondary personality by itself, then, it is to be understood that self-consciousness and personality are always excluded. This testimony was verified by test instances of subconscious perception of visual and auditory images of experiences occurring in my presence.

"4. Part played by the secondary consciousness in (a) normal mentation. The hypnotic self testified that the thoughts of the secondary consciousness do not form a logical chain. They do not have volition. They are entirely passive and have no direct control over the subject's voluntary actions.

"(b) Part played by the secondary consciousness in absent-mindedness. (1) Some apparently absent-minded acts are only examples of amnesia. There is no doubling of consciousness at the time. It is a sort of continuous amnesia brought about by lack of attention. (2) In true absent-mindedness there does occur a division of consciousness along lines which allow a large field to, and relatively wide synthesis of the dissociated states. The personal consciousness is proportionately restricted. The subconscious thoughts may involve a certain amount of volition and judgment, as when the subject subconsciously took a book from the table, carried it to the bookcase, started to place it on the shelf, found that particular location unsuitable, arranged a place on another shelf where the book was finally placed. No evidence, however, was obtained to show that the dissociated consciousness is capable of wider and more original synthesis than is involved in adapting habitual acts to the circumstances of the moment.

"(c) Solving problems by the secondary consciousness.[4] . . .

"The subject of these observations was at the time in good mental and physical condition. Criticism may be made that, the subject being one who had exhibited for a long time previously the phenomena of mental dissociation, she now, though for the time being recovered, tended to a greater dissociation and formation of subconscious states than does a normal person, and that the subconscious phenomena were therefore exaggerated. This is true. It is probable that the subconscious flora of ideas in this subject are richer than in the ordinary individual. These phenomena probably represent the extreme degree of dissociation compatible

---

[4] The statement of the hypnotic self regarding the part played by the "secondary consciousness" . . . [is] given in [Prince, op. cit., 167].

with normality. And yet, curiously enough, the evidence tended to show that the more robust the health of the individual, the more stable her mind, the richer the field of these ideas."

Of course it is a question how far the findings in a particular and apparently specially favorable subject are applicable to people in general. I would say, however, that I have substantially confirmed these observations in another subject, B. C. A., when in apparent health. In this latter subject the richness of the fringe and what may be called the ultra-marginal region in conscious states is very striking. The same is true of O. N.[5] Again in psychas-

---

[5] This subject . . . is practiced in introspection and can differentiate her memories with precision. She distinguishes "two strata" in her mental processes (an upper and lower). The "upper stratum" consists of the thoughts in the focus of attention. The lower (also called the background of her mind) consists of the perceptions and thoughts which are not in the focus. This stratum, of course, corresponds with what is commonly recognized as the fringe of consciousness, and, as is usual, when her attention is directed elsewhere she is not aware of it. She can, however, bring this fringe within the field of attention and then she becomes aware of, or rather remembers, its content during the preceding moment. To be able to do this is nothing out of the ordinary, but what is unusual is this: by a trick of abstraction which she has long practiced, she can bring the memory of the fringe or stratum into the full light of awareness and then it is discovered that it has been exceedingly rich in thoughts, far richer than ordinary attention would show and a fringe is supposed to be. It is indeed a veritable coconsciousness in which there goes on a secondary stream of thoughts often of an entirely different character and with different aspects from those of the upper stratum. It is common for thoughts which she *has resolutely put out of her mind as intolerable or unacceptable, or problems which have not been solved, to continue functioning in the lower stratum without entering awareness.* (Practically similar conditions I have found in B. C. A., and Miss B., though described by the subjects in different phraseology.) She can, however, at any time become aware of them by the trick of abstraction referred to, and sometimes they emerge apparently spontaneously and suddenly replace the "upper stratum." (For instance, to take a sensational example, on one occasion in the midst of hilarity while singing, laughing, etc., she suddenly became depressed and burst into tears. What happened was this: It was a sorrowful anniversary, and in the "lower stratum" sad memories had been recurring during the period of hilarity. These memories had come into consciousness early in the morning, but she had resolutely put them out of her mind. They had, however, kept recurring in the lower stratum, and suddenly emerged into the upper stratum of consciousness with the startling effect described. More commonly, however, the emergence of the lower stratum is simply a shifting play of thought. It is interesting to note that censored thoughts and temptations are apt to go into the lower stratum and here with their affects continue at play. *These sometimes reappear as dreams.*) In hypnosis also the content of the lower stratum can be distinctly recalled.—*Ibid.,* 174-175.

thenics, suffering from attacks of phobia, association, or habit psycho-neuroses, etc., I have been able to recover, after the attack has passed off, memories of conscious states which during and preliminary to the attack were outside the focus of attention. Of some of these the subject had been dimly aware, and of some apparently entirely unaware (i.e., they were coconscious). For the former as well as the latter there followed complete amnesia, so that the subject was ignorant of their previous presence, and believed that the whole content of consciousness was included in the anxiety or other state which occupied the focus of attention. Consequently I am in the habit, when investigating a pathological case, like an obsession, of inquiring (by technical methods) into the fringe of attention and even the ultra-marginal region, and reviving the ideas contained therein, particularly those for which there is amnesia. My purpose has been to discover the presence of ideas or thoughts which as a setting would explain the meaning of the idea which was the object of fear (a phobia), the exciting cause of psycho-neurotic attacks, etc. To this I shall presently return.

If all that I have said is true, it follows that the . . . field of conscious states as a whole comprises the focus of attention plus the marginal fringe; and besides this there may be a true subconscious ultra-marginal field comprising conscious states of which the personal consciousness is not even dimly aware.

The Rôle of Meaning in Moods

MORTON PRINCE, *The Unconscious*, 360-362, 331-337, 365-367 (copyright, 1921, by The Macmillan Company); reprinted by permission

However, whatever be its conscious constituents, obviously meaning must be derived from antecedent experiences and without such experiences no idea can have meaning. If, then, antecedent experiences determine the meaning of the idea, it is *theoretically* possible, particularly with insistent ideas, that the conscious elements involved in meaning are, with many ideas at least, only part and parcel of a larger complex which is for the most part unconscious. That is to say, a portion of this complex—perhaps the larger portion represented by the residua of past experiences—would, under this hypothesis, be unconscious while certain elements would arise in consciousness as the meaning of a given idea. Under such conditions a hidden subconscious process would really determine the conscious setting which gives the meaning. The whole setting would be partly conscious and partly hidden in the unconscious. Such a mechanism may be roughly likened to that of a clock, so far as concerns the relation of the chimes and hands to the works concealed inside the case. Though the visible hands and the audible chimes appear to indicate the time, the real process at work is that of the hidden mechanism. To inhibit the chime or regulate the time rate the mechanism must be altered. And so with an insistent idea: The unconscious part of the complex setting must be altered to alter the meaning of the idea. Of course the analogy must not be carried too far as in the case of the clock the chimes and hands are only epiphenomena, while conscious ideas are elements in the functioning mechanism.

Such a theory would afford an adequate explanation of the psychogenesis and mechanism of certain pathological ideas. At any rate, it is plain that an explanation of such ideas must be sought, on the one hand, in their meanings and in the antecedent experiences to which they are related, and, on the other, in the processes which determine their insistency or fixation. . . .

No psychological event, any more than a physical event, stands entirely isolated, all alone by itself, without relation to other events. . . . For example: a husband good humoredly and thoughtlessly chaffs his wife about the cost of a new hat which she exhibits with pride and pleasure. The wife in reply expresses herself by an outburst of anger which, to the astonished bystander, seems an entirely unjustifiable and inexplicable response to an entirely inadequate cause. Now if the bystander were permitted to make a psychological inquiry into the mental processes of the wife, he would find that the chaffing remark had meaning for her very different from what it had for him, and probably also for the husband; that it meant much more to her than the cost of that hat. He would find that it was set in her mind in a number of antecedent experiences consisting of criticisms of the wife by the husband for extravagance in dress; and perhaps criminations and recriminations involving much angry feeling on the part of both, and he would probably find that when the hat was purchased the possibility of criticism on the ground of extravagance passed through her mind. The chaffing remark of the husband therefore in the mind of the wife had for a context all these past experiences which formed a setting and gave an unintended meaning to the remark. The angry response, therefore, was dictated by these antecedent experiences and not simply by the trivial matter of the cost of a hat, standing by itself. The event can only be interpreted in the light of these past conserved experiences. How much of all this antecedent experience was in consciousness at the moment is another question which we shall presently consider.

I have often had occasion to interpret cryptic occurrences of this kind happening with patients or acquaintances. They make quite an amusing social game. (A knowledge of this principle shows the impossibility of outsiders judging the rightness or wrongness of misunderstandings and contretemps between individuals—particularly married people.) To complete the interpretation of this episode of the hat—although a little beside the point under consideration: plainly the anger to which the wife gave expression was the affect linked with and the reaction to the setting-complex formed by antecedent experiences. To state the matter in another way, these experiences were the formative material out of which a *psychological torch* had been plastically fashioned ready to be set ablaze by the first touch of a match—in this case the chaffing remark or associated idea. This principle of the setting, which gives meaning to an idea, being the conserved neurograms [*supra,* p. 205] of related antecedent experiences is strikingly manifest in pathological and quasi-pathological conditions. I will mention only two instances.

The first, that of X. Y. Z., I shall have occasion to refer to in more detail in connection with the emotions and instincts in a later lecture.[1] This lady, on the first night of her marriage, felt deeply hurt in her pride from a fancied neglect on the part of her husband. The cause was trivial and could not possibly be taken by any sensible person as an adequate justification for the resentment which followed and the somewhat tragic revenge which she practiced (continuous voluntary repression of the sexual instinct during many years). But the fancied slight had a meaning for her which did not appear on the surface. As she herself insisted, in attempted extenuation of her conduct, "You must not take it alone by itself but in connection with the past." It appeared that during the betrothal period there had been a number of experiences wounding to her pride and leading to angry resentment. These had been *ostensibly but not really forgiven.* The action of her spouse on the important night in question had a meaning for her of a slight, because it stood in relation to all these other antecedent experiences, and through these only could its meaning (for her) be interpreted. As a practical matter of therapeutics it became evident that the cherished resentment of years and the physiological consequences could only be removed by readjusting the setting—the memories of all the antecedent experiences with their resentment.

---

[1] [Prince, *op. cit.*, 462.]

The second instance was a case of hysteria of the neurasthenic type with outbreaks of emotional attacks in a middle-aged woman. It developed immediately, in the midst of good health, out of a violent and protracted fit of anger, almost frenzy, two years ago, culminating in the first emotional or hysterical attack. Looked at superficially the fit of anger would be considered childish because it was aroused by the fact that some children were allowed to make the day hideous by firing cannon-crackers continually under her window in celebration of the national holiday. When more deeply analyzed it was found that the anger was really *resentment* at what she considered unjustifiable treatment of herself by others, and particularly by her husband, who would not take steps to have the offense stopped. It is impossible to go into all the details here; suffice it to say that *below the surface* the experiences of life had deposited *a large accumulation of grievances* against which resentment had been continuous over a long series of year. Although loving and respecting her husband, a man of force and character, yet she had long realized she was not as necessary to his life as she wanted to be; that he could get along without her, however fond he was of her; and that he was the stronger character in one way. She wanted to be wanted. Against all this for years she had felt anger and resentment. She had concealed her feelings, controlled them, repressed them, if you will, but there remained a general dissatisfaction against life, a "kicking against the pricks," and a quickness to anger, though its expression had been well controlled. These were the formative influences which laid the mine ready to be fired by a spark, feelings of resentment and anger which had been incubating for years. Finally the spark came in the form of a childish offense. The frenzy of anger was ostensibly only the reaction to that offense, but it was really the explosion of years of antecedent experiences. The apparent offense was only the manifested cause, symbolic if you like so to express it, of the underlying accumulated causes contained in life's grievances.[2] After completion of the analysis the patient herself recognized this interpretation to be the true meaning of her anger and point of view.

Similarly in everyday life the *emotional shocks* from fear in dangerous situations, to which most people are subject and which so often give rise to traumatic psychoses, must primarily find their source in the psychological setting of the perception of the situation

---

[2] Prince: "The Mechanism of Recurrent Psychopathic States, with Special Reference to Anxiety States," *Jour. Abn. Psychol.*, June-July, 1911, 153-154.

(railroad, automobile, and other accidents). This setting is fashioned from the conserved knowledge of the fatal and other consequences of such accidents. This knowledge, deposited by past mental experiences—that which has been heard and read—induces a dormant apprehension of accidents and gives the meaning of danger to a perception of a present situation, and in itself, I may add, furnishes the neurographic fuel ready to be set ablaze by the first accident.[3] . . .

[True], the bringing to light associated memories of past experiences cannot positively demonstrate that those experiences take part as the causal factor in a present process. It can demonstrate the sequence of mental events, and, therefore, each successive link in a chain of evidence leading to the final act; or it can demonstrate the material out of which we can select with a greater or less degree of probability the factor which, in accordance with a theory—in this case that of subconscious processes—seems most likely to be the causal factor. Thus in the analysis of a bacterial culture we can select the one which seems on various considerations to be the most likely cause of an etiologically undetermined disease, but for actual demonstration we must employ synthetic methods; that is, actually reproduce the disease by inoculation with a bacterium. So with psychological processes synthetic methods are required for positive demonstration.

We have *available synthetic methods in hypnotic procedures.* These give, it seems to me, positive results of value. . . .

To take simple examples, and to begin with a hypothetical case, but one which in practice I have frequently duplicated: A subject is hypnotized and although, in fact, the day is a beautifully fair one we point out that it is really disagreeable because the sunshine is glowing and hot; that such weather means dusty roads, drought, the drying up of the water supply, the withering of the foliage, that the country needs rain, etc. We further assert that this will be the subject's point of view. In this way we form a cluster of ideas as a setting to the weather which gives it, fair as it is, an entirely different and unpleasant meaning and one which is accepted. The subject is now awakened and has complete amnesia for the

---

[3] *Ibid.*, p. 152. It is interesting to note that statistics show that traumatic psychoses following railway accidents are comparatively rare among trainmen, while exceedingly common among passengers. The reason is to be found in the difference in the settings of ideas of accidents in the two classes of persons. It is the same psychological difference that distinguishes the seasoned veteran soldier from the raw recruit in the presence of the enemy.

hypnotic experience. When attention is directed to the weather it is found that his point of view, for the time being at least, is changed from what it was before being hypnotized. The perception of the clear sky and the sunlight playing upon the ground includes secondary images of heat, of dust, of withered foliage, etc., such as have been previously experienced on disagreeable, hot, dusty days, and some of the associated thoughts with their affects suggested in hypnosis arise in consciousness; perhaps only a few, but, if he continues to think about the weather, perhaps many. Manifestly the new setting formed in hypnosis has been switched into association with the conscious perceptions of the environment and has induced the secondary images and associated thoughts, emotions, and feelings which give meaning. But it is equally manifest, though many elements bubble up, so to speak, from the unconscious setting into consciousness, that most of this setting remains submerged in the unconscious.

The significance of meaning in the moods of daily life as well as of abnormality, thus brought out by Dr. Prince, is paralleled by the rôle of meaning in the functions of language, so important in both abnormal and normal psychology. *Cf.* the selection which follows.

Meaning and the Functions of Language

HENRY VAN DYKE, "The Fringe of Words," *Yale Review*, 12: 78-81, 82-83 (1922)

It is idle to say that there is no essential difference between this language [of poetry] and the language of prose. There is a vital difference which we feel instinctively. It is more than the charm of metre. It is something in the choice of words, in their power of evocation, which makes the language, not in the old sense, but in the true sense, poetic diction.

Now, what is that magical something, so easy to perceive, so hard to define? . . . I knew that there was a difference between prose and poetry, something more than the difference betwen free rhythm and musical metre, but I could get no suggestion of its nature until one day, some twenty years ago, I came upon certain passages in "The Principles of Psychology," by William James.

"Knowledge *about* a thing," wrote this acute philosopher, "is knowledge of its relations. Acquaintance with it is limitation to the bare impression which it makes. Of most of its relations we are only aware in the penumbral, nascent way of a 'fringe' of inarticulated affinities about it. In all our voluntary thinking there is some topic or subject about which all the members of the thought revolve. . . . Relation to our topic or interest is constantly felt in the *fringe,* and particularly the relation of harmony or discord, of furtherance or hindrance of the topic. When the sense of furtherance is there, we are 'all right'; with the sense of hindrance we are dissatisfied and perplexed, and cast about us for other thoughts. Now, any thought the quality of whose fringe lets us feel ourselves 'all right,' is an acceptable member of our thinking, whatever kind of thought it may otherwise be."

These propositions, and others akin to them, William James expanded through many pages and illustrated with curves and cubes and straight lines and other geometrical figures, after the approved but somewhat bewildering method of modern psychologists. But the idea that caught and held my attention, according to the very doctrine which Mr. James set forth, was something that lay beyond "the limitation of the bare impression," something in the region of relations and affinities, the country of the "fringe."

If it be true, I said to myself, that things and thoughts have these fringes, these suffusions, these psychic overtones about them, may not the same be true of words, which are the symbols of thoughts and the images of things? Certainly words carry with them a subtle yet perceptible atmosphere of relations and suggestions beyond their literal meaning, a personal aura, as it were, derived sometimes from their sound (for the real word is always something heard, of which the written letters are only a conventional sign), or coming it may be from their associations, or a dim remembrance of their origin in some ancient tongue; or gathered from their use in human intercourse, and clinging to them, like "the odors of the valleys" which de Guérin's young Centaur perceived about his mother when she returned from her roaming in the outer world to their cave among the mountains. This indefinable power of suggestion and evocation in words is their magic, their secret of interpretation and revelation, the hidden source from which their color and their fragrance rise like an exhalation.

It seemed to me at the time that this idea might be a clue to lead me through the labyrinth of discussion about the nature of the diction proper to poetry, and bring me at least a little nearer to the truth. I disfigured (or enriched) the margin of a page in Professor James's valuable text-book with a written note: "Poetic language—its value and beauty derived from these fringes of words." Since then I have thought much about the suggestion, and tried to test it by application to various poems, in order to discover what truth it contained, and what were the limitations to be observed to prevent it from exaggerating itself into a falsehood.

Of course, the reader trained in the subtleties of thought and the niceties of expression is aware of these limitations, reservations, and exceptions before they are stated, and takes them for granted without discussion. For example, that some words have more, some less, and some very little of this fringe, this *aura* of suggestion, about them; that the effect even of the richest words depends a good deal on the intelligence and sensitiveness of the listener or the reader, and that some men are born color-blind to language, and others in the glare of the electric light achieve color-blindness; that a considerable part both of excellent prose and of admirable verse is written in very plain and simple words which derive what Sir Walter Raleigh calls their "bare intolerable force" from the way in which they are used, the order in which they are arranged, or the stark sincerity with which they express a deep and powerful feeling; that the central elements of poetry, strong emotion and vivid imagination, are more important than verbal magic and musical charm; these are propositions which every sensible man will admit without argument.

But after these limitations are accepted, what remains of value in this suggestion of the fringe of words as a thing to be considered in poetry? I think there remains a two-fold truth, one side of which raises a barrier against bad diction, while the other indicates the way to language which will clothe the poet's thought in beauty.

There are words which are distinctly non-poetic—scientific terms; technical phrases of law or business; mere colloquialisms, like "Oh say"; and ancient *clichés* of imagery which have been worn smooth by much handling. There are also words which, by reason of ludicrous or trivial associations, are positively anti-poetic, because they break the "stream of thought" and create that "sense of hindrance" which, as William James says, leaves us "dissatisfied and perplexed." This is why some of the verses of the Impressionists and the Vers Librists are so hard to read and so impossible to remember. They are like packs of firecrackers, exploding in a series of violent concussions. Or they are like dull rivers, laden with absurd débris, trailing through a region of backyards and scrap-heaps. . . .

On the other side, there is a kind of language which by virtue of its fringe of associations belongs to poetry, and has a singular power to enhance its beauty and to deepen its meaning. It is in this diction that the finest passages, the most memorable lines, are written. Sometimes it is by the succession or stately ordering of rich phrases that the effect is produced, like the unrolling of a splendid tapestry. Sometimes it is by a single touch that the imagination is evoked and the passage irradiated. This is what Tennyson meant, and illustrated, in his fine poem "To Virgil":

All the charm of all the Muses often flowering in a lonely word.

In Shakespeare's thirtieth sonnet is another example:

> When to the sessions of sweet silent thought
> I summon up remembrance of things past.

In prose the meaning is simply this: "While I am quietly thinking I begin to recollect past events." But in poetry sweet silent thought is holding the sessions of her court, and remembrance is summoned as a witness.

In "Samson Agonistes," Milton puts these words into the mouth of old Manoa, standing by the dead body of his mighty son:

> Nothing is here for tears, nothing to wail
> Or knock the breast; no weakness, no contempt,
> Dispraise, or blame; nothing but well and fair,
> And what may quiet us in a death so noble.

What a magic there is in that word "quiet," with its reminiscence of the Latin *requiescat,* and of the verse in the Psalms, "Then are they glad because they be quiet; so he bringeth them unto their desired haven."

On the basis of the foregoing discussion by Dr. van Dyke, it would seem to be a requisite of effective language, whether scientific or artistic, to have every word and every arrangement of words represent the largest possible number of associations favorable to the view of the writer and the smallest possible number of associations unfavorable to that view.

Thus unnecessary words would give opportunity for confusing associations to enter, while too great condensation would not allow time for the desired associations to come up.

Again, *repetition,* of words and phrases, would have to avoid the extreme of absurd meaninglessness (as when we say a word over and over until its new-found absurdity makes us laugh), while effectively playing upon associations already successfully aroused.

CHAPTER IX

SYMBOLISM

The Nature and Occurrence of Symbolism

A

H. L. HOLLINGWORTH, *The Psychology of Functional Neuroses,* 55 (Appleton, 1920)

Ordinary perception is . . . largely a process of reacting to "cues" in the same way as if the "wholes" were present. The learning process represents a similar result—the child learns to react to the sight of the candle flame in the way in which he previously reacted to the total situation of seeing the flame, reaching for it, and experiencing the pain of the burn. Language also is based on the disposition to react to a part of a total experience instead of requiring the presence of the whole. This is the way in which a word comes to have *meaning.* This is the origin of the *concept.* Such a process is in fact the essence of *symbolism,* and symbolism in all its forms seems to be nothing more than this.

B

KNIGHT DUNLAP, "Sleep and Dreams," *Jour. Abn. Psychol.,* 16: 206-207 (1921)

A symbol is something which has become definitely associated with anything else, as, for example, the name of a man with his appearance or personality. The most conspicuous symbols, however, are those which have become associated with systems of objects, with classes or genera, or with abstract principles. Thus, the flag is the symbol of the nation, associated in common thought with not only the name, but many other characteristics of a people: the six-pointed star is a symbol of "perfection": and the rose is the symbol of silence or secrecy. The history of religion, and consequently of art, is full of symbols, developed in part as an efficient means of calling attention to certain facts of life and certain articles of faith, and in part as a means of secret communication between members of a select group. Much of this symbolism is unknown to the average man, but every one has a vast range of associations of a similar nature. To one man, his collection of golf clubs is a symbol of recreation. To another a certain journal is a symbol of anarchy and deadly civic danger, and so on. In other words, these particular objects have become associated with a certain condition of things, or with certain principles, so that the thought of the one associate leads by normal progress to the thought of another.

As a matter of fact, any pair of associated terms stand in exactly the same psychological relation to each other as symbol and thing symbolized, and it is impossible to draw a line sharply around a group to be exclusively designated as "symbols."

The occurrence of symbols in associative thinking is therefore not a source of especial difficulty for explanation, but merely a typical case of the general process. It is intelligible that a man who feels in need of recreation should think of a certain new golf club he has not yet tried out: the club is for him the symbol of recreation, associated definitely with the whole situation. Nor is there anything more surprising in the fact (to cite an actual case) that a young woman who has been facing serious temptation, and has been emotionally excited about the situation during the day, should dream of an anchor, the symbol of her religious training, consciously associated through hymns, sermons, and miscellaneous religious training, with a force sustaining her against temptation. In the same way, in dreams due to worry over a situation involving a definite individual, another individual associated with the first— through similarity of names or any other common associative link— may appear as the "symbol" of the first.

C

C. B. Burr, *Practical Psychology and Psychiatry*, 58-61, 64-66 (Davis, 1921)

From every object visually examined springs a concept more or less perfectly defined, or an emotion directly related to its physical properties, its correspondences, its uses, its origin, or its value, as well as many an indirectly related concept which its form, its purpose, its resemblances, bring into being. Every object in nature is in a poetic sense endowed with the instincts, capacities, and sentiments of the human family, and the terms descriptive of regional and special anatomy, or physiological and psychological processes, are transferred to inanimate objects. The oak suggests sturdiness, ruggedness, and strength of character. It has *limbs, trunk,* and *heart.* A fellow-citizen of rugged character, dependability, and strength of purpose is said to possess a *heart of oak.* Spring foliage represents inexperience (verdancy) ; brown and yellow, decay (the sere and yellow leaf). Stone is a symbol of hardness, and there are correspondingly *hearts of flint.* The ascent of a river and the exploration of a cave are begun from the *mouth.* The volcano *vomits* forth its lava stream, and the earth *clothes* itself in a green garment. There is the family tree derived from the symbol of trunk (progenitor), offshoots and branches (near and remote relatives). One goes to the *root* of a subject, even as the tap root penetrates deeply the soil. The position "up a tree" is embarrassing and difficult, as many a cat has discovered.

The hills are a symbol of hopefulness and sustenance. "I will lift up mine eyes unto the hills from whence cometh my help." The sea is represented by Schiller as *laughing* and *inviting to the bath,* and in its tempestuous moments it distinctly says to a not unduly imaginative friend of mine "I am coming to get you." Every region has its *twin* lakes; there are in the Yellowstone Park *Teton* Mountains; America has its *backbone;* Michigan has its *thumb;* Italy, its *toe* and *heel.* There are the *lap* and *bosom* and *womb* of nature as well as the *bowels* of the earth, the *nose* of the ship, the *face* of the cliff, the *brow* of the hill. In Scripture imagery the deserts shall *rejoice* and the wind is endowed with volition. It "bloweth where it listeth." There is resurrection of truth crushed to earth. . . . Human sympathy has *breadth,* affection *depth,* folly *height.* A character is spoken of as *well rounded;* sarcasm, as *pointed.* Duty *calls,* happiness *rains,* the stone has a *face,* and the elements on occasions display *anger.* Dispositions are *sweet* and *sour;* certain forms of jesting leave a *bitter* taste. . . . Certain characters are designated as *flabby* and certain heads as *soft.* The sun *rules* by day, the moon and stars by night, and the moon *governs* the tides. . . .

The Klang association, that of words of the same sound as pronounced, but of different signification, is the occasion of much embarrassment and inconvenience to the susceptible Take, for example, through the word "bear," the suggestion of a burden physical or mental, parturition, a wild animal, and, because of sound association through "bare," that of nudity. The word "ball" suggests the national game, the tango, a bearing in a wheel, its unrelated "bawl," the cry of an infant, and milk of magnesia. The word "grip" suggests a fraternal order, friendship, poverty, disease, and death. The right and left associations are, as everybody knows, among the most common, the left implying the negative, neglected, and insincere; the right, the positive, straightforward, and dependable. Such associations as those above mentioned are universal. They insistently obtrude themselves into thinking like Banquo's ghost at the table of Macbeth. In health they are for the most part ignored and are the source of no particular discomfort. In mental disease, on the contrary, they become the bases for distressing word obsession.

Dementia præcox, the paranoid, hysteric, and hysteroidal states furnish the best examples of such obsession. A suppressed sexual experience in early life, the complex of the Freud school, not rarely supplies the groundwork for painful, provoking, and persistent mental hammering and determines morbid conduct in pronounced degree. . . . The symbol of the serpent is as old as mythology. A black snake mentioned by one referred to the person of a brunette male acquaintance. The delusion of fatherhood in an unmarried virgin had its origin in playful contact with another little girl in childhood. Poppies and the fig-leaf are mentioned by those whose thoughts frequently revert to the sexual apparatus. Green pastures symbolize to one that which is fed upon as well as that which produces. The "corner of Pine Street and Broadway" was translated as indicating first sexual pining, second the "broad way" which leadeth to destruction, or in her language "where any old thing might happen." The color green affronted one patient because of the intimation of lack of worldly wisdom. . . . Blackberries may be avoided because seedy; spoons upon the table are looked upon as a reflection. . . . Prunes suggest prudery. (Prunes and Prisms.)[1]

---

[1] ["Apropos of nothing, he asked the examiner what he thought of the guilt of Tucker, executed for the murder of Mabel Page. He himself seemed to have considerable doubt as to whether Tucker merited his end, which he rationalized as follows: If one spells out the name of Tucker, the first letter is T. This is symbolic of China, whose principal export is 'T.' This indicates that Tucker was composed, 'a big sixth of him,' according to the first capital letter of his name, of 'Chinese corpuscles,' i. e., that he had much of the Chinese character in him. But the Chinese are characterized by conscientiousness and so Tucker, having so strong an element of this quality in him, would not be likely to be guilty of the act for which he suffered, unless, indeed, the other letters of his name should offset the good influence of the first one. R represents riches, money, a 'driving principle,' that might operate for evil. E is for English, French Protestantism, i. e., bigotry of narrowmindedness. K he brought into connection with uck, Kentucky, hot Southern blood, passion. C, on

Symbolism and Psychoanalysis

Frederic Lyman Wells, "On Formulation in Psychoanalysis," *Jour. Abn. Psychol.*, Oct.-Nov., 1913

An insufficient distinction seems to have been drawn between two kinds of symbolism that I shall try to illustrate concretely. If one contemplates a well-grown oak tree, one may naturally think of its similarity to the growth of the British Empire. The oak tree becomes to him, for the nonce, a symbol of the British Empire. But the development of the British Empire has no direct causal relation to the growth of the oak tree. Britannia did not create the oak tree to see how she looked, as nature is said to have created Goethe. The "enmity" between oxygen and fluorine, which alone of all elements forms no compound with it, and drives it out of its stable union with hydrogen, to form ozone and hydrofluoric acid might very conceivably suggest to one the hatred of Hannibal for the Romans, or the usurpation of Igraine by Uther Pendragon. In this way the one may always be said to symbolize the other. But psychoanalysis uses the term to mean much more than this; not only that the one idea has certain grounds for association by similarity with the other, but that it is actually a genetic expression of the other. That is, one dreams that he is near the summit of a mountain, down which there flows a gushing waterfall; he is thirsty, but does not drink. It needs no highly colored imagination to associate this episode with *any* deep-seated trend, wish, if you like, that has to be kept in the background, and even to dovetail minute features of the one into features of the other; but it is a very rash step further to say that these detailed features of the one are *therefore* genetically determined by the other.

---

the other hand, represents Christiania, conscience, conscientiousness, a good influence.

"The mental process in instances like the above might be described as an 'over-identification' of language symbols with the things they represent. For example, the idea of debasement becomes so closely identified with 'walk on,' that wherever a process denoted by 'walk on' occurs, it carries with it this idea of debasement. In Will-i-am, the language symbol of *will* is so over-identified with the process of volition, that, when the symbol occurs in a common name, this name carries with it special powers of volition."—Frederic Lyman Wells, *Mental Adjustments*, 67-68 (Appleton, 1922).

For more examples of symbolism, *cf.* Dr. Wells' pp. 71*ff.* Further views on the Nature and Occurrence of Symbolism may be found in the works of Jung, Ranke, and Silberer.]

The fact of contiguity in free association is not sufficient to establish one event as symbolic of another in the sense of genetic expression. This is attested by the numerous symbolisms in which it is not possible that one should be the genetic expression of the other. Such instances as the above are supplemented by cases where differential symbolism is clearly marked. . . . Various snatches of music may become definitely associated in one's mind with certain ideas, and one is often astonished on learning afterwards how different are the ideas conveyed in their original names.

Is it not better to freely admit that we have no objective criterion of genetic expression in dream and much other symbolism, but that the length to which one is willing to go in accepting such interpretations is a matter of personal equation? When, as Ernest Jones remarks, the chief character of the "Servant in the House" is called *Manson,* the proposition that the name represents "son of man" is convincing to most of us; we should assume it without so much as inquiring whether such an idea was really present in the author of the play. Again, when I forget to bring away a five-thousand-ohm coil that I need, some of you would doubtless be inclined to regard this as determined in large part by a wish to get rid of some other species of "resistance." Others would scarcely accept this view, and no objective grounds could be adduced for doing so. The most extreme cases of this nature are, perhaps, to be found in the analyses of the "free selection" of numbers. That it is possible, through various analytic sinuosities, to relate these choices to special trends in the individual, serves, of course, to discover the special trends, but should not be offered as proof that these trends were productive in the selection of the numbers involved. . . .

Analysis is concerned with the discovery of trends and their genesis, and is in no way dependent upon the attachment of any special significance to something from which in free association these trends are more or less indirectly derived. The essential thing is that *a* was associated with *b* and then to *c,* which leads us further to know the existence of *d;* not that *a* as a dream-phenomenon was the symbolic product of *b, c* or *d,* which it need be neither in theory nor fact. . . .

The value of an *association* in determining a symbolism, depends upon the fixity and invariability of that association. *Cat* is a symbol for a certain animal, because it regularly represents to us that animal. If in the content of myths, dreams or schizophrenia, an object is represented performing functions unequivocally attached to another object, the first object may be regarded as symbolic of the second; the air, for example, as symbolic of the procreative

principle. . . . Such are the evidences by which symbolism is determined; it depends on one's self how strong they must be before
symbolism is accepted as "convincing."

Symbolism and Synæsthesia

FREDERIC LYMAN WELLS, "Symbolism and Synaesthesia," *Am. Jour. Insan.*,
75: 481-483, 485-488

[According to many psychoanalysts,] . . . in such manner and
to such extent as a symbol represents its primary idea, it is "identified" therewith. In so far as a certain symbol always represents
the same primary idea and no other, it is "constant." In so far as
a symbol is shared by many persons, it is "pervasive." Symbolisms
also differ in their relations to consciousness. There may be full or
no consciousness of connection between a symbol and its primary
idea. Those with no such consciousness have been classified as
"dissociative symbols." Some psychoanalytic writers consider that
the term symbol should itself be restricted to such cases.

A high degree of constancy and pervasiveness is ascribed by
psychoanalytic writers to symbolisms of this class. It has been
questioned if these features should be wholly accounted for in terms
of individual experience, or if some conception of inherited or
otherwise extra-experiential associations should be considered to
underlie these particularly constant and pervasive symbolisms.
The latter view makes comparatively little headway so far as psychoanalytic symbolisms are concerned. There has been indicated,
however, a mechanism of extra-experiential associations, occasionally having the character of symbolisms, not excluded by the more
accepted experiential mechanism, which it may at times reinforce.

Pathological studies give evidence of definite associations between
two ideas not associated in previous experience. This is indicated
when, e. g., the sound of a tuning fork elicits hallucinations of
different words or phrases. The hallucinations are not confounded
with the tone of the fork, but are strictly associations thereto. The
content is often complex, consisting of many vocables, or words,
and elaborate pictures. In these cases the stimulus does not regularly elicit the same hallucination, the latter being inconstant.
Their status appears that of psychotic symptoms only. Goldstein
(*1*) alludes to happy and melancholy misperceptions induced by the
same stimulus according to the condition of a manic-depressive case.
Such constant relations as do appear between the hallucinations
and the inducing stimuli are, as Goldstein points out, of a formal

character. The hallucination comes when the stimulus comes and does not, as a rule, persist longer than the stimulus lasts. Correspondence in the rhythm of stimulus and hallucination is noted by both Goldstein (2) and Sokolow (3). In the observations of Chvostek (4) and of Goldstein (5), the quality of the hallucinated voice is also affected by the quality of the inducing stimulus. In Sokolow's (6) case cold stimuli elicited sound hallucinations of higher pitch than warm ones, which he thinks may be because the cold differed more from the body temperature than the warm stimuli he used. Auditory hallucinations have also been induced through direct application of electric current, as observed by Moravcsik (7) and Jolly. Here belong also the visual hallucinations (induced in alcoholic cases by pressure on the eyelids with fingers) to which Liepmann (8) called attention. Bechterew (9) reports similar observations with the interrupter of a coil.

These induced hallucinations have scarcely the status of symbolisms, not being identified in any way with the inducing stimulus. They appear to be kept separate, which also takes them out of the category of illusions. They simply show coercive association between two mental processes, independently of special connection experienced between them.

The synaesthesias proper are more relevant. Bleuler (10) finds that like the induced hallucinations, the synaesthesias begin and end with the primary sensation. In the case reported by Downey (11), the synaesthesia appears to last longer than the primary sensation. Synaesthesias differ from the above induced hallucinations in that while the induced hallucinations are very inconstant, the synaesthesias are very constant. This is indicated by Bleuler's (12) reinvestigation of his material, 13-15 years after the original observations. There was only some decrease in the facility and intensity with which the phenomena appeared, in which agreement with Flournoy is cited. The synaesthesias offer groups of associations which persist with hallucinatory coerciveness in those subject to them. Bleuler (13) remarks that he can sometimes recall names from the visual synaesthesia (photism), when he has forgotten the auditory impression.

Bleuler generalizes from his material, 76 cases in all, to observe the continuity of the photism series, corresponding to the continuity of the inducing sounds. The musical scale gives such a series, for example, from black to white through red or gray. Transition forms of vowels give transition forms of colors. Overtones, which certainly form no regular color associations through conscious experience, may appear in the photism even though not consciously perceived in the inducing stimulus. A scale from yellow through red and brown to black is especially frequent for musical tones. For noises, red is nearly absent, blue and green are very rare. In general, high notes induce sharply defined photisms with pointed forms. A whistle beginning low and rapidly becoming high may thus appear in the photism as a wedge whose base represents the low period of the tone. In the photisms not from sound, but from skin and general sensibility, violet is absent, brown and green are very rare.

The following examples of synaesthetic phenomena are noted by observers of individual cases: Among complex sensations of taste induced by vocal complexes of spoken words, Pierce *(14)* reports the word *parlor* to represent honey on bread; *loud,* a boiled new potato; *grin,* French toast, or fried bread. Among nonsense syllables, *zaf* is a meat flavor, salty, hard, like corned beef. *Hes* is small particles, minced meat. *Dep* is roast beef well done. More elementary stimuli induce sensations as follows:

Tuning-fork of 256 vibrations, as if warm air were resting upon the tongue.

Tuning-fork of 512-1024 vibrations, warm and clear, sweet.

On the piano, A_2-E_1, like toast soaked in hot water.

E_1-F, sweet, rather strong, like licorice, a troche.

F-g. mild, gravy-like.

g-c^4, banana, smooth, slippery.

c^4-c^5, thin, insipid.

On the violin, lowest three notes, troche flavor.

From there up, grows sweeter, loses strength, becomes clear, delicate and sweet in flavor. The rubbing of a nail or file evoked a temperature experienced in the mouth, this being hot or cold according to the kind or degree of scraping. . . .

A "spectral octave" in the case of an accomplished musician is reported as follows *(18)*:

Red.	Orange.	Yellow.	Green.	Blue.	Violet.
C G	D	A	E	B	F♯

A case in which pain sensations evoke color perceptions is noted by Coriat *(19)*. Testing pain spots with a hair aesthesiometer showed an increase in the intensity of a red sensation as the stimuli were increased by shortening the hair. The subject reported different colors to be evoked by different types of pain. A "hollow" pain gives a blue color; a shooting neuralgic pain, a white color.

There is observed a tendency of the synaesthesias to run in scales, which are proportional to the scales of the primary stimulation.

This argues against their originating in associations of adult or infantile experience. Other evidence of the same probable import is that they may have different affective quality from the primary, inducing sensation, as noted by both Bleuler and Downey. To the former, words with *io* are unpleasant in sound, but agreeable in their induced photisms. Bleuler observes that the photisms are generally localized not in the visual, but in the auditory field. Downey's case (*15*) of colored gustation localizes the photisms in the mouth.

Bleuler (*20*) regards the synaesthesias as originating endogenously, but not in associations. He considers them rather as cases in which the specific energy of the sensory nerves is not wholly "specific." He rejects the supposition that activities of one sensory center are transmitted to another sensory center. The regularity of the synaesthesias speaks rather for a general property of the cerebral substance to respond with all its various specific qualities to the stimuli through different end-organs. As a rule, only one of these (the primary sensation) is in the foreground; the others come to awareness not at all or as synaesthesias.

Under these conditions, association would be promptly established between a sound and a color always perceived with it, as well as separately. Such association, while not innate, is governed by innate factors, and not by external experience.

Downey (*21*) comments in another paper on expressions in language that counterfeit synaesthesia, but differ therefrom in being inconstant, unsystematic, and having rational associations near the surface. It is not synaesthesia to speak of red war, black looks, weather clear as a bell, clear blue optimism. Sometimes these counterfeit synaesthesias, *synopsies secondaires, provoquées* of Flournoy, acquire relative constancy. Bleuler mentions how a black and yellow pattern symbolizes Wednesday to him, through the pattern of the travelling bag of an aunt who visited his home on Wednesdays. On the other hand, the English use of *blue* to denote melancholy is contrary to the commoner associations of the color in life. A synaesthetic origin might be ascribed thereto, as Bleuler seems to think. Bleuler's (*22*) observation that the photism of bitter is almost always "dark brown to black" may be the essential determinant of the figure "dark brown taste."

A tendency has been variously observed for numbers to arrange themselves in a definite pattern of visual imagery. Sometimes learned associations, as of the clock-face, appear to govern these. Again, these so-called "number forms" appear to resemble synaesthesias, in that a connection between the ideas is established independently of the will, extending as far back as memory, and constant. Bleuler (*23*) speaks of them as "instinctive." Heredity for number forms is postulated by Galton (*24*) and for synaesthesia by Calkins (*25*). This is good evidence of innateness if the same secondary sensations are inherited. Myers (*26*) brings out that this is not always evident with synaesthesia, members of a family disagreeing in the color attaching to a given sound.

Lowie (*27*) has connected this general class of phenomena with the facts of pervasiveness in the symbols of myths and legends. He is impressed with the hereditary character of the number of forms. Since primitive communities are made up largely of blood-relatives, symbolic meanings could grow upon numbers in this way. The same naturally applies to the more strictly synaesthetic phenomena.

Both synaesthesias and mechanisms of autistic thinking form associations foreign to the waking consciousness of ordinary life. The associations of synaesthesia, however, are restricted to the more elementary patterns of sensory qualities. They are not adequate to account for the types of symbolism common to mythology, dreams and psychoses. Brown may represent bitter, vanilla may represent green, but the gulf between these associations and such complex symbolisms as snake for phallus, air for male principle, water for female principle, is greater than most imaginations are prepared to leap. And it is only for the synaesthetic type of association that even slight evidence for hereditary transmission is adduced. If such transmission operated on higher levels, evolution would be expected to transmit, in consciousness, useful ideas, such as of mathematical relations, rather than an unconscious full of ideas generally harmful if acted upon. Artistic mechanisms are capable of accounting for the entire body of "archeopathic" symbols on an experiential basis, and there is evidence for but little of it being accounted for in other ways.

It is a growing conception that a great deal of "higher mental process" goes on in the mind of which the main personality is as little aware as it is of many normal organic processes. This thought, below the level of awareness, consists, like the thought of which we are aware, in the association and elaboration of experiences. But, whereas the thought of awareness is, in the normal mind, mainly governed by the logic of experience, that below the level of awareness is quite free from these restrictions and is "autistic" in Bleuler's (*28*) sense of the term. In this way, associations and symbolisms are formed which are not present to the conscious level of the mind. In the psychoses, these ideas do come to consciousness, dominate it, and give rise to delusions. They also come to the surface in the dream, where they give rise to symbolism that has been amply recorded (*30*). The two levels of thought are less distinct in the savage and in childhood than in more developed life. Whatever community exists between psychotic and primitive ideas (how much one sees depends a good deal on the selection of material) is due to regression in *modes* of thought. There is a regression to modes of thought which more characterize primitive man, but not to special topics of thought. If the topics of thought, the precise ideas associated, do happen to correspond, this is because the primitive kinds of association (similarity, contiguity) lead in like directions for everyone. The ideas which are associations by similarity for the savage or·child are associations by similarity for all. The community appears, not from a transmission of definite ideas through the ages, but because the same associative laws are operating upon the same general class of experiences (*29*).

REFERENCES

1. Goldstein, *Arch. f. Psychiat.*, 43: 499-500 (1908).
2. *Ibid.*, 497-500.
3. Sokolow, *Arch. f. Psychiat.*, 55: 465 (1915).
4. Chvostek, *Jahrb. f. Psychiat.*, 11: 274-282 (1893).
5. Goldstein, *Arch. f. Psychiat.*, 43: 497-498 (1908).
6. Sokolow, *Arch. f. Psychiat.*. 471 (1915).
7. Moravcsik, *Centralblatt f. Nervenk, u. Psychiat.*, 29: 210-211 (1906). *Cf.* also Chvostek, *op. cit.*
8. Liepmann, *Arch. f. Psychiat.*, 27: 203 ff. (1895).
9. Bechterew, *Centralblatt f. Nervenk, u. Psychiat.*, 20: 505 (1897)
10. Bleuler, *Zt. f. Psychol.*, 65: 16 (1913). Further references by this name only are to this article.
11. Downey, *Am. Jour. Psychol.*, 22: 528 (1911).
12. Bleuler, 13.
13. *Ibid.*, 12.
14. Pierce, *Am. Jour. Psychol.*, 18: 341-352 (1907).
15. Downey, *Am. Jour. Psychol.*, 22: 530-535 (1911).
16. Myers, *Brit. Jour. Psychol.*, 4: 231-232-235 (1911).
17. *Ibid.*, 7: 115 (1914-1915).
18. *Ibid.*. 114.
19. Coriat, *Jour. Abn. Psychol.*, 8: 110-111 (1913-1914).
20. Bleuler, 35.
21. Downey, *Jour. Philos.*, 9: 440-448 (1912).
22. Bleuler, 28.
23. *Ibid.*, 6.
24. Galton, *Inquiry Into the Human Faculty,* 118 (1883).
25. Calkins, *Am. Jour. Psychol.*, 7: 97 (1895-1896).
26. Myers, *Brit. Jour. Psychol.*, 4: 238 (1911).

27. Lowie, *Am. Jour. Sociol.*, 31: 217-229 (1915).

28. Bleuler, *Jahrb. f. psa. u. psp. Forsch.*, 4, (1), 1-39 (1912).

29. "Because the sleeping mind looks at things in the same . . .
     relatively simple, naive way as the waking mind of primitive
     man" (Silberer).   "The stereotypy is due to the uniformity
     of the fundamental and perennial interests of mankind"
     (Ernest Jones).

[30. Wells, *Psychoan. Rev.*, 5: 47-63 (1917)].

CHAPTER X

WISHES, SENTIMENTS, COMPLEXES, SYSTEMS

The Concept of the "Wish"

A

FREDERIC LYMAN WELLS, "On Formulation in Psychoanalysis," *Jour. Abn. Psychol.*, Oct.-Nov., 1913

. . . In formulating theories for scientific judgment we must not allow our phraseology to be regulated by autistic fancies, but recognize that in language we are utilizing an important function of paramountly social significance. . . .

The primal difficulty with the psychoanalytic use of the term *wish* is its well-nigh universal interpretation as a process of high mental level. The psychoanalytic commonplaces of *unconscious wish, wish unacceptable to the main body of the personality,* are to most of those who hear them, contradictions in terms. (To wish a thing means to desire it consciously,) and with the main body of the personality.

It is not in the least denied that the processes described in these terms exist, and their recognition is most important; but beware the consequences of new psychological wine in old linguistic bottles. We certainly know that the mental organism is not a close-knit, well-disciplined absolute monarchy, whose every member responds fatally to direction from the highest levels; rather is it a loosely gathered democracy, often with most liberal notions of State Rights. Seldom, indeed, is it altogether united on single questions of policy. The majority of the *Ichkomplex* may be able to enforce its decrees only with difficulty against a riotous minority; which, if it be a sufficiently well-organized complex, may split off and set up a local government of its own; or even seize the reins of the central authority, and carry on according to its own schizophrenic inclinations.

It is thus a far from infrequent experience that one may wish for a thing at the highest level of the personality, and at the same time be wholly conscious of other considerations that oppose it, and make the striving for its object less effective. Still others may, it is thought, be unconscious, and psychoanalysis formulates them all in terms of wish and counter-wish. So firmly fixed, however, is the concept of wish as the expression of the organic "majority," that its persistent employment in the psychoanalytic sense only confuses those who want to comprehend it and encourages those who do not. . . .

One occasionally observes a psychoanalytic writer to use the terms *trend* or *tendency* as the entire equivalents of wish, and it would be well if they largely replaced it. . . . When all levels of the personality are united, if they ever are, in the direction of a given trend, there is not only the conscious wish therefor, but all reactions of the organism are definitely ordered towards it. In so far as instinctive trends conflict, and there is a division of organic policy, in so far are the biological reactions of the personality not consistently ordered towards the paramount end, but disturbed by reactions the expression of other tendencies inconsistent with it. . . .

In fine, we know introspectively that we may heartily wish at one level what is less advantageous at another. But far deeper is our knowledge, from the observation of behavior, that we sometimes react in accordance with certain definite trends, and sometimes against them. Therefore, let us formulate our conceptions of the divisions in personal tendencies not statically in terms of wish and counter-wish, which are at best only secondary inferences below the level of introspection, but dynamically in terms of trend and counter-trend, which are the ultimate criteria of the wish, and are present objectively at all levels of behavior. . . .

B

EDWIN B. HOLT, *The Freudian Wish*, 4 (Holt, 1915)

The wish is any purpose or project for *a course of action,* whether it is being merely entertained by the mind or is being actually executed; a distinction which is really of little importance. We shall do well if we consider this wish to be, as in fact it is, dependent on a *motor attitude* of the physical body, which goes over into overt action and *conduct* when the wish is carried into execution.

Sentiments and Their Significance

MORTON PRINCE, "Miss Beauchamp—The Theory of the Psychogenesis of Multiple Personality," *Jour. Abn. Psychol.*, 15: 74-76 (1920)

By "sentiment" I mean an object, or idea of some object, which has been organized by experience with one or more emotional *dispositions*. As an emotional disposition is an instinct or part of an instinct, a sentiment is an idea structurally organized with one or more instincts from which it derives its motivating force. Thus the idea of mother may be organized with the instincts possessing the emotional dispositions of tender feeling, reverence, etc., that of God with tender feeling, awe, subjection, etc. Sentiments, then, become complex units in the structure of the mind. . . .

But this is not the whole story of a sentiment; it is too schematic. A sentiment is a product of the growth of the mind and organized by experiences. This means that it has its roots in a greater or less number of antecedent experiences related to its object. It is a growth from these roots. . . . They as a setting or context give it meaning, just as every idea is dependent upon its setting for its meaning. This is very neatly shown by a study of pathological sentiments, such as the phobias. Practical examination of these sentiments shows that they are so strongly and intimately rooted in a complex of antecedent experiences that the origin and true meaning of the phobia can often only be understood by bringing to light these experiences. They furnish the viewpoint and attitude of mind towards the object of the sentiment. Nor can you kill a sentiment except by killing these roots; that is without changing the setting, which means the viewpoint. Alter the setting and you alter the point of view, the attitude towards the object, and then destroy the sentiment. . . .

It is hardly possible to overestimate the part played by sentiments in the determination of personality and character and hence in alterations of personality. Upon the sentiments, among other things, largely depend the habits of thought, the behavior, and reactions of the individual to the environment, and, therefore, those traits which we select as particularly marking the character of the personality.

The Nature of the Complex as Compared with the Sentiment

A

W. H. R. Rivers, *Instinct and the Unconscious*, 85, 87-89 (Cambridge, 1922)

Bernard Hart, who more than any other English writer has made the psychology of the unconscious part of general knowledge, has greatly extended the meaning of the term and uses it for any "emotionally toned system of ideas" which determines conscious behaviour, taking the hobby as his special example, while he also instances political bias as a complex. During the war the term has come to be used very loosely. Worries and anxieties arising out of recent and fully conscious experience have been spoken of as complexes. In fact, the word is often used in so wide and loose a sense that my own tendency at present is to avoid it altogether, and this course will have to be followed in scientific writings unless we can agree upon some definition which will make the term "complex" really serviceable as an instrument of thought. I propose now to do what I can towards the formulation of such a definition.[1]

In the broad sense which Hart proposes for "complex," the term becomes almost identical with the "sentiment" of the orthodox psychologist. Used in this definite sense, the term and concept of "sentiment" are among the most recent and valuable acquisitions of psychology, but in my opinion it will only tend to confusion of thought to include in one category sentiments and the bodies of suppressed experience to which I should like to see the term "complex" limited, if it is going to be used at all.

It may perhaps help to make clear how I distinguish sentiments from complexes if I illustrate by similar products on the sensorimotor level. Such an experiment as that of Head [2] shows that certain forms of protopathic experience, such as the radiation and reference of sensation in space, are suppressed while other elements are fused with later developed forms of sensation to make up the normal modes of sensibility of the skin. Let us consider for a moment what we mean when we speak of the sensibility for cold. We mean that the skin is endowed with "something" which, when a body

---

[1] [Tansley states that "the whole of Hart's use of the term is implicit in Jung's original treatment."—*The New Psychology*, 6 (Dodd, Mead, 1924).]

[2] [*Cf.* the present volume, pp 139 *ff.*]

with certain physical properties touches the skin, determines both our experience of cold, and the special kind of behaviour which is adapted to this experience. What we mean by sensibility is thus comparable to the "something" in our mental constitution which determines that when we read in the paper of a certain event, we experience the special kind of affect and special tendency to behaviour, which determine the relation of that event to our political conduct, which help, for instance, to determine how we shall vote at the next election. This "something" which thus determines our feelings and conduct is what the orthodox psychologist knows as a sentiment.

We have seen that the sensibility of the normal skin is produced by the process of fusion of different kinds of tendency and experience. This fusion is a process of a wholly different order from the suppression by which certain features of early experience have been put out of activity. The whole process of development of cutaneous sensibility which is made clear and intelligible by distinguishing suppression from fusion, and by defining the proper place and share of each, would be hopelessly obscured if we confused the two very different processes of suppression and fusion under one heading. And yet this is what in my opinion has been done by Bernard Hart when he includes under the term "complex" the highly complicated product of fusion, which by other psychologists is called a sentiment, and the suppressed experience which probably, indeed certainly, enters into the process of fusion, but only as one of its elements. Using the terms as I propose, both complex and sentiment determine thought and conduct, but differ from each other profoundly in other respects. They differ first in complexity, the sentiment being far more complex in its nature than the process which has been denoted according to this feature.[3] Secondly, to use the special terminology of this book, the sentiment is a far more epicritic product than the complex. The sentiments are features of the mind which take part in the most finely graduated processes and are connected with discrimination of the most delicate description. The complex, on the other hand, being the result of suppression always partakes in some degree of the crude "all-or-none" character which we have been led to associate with suppression. Months or years may pass without its showing any effects at all and

---

[3] It is very unfortunate that the complex should have been so named. Its two characteristic features are its relation to the unconscious and its affective importance, and a suitable term should have reference to one, if not to both, of these features.

then it may reveal its presence by some profound and far-reaching disturbance of the mental life.

Lastly, it is not without importance that the sentiment is an absolutely necessary and constant feature of the normal mental life. Most of our sentiments come into action daily and influence the behaviour of every moment of the life of every day. The complex, on the other hand, in the sense in which I should like to use the term, has essentially a pathological implication. It is not only a result of suppression, but the product of independent activity of the suppressed content, whether accompanied by alternate consciousness or wholly within the region of the unconscious. There is, of course, no hard-and-fast line between the healthy and the morbid, and it is possible, if not probable, that the complex will in some cases shade off into the sentiment, but I believe it is useful that pathology shall have its own terms and concepts. I believe that it will be best to reserve the term "complex" for products which partake, in some degree at any rate, of a morbid quality and that nothing but confusion can result from the inclusion in one category of definitely pathological processes and such absolutely normal and necessary processes as the sentiments.

B

W. S. TAYLOR; adapted from "The Nature of the Complex as Compared with the Sentiment," *Psychol. Rev.*, 33: 68-69 (1926)

Rivers' suggestion in the foregoing paragraph that in some instances the complex will shade off into the sentiment brings out an important case of the principle of *relativeness*,[1] as that principle is so often found in human problems. For it becomes clear as one observes the workings of meanings which lie beyond "the fringe" of consciousness, and the "bubblings up" of elements from subconscious systems into consciousness, that no hard and fast line can be drawn between all sentiments and all complexes. Between the extremes of the descriptive scale, the difference is sharp in accordance with Rivers' definition; but there are plenty of borderline cases in the series.

Also, we should note that, apparently due to the inevitable narrowness of "the field of consciousness" (however this label be interpreted), a very richly constituted sentiment has so many "roots" in experiences conserved beyond the scope of immediate awareness, that such a sentiment, by its very cumbersomeness, so to speak, must function in a manner strongly resembling the behavior of a complex.

---

[1] *Cf.* Prince, *The Unconscious*, 418-422.

This is true, for example, of a mother's sentiment of parental affection for a child that has recently died. No one of the "neurograms" recording experiences with that child is dissociated from her main consciousness; all those memories, let us say, are fully available to her normal consciousness. Yet the *mass* of such associations, strongly welded together and associated with the emotion of grief, but with only a few of the elements of the sentiment in position at any instant for effective inhibition, functions in the crude mass fashion characteristic of a complex. This situation continues, until, through reflecting on the incidents of the child's life, one by one, the mother associates them with other elements, such as her philosophy, and the pleasures she meets in her daily life. Thus she "re-sets" the elements of that sentiment, freeing them from their bondage to a common emotion. The result is that those elements (now really constituents of new sentiments) no longer are set to produce together a single emotion in excessive quantity.

Again, a very frequently practised habit may easily function after the pattern of a complex. A good example is the oft-cited instance of the ex-soldier, who, in carrying a kettle of soup across the street dropped it mechanically when some wag bawled out "Attention!" Here it would seem that the "Attention" pattern is so well-traced or impressed within its own limits, that *relative* to the connections between it and properly inhibitory patterns that "Attention" pattern is dissociated.

Experimental Tests of Connection between Complex-Systems and the Main Consciousness

MORTON PRINCE, *The Unconscious*, 481-484 (copyright, 1921, by The Macmillan Company); reprinted by permission

The psychogalvanic reaction as physical evidence of actual subconscious emotional discharge.—This reaction may be also used to demonstrate that subconscious processes may actually give forth emotional impulses without the ideas of those processes entering the personal consciousness.

I may be permitted to cite here some experiments,[1] which I made with Dr. Frederick Peterson, as they leave the minimum of latitude for interpretation and come as close as possible to the demonstration of emotional discharges from processes entirely outside of

---

[1] *Jour. Abn. Psychol.*, June-July, 1908.

awareness. Such a demonstration is important for the theory of subconscious conflicts.

The experiments were undertaken in a case of multiple personality (B.C.A.) with a view to obtaining the galvanic phenomenon from coconscious states. This case offered an exceptional opportunity to determine whether the galvanic reaction could be obtained in one personality from the dissociated complexes *deposited by the experiences of the second alternating personality for which there was complete amnesia on the part of the first.* These dissociated experiences, of course, had never entered the awareness of the personality tested, who, therefore, necessarily could not possibly recall them to memory. With the information furnished by the second personality, it was easy to arrange test words associated with the emotional ideas of the experiences belonging to this personality and unknown to the one tested.

Similarly it was possible to test whether galvanic reaction could be obtained from complexes—from subconscious complexes—the residua of forgotten dreams, as in this case the dreams were not remembered on waking. An account of the dreams could be obtained in hypnosis. The dreams were therefore simply dissociated.

Again we could test the possibility of obtaining reactions from subconscious perceptions and thoughts which had never arisen into awareness. The required information concerning these perceptions and thoughts could be obtained in this case in hypnosis.

Now we found that test words which expressed the emotional ideas belonging to a forgotten dream gave, in spite of the amnesia, very marked rises in the galvanic curve. The same was true of the test words referring to dissociated experiences belonging to the *alternating* personality for which the tested personality had amnesia, and of the subconscious perceptions. For instance (as an example of the latter), the word *lorgnette,* referring to a subconscious perception of a stranger unnoticed by the conscious personality, gave a very lively reaction.

Further, pin pricks, which could not be consciously perceived owing to the *anesthesia* of the skin, gave strong reactions.

Now here in the first two sets of observations were emotional effects apparently obtained from what were very precise complexes which were definitely underlying, in that they never had been experienced by the personality tested and therefore could not come from memories, or from associations of which this personality was aware. They could only come from the residua of a personality which had experienced them and which was now "underlying." That these experiences had been conserved is shown by the recovery of them in a hypnotic state, and by their being remembered by the secondary personality. Even the pin pricks, which were not felt on account of the anesthesia, gave reactions. It could be logically inferred, therefore, that the galvanic reaction was due to the activity of subconscious complexes, using the term in the narrow and restricted sense of conserved residua without conscious equivalents. But the conditions were more complicated than I have described. There was in this case a veritable coconscious personality, a split-off, well-organized system of conscious states synthesized into a personal consciousness—two foci of self-consciousness. Now the coconscious personality with its large system of thought had full memory of all these amnesic experiences; it remembered the dreams and the experiences of the second personality, and perceived the pin pricks. Hence we concluded that the galvanic phenomena were obtained from the memory and perceptions of this coconscious personality.

This demonstration of an actual physical discharge is proof positive that an emotional process can function subconsciously. This being so, *it only needs this discharge to come into conflict with some other process, conscious or subconscious, for one or other phenomenon of conflict to be manifested.*

Association Systems

Morton Prince, *The Unconscious*, 283-286, 290-291, 294-296 (copyright 1921, by The Macmillan Company); reprinted by permission

In contrast with the limited group of fixed ideas, organized with one or more emotions (i. e., instincts) I have been describing, are the large *systems* of complexes or associated experiences which become organized and fairly distinctly differentiated in the course of the development of every one's personality. In many, at least, of these systems there will be found a predominant emotion and certain instinctive tendencies, and a predominant feeling tone—of pleasure or pain, of exaltation or depression, etc. It is quite possible that careful investigation would disclose that it is this conflicting affective force which is responsible for the differentiation of one system from another with opposing affects and tendencies. The differentiation of such systematized complexes is of considerable practical importance for normal and abnormal personality. Among such systems may here be mentioned those which are related to certain *subjects* or departments of human experience, or are related in *time,* or to certain dispositions or *moods* of the individual. The first may be called *subject* systems, the second *chronological* systems, and the last *mood* systems.

1. *Subject systems:* I find myself interested, for instance, in several fields of human knowledge; (a) abnormal psychology; (b) public franchises; (c) yachting; (d) local politics; (e) business affairs. To each of these I give a large amount of thought, accumulate many data belonging to each, and devote a considerable amount of active work to carrying into effect my ideas in each field. Five large systems are thus formed, each consisting of facts, opinions, memories, experiences, etc., distinct from those belonging to the others. To each there is an emotion and a feeling tone which have more or less distinctive qualities; these coming from the intellectual interest of abnormal psychology differing qualitatively from those of the "joy of battle" excited by a public contest with a railroad corporation or gas company, as it does from that of the exhilarating sport of a yacht race, or from the annoying and rather depressing care of business interests; and so on.

These five subject-complexes do not form independent automatisms or isolated systems which may intrude themselves in any conscious field, but comprise large associations, memories of experiences in a special field of thought. Within that field the ideas of the system are no more strongly organized than are ideas in general; but it can be recognized that the system as a whole with its affective tones is fairly well delimited from the other complexes of other spheres of thought. It is difficult, for certain individuals at least, to introduce the associations of one subject-complex into the focus of attention so long as another is invested with personal interest and occupies the attention of consciousness. They find it difficult to switch [1] their minds from one subject to another and back again. On the other hand, it is said of Napoleon that he had all the subjects of his experiences arranged in drawers of his mind, and that he could open each drawer at will, take out any subject he wished, and shut it up again as he wished. Ability of this kind involves remarkable control over the mind and is not given to all. . . .

2. *Chronological systems* . . . are those which embrace the ex-

---

[1] The switching process is an interesting problem in itself. (*Cf.* Max Levy-Suhl: "Ueber Einstellungsvorgänge in normalen und anormalen Seelenzuständen." *Zeitschrift für Psychotherapie und Medizinische Psychologie*, Bd. 11, Hft. 3, 1910.) An example is the well-known psychological diagram which may be perceived at one moment as a flight of steps and at another as an overhanging wall, according as which perception of the same line is switched in.

periences of certain epochs of our lives rather than the subject material included in them. In a general way events as they are successively experienced become associated together, and with other elements of personality, so that the later recollection of one event in the chain of an epoch recalls successively the others. Conversely a break in the chain of memory may occur at any point and the chain only be picked up at a more distant date, leaving between, as a hiatus, an epoch for which there is amnesia of reproduction. This normally common *amnesia affords confirmatory evidence* of the associative relation of successive events. Involving as it does the unimportant and unemotional experiences as well as the important and emotional—though the former may be as well conserved as the latter—it is not easy to understand. The principle, however, plays an important part in abnormal amnesia particularly, but not necessarily, where there is a dissociation of personality.

The epoch may be of a few hours, or it may be of days, of months, or years. The simplest example is the frequent amnesia for the few hours preceding a physical injury to the head resulting in temporary unconsciousness. In other cases it is the result of extensive dissociation effected by suggestion (e. g., in hypnosis), or psychical trauma including therein emotional conflicts. Thus, to cite an experimental example: Miss B. is troubled by a distressing memory which constantly recurs to her mind during the twenty-four hours. To relieve her I suggest that she will completely forget the original experience. To my surprise, though the suggestion is limited to the experience alone, the whole twenty-four hours are completely wiped out of her memory. She cannot recall a single incident of that day. The whole epoch which had associations with the memory is dissociated. . . .

3. *Disposition or Mood systems.*[2] Among the loosely organized complexes in many individuals, and possibly in all of us, there are certain dispositions toward views of life which represent natural inclinations, desires, and modes of activity, which, for one reason or another, we tend to suppress or are unable to give full play to. Many individuals, for example, are compelled by the exactions of their duties and responsibilities to lead serious lives, to devote themselves to pursuits which demand all their energies and thought and which, therefore, do not permit of indulgence in the lighter enjoyments of life; and yet they may have a natural inclination to partake of the pleasures which innately appeal to all mankind and

---

[2] [For the striking operation of such systems through waking from sleep, *cf.* Robinson's *Readings*, 360.]

which many actually pursue; in other words, to yield to the impulsive force of the innate disposition, or instinct, of play. But these desires are repressed. Nevertheless the longing for these pleasures, under the impulses of this instinct, recurs from time to time. The mind dwells on them, the imagination is excited and weaves a fabric of pictures, sentiments, thoughts, and emotions the whole of which thus becomes organized into a systematized complex. . . .

It may be interesting to note in passing that the well-known characteristics of people of a certain temperament, in consequence of which they can pursue their respective vocations only when they are "in the mood for it," can be referred to this principle of complex formations and dissociation of rival systems. Literary persons, musicians, and artists in whom "feeling" is apt to be cultivated to a degree of self-pampering are conspicuous in this class. The ideas pertaining to the development of their craft form mixed subject and mood complexes which tend to have strong emotional and feeling tones. When some other affective tone is substituted, organized within a conflicting complex, it is difficult for such persons to revive the subject complex belonging to the piece of work in hand and necessary for its prosecution. "The ideas will not come," because the whole subject complex which supplies the material with which the imagination is to work has been dissociated and replaced by some other. Certain elements in the complex can be revived piecemeal, as it were, but the complex will not develop in mass with the emotional driving energy which belongs to it. Not having their complexes and affects under voluntary control it is necessary for such persons to wait until, from an alteration in the coenesthesis or for some other reason, an alteration in the "feeling" has taken place with a revival of the right complex *in mass.*

CHAPTER XI

CONFLICT AND SOME OF ITS MANIFESTATIONS

In an earlier selection in this volume, in connection with Some Fundamental Psychological Conceptions, Professors Smith and Guthrie discussed the interaction of stimulus-response mechanisms (*supra*, pp. 130 *ff.*). In such interaction, apparently, we have the fundamentals of conflict.

The operation of conflict also, was at least implicit in many of the topics treated under the headings of Emotion, Dissociation, Symbolism, Wishes, Complexes, and Systems. The selections which follow are more specific instances of the same principle. Still further manifestations of conflict will appear on later pages.

The Nature and Types of Conflict

MORTON PRINCE, *The Unconscious*, 454-456, 489-492, 460-461, 467-481 (copyright, 1921, by The Macmillan Company) ; reprinted by permission

When an emotion is aroused a conflict necessarily occurs between its impulse and that of any other existing affective state, the impulse of which is antagonistic to the aim of the former. Consequently instincts and sentiments which, through the conative force of their emotion, tend to drive the conduct of the individual in a course in opposition to that of a newly aroused emotion (instinct) meet with resistance. Whichever instinct or sentiment, meaning whichever impulse, is the stronger necessarily downs the other ; inhibits the central and efferent parts of the process—ideas, emotions and impulses—though the afferent part conveys the stimulus to the central factor. Thus processes of thought to which the inhibited sentiment or instinct would normally give rise, or with which it is systematized, are likewise inhibited and behavior correspondingly modified. These statements are only descriptive of what is common experience. If one recalls to mind the principal primary emotions (instincts) such as the sexual, anger, fear, tender feeling, hunger, self-abasement, self-assertion, curiosity, etc., this is seen to be an obvious biological truth.[1] Fear is suppressed by anger, tender feeling, or curiosity (wonder), and *vice versa;* hunger and the sexual instinct by disgust.

What is true of the primitive instincts and their primary emotions is also true of compound instincts (emotions) and of sentiments, i. e., ideas about which one or several emotions are systematized. We may, therefore, for brevity's sake, speak of a conflict of ideas or sentiments or emotions or instincts indiscriminately. In other words, *any affective state may be suppressed by conflict with another and stronger affective state.* A timid mother, impelled by the parental instinct, has no fear of danger to herself when her child is threatened. The instinct of pugnacity (anger) in this case not being antagonistic (in conflict) is not only not suppressed but may be awakened as a reaction to aid in the expression of the parental instinct. *Per contra,* when anger would conflict with this instinct, as when the child does wrong, the anger is suppressed by the parental instinct. Conversely, the sentiment of love for a particular person may be completely suppressed by jealousy and anger. Hatred of a person may expel from consciousness previous sentiments of sympathy, justice, pity, respect, fear, etc. The animal under the influence of the parental instinct may be incapable of fear in defense of its young, particularly if anger is excited. Fear may be suppressed in an animal or human being if either is impelled by great curiosity over a strange object. Instead of taking to flight, the animal may stand still in wonder. Similarly in man, curiosity to examine, for example, an explosive—an unexploded shell or bomb—inhibits the fear of danger often, as we know, with disastrous results. The suppression of the sexual instinct by conflict is one of the most notorious of the experiences of this kind in everyday life. This instinct cannot be excited during an attack of fear and anger, and even during moments of its excitation, if there is an invasion of another strong emotion the sexual instinct at once is repressed. Under these conditions, as with other instincts, even habitual excitants can no longer initiate the instinctive process. Chloe would appeal in vain to her lover if he were suddenly seized with fright or she had inadvertently awakened in him an intense jealousy or anger. Similarly the instinct may be suppressed, particularly in men, as every psycho-pathologist has observed, by the awakening of the instinct of self-subjection with

---

[1] I follow in the main McDougall's classification as sufficiently adequate and accurate for our purposes.

its emotion of self-abasement (McDougall) with fear, shown in the sentiments of incapacity, shame, etc. The authors of *"Vous n'avez rien à déclarer"* make this the principal theme in this laughable drama. Indeed the principle of the suppression of one instinct by conflict with another has been made use of by writers of fiction and drama in all times. . . .

In the heat of anger the mind is dominated by the particular object or thought which gave rise to the anger, or by anger exciting associated ideas. Conflicting memories and correlated knowledge that would modify the point of view and judgment and mollify (inhibit) the anger are suppressed and cannot enter the focus of attention. Further, a person in such a state may not perceive many ocular, auditory, tactile, and other impressions coming from the environment; he may not see the people about him, hear what is said, or feel what is done to him, or only in an imperfect way. All these sensations are either actually inhibited or prevented from entering awareness (dissociated) by the conflicting conative force of the emotion. In other words there is a dissociation (or inhibition) of consciousness and consequent contraction of its field to certain emotional ideas. . . .

When this same general contraction of the field of consciousness, effected by the repressing force of emotion, reaches a certain acme we have a pathological condition—the *hysterical state*. The field of consciousness is now occupied by the single dissociating idea or complex of ideas with its emotion that did the repressing—a condition of mono-ideism. All other conscious processes are inhibited or dissociated. When the complex is an intensely emotional one, its nervous energy, now unbridled, is free to discharge itself in many directions, perhaps producing convulsive phenomena of one kind or another.

To attribute these effects of emotion to repression *from conflict* is only to express the facts in different terms. But it would be often an over-emphasis to describe what takes place as a specific conflict between particular sentiments. It is often rather the discharge of a blind impulsive force in every direction which, like a blast of dynamite, suppresses or dissociates every other process which might come into consciousness and displace it. . . .

The repressions resulting from conflict which we have just been considering have been of a temporary nature lasting only just so long as the conflict has lasted. It is instructive to note that just as an instinct can be cultivated until it becomes a ruling trait in the character, so it can be permanently repressed, or so intensely repressed that it cannot be awakened excepting by unusual excitants or under unusual conditions. Such a persisting repression may be brought about either directly by volitional conflict or indirectly through the cultivation of antagonistic sentiments. The cultivation of an instinct is a common enough observation. Every one can point to some one of his acquaintance who has so fostered his instinct of anger or fear, has so cultivated the habit of one or the other reaction that he has become the slave of his emotion. Conversely, by the conative force of the will, and still more successfully by the cultivation of appropriate moral and religious and other sentiments, and complexes or "settings" systematized about those sentiments, a person can inhibit any instinct or any sentiment organized with that instinct. A bad-tempered person can thus, if he chooses, become good-tempered; a coward, a brave person; a person governed by the instinct of self-subjection can repress it by the cultivation of sentiments of self-assertion, and so on. The complete repression of unchristian instincts and sentiments is the acquired characteristic of the saintly character. The cultivation and repression of character traits and tendencies along these lines obviously belong to the domains of the psychology of character, social psychology, and criminology. But the persisting repression of at least one instinct—the sexual instinct—may take on pathological significance [2] while that of sentiments may lead to pathological dissociation and to the *formation of disturbing subconscious states*. To this latter type of repression we shall presently return. . . .

Thus far we have been considering conflicts between sentiments and emotional processes which have been in the full light of consciousness. But in previous lectures we have seen that ideas with strong emotional tones may be dissociated and function below the threshold of consciousness as coconscious processes. It is theoretically possible, therefore, that conflicts might arise between a dissociated coconscious sentiment and one that is antagonistic to it in consciousness. To appreciate this theoretical condition let me point out that there is one important *difference between the ultimate consequences of the repression of an instinct and of a sentiment.*

---

[2] The repression of the sexual instinct and of sexual wishes plays the dominant rôle in the Freudian psychology. If a wish may be correctly defined psychologically as the impulsive force of a sentiment striving toward an end plus the pleasurable feeling resulting from the imagined attainment of that end, i. e., the imagined gratification of the impulse, then the repression of a wish belongs to the phenomena of repressed sentiments rather than of primitive instincts. This distinction, I think, is of some importance, as will appear when we consider subconscious sentiments.

If an instinct is repressed (it being only an innate disposition) it ceases to be an active factor in the functioning organism. It is inhibited. A stimulus that ordinarily suffices to excite it fails to do so, and it may respond only to an extraordinarily powerful stimulus, or perhaps none will awaken it. Thus abstinence from food fails to awaken a sense of hunger in a person who has lost this instinct for any reason, even though appetizing food be placed before him.[3] Similarly anger, or fear, or tender emotion, or self-assertion, or disgust, in certain persons cannot be awakened excepting by very unusual stimuli. In other words, the psycho-physiological reflex is completely or relatively in abeyance just as much so as is an organic reflex (e. g., the knee-jerk) which has been inhibited. Normally, of course, it is rare for an instinct to be absolutely inhibited excepting temporarily, as has been explained, during a conflict with another instinct. In certain pathological conditions (e. g., dissociated personality), almost any instinct may be persistently inhibited. In normal conditions there is, however, one exception, namely the sexual instinct, which, as we have seen from instances cited, may be inhibited during long periods of time. In women this inhibition is common and is effected, as I believe, by the subtle and insensible influence of the environment of the child and by social education, in other words, by the social taboo. Wherever inhibition occurs observation would seem to show that the psycho-physiological function has ceased to take part in the functioning organism.

With sentiments, however, the case stands differently. A sentiment, being an idea about which a system of emotional dispositions has been organized, when repressed by conflict, or when simply out of mind, whether capable of reproduction as memory or not, may, like all ideas, still be conserved, as we have seen, as an unconscious neurogram. As we have also seen, so long as it is conserved it is still a part of the personality. Even though repressed it is not necessarily absolutely inhibited but may be simply dissociated and then be *able to take on dissociated subconscious activity*. As a subconscious process the idea continues still organized with its emotional dispositions, and the conative forces of these, under certain conditions, may continue striving to give expression to the idea. . . .

1. This being so, it having been determined that *under certain conditions* any conserved experience may become activated as a dissociated subconscious process, it is *theoretically* quite possible that the impulses of an activated subconscious sentiment might come into

---

[3] A distinction should be made between hunger and appetite. Food may excite appetite, although hunger has been appeased.

conflict with the impulses of a conscious process—the two being antagonistic. The resulting phenomena might be the same as when both factors to the contest are in consciousness. In such a conflict if the impulsive force of the subconscious sentiment is the stronger the conscious ideas, sentiments, and feelings—in short, the conscious process—would be repressed, and *vice versa*. Or if the subconscious sentiment got the worst of the conflict and could not repress the conscious process, the former, being dissociated and an independent "automatic" process, might theoretically induce various other phenomena in the effort to fulfil its aim. If it could not directly overcome the impulses of the conscious process it might circumvent the latter by inducing mental and physiological disturbances which would indirectly prevent the conscious impulses from fulfilling their aim; e. g., inhibition of the will, dissociation or total inhibition of consciousness, amnesia for particular memories, motor phenomena interfering with normal activity, etc. The subconscious sentiment engaging in such a conflict could be excited to activity by any associative antagonistic idea in consciousness. It should be noted that the subject being entirely unaware of the subconscious process would not know the cause of the resulting phenomena.

2. Now, in fact, *such hypothetical conflicts and phenomena are actually observed* in very neat and precise form *under experimental conditions,* particularly in pathological or quasi-pathological subjects. These conditions are particularly instructive as they allow us to clearly recognize the subconscious character of the conflicting process and detect the exact sentiment concerned therein.

The following experiment illustrative of such a conflict between a conscious and subconscious process I have repeated many times in one subject with the same resulting phenomenon. It has been demonstrated on several occasions to psychologists and others. On the first occasion when the phenomenon was observed it was entirely spontaneous and unexpected as also has since been frequently the case.

B. C. A. [a case of multiple personality, somewhat similar to the case cited above, p. 87] in one phase of alternating personality (B) was asked to mention a certain complex of ideas which was known to have been organized about a distressing "sentiment" in another phase (C) causing considerable unhappiness. This sentiment included a strong emotion of pride in consequence of which she had in the C phase intense objections to revealing these ideas. As she herself said, she "would have gone to the stake first." Phase B has no such sentiment, but on the contrary the ideas in question were only amusing to her.[4] In phase B, therefore, she not only had no objection to revealing the sentiment distressing to C but desired for therapeutic reasons to do so. In accordance with this difference of sentiments the difference in the attitude of mind in the two phases toward the same experience was quite striking. The impulse in the one was to conceal the experiences and sentiment, in the other to divulge them.

Now, in reply to an interrogatory as to what was distressing in the C phase, B begins to mention the sentiment. At once, and to her astonishment, her lips and tongue are tied by painful spasms involving, also, the throat muscles. She becomes dumb, unable to overcome the resistance. She struggles in vain to speak. When she gives up the struggle to pronounce the forbidden words she speaks with ease on other subjects saying "something prevented me from speaking." Each time that she endeavors to turn State's evidence and to peach on herself, the same struggle is repeated. When she persists in her effort, using all her will-power, the effect of the conflicting force extends to consciousness. Her thoughts become first confused, then obliterated, and she falls back in her seat limp, paralyzed, and apparently unconscious. The thoughts to which she strove to give expression have disappeared. She now cannot even will to speak.

But she is not really unconscious, it is only another phase; there is only a dissociation or inhibition of the consciousness comprising the system of ideas making up the B phase and an awakening of another restricted system. When automatic writing is tried, it is found that a limited field of consciousness is present in which are to be found the ideas which opposed the resistance. A precise statement of the opposing factors (volition) which offered the resistance and brought about the conflict, the spasm of the vocal apparatus, and finally inhibition or dissociation of consciousness, is obtained from this dissociated restricted field.[5]

This phenomenon carries its own interpretation on its face and

---

[4] Note that the same idea forms different sentiments in different phases or moods, according to the emotions with which it is linked. In this case, in phase C, it is linked with mortification, self-abasement, possibly anger, pride, and feelings of pain and depression; in phase B, with joyful emotions and feelings of pleasure and excitement. Also note that the former sentiment, although out of mind at the time of the observation, is conserved in the unconscious.

[5] At first the subject (B) had no anticipation or supposition that such a conflict would occur. Later she learned after repeated experiences to anticipate the probable consequences of trying to tell tales-out-of-school.

cannot be doubted. Certain sentiments, for the moment dormant and outside the focus of awareness of the subject, are "struck" or stimulated by memories within that focus. The conative force of the conscious wishes to which the subject seeks to give expression meets with the resistance of a similar and more powerful force from the previously dormant sentiment. The latter carries itself to fulfilment and *controls the vocal apparatus at first, and then, finding itself likely to be overcome by the will-power of the personality, annihilates the latter by the inhibition and dissociation of consciousness.*

Various forms of the same phenomenon of conflict with subconscious processes I have experimentally demonstrated in Miss B. and O. N. Spontaneous manifestations of the same have also been frequently observed in all three subjects. In the published account of Miss B.[6] numerous examples are given. I will merely refer to the attacks of aboulia, the dissociations of consciousness and inhibition of thought, and of speech resulting in stuttering and dumbness, the inhibition of motor activity, the induction of systematized anesthesia and alexia, etc. In the prolonged study of the case I was the witness, I was going to say, of innumerable exhibitions of such manifestations, and the book is replete with examples of conflicts between opposing mental processes. B. C. A. in her account, "My Life as a Dissociated Personality," [7] has described similar spontaneous phenomena. It is worth noting in this connection that the commonplace phenomena of systematized anesthesia (negative hallucinations) may be induced by conflict with a subconscious process motivated by strong emotion. Thus Miss B. in one of her phases could not see the writing on a sheet of paper which appeared blank to her; on another occasion she could not see the printing of the pages of a French novel which she therefore took to be a blank book, nor could she see a bookcase containing French books.[8] The subconscious conflicting ideas were motivated by anger in the one case and jealousy in the other. That the conflicting ideas in this case were elements synthesized in a large dissociated system or subconscious self in no way affects the principle, which is that of conflict between processes. The conflicting process in such conditions is a more complex one, that is all. Undoubtedly the systematized anesthesia, so easily induced by hypnotic suggestion and which has been made the subject of much study, may be explained on the

---

[6] *The Dissociation*, see Index: "Subconscious ideas."
[7] *Jour. Abn. Psychol.*, October-November, 1908.
[8] *The Dissociation*, p. 538.

same principle, although the affective elements are not so obtrusive. The conflict is between the personal volition of the subject to see the marked playing-card, if that is the test object used in the experiment, and the suggested idea not to see it. The latter wins if the experiment is successful and inhibits the perception of the card—i. e., dissociates it from the focus of awareness. (The emotional tones involved are obscure; possibly they are curiosity on the one hand vs. self-subjection on the other.)

The *unconscious resistance to suggestion* is probably of the same nature. Every one knows that it is difficult to hypnotize a person who resists the suggestion. This resistance may come from a counter auto-suggestion which may be entirely involuntary, perhaps a conviction on the part of the subject that she cannot be hypnotized, or an unwillingness to be—i. e., desire not to be hypnotized or fear. The same is true of waking a person from hypnosis. In other words, an antagonistic preparedness of the mind blocks involuntarily the suggestion. A very pretty illustration is the following: H. O. discovered that she could easily and rapidly hypnotize herself by simply passing her own fingers over her eyelids, but she could not wake herself out of hypnosis. She then discovered that, if she first gave herself the suggestion that she would wake when she desired, she could quickly do so. Likewise, if she suggested to herself that she could not hypnotize herself the customary procedure was without effect. Though this observation is a common phenomenon the rapidity and ease with which the phenomenon was demonstrated were as striking as it was amusing to watch her struggle to awake when the preparatory anticipatory autosuggestion had not been given.

In O. N. *more complicated phenomena* induced by conflicts with subconscious complexes have been equally precise and striking. In this subject I find, as the result of repeated observations, that, in order that a suggestion, that is antagonistic to a preëxisting attitude of mind possessing a strong feeling tone, shall not be resisted in hypnosis, it must be first formally accepted by the personality *before* hypnosis is induced. If this viewpoint is not performed, after hypnosis is induced the blocking attitude cannot be altered. Practically this means that the subject shall *bring into consciousness and disclose ideas* with which the intended suggestion will conflict and shall modify them voluntarily. This she does by first candidly accepting a new point of view, and then, secondly, by a technical procedure of her own, namely, by preparing her mind not to resist in hypnosis. This procedure, briefly stated and simplified, is as follows: she first says to herself, "I will 'take out' that [resist-

ing] idea." Then she arranges in her thoughts the ideas of acceptance which she will substitute. Then she puts herself into a state
of abstraction (hypnosis) and *suggests to herself* that the resisting
idea *is* taken out and that my intended suggestion shall be her viewpoint. Even then, sometimes, when the resisting idea is one hark-
ing back to a long past period of life and belonging to a patho-
logically organized "mood," known as the "b mood" or state, the
acceptance of the suggestion may be ineffectual. Under these circumstances and *when the hypnotic dissociation is carried too far,*
so that the hypnotic state is reduced to the "b mood," the previously
auto-suggested acceptance of the idea by the patient is thereby ostra-
cized from the hypnotic field and is unable to play its part and
have effect. So much by way of explanation.

Now when the precaution has not been taken to see that any resisting idea has been "taken out" and when the intended suggestion
has not been accepted, one of the following phenomena is observed:
(1) the hypnotic personality when the suggestion is given becomes
"automatically" and unconsciously restless, endeavors, *without
knowing why,* to avoid listening, and to push me away, shifting
her attitude and struggling to withdraw herself from contact or
proximity—all the time the face expressing hostility and disapproval
in its features; or (2) complete obnubilation of consciousness supervenes so that the suggestions are not heard; or (3) the subject
suddenly wakes up. The last frequently happens as often as the
suggestion is repeated; and yet in hypnosis (and also, of course,
when awake), the subject is unaware of what causes the resistance
and the resulting phenomena. But if now the subject is warned
of what has occurred and accepts the suggestion by the procedure
mentioned (unless the "b mood" I have mentioned recurs), the
resistance and other phenomena at once cease and the suggestion
takes effect. Thus in this case the conflicting ideas can always be
precisely determined and the conditions of the experiment arranged
at will and the results controlled. It is obvious that all three phenomena are different modes by which the subconscious idea resists
the suggested idea and accomplishes its aim.

3. *In entire accordance with the experimental results are certain pathological disturbances* which from time to time interrupt
the course of everyday life of this subject, O. N. These disturbances consist of one or more of the following: a dissociative state
in which the pathological "b mood" is dominant; a lethargic state;
twilight state; complete repression of certain normal sentiments
and instincts; complete alteration of previously established points
of view; morbid self-reproach; nervousness, restlessness, agitation;

anger at opposition; indecision of thought, etc. Now, whenever such phenomena recur, with practical certainty, they can always be traced by the use of technical methods to a conflict with a turbulent sentiment (in which strong emotional tones are incorporated) previously lying dormant in the unconscious. Sometimes the turbulent sentiment can be definitely traced to childhood's experiences. Very often it has been intentionally formed and put into her mind by the subject herself for the very purpose of inducing the repression of other sentiments, to which for one reason or another for the time being she objects, and of changing her habitual point of view.

Her method of artificially accomplishing this result is exceedingly instructive. It is similar to the auto-suggestive process I have described in connection with the hypnotic experiments. Having first prearranged her psychological plan, she proceeds to put herself into abstraction and to "take out", as she calls it, her previous sentiment (or instinct) and substitute an antagonistic sentiment. When she comes to herself out of abstraction, the previously objected to sentiment has completely vanished. If it is one concerning a person or mode of life, she becomes completely indifferent to that person or mode of life as if previously no sentiment had existed. If an intimate friend, he becomes only an acquaintance toward whom she has entirely new feelings corresponding to the new sentiment; if a physician, nothing that he says has influence with her, her new feeling, we will say, being that of resentment; if a mode of life, she has lost all interest in that mode and is governed by an interest in a new mode. Even physiological bodily instincts have been in this way suppressed. She has indulged this psychological habit for years. Again and again when she has exhibited these, and still other, phenomena, I have been able to discover their origin in this auto-suggestive procedure.

Some of the other phenomena I have just mentioned are more likely to be traced to *autochthonous conflicts between everyday ideas* —dissatisfactions with actual conditions of life, and wishes for other conditions, unwillingness to forego the fulfilment of certain wishes and accept the necessary conditions as they exist, etc. The natural consequence is restlessness, agitation, anger, indecision, etc. The dissociation of personality, with the outcropping of the "b mood," follows—a conflict due to the excitation of certain childhood complexes, conserved in the unconscious and embracing sentiments in which are incorporated the instinct of self-subjection or abasement. This "b mood" is a study in itself. The self-reproaches are, I believe, also traceable to this instinct.

Conflicts may even occur between two processes, both of which are subconscious and therefore outside of the awareness of the subject. Thus, in B. C. A. I have frequently observed the following: while the right hand has been engaged in automatic writing, the left hand, motivated by a subconscious sentiment antagonistic to the subconscious ideas performing the writing, has seized the pencil, broken it, or thrown it across the room. The two conflicting systems of thought, each with its own sentiments and wishes, have been made to disclose themselves and exhibit their antitheses and antipathies.

The principle of emotional conflict and the phenomena we have outlined enable us to understand the mechanism of prolonged reaction time and blocking of thought observed in the so-called "word association tests." These tests involve too large a subject for us to enter upon them here. Let it suffice to say that when a test word strikes an emotional complex the response of the subject by an associated word may be delayed or completely blocked. The emotional impulse which inhibits the response may come from an awakened conscious or subconscious memory.

"Censorship"

EDWIN B. HOLT, *The Freudian Wish*, 13-16 (Holt, 1915)

The more rational wishes, which in ordinary waking hours are strong enough to hold the morbid wish in abeyance, constitute the individual's recognized character. It is they, or the mechanisms that embody them, which need the recuperation of sleep; it is they which "go to sleep." Whereupon the wishes which have been held in idleness, and are therefore not fagged, are able to exercise themselves in opposition to the upper group. But sleep is partial and of varying degrees, and a dream contrary to the person's habitual and normal attitude cannot be put through without arousing the upper group, which then reacts with just the same emotions that it would have in face of the actual waking contemplation of the unlovely wish executed. As is well known, the upper group is often completely aroused by such a dream, and the dreamer finds himself wide-awake and under strong emotional strain. Freud calls this upper group of wishes, which is always the prevailing character of the individual, the "censor." Thus a person who has suppressed wishes, and very few have not, has the rudiments of double, or indeed of multiple, personality—a thing which in practical morals has often been shrewdly noted. In fact, Freud has amply demonstrated that "possession of devils" is not merely a literary figure of the New Testament.

To the question, then, whether a person "wishes to have a painful dream," Freud's answer is, of course, No. But the submerged part of a personality contains many wishes which the better portion ordinarily holds in check, but which, if they succeed in realizing themselves even in a dream, arouse the upper personality to feelings of horror and remorse. This view, so far from being novel or subversive, fits at once into the picture which the most ancient moralists have given us. A fearful dream is an exact counterpart on the plane of imagination, of what only too often happens in actual waking life: a person's lower self "gets the better of him," he commits an evil deed, instantly "comes to himself" again, and suffers an agony of remorse. Unmistakably one of his selves wished the evil and did it, while another self surveys the result with consternation. Again the same thing happens in revery, where the upper self (censor) is somewhat relaxing its vigilance: many a man in revery contemplates deeds and projects which he would not let himself carry out, or even think of, in moments of complete alertness. But such revery is an instructive indulgence, for it is a perfectly just psychological observation that, "As a man thinketh in his heart, so is he." It might also be called Freud's motto. The suppressed motives gain currency if thus exercised, and by just so much are amalgamated with the upper self and become a part of it. The "still small voice" is the popular but just designation for the protest of the semi-dormant upper self when, in revery, fancy, or imagination, lower impulses have succeeded in intruding on the field of consciousness; and I know of no more cardinal doctrine for the cultivation of moral character than that of the still small voice. But of this later. Our point here is that the sole difference between dreams, revery, and waking life is in the *degree* of vigilance exercised by the censor. In dreams the censor is most relaxed, and evil wishes which at no other time would be tolerated can then express themselves.

"Repression" and Amnesias

A

H. E. WINGFIELD; adapted from *An Introduction to Hypnotism*, 122-124
(Baillière, 1920)

Like many others, a friend of mine received during the war a tremendous shock, so painful that he could not bear to think of it. He soon found that if anything tended to remind him of it, he experienced an intense emotion of horror before the memory of the actual event was anything like realized, and at once he voluntarily turned his thoughts away and refused to think of the subject. Soon this turning away became habitual, and the result then of being reminded of the event was an immediate emotion of horror, followed at once by an instinctive, half-conscious withholding from all thought of the incident. It was much like knowing that a picture was there and refusing to look at it. Eventually the emotion of horror when aroused acted as a kind of danger signal. He seemed to feel rather than know what was coming, that the incident which gave rise to it was on the verge of being fully remembered; but he instantly repressed it, and drove it out of his mind. What struck me chiefly was the enormous strength of the remembered emotion compared with the extreme weakness of the memory of the incident. The emotion he could not prevent; the memory of the event he could repress quite easily.

Whilst in adult life very few can repress a memory completely, in child life the experience appears to be much more easy. I imagine that a child who has passed through some really painful experience reacts in much the same way as my friend did. When reminded of it he experiences at once the emotion, and pushes the incident out of his mind. But with constant repetition this process may, in the child, be completely automatic. If anything tends to recollection of the incident, the emotion arises first, and, instantly and automatically, the memory of the occurrence is repressed.

The result is that in after life, should anything tend to remind him of the incident, he will at once be seized by the emotion (which he cannot repress), but will remain in complete ignorance of its cause, since the memory of the latter is automatically repressed. The emotion will constitute a symptom; and hence we see that the symptoms induced by a repressed memory are simply the recalled emotions, sensations, or impulses which occurred with the original incident. In the case of a simple uncomplicated repression, if the sufferer can be made to recall to consciousness the original event, the whole of the symptoms caused by it vanish, and, as the examples which I give below show, vanish immediately—practically in a moment of time.

The newly recalled memory, which is often intensely vivid, at once takes its place among the ordinary painful memories, and behaves like them in that they produce no unpleasant symptoms. Like these, too, it begins gradually to fade away, until eventually it remains a mere dim recollection, harmless, and scarcely even painful, as the lapse of time gradually weakens it.

B

MORTON PRINCE, *The Unconscious*, 508-509, 512-513, 510-511, 513-514 (copyright, 1921, by The Macmillan Company) ; reprinted by permission

It is a general rule that when a person passes from a condition of extreme dissociation to the normal state there is a tendency for *amnesia* to supervene for the previous dissociated state (multiple personalities, epileptic and hysterical fugues, hypnotic and dream states, etc.) Likewise in every-day life it frequently happens, when the dissociation effected by emotion results in an extremely retracted field of consciousness, that, after this emotional state has subsided and the normal state has been restored, memory for the excited retracted state, including the actions performed, is abolished or impaired. Even criminal acts committed in highly emotional states (anger, "brain storms," etc.) may be forgotten afterwards. In other words, in the normal state there is in turn a dissociation of the residua of the excited state. The experiences of this latter state are not lost, however, but only dissociated in that they cannot be synthesized with the personal consciousness and thereby reproduced as memory. That they may be still conserved as neurographic residua is shown in those cases suitable for experimental investigation where they can be reproduced by artificial devices (hypnotism, abstraction, etc.).

Thus B. C. A. could not recall a certain emotional experience although it made a tremendous impression upon her, disrupted her personality, and induced her illness. In other respects her memory was normal. Janet has described this amnesia following emotional shocks, notably in the classical case of Mme. D. . . .

Certain types of pathological amnesia answer to the Freudian mechanism or some modification of it. Certain amnesias undoubtedly follow deliberate wishes to put certain experiences out of mind, just as they follow hypnotic suggestions that they shall be forgotten. A very neat example is that of the observation previously given [Prince, *op. cit.,* p. 74] of the subject who, in a moment of despair and resentment against criticism, expressed a wish to forget her own marriage name, and lo! and behold! on waking the next day she found she could not recall it. But amnesias of this kind differ in an important respect from the classical amnesias of hysteria. In the latter variety the dissociation is so extensive that reproduction cannot be effected by any associated idea of the personal consciousness; for reproduction another state of consciousness (hypnosis, alteration of personality, etc.) with which the forgotten experience is synthesized must be obtained or the subconscious must be tapped. In the former variety although the reproduction cannot be effected through an idea with which it stands in affectively painful association, it can be by some other indifferent idea or complex with which it is systematized. For instance, in the case of the phobia for the ringing of bells in a tower which we have studied,[1] the original episode could not be recalled in association with the object of the phobia, notwithstanding that this object was an element in the episode, but it was readily recalled in association with contemporary events of the subject's life. In the case of C. D., who had experienced a painful episode of fainting the same amnesic relations obtained.

On the other hand there are other forms of amnesia which the *Freudian mechanism is totally inadequate to explain,* or of which it offers only a partial explanation. I refer to the persisting amnesias of reproduction exemplified by much of the common forgetfulness of every-day life (often due to dis-interest) ; by the amnesias for whole systems of experiences in hypnotic states, in different phases of multiple personality, fugues, and deliria; by certain retrograde, general, and continuous amnesias of hysteria, alcoholic amnesia, etc. . . .

If expressed in the following form I think the theory would equally well explain such amnesias, be in conformity with certain known hypnotic phenomena and, perhaps, be more acceptable : An experienced desire not to face, or think of, i. e., to recall to memory, a certain painful experience is conserved in the usual way. When an attempt is made to recall the episode *this desire becomes an active*

---

[1] [Prince, *op. cit.*, 389-410.]

subconscious process and inhibits the memory process. The analogue of this we have in post-hypnotic amnesia induced by suggestion. In the hypnotic state the suggestion is given that the subject after waking shall have forgotten a certain experience, a name, or an episode. After waking the conative force [2] of the suggested idea, functioning *entirely subconsciously* (as there is complete forgetfulness for the hypnotic state), inhibits the memory of the test experience in that there is found to be amnesia for the latter. One may say there has been a subconscious conflict followed by inhibition of one of the belligerents. That antecedent thoughts of the individual can likewise become activated as subconscious processes and come into conflict with other processes and inhibit them, thus preventing them from becoming conscious, we have already seen. The antagonism of the motives in the two processes is often obvious. . . .

Let us note . . . that reproduction is a synthetic process which requires some sort of dynamic association between the neurogram underlying an idea present in the personal consciousness and the conserved neurograms of a past experience. From this view we may in the future find the explanation of amnesia (resulting from the dissociative effect of emotion) in the configuration of the physical paths of residua traveled and engraved by an emotional experience. The emotional discharge may have prevented an associative path of residua being established with the dissociated experience.[3]

---

[2] Probably derived from the "will to believe," the desire to please the experimenter, or other elements in the hypnotic setting. The conception of a "censor" or desire to protect the personal consciousness from something painful is an unnecessary complication.

[3] T. Brailsford Robertson, in a very recent communication on the "Chemical Dynamics of the Central Nervous System" and "The Physiological conditions underlying heightened suggestibility, hypnosis, multiple personality, sleep, etc." (*Folia Neuro-Biologica*, Bd. VII, Nr. 4/5, 1913), has attempted to correlate these conditions and also amnesia (as one of their phenomena) with the isolation of paths "canalised" by auto-catalysed chemical reactions. These processes he concludes, from previous studies, "underlie and determine the activities of the central nervous system (and therefore the physical correlates of mental phenomena)." (See Lecture V, p. 124.)

[For more detailed discussion of the different processes which other writers often group under the term "forgetting," *cf.* T. H. Pear, *Remembering and Forgetting*, 165-177.]

General Manifestations of Conflictful Dissociation

J. A. HADFIELD, *Psychology and Morals*, 118-119 (Methuen & Co. and Robert M. McBride, 1923) ; reprinted by permission.

A repressed complex manifests itself in *conduct,* in *physical symptoms,* in *moral diseases,* or in *dreams.* By following any of these paths, therefore, we may track down the complex.

An illustration at hand exemplifies all of these. A lady protests that she and her husband are most devoted to each other, and to all outward appearances they seem to be so. Yet it was obvious to a psychologist that the opposite was the truth, from four casual incidents—first, she forgot to meet the train by which he was returning after a week's absence; secondly, she dreamt that some harm had come to him; thirdly, she had a habit of unconsciously removing her wedding ring on and off her finger as she talked ; and, fourthly, she protested her devotion over-much. The first incident showed her indifference, the second and third her repressed wishes, the fourth her attempt to hide her true feelings. This diagnosis was confirmed, for it turned out that she was all the time in love with another man. Unconscious signs like these tell us more about the real character than conscious speech.

Behavior Compensatory for Unsolved Conflicts

A

BORIS SIDIS, *The Causation and Treatment of Psychopathic Diseases,* 334 (Badger, 1916)

[In many cases] when a fear becomes annoying, troublesome, and uncontrollable the patient calls up some other fear replacing the present fear which has occupied the field of attention. This forms a relief to the patient. This process often helps in the spreading of the psychopathic state to other mental systems. Temporarily, however, there is some relief. Many a patient who has learned the value of this method employs it as a subterfuge to escape the terrors of facing his fear systems.

B

IRVING J. SANDS and PHYLLIS BLANCHARD, *Abnormal Behavior*, 39-40 (Moffat, Yard, 1923)

Although fear in its open expression has not been given full recognition as a factor in the causation of anti-social behavior, the feeling of inferiority (which after all may be conceived to have its origin in the fear aroused by a sense of inability to cope with one's fellows and one's environment), and its compensatory will to power has been credited with causing misconduct in many cases. A striking example was given by Dr. Frankwood Williams not long ago,[1] and may well be quoted here.

It is the story of a western desperado, who had terrorized the country, and whose exploits were famous over a broad territory. When finally captured, instead of the imposing mass of brawn and muscle which the stories of his deeds would have led one to expect, there was brought to the jail a puny little man, insignificant in both size and bearing. The psychiatrist, by virtue of his insight into mental mechanisms, was soon able to obtain a light on this strange phenomenon. The boyhood history of the desperado was that of the undersized boy, who was tormented by his fellows until he longed for some method of evidencing his superiority. Out of the fear that he might always find himself thus at the mercy of others was bred the desire to have them at his mercy, in order to attain the certainty of his own ability to command the situation. And so he chose the career of a terrorizing bandit in order to satisfy this irrepressible desire.

C

J. A. HADFIELD, *Psychology and Morals*, 36-37 (Methuen & Co. and Robert M. McBride, 1923); reprinted by permission.

We over-compensate when, in order to hide our complex, we "go to the other extreme." A lady may spontaneously protest her devotion to her husband so strongly that one knows there is domestic trouble. The middle-aged man, who, at the beginning of the war, went about protesting that there was nothing he desired more than that he was young enough to go to the front, was really displaying his cowardice, as was proved when men of his age were called up. The man who is always inviting frank criticism is

---

[1] In an address at the National Conference of Social Work. June, 1922.

excessively annoyed when you give him what he asks instead of the flattery that he really wants. The man who, being criticized, says "I don't care a *hang* WHAT people say" shows by the vehemence of his protest how much he does care. The very excess of their protest is the strongest proof of their addiction to such failings. Over-compensation is the method by which we try to disguise our nature, but, like the lark fluttering with agitation over her nest, we exhibit most flagrantly the very thing we would hide. . . .

Deference to others is often assumed by those who wish to avoid the humiliation of a snub; it reveals a phantasy of pride that cannot bear to be wounded, and therefore avoids the risk by an assumed humility. We often depreciate our work in some trifling point, in order to call attention to its otherwise perfect character.

D

ALFRED ADLER, *Individual Psychology*, 10-12 (Harcourt, Brace, 1924)

Let me, on the basis of another case, one which must have happened innumerable times, discuss . . . the positing of goals by nervous people. A remarkably gifted man who by his amiability and refined behaviour had gained the love of a girl of high character, became engaged to her. He then forced upon her his ideal of education which made severe demands upon her. For a time she endured these unbearable orders but finally put an end to all further ordeals by breaking off relations. The man then broke down and became a prey to nervous attacks. The individual-psychological examination of the case showed that the superiority-goal in the case of this patient—as his domineering demands upon his bride indicated—had long ago pushed from his mind all thought of marriage, and that his object really was to secretly work toward a break, secretly because he did not feel himself equal to the open struggle in which he imagined marriage to consist. *This disbelief in himself* itself dated from his earliest childhood, to a time during which he, an only son, lived with an early widowed mother somewhat cut off from the world. During this period, spent in continuous family quarrels, he had received the ineradicable impression, one he had never openly admitted to himself, that he was not sufficiently virile, and would never be able to cope with a woman. These psychical attitudes are comparable to a permanent inferiority-feeling and it is easily understood how they had decisively interfered in his life and compelled him to obtain prestige along other lines than those obtainable through the fulfilment of the demands of reality.

It is clear that the patient attained just what his concealed preparations for bachelordom aimed at, and what his fear of a life-partner, with the quarrels and restless relationship this implied, had awakened in him. Nor can it be denied that he took the same attitude toward both his bride and his mother, namely the wish to conquer. This attitude induced by a longing for victory has been magnificently misinterpreted by the Freudian school as the permanently incestuous condition of being enamoured of the mother. As a matter of fact this reinforced childhood-feeling of inferiority occasioned by the patient's painful relation to his mother, spurred this man on to prevent any struggle in later life with a wife by providing himself with all kinds of safeguards. Whatever it is we understand by love, in this particular case it is simply *a means to an end* and that end is the final securing of a triumph over some suitable woman. Here we have the reason for the continual tests and orders and for the cancelling of the engagement. This solution had not just "happened," but had on the contrary been artistically prepared and arranged with the old weapons of experience employed previously in the case of his mother. A defeat in marriage was out of the question because marriage was prevented.

Although we consequently realize nothing puzzling in the behaviour of this man and should recognize in his domineering attitude simply aggression *posing as love,* some words of explanation are necessary to clear up the less intelligible nervous break-down. We are here entering upon the real domain of the psychology of neuroses. As in the nursery so here our patient has been worsted by a woman. The neurotic individual is led in such cases to strengthen his protections and to retire to a fairly great distance from danger.[1] Our patient is utilizing his break-down in order to feed an evil reminiscence, to bring up the question of guilt again, to solve it in an unfavourable sense for the woman, so that in future he may either proceed with even greater caution or take final leave of love and matrimony! This man is thirty years old now. Let us assume that he is going to carry his pain along with him for another ten or twenty years and that he is going to mourn for his lost ideal for the same length of time. He has thereby protected himself against every love-affair and permanently saved himself from new defeat.

He interprets his nervous break-down by means of old, now strengthened, weapons of experience, just as he had as a child refused to eat, sleep or to do anything and played the rôle of a dying person. His fortunes ebb and *his beloved carries all the*

---

[1] *Cf.* "The Problem of Distance" [Adler. *op. cit.*].

stigma, he himself rises superior to her in both culture and character, and lo and behold: he has attained that for which he longed, for he is the superior person, becomes the better man and his partner like all girls is the guilty one. Girls cannot cope with the man in him. In this manner he has consummated what as a child he had already felt, the duty of demonstrating his superiority over the female sex.

We can now understand that this nervous reaction can never be sufficiently definite or adequate. *He is to wander through the world as a living reproach against women.*[2]

Were he aware of his secret plans he would realize how ill-natured and evil-intentioned all his actions have been. However he would, in that case, not succeed in attaining his object of elevating himself above women. He would see himself just as we see him, falsifying the weights, and how everything he has done has only led to a goal previously set. His success could not be described as due to "fate" nor assuredly would it represent any increased prestige. But his goal, his life-plan and his life-falsehood demand this prestige! In consequence it so "happens" that the *life-plan remains in the unconscious,* so that the patient may believe that an *implacable fate* and not a long-prepared and long-meditated plan for which he alone is responsible, is at work.

E

ROBERT D. GILLESPIE, "Folie à Deux: Dual Organ Inferiority, Religious Conversion, and Evangelism: Conflict, Psychosis, and Adjustment," *Jour. Neur. & Psychopath.,* 3: 269-273 (1922)

Instances of "folie à deux" are not very common; but there are other psychopathological reasons for recording the following two cases. They are brothers, who both suffered from physical defects; they had the same family environment, of course, and enjoyed it together until they grew to manhood; they both developed a manic-depressive psychosis about the same time; they both made an adjustment recognizably abnormal; and they both looked upon their psychosis as a religious experience, and regarded themselves as converted thereafter. But in the one case the psychosis was essentially of the manic type, in the other it was depressive; in the one the psychosis has recurred, in the other there has been no marked recurrence; and their respective adjustments are markedly in

---

[2] The paranoidal trait is recognizable. *Cf.* "Life-lie and Responsibility in Neurosis and Psychosis" [Adler, *op. cit.*].

contrast, the differences in their adjustments closely paralleling the differences in their types of psychosis. Moreover, they have remained closely associated all their lives; and if we divide their existences into two periods, the one ending with the onset of the psychosis in each, the other beginning with their recovery, we find an obvious change in their relationships to each other; so much so that he who was formerly the leader in their enterprises is now content to follow the other.

If we examine the mechanisms in their psychoses, we find them complementary, the one mental history representing chiefly the positive, the other the negative, aspect of the same process; or if we adopt the terminology of Adler, we may say that they represent respectively the "masculine," or aggressive, and the "feminine," or submissive, sides of mental make-up. It is in fact as an illustration of the usefulness of Adler's conception of the "neurotic constitution" that these cases seem principally of value. Nature has in them performed a psychological experiment *in vivo,* and we find the elements which Adler has had the skill to discriminate in all of us, separated from each other, and exhibited, not in phases of the same personality, but in two different personalities; while the experiment is controlled by having the environment, as far as possible, the same in each. In each of them also, the significance of the father for the psychosis and for the adjustment is well seen.

The elder brother A. was born in 1868, B. in 1876. Their father was a man of strong religious prejudices and brought up his sons in the strict tenets of his faith. His father, in turn, had been a ring-leader in certain disturbances of religious origin in the early part of the century. Their mother became demented at the age of 68. Otherwise there was no known nervous or mental illness in the family. B. suffered from infantile paralysis, and his right arm remained paretic. A. had pleurisy at the age of 16. Both were delicate boys; but there were no other outstanding illnesses. A. was, as a rule, cheerful and good-natured, but easily depressed; softhearted and generous. He was musical, clever at his work, and tended to be over-energetic. He was an active member of societies, but always in the subordinate, less honored, position of secretary or treasurer. Of B. less is known, but he was quiet and studious, and, like his brother, became a clerk. Although the younger, he was accustomed to be the leader in their joint enterprises.

Under the father's influence they became interested in Church work, and all seemed well for a time. But in 1904, at the age of 28, B., who was by this time a small, slightly-built, delicate man, became more and more absorbed in his religious activities, being especially interested in the reform of drunkards. He began to lose his power of concentration and his sleep, became very depressed, agitated, and impulsive, and was admitted to the Royal Mental Hospital, Gartnavel, on June 13, 1904, after a month's illness. There he refused food, was mute and hallucinated, and made three suicidal attempts, on each occasion by burning. It appeared from a statement dictated after recovery that he was in a state of extreme fear (of eternal punishment for masturbation). After the failure of his third attempt at suicide he recovered rapidly, and attributed his recovery solely to "purification by fire." Subsequently he devoted himself to religious work, believing that he had been converted during his psychosis. He is now a whole-time evangelist. He is small, delicate-looking, and very timid in his manner. His conversation is usually coloured by his religious ideas, and he believes it his duty to convert everyone he meets, at the same time subtly indicating his superiority to other men in affairs of the soul. In his relations with his brother, with whom he is associated in his evangelical work, he is very cautious and timid, and even afraid, so that where he formerly led, he now tries to temper his brother's aggressiveness by submissive tact.

His brother A., who at the time (1904) was aged 36, and had just been promoted to a responsible position in a bank, visited B. in hospital, and almost immediately himself developed a psychosis—stupor, followed by hypomania. He was not sent to hospital, as he soon recovered. Thereafter he gradually, more and more obviously as time went on, gave vent to strong ideas against the liquor trade, and ultimately refused to do business with those of the bank's clients who were engaged in it. This led to his reduction, and finally to dismissal—twelve years after the psychotic episode. His dismissal led to a second attack of hypomania, from which he soon recovered; but a further change had taken place in him. He says (in retrospect) that his illness was a religious experience, that he was, in fact, converted, and that he felt he had a "new power," which he likens to that received by the apostles at Pentecost. Ever since his "conversion" he has tended to be unstable, to be at times mildly depressed, but more usually over-active and excitable. Since then also he has become more and more aggressive in his religious ideas, and to his prejudices against drink he added strong anti-tobacco prejudices, which he did not hesitate to display, so that he latterly became not only objectionable to his friends, but a nuisance to the community. Finally, he passed into a third definite attack of hypomania (eighteen years after the first), and it is this which we have had an opportunity of studying at first-hand, and for which he was admitted to the Royal Mental Hospital, Gartnavel, on April 17, 1922.

The symptoms were classical, and need not be recounted. His mental attitude was strikingly aggressive, intolerant, and self-important. To the doctors he was at times condescending, expressing a hope of their speedy conversion; at other times he was imperative and derogatory, calling them always only by their surname, without prefix, and threatening them with crude forms of corporal chastisement. He had no realization of his position, and set about endeavouring to "convert" the other patients, rationalizing his presence in the hospital by saying he had a "mission" there. His pretence at superiority was evident in all his relations; if an epileptic patient refused his ministrations and subsequently had a fit, he rejoiced; if an attendant incurred his displeasure, he referred to him as "poor so-and-so."

His letters to his wife were dictatorial, and his attitude to her on her visits was domineering. He made long dissertations to the medical officer on the necessity of a man's asserting his superiority to his wife. He belittled her education and her relations (one of whom had loaned him a large sum of money). To women in general his attitude was derogatory. "I've never aspersed women in my life," he said, "I'm sorry for them. The devil seems to put more obstacles in their path. The very best people agree with me in this. Remember, this has nothing to do with my wife." For his own father (now dead), on the other hand, he expressed a profound admiration.

Reference to his attacks of pleurisy seldom failed to provoke the remark that the doctor who treated him for it "died of consumption, poor fellow." He was reluctant to admit having had pleurisy (recurrent), but he admitted that on account of it he had not been able to go to evening entertainments even in his youth. Now, however, he declared his lungs to be perfectly sound (he inflicted a slight superficial wound on each side of his chest before admission), but at the same time remarked, "There is no health like spiritual health, brother." His voice also he now declared to be excellent—a formerly existing defect he believed to have been removed by a superficial wound he had made on his neck—and he practised raucously in the ward. He admitted also having had D.A.H. This, curiously enough, he dated from an occasion when he raced two Roman Catholic priests on a bicycle. (He has an intense prejudice against Roman Catholics.) Now, however, he stated his heart was better than ever before.

In this connection, his personal prejudices are striking. Thus he abhors dancing—"sees through the horror of it"—but it appears that in his youth he was unable to attend dances on account of his physical weakness, and he significantly instances the danger of pneumonia after a dance. He gave up smoking, too, because he could not stand it (D.A.H.)—"a nasty taste and a throb at the heart." Alcohol he used only medicinally, and "hated it." It may be suspected that he was afraid or unable to take larger doses.

Complex reaction times in an association test were given with "wife," "command," "children," "great," "wish," and "chest."

Significance of the cases in relation to each other, and to the conception of the development of the psychoses.—In both these men was present a pronounced 'organ inferiority' from an early age, which necessarily imposed restrictions on their social activities. The sense of inferiority produced was very evident in A.'s case (in B.'s we have not had the opportunity of investigating this point), as is shown above, and was further apparent in the remark that he used to scorn himself for "envying his chums' preferment in society." Both were dominated by the family tradition and by the father's personality; and their sense of physical inferiority when they tried to live up to this tradition would tend to produce a conflict; but their solutions of the problem were different. Both, it is true, reacted with a manic-depressive psychosis; but this is dependent probably on their pre-existent type of personality. A. at least was of the moody type. It is when we seek to explain why one reacted with a manic reaction, the other with a depressive reaction, that Adler's conception of the neurotic constitution becomes very useful. He finds in neurotics always this "masculine protest," this desire to be above, the setting of a goal which must be attained. There is also in his conception the masculine-feminine antithesis, so that the goal may be striven for in two ways—directly and aggressively, or indirectly by submission and subterfuge. A. illustrates the first method: he strives by his domineering attitude to assert his superiority. The very things he cannot himself enjoy, the very objects he dare not aspire to on account of physical defects, he accounts pernicious, and makes them pegs on which to hang his detraction of mankind in general and on which to base his own superiority. This tendency to detraction, to the belittling of others, is very obvious in A.'s case; and it is, as Adler has shown, one of the methods by which the neurotic seeks to gain his fictive goal. In B., on the other hand, who illustrates the second, feminine method, the derogatory tendency uses more subtle means. He first identifies himself with the father, and then, from this mountain-top of superior virtue, he proclaims, but gently and insinuatingly, that the rest of mankind are inferior to him. In B., too, in the actual psychosis, the sense of inferiority held the field, and until the solution presented itself, action towards the goal was paralyzed.

In A. the tendency to belittle women, and to dominate his wife, may be explained on the same hypothesis. In his actual psychotic spells the flight from the reality of his physical inferiority is even more pronounced, as is well shown above: his "lungs are excellent"; his "voice is splendid." Another allied tendency, recognized by Adler, the tendency of the neurotic to measure himself with everyone he meets, is in A.'s case also obvious, e. g., his race with the unwitting priests.

It remains to account for the recurrence of the acute psychosis in A., and its non-recurrence in B. This is obviously due to the nature of the solution which each sought from his conflict. B. by assuming a superlative spirituality and a feminine, unobtrusive way of asserting it, found an easy task; but A., who chose to be aggressive and to flaunt his assumed superiority in the faces of his fellows, is bound to receive far more actual kicks than moral halfpence, so that he is repeatedly reminded of reality, and, in face of constant rebuffs, breaks down.

In conclusion, the interpretation on the psychosis by each of them as a process of religious conversion is interesting, especially in view of recent "revivals."

F

STEWART PATON, *Signs of Sanity*, 169–174 (Scribner's, 1922)

The most exasperating and dangerous forms of vanity develop in people who are blindly endeavoring to secure some form of compensation for thwarted capacities and frustrated impulses. Few persons are ever clearly conscious of the forces operating to produce excessive self-esteem. They have no inkling of the undercurrents that may interfere with rational management of self. They only feel that they are hampered, annoyed, or even made frantic by a sense of disappointment, the cause of which they cannot analyze. "The riddle of life" has been well said to be "the riddle of the exorbitant self, which somehow or other must be satisfied."

In the Middle Ages many people tried to satisfy the appeals made by an exorbitant self by taking refuge in monasteries or convents, and there meditating about the salvation of their own souls or the souls of other people. To-day a similar fanatical enthusiasm in pursuit of methods for the gratification of self-esteem results in equally useless efforts at pooling esteem and in idealizing the absurd or degenerate activities of the horde and rabble.

There is another type of person who, discontented with an unregulated self, assumes in self-defense an absurd self-depreciatory attitude. The assumption of a false humility and imagined contrition of spirit affords such an one a gratification that feeds the vanity. But "the Nemesis of docility" usually lies in haughtiness and arrogance. Just try to change the opinion of this apparently humble-minded person and notice how quickly he bristles up when any of his opinions are criticized. Although seemingly as meek as Moses, he is suddenly transformed into a stubborn and often short-sighted creature.

The viewpoint of the anti-vivisectionist illustrates very aptly what may happen to an unbalanced mind without an effort to cultivate a rational independence of many unnecessary checks imposed by primitive instincts upon the higher mental processes. The sloppy sentimentality that questions the right to experiment upon the lower animals for the purpose of obtaining knowledge useful in combating disease in human beings is, in many instances, merely a blind to hide the chaos of conflicting instincts, or, perhaps, cruel impulses disorganizing the personality. The writer has observed the genesis of anti-vivisection interests and views in a number of cases where there has been an attempt, although unsuccessful, to find some satisfactory compensation for thwarted desires and smothered instinctive drives. In one person the buried complexes had been expressed in secret drinking; in another, by serious marital misunderstandings. Again: such study has usually brought out that at some period of life the anti-vivisectionist has shown various anti-social masochistic and even sadistic tendencies, which there has been neither courage nor intelligence to face or recognize. In the more intimate relationships with immediate friends, such people, while claiming that they value the lives of lower animals equally with human lives, frequently display a marked perversity of character and sometimes debasing tendencies. Possibly partly conscious of such cruel tendencies they nevertheless develop fixed ideas as to the cruelties they imagine that others have shown to animals. Without courage to face their own unsolved problems, they transfer most of their interest and sympathy from their family and friends to animals. So also their notions, as in all instances of overvalued ideas, are largely influenced by auto-suggestion. Thus when the idea of cruelty enters, it so completely fills the mind that it cannot be dislodged by argument; indeed, any reference to it serves only to

. fix it in consciousness, and the idea itself acts as a nucleus with power to attract, even from the subconscious field, the various forces that make their view inaccessible to logic. . . . The publicity obsession is doubtless one of the important symptoms of American inadequacy and nervousness. Nervous people, being usually uncertain of the foundations of their own houses, prefer to turn their attention to the premises of others.

G

D. A. HARTMAN, "The Psychological Point of View in History: Some Phases of the Slavery Struggle," *Jour. Abn. Psychol.,*
17: 262-264 (1922)

The reformer of 1830 had a "psychology" as well as has the reformer of today. The historian, to give a true estimate of the work of William Lloyd Garrison, the Abolitionist, should understand the nature of the reformer. Was the realization of the evil of slavery the driving force behind Garrison's efforts, or was Abolition merely one means of expressing a far more general drive? In this connection it is interesting to note that Garrison was a "reformer" before he became an abolitionist. In 1828 he was editor of one of the first "prohibition" papers in the United States, *The Philanthropist.*[1] As late as 1829 Garrison said: "I acknowledge that immediate and complete emancipation is not desirable. . . . No rational man cherishes so wild a vision." [2] Two years later, in the first number of his abolition paper, the *Liberator,* we read: "I shall strenuously contend for the immediate enfranchisement of our slave population—I will be as harsh as truth and as uncompromising as justice on this subject—I do not wish to think, or speak, or write with moderation—I am in earnest—I will not equivocate—I will not retreat a single inch, and I *will be heard!*" [3] Did the fact that few people cared to read *The Philanthropist,* that a prohibitionist in 1830 would not be *"heard,"* account to a certain degree for this change?

As editor of *The Philanthropist,* in 1828, Garrison advocated, in addition to temperance, many other reforms. He fought lotteries, imprisonment for debt, and particularly "the desecration of the Sabbath." [4] Universal peace was another cause to which he was

---

[1] Garrisons', *William Lloyd Garrison,* 1: 80.
[2] Garrisons', *William Lloyd Garrison,* 1: 140.
[3] *The Liberator,* Boston, 1 January, 1831.
[4] Garrisons', *William Lloyd Garrison,* 1: 84.

devoted at this time, and of which he never lost sight during all of his later abolition agitation.

From evidence such as this it would seem reasonable to conclude that Garrison was primarily a reformer, an agitator, and that the abolition of slavery was merely one method of expression for this more fundamental drive.

A study of the factors beneath this drive for social reformation is still more interesting. It is fitting here to submit for the reader's consideration two seemingly significant instances in Garrison's youth.

I. In July, 1827, Garrison, who was then a young man of but twenty-two years, attended a nominating caucus at Boston. Although he had been in the city not more than six months, and knew very few people, he came to the political meeting with a memorized speech in behalf of a man he admired. During the course of the evening, he seized an opportunity to deliver his address. Before he had concluded, however, his memory failed him, forcing him to read from the manuscript the remainder of the eulogy.

A man who had been present at this caucus, a well-known local politician, considered the bold interruption as rather presumptuous on the part of an unknown young workingman, and expressed himself quite freely in the *Boston Courier,* July 2, 1827. Two days later the same paper published young Garrison's reply. The nature of the conclusion of this reply is significant: "It is true my acquaintance in this city is limited—I have sought for none. Let me assure him, however, that if my life be spared, my name shall one day be known to the world—at least to such an extent that common inquiry shall be unnecessary. This, I know, will be deemed excessive vanity—but time shall prove it prophetic." [5]

II. A year later (1828) Garrison wrote the following "prophecy" to a newspaper editor who professed to ignore him: "I have only to repeat without vanity, what I declared publicly to another opponent —a political one (and I think he will never forget me)—that, if my life be spared, my name shall one day be known so extensively as to render private enquiry unnecessary, and known, too, in a praiseworthy manner. I speak in the spirit of prophecy, not of vainglory—with a strong pulse, a flashing eye, and a glow of the heart. *The task may be yours to write my biography.*" [6]

A close study, from the psychological point of view, of the life of this famous reformer may be able to show us that the recognition

[5] Garrisons', *Garrison,* 1: 74-76.
[6] Garrisons', *Garrison,* 1: 100.

of the evil of slavery was not the primary cause that led to his agitation for abolition. As has been pointed out, Garrison had tried other reform activities; prohibition, anti-lottery, universal peace, and the old opposition against "the desecration of the Sabbath." It may be that the desire that his name should "one day be known so extensively as to render private enquiry unnecessary" was a factor of far from minor importance in the character of the man who played a leading part in the struggle that led up to our Civil War. Whether or not the "desire to be heard" was a potent factor in the career of this reformer can be answered by the historian who brings to his aid the results of modern psychology.

A Concept of Compensation and Its Psychological Setting

EDWARD STEVENS ROBINSON, "A Concept of Compensation and Its Psychological Setting," *Jour. Abn. Psychol.*, 17: 383-394 (1923)

It is my purpose in this paper to discuss a certain manner in which conflicts between impulses or tendencies toward action become partially or temporarily resolved. The concept of compensation which I wish to develop appears in the psychoanalytic literature [1] and many of its items are taken into serious account in psychological theory from Herbart to Stout.

(Compensatory behavior may be defined in a very general way as a type of activity which grows out of conflicting and mutually modifying impulses.) The spinster reading over the matrimonial notes in the morning paper, the schoolboy day-dreaming of the swimming hole, the failure orating on the might-have-been, all these manifest activity in which conflicts are being partially resolved, and it takes no exceptional acuteness to reconstruct these several conflicts from the nature of their resolutions. This is the sort of thing which may usefully be subsumed under *compensatory behavior*. Within this general class there are, of course, many varieties of behavior, but before discussing the typical ways in which compensatory behavior varies, it should be profitable to examine the psychological setting of compensation.

A question arises at this point as to the nature of the participants in these conflicts which are at times resolved through compensation. My answer is that they are, in the first place, tendencies toward action and that they are, in the second place, tendencies which vary

---

[1] See Adler, *Organ Inferiority and its Psychical Compensation*, and *The Neurotic Constitution*, both translated.

from mere undetected dispositions toward action of a particular kind to dispositions which have attained anything short of complete, unmodified expression.

That the participants in mental [2] conflicts are impulses toward action seems rather obvious on first thought. It is an obviousness, however, which is not sufficient to prevent so-called psychological discussions of conflict which identify certain of the participating elements with the nature of a world outside of the individual. Now there is a type of conflict which can be described accurately in such fashion. If a man, hurrying across a dark field, bumps against a fence, there is no error in describing this occurrence as a conflict between an impulse, possessed by the man, to reach a certain goal and the quite unpsychological qualities of a fence. But such an event is not a conflict for the psychologist, at least so long as he is acting in a merely professional capacity. Of course, a conflict of a psychological sort arises as soon as the man realizes that the conflict is delaying him or as soon as his reflex, habitual, or rational activities become influenced by the presence of the fence. This simply emphasizes the point that the items in a mental conflict are themselves necessarily mental, i. e., impulses toward action.

There is still another type of conflict some of whose elements are apt to be identified with a world external to the subject. Take the case of a worker striving for a livelihood. It is his persistently present tendency to win as liberal wages as possible. Certain enactments on the part of his employers define rather sharply the limits of his earning capacity. Under such circumstances there *may* arise a conflict of the strictly psychological sort which may be looked upon from a psychological point of view as a conflict between impulses; i. e., as a conflict between this man's attitude toward his family, perhaps, and his recognition of his employer's regulations. But only in so far as both of these are parts of the behavior pattern of the individual, can the situation be subjected to psychological examination. There is a very prevalent inclination in the interpretation of such cases as this to identify one of the tendencies of the man with the nature of the man himself and the other with a world which imposes upon him. Such a view, even though it be motivated by considerations of convenience rather than by misunderstanding, is likely to turn attention away from the very fundamental fact that an appreciation of the mental mechanisms involved in such a

---

[2] I do not use this term as implying one or another level of awareness, but simply as implying something pertaining to mental life in its larger sense.

conflict demands an analysis of the conflict in terms of the facilitative and inhibitory interaction of impulses within the individual.[3]

Of course, the desirability of maintaining such a point of view as I have recommended will vary with the purpose and general standpoint of the investigator. The sociologist, for instance, may find it convenient to talk of conflicts between the family and industrial groups, but such a procedure is hardly to be classed as psychological nor would it prove a substantial basis for more extended *psychological* analysis.

The impulses which participate in mental conflicts may be mere undetected dispositions toward action or tendencies which have reached anything short of complete expression. It has been a more or less traditional practice to differentiate sharply between tendencies toward action which have arrived at partial expression in thought, for instance, and those of which the subject himself may be unaware. Such tendencies, however, are not completely disparate types; they are rather stages in a single continuous variable, and either may enter into mental conflicts and play determining parts in the production of an overt act of behavior. . . . In both cases, tendencies toward action inhibit each other to some degree. The principal difference lies in the fact that in one case one or more of these impulses is not clearly apparent to the subject, while in the other case, the impulses, achieving more nearly full expression, make their nature more evident to the subject.

The next question is concerned with the various ways in which conflicts become resolved, including the case of partial resolution through compensation.

A conflict may result in the effectual inhibition of all but one of its elements. This takes place where these elements are very unequal in strength or where tentative action in one direction so modifies the stimulating situation that a former competition is broken down. The mere fact that the human organism possesses a multiplicity of receptors guarantees a perpetual state of conflict, but many of these conflicts are so promptly resolved because of the markedly uneven strength of their participants that we scarcely think of them as conflicts at all. We may have, on the other hand, a very evident conflict which ends in what for all practical purposes is a complete inhibition of all but one element. This is what takes place when a tentative action in one direction (tentative because

---

[3] In my earlier essay on Compensation ("The Compensatory Function of Make-believe Play," *Psychol. Rev.*, 27: 429-439, 1920), I was plainly guilty of the practice I have criticized in this paragraph.

of competition) suddenly tips the balance of stimulating factors in favor of one line of action. In such a case our emphasis may fall on the conflict aspect of the behavior or upon the completeness of the inhibition of all but one line of action, depending upon our point of view at the time.

Where the impulses involved in conflict are of considerable strength and evenness, the individual is likely to manifest emotional behavior. Under such circumstances the competition of impulses is marked by a widespread activity in many effectors, especially those of the visceral system. Of course, this activity itself expresses a considerable number of impulses, but they are not in direct response to the stimuli arousing the conflict. They grow out of the fact that the impulses which those primary stimuli arouse have inhibitory relations to each other.

Emotional states caused by conflicts do not in themselves express complete resolutions of those conflicts. As a result of emotional activity, however, the individual may by means of movement be put into a new relationship to surrounding stimuli and this new situation may favor one of the conflict's elements more than the others, or it may be so inappropriate that all of these elements lose their force, and the individual turns off, as it were, into a new line of action. Then, too, the emotional activity may supply visceral stimulations which reënforce one of the conflicting impulses or they may supply new stimuli of such importance that those arousing the conflict become, for all practical purposes, neglected.

Under certain circumstances conflict manifests itself in a fluctuating partial expression of its different elements. First one element, then another gets out into action, but these actions do not achieve completion due to the presence of competing impulses. Such conditions of alternating or rotating, tentative activities may be carried out in terms of overt bodily movements, in terms of thought, or in terms of a combination of the two. The conventional discussions of *voluntary deliberation* are concerned mainly with rotating, partial responses which are carried out in thought.

These deliberative states, like the emotional ones, are partial and tentative rather than complete resolutions of conflict. They may lead eventually to completer resolution by essentially the same mechanisms as those noted in the case of emotional activity passing on into conflict resolutions.

When two or more tendencies persistently conflict they are likely to become dissociated. The individual tendencies, that is, come to operate only when the others are partially inactive. A person with two sets of ethical standards, for example, acts now according to one set and now according to the other, and there may be no apparent conflict between the contradictory standards which his behavior represents. This kind of dissociation means simply that two tendencies which at first, or ordinarily, would operate in the same situations become so differentiated or conditioned as a result of experience that each comes to have its own adequate set of stimuli which are not adequate for the other tendency.

It quite frequently happens that a conflict results temporarily or permanently not in the effectual inhibition of all but one tendency toward action and not in the dissociation of competing tendencies, but rather in the formation of a new line of action or tentative action that expresses in modified form all of the essential elements of the conflict. I believe that the term *compensation* may well be employed to designate adjustments of this type.

In some cases this new line of action contains in it little or no evidence of the specific constituents of the conflict which gives it its driving force. There is little in an arduous interest in politics to suggest conflicts in a man's organization concerning his family life, yet such an interest may easily arise out of such a conflict. There is little in scholarship to suggest a conflict between desires for athletic achievement and an awareness of physical limitations, yet such a conflict has without doubt often given an impetus to academic endeavors. Under other circumstances conflicts issue into new lines of action which show their origin quite clearly. The child plays at war as a partial resolution of a conflict between a desire to be a soldier and an apprehension of the impossibility or even undesirability of actually experiencing war. The old man lives over in mere thought reglorified days of a departed youth in compensating for a conflict between a desire for a return of those days and an apprehension that that can never be. In both of these cases the partial resolution of the conflict shows plainly its participating elements. But the difference between compensatory behavior the constituent elements of which are plainly evident and that in which the constituents are less plain is one of degree rather than kind; and this degree is probably dependent upon the amount and direction of the interference among the impulses involved.[4]

It should be kept in mind that compensations are not modified expressions of single impulses, but rather modified expressions of

---

[4] The term *sublimation* is applied by Freud (See *A General Introduction to Psychoanalysis* [translated], pp. 8, 299-300), to those compensatory activities which give a higher and more civilized form of expression to socially dangerous impulses. This distinction is ethical or esthetic, however, rather than psychological.

combinations of incompatible impulses. The fact that the child plays at soldiering expresses not alone his belligerent desires, but also his apprehension of the impossibility of realizing them outside of play. The fact that the old man indulges in reminiscence expresses his apprehension of the irreversibility of time quite as much as it does his desire for a return of the days that are past. In other words, the process of compensation is characterized by the expression of incompatible impulses in a mutually modified form.

Freud and most of his followers, I believe, fail to make this point clear. They describe the manner in which certain impulses arrive at a modified expression due to the presence of competition of some sort, but they do not seem to recognize the fact that one impulse becomes modified only to the extent that another impulse, somewhat incompatible with the first, becomes expressed. It is also true of the second impulse that its expression is modified only to the extent to which the first one is expressed. The neglect of this double or multiple aspect of the inhibitory process is apt to lead to a fallacy quite apparent in the writings of many of those who have taken their cues from Freud. This fallacy grows out of dividing human impulses into two opposed classes: (1) those which are typically tending toward free expression—sexual and egoistic impulses, for example, and (2) those which are typically active as inhibitors— impulses growing out of social experience or whatever comprehensible elements make up the Freudian *censor*. There is, of course, some truth in the intimation made by this dichotomy that certain relatively unmodified tendencies are apt to come into conflict with those which in their present form are largely products of social education. It is equally true, however, that so far as the mechanism of adjustment is concerned either group can be expressed only to the extent to which it inhibits its competitors and inhibitory only to the extent to which it can get itself expressed. Furthermore, there are conflicts between the impulses within each of these groups as well as conflicts between impulses of different groups.

So much for the principal features of mental conflict and its different forms of resolution, including compensation. We may now proceed to the varieties of compensatory behavior.

Conflicts may be resolved through compensation into overt or into purely private ideational behavior. The child who plays his game of fighting or hunting resolves his conflicts into overt acts. As this child becomes older he is likely through social experience, to develop impulses incompatible with overt games of war and the chase before his interest in those topics has shown any evidence of decline. But he will now indulge in fantasy rather than in make-believe play of a more explicit variety. Fantasy, itself, may, of course, change over into the overt behavior of playing, lying, or story telling. It is also true that practically no manifestation of overt compensation is without its imaginal accompaniments and few acts of imagination are without some appreciable effects upon overt behavior.

Perhaps the most characteristically compensatory expressions in human life are carried out in thought. Thinking and imagining are the modified and abbreviated expression of impulses toward action and it is doubtful whether thought would ever have appeared without conflict. It is possible, of course, that verbal expression, in so far as it is overt, arose to some extent independently of conflict, but I can see no explanation for the rise of implicit linguistic or nonlinguistic ideational behavior except in terms of the modification and abbreviation in conflict of fuller expression. Most of us teach that thinking is favored by complexity and instability (to a degree) of sensory-motor organization, but it is not such a common procedure to show that thinking arises out of this complexity and instability only to the extent to which these characteristics favor conflicts between impulses and the production of thought as a considerably modified manifestation of competing impulses. All thinking looked at in this light is, in origin at least, a form of compensatory conflict resolution.

The day-dream or fantasy is generally recognized as a mechanism through which interfering impulses gain modified expression. But more matter of fact trains of thought are also produced through conflict. The principal difference between day-dreaming and thinking in general lies not in any fundamental difference in origin or function, but rather in the different degrees of likelihood that they will pass over into overt behavior without considerable further modification. An acquaintance of mine a good many years ago felt almost equal desires to go into legal and literary work. He chose the law, perhaps as the more certain profession, and soon gave up all of his plans for literary productivity. At the present time, as a successful lawyer, he is in the habit of sitting down in an easy chair after dinner, lighting a cigar, and projecting himself into a theater where his first play is being received with great enthusiasm. This sort of behavior, with its slight likelihood of getting into overt expression, we unhesitatingly call day-dreaming. Suppose, on the other hand, that this man were actually a playwright whose first play was about to be performed. And suppose that he were anticipating the scene of that performance. In this case we should hardly know whether to call his behavior fantasy or thinking. Suppose now that the man, an actual playwright, were dwelling on this anticipated performance of his play and considering just what he ought to say if given a curtain call. Here surely we have thinking. Yet, although these three trains of thought differ in regard to their likelihood of getting over into overt behavior, their fundamental psychological features are the same. In each case there is a conflict the elements of which so check each other that thought rather than action takes place. In the first situation we have a conflict between the impulses of a life devoted to law and the desire to write plays; in the second a conflict between a desire to see a first play performed and an apprehension, (implicit, of course,) that that performance is still a thing of the future; and in the third a conflict between a desire to make a few apt remarks and an apprehension of the fact that those remarks are not yet formulated. While the specific impulses involved in these several conflicts are different, and while their respective applicabilities are different, they are all impulses toward action which are modified and kept in implicit form by the simultaneous presence of other impulses. In all of these cases then we have conflicts temporarily resolved through compensation.

When conflicting impulses limit each other to expression in thought, they need not, of course, remain indefinitely in that form. Indeed the honorable law of dynamogenesis states that wherever we have thinking we have a tendency for that thinking to work over into overt behavior. This overt behavior growing out of thought may still be compensatory or it may represent the more or less complete expression of one set of rival impulses and the more or less complete inhibition of the others. That is, the mere fact that compensation in thought takes place may so change the intraorganic conditions of the individual that a conflict within him, which was at first quite even, is resolved through a pronounced facilitation or inhibition of certain of the competing elements. This is what occurs in voluntary decision.

Compensatory behavior varies also in permanency. We are constantly facing situations giving rise to conflicting impulses which gain compensatory expression. Some of these compensations are relatively temporary affairs. Due either to the fact that the stimulating situation is a temporary one not likely to recur or to the fact that compensatory expression shifts over into more definite action along some one fundamental line certain of these compensations are extremely temporary. There are others which, because of the persistence of certain aspects of the world of stimulation, to the unmodifiability of certain aspects of the individual's behavior pattern, and to the laws of habit, become relatively permanent modes of behavior. There is not a condition of life, with its own peculiar stimuli, but creates and maintains within its individuals typical and more or less permanent compensations.

The play of children, which is certainly compensatory, reflects vividly the conflicts which grow out of the conditions of child life. The child, living in intimate contact with a world of adults (often, too, with a world of fiction), develops impulses to behave in manners which he is taught by his parents and by more concrete agencies are not desirable or possible for him. The conflicts thus created remain until they are finally resolved by changes incident upon his own growth and by changes which practical experience creates in his own impulsive nature. But while he is a child, certain conflicts and certain compensatory resolutions of those conflicts remain as integral parts of his child character. Middle age, old age, great wealth, poverty, health and sickness, and social position, likewise have their typical modes of compensatory behavior.

These considerations suggest the importance of examining the behavior of growing children, of the sick, of laborers, or of any other groups, not superficially, but with an eye for the elements in the conflicts to which much of their behavior gives compensatory expression. Now it is true that many of these compensations, and certainly the impulses at the bottom of them, are difficult to detect. A man's talking, joking, choice of books and of religion, his fantasies and his dreams in sleep all contain rich psychological materials many of which it is practically impossible to tease out of the complexities of his behavior. The psychoanalysts make much of this fact. Indeed they have so emphasized the importance of those impulses which are difficult of detection because of extreme modification in the process of compensation, that they seem in many cases to have lost sight of the desirability of looking into those forms of conduct which are fairly obvious indicators of their impulsive elements. The dreams in sleep are extremely difficult to interpret; prejudiced views are much less difficult. The psychoanalyst somehow seems forced to emphasize the more difficult task. While this is perhaps a praiseworthy hardihood, it does appear that programs of investigation aimed at the more analyzable forms of conflict resolution would tell us more about the individual or group in whom we happen to be interested and, perhaps, make easier the later analysis of more subtle forms of behavior.

While certain compensations become more or less permanently present in certain individuals living in certain surroundings, there are others which persist through generation after generation and become spread throughout the human race. Such compensations grow out of sources of conflict common to all times and all peoples. The fantasy of a future life is one of these. While it differs in its detail from time to time, from place to place, and from group to group, this fantasy seems to be an almost universal compensation for the conflict between the desire to live and have life, and the apprehension of the certainty of death. The desire for physical prowess competing with the apprehension of physical limitations is another widespread source of conflict. This conflict gets compensatory expression through watching the physical feats of the more favored, reading stories of adventure and the like.

These highly persistent types of compensation are likely to become institutionalized. Religion, philosophic systems, art, and sport are, in many of their aspects, institutionalized agencies for compensatory conflict resolution.

Compensations are easily recognized as such when they are in the major key. Fantasies and myths of heroic deeds, for instance, are naturally identified with the almost universal wish to be heroic and the universal apprehension of the difficulties of heroism. But there are also a great many compensations which are distinctly in the minor key. Many a conception of a future life is somber or even terrible, many a folk song and story is tragic in plot. The question arises as to how these things which appeal predominantly to such negative tendencies as fear can be thought of as expressions of conflicting impulses toward action. The answer, I believe, lies in the fact that the negativity of such an impulse as fear implies not a negation of action (fears tend to find expression just as positively as other impulses), but rather a negation based upon the particular quality or direction of that action. If, then, a man can find insufficient excuse for fear or sorrow in his actual world he is quite likely to create such an excuse in his religion, his art, and his sports. Even popularly we recognize this to a degree. It is not infrequent that we hear of persons who seem to get a great deal of satisfaction out of their own misfortunes; and we are all familiar with the woman who thoroughly enjoys a play which sets her to crying, and the young girl who has a *perfectly lovely* time being frightened by the speed of the roller coaster.

The concept of compensation as treated in these pages has extremely wide limits. One may expect, therefore, that it will be objected to on the grounds that, applying to every conceivable psychological act, it is not effective in distinguishing any. I should be quite ready to concede that every psychological act is to some degree compensatory, but there are two reasons why that does not destroy the usefulness of the concept of compensation. In the first place, this concept emphasizes an aspect of behavior (and that is all that is done by attention, habit, and many other categories) which is usually ignored. In the second place, it does label a certain class of acts which most obviously display that aspect. Certain acts we call habits and certain others we do not, yet the distinction is merely of degree. Both classes contain habitual acts, but in one class habitualness is an outstanding feature. The same is true of compensation and compensativeness.

The final point which I wish to consider is the function of compensation. Two functions are performed by this method of adjustment. Through compensation the individual is relieved, to a certain extent, of the stress and strain of conflict. Witness the fact that, when adequate compensation is lacking, there is apt to be a prolonged period of intraorganic activity of a very demanding intensity. Furthermore, compensatory behavior, like any other behavior, alters the individual's relationships to surrounding stimuli, if not as a result of explicit changes in bodily position and the life, at least as a result of a variation in his general set or attitude and his consequently altered susceptibility to different stimuli.

To summarize, compensation is a mode of behavior in which conflicting impulses of something like even strength are expressed in a mutually modified form. From a psychological point of view, the elements in conflict which result in compensatory behavior are always impulses to action. Compensation manifests itself in a variety of ways but the one which is of perhaps most fundamental importance is thinking. Compensation may exist simply as the resolution of a passing conflict or as an habitual mode of resolving some persistent conflict. Certain compensations of this latter type become institutionalized in religion, art, sport and the like. Compensation is important as a means of minimizing the stress and strain of the individual's conflicts, and also as a form of behavior, which like any other form alters the individual's relationship to the surrounding world by bringing about either immediately important physical results or changes of attitude.[5]

---

[5] [Cf. also Herbert Sidney Langfeld, "Conflict and Adjustment in Art."]

The Use of Sleep as "Escape"

MALCOLM M. WILLEY and STUART A. RICE, "The Psychic Utility of Sleep",
Jour. Abn. Psychol., 19:174-178 (1924)

An illuminating bit of evidence, undoubtedly unconscious on the part of its author, that sleep may serve to meet a psychic need, is contained in a popular song which some years ago had considerable vogue:

> Please go 'way and let me sleep;
> Don't disturb my slumber deep,
> For I would rather sleep than eat,
> And sleep to me is such a treat, treat, **treat**!
>
> I never had a dream so nice,
> Thought I was in Paradise.
> Waking up makes me feel so cheap—
> So please go 'way and let me sleep.[1]

It is clear to anyone familiar with the psychology of the unconscious that the appealing motive of this song consists in its reference to the manner in which most individuals are enabled to escape from the harsh, "cheap" conditions of everyday existence to a "paradise" of comfort. Apart from the "catchiness" of the tune, one may reasonably assume that its widespread popularity gave evidence of the universality of this appeal.

A few striking individual cases which have come under the observation of the writers will make the principle of the escape mechanism more clear.

Millard S., the only son of parents of more than average ability, has been known to one of the writers for the past eight years. He is now eleven. The family is economically prosperous, and has been able to give Millard every advantage usually available to a middle-class family. By nature he is a sensitive child, extremely conscientious, and somewhat introverted. From a very early age, in cases of childish misconduct, he has been unable to conceal his guilty conscience. Any trivial violation of the code of behavior which his parents had instilled, has always led to obvious manifestations of mental discomfiture, or even suffering. The striking

---

[1] This should be read in connection with S. Freud, *A General Introduction to Psychoanalysis*, 67.

thing about this case, however, is the method employed in seeking escape from this mental discomfort. The facts are best presented in a statement by the mother:

> When Millard was four years old, he threw a piece of glass at a boy, and the boy happened to be what they call "a bleeder." I guess this frightened Millard nearly to death. Apparently no one saw him do it. He came into the house and said, "I'm tired; I want to go to sleep." I did not know then, of course, what had happened, though he actually looked as though he would fall asleep then where he stood. He was always affected like that when he did anything wrong, and he actually would lie down anywhere, perhaps under the bed, and go to sleep at once, even with his hat and coat on. He always would sleep until I woke him for his next meal. Not infrequently I would be going around the house and find him asleep. Then I would know that he had done something wrong.

It is interesting to notice, in addition, that Millard not only employed this device of escape when he had violated his childish code, but also employed it to escape from any situation which was not pleasing to him. Of this the mother also gives an example:

> I remember the day he was two years old. I took him to have his picture taken. He did not want to go, and all the time they were trying to take him, he kept saying, "I'm tired. I'm tired!", and I thought really he would fall asleep.

A case which is far less striking than that of Millard S., but which is of interest because of the fact that it probably can be duplicated in almost an indefinite number of instances, illustrates the escape principle in slightly different form. Here the escape is not from actual mental conflict, or even from a situation consciously unpleasant, but rather from a condition in which there is lack of stimulation. This condition, in the case to be cited, is merely the routine of uneventful, middle-class married life. It is the escape of a successful young man with an adventurous past, who, unconsciously perhaps, feels fettered by the monotony of a conventional, settled, family existence.

Alfred S. is a young man, 31 years of age, a graduate of an eastern college, and of superior ability. He comes from a family of excellent English stock which migrated to this country in the colonial period. The parents died when Alfred was in his senior year at college. Upon graduation he decided to travel and for nearly five years roamed in various parts of the world,—a carefree, adventurous life. Returning to America just before this country entered the war, he fell in love with a young woman whom he soon married. She was capable, though lacking the incisive mental acumen that characterized her husband. Her life had been far more conventional and her home training had been such that to her marriage was a process of "settling down." A few months after their marriage, Alfred was drafted and waived exemption. He was soon placed in an officer's training camp. His wife remained with her parents. Eventually Alfred was ordered overseas, where he saw active service in the later campaigns on the western front. Following the war he rejoined his wife and obtained a position with one of the oldest and most conservative banking houses in their city. In this position he advanced rapidly in salary, responsibility, and the confidence of his employers. The association with a conservative business, no less than the requirements of an established married life, were in marked contrast to his earlier care-free and wandering existence, as well as to his strenuously exciting months in France.

The couple made their home in a suburb . . . and purchased, when their expanding means permitted, a small home in which the wife took exceptional pride. In all respects the two lived a normal, uneventful married life, broken only by diversions of the sort available to and expected of a young banker. The marriage was conventionally happy in every respect, although there were no children.

About a year after they had moved to that city, the wife went for an extended visit with a former friend. Shortly after her return she was again called away because of the death of her brother. On both of these occasions Alfred remained at his work in the city. Frequently during her absence he invited into his home several friends and it was often late when the group would break up. It was during one of these gatherings that Alfred announced to one of the writers that he thought it strange that while his wife was away he was able to get along with so little sleep, and not feel the need for more. Even when he was alone in the house he would sit up until very late, reading or otherwise occupying himself. "When L. is here," he explained, "I always get dead sleepy by a little after ten, and just have to turn in then. We sit around and talk, and my eyes get heavier and heavier. Now I get along fine on six hours of sleep. I wonder why that is?"

It required only a brief analysis to bring out the fact that Alfred's desire for sleep while his wife was with him resulted from the monotony and routine of an unadventurous marriage. When the wife was away the routine was broken, and Alfred was enabled to return to the psychic freedom of the pre-marriage days. Alfred tacitly admitted the results of the analysis and confessed that settled married life at times palled on him and caused a craving for the excitements he had once enjoyed.

The escape from monotony and the uninteresting which is so clearly evidenced in the case of Alfred is to be seen in the case of almost any college student who is forced to prepare a lesson in a subject that is uninteresting to him. Such a student will spend the early part of an evening drudging at his unpleasant assignment, and complaining that he is so sleepy that the words of the book are meaningless. Yet let companions come to his room for a game of cards, and he will become alert and play with them until the hours of early morning. Numerous students of ours have testified to this. Similarly, having wearily finished an uninteresting assignment, to complete which sleep had to be fought all the while, the student may pick up a novel and read it through at a sitting, with no feeling of drowsiness.

The preceding examples can be supplemented by experiences in the life of every one: an unpleasant task leads to the desire to escape; the sensations of apathy, antecedent to sleep, inevitably follow. It is not at all improbable that the roots of the expression heard on every hand, "You make me tired!" are in the desire to withdraw from the company of individuals whose conversation or personalities are conducive to boredom or irritation. The sequence is: boredom, the desire to escape, the unconscious urge to sleep, the expression of tiredness. The universal acceptance of this expression as a rebuke to individuals whose presence or conversation is consciously or unconsciously annoying, testifies to the adequacy of this analysis.

The various examples which have preceded all serve to indicate that sleep has something more than a physiological value. They testify to its psychic utility as well.

CHAPTER XII

MENTAL REGRESSION

Some Cases of Mental Regression

A

RALPH REED, "A Manic-Depressive Attack Presenting a Reversion to Infantilism," *Jour. Abn. Psychol.*, 11: 361-367 (1917)

The case I desire to report, that of Mrs. A. aged 30, was remarkable in three ways: the storminess of the attack, the apparent completeness of the recovery, and the clearness of the life recapitulation. My facilities for observation were good, since I have known the patient since the age of four, and until her marriage we were much in each other's company. Before marriage she was exceedingly active in sports and social life. She was slightly erratic, and her accounts of an occurrence usually erred on the side of being too highly colored with imaginative detail. She was well-liked by every one and never lacked friends and admirers. She was quite the opposite of what we understand as the shut-in type. Her heredity was good. She had no serious love affairs until she met her present husband, whom she married at twenty-two.

For a period of about one month prior to her marriage she underwent a severe depression. She wept almost constantly, longed for death to relieve her from the responsibility of marriage, and could take but little interest in the wedding preparations. Yet none of this depression was betrayed in the daily letters she wrote her fiancé. She has since told me that her dominating idea was one of physical unworthiness for marriage. She insists that there was no idea of moral unworthiness. Within three days following her marriage all depression had vanished.

After her marriage she suffered many vicissitudes of removal from one city to another, ill-health, periods of financial stringency, etc. She had three children and one miscarriage. She was very passionate, and *coitus interruptus* was frequently practiced, often to her dissatisfaction. But much of the time her husband was neurasthenic and more or less impotent.

About three years ago she lapsed into a severe depression in which I was unable to see her but know it was characterized by a loss of interest in husband and children, marked psycho-motor retardation and a desire to kill herself with a revolver.

Following this depression her condition merged into a hypcmania, during which she talked excessively, expressed everything in the most extravagant and effusive terms, neglected her husband and children, was always down town or paying visits or hastening from one interest to another. During this period she excited her husband's jealousy by a certain free and familiar attitude she took toward her men friends. Seeing her in this state, I recognized it as a definite exaggeration of the naturally intense and active social characteristics I knew so well before her marriage. She gradually grew more restless and discontented, and this condition was not alleviated by the removal of the family to a plantation in the south. Very lonely here, and being ten miles from the nearest physician, she nursed her husband through a severe illness. Almost daily she took long drives into town to see her physician, both for herself and her husband.

The attack of special interest was now initiated. It began with a very vivid dream, the impressions of which seem to have lingered during the following days and merged into the earlier delusions. She dreamed that negroes had broken into the house and, in order to obtain her husband's money, tortured her by thrusting knives and the handles of hay-forks down her throat and into the vagina and rectum. During the next few days she forced her husband to search the house with a revolver again and again to make sure that there were no negroes hiding about. She developed delusions of poisoning. She thought her husband, her doctor, the plantation overseer, and negroes were trying to poison her. She smelt chloroform on her clothes, and said that the overseer had put it there in order to render her unconscious and seduce her. At the local hospital she was violent, destructive, and refused food.

She was brought to me in April of last year by her husband and family physician. Her psychosis lasted from April to September. It displayed lightning-like changes, and at times at first for an hour or two she would seem quite sane and orientated, and again disorientated and confused. Her delusions of poisoning quickly passed away, although for the first few days she would eat nothing unless it was first tasted by myself. There seemed to be at first a marked element of simulation and hysteria present. She gave me the impression that she was deliberately attempting to act crazy, being at first always worse in the presence of myself or her regular nurse.

During her more lucid moments she stated that she had long been unhappy, that she loved her husband no longer, that for years she had suffered from sexual dissatisfaction, that she really loved her family physician, Dr. B., and that a few days before the beginning of her psychosis she had been sexually intimate with the overseer of the plantation, C. W., that she regretted this very much, but that it was the result of her loneliness, her emotional starvation, that perhaps after all it had never occurred, or that if it had she must have been unconscious or chloroformed or crazy to have done such a thing.

I was inclined to accept this confession as probably true, and thought that her psychosis might in part be the result of an attempt to cover by the assumption of irresponsibility her feeling of guilt. She went into some detail with respect to the circumstances of this affair, but continued to assert that she was not clearly conscious of the actual occurrence. Discussion, however, produced no change in her psychosis, and the subject was dropped. She continued destructive, violent, negativistic in the sense of doing everything possible to spite or annoy her nurse, and at times would lie for hours with closed eyes waiting for the nurse to leave the room, when she would instantly get out of bed and accomplish some act of mischief.

After a few days she said that she was not married, that she had no children, that she was going to marry Dr. B. who was in love with her and must be sent for immediately. For several weeks she talked of nothing but Dr. B. Gradually she dropped this topic, and in doing so her talk became more profane, vulgar, and obscene. She now began to make violent homosexual advances toward her nurse. Later she began to masturbate. Her eroto-mania was the most violent I have ever seen, producing at times severe swelling and laceration of the vulva. Narcissistic symptoms were prominent in that she would seize every opportunity of posing before the glass, disrobed if possible.

During these manifestations I recognized a gradual recapitulation of life-time experiences. First she went through, or re-acted, many incidents of her married life. She imitated revivalist preachers she had heard and sung religious songs, then on two or three occasions she had a morning nausea, declared that she was pregnant and went through with the greatest dramatic skill and realistic detail the birth of her children. Finally she took up her girlhood memories. She repeated the slang and catch-words of that day, sang the now forgotten popular songs, and talked much of old friends—in brief she became again in many respects the young girl

I had known before her marriage. Later she reached the period of nursery songs and rhymes, and the childish naughtiness in which she had all along indulged became more marked.

Now more striking infantile characteristics were revealed. She talked very little, and then in a babyish fashion. She asked naïve and childlike questions. She drooled at the mouth constantly, and would rub the saliva over her face. She displayed an incessant curiosity about everything in her environment, handling it awkwardly and attempting to place it in her mouth. She was constantly tearing things apart or taking them to pieces 'to see the insides.' She forgot the use of knife and fork, eating with her fingers and spilling her food. She seemed partially to have forgotten how to walk, falling and bumping against furniture or crawling on her hands and knees. She would sit on the floor and amuse herself for considerable periods of time by tearing books and magazines to pieces. Finally she began to soil the bed, and insert the fingers into the rectum and at every opportunity smear the walls and bed with faeces. She would hold the stool when placed on the closet, but immediately afterwards soil the bed. As she began to recover, these habits were replaced by a mania for taking enemas. The drooling habit also was replaced by a constant childlike spitting. We are all familiar with the interest little children often take in spitting as soon as they learn the trick, and how natural it seems to be for them to use it as a means of defense.

Gradually she seemed to grow up. She no longer denied her marriage, but expressed no interest in husband and children. She seemed rather distraite, indifferent and dazed. After a time she expressed a desire to go to her sister's home. She was then allowed to go to live with her father and sister, just as she had before her marriage. Continued separation from her husband was advised. She now asked for her children, and they were brought to her. She began to correspond with her husband, and after her recovery seemed to be complete they began living together.

I did not see her for some months, and then was surprised at the completeness of her recovery. The anamnesis following recovery may be briefly stated. Her memory for much of the period of her psychosis was lost, particularly for the unpleasant features. For instance, she had no recollection of ever having masturbated at all, either during her psychosis or at any time in her life. She denied having lost any of her love for her husband, but admitted that for some time prior to her psychosis she had been restless and discontented. She was not conscious that her manner toward men during the preliminary hypomania was of a doubtful nature. She denied any erotic interest in her physician but thought that there had been indications that he was interested in her. Because of the loneliness of her situation, the fear that every Southern white woman has of the negro had been somewhat accentuated, and during the few days prior to the onset of her psychosis one or two incidents, perhaps partly imaginary, possibly with some real foundation, had further aroused this fear. With respect to her confession of intimacy with the plantation overseer, which at first misled me into crediting it with a possible etiologic relationship, her total denial of any such incident was convincing. But she did have the idea for some time that he was in love with her and contemplated her seduction. Notwithstanding this belief, she spent so much time in his company that she thought her husband's jealousy was aroused. An interesting detail was the intense hatred of her nurse expressed after her recovery. She accused her of many acts of impatience and abuse. During her psychosis, although she had many opportunities, she expressed no such complaints. Although it may be supposed that her nurse at times lost patience with her (and the patient remembered nothing of the great provocation she herself had frequently given) yet it was evident that her hatred was clearly exaggerated and abnormal.

COMMENT

The possible verification, by direct observation of a regressive psychosis, of Freud's theory of the sexual development of the child is interesting.

The mechanism capable of accounting for the patient's abnormal hatred of her nurse following recovery should be clear.

During her whole psychosis she frequently expressed the belief that she was hypnotized. This was probably an attempt to rationalize what was to her her strange behavior.

It will be noted that Bertschinger's thesis to the effect that recovery may be made possible or facilitated if there exists a suitable social structure between the point to which a psychosis may evolve and real life was ideally realized in the present case.

Notwithstanding her lack of insight, I believe, after reviewing my memories of her whole life, that after her recovery she was more nearly a mentally normal person than she had ever been before. Could this be accounted for by the fact that her psychosis gave her the opportunity for a free catharsis and expression in acts or words of practically a life-time of unconscious or repressed wishes and impulses?

The question of the possibility of recurrence in such a case, and whether a psychoanalysis, made with a view of preventing such a recurrence, would offer too many risks of further upset to be justifiable, is of interest.

B

WILLIAM McDOUGALL, "Four Cases of 'Regression' in Soldiers," *Jour. Abn. Psychol.*, 15: 136-141 (1920)

Of all the remarkable cases of nervous disorder which came under my care during the late war I select for description here four which seem to be properly classifiable as cases of regression. I desire to put these on record, because, among all the wealth of cases presenting an immense variety of combinations of symptoms and conditions, these cases, in which the dominant feature is regression to early childhood, seem to have been comparatively rare, and the nature of the condition and of the processes involved in its onset remain to my mind obscure and deserving of further discussion.

I use the term "regression" in a purely descriptive sense, without meaning to imply any theory of the process or condition. . . .

Case I. M. B. An Australian, 22 years of age, a private in the Australian Army Veterinary Corps. The early history of the case as here presented is very imperfect, having been pieced together from information supplied by relatives and friends and from some scraps of information which accompanied him when he was sent to my ward in Feb., 1918. M. B. was one of a large family all of whom, including both parents, seem to have enjoyed robust health. He was brought up to an active open-air life as a jockey and breaker of horses, in a large racing establishment, and seems to have had the reputation of a daring rough-rider. He spent some months at the front and, after a heavy bombardment of the area in which he was stationed, was admitted to hospital on Nov. 22, 1917, with complete loss of speech or "mutism."

In hospital he quickly recovered power of whispering, but aphonia remained complete. He stated that he had been on active service in France since Nov., 1916. He was sent to a neurological hospital in the London area, which furnished the following notes—"Patient mute—cured in 3 minutes by faradic suggestion on Dec. 8. On Jan. 7 appendectomy for acute appendicitis—good result." In January of 1918 occurred a series of severe air raids over London, and it seems that bombs fell in the neighborhood of the hospital in which M. B. was a patient. The War Office ordered all functional nerve cases to be evacuated from the London area to the provinces. I received some fifty of these cases and was compelled to allow some of them to go temporarily to the ordinary medical wards. Among these was M. B. Before his removal from London he had so far recovered from his operation and his nervous shock that he was permitted to go about London on the omnibuses, seeing the sights in the company of his brother G. B., who reported that, but for his stutter, M. B. seemed perfectly normal at this time and showed no nervousness even in the busy traffic of the London streets.

On the day after admission I saw M. B., but had time only for a casual inspection. I noted that he spoke with a severe stutter and showed some tremor of the limbs. Otherwise he behaved normally. During the second night in this ward he was reported to have become excited and frightened, thinking some one was "after" him, and for some time it was difficult to restrain him from leaping out of bed. On the following day he was transferred to my ward. The transfer is said to have excited him, and he was startled by the noise of some falling object. When I saw him shortly after his arrival in the ward he was in a completely childish condition. He sat in bed alert and lively, like a young child taking a keen interest in new surroundings. He childishly displayed his few bits of property and pointed inquiringly towards various objects. He showed no trace of comprehension of spoken or written language and uttered no sounds other than "Oh sis—sis—sis"; this was frequently repeated and used partly as an emotional expression partly to call our attention to the objects of his curiosity. Given a pencil he made no attempt to write; and he seemed to have little or no understanding of the use of ordinary objects and utensils, most of which he examined with mingled expressions of curiosity and timidity.

All his motor functions seemed to be intact, save that when put on his feet he walked jerkily, with short hurried steps, the feet planted widely apart. As soon as allowed to do so, he slipped down upon the floor and crawled about on his buttocks with the aid of his hand, as some young children prefer to crawl. This peculiarly childish gait and preference for crawling to walking persisted for many weeks.

He could not easily be induced to obey simple commands conveyed by gesture, such as to put out the tongue, seeming to fail to grasp the nature of the command. He displayed no interest in letters and photographs of his relatives and friends which we found in his pockets. He could not or would not feed himself, and was fed with a spoon by the nurse, who, he insisted by gesture, had to taste each spoonful before he would take it, quite in the manner of some "spoilt" infants. He played in a childish manner with various objects, making toys of them, and he quickly adopted and became very devoted to a small doll kept as a mascot by a neighbor in the ward. Physical examination showed no abnormality beyond the scar of the appendectomy operation, and occasional slight tremor of all limbs. The expression of his face consistently conformed to the rest of his behaviour. It seemed at this time as though he had completely lost all the knowledge, understanding and motor facilities that he had acquired since the age of some 12 or 18 months; and that he had reverted to the mode of life, bodily and mental, which is normal to a child of some fifteen months of age.

In the course of a few days it appeared that this summary statement of the conditions was not quite correct. There were a very few facilities and memories which were not entirely in abeyance. When offered a lighted cigarette he smoked it forthwith, and then stuck it, still glowing, behind his ear. Subsequently, he would light cigarettes and then throw the burning match upon the bed or the floor in perfect recklessness. A patient who had command of finger-language engaged him in conversation. M. B. showed some slight comprehension and some slight facility in the use of finger-speech, and by this means a few statements about the persons whose photographs he carried were elicited. But he showed no sustained interest, his statements were fragmentary and random, and after the first few days he ceased to respond at all.

He was shown a picture of a steeple-chase; whereupon he became very excited and animated, straddled across a chair and made as though riding a horse-race, and then by gesture and the help of various small objects gave a vivid description of a steeple-chase upon a miniature course indicated on the floor. Afterwards pictures of horses would always excite him and often would provoke a repetition of this pantomime.

Some weeks later when he had made some progress, but still walked like a young child, he was taken to look on at a swimming bath. He stripped off his clothes, dived in and swam like an expert. These four indications of retained facilities were, so far as I could ascertain, the only exceptions to the general loss of all mental and bodily facilities acquired after the age of some fifteen months.

During the first few weeks subsequent to his admission to my ward, he showed other childish traits, of which the following seem worthy of notice. He slept soundly at night and during the day would pass quickly, almost suddenly, from animation to deep sleep. He wept like an infant, when a nurse accidentally stepped on one of his pictures of horses, and upon other similar occasions. He was sometimes playfully mischievous. His digestion was easily upset; and if he took other food than [liquids] . . . he would complain of pain in the belly, suffer from wind, and would curl up in bed. He was very easily frightened. He shrank in fear from dogs, all furs, a negro patient, the stuffed head of a stag, and from all sudden noises and all loud noises the cause of which was not obvious. This timidity was the main obstacle to progress; for on each occasion of being frightened he relapsed to his completely childish condition and had to begin growing up afresh.

He quickly made friends and became a universal pet in the ward. One man patiently taught him to spell out a few words on a type-writer. He was induced to draw with a pencil, and began to copy pictures in the crude style of a child of 5 or 6 years. He acquired great facility in describing small events of his daily life in gesture language. By March 5 he was using a few vocal sounds to aid his gestures and had progressed a little in many other ways. For example, he had ceased to crawl on the floor, though his gait was still that of an infant just learning to walk. He hummed fragments of melodies as he toddled about the ward. On seeing a picture of dogs and sheep, he grew very excited and described by gesture and with loud whistles how he had driven sheep. In his vocal utter-ances, which by the beginning of April were varied, I seemed to detect vague adumbrations of appropriate phrases occasionally. On April 6 he was frightened by the rumbling noise of beds being moved in the ward above him and promptly relapsed to complete mutism and crawling, with loss of all his gains.

After such relapses his progress was usually more rapid than before, i. e., he quickly regained most of what he had lost in the relapse. In May he began to use certain self-chosen vocal sounds as names for familiar persons and objects. He took a keen interest in childish pictures, showing by gesture recognition of animals and other common objects depicted. He busied himself in the kitchen, helping to wash up and so forth. He learnt some basket making and embroidery and worked keenly at these occupations. One day he wrote "Mick" (his own nickname) spontaneously. About this time he showed new evidence of being on the way to grow up, by trying slyly to kiss some of the nurses.

During this period I made several attempts to change his con-dition by inducing hypnosis and by narcotisation with ether. The hypnotic procedures succeeded only in inducing repose and a som-nolent condition, without further change; and etherisation was no more successful, though he took the ether well and had a tooth removed while under its influence. In this case . . . the main difficulty in applying any psychotherapeutic procedure was the difficulty of getting into any effective contact with the mind of the patient, owing to his failure to understand written or spoken language.

On April 6 the brother with whom M. B. had gone about London in January paid him a visit. M. B. showed no clear signs of recognition, but behaved just as I have seen young children behave on the return after a long absence of some familiar friend, namely, he showed a slight shyness, seemingly a pretense of complete indifference, and after a few minutes began to show his toys to his brother as he would to any friendly stranger.

June 13th. After making considerable progress, working keenly at basket-weaving and embroidery, using a few self-chosen sounds as names of things and persons, and going about freely with childish gait, he relapsed with evidences of pain in right iliac region of abdomen, seemingly quite unable to walk. A few days later his head began to jerk laterally without any apparent exciting cause, owing to spasmodic twitching of both sterno-mastoid muscles. The twitch persisted all day, ceasing in sleep, but recurring on wakening. He made great efforts to hold his head still with his hands. A faradic current, applied to the muscles affected, steadied them and, though he was a little frightened at first, as soon as he realized the steadying effect of the current, he allowed me to push up the strength to a point which must have been painful but which subdued the twitch.

July 2. After making good progress, again relapsed with attack of influenza, on recovery from which he was again quite mute. He has learnt to copy printed words and numbers, but doesn't attach any meaning to them. He still could not use words in counting, but would count a small number of articles by placing them in pairs. He seemed at this time to understand in a very vague way much that was said to him or in his presence.

Shortly after this time, when it was becoming possible to reach his mind in a very imperfect way by the aid of language, he was removed from my care by the Australian authorities, who ordered that he should be returned to Australia. He seems to have continued to progress slowly towards recovery of his adult powers. In January, 1919, about a year after the outset of the regression, he wrote saying that he remembered his various friends in England, but had not known his relatives on arriving in Australia. Still later news seems to show that he has gradually returned to an approximately normal condition. . . .

C

MAURICE NICOLL, "Regression," in H. Crichton Miller, *Functional Nerve Disease*, 102-105 (Oxford, 1920)

All regression, of whatever degree, means some impoverishment of life—that is, of the focussed adaptive life of a normal being. The soldier in the trenches who becomes functionally paralysed renounces his daily life for the time, and withdraws from it by a psychological path. *He does not run away from it physically, but psychically, and the path that is open to him is that of the retracing of his ontogenetic development.*[1] The following case illustrates the movement of regression [described in more Freudian terms]:

CASE 1

Patient, an officer aged twenty, was taken prisoner under doubtful circumstances. He escaped and was interned. Shortly after, he began to lose his sight, hearing, and speech. The conversion of his conflict into the somatic sphere was of the ingravescent type. There was no sudden conversion. Both legs then became slowly affected, and both arms. The right arm, however, recovered soon. Sight, hearing and speech were lost. His condition remained stagnant for many months. When I saw him he could move his right arm freely. His expression was placid and meditative. Transference [rapport] was obtained with difficulty, but once established, he spoke a little. He seemed, psychologically, about twelve years old. During the next three weeks the regressive movement continued until he was psychologically five years old or thereabouts. He called the servants by the names which had belonged to servants who had been in the house when he was five. He called his young sister by the name of his eldest sister, etc. His speech was infantile. He lisped and used phrases and recalled incidents that his mother remembered only with difficulty. He remained at this level of regression for about two weeks. The transference was now very strong, and he slowly "grew up" until he was about seventeen. Here he came up against the periphery of his war experiences, and the progressive movement in his psyche was held up again, there being total amnesia for the war. He had now recovered his speech,

---

[1] In dreams the dreamer is often younger than he actually is—sometimes he goes back to school, sometimes he is a little boy, etc.

his hearing, and his sight, but the left arm and the legs remained paralysed.

In this patient the impoverishment of life was complete, showing that the conflict which he sought to solve by regression, was profoundly painful. The method whereby he solved his problem was pathological. He solved it at the expense of his normal efficiency as an adult being, substituting for the adult relationship to life a relationship that was increasingly infantile,[2] and freeing himself from the anxiety that inevitably arises as regression proceeds, and the forbidden barrier is approached, by converting it into an extensive somatic palsy. It was only toward the end of his return to normal life that anxiety began to appear—that is, when the somatic conversion was lifting and the converted affect was reappearing in the psychical realm.

CASE 2

Patient, aged twenty, a flying officer, crashed and was concussed. Previous to this, his history was as follows: He had crashed twice before in the previous month, and had suffered no physical damage, but his nerve was badly shaken. He began to get feelings of anxiety, became rather sleepless, and had one battle-dream. He took to drinking and carousing in general as a relief.[3] . . .

The Mechanism of Mental Regression

A

WILLIAM McDougALL, "Four Cases of 'Regression' in Soldiers," *Jour. Abn. Psychol.*, 15: 153-155 (1920)

Cases of very complete amnesia were very common among soldiers during the war. I had many such cases under my care. The common type may be characterized by saying that the patient had forgotten, or could not recollect by any effort of will, any particular facts of his previous experience. A soldier in this condition would

---

[2] The . . . expression, "Don't be a baby," contains a true psychology.

[3] Regression had begun. The task of flying became increasingly formidable, and a psychic retreat from it began, with a rise of anxiety. He endeavours to blot out reality by alcohol. From my point of view, whenever the battle-dream begins, the balance has begun to be tilted and regression has set in. The normal direction of the psychic stream has been partly reversed, and the regressive movement preponderates. A pathological condition is therefore present.

be unable to give his name, number or regiment, to say whether or not he was married, where he had lived, or what his occupation had been, or to describe or state any fact of his former life. But he would retain a general understanding of his surroundings, would use common articles normally, and would use and understand language, whether written or spoken, almost normally. Apart from his lack of memory of particular facts, he would behave normally, so that a stranger seeing him going about would notice nothing peculiar. In such cases it was usually an easy matter to restore the memory. If one had clues, a carefully directed conversation sufficed in many cases to effect a sudden or rapid restoration. And if this failed, direct suggestion in hypnosis was almost always successful. In most of such cases there were no complicating bodily disabilities, such as paralysis, anesthesia or contractures.

In the cases described above [M. B., and three others not included here] the amnesia was more profound. There was loss of understanding of language and of the common things and relations of life; and this, in the more extreme conditions of Cases I and IV, went so far that it might be said in general terms that all the functions or facilities acquired or built up after some date in infancy were suspended. In this respect they were comparable to Dr. Sidis' famous case of Mr. Hanna.[1] But in another important respect they differed from this case and also from the common cases of complete amnesia referred to above. Namely, they showed, not only deprivation or suspension of functions, but also positive symptoms; for they reverted to childish modes of functioning, both bodily and mental. Their behaviour afforded ample evidence of a re-animation of infantile modes of functioning which had been superseded and apparently lost or suppressed in the course of growing up from infancy. What is this positive process which results in the addition of these infantile modes of functioning to the picture of wide-spread suspension of acquired functions?

One might suspect that the patient is playing an elaborately sustained part, that, without perhaps having explicitly formulated the intention of doing so, he is acting the part of a young child with more or less skill. I confess that there were moments when, as I stood before one or other of these baffling cases, I was tempted to take this view, so unhesitatingly expressed by some of my medical colleagues. But the deprivation of functions was too real, and the consistency and even the inconsistencies of the "acting" were incom-

---

[1] *Multiple Personality* by Drs. B. Sidis and S. P. Goodhart, New York, 1905. [Described below, p. 447.]

patible with the view. I was driven back to believe that the dispositions to infantile modes of behaviour which had ceased to function in boyhood, had not been transformed as they were superseded, but merely suspended or rendered latent, and that the loss of the higher functions was accompanied by an actual re-animation of these dispositions that had been latent or in suspended animation for some twenty or more years. This would seem to be the essential feature of the process of regression. . . .

I seek to render my conception of regression more definite by likening the nervous system to a tree, which it resembles in the facts (1) that the higher the branches and twigs the more recent was their growth. (2) That the sap and vital energy of the tree seems to tend towards the highest most recently formed parts of the organism, at the cost of the lower branches and stem, in which many potential growths and vital activities lie latent so long as the upper more recent structures are functioning normally. If in a tree these most recently formed parts are injured, if in any way, as by frost or fire, their vital activities are checked or suspended, we observe a new outburst of growth and vital activity in the older more primitive parts, namely, we see buds growing out from those parts. (I do not know if this is true of all trees, but it may be frequently observed in the willow and the lime tree and, I think, many other kinds.) This seems to be truly analogous to the process of regression in the cases described above. The highest or most recently developed parts of the cerebral cortex represent the growing points of the human organism and are analogous to the growing points of the upper branches of the tree. Arrest of their functions is followed by a new outburst of vital activity in the lower older parts, which had been rendered quiescent by the flow of vital or nervous energy to the more recently organized parts. Just as the tree injured at the top puts out new buds below, so the nervous system, when the vital activities of its latest organized parts are arrested, puts out new buds below, i. e. resumes or re-animates its infantile functions. In both cases there is new growth and activity on the lower older plane.

I am informed by a highly competent biologist, my friend Mr. Julian Huxley, that analogous phenomena of a striking kind occur among some of the lower animals; namely, one of these soft bodied creatures, having attained a certain differentiated structure, will, if its more specialised recently formed parts are gravely injured, undergo a process of regression. That is to say, it reassumes an earlier form and mode of growth, becomes infantile again, and proceeds to grow up anew from this infantile form. It looks, then, as though, in these cases of regression in man, we have to do with a process which is not peculiar to man, but is, at least as regards its general type, exemplified in many different parts of the realm of life. For this reason I would regard it as a biological rather than a specifically psychological process, that is to say, as a process which though purposive in a sense, like all biological processes, is not governed by any explicit or conscious purpose. It might perhaps be regarded as the ultimate or extreme consequence of the instinctive shrinking of fear. Fear is the great inhibitor, which determines shrinking, both bodily and mental, from all fear-exciting things and ultimately perhaps from all things. If the fear be sufficiently intense and sustained or renewed, we may imagine this inhibitory or shrinking effect carried so far as to paralyse all the higher functions; and we may suppose that the vital or nervous energy, being withdrawn from those levels of the nervous system concerned in these higher functions, then revitalises older, more primitive, infantile levels of function, finding its outlet through nervous channels organized and active in infancy, but long disused. Fear seems to have played the dominant role in all the four cases described above, and in three of them, an excessive or abnormal timidity persisted, and slight occasions of fear determined in all these three cases immediate relapses after partial recovery.

I can see no sufficient reason to postulate as the root of these regressions any hypothetical incestuous fixation on the mother, or any unconscious desire to return to the womb. Far stronger evidence than has yet been offered of the reality of such fixation would seem to me to be necessary, before we should be justified in seeking an explanation along that line. And even if it were possible to show that a "mother-complex" plays a part in the determination of regression, it would still remain a highly disputable question, whether such a complex contained any sexual component.

B

MAURICE NICOLL, "Regression," in H. Crichton Miller, *Functional Nerve Disease*, 109-111 (Oxford, 1920)

From the neurological—or, more properly, from the psychophysiological—standpoint the conception of regression links up with the central teaching of Hughlings Jackson on dissolution in the nervous system. In diseases affecting the brain, he emphasized the fact that destruction of nervous tissue cannot produce positive symptoms. Whatever positive symptoms appear must be due to the activities of nervous elements that remain intact. The observation, though it may appear obvious on reflection, is still neglected by probably the bulk of neurologists, who still describe the symptoms of nervous diseases in terms of the destructive lesion (negative factor). "I submit that disease only produces negative mental symptoms answering to the dissolution, and that all elaborate positive mental symptoms (illusions, hallucinations, delusions, and extravagant conduct) are the outcome of activity of nervous elements untouched by any pathological process: that they arise during activity on the lower level of evolution remaining." [1]

In this paragraph of Jackson's is contained the key that will unlock the mystery of mental disturbance. The rise of the activity of modes of consciousness different from those of the normal waking state is not a meaningless, inexplicable phenomenon, but is the expression of sublevel functioning. . . .

Jackson postulates various levels of nervous arrangements, progressively more complex in an evolutionary sense, and in speaking of the results of dissolution, of the highest or most evolved cortical level, he says, "There is a defect of consciousness significant of dissolution of the topmost layer along with the *rise of a certain kind of ideation significant of increased activity of the second layer.* The double condition is roughly analogous to ordinary sleep with dreaming." [2]   In mild cases of head injury, with bruising of the pia-arachnoid and consequent local interference in the nutrition of the cortex, an "unfocussed" mental state, corresponding with that observed in patients with pure anxiety states, is not uncommon. From the organic standpoint, such a patient has a partial dissolution of his first level of nervous arrangements; while in the pure anxiety cases, the patient has undergone some degree of psychical regression, and, in place of an adapted discriminative mental function, he has an excess of emotion and a greatly increased phantasy or dream life. [3]

---

[1] *Evolution and Dissolution of the Nervous System*, Croonian Lectures, 1884.

[2] *Ibid.* No italics in original.

[3] For a fuller discussion of the subject, see "Conception of Regression in Psychological Medicine," *Lancet*, June 8th, 1918.

Mental Regression: Its Conception and Types

FREDERIC LYMAN WELLS, adapted from "Mental Regression: Its Conception and Types," *Psychiat. Bull.*, 9: 445-492 (1916)

It is a typical instance of regression when the conventional young woman, disappointed in love, betakes herself to a convent. Regression takes place when fundamental trends of the organism are replaced by trends less fundamental; in this case, the trend of love by that of religion. What one conceives as regression, therefore, depends on what one includes in the fundamental trends. We consider as fundamental the sexual-parental trends, the trends for obtaining food, those for protection against enemies, and the social trends, i. e., those for coöperation with one's kind.

As we know, these trends may interfere with each other, so that one is sacrificed to another. A man who steals bread for his starving family acts against the social trends, but in accord with the familial ones. Reactions like these, where one *fundamental* trend supersedes another, will not come under our conception of regression. It is not regression if a man steals bread for his starving family. It is not regression if he leaves home to fight and die for his country. It is not regression if a girl sacrifices domestic luxuries for the sake of love. It need not be regression if she marries a rich man she does not love, but who will provide better for their children. But it is certainly regression if, unable to accept either solution, she seeks the consolations of religion. Then she is clearly allowing a secondary trend to supersede a fundamental one.

Normal life demands a certain minimum in the meeting of the fundamental trends. A person must meet the economic trends to the extent of self-support. He must meet the sexual trends to the extent of rearing children under the conditions which his group prescribes for so doing. The effective doing of these two things is the mark of mental independence; of a proper degree of "progression," in a well-chosen term borrowed from Keller. When the minimum is not reached, it is sometimes because the person's vital energy has been deflected into wrong channels. It is absorbed by activities which do not serve the fundamental trends. By the mechanism of *Uebertragung,* or *affective transference,* a less important trend may absorb, or *siphon* to itself, the energy of a more important trend; "some women prefer dogs." When a less important trend thus absorbs energy that, for the fullest life of the individual.

should go to the furthering of fundamental trends, this is called *regression*.

A great feature of regression is, that its trends are those which are normal at a less mature stage of the individual's development. As Pfister expresses it,

If inner or outer conflicts obstruct a trend, the course of mental energy is turned back. It is expressed in various other trends. This backward turning is called regression. It is always a reversion to the infantile; and it is either (topically) a re-presentation of childish fancies, feelings and strivings, or (functionally) a renewal of types of behavior which are adapted to an infantile stage of development.[1]

It is, of course, a commonplace that our trends change in character as we grow older. "But when I became a man, I put away childish things." The student has heard of the *transitoriness of instincts*. When an adult exhibits a trend of thought or conduct that would be normal and characteristic in a child, but which his other trends have already developed beyond, he is said to show reversion towards the infantile. For example, day-dreaming is a specially childish characteristic, which is given up for realities in later life. An adult who does much unproductive day-dreaming thus shows a reversion towards the infantile. This kind of regression represents a trend characteristic of a less developed stage of the mind. It might be called *genetic regression*. Sometimes one wants to lay more stress on the regressive trend as a normal feature in primitive *peoples*. This may be further denoted as *atavistic regres-*

---

[1] *Die psychanalytische Methode*, 193.

["Regression is a concept which deserves a special study by itself and a thorough comparison with the uses of the terms reversion, retrogression, retroaction, and atavism; but the scope of one paper does not permit so lengthy a consideration. I would suggest, however, that regression can probably best be defined in terms of the forms of individual behavior. I have already shown that there often are changes of behavior of a temporary nature which can quite well be called regressive. Examination of these will show that this regression is not a complete return in all its details to the behavior of an earlier period of life. It may be quite child-like but it is not exactly the same as the behavior of that person when he was a child because he has since been an adult and when he does for a period act like a child he inevitably carries with him some of the adult forms of behavior. It is thus a matter of dominance, and so I would tentatively define normal *regression* as *the return to predominancᵉ of earlier forms of individual behavior, with a greater or less exclusion of the later acquired forms of behavior.*"—Edmund S. Conklin, "The Definition of Introversion, Extroversion and Allied Concepts," *Jour. Abn. Psychol.*, 17: 379 (1923).]

sion.[2] When a patient thinks someone whose name begins with "T" has Chinese blood in him, that is atavistic regression, because this irrelevant play on the sound of words is to be found in racial as well as individual childhood.

The above view conceives of regression as essentially a reversion to the infantile. To be compared with this is the more *quietistic* conception of it as set forth by Ribot.[3] He lays emphasis rather on regression as representing an economy of energy—"the least possible effort" necessary for adapting to the immediate situation. This is, on the whole, the more fundamental view of it. Regressions are usually expressed through infantile trends, it is true; not because they are infantile especially, but because infantile trends make fewer demands than adult trends on energy and activity. If a blocked trend seeks a more facile representation, this will very likely be one which has previously been a part of the organism, and has left its "neurograms" upon it. It is from this quietistic standpoint that some writers speak of regressions as "shirking" reactions. This is an expressive term, gaining force through the ethical significance it imparts to the fundamental trends. The hermit "shirks" his duties as a member of society. The lovesick nun abovementioned "shirks" the responsibilities of a normal sexual adjustment.

The regressions we shall study here are such as detract, in small or great degrees, from the fulness of the person's adaptation to life. In doing this, regressions become wasteful, even pathological, expenditures of energy. But, as Keller illustrates in the primitive colony from a civilized mother country,[4] a reversion is not pathological unless it interferes with adaptation. As the "mores can make anything right," so can the conditions make anything adaptive. Though, if a convent is really the best solution for the young woman, she is not normal. It is in that they do not help to meet the normal adult environment, that regressions become superfluous, shirking or pathological.

The more fundamental view of regression, as expressed by Ribot, brings us more directly to a large class of trends whose relation to childhood trends is not at once clear. If ever trends stood in the way of all fundamental trends, those of asceticism do so. Asceticism is more facile, "quietistic," in that it lessens the struggle with the environment, but it can hardly be called a direct reversion to

---

[2] *Die psychanalytische Methode*, 203.
[3] *La Vie inconsciente et les Mouvements*, Ch. 4 (1914).
[4] *Societal Evolution*, 276.

the infantile. Nor is the positive desire to suffer pain and humiliation (masochism) an infantile trait as such. "Contrariness" is indeed a fairly distinct trait of childhood; the reader may form his opinion of how far the *negativism,* which is its pathological adult counterpart (as a symptom of dementia præcox), is really a reversion to this infantile characteristic. The same is true of the so-called *nihilistic* ideas in mental disease. If a man of mature years masturbates, that is clearly a genetic regression, because it is expressed in a trend characteristic of childhood. If on the other hand he gives himself to a life of beggary, self-immolation and torture, he is not enacting a part of the normal genesis of human behavior. If the law of parsimony demands that we regard all regressions as reversions to the infantile, symbolism must be called in to help us do it. His sufferings might represent a father's punishments of his child, as we shall later see in more detail. All regression need not appear to us a direct or symbolic reversion to the infantile. The old maid's love for her parrot has the maternal, not the infantile character, but clearly meets our concept of regression.

With these remarks in definition, we may proceed to describe various forms in which regression is manifested.

The chief organic pleasures of life come in the exercise of functions which serve fundamental trends. Such pleasures are involved in the taking of food and in sexual reactions. In that they demand the obtaining of food and of sexual partners, they demand the activity of the organism upon its environment. There is another group of pleasure-giving trends, most prominent in childhood, more or less persistent throughout life, and distinct from the above in two ways. First, they depend essentially on the body itself and do not involve any special control of the environment. Second, their value to the fundamental trends is indirect, very small, or even negative. There has been a tendency to name these reactions *autoerotic,* which is all right if one remembers that *erotic* is Freudian for *hedonic.* But this is often lost sight of, with resulting confusion, if not recrimination. It seems that their features would be better expressed by *autohedonic.* Such features are (1) independence of special conditions outside the body (2) value for organic pleasure only. As they do not serve any fundamental trends, the energy expended upon them is wasted for the purposes of fundamental trends. Thus they come under the concept of regression.

One source of these autohedonic trends is the pleasure derived from special stimulation of body surfaces. They are exemplified by the childish habits of sucking the fingers, biting the nails, picking the nose (Jung). Sadger [5] has been especially interested in them. He calls attention to autohedonic value in tickling and scratching (Jaquet). . . . A variety of instances show "siphoning" of autohedonic value from infantile ticklishness to mature sexuality.[6] Ticklishness diminishes in women with the establishment of regular sexual relationships in marriage. In Iceland, ticklishness in either sex is regarded as a sign of sexual inexperience. Sadger places in the same category the proverbial giggling of adolescent girls, which diminishes with sexual maturity.

The normal destiny of these reactions, at first autohedonic, is later to require an object. Normal persons do not bestow many caresses on their own bodies, but seek to exchange them with the opposite sex; and thus prepare the way for the primary sexual activities.

A perceptible number, however, generally persist into adult life. If one observes a company of adults, preoccupied or at ease, examples of these reactions may easily be seen. One person is rubbing his hands together; another generally strokes his cheek with his fingers; a third twists his legs about each other; a fourth is forever tugging at his mustache. The epidermis does not depend for pleasurable sensations on the lover's touch. The masseur, the manicure, the chiropodist and the barber do their share to preserve this property for it. The "umble" but self-loving Uriah Heep is very aptly endowed by his creator with a habit of scraping his chin with his hand, and writhing. The children's swing survives in the adult rocking chair. . . .

It may be an acquired taste, but that there is genuine sensory pleasure in bathing will be denied by few whose experience qualifies them to speak. In all ages its practice has been refined far beyond the demands of physiological cleanliness. Glaucus informed the rich freedman, Diomed, that at Rome there were persons who lived altogether at the baths. Sumner observes that in Germany, during the Middle Ages the bath was so popular that its indulgence was forbidden as an ecclesiastical penance.[7] Such a usage would, indeed, "overdetermine" the conventional distinction between the sheep and their more odorous fellow-ruminants.

Jung describes an instance of a normally matured sexuality reverting, in a psychosis, to one of these autohedonic forbears. At

---

[5] "Ueber Haut, Schleimhaut, und Muskelerotik," *Jahrb. f. psa. u. psp. Forsch.*, 3: 525-556 (1912).

[6] Ellis, *Sexual Selection in Men*, 16-18 (1905).

[7] *Folkways*, 443.

two years, the future patient would for hours rhythmically push a door to with her head. A little later she began to make indefatigable boring movements with her finger in a hole in the wall. At four years, these reactions seem to have been replaced by masturbation. It was not until after marriage, that upon the death of an overmuch loved child, a similar autohedonic practice reasserted itself. She would make violent rotary movements with her left forefinger upon her temple, as if boring a hole there. This was accompanied by a masturbatory activity of the thighs. The psychosis was a catatonic depression, apparently precipitated by the death of the child. In it, the hedonic affect regressed (siphoned back) from the matured sexual trends. It went partly to the masturbation, and partly to the still earlier infantile epidermal stimulations of the finger and head.[8]

Various observations have been made of the autohedonic value of the excretory trends during infantile life. If, as the individual matures, this affect does not siphon over into the sexual trends, there is a regression from the normal development of the instinctive life. . . .

The most important, and the prototype of all autohedonic reactions, is of course masturbation. Its definition is a matter for casuistry rather than science. From the former standpoint, it may be said to occur "when orgastic sensations are produced in the genital tract by action or mental process of which the individual is aware, and without the contactual stimulus of another living creature." It is normally a stage of sexual development. It represents the period after autohedonism is siphoned away from the trends of diffuse body surface stimulation. The instinctive life has not yet reached the stage of projection to other individuals, when it ceases to be *auto*-hedonism. Relapse into masturbation, or abnormal persistence of it, is thus a regression. Freud has suggested that masturbation may at first serve a useful purpose in completing the transference of the hedonism to the genital tract. . . .

A characteristic feature of masturbation is its accompaniment by a systematized flight of imagery. . . .

The coerciveness of masturbatory ideas leads to their habitual use to drive unpleasant thoughts out of awareness. Like the alcohol that drowns the drunkard's troubles, it is a substitutive reaction, that grows by what it feeds on. . . .

In ordinary masturbation, action upon the body itself is substituted for action upon the environment, which involves greater effort

---

[8] Jung, "Wandlungen und Symbole," *Jahrbuch*, 4: 186-8.

of adaptation. Thus it represents the quietistic feature of regression as well as the infantile one. Psychic masturbation regresses a step further. It cuts out voluntary action altogether, and replaces it with imagination and thought. . . .

The prime feature in all regression is the negation of effort. Who lives in the completest negation of purposive effort? The child, as we saw. But how does it live without its own effort? Because its needs are met for it by its parents. When, therefore, we figure regression in terms of a return to the infantile, we figure it as a return to protection and domination. The typical sources of this protection and domination are the father and mother. The literature of mental regression is actually full of "returns to the father" or "mother," but the words must be understood in this essentially figurative sense. Mother and father are the embodiments of protection and domination. Whatever persons or things play these rôles in the regressive trends, those the subject is said to "identify" with the father or mother, i. e., they become father or mother symbols to this degree of identification. Let us not forget that the subject first identified father and mother with protection and domination. It is only by virtue of this, that father, mother, or their symbols play their special rôle in regressive trends. Again it must be emphasized that the quietistic concept of regression is fundamental to the infantile one. If a little more cumbrous, it is much more accurate, to speak as many now do, of father-representative, father-image, *Vater-imago,* rather than convey the idea that it is the literal parent who is meant.

Even when the parent is identified as such, we must always remember, as Rank tells us, that it is not to the father or mother as the subject now knows them, that the regression occurs. It is to them as representatives and symbols of protection and domination,[9] which they did represent in the subject's childhood, more completely than anything in the later environment can ever represent this protection or domination.[10] The most natural metaphors in the

---

[9] David Copperfield never knew an "actual" father. But, in the sense of protection and domination, Steerforth is a proper father-representative. Observe also David's very mild reaction to Steerforth's part in the abduction of Emily, while he is quite ready to break a vial of wrath over the head of Littimer. The influential rôle of Agnes towards him is that of a "mother-representative"; far more so indeed than that of his actual mother. "There were a pair of babies when she gave birth to this child," as Betsey Trotwood rightly observes.

[10] *Cf.* Rank, *Myth of the Birth of the Hero* (Tr. Robbins and Jelliffe), 67 (1914).

world to represent anything that dominates or protects us are the words father and mother.

With this in mind, his ideas are much easier to assimilate.

Our material related to these points falls into groups as follows: (1) A regression which emphasizes dependence upon, and domination by, some outside influence (naturally symbolized by the "father"-relationship; cf. "paternalistic government"); (2) A similar regression in which the dominant force is figured as "maternal"; cf. *Mother Earth, Mother Nature, Mother Church.* (3) The overcoming of the regressive tendencies figured as a *resurrection* or *rebirth*. In the latter case, the "mother"-representative, from whom the "rebirth" takes place, is quite apt to be figured in a hostile role (Jung's *furchtbare Mutter*). (4) A regression to protection, not only by a mother-representative, but also by a deified culture-hero (founders of religions, Christ). (5) A regression consisting, not in a reversion to the infantile, (i. e., to dependence on a father- or mother-representative,) but in the symbolization of adult trends (usually erotic; "bride of Christ"). (6) The limit of introversion, symbolized by a return to the mother-representative as in (3), but without "rebirth" therefrom.

We take up first regressions to domination, which are regularly represented by the father-relationship. Normal progression involves a gradual freeing from the control exercised over the child by the father, or whoever stands *in loco parentis,* until the matured individual maintains himself independently. Opposed to the achievement of this independence by the individual, are such *trends of submission, deference and dependence* as may, and properly do, characterize his childhood. If such trends become fixed habits in the individual, then he makes, in after life, a "father-image" of any accidental superior, of his fellows, of the world itself. He is oversensitive to praise and blame, fears to oppose rivals, reacts poorly under discouragement; yields readily to enemies, because he has not outgrown the habits of submission that were a normal and necessary part of his childhood.[11] He is "fixated" on an infantile level of development. The power of the world over him is identical with that of the "father"-authority which he has read into the world.

Frequently, this submission to the "father"-authority is not passive but rebellious. An actual father may cling too closely to paternal authority, against the offspring's normal developmental

---

[11] *Cf.* the character "A Weak Man" in Earle's *Microcosmography:* beginning "Is a child at man's estate . . ."

strivings for independence. In response to this, trends of opposition to the father develop. The "convention" of filial duty and affection makes it impossible to know the force or frequency of such opposition in normal life. McDougall remarks that in the Sullan prosecutions, no father was known to denounce his son, but many sons denounced fathers. Freud suggests that the tabu which, in primitive tribes, prevents marriage between persons of the same *totem* originates in a prohibition by the original father, or patriarch, who as ruler of the family would reserve its women for himself. The *totem* animal, he says, is a father-representative. The tabu on intragroup marriage is thus a symbolic regression to "father"-authority. Ferenczi [12] considers hypnosis a state of regression, in which the hypnotizer takes the place of the infantile "father" or "mother." He points out that there are two motives by which one may put the will and thought of another in abeyance: fear and love. Accordingly, there are two techniques of hypnotizing. The operator with the imposing and formidable appearance surely suggests the image which the child creates of the stern and all-powerful *pater-familias* whom it is the highest ambition to believe, to imitate, to obey. Conversely, the lightly stroking fingers, the pleasant, monotonous, somniferous words, are clearly suggestive of ideas associated with the "mother"; "and what does one not do to please her?" . . .

Another trend of regression to dominating influence is shown in delusions of persecution. The patient imagines his happiness to be conspired against and thwarted by others. It is properly considered that delusions, persecutory and otherwise, are split-off portions of the patient's own personality. Delusions of persecution are trends of thought which are opposed to the main personality. If a young man in love deludes himself that an uncle of the girl is working against him, that is because his own personality is quite divided in its desire for the girl. There is a split-off trend in his personality which opposes his getting her. And since his desire for her expresses a fundamental trend, the split-off opposition to it is a regression. But, more than that, the regression is here "projected" upon the uncle, and thus becomes an idea of persecution. It does not go to the bottom of things to call the uncle a "father"-representative; or mother-representative either, if it should be an aunt instead of an uncle. The fundamental thing is the conflict in the progressive and regressive trends of the young man. Father or

---

[12] "Introjektion u. Uebertragung," *Jahrb. f. psa. u. psp. Forsch.*, 442, 443, 457 (1909).

father-representative are simply the nearest objects for the regressive trends to fasten themselves on.[13]

Jung has made a special study of cases in which the influence of the actual father obstructed the patient's adaptations. They are to be viewed from two standpoints: First, as abnormal regressive tendencies on the part of the patient; second, as an exaggerated paternalism in the father, encouraging regression in the child who becomes the patient.

One of his cases was the youngest of five children, and always the father's favorite. At 24 she married an entirely suitable man, against the will of her father. He wished her to marry an adopted child of his; a foundling, who was feeble-minded, and had purulent glands about his neck.[14] She took the father to her home, "because none of the others wanted him." He was a drunkard. Frequent quarrels arose, in which she took the part of the father against the husband. Annoyed beyond endurance, the husband had the father taken elsewhere. For two years the pair lived happily. Then the patient remorsefully took the father back and trouble began again, continuing until the sudden death of the father. Then she began to accuse herself of having sinned greatly in not having married the man her father wished for her. She would get a divorce from her husband if it were not for the children. That is, the early favoritism of the father leads to a pathological affection in his daughter which makes her comparatively helpless against his later selfishness. . . .

Regression is a pervading motive in religion. The present type of it is nowhere better defined than in Christianity, with its great emphasis upon the Fatherhood of God and the infantilism of men. "Except ye . . . become as little children." The concepts of deity are of course projections from the personalities that create them. Jung calls attention to the angry and vengeful character of the Old Testament God (conventional father-attributes) as contrasted with a loving fatherhood in the New (having a more feminine char-

---

[13] If the regressive trend were not projected, it might come as a rationalization that although he loves her dearly, he ought not to marry her, for eugenic, economic, or what not considerations.

[14] Cf. Rank, *Myth of the Birth of the Hero*, 77: "The father who refuses to give his daughter to any of her suitors, or who attaches certain conditions, . . . does this because he really begrudges her to all others. . . . He locks her up in some inaccessible spot so as to safeguard her virginity." And again, the "countless versions of a *new-born boy* of whom it is *prophesied* that he is to become *son-in-law* and *heir* of a certain ruler or potentate . . . in spite of all persecutions . . . on the part of the latter. (*Italics*, author's.)

acter).[15] The regressive element in religion is biologically to be
traced to the long continued helplessness and dependence of the
young human being, that, when it later finds itself in a similar
situation towards the great forces and complexities of life, feels its
condition as again that of a child, and seeks to escape their evil
through a regressive renewal of the protecting powers of its infancy.[16]

---

[15] *Jahrbuch*, 3: 177 (1912).

[16] Freud, *Leonardo da Vinci*, 57.

No better expressions of such regressive ideas are to be obtained than
in religious doctrines and invocations. Nor is it necessary to explore unfamiliar fields to find them. Insofar as they bear upon the present topics,
liberal quota of illustrations are to be had from hymnological material
accessible to everyone. (References are to the numbers of hymns in the
Episcopal *Church Hymnal*, Boston, The Parish Choir (1896).)

From among these invocations showing the regressive trends, nineteen
hymns may be mentioned as especially illustrating motives of an infantile
self-abasement and dependence. They may be enumerated as follows:

Invocation of Father: 276, 333, 414, 502, 513.

Invocation of Son: 7, 10, 12, 36, 85, 202, 234, 335, 336, 345, 394, 603, 606.

Invocation of Holy Ghost: 135.

In these groups, the more distant relationship to the Father comes
out very clearly. Only in 276 is the Father conceived in a spontaneously
loving rôle. This is a hymn for orphans, likening humanity to them;
supplicates the "Father of the fatherless."

The invocations of the Son, on the other hand, are appeals to tenderness
rather than to mercy from wrath. We usually think of sternness as a
Father-attribute, and tenderness as a Mother-attribute; in this sense,
therefore, we can say that Christ has here the rôle of a "Mother"-representa-
tive, as contrasted with Jehovah, a Father-representative. A notable
exception to this is the *Dies iræ* (36), in which Christ has distinctly the
stern "Father"-rôle, here uniformly attaching to Jehovah. In this material, therefore, sternness and tenderness regressions are both represented,
the former usually by the Father, the latter by the Son, but with exceptions in either case.

The tenderness rôle here attaching to Christ attaches in Roman Catholi-
cism to the Virgin Mary, an apter "Mother"-representative. Whichever
of the two figures becomes "loaded" with the tenderness regression, the
importance of the other dwindles.

Self-abasement is put among the instincts by McDougall, but as we see
it here it seems more a rationalization of regressive trends. Pleas to the
Divine Power to be hidden within him, to be covered by the shadow of his
wing, to be fed with the heavenly manna, and the like, come more naturally
from one regarding himself as weak and resourceless. The dominant note
is of melancholy, with self-accusation an occasional minor feature (36, 85,
135). There is special imagery of weakness (335); lost wandering (333);
requiring assistance (414); the world is an unhappy or wicked place
(394, 513), to be escaped from through death, and the attainment of
heaven; death itself, however, pictured as fearful (340, 345, 414). *Evening*

Thus we have seen the regression to stern domination embodied now in the childish ideas of the actual father, and in the adult idea of a heavenly Father; occasionally also in Christ, and in other dominating influences. Authorities conceive these as *father* and *mother* regressions according as the figures that embody them happen to be male or female. Naturally, they are usually the former. One would expect the tenderness regressions to have female embodiments, but the figure of Christ shows amply that this is not necessarily the case.

Female embodiments of sternness regression exist in mythology as they do in real life, but are exceptional in both. Hela, queen of the Norse Hades, is a figure of the sort. The Lilith of the Talmud, the Lamia of the Greeks, the Delilah of the Bible, and the Tiamat of Babylonian legend are examples cited by Jung.

It is commonly observed that the earlier love affairs of men concern women older than themselves. Also, this love is not a matured eroticism, but is a mixture of erotic and filial affection.

> Older than me, but my first one,
> More like a mother she were [17]

In such cases, the man is much more under the influence of the woman than in the matured relationship:

> Showed me the way to promotion and pay . . .

The admixture of filial with erotic components in such an affection is a regression. The youth assumes a childish, subordinate rôle, and puts the object of his affections *in loco parentis*. It is not surprising that there should be reminders of the actual mother in the woman. They are in no way essential. The regression is *not*

---

and *Old Year* hymns have similar characteristics. The anthology contains eighteen *Evening* hymns to five *Morning* ones.

The high admiration in which many of the hymns cited are held, movingly demonstrates how deep-rooted is the trend of melancholy regression in people's souls.

Similar trends are to be especially observed in the following Psalms: 6, 22 (v. 1-21), 25 (v. 16-22), 31 (v. 1-14), 38, 39, 44 (v. 8-26), 56, 69, 88, 90, 102, 130, 131, 143. . . .

Hymn 636 owes not a little of its sublime character to the self-identification with God that takes place after the first stanza. Compare also 81 and 673.

[17] Kipling, *The Ladies.* The verses are a first-rate review of different types of love.

to the "mother;" it is to the principle of tender protection, with which as a rule the mother is most identified.[18] . . .

A similar regression is shown in men who remain single with close attachments to their actual mothers. Such persons come within everyone's observation. Let the demands for affection on the mother's part have been small or great, the son has not made the normal detachment of himself from them. It is wrong to interpret such conduct as sacrifice to a "mistaken sense of duty." That is a surface rationalization. The obeyed sense of duty does not make a mistake. It indicates the direction in which the sum of our trends, conscious and unconscious, most impels us to go. In the presence of economic competence, such attachment to the father's family is an evasion of the normal adjustments to life, and as such, a regression. This is not so clear in women, because they are more dependent on the initiative of men. But it doubtless makes many women repel, or less competent to encourage, advances that would normally lead to marriage.

Case T . . . gives a pathological example of such regression with insufficient detachment from the family. His is an ideal household, consisting of his sister, brother and himself; they are the best brother and sister in the world. His only desire is to get home to his family whom he loves and who love him. The only evidence of a special mother attachment is that his first psychosis, at 36, was precipitated by the death of his mother. . . .

His demeanor under examination was one of exaggerated respectfulness. The examiner, who makes a youthful appearance beside him, is habitually addressed as *Sir*. When the examiner would motion to him to go first, as through a doorway, the patient would in doing so say "excuse me." That is, he reads the "father"-authority into those about him. He makes himself, in the fullest sense, "a child at man's estate."

---

[18] "The presence of the maternal element in the attitude of a woman towards her lover has been recognized by countless writers of romance." McDougall, *Social Psychology*, 394 (1914).

The writer recently observed this trend of *Mutterschutz* in its ultimate form. A young woman, dementia præcox, fancies herself loved by a certain exalted person. She bears children by him. The two are constantly threatened. She is not in danger, being supernaturally protected. The lover has a medicine which makes one very small (*Alice in Wonderland;* Andersen's *Ole-Luk-Oie* "Thursday"). When danger approaches, he takes some of the medicine, creeps into her vagina, and remains there until the danger is past.

> "Mariechen—ich möchte kriechen—
> In dein kleines Herz hinein!"

Case U does not show positive evidence of over-attachment to the actual parents. But at 17, when a shop assistant, he falls in love with his employer's daughter, eight or nine years older than he. This attachment he never outgrows. Apparently it lay deeper than the organic level, for it was unaffected by his later intercourse with prostitutes. He kept trying to meet her, writing to her, watching the windows of her house. She is said to have *feared* him. When she married someone else, he broke down for three or four years. At 26 he obtained a low-grade position (it being noteworthy that he worked at this satisfactorily for twenty-nine years). At about 28 he tried to correspond with her under an assumed name, expecting her but no one else to recognise it. Later, he wrote to her under his own name. When he was 54, and ill, she went to see him. With childish contrariness, he was affected, but blamed her for spoiling his life, and would not shake hands. However, they gradually came into closer contact, and about two years later were married. They tried to live at his home, but the sisters made it too unpleasant for her. She left, but he did not accompany her, feeling obliged to remain with his *mother who was feeble*. The married life has been unhappy with violent disagreements, and inadequate organic relations (*ejaculatio præcox*).

This case shows a distinct arrest in the development of the instinctive life. According to his own account, his wife induced him to marry her against his judgment, and she has since acted independently of him in other important matters of mutual concern. He has not outgrown the infantile attitude towards woman. His preferring to remain by his mother rather than his wife is striking. So far as the information goes, it may have expressed a positive mother attachment that outweighed the marriage, or a more generalized infantile contrariness. It is a regression in either case.

There is a group of motives, common to the lore and usage of many peoples, whose characteristic feature is, that the hero gains new powers or knowledge, through overcoming an enemy (this often by entering within the enemy), or through undergoing and escaping from some confinement or duress. Such a process is elaborately figured as a rebirth in a Brahman ceremony described by Frazer.[19] A householder in performing certain rituals is supposed thereby to become temporarily divine. The first step in the transformation is to be sprinkled with water in representation of semen. Then the man feigned to be an embryo, shutting himself up in a special hut, signifying the uterus. Under his robe he wore a belt, as the navel-

---

[19] *The Magic Art*, 1: 380.

cord; and over his robe a black antelope skin. The robe and the antelope skin represent the amnion and the chorion. If he moved about in his hut, that represented the fetal movements. If in bathing he put off the black skin but not the robe, that was because the child is born with the amnion but not with the chorion.

Comparable to this is a swallowing and disgorging ceremony from Australia. It is part of the pubertal initiation of men. A hut about a hundred feet long, modelled to represent a monster, is built. His swallowing of the young men may be represented by causing them to pass under a scaffold on which stands a man who pretends to swallow a little water as each novice passes. For the disgorging, he projects the water upon the young man's head. After this the youth is circumcised, and must then live for some months inside the long hut that represents the monster's belly. When they return, they are covered with a coating of white chalk, with which their eyes are also sealed. At first they affect to know nothing.[20]

Jung draws a close parallel between the mass-ritual and a rebirth symbolism. In further instructive instance, he mentions a sepulchre of S. Stefano in Bologna. It consists of a chamber or artificial cave, into which one creeps through a very small door. After tarrying there the believer comes out, so to speak, reborn.

Again, the hero escapes an enemy by entering into the enemy's body. Hanuman, making himself very small, slips into the body of a monster seeking to devour him, and comes out whole again. The Chinookan hero, EntsiX, enters the body of an elk, and cuts his stomach to pieces.[21] Hercules does the same with a marine monster. We may recall from a previous citation [22] the hydra who enters the crocodile and kills him. This is there freely made to symbolize the entry of Christ into hell, and his conquest of it thereby.

Again the hero, instead of being simply hidden away to gain power or safety, dies altogether. But, like the phœnix, he is reborn with renewed youth thereby. "That which thou sowest, is not quickened, except it die." The salmon myth quoted by Boas is a good example of such a self-perpetuating hero.[23] Hindu lore expresses a similar idea in the Laws of Manu, where "the husband after conception by his wife, becomes an embryo and is born again of her; for that is the wifehood of the wife, that he is born again by her." In relation to this Frazer [24] quotes a Polynesian rule of

---

[20] Frazer, *Balder the Beautiful*, 2: 240.
[21] Boas, *Chinook Texts*, 119 (1894).
[22] *Jour. Philos.*, 10: 553 (1913).
[23] *Chinook Texts*, 77-87.
[24] *The Dying God*, 188-190 (1914).

royal succession, where a king abdicates in favor of his first son as soon as the latter is born. Naturally, whoever is able thus to rebeget himself achieves a conquest of death. The distinctive features of rebirth may be absent. Then the overcoming of death is figured as a simple resurrection. The resurrections of Christ, Attis, Adonis, Osiris, are examples of this. Odin, hanging on the tree of life, pierced with a spear, achieves knowledge of the runes, and of the mead that makes him immortal.[25]

It has been in the minds of many to regard as the prototype of such conceptions, the sun. "The new born hero is the young sun rising from the waters, first confronted by lowering clouds, but finally triumphing over all obstacles." The sun dies in setting, vanquishes death, and is reborn, or resurrected, in rising again the next day. In a similar sense, the seasonal changes may be figured as an overcoming by the solar hero of a death in winter instead of night. Such a view regards the above legends and usages as symbols of the courses of heavenly bodies. It is natural to ask why such symbolization should take place. It is to be observed that symbolization particularly affects ideas of much interest and distinction. The primitive man could scarcely fail to perceive the importance of the sun to his life, and to read into the moon [26] and stars a good deal more than they possess. One would naturally expect them to be prolific in symbols. By the time these ideas and usages come to our knowledge, their symbolism has long been lost sight of, and they are distorted beyond any immediate recognition. It seems, however, a reasonable theory that the primitive interest attaching to the courses of the heavenly bodies would lead to their readily forming symbols in the regular ways. Thus they would have such symbolic designations as those we have just been describing. These are scarcely more remote from the heavenly bodies than *been among the Philistines, high lonesome, petrified, medzabeargeared,* or *whipped* are from alcoholic intoxication. (*Partridge.*)

Jung, however, and those who agree with him, go much further than this view. They might, indeed, recognize a solar symbolism in many myths. They would not grant that solar or astronomical interest were the *fons et origo* of that symbolism. They would hold

---

[25] Jung, *Jahrbuch*, 3: 218 (1912); 4: 459 (1912). *Cf.* Gering's *Edda*, "Havamal," 105-6, Strophes 138-42.

[26] Possibly after the manner of the negro who compared the sun with the moon, to the great disadvantage of the former,—"Sun only shine in de day time when yo' don't need it; moon shine nights when it does some good." This negro is to be met elsewhere, on more intellectual levels.

that the entire group of conceptions, solar myths and all, are symbols of regression. The hero is not, fundamentally, a sun-representative. He represents the progressional trends of human personality. The prison [27] from which the hero escapes, the monster he fights and overcomes, the death from which he rises again, the "mother"-representative from which he is born again, are not the darkness of night, or the dreariness of winter. They are the regressional trends of human character. The triumph of the hero is the triumph of the progressional trends. And if most of this lore seems to go back to solar myths, this is because the course of the sun is such an exquisite metaphor of that triumph. . . .

It is a common figure of speech to denote a great turning point in either personal or national character as a rebirth, regeneration, or, indeed, resurrection. In every individual, the most important rebirth of this figurative kind is actually that in which the regressive tendencies of childhood are put under our feet by the progression of the fundamental trends. This gaining is true living, and lordly man's up-rising. If this development be figured as a rebirth, it is no great flight of autism to denote an actual or figurative agency through which this rebirth takes place as a *mother*-representative. This is amply attested in Jung's own choice of words. Into his theories of an organic repossession of the "mother" we can not here follow him.

Thus the fabled conquest of mysterious difficulties is carried further back than representing the sun's conquest of winter and night. It represents the triumph of light over darkness in the inevitable and most momentous conflict of men's souls. The chief obstacle to this view is that the cultured man (and presumably the primitive one) does not readily *perceive* this conflict between the progressional and the regressional trends. And how should he come to symbolize what he does not know about? "I feel two natures struggling within me," indeed; yet the struggle is but vaguely felt in consciousness, and only superficially comprehended. The conscious comprehension of the inner struggle is so slight that it hardly seems to give adequate "originals" from which the symbolisms we have seen could be derived. Many properties and effects of the sun are clearly present to our minds, and afford very ready material for symbolic association. Still there is good evidence that trends may be symbolized in consciousness whose originals are not a part of consciousness. The mind may indeed symbolize to consciousness something the main personality does not know about

---

[27] Or other enclosure.

("dissociative" symbolism). Thus the personal interpretation of these myths and usages involves no novel principle of the conduct of mind. It does involve the large extension of a little understood principle. It certainly makes a stronger appeal to the imagination than the simply solar interpretation, and seems to have a higher ethical value.

According to this view, the crucifixion of Christ, the *Ragnarök* of the Northern legends, and the whole group of analogous conceptions, represent to us the death of all that is unworthy in ourselves. With the resurrection, the trends for fuller self-realization are reborn, no longer hindered by the corruption of regressional trends.

To represent this triumph in the god, however, is not to fulfill it in oneself. It is a serious regression if the contemplation of the victory, divinely represented, takes the place of actual striving in the world of men. The worshipper, in raising his god above the pit, falls into it himself. The doctrines of great religions show this, when they hold up a negative conduct of life as an ideal. This is, in Jung's deepest sense, a return to the Mother as an introversion symbol, without prayer or effort to be "delivered from the body of his death." On the contrary, it is in this self-merging with the godhead that the greatest good is sought.[28] The heavens of the great religions are essentially regressive pictures.[29]

---

[28] *Cf.* Hymn 403 (v. 1).

> O Mother dear, Jerusalem,
> When shall I come to thee?
> When shall my sorrows have an end
> Thy joys when shall I see?

[29] We need not go beyond those of Christianity as represented in the invocations quoted. The principal group of hymns to be considered here is dominated by ecstatic passivity. Sacrifices are perhaps necessary here below, but are made joyfully, and more than compensated for hereafter. The frequent visualizations of heavenly bliss are of an unproductive character. They seem largely derived from the Revelations (179, 387, 397, 404). The attitude towards self ranges from the humility of the sheep-symbolism (412, 659; *cf.* Psalm 23), to the extreme but passive self-glorification of hymn 460. Others belonging to this group are 216, 241 (v. 2), 355, 359, 398, 415, 418, 628, 643.

Nothing of significance is noted in regard to the personage invoked. Similar ideas are shown in the Psalms as follows: 1 (v. 2), 23, 24, 33, 44 (v. 1-8), 73, 103, 145.

A small body of hymns shows a lack of affective reaction, happy or melancholy, as well as a lack of self-abasement and self-accusation; there is, on the other hand, great self-abnegation (612, 634), or even self-nullification (632); a Nirvana-seeking reaction. The notion before men-

Shifting the responsibility for action properly shifts the burden of wrong-doing. This is rather a moral regression than a regression of the fundamental trends. It seems to be a fairly pervasive motive to shift the consequences of one's acts to another, through either magic or religion. Frazer devotes a long volume to the "divine scapegoat" motive.[30] . . .

We have now followed the conception of regression as a reversion to the infantile quite as far as it is profitable to do so. We saw first that organic autohedonism represents trends of greater prominence in early life. Passing over to the mental side, we noted the infantile feelings of dependence and subjugation, whether or not combined with desire for tender affection. A regression is shown in the undue prominence of these in adult life. The parents are especially associated with these feelings in the life of the child. Therefore the words *father* and *mother* have come to be used to designate figuratively whatever is an object of these feelings in adult life. Now it is an actual parent; now a divine protector; now a sexual partner loved with partly filial and partly erotic devotion; now it is a superior friend; now it is someone in official authority over us. These latter we call father or mother *representatives*.

But such regression, if carried to its psychological conclusion,

---

tioned, of *entering into*, or merged identity with, the divinity, is represented here (613, 666); also an expression of naïve acceptance of revelation (649). This material all comes from a restricted portion of the anthology, which offers more illustrations than those cited. The invocations are mainly, but not entirely, of Christ.

Three of these hymns showing a balance of affect between joy and melancholy, show also an extreme shifting of action and responsibility for action to the divinity (*cf.* 502). Two of these are much used at funerals (637, 674); the other (605) is not so well known, but a very clear expression of the ideas under discussion.

[30] We may include here certain invocations that lay particular emphasis upon the worshipper's *helplessness*. Hymn 470 recalls the sheep-symbolism. The affective reaction is not prominent (614, 623), or if so, there is a good balance between suffering here and bliss hereafter (341, 363). (These remarks refer wholly to the text of the hymn. In present use, however, it is unwise to consider the affective value of hymns apart from the music which attaches to them, since music has more emotional significance than simple words. Frequently the tune alone is observed by the singer or intelligible to the hearer. There have been several observations of children who, when called upon to repeat the words of songs they have heard, reproduce gibberish. Hymns may thus carry the emotional value of their tunes rather than their words. Hymns somewhat regressive in sentiment seem to derive a dynamogenic value through stirring tunes; as in 311, *Ancient of Days;* 383, *Nicæa;* 460, *Covenant.*)

would inhibit normal mental development. The fundamental, progressional trends come into conflict with the regressional ones, and must overcome them if the personality is to realize itself. Regression must die that progression may be reborn to a more abundant life. We have tried to illustrate a view, more stimulating, indeed, than provable [31] consisting of two parts. First, this conflict is represented in the great body of myths more usually thought to reflect cosmic and seasonal changes. Second, that it is in representation of this soul-conflict that certain historical occurrences become invested with an atmosphere of mystery, and attain the tremendous holds that they have upon the minds of men.[32] All such ideas are thought to derive their appeal to the imagination, as picturing a victory of self-realization over self-abnegation in the supreme conflict of mental life.

When religion is made to rationalize regressional trends, three fairly distinct developments occur. We have considered only the first of these. Its ultimate form is a losing of one's individuality in the divinity, to be merged with, to become one with, the divinity. This implies the abolition of activity in the fundamental trends, and the substitution therefor of a mental state. Thus it is the extreme of introversion. . . .

On p. 326, *supra,* was mentioned a regression "not to the infantile, but in the symbolization of adult trends," usually erotic, particularly to Christ. This can be made clearer only by examples of what is meant. We have illustrated regressions to Jehovah and to Christ as representatives of the feeling that in children goes to parents. Jehovah represents trends usually associated with the father, Christ more often those of the mother. Now we meet instances in which devotion to the divinity is not of the filial but of the erotic type. The attributes assigned to Christ are apparently the best adapted to this role. It is regularly Christ that takes the place of the human love object, but not necessarily so. Like the filial devotion to father and mother representatives, this erotic devotion is a regressional variety of the affective symbolism, as we shall see in more detail. The erotic affects are transferred from their proper place to objects through which they can not be made effective.

---

[31] The concluding words of Jung's study are: "But I look upon science, not as a rivalry in being right, rather as a labor for the broadening and deepening of our mental vision. To those who feel towards science as I do, this work is addressed."

[32] Compare, outside of religions, the belief that Julius Cæsar became a divine being, and the immortality legends attaching to Arthur and Barbarossa.

The best formulation of this transfer the writer has seen, is given in the following verses:

> When upward like a flame of fire
> My thoughts fly searching God above,
> My lips, also, breathe earth's desire
> And whisper but thy name, my love;
> I consecrate myself to God
> That His just will may be my own,
> That He may be my staff and rod,
> Asking for his love alone.
> It is in vain. My human heart
> Turns still to thee its sweet lodestar,
> Tortured and torn by bitter smart
> It lies at thy feet to love or (mar?)
> May God forgive this earthly passion
> And mold it to His heavenly fashion.
>
> Love's burning passion in my breast
> Rages fierce for thee beloved,
> My pulses throb in pain oppressed
> I know I love and am beloved.
> A spectre dread assails my brain
> It whispers your sweet love may die
> I feel the anguish of that pain
> And yet my heart in peace shall lie.
> The thrilling fires of this great love
> They honored mine, they honored thine,
> Transfigured they burn high above
> On earthly dust to flames divine.
> 'Tis God in thee that I adore,
> His name is love forevermore.

Such expressions spare elucidation rather than command it.

Some things distinguish the above from other material we shall present. Its tone is much more elevated. There is very little sensuous or in the least organic about the expressions. This is coordinate, perhaps, to its invoking the Deity instead of Christ. Christ plays a more intimately human role. Also, the main personality recognizes the transfer of affect more clearly than in other cases. There is more insight into it. Of other phenomena Josiah Moses writes: "Unable to express itself naturally, the sexual impulse finds an outlet in a more or less sensuous love of God, Christ or the Virgin Mary." We need not follow this author or his sources through the numerous historical examples. A very good one is that reported by Parkman of Marie de l'Incarnation, in which she heard [33] in a trance a miraculous voice:

> It was that of Christ, promising to become her spouse. Months and years passed. . . . when again the voice sounded in her ear, with assurance that the promise was fulfilled, and that she was indeed his bride. . . . To her excited thought, her divine spouse became a living presence; and her language to him, as recorded by herself, is that of the most intense passion. . . . "O, my Love!" she exclaimed: "when shall I embrace you? Have you no pity on me in the torments that I suffer? Alas! alas! my Love, my Beauty, my Life! Instead of healing my pain, you take pleasure in it.[34] Come let me embrace you, and die in your sacred arms!" . . . "Then, as I was spent with fatigue, I was forced to say: 'My divine Love, since you wish me to live, I pray you let me rest a little, that I may the better serve you,' and I promised him that afterward I would suffer myself to consume in his chaste and divine embraces." . . . Some of the pupils of Marie de l'Incarnation also had mystical marriages with Christ; and the impassioned rhapsodies of one of them being overheard, she nearly lost her character, as it was thought that she was apostrophizing an earthly lover.[35]

It is difficult to know how far towards the organic level such fancies as these may descend. They seem to approach it more nearly in those dealing with the Holy Ghost. We could scarcely expect many instances of the *main personality* picturing to itself bodily caresses from a divine love object. If such persons should merely picture themselves as thus approached, they would be punished for harboring improper thoughts. But if they hallucinate the approach, those about them are more likely to accept it as a real occurrence. One may hallucinate the approach as the Ursuline did the visits of Urbain Grandier. This is not a straight day-dream, integrated with the main personality, but a hallucination, dissociated from it. Then if the hallucinated love object is human, he suffers as Urbain Grandier did. If he is divine, the person thus honored by him is revered. . . .

While these illustrations are concerned with the religion most familiar to us, it may also be true that the circumstances leading to them are more marked in Christianity than elsewhere. The normal

---

[33] *The Jesuits in North America*, 175-7 (1867).

[34] Note the "masochistic component."

[35] There are hymn-writers who court a similar imputation. Among the many interchanges of religious and erotic figures to be found in the anthology, none are clearer than these. They occur especially in hymns: 434 (v. 1, 2); 441 (v. 5); 600 (v. 2, 3, 4); 607 (v. 3); 625 (v. 1, 2, 3); 658 (v. 1, 2, 3, 4). . . .

living out of the sexual trends seems to be interfered with by more tabus among Christian communities. This would especially favor the transfer of energy ordinarily spent through sexual trends. Such transference may take a regressional course. If so, a very direct course for it to take is the affective symbolization of a human by a divine love object, in the ways that have been illustrated.

A third great manifestation of regressional trends in religion is asceticism. We may consider it from two angles; the nature of ascetic practices themselves, and the way they receive their religious motivation.

Asceticism is a negation of the fundamental trends. It aims to suppress them altogether, thus differing from the self-denial which inhibits an impulse now simply that it may be better gratified in maturer years of life.[36] Sumner emphasizes that for this reason the ascetic conduct of life is always conditioned by rationalization. "It is never," he writes, "a primary product of the ways in which unreflecting men meet the facts of life. . . . It is a secondary stage built on experience and reflection. It can never be verified by experience. It purposely runs counter to all the sanctions which are possible in experience." Ascetic reactions are referred, therefore, to trends of "other-worldliness;" a desire to propitiate the ghosts without whom effort is unavailing, and with whom it is unnecessary. It is a pervasive feature of the folkways, and its origin can not be traced to any particular religious system. "Asceticism in a higher civilization is the survival of the life-philosophy of an earlier stage, in which the pain of men was believed to be pleasant to the superior powers." [37]

Let us remember that the superior powers are themselves simply "projections" of trends in the personalities that venerate them. Such superior powers do not find anything pleasant unless it is in some way pleasant to their creators. No rationalization may embark upon the sea of thought without clearance papers and a pilot from instinctive desire. Asceticism runs counter to progressional trends. It does not run counter to those of regression, but is built upon a rationalization of them.

The author of the "Pathological Aspects of Religions" recognizes eight motives for asceticism. Of these, six are instructive examples of rationalization. *a.* In the opposition of good and evil, the good is of the other world, and evil is to be combated by mortifying the flesh. *b.* An angry God is gratified by the self-

---

[36] *Folkways*, 606ff.
[37] "Dear in the sight of God is the death of his saints."

humiliation of sinners. *c.* A desire to compensate Christ for his sufferings in behalf of the human race. Dr. Moses compares this to the self-sacrifice of lovers (cf. Christ as a love-object, above), and cites Baring-Gould that this is the whole cause for the self-maceration of the ascetic: "he joys in his penances, because they ease his soul of his inextinguishable love." *d.* A belief in the imminence of the end of the world, with consequent detachment from earthly affairs. *e.* Satiety with terrestrial pleasures; *e. g.,* great centers of luxury also produce great exponents of asceticism. *f.* Great calamities act as "precipitating causes" of asceticism. But these motives for ascetic conduct would not be accepted by the main personality save through a deeper predisposition towards it. The remaining two motives go deeper. *g.* The privations of primitive life induce, especially in neurotic persons, trances and similar dissociated states. Thus Pfister quotes the case of Christine Ebner (1277-1357), who, after two years of self-torture, falls into sensual visions, in which she feels herself embraced by Christ, and receives a child from him.[38] Dr. Moses thinks that people would inflict privations upon themselves with a view to inducing such states, which are not only pleasant in themselves, but increase one's standing in the community. Their fellows would consider such states supernatural, and have special regard for those who were thus visited. This motive would operate more to sustain asceticism than to originate it. Lastly, *h.* There is the temperamental passivity of many individuals to whom asceticism is simply an easy way of avoiding life's conflicts. Here, of course, Dr. Moses meets the basal concept of regression. Such passivity leads naturally to introversion of varying grades, and covers the contemplative type of asceticism well enough. But it scarcely leads to the active and violent self-tortures [39] which are included in the concept of asceticism.

Nor is the purposeful induction of dissociated states (*g,* above) the simplest motive of voluntary suffering. There is not infrequently observed in the human mind a powerful trend towards the suffering of physical or mental pain, stripped of all rationalization and of all purposeful reflection. This trend is called *masochism.*

Historically, and in its narrower sense, masochism is a feature of erotic reactions. It is a delight in pain and humiliation inflicted by the love object. Correlated to it is a trend called *sadism,* which means a delight in inflicting pain and humiliation upon the love

---

[38] *Die psychanalytische Methode,* 483-4.
[39] *Cf.* Lecky, *Hist. Eur. Morals,* 2: 107-116 (1897).

object. It has been pointed out that selection accounts for some degree of these traits. In primitive times, both physical and mental masterfulness contribute to erotic success in men; women of rebellious or too independent spirit would be cast out if not killed by their stronger partners. Thus women come to despise men who do not dominate them. Sumner records that with some Australian girls, honor requires that they be knocked senseless and carried off by their future husbands. "Eskimo girls are shocked to hear that European women publicly consent in church to become wives." In more cultivated times, greater variations from these types can occur. Men of masochistic disposition become the henpecked husbands of masterful wives. When the abnormality is more pronounced, grotesque perversions occur. The man can experience no gratification except under extreme humiliation and indignity at the hands of his partner.

McDougall refers masochism to the instinct of self-abasement, "operating with abnormal intensity under the special conditions of the sexual relation." This defines masochism in its narrower, erotic sense. But, by the same token, anything which brings the instinct of self-abasement into play, will call forth "masochistic" reactions, whether or not the situation be sexual. We may, if we understand him rightly, group the manifestations of active asceticism, together with those of masochism, all together under the instinct of self-abasement. They give, indeed, strong grounds for conceiving an innate tendency of self-abasement.[40] In abnormal individuals, strong excitements like those of religion and eroticism, bring out perverse exaggerations of this tendency.

Ascetic self-tortures are, in fact, masochism plus a rationalization that harmonizes them with religion. In eroticism they need no rationalization. The enduring of pain for pain's sake is a contradiction of the fundamental trends, outside its limited rôle in love. As such, it is a regression.

When Pfister speaks of the "masochism of many ascetics," and the "masochistic death-wish" in one of his cases, he plainly takes the same view.

The ordinary rationalizations [41] of asceticism and masochism take strength and guidance from an inherent tendency of self-abasement. The general tendency of self-abasement is against

---

[40] McDougall, *Social Psychology*, 64-66 (1914).

[41] [Rationalizations, that is, in the sense of false professions of motives: suppressing the true motives when they are objectionable, while professing other and more socially acceptable ones to be the real motives.]

progression, and in the direction of regression. The above rational-izations of self-abasement bolster this regressive tendency up against the progressional, self-assertive trends. There are two more rationalizations that operate in the same way. One of them is self-accusation. The subject covers his instinct for abasement by a fancy that he is wicked and despicable. He fancies pain as pun-ishment in expiation of offences he has committed. "The remem-brance of them is grievous unto us; the burden of them is intolerable." [42]

This self-accusation is often combined with imagery of weakness and dependence, such as was noted on p. 325, *supra*. The imagery of weakness and dependence is itself a rationalization of self-abasement, as was there said. Self-accusation rationalizes the need for help, in turn. For example, the prayer for help must often fail. Then the preservation of faith is made easier by the self-imputation of great wickedness. The sinner meets disaster, or does not receive prayed-for help, not because there is no God to hear his prayers, but because he is unworthy that they should be answered. [43]

[Similarly], self-accusation rationalizes masochistic self-torture by picturing it as an expiation of offenses. Frazer [44] cites a number of primitive usages in which being beaten not only absolves from sin, [45] but confers various physical and mental advantages. In this connection it may be remarked that the interpretation which is given to such a practice at the time of observation is not necessarily the idea in which it originated. Thus in a Hungarian superstition, barren women are fertilized by being struck with a stick which has

---

[42] Self-accusation does not play so large a part in the anthology as in some portions of ritual, like the Litany. Examples from the anthology are as follows:

82, 201, 219, 529 (esp. parts I and III).

[43] In the Psalms, which show frequent self-depreciation or self-abnegation, self-accusation is nearly absent. It appears in Psalms 90 and 130. Psalm 59, verse 3, contradicts the idea: "not for my transgression, nor for my sin, O Lord."

An interpretation of this difference is possible in the light of contem-porary experience with mental disease. It has been noted that the topics of morbid self-accusation are generally "loaded" with their affect from a feeling of guilt for autoerotic reactions. It is probable that under the *mores* in which the earlier invocations (of the Psalms) were produced, sexual relations were among religious persons freer than in the later times. The greater sexual suppressions ensuing later could give rise to increased autoerotic tendencies. These find a natural reflection in the increased religious self-accusation that we see.

[44] *The Scapegoat*, 263-4.

[45] *Cf.* the conclusion of the Flatterer episode in *Pilgrim's Progress*.

been used to separate pairing dogs. Here it is less the beating than the magical properties inherent in the particular stick. The masochistic element is subordinate to that of sympathetic magic. Succeeding ages, however, could easily modify this practice so that any kind of stick might be used. The subsequent observer would entirely miss the reasoning processes by which the custom originated. . . .

Self-abasing tendencies are shown in masochistic fancies and imaginations as well as in masochistic acts. The striking thing about masochism appearing in fancies is, that as a product of imagination, there is no question of compulsion or duress from the environment. The mind is simply pursuing its own inclinations for suffering. . . .

To St. Theresa is attributed a vision of "a kind of low oven, pitch dark, miry, stinking, full of vermin, where sitting and lying were alike impossible; where the walls seemed to press in upon the sufferer—crushing, stifling, burning."[46]

As this was the "place she merited in hell," a rationalization is still present here. . . .

The active self-abasement we have considered shows itself in a tendency to suffer pain and indignity. We have seen that this may be either self-inflicted, as in the self-torture of the ascetic, or it may require to be inflicted by another, as in typical masochism. A fair distinction between asceticism and masochism would be when the "discipline" is self-inflicted, to call it asceticism; and masochism, when it must be inflicted by another. Both rest upon the same foundation in self-abasement. Masochism becomes to active asceticism exactly what heterosexuality is to autoerotism. Any form of erotic desire may be expressed in conduct, or merely imagined. The same is true of asceticism and masochism. Some religious fanatics inflict suffering upon themselves. In other cases they are merely imagined, as in St. Theresa's vision of her place in hell. . . .

Such exaggerations of the self-abasing trends are not compatible with the demands of normal progression. They belong, therefore, to psychopathology. We noted some of its more normal grades in the henpecked husband, or the wife who submits unnecessarily to great marital abuse. Outside of this sphere, we have seen it in the reversions to the infantile. The self-abasing trends properly excited in early childhood by father or mother, persist into adult

---

[46] Josiah Morse, "Pathological Aspects of Religions," *Am. Jour. Relig. Psych. & Educ.*, 2: 93 (1906).

life. Competitors in the struggle for existence become "father-representatives." Habits of self-effacement develop which are of grave hindrance to normal success. Sometimes a not abnormal grade of this self-abasement combines with other and more fundamental trends to form a powerful motive, to which recent history has given particular social significance. This motive is that which tends to inhibit a group's defense of itself against the organized hostility of another group. It has now so well identified itself with the term *pacifism* that it may properly be thus denoted in the remarks to follow.

The instinct of pugnacity, as McDougall calls it, grows out of conditions in which the organism must contend with other organisms for the realization of fundamental trends. Organisms that would prevent its realizing fundamental trends are enemies, and if it would live, it must destroy or drive them away. A tiger that bowed itself to the tramp of the elephant would show as pathological behavior as the amoeba that spread itself out over poison.

The reactions of animals towards enemies are to get away from them or to attack them. Which of these is done depends on the balance of their trends, as well as the nature of the enemy. A dog will fight for a bone, or a she-bear for her cubs, where either would slink away if these were not involved. Special adaptations, used in self-defense only, are seen in the hedgehog, turtle, skunk, and opossum.

All natural reactions of animals under threat of injury are such as should help the animal to escape the injury. The animal has certain behavior patterns that help it in its ordinary dangers. No animal could survive in a natural environment without such behavior patterns. If it is exposed to novel dangers, which it has no instinctive behavior patterns to meet, its reactions will not be adequate. They may even give the appearance of passive acceptance, like Ambrose Bierce's opossum on the approach of a flood. It has been said that a frog placed in very gradually heating water was thus killed without making an attempt to escape.

The attempts to escape injury are parts of the progressional trend of self-preservation. Regression from these begins where no attempt is made to escape injury, though the animal has behavior patterns fitted to do so. We have seen human developments of this in asceticism and masochism. In the animal world, the "belabored hound beneath his master's lash" is a commonplace figure, yet the dog has well-defined instincts for flight or attack with things that would injure him. An animal that, physically able to escape, passively accepts injury, or that runs away from something that its kind rather attack, shows a regression from the trends of self-preservation or pugnacity.

The trend of self-preservation is clearly sacrificed to social trends in war. Since we regard the social trends as fundamental, this sacrifice of self-preservation is not what we call regression; we exemplified this at the opening of the present paper. The sacrifice of self for group is a normal tendency, built up under natural selection. . . .

The adaptive system that is normal in the plant kingdom is regressional for animals. In men, a great part of psychopathology is regression; most of regression is pathological in origin or effect. Like fever, it is a defense mechanism; but again like fever, it uses up energy that in health would go elsewhere.

Normal versus Abnormal Regression

EDMUND S. CONKLIN, "Definition of Introversion, Extroversion and Allied Concepts," *Jour. Abn. Psychol.*, 17: 372-373 (1923)

The existence of a healthy form of regression has not I think been given sufficient consideration. Perhaps it should be reinforced by a few examples. Hall long ago pointed out the peculiar table-land nature of the college years of adolescence.[1] Here the youth may rise to the greatest heights of human conduct and within a short time regress with equal ease to the most banal of puerilities. Such great variations of conduct are the daily observation of all who teach the college youth. The antics of grown men at the conventions of some fraternal organizations is so like that of my neighbor's children parading around in fantastic costumes of their own creation and cutting up didos of their own invention that I think there can be no doubt of the regressive nature of this form of adult behavior. Patrick has shown [2] most convincingly the regressive or reversionary nature of our plays and games, of our dancing, and even of our enjoyment of movie comedians. A fairly well known orator has made much of a personal experience in which he actually went back to his old childhood home, to live once more as he did in infancy, to say his prayers at his mother's knee, and be tucked in once more and receive the good-night kiss. I suspect that in the devotional life of many religious adults there is a regression to a childhood attitude of mind, they come with the

---

[1] Hall, G. Stanley, *Adolescence*, 2: 402.
[2] Patrick, G. T. W., *Psychology of Relaxation*.

submissive attitude of the penitent child into the presence of their God conceived as a great father. From all these there is a normal rebound in the healthy mind back to the condition of life common to that individual. The college man swings back from his puerilities, the lodge man hurries back to his business, the sportsman returns to his duties, the orator to his platform and the religious devotee to the mundane world. These minds are regressively flexible and uninhibited, and because of that they are normal. When the morbid mind suffers a regression it cannot return so easily if at all. Fixations and conflicts incapacitate the individual and there is a "flight into disease" or a "flight into reality," both phrases meaning a regression from which there is no voluntary recovery. "Flight into disease" indicates a regression with abnormal introversion conspicuous. "Flight into reality" indicates a regression with an exaggerated or distorted extroversion. That flexibility which characterized the normal mind and made possible the unimpeded return from temporary regression has here disappeared.[3]

---

[3] [For further consideration of Regression, especially with reference to the functional nervous disorders, cf. Donald Elms Core, *Functional Nervous Disorders.*]

CHAPTER XIII

DISTURBANCES OF SENSATION, OF ORGANIC FUNJTIONS, AND OF EMOTION

It is only for convenience that this and the immediately following chapters dealing with the manifestations of Dissociation
show a somewhat arbitrary classification of the phenomena.
Functional Anæsthesias, with which the present section deals,
are intimately related to the functional motor disorders, *e.g.*
These symptoms are the manifestations of underlying mechanisms, not entities.

Highly illuminative of basic principles of abnormal psychology are the phenomena of functional anæsthesia. Did space
permit, Professor Pierre Janet's masterly description of these
phenomena, as found in his volume, *The Mental State of Hystericals,*[1] would be included here. The topic is touched, however, at different points in the present volume, especially by
Dr. Prince on p. 253. There he describes the way in which
stimuli applied to anæsthetic skin areas on the hysteric do not
reach his or her consciousness at the moment, and yet, under
special conditions later, can be shown to have been registered
somewhere so as to be definitely recallable. Professor Janet
depicts the varieties of such phenomena, and their conditions,
in the passages mentioned. In further pages of his work,[2] he
describes phenomena of organic anæsthesia, including losses of
consciousness-of-existence, the knowledge of which side of the
body is being affected in any manner (including allochiria[3]),
and loss of sensations of hunger, thirst, excretion, generation,
kinæsthesis, temperature, and vision.

---

[1] Pp. 3-13, xvi, 13-25, 27-30, 42-56 (Putnam, 1901).
[2] *The Mental State of Hystericals,* 56-74. *Cf.* also *The Major Symptoms
of Hysteria,* 160-174, 182-207.
[3] *Cf.* J. W. Bridges, *An Outline of Abnormal Psychology.*

Relation between Anæsthesia and Amnesia

PIERRE JANET, *The Mental State of Hystericals*, 111-116 (Putnam, 1901)

We believe it necessary to insist in certain cases on the modifications of sensibility, which have more influence on memory than is thought. As we said, in beginning this chapter, one of the cases of amnesia that most struck us was that of a patient at the Havre hospital, whom we described by the name of Rose. She had in her remembrance an indisputable lacuna of three months' duration, which is unusual and indeed quite rare. Unlike the cases of the patients of whom we have just now spoken [omitted], it was not sufficient to hypnotise her in any kind of way, to recover her remembrances; but despite all our attempts, prolonged during six weeks, we could not succeed in making her recover the memory of that long period.[1] This woman presented, as it frequently happens with very ill hystericals, a somnambulism very unstable, continually changing, with occasional spasms and small convulsive accidents.[2] One day, as she was in one of those accidental somnambulic states, she said to us spontaneously: "You have often asked me what had happened to me in the months of August and September. Why could I not answer you? It was so simple. I know well now that I did this, that," etc.[3] The remembrance of the three forgotten months had entirely come back, as we could verify. As soon, however, as this somnambulic state changed, and the subject entered the waking state, or any other somnambulic state, those remembrances disappeared again completely. We tried to discover what there might be unusual in this state, and were struck with a discovery which we still think interesting. In this particular som-

---

[1] It is well to say that I did not know then, as I do to-day, the use of automatic writing, which would probably have given me other results.

[2] [Prof. Janet follows "the classical distinction" between *stigmata* and *accidents*. By *stigmata* he means such symptoms as are, in general, "essential" ("characteristic of the disease") and "permanent" (lasting as long as the disease does). Such symptoms are "doubtful" to the patient; he "cannot tell exactly from what he is suffering." *Accidents*, on the other hand, is a term applied to the symptoms that are "superadded, in a way, to the disease to which they do not necessarily belong; they are transient, or, at most, periodical . . ." Further, they are definitely "painful to the patient, who [in those respects] knows exactly what most torments him."—Following Pierre Janet, *The Mental State of Hystericals*, xvi.]

[3] *Automatisme psychologique*, 1889, p. 94.

nambulism, which brought back her remembrances, Rose suddenly recovered the tactile and muscular sensibility of her whole right side, while in all her other states she was continually an entire anæsthetic. On the other hand, thanks to some information we were fortunate to obtain, we were shown that Rose was sensitive on the right side and on the left hemianæsthetic during the whole period of those three months the remembrance of which had been lost. The accidental restoration, we confess, of the same state of sensibility had been accompanied by the restoration of all the remembrances of that period. Facts of this kind have, we think, been often pointed out. We shall especially recall the extraordinary observation of Louis V., which numerous authors have collaborated.[4] This celebrated patient presents five or six different personalities, or rather five or six different conditions of memory, each characterised by remembrances and determined amnesias. In each of these states of remembrance, he had a particular state of sensibility, and it was enough, when possible, to re-establish artificially such or such state of sensibility to cause immediately the corresponding state of memory to appear. We establish with this patient and with many others a close relation between the state of sensibility and the state of memory, such as we met in observing the somnambulic states of Rose.

We have tried to verify this relation experimentally by producing well-determined anæsthesias, and by seeking their influence on equally well-determined remembrances. We thus succeeded, we think, in establishing certain facts which do not seem to us devoid of interest. Very often,—we do not say always,—when an hysterical has completely lost a certain sensibility, she has at the same time lost the faculty of perceiving the images which depend on that sensibility. Thus, a patient whose observation we formerly recorded was attacked by a complete dyschromatopsia, and could not, with either one eye or the other, perceive any colour. It was therefore impossible for us to cause her to experience any colour-hallucination; she saw, she said, the flowers and objects we suggested to her for seeing, but she saw them grey and white.[5] She had at

---

[4] H. Bourru et P. Durot, *Variations de la personalité*, 1888; especially p. 123 *et seq.* See in the same work a certain number of analogous observations.

[5] M. Paul Richer was the first, I believe, in calling attention to this phenomenon: *Études cliniques sur la grande hystérie*, 1885, p. 707; but he established his observation on a woman who was only achromatopsic in one eye, which makes the psychological interpretation more difficult. For a complete discussion of these experiments, see *Autom. psych.*, pp. 96 and 152.

the disposal of her personal perception the images of the colours no longer than their sensations. Sometimes, also, we can make a verification in an inverse sense; if you suggest very strongly to a subject that he feels a certain tactile sensation, a kind of tickling, for example, in an anæsthetic member, the suggestion sometimes succeeds, and the subject complains of being tickled. At this moment you can establish, by pinching the arm, that the tactile sensibility has wholly returned to that member. The image could not have been evoked without bringing back at the same time into the personal consciousness the sensation itself. These experiments may be varied indefinitely, and in most cases, you establish a sort of law of quite a regular application. The sensations and images of the same species seem assured; they are present or absent in the personal perception at the same time. If we take up again the schema which has already served, as . . . [in the figure], we can

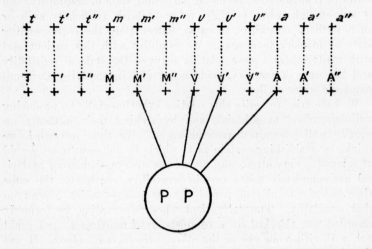

at each elementary sensation T T′ T″ M M′, etc., associate the corresponding images tactile t t′ t″, muscular m m′ m″, visual v v′ v″, and auditive a a′ a″, and we shall then read the graphic expression of the following fact: Personal perception, P P, when it seizes upon the sensations M′ V V′ A, is at the same time capable of seizing upon the associated images m′ v v′ a; on the contrary, by neglecting the sensations T T′ T″, it loses at the same time the images t t′ t″. In a word, certain amnesias seem to be dependent on the anæsthesias. It would then be the abrupt variation of the state of sensibility that would determine the localised amnesias.

In certain cases, this explanation sums up the facts very exactly. The hysterical, unable, because of the retraction of the field of consciousness, continually to gather up in one and the same personal perception all the sensations and images, seems, in order to perceive them, to choose now the one, now the other. She has a very unstable personal perception. Ordinary men, says Professor Charcot, are auditives, visuals, or motors; some belong to the indifferent type. We think that it might perhaps be necessary to admit for hystericals one more type, the alternative type; for they pass naturally or artificially from one to the other; they are, for instance, visuals when awake, and motors when in the somnambulic state. A patient, Lucie, whom we formerly described,[6] answered absolutely this description: She naturally, according as she took to such or such type of thought, possessed or lost such or such category of remembrances.

However just these remarks may be in certain particular cases, we think they are far from solving entirely the problem of the localisation of amnesias. In fact, it is easy to understand that the disappearances and returns of remembrances take place usually in a much more complicated manner. The disappearance of a certain sensation and image may possibly not be the cause of all the forgetfulness which the preceding theory might indicate. Substitutes may present themselves; the same remembrance—that of a person, for instance, may be represented in the mind by images of a different nature, auditive images of the sound of voice, visual images of the face, etc. The name, alone, of this person may suffice to recall her to our mind when we have lost the visual image of her face, and very often the forgetfulness which any anæsthesia must bring about is compensated for and becomes somewhat manifest. On the other hand, certain images play, in our remembrances, too important a part. They serve in some sort as a rallying centre, around which all the other remembrances are coördinated, and the loss of those images, when it takes place, brings with it considerable amnesias, with little connection, apparently, with the anæsthesia that produced them. We may add, finally, that this association of the images and sensations, like that of the tactile sensations and movements, is an habitual association, very general, which, however, is not necessary, and which, in certain cases, may be broken; so it will be understood why we consider this explanation of amnesia as particular and limited to certain particular cases.

These studies on some particular forms of amnesia are, therefore,

---

[6] *Autom. Psych.*, p. 104.

far from being complete, for the phenomenon is extremely complex and variable. They only confirm our general conclusion, explaining to us how personal perception, incapable of connecting all the elements with the whole personality, neglects perceiving such or such category of images. They show us that sometimes one may suspect why such a group of remembrances is especially overlooked; but they show us, also, that many complex and imperfectly known influences intervene to determine this choice.

Eye Symptoms and Emotion

W. S. INMAN; an abstract by Alfred Carver, in *Jour. Neur. & Psychopath.*, 2: 386-387 (1922), of W. S. Inman's article, "Emotion and Eye Symptoms," *Brit. Jour. Psychol.* (*Med. Sect.*), 1921, ii, 47.

"It is the object of this paper to show that the eye rarely produces other than ocular symptoms unless the patient is emotionally unstable, and that he frequently is relieved, not by glasses but by suggestion, or else by some adjustment of the inner life unknown to the oculist." Inman shows that the frequency and intensity of headache and other symptoms complained of by patients sent to an oculist have no relation to the degree of strain which the error of refraction produces, and that this error, itself often insignificant, is only brought to light when the patient complains for reasons which really are unconnected with it. The symptoms complained of make their appearance during some period of emotional stress— though the patient is oblivious of this fact—and usually disappear with their emotional cause.

Inman gives many good examples of this from his own practice. The result of a questionnaire in a hundred consecutive cases which came to him for glasses further supports his view that the mental state of the patient, not the error of refraction, determined the onset of symptoms. Inman then deals with the emotional factor in glaucoma, unequal pupils, watering of the eyes, and squint. Squint, originating as it does in such early years, was a particularly difficult subject to investigate; but after closely inquiring into 150 consecutive family cases of squint, Inman arrives at the following conclusion. Squinting is definitely related to left-handedness and stammering, and all are traceable to faults in the child's upbringing. Generally they express a rebellion against a harsh or oppressive regimen, though sometimes their object may be to gain a privilege otherwise inaccessible. These neurotic manifestations do not occur in the offspring of a really happy and well-balanced marriage, where the parents themselves are presumably free from troublesome fixations and the attendant conflicts.

Of interest in connection with the subject of functional anæsthesias are the many phenomena of this sort that resulted from the war.[1]

Possibility of Error in Identifying Functional Disorders

MABEL WEBSTER BROWN, *Neuropsychiatry and the War*, Supplement I, 9 (War Work Committee, Nat. Com. Ment. Hyg., 1918). This report is by A. Ninian Bruce, *Rev. Neurol. & Psychiat.*, 15: 332, Aug.-Sept. 1917; after Maitland, E. P., and Campbell, Kenneth, "Case of Temporary Blindness," *Brit. Med. Jour.*, 360, *Sept.* 15, 1917

In considering functional disorders, however, such observations as the following should not be overlooked:

A sergeant, aged 49, was admitted to hospital with a temperature of 101.2°, and blind. He complained of some headache. Both fundi were healthy, the media were clear, and no thickening of the retinal arteries could be seen. The temperature slowly fell to normal in eight days, when *pari passu* with the reduction of temperature his vision began to improve, and fourteen days after admission he could see well enough to read a newspaper. He later returned to duty.

The usual causes of blindness unconnected with visible eye changes are hysteria, uremia, and acute retrobulbar neuritis. The case bore some relation to the last, but the pupils were undilated and normal in action, there was no pain on movement of the eyes, nor pain on pressure applied over the globes.

The case was considered to be due to some toxic condition of the blood, which caused either anæsthesia of the rods and cones of the retina, or of the neurons of the visual cortical centres.

Disturbances of Organic Functions and Emotion

Prof. Pierre Janet, in his work, *The Major Symptoms of Hysteria*,[2] describes the astonishing variety of abnormal phenomena of alimentation and respiration that are found in some

---

[1] *Cf.* especially E. E. Southard, *Shell-Shock and Other Neuropsychiatric Problems*, cases 318-370.

[2] 227-269.

mental cases. Dr. Tom A. Williams has an article on "Mental Causes in Bodily Disease: The Most Frequent Cause of . . . 'Nervous Indigestion.' " [1] Dr. Morton Prince, in *The Dissociation of a Personality*,[2] observes the occurrence of functional aches and pains. Hugo Münsterberg gives many instances of similar phenomena in his volume, *Psychotherapy*. Because of the intimate relationship of such occurrences to the topics preceding and to those that follow, only a few instances will be included here.

A

TOM A. WILLIAMS, *Dreads and Besetting Fears*, 51-64 (copyright, 1923, by Little, Brown & Co.)

Anxiety is merely chronic fear. It affects the bodily functions in a similar way. The sources of the anxiety are not always apparent to the patient. There are several reasons for this. One is the complexity arising from the failure of the circumstances which arouse the anxiety to lend themselves readily to a clear grasp of their import. The preoccupation by the anxiety, which might lead to a discovery of its causes if scientifically directed, is usually a mere worrying repetition of the fact that one is anxious and not an investigation of circumstances at all.

A second reason militating against an understanding is the patient's reluctance to face honestly what he feels might be discreditable. A third is a tendency to be carried away by the feelings and a lack of power to pause for a logical judgment.

To this tendency is given the name of suggestibility. It is highly developed in primitive people and in children. It is subdued or diminished in proportion as one is trained into habits of logical thinking, more especially where the management of the emotions is concerned.

Many seeming exceptions occur to this statement. Examination of these shows that the training of these persons has succeeded only concerning a portion of their activities, such as, for instance, those concerned with their occupation. Many a man of highest acumen in the scientific world or in business is the easy prey of the suggestions of the salesman or of the medical charlatan. The present

---

[1] *Cf*. Bibliography.

[2] 21.　*Cf*. also Roland C. Travis, "A Study of the Effect of Hypnosis on a Case of Dissociation Precipitated by Migraine."

vogue of spiritualism is a striking instance of the muddled reasoning of thousands of persons who in daily life conduct their affairs
in a tolerably intelligent fashion. Their fall is not entirely due
to ignorance of the operations of the mind and the effect of feeling
upon thought. It is often a willing blindness motivated by wishes
of which the person is quite aware, but of the relation of which to
his thinking he is not appreciative.

Self-preservation is fundamentally the strongest of motives, and
fear of death or of the disability which will prevent livelihood is
not confined to immediate emergencies but may be a prolonged
sentiment expressing itself in what we call anxiety. That is why
the bodily functions are so frequently the center of preoccupation in
states of anxiety. And it must be remembered that emotions distressing in themselves repercuss in different ways in different
people so as to give rise to different bodily sensations. One person
may shiver along the spine, another may palpitate, another choke,
another urinate, another vomit, in another the hair may stand on
end, in another the skin may be suffused with a flush in some part
of the body or face. The mouth may become dry, the intestinal
movements may stop, the secretion of gastric juice may be arrested,
a cold sweat may break out, the patient may tremble, he may even
drop to the floor, or become unable to move or speak, with thinking
almost arrested. The consciousness of any of these bodily states
may lead to anxiety concerning the whole body or only of the
function which seems affected.

For instance, a person having experienced digestive distress because of an emotional upset falsely attributes it to disease originating in the stomach. Then he becomes preoccupied about what he
should or should not eat. His trepidation at meals serves to increase the very anxiety which is the cause of his poor digestion.
Hence, he restricts his diet more and more, inadequate nutrition
follows and with it lowered interest in external affairs, as well as
less resiliency with which to rebound from his dread of his stomach.
Professor Dejerine has shown how readily we can dissipate the
anxiety of these patients concerning their digestive function by
proving to them that they can digest food, and do gain weight.

I append an example from my own experience in which the element of anxiety was minimal and in which the factor of suggestion
was the most important feature; this was because the patient was
unusually young. However, youth in itself is not an effectual bar
to a perversion of ideas, even when an instinct so powerful as that
of alimentation is concerned; a physician recently called me to see
a child three and a half years old, in whom existed a similar mech-

anism on account of which the child would refuse its food. This latter child was cured without hospitalization, by alteration of the morale of the household concerning it.

A child aged eleven was referred by a gastroenterologist, who had been treating her because of dyspepsia and a capricious appetite. During the preceding three years she had left school three different times because of her health. The only occasion on which any definite disease had occurred was six weeks before she was sent to me, when she had a slight operation for an infected corn. After this she had been dieted, and seemed to improve for about two weeks; but during the week preceding my consultation she had lost one and a half pounds.

Upon going to bed she felt sick and weak, and pains shot all through her. She had had a constant headache for several months. When she felt ill she was very peevish, and she was homesick for her playmates, as she had made no friends in Washington, where she had only been a few months. Instead of playing she sat and lay about most of the day, feeling too tired to fetch her books for reading, of which she was formerly very fond. She had also been fond of games formerly. She had had glasses since the age of eight, but had not worn them until lately. Her appetite was very poor.

The mother had been very conscientious in her upbringing; and this had reacted on the child, before whom far too much attention had been shown regarding both manners and physical welfare. Conversation before her would frequently concern the appropriateness of different foods and their digestibility; and the atmosphere of the home was one of solicitude about the child's health.

As an infant she was not retarded; she had been apt at school except in writing, when her hands would jerk; but they did not do so in sewing, at which she was skillful. Her bad writing in school disturbed her, and she would become "hysterical." Respiratory infections were easy and frequent, as was the case with her father. Perhaps this was accountable to mouth breathing; for this adenoidectomy was performed when she was eight.

We were dealing with a case of "hysterical nosophobia," by which is meant a fear of disease implanted by suggestion, a matter very easy in young children and uncritical people in general. But it is quite exceptional for food and appetite to be the subjects of a phobia in so young a child, for in the child the vegetative functions and instincts are usually paramount.

She was sent to the hospital on account of the nosophobia from which she suffered, the result of too much sympathy at home.

When her parents left her she wept bitterly, but was soon relieved by a little "jollying." She promised that she would try to behave properly if her parents were allowed to visit her. The promise that they might do so stopped the weeping for twenty-four hours. The visit was postponed, however. She was encouraged to play with another little girl patient; and this she came to enjoy so much that she ceased to ask to go home. When she was quite contented and happy she was allowed to return home, where she has remained well ever since.

The treatment in hospital consisted of creating an atmosphere around the little patient designed to show her how trivial were her own preoccupations about what she could eat as compared with the real suffering and disabilities of the patients around her in the ward. Of design she was placed in the open ward in preference to a private room. She was shown to what a degree her feelings and behavior were under her own control, and no solicitude was shown about whether her food would agree with her or not.

It is not possible to set down in detail the numerous measures used to destroy the inconvenient suggestions to which she had been subject so long. While the therapeutics inevitably contained a modicum of suggestions, yet the end worked for was always the giving of a rational understanding to the little patient of why her symptoms had occurred and how to prevent them in the future. In other words, the *modus operandi* was persuasion and reëducation. Toward this the hospital furnished a valuable aid, not merely because it was a hospital, but because the nurses were intelligent coadjutors of the case. The child had been too much derationalized to have been manageable by office consultations alone unless the mother had been able to collaborate, which she could not,—not from lack of intelligence or conscientious desire, but because she had not understood the psychological mechanism of the daughter's illness. The mother's reëducation was much more readily effected when uncomplicated by the child's presence. Its success was shown by her successful management of the child when she returned home.

Preoccupation by the function of the heart is a very frequent source of anxiety. This may be purely emotional, the patient being dominated by the suggestion that his heart flutterings indicate disease.[1] His fear is to be dealt with according to the principles set forth in this book. But not infrequently there are physical factors which disturb the beating of the heart. These may be tri-

---

[1] See case in Chapter VII [Williams, *op. cit.*]; also that on p. 98 [*ibid.*].

fling both as regards the heart itself, and as regards the patient's general health. But the sensations referred to the heart are nevertheless alarming, so that the physician has to deal then with the anxiety state now under discussion. Sometimes again the physical state is less trifling and there may be irregularities of rhythm, increase of rate or actual inadequacy for extra effort of the heart.

In certain of these instances, too, it is not the slight discomfort from such conditions as these that incommode the patient, but the anxiety that he feels concerning them. Sometimes this is the product of medical suggestion, which leads him to suppose that the condition of his heart is more serious than is the case. This may occur even when the patient is assured to the contrary, through a physician's mistaken policy of trying to minimize to the patient's mind the condition present.

For example, a man was referred to me because of anxiety regarding an acceleration of the heart with accompanying unpleasant sensations whenever he walked a few blocks. He had seen three eminent heart specialists, all of whom had assured him of the soundness of his heart. This assurance in no way diminished his fear of death, a fear which occurred upon any exertion. He felt that there must be something that the physicians were trying to conceal. It was only when the admission was made that there must be an unbalance of the mechanism which accelerates the heart that he was able to reconcile himself to his condition and go about his work with due precaution and without undue anxiety. What was done was to remove from his mind the fear of the unknown. "Better a dreadful certainty, than an uncertain dread." But the certainty was not so awful in this case.

In young people, anxious preoccupation as regards the health of the generative organs is a not infrequent upshot of the observation of their functioning. This psychic weakness is pandered to by harpies who advertise remedies for conditions which are often merely physiological. The anxiety fostered in this way may become so intense as to lead to suicide. Fear of the consequences of masturbation is a happy hunting ground for these charlatans.

Dread of impotence is not an uncommon source of anxiety in older men. I have had several occasions to dissipate this in men about to be married, or even soon after marriage, where some accident has aroused an anxiety so intense as to inhibit the proper performance of the sexual act. In women such preoccupations are less frequent, but they are more apt to be anxious concerning such diseases as cancer.

This fear of the genital function is sometimes the foundation of a social fear formerly much more prevalent than now. It expresses itself as extreme diffidence in relation with persons of the opposite sex. Of course it has received enormous intensification from ethical doctrines which taught that woman was an unclean thing and denied her a soul, and which asserted that carnal relations with her were an evil, even though necessary. The ideal to be sought was celibacy. So extreme became the obsession that in the Greek monastery at Mt. Athos not even female animals were permitted upon the place. This absurdity was satirized by Shakespeare in his first play, "Love's Labour's Lost."

The same sentiment among women was strongly pervasive during the nineteenth century in Great Britain, and was exquisitely ridiculed by Tennyson in "The Princess." But ridicule of this kind does not reach persons seriously affected by this obsession. Far more powerful as an instrument of moral help has been the diffusion in our day of information concerning the physiology of reproduction. This, in conjunction with the great expansion of the freedom of young women, is rapidly putting an end to fears of this kind.

Dreads and fears of tuberculosis, syphilis, and other contagions are not uncommon in our day of widespread information about the way infection is spread. They only parallel the intense terror of leprosy,—so graphically portrayed by Lew Wallace in "Ben Hur,"—plague and other epidemics of the Middle Ages. They are to be dealt with on the principles which will be apparent to every reader of this book.

B

Boris Sidis, *Symptomatology, Psychognosis and Diagnosis of Psychopathic Diseases,* 368-371, 373-375 (Badger, 1914)

Mrs. L., sixty years of age; married. Family history is good. Parents died of old age; brother died of apoplexy. Patient had one daughter who died some fifteen years ago.

The patient complains of sensitiveness of the stomach, of kidney trouble, and of nervousness. During the attacks of nervousness she is restless, sleepless, and is undergoing "death agonies." The suffering is so intense that, in spite of her religious scruples, the thought of suicide forces itself on her mind. She has an insistent fear of getting insane; the fear is so intense that she paces the floor night after night, like an animal in a cage.

She is unable to eat and hardly drinks anything when the attack is on. If she attempts to eat, she rejects it immediately. "While my brain is perfectly clear to take up any intellectual pursuit, if I attempt, for instance, to purchase anything in the way of apparel, my brain gets on fire and I walk the floor in a frenzy of excitement, not having the least idea as to the choice I should make. I am not able to sleep or eat, and what little food I eat does not digest. Although so disabled in judgment as to myself, my friends often come to me to aid them in their decisions in matters of apparel, because they value my judgment, which is perfectly cool, when I am deciding for them."

Though the oculists do not find anything special the matter with her eyes, she complains of weakness and occasionally of complete darkness settling on the eyes, at first in the form of a mist, and then, becoming denser, ends in total darkness, a form of functional amblyopia. She also complains of severe headaches,—the head feels at first dizzy, sore, painful, throbbing, and hot, as if it were on fire. Patient also complains of trophic disturbances, of a dry skin, of swellings and rashes on the body. For years she has been suffering from those trophic disturbances which she terms "erysipelas."

When the attack sets on, the patient becomes greatly depressed,— the hands and the feet are cold; the bowels are constipated; there is irritation of the bladder; tinnitus aurium is present; there is a feeling of pressure in the head with dreams of a distressing character; then the headache grows in severity and becomes throbbing. After a time trophic disturbances appear, such as rashes in the form of "pimples and swellings," with œdema of the legs, of hands and eyes.

Now and then the patient has seizures of coughing spells, and has insistent fears of some impending lung troubles. Occasionally she has epileptiform attacks with slight tonic and clonic convulsions, accompanied with unconsciousness or semi-consciousness. Some years ago she used to have "attacks of helplessness," and even of complete paralysis. She also suffered from tingling sensations in the extremities, "numbness all over," becoming fully anæsthetic over the whole surface of the body.

An examination of the patient shows her to be greatly emaciated; poorly nourished; skin is dry and crackling. There are a few macules and papules, a few wheals and remnants of dried-up vesicles and blebs. Near the margin of the mucous membranes some fissures and excoriations are found in various stages of healing and crusting. The tongue is coated, furred and there is a heavy smell from the mouth. The lungs are in good condition. The heart-beat is irregular, aortic second sound is slightly accentuated. Patellar reflexes are greatly exaggerated. The eyes do not accommodate well,—the left eye is somewhat defective in convergence during the act of accommodation. Pupillary reaction is rather sluggish. The tympanic membrane of the left ear is slightly thickened, and hearing is defective on the left side. She also suffers occasionally from noises, "buzzing in the head" and dizziness.

Motor activities and sensitiveness to all forms of sensory stimulations are in good condition. No œdema could be found, except a slight puffy condition below the eyes. Several examinations of the urine showed the latter free from any trace of albumin. Patient can see well, but she gets easily fatigued when reading or sewing,— a darkness then comes over her, and everything seems to be enveloped in a mist which is getting heavier and thicker. Field of vision is normal. No reversion of the color field is present.

Memory for present and past events is excellent. Attention is good, but she cannot keep her attention for any length of time; she then begins to complain of fatigue and sometimes gets an attack of severe headache. Intellectual powers are well preserved, and, in fact, are quite vigorous. Patient is well educated, writes well and has a deep interest in philosophical, especially in theological problems.

Hypnagogic and hypnapagogic hallucinations are well developed; field of vision on closure of the eyes is very rich in colors. Sleep is greatly disturbed, she suffers from insomnia, and when she falls asleep she has quite elaborate dreams, often of a distressing character. Once she had a visual hallucination of her daughter, and another time she had the peculiar hallucination of the reality of the presence of her daughter, who did not appear to the "bodily senses," but to the "inner mental vision," a form of pseudo-hallucination. She has a yearning after something, she does not know what, and is in constant fear of losing her mind. . . .

A psychognostic examination by the hypnoidal states revealed the following data:

When at the age of five, the patient happened to see an insane woman in a maniacal condition. The image of that woman never left the patient's thought, conscious or subconscious, so deeply was her mind impressed with that event. She was greatly frightened and the thought kept recurring: "Do little girls get insane?" Since that time she became possessed by the fear of insanity. In her ardent imagination she actually felt that she was getting insane.

When asked about her dreams, the patient was unable to tell anything, but in one of the deeper hypnoidal states she remembered that she used to dream about that insane woman standing near her bed, bending over her and even touching her. Many times she was in such agony of fear that she wanted to cry out, but was unable to do it. When she woke up, she cried in great terror. When the patient gave birth to her child, she was afraid the child would get insane; many a time she even had the feeling, as if the child was insane.

Thus the fear of insanity is traced to an experience of early childhood, an experience which, having become subconscious, is manifesting itself persistently in the patient's consciousness.

The patient's parents were very religious, and the child was brought up not only in the fear of God, but also in the fear of hell and the devil. Being sensitive and imaginative, the devils of the gospel were to her stern realities. She had a firm belief in "diabolical possessions" and "unclean spirits." The legend of Jesus exorcising in the country of the Gadarenes unclean spirits, whose name is Legion, was to her a tangible reality. She was brought up on brimstone and pitch, with everlasting fires of the "bottomless pit" for sinners and unbelievers. In the hypnoidal state she clearly remembered the preacher who used every Sunday to give her the horrors by his picturesque descriptions of the tortures of the "bottomless pit." She was in anguish over the unsolved question: "Do little sinner-girls go to hell?" This fear of hell made the little girl feel depressed and miserable, and had poisoned many a cheerful moment of her life.

What a lasting effect and what a melancholy gloom this fear of ghosts and of unclean spirits of the bottomless pit produced on this young life may be judged from the following facts:

When the patient was about eleven years old, a young girl, a friend of hers, having noticed the patient's fear of ghosts, played on her one of those silly, practical jokes, the effects of which on sensitive natures are often disastrous and lasting. The girl disguised herself as a ghost in a white sheet and appeared to the patient who was just on the point of falling asleep. The child shrieked in terror and fainted. Since that time the patient suffered from nightmares and was mortally afraid to sleep alone; she passed many a night in a state of excitement, frenzied with fear of apparitions and ghosts.

When about the age of seventeen, she apparently freed herself from the belief in ghosts and unclean powers, but the fear acquired in her childhood did not lapse, it persisted subconsciously and manifested itself in the form of uncontrollable fears. . . .[1]   She

---

[1] "Every ugly thing," says Mosso, "told to the child, every shock, every fright given him, will remain like minute splinters in the flesh, to torture him all his life long.

"An old soldier whom I asked what his greatest fears had been, answered

was afraid to remain alone in a room especially in the evening. Thus, once when she had to go upstairs alone to pack her trunks, a gauzy garment called forth the experience of her ghost-fright,— she had the illusion of seeing a ghost and she fell fainting to the floor.

When about the age of eighteen, she began to teach mathematics in a school and worked hard . . . and worried much over her prospects of advancement. It was from that period that her headaches date as well as her first attack of nervous prostration.

When she got married, the duties of housewife and of social relations made life still more strenuous. Motherhood served only to increase the nervous strain and anxiety all the more so as her child was constantly ailing up to the age of five. After years of devotion and of motherly self-sacrifice she succeeded in bringing up her daughter, who became the very soul of the patient's being.

What a fearful blow it must have been to this frail woman when her only daughter, in the full bloom of her young womanhood, at the age of twenty, began to ail, to sink in health, and was declared an incurable case of tuberculosis! Day and night did the unfortunate mother watch in anguish over her only child. She actually lived through the distressing cough, the gastric and trophic disturbances, the loss of appetite, the nausea, the inability to retain food, the weakness, the helplessness, and the complete prostration of her daughter who did her best to cheer her poor, suffering mother, who, with an aching heart, eyes blinded with tears and with a mind distracted by anguish and anxiety, felt her head in a whirl; choking sensations, darkness, fainting spells began to seize on her, spells of darkness against which she struggled in throes of convulsions.

In one of the hypnoidal states I happened to press on the throat, accidentally producing choking sensations, when the patient began to feel faint and, losing consciousness, became convulsed with epileptiform tonic and clonic contractions. The state of unconsciousness, or semi-consciousness or of "Dämmerzuslände," lasted about twenty-five seconds, the patient coming back with a deep sigh

---

me thus: 'I have only had one, but it pursues me still. I am nearly seventy years old, I have looked death in the face I do not know how many times; I have never lost heart in any danger, but when I pass a little old church in the shades of the forest, or a deserted chapel in the mountains, I always remember a neglected oratory in my native village, and I shiver and look around, as though seeking the corpse of a murdered man which I once saw carried into it when a child, and with which an old servant wanted to shut me up to make me good.' " Here, too, subconscious experiences have persisted throughout lifetime.

and with no memory of what had taken place during the attack. I was thus enabled to reproduce at will the original attacks.

The patient told me that with all her "faith in the Lord" she rebelled against "Providence." "I have blasphemed the Lord,—He is not as good as a loving mother."

The daughter passed away in the arms of the mother, who from that time on had been living through the disease of her child with all the symptoms of trophic disturbances and death agony, but much more complicated and intensified by the agony which she herself had then undergone. Dress, receptions, visits became painful to her, because of the daughter with whom all those enjoyments had been associated. The whole life experience of that period of anguish has persisted in her subconsciousness and has been forcing itself with all its vehemence on the patient's personal self. All those symptoms, however, disappeared during the treatment.

Thus the whole symptom-complex of the disease could by means of the hypnoidal states be traced to dissociated, submerged, subconscious experiences, or to subconscious sets of systems, coming in the form of attacks of insistent mental states, or of recurrent psychomotor states, now meaningless, harmful, psychopathic.

CHAPTER XIV

FUNCTIONAL MOTOR ABNORMALITIES

FUNCTIONAL PARALYSES AND CONTRACTURES

Definitions and Characteristics

A

PIERRE JANET, *The Mental State of Hystericals*, 166-167, 325-335 (Putnam, 1901)

Usually, when the members of an hysterical are attacked by an anæsthesia, quite complete, tactile, and muscular, affecting the entire limb, the troubles of motion are more emphasized than in the preceding cases [omitted]. They take a very special aspect, one which raises some of the most interesting problems of psychology.

This alteration in the movement of the anæsthetic members was long ago pointed out by MM. Ch. Bell, Duchenne, and Briquet, but it seems to us that the most complete description of it, the most precise, was given by M. Lasègue,[1] and it is for this that we propose designating this ensemble of rather complex phenomena under the name of syndrome of Lasègue.

Let us first sum up the essential facts which constitute this syndrome.

1. The subject is incapable of effecting any movement on the anæsthetic side without the help of sight.

2. In certain experiments, the movement begun with the help of sight may be continued without this help.

3. Visual images, or even the tactile sensation, may take the place of visual sensation, provided they teach the subject the position of his limb at the beginning of the movement.

4. This characteristic does not seem to trouble the subject, who, during his normal life, performs all the movements without any complaint.

---

[1] Lasègue, "Anesthésie et ataxie hystériques," *Études médicales*, ii., p. 25.

5. If you raise the subject's arm without his seeing it, this arm will remain immovable in cataleptic postures.

6. Movements may be obtained without the help of sight, but they are subconscious, and the subject does not know of them. . . .

The principal fact is the loss of motion without the help of sight. . . .

In view of other discussions included in the present volume, Professor Janet's interesting explanation of this syndrome [2] is omitted.

"There will be *paralysis*," says M. Paul Richer, "every time the muscular fibres shall have lost the faculty to shorten under the influence of the ordinary stimulants used in the case. . . . Contracture is defined as follows: a motor-impotence, accompanied by a persistent and involuntary rigidity of the muscles, without notable modification through the electric reactions and without alteration in the texture of the muscular fibre itself." [3]

In a word, in paralysis the members fall back flaccid, the muscles are soft and relaxed; in contracture the members keep a fixed position, which it is difficult to modify; the muscles are hard and contracted; but in either case the subject has equally lost the power of moving his limbs by an effort of his will. These two phenomena, then, resemble each other by a principal characteristic; they alternate and intermingle closely; they are produced in the same conditions, present the same varieties, and raise the same problems. Certainly, in a complete clinical study, these two accidents should be distinguished and analysed separately; but, since we wish to make here simply a general review of psychological phenomena which accompany hysterical conditions, we have thought it well to consider paralyses and contractures in one and the same study.

Paralyses and contractures are among the most interesting symptoms in hysteria; they often constitute alone very painful and very enduring infirmities; they are often a cause of errors of diagnosis and of questionable surgical interventions.[4] They become mixed up with many other phenomena of the disease. When a hysterical complains of pains, of difficulty of motion, speech, deglutition, of digestive or even respiratory disturbances, it is not rare to discover, here or there, a contractured muscle which provokes and keeps up the symptoms. On the other hand, the study of these facts has had a great historical importance, for it has given birth to the first

---

[2] *Op. cit.*, 168-188.

[3] Paul Richer, *Paralysies et contractures hystériques*, 1892, p. 1.

[4] Charcot, *Arch. de neurol.*, 1892, iii., p. 275.

exhaustive works on the psychical conditions of the neuroses, namely, to the Charcot lectures of 1884-1885. This study is still to-day far from being concluded, and it gives rise to curious psychological problems, which are far from being solved. We do not, therefore, pretend in any way to explain all hysterical paralyses; we put aside, as we have always done, the simply organic phenomena which may intervene, and we speak only of a group of paralyses, those which may be justly considered as cerebral—namely, as psychologic. Even in regard to the latter, we shall be content to offer a résumé of some descriptions and a few hypotheses which seem to us to be legitimately applicable, not to all, but to a few of the observed facts.

Paralyses and contractures are very varied, but it is interesting to notice that they almost always find a place in groups already known. They present the same varieties and may be ranked in the same classifications with all the other phenomena already described, such as anæsthesias and amnesias.[5] They may be *systematic, localised,* or *general.* We shall insist especially on the first, which, from our point of view, are particularly important.

1. Let us, then, first examine the *systematic paralyses.* It seems to us certain that in many cases the patients have not wholly lost all the movements of a limb; they have simply lost the power of effecting such or such category of movements, while they have well-nigh completely preserved the power over others. Certainly, in cases of this kind, there may sometimes be established a general weakening of all the movements, even of those that are preserved. This enfeeblement, which, besides, does not exist in all cases, is related to the common amyosthenia of hystericals. Yet is there none the less a very appreciable difference between the preserved movements and the lost movements, since the first, although enfeebled, still exist, and the second no longer exist at all. This loss of certain movements is not due to the complete paralysis of such or such muscle, for all the muscles are able to work in other movements. It is certain combinations, certain systems of muscular contractions, that have disappeared. It is for this reason that such paralyses have often been described under the name of systematised paralyses. M. Babinski, in publishing very interesting examples of these phenomena, observes that the word "systematic" would be a better term.[6] He recalls that to systematise designates an act,

---

[5] *Automatisme psychologique,* p. 335.
[6] Babinski, "Paralysies hystériques systematiques," *Bulletins de la Société médicale des hôpitaux,* 28 octobre, 1892.

"bringing facts back to a system," and that systematic applies simply to things which belong to, which relate to, a system. Although there is no great difference between the two terms, we acknowledge the correctness of this observation, and we designate these phenomena by the name of systematic paralyses.

The most known and the clearest among these systematic paralyses are the disturbances of the walk indicated by MM. Charcot and Paul Richer in 1883,[7] and described in 1888 by M. Blocq under the name "astasie-abasie." M. Blocq to-day brings together under the name of dysbasias an ensemble of disturbances of the walk of which the astasia-abasia is the type. "It is," says this author, "a morbid state in which the impossibility of the vertical posture and of the normal walk contrasts with the integrity of the sensibility of the muscular strength and the coördination of the other movements of the legs."[8] The patient, lying on his bed, can raise his legs, bend his knees, resist movements communicated in a way absolutely normal, apparently; but if he tries to rise, to stand, to walk, his legs give way under him.

In some cases particularly curious, the subject retains the power of jumping, dancing, walking on all fours, hopping on one foot, etc. He is paralysed in only one single act, normal walking.[9] This (syndrome), as may be readily seen, is very varied; at one time it is pure, as in the preceding paralytic form; at another it is accompanied with other phenomena. This motor incoördination, accompanied with sharp pains, may, in very rare cases, simulate tabes.[10] Sometimes it is found that the subject, at the moment when he tries to walk, experiences an emotion, an anguish analogous to that which would drive an agoraphobe to cross a public square, and gives to the syndrome a clinical aspect comparable to that of obsessing ideas; it is the emotive dysbasia of MM. Dinswanger and Séglas.[11] In other cases may be observed phenomena of aboulia, indicated by M. Régis. It is no rare thing, moreover, to find the dysbasia accompanied by systematised chorea, which may be considered, as we have demonstrated in the preceding paragraph, a veritable,

---

[7] Pour la bibliographie et la description complète de ce syndrome, cf. Paul Richer, op. cit., p. 48; Paul Blocq, Les troubles de la marche dans les maladies nerveuses, 1892, p. 55; et la thèse récente de Pierre Jolly, Contribution à l'étude de l'astasie-abasie, p. 9 (Lyon, 1892).

[8] Paul Blocq, Archives de neurologie, 1888, and op. cit., p. 56.

[9] Pitres, Leçons sur l'hystérie, i., p. 459.

[10] Ibid., p. 471.

[11] Séglas, "De l'abasie et de l'astasie émotives,' Médecine moderne, 1891, No. 24.

fixed idea. Rem., paralysed for ordinary walking, can, however, walk on tip-toe, as if she were in constant fear of crushing fragile objects. Finally, MM. Weill and Pierre Jolly have noticed [12] that the dysbasia of certain patients may be instantaneously stopped by compressing certain parts of the body. This fact recalls the influence of certain sensations meant to stop or provoke the automatic phenomena of hysteria.

Besides the astasia-abasia, other systematic paralyses are known, less frequent perhaps, but quite as significant. A patient described by M. Babinski could stand up and walk but was altogether unable to execute voluntarily the elementary movements of flexion or extension of the foot, leg, or toes.[13] It is a systematised paralysis of all the general functions of the lower leg, with the exception of that of walking; it is the reverse of abasia.

By a delicate analysis of certain cases of facial paralysis, the same author was able to demonstrate another systematisation. The movements of the commissures of the lips are very easily executed on both sides when the subject is requested to put each side into movement separately, but when the patient speaks or tries to whistle there is but one side of the face, the left, that normally contracts. The commissure on the right side remains immovable. "There is here a contrast between the integrity of a system of movements which one muscular group is called upon to execute and the abolition of some other system of movements, the execution of which is entrusted to this same group of muscles." [14]

The disorders which have been described by the name of external ophthalmoplegias of hystericals [15] seem to be of the same kind. The patients seem to have lost the power of effecting alone a certain movement of the eye, a look to the right, for example; but it may be proved that, in many circumstances, this movement may nevertheless be effected. As a general thing the question here is not of systematic paralysis; it is only a question of the opposition between the voluntary movement and the automatic movement, which we shall find again in many other paralyses.

We shall, rather, point out as systematic paralysis certain forms of hysterical mutism. "Certain people are dumb without being aphonic, others are aphonic without being dumb. One patient may

---

[12] Weill, *Archives de neurologie*, 1892, p. 89; Pierre Jolly, *op. cit.*, p. 23.

[13] Babinski, *Soc. médicale des hôpitaux*, 8 juillet, 1892.

[14] Weill, *Archives de neurologie*, 1892, p. 89; Pierre Jolly, *op. cit.*, p. 23.

[15] Ballet, *Revue de médecine*, 1888, pp. 337, 513; F. Raymond et E. Koenig, "Sur la dissociation des mouvements oculaires chez les dégénérés hystériques," *Annales d'oculistique*, juillet, 1891.

be able to blow and whistle; he has only lost the motor-representa-
tions necessary to put into play the mechanism of the articulate
word." [16] "A patient is absolutely dumb," says M. Babinski, likewise, "and yet tongue and lips move easily to accomplish functions
which do not belong to language." [17] A patient of M. Oppenheim's
can no longer speak, but utters cries of pain when pinched; she
can also sing aloud.[18] A child, of whom MM. Breuer and Freud
relate a most interesting fact, "was a little frightened at night; she
cannot speak, and tries to recall a prayer to recite. Just at that
moment she cannot find in her memory any other except a child's
prayer in English. This child remained dumb for a year and a half;
she can neither speak, nor write, nor even understand her mother
tongue, but she understands, speaks, and writes English. Is not
this a fine case of systematic mutism?" [19]

The same characteristic, the same systematisation, may be met
with, to my thinking, in contractures.

"There are [as we have said before] *systematic contractures*—
that is to say, contractures in which all the muscles of the arms or
hand are not exactly contractured, to the highest degree, but in
which only some are more or less contractured, so as to give to the
limb an attitude equally rigid but expressive. The arms, for example, might remain contractured in a menacing or a praying
posture." [20] We related the example of a woman who lifted her
fist against her husband and who, by a celestial punishment, is
keeping her arm contractured in the position of dealing a blow
with the fist. We presented, also, as of the same kind, Lem's case.
This young man, sailor on a merchant-vessel, who already had had
hysterical accidents, received upon the chest and abdomen the shock
of a barrel rolling on the deck. He was not hurt but he remained
bent forward by a permanent contracture of the muscles of the
abdomen and thorax. He had kept this position for six weeks, when
Dr. Pillet, chief physician of the hospital, showed him to us. We
may now add other examples. Margaret has had for a year her right

---

[16] Charcot, *op. cit.*, iii., p. 427; *cf.* Blanche Edwards, *De l'hémiplégie*,
p. 103.

[17] Babinski, *Migraine ophthalmique hystérique*, p. 4.

[18] Oppenheim, *Thatsächliches und hypotetisches ueber das Wesen der
Hysterie*, October, 1889, p. I; même observation par Gerhardt de Wurtz-
burg, P. Richer, *op. cit.*, p. 207.

[19] Breuer et Freud, "Ueber den psychischen Mechanismus hysterischer
Phänomene," *Neurologisches Centralblatt*, E. Mendel, 1893, Nos. 1 and 2,
extract p. 6.

[20] Breuer et Freud, *op. cit.*, p. 2.

hand contractured in the position of a hand that holds a needle. Justine, in circumstances which we shall study [omitted], had her hands contractured in the position a pianist would give them in trying to stretch an octave. Many other examples are of the same sort, and would show us that systematised contractures are not only met with in experiments of suggestion, but that they are often produced in a natural manner.

We have, in a general way, seen in these systematic conditions something analogous to the characteristics already studied in respect to the anæsthesias and amnesias of the same kind. The limb is not entirely paralysed or contractured in a brutal manner, it is a function, and above all an intelligent function, of the limb, which acts separately from the others. There is a delicate distinction made which awakens the idea of a selection of a thought, rather than of a gross lesion of the organism.

2. Localised paralyses do not affect an isolated muscle, but a member or part of a member; they are complete and suppress to the same degree all the movements of this member. Most of these cases of hysterical monoplegias have found their résumé in Miura's work.[21] Generally, these monoplegias develop after a traumatism, or an accident befalling a particular member. Immediately after the accident, or oftener after a certain period, which has been justly called *period of meditation,* the member becomes more or less completely inert.

"As the traumatic action we speak of is often very slight—said M. Brodie, already in 1837—and in apparent disproportion with the effects produced, the latter are often badly understood, badly interpreted; they are taken for something very different from what they are in reality." [22] M. Charcot has shown how this most important diagnosis should be made.[23] He insisted, in the beginning, on the absence of fever, and on the ordinary absence of trophic lesions and of reaction of degeneration, which, in a paralysis of organic origin, should manifest themselves in a few days. He insisted on the preservation of tendon-reflexes, and, above all, on the repartition of the anæsthesia. These anæsthesias in geometrical segments do not correspond to anatomical regions supplied by a nerve-trunk, but to entire organs such as they are conceived and

---

[21] Kinnosuke Miura, "Sur trois cas de monoplégie brachiale hystérique," *Archives de neurologie,* 1893, i., p. 321.

[22] Brodie, *Illustrative Lectures of Certain Local Nervous Affections,* London, 1837.

[23] Charcot, *op. cit.,* iii., pp. 288, 293, 302.

limited by popular custom.[24] They have the shape of a vest-sleeve, of a leg of mutton, of a cuff. It is not only the arm supplied by the brachial plexus that is insensible and paralysed; it is also the region of the shoulder, which indeed depends on the cervical plexus. The thigh and the buttock are attacked, but the sacral region and the genital region are respected, a fact which does not occur in spinal paralyses.[25] These characteristics present, it is true, some exceptions and irregularities. Atrophies and even disturbances in electric reactions have been pointed out.[26] Hysterical monoplegias, in which sensibility has been preserved, have also, though rarely, been demonstrated. M. Miura [27] pointed to a case in 31, that of Roug, which was this year the subject of one of M. Charcot's lectures. These exceptions are rare. A hysterical monoplegia has generally a special aspect; one is particularly struck by its complete insensibility, its loss of tactile and muscular sense; the indifference of the subject who has no longer any consciousness of the existence of his arm, "who has forgotten it, who has lost it." This attitude of the subject is scarcely seen outside of hysteria.

It is useless to insist on *contractures localised* in such or such organ. The contractures of legs, arms, the coxalgias, the contractures of the thorax with respiratory disturbances, the stiff-neck, the contracture of the masseters, glosso-labial spasm, blepharospasm, the troubles of ocular accommodation, the spasms of the viscera, principal among which is the pharyngo-œsophageal spasm, are well-known phenomena.

We only regret not being able to study here in detail the observations which lead us to suppose the existence of a spasm of the diaphragm. [Hysterical meteorism is not always due to a paralysis of the tunics of the intestine; it often depends in a large part on spasmodic phenomena that take place in the diaphragm.] This is the opinion maintained by M. Talma, of Utrecht, then by M. Bernheim, which to us appears, in great part, very exact. "Certainly," says M. Bernheim, "the mechanism of this swelling is not made quite clear; for the pathological lowering of the diaphragm by a pleural exudate does not usually produce so notable an increase of the circumference of the abdomen. Perhaps there is also required a particular state of the abdominal musculature which loses its tonicity and allows itself to be distended by elasticity like an india-

---

[24] *Stigmates mentaux de l'hystérie*, p. 12.
[25] Souques, *Syndromes hystériques stimulateurs*, p. 80.
[26] *Cf.* P. Richer, *op. cit.*, p. 9.
[27] Miura, *op. cit.*, p. 326.

rubber ball?" [28] But it is evident that the diaphragm plays a great rôle in this phenomenon. The astonishing rapidity with which, by a simple suggestion, one can produce the swelling out or lowering of the abdomen without there being any passage of gas; the lowering of the diaphragm and of the inferior lobe of the lung on the axillary line established by percussion during meteorism, the disturbances of the breathing which become only higher costal after a few deep inspirations have produced the phenomena—show us the correctness of this interpretation. We shall add that with a patient, M., we have demonstrated that all phenomena which depend on the diaphragm, such as laughter, sobbing, hiccough, could not be produced during the meteorism, and if they were brought about through suggestion the abdominal swelling would disappear. It is useless to point out the rôle which these diaphragmatic spasms play in the "phantom-tumors," and in imaginary pregnancy.

3. The paralyses, more or less general, which are not confined to one limb, but which take the hemiplegic and paraplegic forms, or, in exceptional cases, a quadriplegic form,[29] present about the same characteristics as the preceding forms; yet it seems to us that they should be distinguished from them, for, in certain cases, they cannot be interpreted in the same way. Facial paralysis is met with, as MM. Ballet and Babinski [30] have shown, but it is much more rare in the hysterical hemiplegia than in the organic hemiplegia. The energy of the non-paralysed side is not affected. It remains intact, or even increases sometimes instead of diminishing, as in organic paralyses.[31] In short, one may establish here, in a supreme degree, the great characteristic of hysterical paralyses, of anæsthesia, and even of the amnesia of paralysed limbs. "The patient sweeps the ground," said M. Todd. "He drags his limb after him," said M. Charcot; "he may be designated by the name helcopode." "He drags his leg," says M. Blocq, "as if it were a foreign body fastened on him without his knowing it." [32]

---

[28] Bernheim, *Hypnotisme, Suggestion*, 1891, p. 187.

[29] P. Richer, *op. cit.*, p. 177.

[30] Babinski, "Paralysie faciale hystérique," *Bulletins de la soc. méd. des hôpit.*, 28 juin, 1892; Blanche Edwards, *De l'hémiplégie dans quelques affections nerveuses*, 1889, p. 163.

[31] Féré, *Sensation et mouvement*, 1887, p. 28; Pitres, *op. cit.*, p. 204.

[32] Blocq, *op. cit.*, p. 82.

["We cannot help therefore being somewhat surprised and ill-humoured when we attend a paralyzed hysterical. These patients vex us with their calm indifference and inertia. One of their limbs being out of use does not appear to incommode them; they think it quite natural to walk with but one leg, and do not make the least effort to use the other leg. It was just

Contractures appear to us *general* when all the muscles of one limb are contractured to the highest degree, so as to give to the limb a regular posture, always the same, determined by the unequal force of the different antagonistic muscles.)The lower limb is stretched out, adducted, and slightly rotated inwards, the foot, in equinovarus, slightly bent inwards, with the toes much flexed. The position of the upper limb is more open to dispute. M. P. Richer gives as the most regular form the forearm flexed on the arm. We have much oftener observed, in general contracture, the arm held tight to the body, the forearm extended and slightly rotated inwards, the fist clinched without the position of the thumb presenting anything very characteristic. These positions are very frequent; for contractures, even systematised, have often, at the end of a certain variable length of time, and according to the subjects, a tendency to become general and the limbs assume then a regular position.

---

this that determined the famous distinction Charcot made between the helicopode and helcopode gaits. While the person affected with organic hemiplegy labours hard to move his restive limb forward, the hysterical drags hers after her like a cannon-ball. She almost despises it, and she wants to beat it, calling it 'an old stump,' like a patient Professor James has described. (William James, 'Notes on Automatic Writing,' *Pro. Soc. Psy. Res.*, March, 1889, p. 552 and in *The Principles of Psychology*, 1890, I, p. 377.)

"This conduct corresponds to a very special mental trouble. If you question such persons, you find that they seem not to have kept the remembrance of their limb, they do not know any longer what this paralyzed limb used to do and they can no longer make the efforts of imagination necessary to conceive it. Féré was one of the first who insisted on this point. 'After having shut the patient's eyes,' he says, 'I ask her to try to represent to herself her left hand executing movements of extension and flexion. She is not able to do it. She can represent to herself her right hand making very complicated movements on the piano, but on her left, she has the sensation that her hand is lost in empty space. She cannot even represent to herself its form. (Ch. Féré, 'La Pathologie des Émotions,' 1892, p. 143.) I have verified this remark more than twenty times. This lack of representation and memory of the paralyzed limb is one of the most typical things; many authors have remarked it. Here is the statement of an English author, Dr. Bastian, who, by the way, has quite another conception of hysteria than we; 'When I ask her if she can imagine that she touches the tip of her nose with her left finger, she immediately answers: "Yes." If I ask her to imagine the same movements with the paralyzed hand, she remains hesitating and at last answers: "No." She can imagine herself playing on the piano with her left hand but not with her right hand.' (Charlton Bastian, *Various Forms of Hysterical or Functional Paralysis*, 1893, p. 15.)"—Pierre Janet, *The Major Symptoms of Hysteria*, 174-176 (copyright, 1920, by The Macmillan Company); reprinted by permission.]

It is none the less true that at the beginning, and often for a considerable time, the diverse forms of contractures are quite distinct from each other.[33]

B

E. E. SOUTHARD, "General Reviews and Summaries—General Psychopathology," *Psychol. Bull.*, 16: 195-196 (1919)

That theorist who shall go very profoundly into the nature of shell-shock will have to reckon not only with the "weak spot" and *"ante bellum* trend" hypotheses, but he must take account of the fact that the symptoms are so often on the same side as the explosion. In some cases it would seem as if the muscles on the side of the body where the explosion occurred were paralyzed (and the overlying skin rendered anæsthetic), whereas the muscles on the other side of the body were thrown into contraction,—almost as if the part opposite to the explosion was trying to run away therefrom, while the parts near to the explosion were transfixed upon the spot. The behaviorist must gain a great deal to his purpose from this group of cases with asymmetrical symptoms on the two sides of the body. Especial attention should be given to the work of Babinski. Whatever the truth of his contention that the so-called reflex disorders are incurable by suggestion (other authors, notably Roussy, seem to have been able to cure by suggestion certain cases that Babinski calls "reflex"), nevertheless, the theoretical contribution of Babinski upon the nature of these so-called reflex disorders must certainly be conceded. According to Babinski, these ideas simply conform to points made years ago by Charcot and Vulpian, but neglected by later workers. Babinski's main point is that in certain stages of chloroform anæsthesia unsuspected conditions of the nervous system can be brought out. Whereas it has been thought that anæsthesia ought in general to reduce the reflexes and whereas this is in general true, nevertheless there is a phase whilst going under and coming out of chloroform anæsthesia in which the reflexes may come out in excess. Let us suppose a patient whose knee jerks are perfectly equal in the waking life; let him be chloroformed, and one of the knee jerks early in the anæsthetization becomes very much exaggerated or even polykinetic. How is this to be explained? No doubt, the anæsthesia has removed the normal downstream of inhibitory influences which physiologists for many years have attrib-

---

[33] [*Cf.* also Pierre Janet, *The Major Symptoms of Hysteria,* 131-158 177-178; his volume, *The Mental State of Hystericals,* 188-197; and Tor A. Williams, in *Jour. Abn. Psychol.,* 7: 99*ff.*, 161*ff.*]

uted to the brain. In short, Babinski by chloroform anæsthesia is producing an effect not in any wise logically different from the exaggerated knee jerks produced after cutting through the spinal cord. In both instances the downstream of inhibitory influences from the cerebrum has been cut off. In this way Babinski feels that he has shown the existence of functional differences on the two sides of the body which could not be demonstrated in normal life. The reviewer cannot here do justice to these contentions which ought to be read by the psychologist in the book by Babinski and Froment on *Hysteria.*

One of the most striking illustrations of the Babinski theory is to be found in an article by Monier-Vinard.[1] Monier-Vinard had to do with certain cases of tetanus, the victims of which had apparently entirely recovered after a period of some weeks. For certain reasons, it became desirable to operate upon these men for orthopedic defects. To the astonishment of the observer, under chloroform these men redeveloped tetanus and showed a degree of rigidity in anæsthesia which was highly alarming. Upon removal of chloroform these rigidities disappeared, only to reappear upon further chloroforming. The only hypothesis ready to hand is that although these cases were clinically cured of their tetanus, nevertheless there was within their nervous systems a tendency to hypertonus. This tendency to hypertonus was counteracted, no doubt, by the normal downstream of inhibitory influences from the cerebrum, and it was this normal downstream that had been interfered with by the chloroform anæsthesia. Here then, we have laid down for us the basis of an ingenious hypothesis concerning concealed functional disorders. Suppose we apply this hypothesis to the cerebral cortex itself: we can well get an image of what may be the basis of, let us say, so delicate a disease as the fixed idea. Far be it from the compiler to insist that this is the true account of the basis of a fixed idea or of any similar notion in the psychopathic field. It appears, however, as if a new weapon was in the hands of the psychopathologist. Let us suppose alcohol to work upon a man with certain inhibited tendencies (tendencies which Freudians might like to call repressed), the alcohol might work after the manner of the chloroform anæsthesia in the Babinski cases, and the special tendency be released precisely like the exaggerated knee jerk under chloroform.

Prof. Pierre Janet, in his classical work, *The Mental State*

---

[1] See case 280 [in the writer's volume, *Shell-Shock* . . .]

of Hystericals,[2] explains the functional paralyses and contrac
tures in terms of their dependence upon psychological phenomena in the form of fixed ideas which, requiring some of
the personality for their existence, are very frequently subconscious, ideas for which there is amnesia, thus weakening
the remaining personal consciousness.[3]   These pages [4] are distinctly worth the attention of the advanced student.   But as
patterns of dissociation have already been illustrated, and
underlying mechanisms are taken up elsewhere in the present
volume, we should forego their further consideration at this
point.

Functional Paralyses and Contractures in Children

A

ÉLIDA EVANS, *The Problem of the Nervous Child*, 223-228 (Dodd, Mead,
1922)

"I will make her cry for it," I heard a fifteen-year-old girl say,
when her apparently very firm and wise mother insisted upon more
modest dress and sensible heels. The girl had found that, by showing resentment, by living apart from the family circle during the
day and not speaking, she could make her mother suffer and even
cause her to shed tears.

THE HAND OF THE TYRANT

Another case of tyranny in an eleven-year-old girl managing her
mother was a girl with an apparently paralysed left hand, which she
refused to use. She was an only child, fat, over-grown and indolent.
Her father was a working-man. Her mother had indulged the girl
in every possible way, until she was very weak in character. She
dressed and undressed her daughter, arranged her hair and cooked
all meals to suit her special taste. At ten years of age the doctors

---

[2] 336-365.

[3] Prof. Janet's discussions in the same connection, also, of subconscious
perception by hysterical subjects, are very interesting. Important, too,
are his presentations of the abulias (117-149), attacks (366-412), "somnambulisms" (413-453), deliriums (454-483), and modifications of the
character (198-224), as observed in hystericals.

[4] Including preceding footnote.

had treated her for a cold and advised the removal of adenoids and tonsils. The operation was performed in a hospital, and the girl spent the following night there. It was the first time she had ever suffered pain or met a situation where she was not "babied" by the indulgent mother. After the operation the doctors and nurses did not notice anything unusual about the patient, and the patient declared after the operation the nurse had "walked" her to the bathroom. But when the mother came in the afternoon to take the girl home, it was found she did not move her left side. Arm and leg seemed paralysed. The patient was moved home after a few days, and the left foot and leg soon regained normal activity. The arm also was moved freely but not the hand. She doubled up her left elbow, and kept the folded hand on her chest, the fingers tightly closed. As she talked with me, she laid the closed left hand in her lap, pulled open the fingers, caressing them, and playing with them as if with a doll. I took her mind off her hand and engaged her in conversation about a circus, describing the trained animals. As she became interested, she opened and moved her left hand. It looked relaxed and natural. At other times it looked rigid and strained.

At the fourth visit I gave her a box of building blocks, formed so as to be dove-tailed together and requiring two strong hands to unite them. I first built a bridge with them. Then I suddenly remembered an important letter I had to write, and left her seated with the blocks on the floor in the farther corner of the room. She worked with one hand for a while, but, as she became more interested, the left hand opened and worked with the right. I called her attention to this fact and spoke in flattering terms. "Yes," she said, "sometimes it opens, but I have to move it three times, like this." She made a pawing motion. I took the left hand in mine. Instantly it closed, or she closed it, and could not be induced to open it again. I could not possibly pry her fingers open, without using such force as to break them. They seemed made of iron.

Opposition arouses opposition but does not remove its cause, so we must work to arouse the desire in the patient. This girl was fond of playing cook. She was told how to cook her father's supper consisting of fried eggs and mashed potatoes. She was very fond of her father and very anxious to prepare his supper, but she needed two hands to peel and mash the potatoes and break the eggs for frying. The mother was instructed to keep out of the kitchen, but to peep in occasionally and see what was happening. The girl was using both hands in peeling and mashing the potatoes and in cooking the eggs, although the left one, from not being used as much as the right one, was working awkwardly and weakly. She became quite excited at this first cooking adventure, and ordered her mother to set the table, but cut the bread and put the finishing touches on the meal herself. When she cooked or did anything else for her father, she used her two hands, but would never do so for her mother, refusing to make her bed, dust the furniture or dress herself. She thus showed a strong father complex, a topic which is discussed in another chapter.

Most interesting were the unconscious thoughts brought out in the analysis. In her dreams she was a princess and in her left hand she held a beautiful golden sceptre such as she had seen in a moving picture; or she was a teacher in school, holding a pointer in her left hand and telling the class that when she moved the pointer, they were to change from one side of the room to the other, all excepting the history class, which must sit still. This was interpreted to mean that she did not want the course of her own personal history to change. Unconsciously she wanted to reserve her left hand to command others and point out what they were to do, but not to do anything with it herself.

After a few months of analysis a new environment was selected with a cousin living in the country among the mountains, where there was rough, uneven walking, and where mountain climbing sometimes needed the use of two hands. In the unconscious thoughts brought out in the analysis, the girl had seen that she must conquer her desire to be wilful and babyish, which she evidently was in using her left hand to tyrannize over her mother, and then her left hand would want to work with her right. She went to the mountains, unaccompanied on the train and full of good resolutions to try her best to grow up and be a fine young woman of whom her father would be proud. She remained there five months, using both her hands all the time (the left improving in efficiency even to the extent of allowing her to row a boat), but when she returned to her mother and former playmates, the old temptations reappeared, partly, in her mother's treatment, partly in the shut-in conditions surrounding a child in her own home. A little more help from further analysis was needed to start this girl again in different habits of thought, after which she finally abandoned her wish to be continually a child.

B

H. ADDINGTON BRUCE, *Psychology and Parenthood*, 227-229 (Dodd, Mead, 1919)

Consider, also, the case of a little Chicago boy who had fallen out of a play-wagon and hurt one of his arms. The injury was in reality very slight; but his mother, becoming greatly alarmed, declared her belief that the doctor would say the arm was broken. What the doctor—D'Orsay Hecht, of Northwestern University Medical School—did say was that a few applications of witch-hazel would speedily remedy matters.

The mother, nevertheless, insisted on bandaging the arm, talked of having an X-ray examination, and broadly hinted that a wrong diagnosis had been made. Within a few days, as Doctor Hecht had expected, all signs of injury disappeared. But now the boy complained that the hand of the injured arm felt stiff; and, in a day or so, his mother reported that both hand and arm were paralysed.

This was the situation when, passing along the street one day, Doctor Hecht was astonished and amused to see his "paralysed" patient romping with a number of children, quite as if nothing were the matter with him. He used his injured arm freely, pushed and pulled his playmates, and was pushed and pulled around by them.

"Ah," thought the physician, with a feeling of relief, "evidently this youngster is going to give no more trouble."

He was mistaken. Within a week the mother sent for him, reporting that her boy was suffering agonies, that he could not eat, and that his arm had become contracted at the elbow. In fact, on visiting the boy he found that at every attempt to flex the arm the little fellow screamed with pain.

But on his next visit, when the child chanced to be asleep, Doctor Hecht noticed that there was then no contracture of the arm, and that he could move it without disturbing the boy in the slightest. So soon, however, as he awoke, the contracture returned, and he wailed and shrieked when his arm was touched. To the astonished mother, the doctor said:

"I see what the trouble is. Your son needs a certain kind of treatment that I can administer only at my office. Bring him there as soon as possible."

The treatment in question consisted in the application of a succession of slight electrical shocks, just painful enough to be felt. These, the doctor assured the boy, would cure him completely.

"If they do not," said he, "your mother must bring you back, and I will give you a stronger treatment next time. I don't think, though, that that will be necessary, do you?"

And, in point of fact, no second treatment was needed. From that moment the boy ceased complaining of his arm, the contracture and paralysis entirely disappeared, and he was like any normal, healthy child.

TICS AND TREMORS

Tics

PIERRE JANET, *The Major Symptoms of Hysteria*, 119-122, 125-128, 135-137 (copyright, 1920, by The Macmillan Company), reprinted by permission; *The Mental State of Hystericals*, 489 (Putnam, 1901)

You[1] all know the commonplace phenomenon of *tics,* which is to be met under so many circumstances; I advise you to keep the French word because I do not find in the English language a good translation. You must not fancy that all tics are hysteric. There are some epileptic tics, and even oftener, psychasthenic tics. . . .

[Hysteric] tics are essentially constituted by little movements of the face, head or limbs, which appear at random, without any relation either to the present circumstances or the consciousness of the patients. This name is generally reserved for rather sudden little movements of short duration, and other terms are used when the same involuntary movements have a greater extent. These little muscular shakes may present themselves in all parts of the body. You may especially notice them in the face; they constitute grimaces of a thousand kinds, affecting the eyes, the nose, the mouth. The patient puckers his forehead in various ways, raises or lowers his eyebrows, winks, looks sideways by starts; he makes his nostrils tremble, closes or opens them too much. A very interesting patient, whom we shall study with more detail to-day, blows violently through his left nostril. Others seem to wipe their noses or to sneeze; their lips suddenly draw to the one side or the other, stretch forward or shrink backward, or else are continually bitten— the upper lip as well as the lower one. The tics of the neck have been brought into notice by being described under the name of psychic stiff neck; involuntarily and suddenly the patient inclines his head towards one shoulder, or throws it back, or bends it for-

---

[1] *The Major Symptoms of Hysteria*, 119-122 (copyright, 1920, by The Macmillan Company); reprinted by permission.

ward, or turns it on its axis. He repeats these movements every two or three seconds in a way which it is impossible to explain or justify by any present reason.

I do not speak now of the tics related to the visceral functions such as the alimentation or breathing tics; I at once pass on to the tics of the limbs. In these the arms, the hands, seem to have taken strange habits; they rise suddenly or move backwards; the shoulders are shaken convulsively; the legs, instead of regularly performing the act of walking, every moment interrupt it by a strange little shake of the knee or foot or toes. These little movements, which have innumerable forms, of course impede every action of the arms, and when they occur in the waking state, they often make walking almost impossible.

Let us proceed at once, in order not to interrupt the description, to the same kind of involuntary and useless movements that have a greater extent and, for that reason, have been called *choreas*. This distinction is not essential at the bottom, and must not prevent us from putting all the motor agitations in the same group. The first choreas that physicians decidedly connected with hysteria were the *rhythmical choreas,* thus called because the movements were repeated regularly at determinate intervals, like those of a pendulum. This kind of rhythmical movements occurs very often in the hysteric fit; it constitutes those complications of the simple fit which I have pointed out to you. Very often the patients, without recovering consciousness, cease their emotional manifestations to indulge in some odd and perfectly regular gymnastics.

One of the most commonplace is the salute, which Charcot described; the patient, lying on her bed, sits up, bends her head and body forward, sometimes low enough to touch her knees, as if she were making a salute, then suddenly throws herself back till her head falls on her bed. After a moment, she begins again; she may thus make this salute twenty or forty times a minute for hours together. Others have malleatory movements of the arm or leg; you would think they strike regularly with a hammer. Others again have saltatory movements; either when lying or when standing, they appear to jump or dance regularly. Besides these definite classified movements, there are hundreds of others which have no definite name; this one clinches her fists and suddenly brings them together towards the middle of her body, then separates them, and begins again indefinitely; another turns her right wrist as if it were fixed to a wheel, and so forth indefinitely. In all such acts there is always the same rhythmical regularity; Charcot quoted, in reference to this, the sentence in Hamlet: "Though this be mad-ness, yet there's method in it," and wished a ballet-master might observe and write down the strange and regular movements of the patients. . . .

There [2] are, in fact, two categories of hysterical accidents, which in particular can be easily distinguished by examining tics or spasms. Some take place *when the subject thinks of it;* they disappear when the subject's attention is diverted or when he falls asleep. Those may easily be connected with an idea. But very often it happens that the morbid movement is produced even *when the subject does not think of it;* the spasm persists despite the mind's diversion, sometimes despite sleep. . . . When [3] we come to motor disturbances, that insensibility which is called hysteric anæsthesia begins to intervene. It may present itself in two ways; sometimes it is systematic and bears only on the movement that constitutes the tic or the chorea. The subject does not feel that he moves his forehead, or that he strikes his bed regularly with his hand, but he feels the other things, and in particular, is able to tell you that somebody seizes his hand while he is performing the choreic movement. Notice this systematic anæsthesia, which will become more and more important. Sometimes the anæsthesia is more important, and the whole of the limbs affected with a tic or a chorea is insensible. For instance, one of the subjects to whom I alluded used to turn his right hand in a circle and had a see-saw movement in his right foot; the whole of his right side was nearly insensible.

These anæsthesias, this kind of unconsciousness, must play a certain part in the diagnosis; you will not meet again with the same characteristics in the same degree in tics of another nature, particularly in the tics of the psychasthenic. With the latter, the tic, while appearing involuntary, is accompanied by a great deal of consciousness and attention. The subject performs his tic when he thinks of it, when he directs his attention to the organ and tries to keep it motionless. It seems that, with these patients, attention increases the tic instead of diminishing it. Inversely, you may observe that distraction sometimes has a good effect. When the subject forgets his disease and his mind is absorbed by something else, he leaves off performing his tic. You see that with him the tic is conscious, that it is in connection with thoughts the subject possesses. There is, therefore, no anæsthesia in this case. The subject feels his movement very well and all that passes in the dis-

---

[2] *The Mental State of Hystericals*, 489 (Putnam, 1901).
[3] Pierre Janet, *The Major Symptoms of Hysteria*, 125-128, 135-137 (copyright, 1920, by The Macmillan Company); reprinted by permission.

eased limb. With the hysteric, the movement is impeded by attention; it develops, becomes more complete and regular in a state of distraction; it is much oftener accompanied with anæsthesia.

These characteristics, which serve to make the diagnosis, also enable us better to understand the nature of the phenomenon. In fact, the tic and the choreic movement are much more intellectual phenomena than they appear to be. We notice many mental phenomena at their beginning exactly as at the beginning of somnambulisms. One has had an accident to his face or eye, another a pain in his teeth; the man who constantly blew through one of his nostrils had had for a long time a scab in his nose, consequent upon a bleeding at the nose. All the patients who have had mental stiff necks had had some moral impression relating to a movement of the head. A girl I am attending now felt very dull at home; she worked all day long by a window that looked out into the street. Her strongest desire was to leave her monotonous work and go out into the street at which she constantly looked. At every moment she lifted her eyes from her work and turned her head to the left in order to see what was going on in the street. She gradually felt that her head constantly turned to the left, and even maintained that her hat was too heavy on that side. An absurd diagnosis, the application of a plaster bandage, had singularly aggravated her state, and now she has a bad mental stiff neck on her right side.

These ideas, these more or less definite mental phenomena which existed at the beginning, persist throughout the development of the tic or the chorea. Let us return to a singular story, which I have often related. It tells how the rhythmic chorea of that girl of sixteen had begun, who kept on turning her right wrist and regularly raising and lowering her right foot. One evening, on the eve of the quarter-day, she had heard her parents, who were poor workpeople, bewailing their poverty and the difficulty they had in paying their landlord. She was very much moved, and from that time she had at night a kind of somnambulism, during which she tumbled and tossed in her bed and repeated aloud: "I must work, I must work." Now, what was the work of this girl? She had a singular trade, which was to make dolls' eyes, and, for this purpose, she worked a lathe by treading a pedal with her foot and turning a fly-wheel with her right hand. During her nocturnal somnambulism, she made this movement of the hand and of the foot, but this movement was evidently accompanied with a corresponding state of consciousness, since she repeated aloud: "I must work." It was a simple somnambulic action, like all those we have studied. On awaking, she no longer has any recollection or consciousness of her dream, but the movement continues exactly the same on her right side. Is it not likely that it is still accompanied with a state of consciousness of the same kind?

We can make this state of consciousness evident by certain experiments which we know now how to effect. By hypnotizing the subjects, you find again dreams that account very well for the continuation of the tic. For instance, a young woman comes to complain of a pretended vertigo; it appears that, in the street, every hundred steps, she feels herself as it were precipitated forward, that she suddenly takes a leap and has often fallen while taking it. What a strange vertigo! In a state of induced somnambulism she relates to us what follows: Once she went to her parents, who sharply reproached her for her irregular conduct. On going out of their house, she took a resolution that simplifies many things,—she made up her mind to commit suicide, and in a dream, of course, for she was, happily for her, hysteric to a high degree—she fancied she had got upon the parapet on the bank of the Seine, took a leap, and was awakened by a fall to the ground. In all such cases, the existence of a system of images that works unknown to the subject is undeniable. . . . Let us try, with our sound limbs, to copy the attitude of a rhythmic chorea and register our movements accurately. You will find that you are much more awkward than a hysteric person, and that, unless you have practised specially to this end, you cannot obtain the same regularity. Try to keep your arm in the position of a hysteric contracture and describe the movement of the arm; you will remark that you have not the same perseverance or courage as the patient. After a short time, your arm trembles and is displaced, while the hysteric contracture has not changed. If therefore we suppose there is a psychic action in these hysteric phenomena, it must be acknowledged that this action is not identical with ours, but that it is performed in other conditions.

Here is my hypothesis; think of it what you please; the actions that are manifested by muscular movements present different degrees of perfection corresponding to the development and systematization of the consciousness that accompanies them. These degrees of perfection are manifested first of all by psychological characteristics of the action, delicacy, harmony, usefulness of the act, but it is also manifested by properties of the movements themselves. The muscular movement of a draughtsman's hand is not the same as the muscular movement of a dog's or a crocodile's paw. There are some particular physiological properties accompanying the perfection of the act. Some are known: the rapidity of the contraction is much greater, and in particular the rapidity of the decontraction, of the fall of the muscle, is much more considerable. In the muscles of the lower animals, the contraction takes place slowly and disappears slowly. We see also the same modifications of the muscular contraction brought about by fatigue. By repetition, muscular contraction changes, becomes slower, has a long period of decontraction as in the case of lower animals. I even think—excuse the temerity of these suppositions—that there must be in these different muscles and in these different states of activity of the muscle some anatomical differences. Great stress has been laid recently on the two organs that exist in the muscular fibre: the fibrils which give short contractions, and the sarcoplasm which gives long and permanent contractions. The latter predominates in the smooth fibres of the viscera, the former in the striated muscles of the voluntary movements. I suppose that it will be possible later on to observe some modifications in the proportion of these two substances in the muscles of different animals according to their state of evolution, and in the different states of the same muscles in rest or in fatigue, for instance.

Now action, by becoming unconscious in hysterics, by separating from consciousness, loses something of its dignity, retrogrades in a manner and assumes an appearance that recalls the action of the visceral muscles, the action of the lower animals, and the movements of the fatigued muscles, as if the activity of the sarcoplasm prevailed over that of the fibrils. This is what, in my opinion, gives to the subconscious actions of the hysteric those abnormal characteristics we saw in tremors and contractures.

A Regressive Tic

OSKAR PFISTER, *Psycho-Analysis*, 68 (Kimpton, London, 1922)

. . . In the case of a girl who had the habit of moving the skin of her forehead every two or three minutes, she then felt a strong tension at the ear and adjoining parts. When she was small her father used to tilt her head gently back by holding this part, in order to kiss her. She wore a bonnet to protect her head and the upper part of the ears. Later on, when she had become estranged from her father, she was attracted towards a dentist. The tension which she feels in her ears reminds her of the dentist's chair, which presses the head slightly. Finally, when she was seventeen, she was taking a walk with some girl friends when they were met by some rough boys, one of whom seized her from behind and took her head by the same part so as to kiss her, laughing as he did so. The young girl suffers under the estrangement from her parents, with whom she is on bad terms on the pretext that they show her no love. She likewise complains of the coldness of her fiancé. Her nervous tic signifies: "Ah, if I were only back in the time when my father used to caress me, when I was safely guarded from shock, when he who replaced my father in my affections used to treat me with kindness and friendship, when a young man kissed me ardently." As we see, it is a moral conflict which has determined a regression in this case of hysteria, and I may say at once that, in order to bring about the disappearance of this tic, it was necessary, after the revelation of the circumstances that had caused it, to get the girl to abandon her attitude of hatred to her surroundings and her desire to play the little girl.

A Case of "Shaking Spells"

BORIS SIDIS, *Symptomatology, Psychognosis and Diagnosis of Psychopathic Diseases*, 366-368 (Badger, 1914)

M. L., nineteen years of age. Family history is negative, his parents died when the patient was young, and he was left without kith and kin, so that no data could possibly be obtained.

Physical examination is negative. Field of vision is normal. There are no sensory disturbances. The process of perception is normal, and so also is recognition. Memory for past and present events is good. His power of reasoning is quite limited, and the whole of his mental life is undeveloped, embryonic. His sleep is sound; he dreams little, wets his bed since childhood. Digestion is excellent; he can digest anything in the way of eatables. He is of an easy-going, gay disposition, a New York "street Arab."

The patient complains of "shaking spells." The attack sets on with tremor of all the extremities, and then spreads to the whole body. The tremor becomes general, and the patient is seized by a convulsion of shivering, tremblings, and chattering of teeth. Sometimes he falls down, shivering, trembling and shaking all over. The seizure seems to be epileptiform, only it lasts sometimes for more than three hours. The attack may come any time during the day, but it is more frequent at night.

During the attack the patient does not lose consciousness, he knows everything that is taking place around him, he can feel everything pretty well; his teeth violently chatter, he trembles and shivers all over, and is helpless to do anything. There is also a feeling of chilliness, as if he is possessed by an attack of "ague."

The seizure does not start with any numbness of the extremities, nor is there any anæsthesia or paræsthesia during the whole course of the attack. With the exception of the shivers and chills the patient claims he feels "all right."

Patient was put into a deep hypnoidal condition. There was some catalepsy of a transient character, but no suggestibility of the hypnotic type. In this hypnoidal state it came to light that the patient "many years ago" was forced to sleep in a dark, damp cellar where it was bitter cold. The few nights passed in that cold cellar he had to leave his bed, and shaking, trembling, shivering and chattering with cold he had to go to urinate, fearing to wet his bed, in expectation of a severe punishment.

The patient, while in that intermediary, subwaking hypnoidal state, was told to think of that dark, damp, cold cellar. Suddenly the attack set on,—the patient began to shake, shiver and tremble all over, his teeth chattering, as if he was suffering from great cold. The attack was thus reproduced in the hypnoidal state. "This is the way I have them," he said.

During this attack no numbness, no sensory disturbances, were present. The patient was quieted, and after a little while the attack of shivering and cold disappeared. The room in which the patient was put into the hypnoidal state was dark, and accidentally the remark was made that the room was too dark to see anything; immediately the attack reappeared in all its violence.

It was found later that it was sufficient to mention the words "dark, damp, cold" to bring on an attack even in the fully waking state. We could thus reproduce the attacks at will,—those magic words had the power to release the pent-up subconscious forces, and throw the patient into convulsions of shakings and shiverings, with feeling of cold and chattering of the teeth.

Thus the apparent epileptiform seizures, the insistent psychomotor states of seemingly unaccountable origin, were traced *to dissociated, subconscious systems, now lapsed and meaningless in the patient's present environment and life reactions. They are recurrent reversions, atavistic manifestations of lapsed, now meaningless groups of psychomotor reactions.*[1]

---

[1] [A very interesting case of attacks of tremors simulating epilepsy is found in Boris Sidis' *Symptomatology, etc.*, 329-338.]

SPEECH DISORDERS

Examples from History

PIERRE JANET, *The Major Symptoms of Hysteria*, 209-210 (copyright, 1920, by The Macmillan Company); reprinted by permission

In antiquity certain impairments of speech had already been noticed, the rapid evolution and the surprising cure of which seemed unaccountable. The following observation made by Hippocrates appears to relate to a hysterical accident: "The wife of Polemachus, having an arthritical affection, felt a sudden pain in her hip, as her menses had not come; having drunk some beet-root water, she remained voiceless for the whole night until mid-day. She could hear and understand; she showed with her hand that the pain was in her hip." This description seems to contain everything, the stopping of the menses, the arthritic disturbances, which are probably disturbances of motion, the preservation of the perceptions of speech, and the dumbness. It is not necessary to remind you of the story of Crœsus's son, the dumb young man who suddenly recovers his speech to cry: "Soldier, do not kill Crœsus."

We may pass on to modern times, and remind you of all the stories of dumbness in possessed people and ecstatics. I have already alluded to Carré de Montgeron's work on the "Miracles of Deacon Paris," in which you can read the case of Marguerite Françoise Duchesne. After a fit of lethargy which lasted seven or eight days, there appeared a nearly total loss of voice. She was deprived of everything, even of the power of complaining. A month afterwards, she recovered her hearing and sight, but it was not the same with her voice, which was never restored to her. In the nineteenth century, such cases become more numerous. The English surgeon Watson boasted of having, through an electric treatment, restored the power of speech to a young lady who had been voiceless and dumb for twelve years. Briquet, Kussmaul, Revillod, Charcot, and Cartaz insisted very strongly on these phenomena, which are now well-known in their ensemble.[1]

---

[1] *Cf.* Janet, *op. cit.*, 208-219.

Occurrence Today

SMILEY BLANTON, "Speech Disorders as a Psychiatric Problem," *Jour. of Oralism and Auralism;* "The Medical Significance of the Disorders of Speech," *Jour. Am. Med. Ass'n.,* 77: 375 (1921)

Emotion [1] registers itself through changes of muscle tension in the speech mechanism. The diaphragm may be said to be the safety valve of the body; through giggling, crying, screaming, laughing and speech are the emotional tensions siphoned off. . . .

Oral surgeons and laryngologists see a great many speech disorders that are due to abnormalities in the peripheral organs, such as cleft palate, malformed arch, poor occlusion, etc., such cases naturally going to those who specialize in this field. When, however, we study an unselected series of speech disorders in adults and in children, we find that perhaps not more than ten or fifteen per cent are caused by abnormalities in the peripheral organs. The rest are due to functional causes. A study of these causes takes us into the realm of psychology and of psychiatry.

Much light was thrown upon the cause and nature of speech disorders through a study of these conditions occurring in soldiers who had nervous breakdowns at the front. Most of these cases had a speech defect. Sometimes the speech condition cleared up in a few days, but in about five per cent of cases the condition became fixed and there are still many ex-service men who have disorders of speech. These disturbances of speech were caused in some cases, partly by the physical shock of high explosives, but more often the cause was to be found in emotional strain and shock.

The primary object in treating these cases is to re-educate them so that they can go back and take their places in the world; the training of the speech mechanism is a secondary factor. The re-education of the personality is the primary thing in these cases. The stuttering is only a symptom of the anxiety, fears, and lack of emotional poise. The inadequacy of breathing exercises, of vowel or consonant training, and of elocution alone is evident. Of course, the hysterical symptoms can be cured through suggestion, whether this takes the form of breathing exercises, elocution, Christian Science, or what-not, but curing such symptoms by suggestion leaves the personality difficulty untouched. . . .

---

[1] "Speech Disorders as a Psychiatric Problem," *Jour. of Oralism and Auralism.*

About one hundred cases of speech disorders have passed through the speech clinic which I have at the U. S. Veterans' Hospital No. 37 at Waukesha, Wisconsin. The diagnoses made on these cases after a thorough study not only by myself, but by the entire staff, were as follows:

Hysteria	58%
Anxiety Neurosis	19%
Neurasthenia	6%
Constitutional Psychopathic Inferior (usually with hysteria as the mechanism causing speech disorder)	5%
Traumatic Neurosis	4%
Psychasthenia	2%
Mental Deficiency (the mechanism causing the speech disorder, hysteria)	2%
Manic-Depressive Insanity	1%
Hyper-thyroidism	1%
Case of stuttering following apoplexy	1%
Organic Nerve Lesion	1%
	100%

Some writers [2] have maintained that the neurasthenia and other troubles were caused by the stuttering, and not the cause of stuttering. This we feel to be a fallacy, owing to several factors which I will present. Since the war stuttering has been studied, the fact has been brought out that the same type of temperament was present before the stuttering was developed as was shown after, and that the temperament and the hereditary factors are virtually the same in those individuals who stuttered, but who never experienced war, and in those who stuttered owing to strain in service, but who saw no active service under fire at the front, and in those who stuttered previous to service, but relapsed under the strain, and in those who did not stutter previous to experience under shell fire and in fighting.

In the comparison of forty soldiers with 200 schoolchildren from 1 to 18 years of age, some interesting facts are brought to light. A comparison of the personality showed that 13 per cent. of the children, and 9 per cent. of the soldiers were classed as showing no marked variation; 52 per cent. of the children showed marked inferiority feelings, showing themselves either in timidity or in over-compensations by extreme boldness; 54 per cent. of the soldiers came

---

[2] "The Medical Significance of the Disorders of Speech," *Jour. Am. Med. Ass'n.*, 77: 375 (1921).

in this class; 35 per cent. of the children and 34 per cent. of the soldiers were markedly moody, either of the temper, sulky, depression, or of the hypomanic types. In addition, 5 per cent. of the soldiers were apathetic and dull; none of the children were so classed. Whether this is a true variation or a mistake in classification in the group of schoolchildren would probably be demonstrated in a study of a larger group.

A study of the variation shown in the symptom of stuttering itself is indicative of its functional etiology. Of the children, twenty-two were worse at school than at home; two were worse in town than in the country; one was worse on vacations; five varied with their physical conditions; sixteen were given to complete remissions in stuttering; one stutters only in school; one stutters only in Polish; one stutters only in speaking to his father; one never stutters while at play; one never stutters with members of his own sex; one gets worse at intervals of three or four days; one is markedly worse after sleep, even a short nap; one is worse after an operation for adenoids and tonsils (undertaken to cure the stutter); one stuttered for three weeks only, and so on with such variations for virtually the entire group. Among the soldiers, six began to stutter with service at the front (five of these began with aphonia); seven were stutterers who relapsed with service at the front; one who had stuttered severely had a complete remission while at the front, until he got up into Germany and became homesick; six who had stuttered previously relapsed with service in this country (such as a fight, a runaway horse, and a close shave with an explosion); one relapsed with the draft, and one relapsed with influenza. Many of these men have trouble at the telephone, although they do not have any trouble if the receiver is closed, but begin to stutter immediately when it is opened.

If brain congestion or defective auditory imagery or malocclusion of the arch or infected tonsils were the primary cause of stuttering, rather than results or merely accompanying disorders, what part is played by the movement of the hand of a second person in the connecting of the telephone? The only real change is the knowledge of a third person listening over the wire.[3]

---

[3] ["What is the problem of stuttering?" This question is discussed further in an article under that title by Margaret Gray Blanton and Smiley Blanton (cf. Bibliography). An exceedingly interesting study is Herbert Austin Aikins' "Casting Out a 'Stuttering Devil.'" Cf. also Tom A. Williams, *Dreads and Besetting Fears*, 39-50. Aphasia of the functional type is described in Janet's *Major Symptoms of Hysteria*, 219ff.]

CHAPTER XV

FUNCTIONAL MOTOR ABNORMALITIES (CONTINUED)

THE PSYCHOLOGY OF ERRORS

Related closely to the chapter on Conflict, and therefore to Professors Smith and Guthrie's discussion, above,[1] but also to be understood in part through the chapter on Dissociation, are the phenomena of "lapses."

Errors as Wish Fulfilment

A

SIGMUND FREUD, "The Psychology of Errors," *A General Introduction to Psychoanalysis*, 10-12, 39-41 (Boni & Liveright, 1921)

We begin with an investigation, not with hypotheses. To this end we choose certain phenomena which are very frequent, very familiar and very little heeded, and which have nothing to do with the pathological, inasmuch as they can be observed in every normal person. I refer to the errors which an individual commits—as for example, errors of speech in which he wishes to say something and uses the wrong word; or those which happen to him in writing, and which he may or may not notice; or the case of misreading, in which one reads in the print or writing something different from what is actually there. A similar phenomenon occurs in those cases of mishearing what is said to one, where there is no question of an organic disturbance of the auditory function. Another series of such occurrences is based on forgetfulness—but on a forgetful-ness which is not permanent, but temporary, as for instance when one cannot think of a name which one knows and always recog-nizes; or when one forgets to carry out a project at the proper time but which one remembers again later, and therefore has only for-gotten for a certain interval. In a third class this characteristic

---

[1] Pp. 130*ff.*

of transience is lacking, as for example in mislaying things so that they cannot be found again, or in the analogous case of losing things. Here we are dealing with a kind of forgetfulness to which one reacts differently from the other cases, a forgetfulness at which one is surprised and annoyed, instead of considering it comprehensible. Allied with these phenomena is that of erroneous ideas—in which the element of transience is again prominent, inasmuch as for a while one believes something which, before and after that time, one knows to be untrue—and a number of similar phenomena of different designations.

These are all occurrences whose inner connection is expressed in the use of the same prefix of designation.[1] They are almost all unimportant, generally temporary and without much significance in the life of the individual. It is only rarely that one of them, such as the phenomenon of losing things, attains to a certain practical importance. For that reason also they do not attract much attention, they arouse only weak affects. . . .

But . . . are there not very important things which under certain circumstances, and at certain times, can betray themselves only by very faint signs? I could easily cite a great many instances of this kind From what vague signs, for instance, do the young gentlemen of this audience conclude that they have won the favor of a lady? Do you await an explicit declaration, an ardent embrace, or does not a glance, scarcely perceptible to others, a fleeting gesture, the prolonging of a hand-shake by one second, suffice? And if you are a criminal lawyer, and engaged in the investigation of a murder, do you actually expect the murderer to leave his photograph and address on the scene of the crime, or would you, of necessity, content yourself with fainter and less certain traces of that individual? Therefore, let us not undervalue small signs; perhaps by means of them we will succeed in getting on the track of greater things. . . .

A. Maeder tells of a lady who, the day before her wedding, forgot to try on her wedding dress and to the despair of the dressmaker only remembered it later in the evening. He adds in connection with this forgetfulness the fact that she divorced her husband soon after. I know a lady now divorced from her husband, who, in managing her fortune, frequently signed documents with her maiden name, and this many years before she really resumed it. I know of other women who lost their wedding rings on their honeymoon and also know that the course of the marriage gave a mean-

---

[1] "Fehl-leistungen."

ing to this incident. And now one more striking example with a better termination. It is said that the marriage of a famous German chemist did not take place because he forgot the hour of the wedding, and instead of going to the church went to the laboratory. He was wise enough to rest satisfied with this one attempt, and died unmarried at a ripe old age.

Perhaps the idea has also come to you that in these cases mistakes have taken the place of the *Omina* or omens of the ancients. Some of the *Omina* really were nothing more than mistakes; for example, when a person stumbled or fell down. Others, to be sure, bore the characteristics of objective occurrences rather than that of subjective acts. But you would not believe how difficult it sometimes is to decide in a specific instance whether the act belongs to the one or the other group. It so frequently knows how to masquerade as a passive experience.

Every one of us who can look back over a longer or shorter life experience will probably say that he might have spared himself many disappointments and painful surprises if he had found the courage and decision to interpret as omens the little mistakes which he made in his intercourse with people, and to consider them as indications of the intentions which were still being kept secret. As a rule, one does not dare do this. One would feel as though he were again becoming superstitious via a detour through science. But not all omens come true, and you will understand from our theories that they need not all come true.

We may certainly put it down as the conclusion of our labors up to this point that errors have a meaning, and we may make this conclusion the basis of our further investigations. Let me stress the fact once more that we do not assert—and for our purposes need not assert—that every single mistake which occurs is meaningful, although I consider that probable. It will suffice us if we prove the presence of such a meaning with relative frequency in the various forms of errors. These various forms, by the way, behave differently in this respect. In the cases of tongue slips, pen slips, etc., the occurrences may take place on a purely physiological basis. In the group based on forgetfulness (forgetting names or projects, mislaying objects, etc.) I cannot believe in such a basis. ' There does very probably exist a type of case in which the loss of objects should be recognized as unintentional. Of the mistakes which occur in daily life, only a certain portion can in any way be brought within our conception. You must keep this limitation in mind when we start henceforth from the assumption that mistakes are psychic acts and arise through the mutual interference of two intentions.

B

JOHN B. WATSON, "The Psychology of Wish Fulfilment," *Sc. Monthly,*
3: 479, 481-482 (1916)

In waking moments we wish only for the conventional things which will not run counter to our social traditions or code of living. But these open and above-board wishes are not very interesting to the psychologist. Since they are harmless and call for the kinds of things that everybody in our circle wishes for, we do not mind admitting them and talking about them. Open and uncensored wishes are best seen in children (though children at an early age begin to show repressions). Only to-night I heard a little girl of nine say: "I wish I were a boy and were sixteen years old—I'd marry Ann" (her nine-year-old companion). And recently I heard a boy of eight say to his father: "I wish you would go away forever; then I could marry mother." The spontaneous and uncensored wishes of children gradually disappear as the children take on the speech conventions of the adult. But even though the crassness of the form of expression of the wish disappears with age, there is no reason to suppose that the human organism ever gets to the point where wishes just as unconventional as the above do not rise to trouble it. Such wishes, though, are immediately repressed; we never harbor them nor do we express them clearly to ourselves in our waking moments. . . .

In social gatherings where there is some slight emotional strain and the customary control over speech is off, we find numberless examples of the expression of the suppressed wish. If we were to make a tabulation of such slips met with in a single week, the list would be long. Most of the slips reveal too much to be put down in print. But I can mention some of the types usually met with.

An elderly bachelor, the friend of the family, squires his friend's wife to a dance. He introduces her as "Mrs. S." (giving her maiden name instead of her married name, "Mrs. J."). If taxed with possessing the wish that the woman were single so that he might have another chance, he would indignantly deny that any such thought had ever crossed his mind. This is probably true in the sense that had any such wish crossed his mind in his ordinary waking moments it would have been put down immediately—repressed. It is rather interesting to note in the above case, which is an actual one, that later in the evening the "Mrs. J." referred to, after having danced with a man other than her escort, shortly afterwards introduced her partner as "Mr. J." (her husband)!

It is of course unusual to find material so readily as this. I noted another and common type of slip the same day as the above. A woman of my acquaintance had to go to the . . . station to meet three girl friends *en route* from Boston to Washington. She decided to buy some flowers for each of them. I went to the florist shop with her and to my surprise she purchased only two bouquets, saying: "A likes violets, but B is fond of orchids." When we reached the sidewalk I asked her why she disliked "C" so much. "Why do you think I dislike her?" she asked. "Because," I said, "you have done all in your power to annihilate her—you have forgotten to purchase any flowers for her." She showed confusion but gracefully admitted that I had saved her from making a serious *faux pas*. To take revenge, however, she gave me my just deserts by saying: "I can't bear to be around a man who has your view of life." (She afterwards admitted, however, that "C" had been for many years a thorn in the flesh.)

Slips are often expressive of wishes which bear on the pleasanter side of life. I mislay my cane and umbrella, both of which I prize highly, and find that I left them at the house of a friend where I last had dinner and a game of bridge. The wish shortly to visit so pleasant a place again is very clearly implied. To take a single final example in this connection: Only a moment ago it was necessary for me to call a man on the telephone. I said: "This is Dr. John B. Watson, of the Johns Hopkins Hospital," instead of Johns Hopkins University. One skilled in analysis could easily read in this slight slip the wish that I had gone into medicine instead of into psychology (even this analysis, though, would be far from complete).

Slips of the pen are just as numerous and just as interesting revealers of hidden character as are slips in speech. It is in dreams, however, that we get our most interesting and valuable material for analysis.

C

EDWIN B. HOLT, *The Freudian Wish*, 35-37 (Holt, 1915)

In view of the only too obvious and universally acknowledged fact that a man's general trend of conversation, like his deeds, expresses his character, it is amusing to see with what incredulity persons will often receive the statement that the finer details of speech and action (such as "slips of the tongue" and the previously mentioned "slips of the pen") are significant as well. A man once even argued with me that the manner of a hand-shake possessed no significance. And *lapsus linguæ* are often accounted one of the pet absurdities of the Freudians. Once in going to make a call on Mrs. A. I had to pass the house of Mrs. B., who was sitting on her front verandah. I am always irritated by Mrs. B. and at this time was feeling particularly out of patience with her because she had not shown herself very neighborly during a recent illness of Mrs. A. But I like Mr. B. immensely and wish to "keep in" with the family; so that I had to nibble Mrs. B.'s bait and spend an impatient half-hour on her verandah. When I arose to go I undertook to be amiably untruthful and to say, "I'm so glad that you were out on the verandah as I was going by." But my treacherous lips actually brought out, "I'm so sorry that you were," etc. The reader may be skeptical as to the cause of this slip; but Mrs. B. was not, and did not invite me to her house for over a year; as served me quite right.

D

R. H. Hingley, *Psycho-Analysis*, 126-128 (Methuen & Co. and Dodd, Mead, 1922); reprinted by permission.

But Freud has gone even further and analysed cases where apparently arbitrary numbers have arisen in the mind, and shown that they are determined by definite psychical causes. But such instances usually demand more skilful analysis, and, to persons unversed in the science seem far-fetched and improbable.

The analysis of cases of forgetting of proper names is usually less difficult, but at the same time often rather more complicated than the simple and perhaps rather obvious examples we have already cited. For this reason they provide a particularly useful exercise. Freud, at the beginning of his book, and Jones in the chapter we have referred to, both give a detailed examination of such instances. The following case may possibly prove helpful in the investigation of this type of experience. On no less than three occasions since returning from active service I have endeavoured to recall the name of a certain French village where I lived for two months, and in addition to this, I had lived in another village only two miles away and had been in constant communication with it for another five months. On each occasion I was compelled to refer to a map, and even then there was a strangeness about the name, though there could be no possible doubt as to its correctness. My memory for names is usually good. Why then, did I forget the name Grévillers? Before analysing this instance it should be said that my memory of the name was partly determined by a vague visual image of the spelling, and partly by an auditory image of its common English pronunciation, and scarcely at all by its proper French pronunciation which was rarely heard. It was commonly referred to as Greyvillers or Grave-ill-ers. The nearest I could get in attempting to recall the name was Etretat or Etaples, both of which places I was perfectly aware are many miles away, the only similarity in these names being the first vowel sound, though I found it an easy matter to establish connexions by association between them and Grave-ill-ers, as follows: Etretat, Etre = to be, "To be or not to be, that is the question" (Hamlet). The connexion with "graves" is obvious. The second part of the word, etat, aetat (Latin), generally found on tomb stones, and in obituary notices; Etaples, common pronunciation, "ate aple," reminds me of the penalty on Adam's disobedience (*see* Gen. ii, v, 17). The connexions are obvious, though I am bound to say that I am not aware of any morbid interest in death.

Turning now to the forgotten word itself, and taking first the part that was most obscured, *ill.* At once there comes to my mind the only illness that has been of any consequence in my life. But it certainly cannot be described as grave, nor was I ever under the impression that it could. Possibly my fear was that it was not grave enough to enable me to escape from an impending situation that I could not help but regard with some degree of foreboding. Of course I was not aware of this at the time, but when I review the course that the illness took, the two partial recoveries that I made, when I over-hastily took up my work in such a way that it was almost certain to aggravate the trouble, when I remember that I did finally manage to evade the dreaded situation, I am bound to admit that the "unconscious wish" to be ill had no small bearing on the course of the trouble. There are several other facts which point in the same direction. Such an experience one does not usually regard with pride. Taking now the first syllable of the word, Gré, my associations are, malgré, mal—ill. Gré—wish, liking, pleasure. Already sufficient associations have been given to show that the significance of the word Grévillers is overdetermined as "desired illness." Similarly if I take the syllables, villers, the associations lead back to an incident, which even now I cannot help regarding with some degree of repugnance.

Criticism of the Freudian Doctrine of Errors

A

A. A. Roback, "The Freudian Doctrine of Lapses and Its Failings," *Am. Jour. Psychol.*, 30: 274, 277-280, 288-289 (1919)

Whether Freud's interpretation of lapses constitutes an integral part of his system or not, of one thing we are certain, and that is the growing importance of that phase of psychology as throwing light on everyday occurrences, which, insignificant in themselves, are often the vehicles of portentous events.

We seldom notice a slip unless it assumes the proportions of a blunder. Sometimes we are prone to attach an ominous significance to such an occurrence, which fact might account for the halo of mystery surrounding the subject in semi-intellectual spheres. Aside from that, however, there is something fascinating about a situation where one acts, as it were, in spite of himself. It is our intention to say one thing, yet we say another. We purpose writing a certain word or phrase; our fingers, however, execute a set of movements other that those intended. What is at the root of this mischief? . . .

The only case of a *lapsus calami* where the larger negative form "unhappy" was substituted for the intended word "happy" is given by Ernest Jones [1] who was told by a lady that an "old friend in writing to her closed the letter with the curious sentence, 'I hope you are well and unhappy.'" According to Jones, "the slip of the pen was evidently determined by his dislike at the thought of her being happy with some one else" as he had entertained hope of marrying her himself. Even this solitary case pointing apparently to the operation of a wish complex may easily be explained by supposing that the slip was occasioned by the conflict not of *two wishes* —the one censored and the other primitive—but rather by the interference of a *wish* and a *fact,* the mental attitude corresponding to the expression, "I hope you are well and happy, though I am unhappy." In other words, the antithesis is not between two states in the future, but between the future and the present. There is no need of positing even here a hidden wish mechanism. Most likely, the writer was actually thinking of his unhappy condition at the time he was concluding his letter, and the various imaginal elements

---

[1] E. Jones: *Papers on Psycho-Analysis*, 63.

that went to make up his mental attitude, were probably synthetized by the word "unhappy."

There are, nevertheless, two or three accounts of a *lapsus linguae* in Freud's (Brill) *Psychopathology of Everyday Life* that we can become reconciled to, but only after definite qualification.

Brill relates of an admirer of Roosevelt who remarked to his host on the occasion of an evening dance, "You may say what you please about Teddy, but there is one thing he can always be relied upon; he always gives you a square *m*eal." [2] What he was about to say was a "square *d*eal," but the guests had reason to be disappointed in the hospitality of the host, and this embarrassing slip gave away the situation.

We have no difficulty here in accepting Brill's implication, provided it is admitted, on the other side, that the speaker had been *thinking* of the word "meal" that evening and probably the idea came up several times and, that too, suffused with emotion, as in the case of every hungry man. Hence there was with him what we should call a "predisposed attitude." Now the fact that square is used with both meal and deal, and that the two words are so similar in sound much helped the "predisposed attitude" to bring the association and finally the unfortunate slip.

In the same way also is it understandable that a person who entertains high ideas of his importance would sometimes substitute an "I" when he is referring to other people, especially those he looks up to. Here we may say that a "prepotent attitude" (congenital) is at the root of such lapses. . . .

[Freud] takes two pages to account for a slip of his that could be done to much better advantage in a few lines. Here is the instance. Wishing to draw some money from the bank, he glanced at his account, and finding that it was 4380 crowns, he decided to bring it down to the round sum of 4000 crowns. Upon making out the cheque, however, he noticed that he had written 438 instead of 380 crowns. [3] Common sense and experimental evidence [4] would lead us to believe that while his attention was occupied with something else, the determining tendency to subtract 380 was in abeyance. Hence his action incorporated the elements of perception of the figures and the marginal idea of subtraction. Some figure was to go. Now in a number like 4380, what impresses one is the 438, not the cipher. The 438 is like a unit. It has more significance,

---

[2] *Loc. cit.*, p. 102.
[3] *Loc. cit.*, pp. 122-123.
[4] *Cf.* A. A. Roback: "The Interference of Will-Impulses," 91*ff*.

besides the 0 comes at the end, and in many of our computations, for instance, in division, we have occasion to lop off the cipher at the end. Under the determining tendency to subtract mentally, this mathematical stereotyped act reinstated itself and the 0 was disregarded making the number 438, which was promptly copied on the cheque.

In the opinion of the writer, this explains amply what has taken place psychologically, but Freud naturally must introduce a whole series of numbers and weave into his material several interesting, though irrelevant, stories to account for such a comparatively simple operation. . . .

As a methodological principle in the study of lapses, the writer would lay down the rule that first the word, sentence, or sentences preceding or following are to be examined, then we must look into possible associations that may have determined the mistake; only in default of such clues, would it be legitimate to hunt for a new principle of explanation. . . .

In the Psychopathology of Everyday Life, there are a number of acute observations, but in a great many statements there is neither rhyme nor reason, and in general Freud's doctrine must be taken *cum grano salis.* To be consistent, he should hold that *a workman who misses his step on a high scaffold and falls into space has a secret desire of ending his life; for in what way is the psychological mechanism of such a slip any different from others that bring no grave consequences with them?* . . .

Much of our illness is due to what is ordinarily spoken of as thoughtlessness. . . . Yet we shall have a difficult task finding the man who may be said to invite illness, however unconsciously, unless as very rarely happens, when illness is a boon alternative as compared with some greater evil that may be in store for him.[5] As a rule, however, there does not seem to be the slightest motive for wishing to fall ill or for courting death. . . .

The principle of *determinism* which forms the background of the Freudian theory of lapses is sound, of course, *per se.* No scientist

---

[5] *Cf. A German Deserter's War Experience,* 163 . . . "We were especially forbidden to make use of woolen blankets, because the French were infected with scabies. 'Scabies' is an itching skin which it takes at least a week to cure. But the order had a contrary effect. If one was the owner of such an 'itch blanket' one had a chance of getting into the hospital for some days." . . . "In the evening we took some of the forbidden blankets, hundreds of which we had captured that day . . . everybody wanted to get the 'itch', however strange that may sound."

would deny that the writing lapse is conditioned by certain physiological or psychological antecedents.

B

LYDIARD H. HORTON, "Mechanistic Features in the Dream Process," *Jour. Abn. Psychol.*, 14: 181-182 (1920)

While engaged in writing this paper I read on the editorial page
of the *New York Times,* July 12, 1921, the following: "I, William
Howard Taft, do solemnly swear that I will . . . faithfully and
impartially discharge and perform all the duties incumbent upon me
as Chief Justice of the United States . . . and that I will well and
faithfully discharge the duties of the office on which I am about
to *tener."* (Italics mine). . . .

We turn to the mechanistic layout of the linotyper's operation.
We note that he operates a keyboard with an arrangement of letters
somewhat like that of the standard typewriter. In explaining the
word *tener* we have only four keys to consider, the three consonants
T, N and *R,* and the vowel *E,* which appears twice. Now we notice
that the consonant *N* occupies a solitary position in the bottom row
of keys. *E, R,* and *T* are side by side in the order named in the left
top row. A mix-up is very likely to occur under these circumstances
since the reaction is not "spaced out" by need of deliberation in
shifting the position of hand and fingers. Further we find internal
evidence indicating that the finger operating the letter *T* has been
facilitated by recent movements, whereas the right hand has been
more or less resting. Therefore, when it comes to the word *enter*
which is the stimulus idea, *T* gets ahead of the game. *N* slips in
after the first *E* as it should, having formed a union at the start of
the reaction. In the same way, we may regard the reaction as an
inversion between syllable *EN* (represented by *E* alone in left hand)
and *T.* Their positions are interverted by reason of the inertia of
the letters *N* and *E* and owing to marked facilitation of the
letter *T*.[1]

---

[1] [*Cf.* also Meyer Solomon, "Psychopathology of Everyday Life, A
Critical Review of Dr. Sigmund Freud's Theories"; A. Wohlgemuth, *A
Critical Examination of Psycho-analysis,* 198*ff;* J. Laumonier, *Le Freudism
Exposé et Critiqué.*]

AUTOMATIC WRITING

Nature and Significance

ANITA M. MÜHL, "Automatic Writing as an Indicator of the Fundamental
Factors Underlying the Personality," *Jour. Abn. Psychol.*,
17: 166-183 (1922)

PART I

. . . Automatic writing in its simplest form is script which the
writer produces involuntarily and in some instances without being
aware that he is doing it, even though he be in an alert waking
state.[1] Automatic writers may be divided into two classes: those
who can write only while being consciously distracted and stimulated, and those who can write only while relaxed and with the
attention fixed. These two groups may be further subdivided into
subjects who at the moment of writing have no idea what the hand.
is recording and those who at the moment have ideas corresponding
to the ones recorded, but which seem to flood the mind without
volition and without logical association toward the normal mental
processes. The writing is the manifestation of dissociated ideas
of which the writer is not aware. Very frequently the subject has
no idea what causes him to do the writing and he may be accredited
with mediumistic possession, and supernatural powers so that he
may even begin to believe that he has "psychic tendencies."

However the material produced by the person doing automatic
writing is entirely endogenous. The subject matter presented generally comes from the paraconscious [2] though the fundamental
traits found in the unconscious [3] often exhibit themselves in some

---

[1] ["Often even after reading the script his memory remains a blank."—
Morton Prince, *The Unconscious*, 27 (Macmillan, 1921).]

[2] [The paraconscious, for Dr. Mühl, means "that state in which ideas
and images are beyond the field of awareness but which are not too
difficultly recallable. If the ideas and images of the paraconscious are
dormant then we have a state which was formerly described as the fore-
conscious and the subconscious; if the ideas and images are active and
independent then we have a state which has been called the coconscious."—
Loc. cit., 162-164.]

[3] [By the unconscious Dr. Mühl means two things:

(a) The personal unconscious, or "that state in which the records
of the experiences of our lives are retained and conserved, no matter
in what condition they were impressed; whether in normal consciousness,
in the hypnotic state, in dissociated personality, or in hysterical crises.

of the productions, masquerading as individual personalities. Some of these personalities—those of the secondary type—are concomitant with the original or primary personality and are fully aware of all that the waking or normal personality does, feels, and thinks, and so they have an enormous advantage over the poor normal who has not the faintest idea what any given secondary personality may be up to. These secondary personalities may make records which appear to be exact reproductions of the handwriting of persons who have died and it is this type of individual who is often unsuspectingly exploited by the professional and unscrupulous so-called "psychic."

These cases of apparently authentic communication in the handwriting of deceased individuals have been the inciting factor of numerous psychical research experiments. It is interesting to note in this connection that W. A. Melcher in his discussion on "Dual Personality in Handwriting" says that attempted voluntary changes in handwriting as for purposes of disguise would not produce any marked effects especially in those details which were not known to the writer, but in the case of dual or multiple personality it is different, for here the writing lacks the features of voluntary disguise and it is necessary to go beyond physical and pictorial details and search the writing for the involuntary and uncontrollable discriminating marks shown by the writer. The disinterested handwriting expert using all scientific methods available can determine correctly whether or not the writings are the records of two different individuals or the same one. In this way there is provided a physical means of proving that the writing is not that belonging to another person who supposedly has taken possession of the writer.

These complexes . . . are not readily accessible and recallable," though containing elements compatible as well as elements incompatible with "the civilized conscious personality," not only because of being kept in the unconscious "by the direct utilization of energy, but also because once having reached there they may lose the necessary intensity which would enable them to reach the conscious state. . . . Put very simply the personal unconscious is the individual's mental lumber room."

(b) The genetic unconscious, "which constitutes the haziest part of the background, and is that state in which the instincts of the development are impressed. These instincts while influencing the individual's reaction are beyond any form of recall. It is thus seen that although the conscious, paraconscious and personal unconscious are capable of affecting each other reciprocally, the genetic unconscious while exerting an influence on the preceding states, can never be influenced by them because it represents the residual left in the wake of a development for which our present powers of interpretation are wholly inadequate."—*Ibid.,* 164.]

The surprising and unexpected variety of material produced by the subject is simply amazing. Latent talents of which the writer is in complete ignorance of possessing may be demonstrated, such as, writing poetry or stories; composing music; illustrating and designing. The writer may record lurid, criminal stories well worked out in detail though in the normal personality all traits of criminality and cruelty appear entirely lacking, thus suggesting the "Universal Kriminell" trend. Another writer may reveal personalities claiming to be delinquents and prostitutes, thus showing polymorphous perverse sexual instincts which would quite horrify the normal personality. The writer may fluently express ideas in a foreign language which he has forgotten he has ever heard. The subject may display a sudden facility for using the opposite hand or of using both together and may even produce two personalities simultaneously each making use of a different hand and each representing a different sex, thus showing a distinct bi-sexual trend.

The set of experiments reported by Downey and Anderson in 1915 showed conclusively that a person could read, write or calculate consciously and could produce records at the same time automatically from the paraconscious, thus showing that two streams of thought could take place at the same time. Prince through a reverse process demonstrated by means of a clever set of experiments that the active paraconscious could function simultaneously with the conscious and could even perceive and do elaborate computations correctly, totally independent of the conscious. The chief thing to bear in mind is the fact that not all the material produced automatically is necessarily symbolical and that much of it is merely an autographic record of ideas, images or experiences absolutely intact. The variety of material is almost limitless, but in the two cases I am discussing, both show distinctly a bisexual trend, while one beautifully illustrates the polymorphous perverse sexual, and the other the "Universal Kriminell."

PART II

The two subjects to be discussed both have the same first name and their life histories are quite similar though they do not even know of each other's existence. For the first of the two cases, I am very greatly indebted to Dr. Winifred Richmond who is a personal friend of the subject and who turned over to me her records and such information about the writer as was available. This case was reported by Dr. Richmond at one of Dr. G. Stanley Hall's seminars at Clark University in 1919 but was never published.

The second case is that of a personal friend of my own and for this reason I am somewhat handicapped in presenting both history and a statement of the records as I have promised to withhold certain material.

I.   Violet X—

Little can be told of the family history except that the parents were Scotch and that the father died at the age of sixty.   The mother is a "chronic worrier."   There are two younger sisters who are healthy and are not dominated by intellectual interests as is their sister.

Violet X— was born in New England and lived a normal healthy life as a child.   She had excellent schooling, graduating from a college for women.   She had no illnesses and never considered herself nervous or hysterical.   In college she had the usual courses in psychology but knew practically nothing about abnormal psychology. She had been specially interested in sociology and had done some social service work in Boston.   She was a teacher of English and later married a professor of English in a western town.   She had a fine intellect and a charming personality.

Just previous to the time of her automatic activity she had worked very hard and had begun to feel run down.   The physician she consulted told her she was overtired and had some slight cardiac disturbance.   Aside from this condition of fatigue she appeared to be normal physically and mentally.   One day when in this state of fatigue, it was discovered that the Ouija Board was working unusually well for Violet X— and Dr. Richmond was prompted to test her ability to write automatically.   This started a series of records which were obtained during a period of several months.   The first attempts were not so brilliantly successful, but with repeated attempts a marvelous facility for writing developed and with this an increased tendency to dissociate appeared which finally became so alarming that the experiments were abruptly terminated.

During the period of experimentation no less than seven distinct recurring personalities emerged, together with several minor ones. Each had a name and a handwriting more or less individual.   Each spoke of herself or himself in the first person giving detailed answers to questions, coherent accounts of themselves and admonitions and advice to the experimenters.   Half a dozen different personalities might come at one sitting, interrupting one another unceremoniously, and sometimes even rudely.   The personalities, once established, would often appear when called, coming with the remark: "So and so is here, what do you want?"   Miss Violet X—

maintained the same attitude as the other experimenters questioning or replying to what the hand was writing. Any levity on the part of the subject or the others was apt to call forth scathing remarks from the secondary personalities. Miss X— with one exception retained her own personality and was fully aware of what was going on, although she by no means always knew what the hand was writing; but as will be seen, her behavior was different when the different personalities were asserting themselves. In the following account it must be remembered that they appeared at different times throughout the several months of the experiment and that often several came at one sitting; but they shall be taken up, one at a time.

The first of these personalities to appear and the one who appeared most frequently and had the most to say was Annie McGinnis. Annie immediately drew a portrait of herself and it was a very clever picture. (In her normal personality Miss X— could not draw at all.) Annie's story as she told it at various intervals is the following. Annie was a poor girl who had fallen through no fault of her own, but had been led astray by a man who had promised her food and shelter and an easier life. After that she became a prostitute and finally died in giving birth to a child; she suffered greatly because of her sins and wandered aimlessly about until she found Miss X— with whom she took up her abode "because," as she said, "you are so good, I love to be with you." Annie true to type was coarse, rude, quick-tempered, resentful, reckless and passionate. Whenever she appeared she took charge in a whirlwind fashion and if she happened to be in a good humor, she was a great blarney. Whenever Annie appeared, Miss X— would be seized almost as though with a convulsion; her arm would stiffen and the fingers would grip the pencil tightly and write in a coarse, flowing hand; or her feet would pound on the floor while the arm would bang itself on the table with enough force to cause considerable pain. The pounding occurred, Annie said, when she thought of what men had done to her. Annie hated men with large capital letters and often after one of the male personalities had been recording she would obliterate all traces of these records by scribbling over the entire paper.

During Annie's appearance, Miss X— often was observed to have a peculiar expression on her face which grew more marked toward the latter part of the experiment. Her eyebrows were raised and she looked almost frightened. Sometimes she would grit her teeth and press her lips together firmly.

Mary Patterson was the next personality. Her handwriting was very much like Miss X—'s normal writing. She used the best English and in general was more like Miss X—'s primary personality than any of the others. She came quite seldom and when she did she was apt to be rather rudely ousted by some of the more aggressive ones. Mary declared she was Miss X—'s most familiar spirit.

Mary Minott was a third personality. She described herself as a cosmopolitan and very talented. She hated Mary Patterson and called her a prig, full of puritanical notions. She would bitterly upbraid Miss X— for preferring Mary Patterson to her. She insisted that if Miss X— would only listen to her she would make her a famous designer, and to prove it she designed a number of beautiful dresses (Miss X— normally could not do this at all). Mary Minott had a perfect passion for designing gowns and she had talent that amounted almost to genius.

A fourth personality, persistent and always unwelcome to Miss X— was Alton. Unlike the others, he was no myth but a friend of her fiancé, whom she had met the previous summer. He wrote the most sentimental things and seemed to try to dissuade her from marrying the man to whom she was engaged. Alton was always urging Miss X— to give herself up to mediumship saying that the spirits of both the dead and the living could speak through her. He admitted that it was sometimes dangerous but felt he could guard her from harm.

Miss X—'s father was the other personality who purported to be dead, as he actually was. This personality assumed the actual handwriting of her father. He did not appear often and then only made hurried remarks about family affairs.

A sixth interesting personality labeled himself simply "the Spirit of War and Desolation." This spirit sounded dreadful warnings (it was just prior to America's entry into the war) and urged Miss X— to work for the Red Cross. This personality alternately urged Miss X— to give up automatic writing and to take up the study of mediumship for which she was told she had rare talent.

The last personality to develop and the one who finally caused the disruption of the experiment, called himself merely "Man." In the beginning he was not at all distinct, neither with regard to handwriting nor to the content of what he wrote. At first he would break into some other conversation with totally irrelevant remarks and when questioned would give only ambiguous answers or none at all. Finally however he identified himself as man and would alternate with Alton, but he developed such an antipathy toward

Alton that he succeeded in banishing him altogether. He also
fostered an intense dislike for Annie McGinnis who hated him in
return in letters two inches high. She considered him the incarnation of all her enemies. "Man" tried to banish her, but nothing
could banish the flippant and irrepressible Annie and she took
particular delight in scribbling all over the things he had written.

These two personalities now had the field pretty much to themselves and "Man" became more and more persistent and dominating.
A change began to come over Miss X—when he was in control.
She first mentioned it herself, saying: "I feel different when 'Man'
is present than I do with any of the others; there is a feeling
of power and vigor and I don't want to sit still, I want to run or
express myself in some vigorous physical way." "Man" soon expressed an interest in dancing and would fill sheet after sheet
with marks produced through rhythmic motion of the pencil, becoming more and more energetic as time went on. He would write
occasionally—"Let's dance, Violet." Miss X— began to say she
believed she really could dance spontaneously if she would give herself up entirely to the feelings, but she was always a little afraid
to try.

Toward the end of the experiment some three months after it
was begun, Miss X— was writing quietly one evening when "Man"
came and as usual began to dance. In a moment Miss X— spoke
loudly and said—"Oh—I want to dance—I believe I can dance"
and getting to her feet she began to sway rhythmically back and
forth. The swaying became more and more violent, her arms began
to wave and her feet to execute a curious shuffling movement. Suddenly her body gave a violent wrench and she cried out in a sharp,
high voice. Her face depicted the emotions of a tremendous struggle, ecstacy and terror contending for expression. She was taken
to a couch by the experimenters, where for about ten minutes she
remained stiff and moaned in an unnatural voice. Gradually she
resumed her natural speaking voice, relaxed and returned to normal
and though rather terrified by the experience, she was able to
discuss what her feelings were. She said she tried to control the
movements and suddenly realized she couldn't—it was as if something were making her do it and she couldn't stop. She declared
she was in fear of losing herself and of another personality gaining
control. She said: "I wanted to give myself up to it and yet I
didn't want to. I can't describe it, but I felt as though I were two
people."

After this experience, Miss X— was strongly dissuaded from
trying anything more, but she did try it a few times and always

"Man" came, telling her he represented all the vigor and love of action in her. He always wanted to dance. After this came her marriage and the automatic writing was largely forgotten for several months, but one day when she was alone she decided she would try it again. This time Mary Patterson, "the most familiar spirit" came and explained that all the other personalities were completely submerged and lacked sufficient intensity to be able to express themselves. After this no further attempts were made.

Miss Violet X— was tremendously interested in all the manifestations and introspected carefully and sincerely. She felt that none of them expressed things outside her own experience except Alton, who was a real person. However after repeated attempts at analysis, Miss X— recalled a conversation with her mother after her meeting with Alton which satisfactorily accounted for the genesis of his remarks, and after this explanation he gradually disappeared.

Miss X— felt that Annie McGinnis was entirely explicable. She had been strongly impressed in her experience in social work with the idea that only the accident of birth and training had saved her from such a life as that led by some of the girls of the lower economic classes. Annie was, in part, the systematized expression of ideas, once acutely conscious but largely relegated to the paraconscious where they continued active, and she was also the means of expressing the polymorphous perverse sexual tendencies of the personal unconscious. She further illustrated a distinctly compensatory trend for her expressions of hatred for men were probably the outcome of the ambivalent opposite emotional tendency.

"Man" undoubtedly represented the bisexual trend of the subject and came, if not wholly, at least to a great extent from the personal unconscious. His desire to dominate, as well as the assertive and very aggressive tendencies manifested, appear much more instinctively masculine in character than feminine. The power and vigor of expression as well as the greater freedom from repression in this personality seem to be evidence of the same phenomenon.

II. Violet Z—

The family history in this case is of considerable interest. The father's maternal grandmother who lived to be past a hundred had the ability to do automatic writing. The father himself of Scotch and Dutch ancestry has always been a very unpractical business man and though once in good financial circumstances, met with many reverses. His particular interest has been tracing the origin of religions and he has written a book on the subject. He has been so engrossed in his researches that he has paid too little attention to his children. The mother was of Welsh and English descent and was a lovable, sweet, dignified woman whom every one admired. She met her husband at college and they were married during their Senior year. She could do automatic writing and was thought to have the power to be a Spiritualist Medium. She however did not believe this, and told her husband,—who was then interested in spiritualism—that after she was "in spirit land" she would not communicate with him. She died when Violet Z— was eight years old. Mr. Z— feels that he has talked with his father and many dead friends, but *never* with his wife. Violet Z— has an older sister and brother, both very bright. The brother has always been erratic—has been an actor and a newspaper man. The sister did very well in school and was bright in college. She was witty, attractive and delightful. Up to her sophomore year Violet's sister was cook, housekeeper, mother, and chaperone all in one, as they had no maid. Toward the end of her second college year she began to suffer with thyroiditis and had to go to a hospital for many months, and the rôles of the sisters became reversed.

Violet Z— herself is now [1922] about 26 years old. She was a seven months baby. As stated above her mother died when she was eight and she remembers her mother as a very pretty lady who lived with them—not so much as a mother, although she was deeply attached to her. Violet Z—'s childhood was normal and she had good health. She dearly loved to play with dolls, but on the other hand she was a bit of a tom-boy too, for she enjoyed romping and playing out of doors and was frequently up to some sort of mischievous pranks. She started going to school at the age of six. In spite of her liveliness at home and among her intimate playmates, among strangers, she was quite shy and timid and made few friends. As a child Joan of Arc and Florence Nightingale were the two characters who most appealed to her. She was never so brilliant in high school as her sister and her shyness increased.

When she started to college she was absolutely ignorant of all sex matters, as she had received no instruction. The following summer, after having studied Biology for a term and still not understanding the reproductive functions, she had these phenomena explained to her while visiting a friend in the country. Her whole college course was shadowed by worrying about her sister who became ill. She had a great many additional responsibilities added to her usual ones and she began to lose her remarkable endurance. Whereas she had always been even tempered, happy and sunny in disposition, she now began to show slight signs of irritability and of being inclined to worry.

It was during her sophomore year that she met the man she eventually married. After her marriage her husband was unable to keep a position for more than a short time, and she had to help with their support by teaching. She had a miscarriage and was very ill. At present her husband is doing splendidly and they have bought a new home. A baby was born about six months ago and Violet Z— got along fairly well afterwards, though the child had to be taken with instruments.

She first began to do automatic writing during her freshman year in college and started it simply because she knew her mother had written and thought she would try. She was delighted to discover she could do it and soon was entertaining her more intimate friends with her performances. She always preferred having the room quiet and always maintained a rather listless attitude toward the whole procedure. Her automatic activity differed from that of Violet X— in that it never produced a recurring personality and also in that it did not cease after her marriage, for the most remarkable record she accomplished was made just a few months ago.

The first of the stories and one that was written all in one evening concerned the phenomena attending the death of a person calling himself William Young. The working out of the plot covered sheets and sheets of foolscap paper and the tale was profusely and cleverly illustrated. (Violet Z— like Violet X— could not draw *at all* voluntarily.) William Young was born in England over a hundred years ago (he was forty-five when he died and he said he had been dead over fifty-five years). He lived in a small coast town which he said was called X— and he drew a map on which he located the place. This was verified in an atlas and it was further found that the map was very accurate. None of the group present has any conscious knowledge of ever having heard the name of the town before. William gave as his occupation, that of butler in a wealthy family. He drew a magnificent picture of himself in his livery. His brother, several years younger and not so successful as himself, was a carpenter by trade. Both he and his brother were in love with an attractive young woman who was a maid in the same residence where William was butler. She preferred William and they became engaged one early summer. This angered the brother and made him very resentful toward William but he attempted to mask his feelings and he made a picnic in honor of the engaged couple, inviting the members of the family and some intimate friends.

At this stage of the story several sheets of foolscap paper were covered with illustrations depicting the picnic grounds in a shady nook near a spring. The ground was covered with wild flowers. Great care was given to drawing the details of the lunch; the cloth spread on the ground, the cutlery, the baskets of food and ale were all portrayed, while special attention was directed to the seating arrangements and the places where he, his brother and the girl sat were carefully marked. The party proceeded hilariously for a time, but presently as William ate an onion his brother passed him, he suddenly appeared to strangle, and died most unexpectedly.

The merrymakers were utterly stunned over the tragedy and the young woman was quite wild with grief. Great perplexity prevailed when it was attempted to fix the cause of death, for William had always been strong and robust and was supposed to be in the best of health, but finally it was decided he must have had a weak heart of which no one had been aware and that he had really died of heart trouble.

At this point of the story, the writing became agitated and the words simply poured themselves on to the paper. William assured us that instead of dying from any normal cause, he had been foully murdered by his brother who was so intensely jealous of him that he decided to put him out of the way. He wrote over and over— "it was just one drop that he put in the onion that did it"—but what the drop of poison was William did not know.

His betrothed after a suitable period of grieving, married the wicked brother who contrary to all the laws of fairy tales, prospered and lived with his bride, happily ever after. William showed considerable emotional distress over the fact that the murder had never been discovered and that his criminal brother had never been brought to justice.

We tried by various methods to discover if Violet Z— had ever read or heard of such a tale, but she was unable by any means attempted to recall anything even faintly resembling it. However undoubtedly she had heard or more likely read of it; for the geographic details were so accurate that they could not have been fabrications.

The second story written on another occasion claimed to come from a Charles You. The beginning of this story was quite amusing, for as the hand commenced writing, some one asked, "Who is writing?" and the hand replied *"You."* This naturally caused considerable mirth and about ten times in reply to the same question, the hand wrote, each time in larger script, more emphatically and apparently quite peevishly, *"You."* Finally some one said: "Well, what is your other name?" and the reply this time was, "Charles You."

Charles You was a scientist in the employ of the German Government who had been sent to China to make an important geological survey in the interior. He was accompanied by an assistant and all went well for a while until one day they had a quarrel which ended in a bitter fight. The assistant who had about the same amount of strength, triumphed and left his adversary in a state of unconsciousness, taking with him important data which had been collected. You, however, had been injured during the fight, in his foot and was unable to move for some time after regaining consciousness. Owing to lack of proper medical attention an infection started in the foot which finally developed into a general septicæmia and which was the cause of his death.

The only illustration in this story was so remarkable that I feel inclined to describe it in detail. In discussing the foot injury and subsequent infection a most accurate picture was drawn of the bones of the human foot and leg—not a tarsal nor a metatarsal was omitted and they were placed in perfect juxtaposition. I happened to be studying anatomy at that time and consequently I was much impressed by the perfect correctness of the production. Violet Z— had studied zoology but the only occasion she had of seeing the bones of the foot was in the skeleton which adorned the biology laboratory and she never consciously paid any attention to it. The accurate image was impressed in the paraconscious however where it was stored for further use, even though the perception in its passage through had evoked no response in the conscious state. When Violet Z— was asked to make a *conscious* effort to draw what she had automatically done so perfectly, she was utterly unable to draw anything that in any way resembled that part of the skeletal anatomy.

The third story concerned an unnamed prisoner who had escaped from the penitentiary where he was serving a long sentence for having assaulted a man and who had traveled to the far north. He drew numerous maps in great detail and showed the desolate strip of land where he was isolated. He had reached his destination by means of a small water craft and had taken some provisions with him. He was soon caught in the freeze-up and had to build himself a small snow hut. Here he was existing, but he said he did not think he had enough provisions to last him until relief would come in the late spring and he thought he would probably die of starvation and exposure. As in the case of William Young recourse was had to an atlas and again it was discovered that the map was accurate and that the place indicated was beyond the regions of habitation. This ability to draw maps is interesting, for in her normal state of consciousness she has no interest in geography.

The next case was that of a person who was confined to an insane asylum through the misrepresentation of some relatives who took this means of getting control of the man's fortune. He had had a number of unusual experiences and had been the victim of some political plots and after he was in the hospital, the mere recital of the things that had really happened, caused him to be considered paranoid. The recital ended with a pitiful plea—"Please help me, for I am sick physically and can't live long and if I stay here much longer I shall really go mad."

A number of interesting writings followed, all dealing with some phase of criminality, such as embezzling, forging or larceny. The criminal productions were all made before Violet Z—'s marriage. As in the case of Violet X—, after marriage, she had so many duties and cares that the writing was neglected. However in January of this year I saw her again and as of old we decided to amuse ourselves with the automatic writing. Violet Z— sat at the table and made some incoherent records with her right hand. The facility for smooth production seemed to have been lost. At last becoming impatient, I put the pencil in her left hand and said, "Let's see what that will do!" Almost immediately the left hand (which she ordinarily cannot use for writing) began to fly across the paper and the resulting records were perfectly coherent. Then I decided it would be fun to see what would happen if I put a pencil in each of her hands. There seemed to be a momentary quiver in each arm and then both hands began writing simultaneously, each hand recording a different message and each denoting a different sex. The left hand wrote in small characters and claimed to be representing a girl by the name of Aneta Glane who expressed admiration for Violet Z—. The right hand wrote in bold flourishing style under the name of Daniel Raun and was pompous and boastful. After some time the left hand wrote: "If you will help me I can write better," while *simultaneously* the right hand recorded "I would like to let you but I am stronger and I hinder." The last thing written was, "I want to be strong, but I am weaker"—with the left hand while the right hand pranced all over the page in huge letters saying, "Good, good—Good—GOOD!" This closed the set of experiments with Violet Z— for she was shortly after taken ill with influenza and I returned to Washington before she was well enough to attempt any more writing.

The criminal trend is so marked in these records that little comment should be needed and yet there is one remarkable feature that should be emphasized. In each story, the degree of the criminal phase decreases. The first tale deals with first degree murder—a cold, premeditated and deliberate deed which goes unavenged. The second deals with an indirect murder—the death resulting due to neglect of the adversary's condition after the fight. The third concerns a man who has escaped from prison where he is serving a long sentence for assaulting another and it shows him likely to pay the final penalty through retribution. The fourth case deals with criminal persecution and the others in lesser crimes of embezzling, forging and thieving. It is interesting to note that the criminal element finally disappeared and was absent in the last experiment.

In view of the history (the authority of the sister, the greater ability she displayed in school, her popularity and lastly the illness which threw the responsibility on Violet Z—), the parallel incidence in the stories of William Young and Charles You of the subservient character eliminating the dominating personality is quite significant. Consciously she was aware of no resentment toward the sister and would have been annoyed had such a feeling been ascribed to her, but the paraconscious did protest and the automatic activity gave vent to her disapproval. The expression of Aneta Glane's commendation of Violet Z— as well as Annie McGinnis' approval of Violet X— suggests a narcissistic trend.

The bisexual element in Violet Z—'s case shows up especially well in the last set of records. Here we have both sexes striving for dominance, the left side illustrating the female and the right hand the more energetic and vigorous male characteristics.

PART III

In Part I a number of facts were discussed which appeared pertinent to a study of these cases of automatic writing. In Part II, the cases themselves were presented and the more important phases were emphasized. An attempt will now be made to briefly summarize the points which have been illustrated.

1. Automatic activity and dissociation constitute a reversible reaction. The greater the tendency to automatism the greater the danger of dissociation. Violet X— as she attained her greatest proficiency in writing also came very near to having a complete cleavage of the personality. This was when "Man" insisted she should dance.

2. The Paraconscious is the chief abode of automatic activity and may consist of dominant and active states, the latter of which are apt to produce personalities which are concomitant with the

original personality. Mary Patterson knew all about Violet X—and what she thought and did—on the other hand, Violet X— knew nothing of what Mary Patterson thought. Annie McGinnis also knew what Violet X— thought and also what the two personalities "Man" and Mary Patterson thought.

3. The Personal Unconscious besides being the zone where the impressions of the most deeply repressed and lost experiences are left also contains the elemental instincts of the personality and may so color the paraconscious activity as to suggest many unusual trends.

4. The two cases are of interest in that they illustrate on the one hand Stekel's theory that we have universal criminal impulses and on the other hand Freud's theory that we all have polymorphous perverse sexual tendencies, and that both show the bisexual disposition of the individual.

5. These cases further confirm Prince's experiments that the Paraconscious may act on its perceptions and function independently of the conscious. The drawing in the story of Charles You, of the skeleton of the foot is one of the corroborative pieces of evidence of this principle.

There are two questions which have suggested themselves during the preparation of this paper, but the scope of this article is too limited to allow of more than a brief statement of them. The first is a problem for the neuro-physiologist and concerns itself with habit formation. The last record discussed showed a hand that had not been accustomed to writing, suddenly exhibiting this activity independent of the simultaneous writing of the other hand. The neuro-muscular apparatus which controls this is apparently all connected—and an energy of some kind functions it, but of what character is it? Is it merely an overflow phenomenon or is it an independently functioning phenomenon?

The second question is one for which the psychiatrist will have to find the answer. If it is seen that a certain tendency to dissociation in a given person exists and that in the secondary personality developed there is a suggestion of latent abilities and talents—would it not be worth while to deliberately break up the synthesis of the mental states and resynthesize the subject into a more culturally successful and economically efficient individual by means of either hypnotism or analysis, or both combined.

In conclusion I should like to state that in view of the evidence offered, I believe I am justified in assuming that automatic writing is an indicator of the fundamental factors underlying the personality and that it may be considered an especially valuable instrument in the study of mental disturbances of psychogenic origin, to reveal the predominating elements of the patient's mental make-up.

NOTE. I wish to most especially express my appreciation to Dr. Winifred Richmond for permitting me to use the case of Violet X—, and for the unfailing encouragement and helpful suggestions she has offered during the preparation of this paper. I also wish to thank Dr. Johan Liljencrants and Dr. Nolan D. C. Lewis for the constructive criticisms they have made and on which I have acted. I further wish to express my indebtedness to the authors of the following books and articles, in whose works I have found many valuable ideas which have been of great assistance to me in the writing of this article.

1. ADLER, ALFRED. *Study of Organ Inferiority and Its Psychical Compensation,* Nerv. Men. Dis. Monograph Series No. 24. Trans. by Smith Ely Jelliffe.

2. ANGELL, E. B. "A Case of Double Consciousness,—Amnesic Type, with Fabrication of Memory." *Jour. Abn. Psychol.,* Oct., 1906.

3. "B. C. A. My Life as a Dissociated Personality." *Jour. Abn. Psychol.,* Oct., Nov., '08; Dec., '08; Jan., '09.

4. BLEULER, DR. PROF. E. *Die Ambivalenz.* Abstracted by C. R. Payne, *Psychoan. Rev.,* Vol. 2, 1915.

5. BLEULER, HANS. "J. P. Jakolsen's 'Niels Lyhne' and the Problem of Bisexuality." Abstracted by J. S. Van Teslaar, *Psychoan. Rev.,* 1915, Vol. 2.

6. BURROW, TRIGANT. "Notes with Reference to Freud, Jung and Adler." *Jour. Abn. Psychol.,* 1917-18.

7. CARRINGTON, HEREWARD. "Freudian Psychology and Psychical Research. (A Rejoinder.)" *Jour. Abn. Psychol.,* May, 1915.

8. CORIAT, ISADOR H. "Experimental Synthesis of Dissociated Memories in Alcoholic Amnesia." *Jour. Abn. Psychol.,* Aug., 1906.

9. IBID. "The Lowell Case of Amnesia." *Jour. Abn. Psychol.,* Aug., Sept., 1907.

10. CORY, CHARLES E. "A Divided Self." *Jour. Abn. Psychol.,* 1919.

11. IBID. "A Subconscious Phenomenon." *Jour. Abn. Psychol.,* 1919.

12. DEWEY, RICHARD. "A Case of Disordered Personality." *Jour. Abn. Psychol.,* Oct., Nov., 1907.

13. DONLEY, JOHN E. "On Neurasthenia as a Disintegration of Personality." *Jour. Abn. Psychol.,* Vol. 1, June, 1906.

14. DOOLEY, LUCILE. *Psychoanalytic Talks* [to be published], 1921.

15. DOWNEY, JUNE E., and ANDERSON, JOHN E. "Automatic Writing." *Am. Jour. Psychol.,* April, 1915.

16. FOX, CHARLES D. "Report of a Case of Dissociated Personality, Characterized by the Presence of Somnambulistic States and Ambulatory Automatism." *Jour. Abn. Psychol.,* Aug.-Sept., 1909.

17. FREUD, SIGMUND. *Three Contributions to the Theory of Sex.*

18. GOLDSCHMIDT, RICHARD. "Experimental Intersexuality and the Sex Problem." *Am. Naturalist,* Dec., 1916.

19. GAVER, EARL E. "A Case of Alternating Personality, Characterized chiefly by Ambulatory Automatism and Amnesia with Results of Hypnotic Experiments." *Jour. Am. Med. Ass.,* July 4, 1908.

20. HART, BERNARD. "The Conception of the Subconscious." *Jour. Abn. Psychol.,* Feb.-March, 1910.

21. IBID. *The Psychology of Insanity.* (Cambridge, 1916.)

22. HYSLOP, JAMES H. "Apparent Subconscious Fabrication." *Jour. Abn. Psychol.,* Dec. '06.

23. JAMES, WM. *The Principles of Psychology.* (Holt.)

24. JANET, PIERRE. *L'hysterie Maladie Mentale.* Abstracted by Charpentier in the Journal de Psychologie, 1908.

25. IBID. "On the Subconscious." *Jour. Abn. Psychol.,* Vol. 2, 1907.

26. JASTROW, JOSEPH. "On the Subconscious." *Jour. Abn. Psychol.,* Vol. 2, 1907.

27. KEMPF, E. J. *The Autonomic Functions and the Personality.*

28. LILJENCRANTS, JOHAN. *Spiritism and Religion.* Devin Adair Co., New York, 1918.

29. LONG, CONSTANCE. "An Analytical View of the Basis of Character." *Psychoan. Rev.,* 1920.

30. LODGE, OLIVER. "Evidence of Classical Scholarship and of cross-correspondence in some new Automatic Writings." *Pr. Soc. for Psych. Res.,* 1911, Vol. 25.

31. MAYER, EDWARD E. "A Case Illustrating So-called Demon Possession." *Jour. Abn. Psychol.,* Oct., Nov., 1912.

32. McDOUGALL. "The Physical Basis of Mental Dissociation." 13 *M. J.,* Oct. 24, 1908.

33. MELCHER, WEBSTER A. "Dual Personality in Handwriting." *Jour. Am. Inst. Crim. Law and Criminol.,* Aug., 1920.

34. MITCHELL, T. W. "A Study in Hysteria and Multiple Personality with Report of a Case." *Pr. Soc. Psych. of Res.,* Nov., 1912.

35. IBID. "Some Types of Multiple Personality." *Pr. of Soc. for Psychol. Res.,* Nov., 1912.

36. IBID. "Psycho-Physical Discussion of Multiple Personality." *Pr. Soc. Psych. Res.,* Nov., 1912.

37. MOLL, ALBERT. *Hypnotism.* Scribner and Welford, N. Y.

38. MONTIETH, M. E. "Automatic Writing, its Uses and its verification." *Nineteenth Century,* Vol. 83, 1918.

39. MÜNSTERBERG, HUGO. "A Symposium on the Subconscious No. I." *Jour. Abn. Psychol.,* Vol. 11, 1917, Apr., May.

40. O'MALLEY, MARY. "Certain Pluriglandular Anomalous Functions Associated with Psychopathic Sexual Interests." *Jour. of Nerv. Men. Dis.,* Vol. 48, 1918.

41. PFISTER, OSKAR. "Die Psychologische Enträtselung der Re-

ligiösen Glossolalie und der automatischen Kryptographie." *Jahrbuch für Psychoanalytische und Psychopathologische Forschungen,* Band 3.

42. PIERCE, WALTER FRANKLIN. "The Doris Case of Quintuple Personality." *Jour. Abn. Psychol.,* Vol. 11, 1916-17.

43. PILLSBURY, W. B. *The Fundamentals of Psychology* (Macmillan, 1916).

44. PRINCE, MORTON. "Coconscious Images." *Jour. Abn. Psychol.,* Vol. 12, 1917-1918.

45. IBID. "Experiments to Determine Coconscious Ideation." *Jour. Abn. Psychol.,* April-May, 1908.

46. IBID. "Hysteria from the Point of View of Dissociated Personality." *Jour. Abn. Psychol.,* June-July, 1907.

46a. IBID. *The Dissociation of a Personality.* (Longmans, 1906.)

46b. IBID. "Miss Beauchamp: The Theory of the Psychogenesis of Multiple Personality." *Jour. Abn. Psychol.,* June-Sept., 1920.

46c. IBID. "The Structure and Dynamic Elements of Human Personality." *Jour. Abn. Psychol.,* Dec., 1920, March, 1921.

47. IBID. "The Subconscious Setting of Ideas in Relation to the Pathology of the Psychoneuroses." *Jour. Abn. Psychol.,* Vol. 11, 1916-1917.

48. IBID. "On the Subconscious." *Jour. Abn. Psychol.,* June-July, 1907.

49. PRINCE, MORTON, and PETERSON, FRED. "Experiments in Psycho-Galvanic Reactions from Coconscious Ideas in a Case of Multiple Personality." *Jour. Abn. Psychol.,* October, 1906.

50. PRINCE, MORTON. *The Unconscious* (Macmillan, 1914).

51. IBID. "The Unconscious." *Jour. Abn. Psychol.,* Oct.-Nov., '08; Dec., '08; Jan., '09; Feb.-March, '09; Apr.-May, '09.

52. IBID. "The Psychogenesis of Multiple Personality." *Jour. Abn. Psychol.,* 1919.

53. PUTNAM, J. J. "Freud and His Work." *Jour. Abn. Psychol.,* 1909-10.

54. IBID. "The Work of Sigmund Freud." *Jour. Abn. Psychol.,* 1917-18.

55. RIBOT, THEODORE. "On the Subconscious." *Jour. Abn. Psychol.,* Vol. 11, 1907.

56. ROSENSTEIN, GASTON. "Die Theorien der Organminder Wertigkeit und der Bisexualität in ihrer Beziehungen zur Neurosenlehre." *Jahrbuch für Psychoanalytische und Psychopathologische Forschungen,* Band 2.

57. SIDGWICK, MRS. HENRY. "A Reply to Dr. J. Maxwell's Paper on 'Cross-Correspondence and the Experimental Method,'" *Pr. Soc. Psych. Res.,* Vol. 26, July, 1913.

58. SIDIS, BORIS. "A Clinical Study of a Dream Personality." *Jour. Abn. Psychol.,* Vol. 12, Aug., 1918.

59. IBID. *Multiple Personality.* 1905.

60. IBID. *Psychopathological Researches; Studies in Mental Dissociation.* D. E. Stechert, New York, 1902.

61. STEKEL, WILHELM. *Die Sprache des Traumes.*

62. TROLAND, LEONARD. "The Freudian Psychology and Psychical Research." *Jour. Abn. Psychol.,* Feb., March, 1914.

63. VERRALL, MRS. A. W. "A Series of Automatic Writings." *Pr. Soc. Psych. Res.,* Vol. XX, Oct., 1906.

64. WHITE, WM. A. *The Foundations of Psychiatry.* Nerv. & Ment. Dis. Mono. Ser., No. 32, 1921.

65. IBID. "The Unconscious." *Psychoan. Rev.,* Vol. 11, 1915.

Uses and Mechanism

ANITA M. MÜHL, "The Use of Automatic Writing in Determining Conflicts and Early Childhood Impressions," *Jour. Abn. Psychol.,* 18: 1-7 (1923)

INTRODUCTION

In a previous article, "Automatic Writing as an Indicator of the Fundamental Factors Underlying the Personality," [1] I discussed the psychological factors involved in producing the dissociation phenomenon known as automatic writing and reported two cases illustrating bisexuality, polymorphous perverse sexual tendencies and criminal trends, besides other traits, but these cases had merely been observed and no special analysis had been attempted as neither subject was a patient.

In part three of that paper I presented two questions which had suggested themselves in the course of the construction of the article, one of which I am prepared to answer myself—I refer to the one which was phrased as follows: "If it is seen that a certain tendency to dissociation in a given person exists and that in the secondary personality developed there is a suggestion of latent abilities and talents, would it not be worth while to deliberately break up the synthesis of the mental states and resynthesize the subject into a more culturally successful and economically efficient individual by means of either hypnotism or analysis or both combined?" Case number three of this series will give a fair idea of what can be done with material of this kind.

Furthermore, in my concluding paragraph I made the statement that I felt automatic writing could be considered an especially valuable instrument in the study of mental disturbances of psycho-

---

[1] *Jour. Abn. Psychol.,* July-Sept., 1922. [Also cited here (preceding selection).]

genic origin to reveal the predominating elements of the patient's mental make-up—but I then had no idea just how valuable I was to find it.

I can now definitely state that it may be used as a successful adjunct to psychoanalysis, first to hasten the solution of the conflicts and second to minimize the problems of transfer and resistance. Once succeeding in getting the patient to "automat," the unconscious gives up its material much more readily and for some reasons a patient seems to accept her unconscious problems with much less disbelief when she sees them on paper written by herself, rather than if she merely utters them verbally. The patient may write just simple words, or only nonsense syllables but even so each of these by means of association will generally go back to conflict material. Frequently by proper questioning, the entire conflict nucleus will be recorded in so many words. This occurred in several of my cases.

Even more important in my opinion than the aid to locating conflicts is the value in helping us investigate the child's personality trends, with its wonderful maze of curious whys, its odd resentments (odd to adults), its wealth of play fancies and activities and above all its attitude toward grown-ups. In two of my cases I was able to get out whole blocks of early childhood activities (too young for the patient to remember anything about, but corroborated by the parents) and the incidents were described in detail.

In some personality studies I was making I found that I had to hurry in order to finish all the material I had begun. I had reached a standstill in several of the analyses, a condition which threatened tedious and prolonged work in order to bring them to a satisfactory conclusion. More as a diversion than anything I attempted to get my patients to automat and much to my surprise it was highly successful. This induced me to try it on others and it was in this way that I managed to collect twelve good new cases of automatic writing, three of which I am reporting in this series.

In one case the automatic productions helped to clear up two fears that analysis had not reached and which went back into very early childhood, in another it was the means of bringing to the surface deeply rooted resentments and establishing a better understanding of self and environment, while in the third it did not only these things but it uncovered a really fine hidden talent and made it possible for a path to be blazed from the unconscious so that it became a part of the conscious life.

PHYSIOLOGICAL THEORIES OF AUTOMATIC WRITING

Although the psychological explanation of automatic writing has been established satisfactorily (for some of us, at least) the physical mechanism involved in the phenomenon of automatic writing apparently remains a much neglected problem. A few months ago I sent a little note to the psychology departments of one hundred and ten universities and colleges, asking if they knew any references regarding the physical aspects. Of the one hundred, seventy-five responded. Most of the writers had not been interested in the subject but some did suggest various references from which the following ideas ars assembled.

In order to understand the queer neuro-physiological pranks of automatism we have to take into consideration some of the factors involved in the production of normal voluntary writing. Wyczolkowska has shown that there are five stages in the evolution of automatic writing by children leading to the normal writing habit. The first appears from two to two-and-a-half, in which the child produces a chaos of straight and concentric lines limited only by the edges of the paper. The second stage comes from two-and-a-half to three and in this waving lines of long phases but small amplitude are recorded either in horizontal, perpendicular or circular directions. The third is seen in three to five year old children in which the amplitude of the curves is increased; the fourth period shows zig-zags in unconscious imitation of letters and symbols of the writing of various languages [2] and in the fifth there appears conscious imitation of writing interspersed with a mixture of the previous symbols. This is of real interest because as everyone who has done much work with automatic writing knows, the foregoing program is the one followed by adults who are not facile "automaters" to start with.

It is during the scribble or uncontrolled writing period that the child uses the trial and error method of attaining maximum results with minimum difficulty and so if she attempts to write with her left hand (if she is normally right-handed) she will be apt to try mirror writing, as symmetrical movements of both sides of the body will initiate this particular activity according to the method of least resistance.

Up to five according to Jastrow the child's visual center is undergoing its elementary education. Apparently after that the visual imagery seems more stabilized and it is also at about this time that

---

[2] [I.e., such as the child sees?]

the child begins to bring this factor into play in its attempts at writing. I have mentioned that the initial attempts at automatic writing are suggestive of the child's early scribble period—is it then so remarkable that the child's associations to this period (the record of its happenings) should be easily tapped through judicious limitation of the automatic activity to the associations at certain age levels of the patient?

Klages says that control in writing may arise either from mastery of impulse or from excessive inhibition; then, if that is so, in involuntary writings we might expect loss of control of impulse or release of inhibition and it appears we are dealing not with one or the other alone but with both.

These two factors could account for bi-manual dissimilar records being produced at the same time if we can accept the idea of a two sided neuro-physiological mechanism being set for writing activity. In order to make this appear plausible we will have to take into consideration some of the ideas concerning handedness.

Gould tells us that the education of left-handed children in whom with long training and habit the naturally placed dextrocerebral center is changed to the opposite side we have a demonstration that "no inherent neurologic or physiologic law governs the location of the cerebral center or its peripheral outworking." It seems to me however that it is quite possible that there are at all times two such oppositely placed centers one of which is normally completely inhibited. I have several reasons for thinking this. (1) Movements of symmetrically placed parts of the body tend to produce symmetrical movements,—that is if one arm moves there is a tendency toward or an imagined movement of the other arm, generally inhibited. Slight as this imagined movement may be still it will produce initial muscular movements even though they are so insignificant as to be unobserved. Naturally they will be recorded in the corresponding opposite half of the brain. If the impulse is initiated by a "motor" image then there will be a reversed record left in the brain in case of the inhibited left side (a motor image demanding writing with the left if the right hand is writing normally); if on the other hand it is initiated by a visual image, then there will be the same type recorded as made with the opposite hand. This in itself could explain the frequent interchange of normal and mirror script employed by the left hand in right-handed individuals in automatic productions. (2) Sherrington has shown by experiment that the cerebral seats of the right-eye and left-eye visual images are separate, one for each hemisphere, and that ordinarily the binocular vision we attain is due to a synthesis of a left-eye with a right-eye sensation. (3) Gould says that the people, who are definitely "handed" are also definitely "eyed"—that is, the eye corresponding to the most skilled and used hand is the dominant eye and its image is the preferred one in the fusion-pattern which would suggest a slight difference in the recording time of the two halves of the brain. If this is so we have the physical root of dissociative tendencies in the physiological phenomenon and it is not at all amazing that dissociative material can be demonstrated in so many average "normal" individuals.

Given these various sensory areas (one for each side of the brain) visual writings, auditory and kinesthetic, all connected with its motor area by association we have the stage set on both sides; then why do not the two sides act synchronously? We do not definitely know how far back the inhibition of one side in preference over the other in making graphic symbols goes, but one side *generally is* inhibited. Now suppose we release this inhibition. What happens? The current is on, and the apparatus works, but how account for the facility of action in a group of muscles not accustomed to do this work? I have said that motion in like members tends to be symmetrical and that though one is inhibited the feeling of the movement is imagined for the other side and therefore tends to set up a certain pathway of reaction kept quiescent by inhibition.

Sherrington says, "The most striking thing that we know of inhibition is that it *is* a phenomenon in which an agent such as in other cases excites or increases an action going on in this case stops or diminishes an action going on. Now, the activity of a tissue can be lowered or abolished by production in it of deleterious changes such as exhaustion or in the highest degree, death. But there is no evidence that inhibition of a tissue is ever accompanied by the slightest damage to the tissue; on the contrary it seems to predispose the tissue to a greater functional activity thereafter." [3]

If inhibition predisposes to a greater functional activity, then if the inhibition is removed, and coincidentally there is diminution of the control of impulse, what is to prevent this neuromuscular apparatus which has an imaginary knowledge of how it feels to write from practically demonstrating its ability? This would explain writing the same thing as the other hand; but would it explain the writing of dissimilar things with both hands? If we take into consideration the physical basis for dissociation which I mentioned

[3] Charles S. Sherrington, *The Integrative Action of the Nervous System,* 194 (Yale, 1911).

before, I believe it could; it would simply indicate a more complex type of splitting.

There is another phenomenon exhibited by one of my patients for which I should like to find the counterpart of the psychological explanation in the physical, and that is the little trick practiced by this young woman of writing forward normally on one line, dipping down at the right margin and writing mirror-wise on the next line, again dipping down at the left margin and writing forward, etc., without ever taking her pencil from the page. The explanation may be very complex, or it may be one of simple convenience, as a very charming young woman I met recently suggested. She said she had often drafted letters after going to bed and as it was perfectly dark and she couldn't see, it would be much easier when she felt she was coming to the end of a page to dip down and write backward to the opposite margin than it would be to take her hand up and locate the correct spacing at the opposite edge.

However, there is another possible explanation. Stern indicates that perception of position is an outgrowth of experience through association of determined visual impressions with certain movements of the body and that the child generally produces and interprets with ease given forms in any position because fusion of form and position has not taken place. Janet says reversal of position in the visualization of a situation could account for certain illusions of orientation, and Downey tells of a natural right-handed mirror writer who memorized a printed page and in reciting it orally read from a reversed memory visual image.

Case number two of this series, who so dearly loved to write every other line mirror-wise, used mirror imagery as a child in play activities, and it is probably this practice of recklessly juggling spatial perception which gave her the ability to reverse images as she automatically wished; and this, plus the convenience of not taking her pencil from the paper, caused her to adopt the particular mode of writing in which she indulged.

In looking over my numerous records and observing the graphic characteristics I found that by attempting to interpret the script in itself according to the tables in Downey's book on graphology and then comparing the results with my analytical material that there was a remarkable coincidence of findings in determining the emotional state for the period of the unconscious revealed through the writing. This does not mean that graphology will or can replace analysis but it does mean that an open minded individual wishing to use every means available to help the patient, can interpret automatic graphic characteristics in such a way as to obtain valuable clues to unconscious reaction patterns.

Summing up the physical characteristics then, we may suggest (1) that in automatic writing in which the subject does not see the page the kinesthetic and auditory stimuli (from the record pencil) set up a train of associations which react with the corresponding visual image and writing centers to produce material from the automatic zone; (2) that if the normally unused writing side does produce records it is probably due to the sudden entire release of inhibition in a completely set neuro-physiological mechanism; (3) that alternate mirror [4] and normal script may be due to the ability to reverse images, a characteristic resulting from the period where the child pays no attention to the perception of position or that it may just be an automatic reversal of the control movement of an old habit which functions in a novel way.

An Experiment in Veridicality

BORIS SIDIS, *Symptomatology, Psychognosis and Diagnosis of Psychopathic Diseases,* 240-241 (Badger, 1914)

[A subject Sidis had been testing] was again put into the hypnotic state and was suggested to see a flower. On awakening he claimed he saw a flower and smelled it in an indifferent, perfunctory fashion. The subconscious was then tested by automatic writing and the writing was to the effect that he saw it: "I see a flower." The subconscious then had also the same hallucination. A series of similar experiments was carried out with the same results. *The subconscious claimed in automatic writing that the suggested hallucination was real.*

The subject was again put into hypnosis and was given the suggestion that he would see a watch on awakening, but here I made some modification. "When you wake up you will be sure to see a watch," I said emphatically. "Look here; I want you to write what you really see and not what you do not see." When awake he saw a watch, but he immediately wrote: "I do not see anything." *Here the subconscious disclaimed the suggested hallucinations which it had claimed and insisted on before.*

Rehypnotized, he was given the suggestion that on awakening he would see three watches. He was awakened and a real silver watch

---

[4] [On Mirror Writing, *cf.* Justin Keyser Fuller, *The Psychology and Physiology of Mirror-Writing.*]

was put before him; the other two were hallucinatory. He claimed he saw all three. Meanwhile, in automatic writing he wrote: "One silver watch, real, the others golden, not real; nothing there." A series of similar experiments was made and with the same results. *The automatic writing disclaimed the hallucinations, although before, under the same conditions, it most emphatically insisted on their reality.*

The subject was put into hypnosis and a post-hypnotic suggestion was given to him that he would see his wife and child. When awake he began to smile, and when asked why he smiled he said: "I see my wife and child"; but he wrote: "I see nobody." When put again in hypnosis he still continued to smile and said: "I see my wife and child"; but he wrote (in hypnotic state): "I do not see them really; I see nothing; I see my child, but I really see nothing." "What do you mean," I asked, "by 'I see my child, but I really see nothing?'" To which he replied: "I mean that I see my child in my mind only, but *'honest'* I don't see anything."

Automatic Speech

EDMUND PARISH, *Hallucinations and Illusions,* The Contemporary Science Series, 261-265, 270-271 (Walter Scott, 1898)

The complete correspondence between automatic writing and automatic articulation will be best shown by the following parallel table [on page 432].

[This] view is not only theoretically tenable, but finds further support in medical observations on hallucinated patients. Thus Moreau [1] observed an insane patient who, when under the influence of hallucinations, moved his lips, and therefore was no doubt softly uttering the words which he heard from imaginary voices.

Michel [2] reports the remark of a patient that his auditory hallucinations—the words which forced themselves upon him—accumulated in his mouth, so that his saliva was impregnated with them. Hoppe [3] cites the case of a lunatic with persecution-mania, whose auditory hallucinations (consisting of abusive language) were accompanied by a twitching in his head, and who also declared that he perceived a gentle plucking in his mouth, and especially in the

---

[1] Moreau (de Tours), *Du Haschisch,* etc.
[2] Michel, *Gazette des hôpitaux* (1864); *vide supra,* p. 28, Note 1.
[3] Hoppe, *Erklärung der Sinnestauschungen,* p. 217.

RESULTS

In automatic action of the muscular writing-apparatus.[1]

1. Up and down strokes without recognisable meaning.

2. The hand writes the same word or sentence over and over again. (Occurrence of mirror-writing, anagrams, etc.)

3. The hand writes sentences, often long and complicated, belonging to the subliminal consciousness.

4. The hand writes what the person is consciously thinking; but the person does not consciously or intentionally influence the writing.

5. The hand writes automatically, but the conscious train of thought on the part of the subject influences the character of the communication.

In automatic action of the vocal organs.[2]

1. Inarticulate sounds without recognisable meaning; when vigorously uttered, objectively perceptible as *vociferation,* or ecstatic "speaking with tongues"; when the utterance is feeble, subjective perception of "confused noise,"—"many voices talking at the same time."

2. Subjective perception: The same word or sentence heard over and over again, *e.g., "Onkel August," "hepp, hepp,"* "Do not eat," "Kill your child," or strange words, as, *"Lolch-graf,"* etc.

3. Subjective perception: Hearing of strange voices: "Thoughts are made for me." (This case sometimes develops out of the former).[3] Objective perception: somnambulistic prophecy.

4. Subjective perception: Audible thinking, double thinking. Objective perception: attacks of chattering; Friedreich's coördinated memory-spasms.

5. The patient is able to direct the voices at pleasure.

---

[1] *Cf.* the series of articles by F. W. H. Myers in *Proc. S. P. R.*

[2] Compare *"A Case of Psychic Automatism,* including *Speaking with Tongues,* by Albert Le Baron, communicated by William James, *Proc. S. P. R.,* Vol. xii., pp. 277 *et seq.*

[3] Ball, *Maladies mentales,* p. 67. Also the hallucinatory "running commentary" on conscious thoughts mentioned, *e.g.,* by Ziehen, *Psychiatrie.*

epiglottic region. With this may be compared Hoppe's observations on himself : [1]

"I was suffering from a slight inflammation of the left ear, and was lying in bed, on my left side, prepared to go to sleep. In consequence of the pressure and the pulsation I heard the secretion in the left ear moving with a slight crepitation. It occurred to me to imitate this noise articulately; I therefore gave the necessary impulse to the articulatory muscles and very soon my imitative articulatory motions were produced with extreme rapidity, while I heard them in my ear, and *felt them in my mouth."* . . .

According to Séglas,[2] a patient said, "When I think, I cannot help speaking, or I should choke. Even if I do not speak aloud, if you watch carefully you can always see my lips moving; but this is still more the case when I hear voices out of my belly." Further material in abundance is to be found among the cases discussed in the article of Klinke's already cited.[3] In one patient frequent movements of the lips were noticed, as though he were talking to himself; another denied that he was forced to repeat what he heard, but felt his tongue becoming heavy, etc. . . .

Not satisfied with all these arguments, I have tried experiments in order to produce automatic articulation. From the series of experiments, which (so far as any automatic articulation took place at all) for the most part yielded positive results, the following example may be given.

A. having been hypnotised, these directions were given him (carefully written out beforehand, so as to avoid any unintentional suggestions connected with *hearing*) :—"You are aware that no thinking is possible, except in words. When I wake you, after a time, you will articulate all your thoughts very forcibly. You will only do this until I give you an order to the contrary. You will articulate all your thoughts very forcibly, but you will not notice that you do so; you will not be conscious of moving your epiglottis, your tongue," etc. I expected speech as a result of this suggestion. This did not take place. On the contrary, after A. had been awakened, he assumed, almost immediately, a *listening* attitude. *His expression showed intense expectation; his look was directed sideways.* After a considerable pause, he remarked spontaneously, "Tell me,

---

[1] *Op. cit.*, p. 229.

[2] "L'hallucination dans ses rapports avec la function du langage; les hallucinations psychomotrices," *Progrès médical*, 16e année 2, série viii., Nos. 33, 34.

[3] [Klinke, "Ueber das Symptom des Gedankenlautwerdens," *Arch f. Psych.*, xxvi.]

do you think there is any one in the room?" "Yes, you and I."
"But is there no one else?" He cast his eyes searchingly about the
room, and once more assumed a listening attitude. In order not
to suggest to him any ideas having reference to this matter, and to
leave him uninfluenced, in view of future experiments, no further
questions were put to him.

From all this, it would appear that the greater number of the
"voices," if not all, are caused (in flat contradiction to Cramer's
theory) by automatic speech on the part of the percipient. As in
all automatism, we must assume here, as in genuine hallucinations,
a dissociation, a splitting off, even in those cases where the hallucinatory perceptions form the only symptom visible to the observer.[1]

---

[1] [On Functional Motor Abnormalities, *cf.* also Morton Prince, *The Unconscious*, 87-90, 96-97, 101-103, and the Index to his *Dissociation of a Personality;* William Healy, *Mental Conflicts and Misconduct*, 17, and cases
cited in that work; and the article by Tom A. Williams, cited below (p.
731ff.), "Studies of the Genesis of the Cramp of Writers and Telegraphers."]

CHAPTER XVI

DISSOCIATION OF PERSONALITY

As already indicated, the total neural organization whose functioning constitutes an individual can be dissociated in a great variety of shapes. In many of these the dissociated elements function very independently. Sidis describes this class of phenomena as follows:

The Functioning of Dissociated Subconscious Elements

A

BORIS SIDIS, *Symptomatology, Psychognosis, and Diagnosis of Psychopathic Diseases,* 316, 317-318, 391, 394 (Badger, 1914)

One point is worth while emphasizing, and that is the fact of *recurrence,* so highly characteristic of the activity of dissociated subconscious states. . . .

This characteristic of *recurrence* is of great importance in psychopathology, as it brings the subconscious activities under one perspective view, gives an insight into their nature and mode of manifestation; and *from a biological standpoint brings them in line with the mode of action of the lower mental types, which respond to special stimuli of the external environment with the same amount and quality of sensori-motor reactions.* . . .

Another important and striking trait of the dissociated states is the *violence,* I would almost say the vehemence, with which they become manifested; they reveal an amount of energy which similar states do not possess in the normal condition, when the personal consciousness is in active relation with the external environment. The energy displayed is more than the individual is capable of putting forth under ordinary conditions of life.

The *sudden, mysterious onset* of subconscious states, foreign to the whole character of the individual, as well as the *sudden display of energies,* until now unsuspected in the person, make those states appear as mystical in the eyes of the populace and the superstitious. No wonder that the church has regarded subconscious activities as supernormal and miraculous, and either ascribed them to divine powers, or to satanic agencies, demoniacal possessions and obsessions. In our own time we have men devoting time and energy to the investigation of the supernormal nature of subconscious phenomena.

In my previous works on the subject I have discussed the energy and violence of the eruption of subconscious forces as due to *lack of inhibitions.* This follows frcm the very nature of dissociation. Dissociated subconscious systems being released from all relations with other systems and groups of mental elements, being let loose, so to say, from all associative bonds, will naturally display an amount of energy, unusual for similar systems under the normal conditions of mental association. . . .

[Any such] pathological focus underlying the total morbid symptom-complex can be proven, by various methods, to be *detached,* or as it is termed, *dissociated,* from the patient's normal mental life. In the course of time, if it persists and keeps on growing and proliferating, it may become organized into a parasitic cancerous growth, sapping the vital energies of the normal personality.

This *parasitism* is well brought out in the attitude of the patient, especially in psychoneurosis, towards those morbid manifestations. He regards the whole symptom-complex as foreign to his personality. "When the attack is on," one patient tells me, "I am conscious of everything, and still I have no control." "Something has happened," says another patient, "over which I have no control." "What a fool I am to be troubled by such nonsense; but I cannot help it when it comes." . . .

During the predominance of the recurrent states, the *sense of reality* is affected, since the subconscious or dissociated mental states come with an almost uncontrollable insistency and intensity of the sense of their reality. This is especially true of the highly developed and fully systematized *complex recurrent mental states.* This affection of the sense of reality is still more enhanced by the suddenness and violence of the subconscious eruption.

This topic, the Functioning of Dissociated Subconscious Elements, really includes all the phenomena of "lapses," functional obsessions, and automatic writing, also much that comes under the topic of dreams, and many anomalies of emotion, perception, thought, and action. Many of these, with their mechanisms, are treated elsewhere in the present volume. Their most effective presentation is to be found in the pages of Dr. Morton Prince's work, *The Unconscious*. They constitute a class of important phenomena, fortunately, that can be produced artificially and studied very conveniently in the classroom, as Professor Wesley Raymond Wells has made clear recently.[1]

---

[1] "Hypnosis is often used for class demonstration and experimental purposes in courses in abnormal psychology. So many specific aspects of abnormal psychology may be quickly and concretely illustrated by means of hypnosis that a course would be very incomplete without actual experiments. In fact, it is historically correct to say that scientific abnormal psychology had its origin in experiments in hypnosis, for hypnosis makes possible the production under controlled laboratory conditions of abnormal mental processes such as occur in hallucinations, functional blindness, deafness, and paralysis, cutaneous anæsthesia and hyperæsthesia, and a host of other symptoms of the psychoneuroses. Especially significant in this connection is the work of Liébeault, Bernheim, and Charcot. The extent to which hypnotic phenomena may be profitably drawn upon in abnormal psychology is well illustrated by the contents of one of the best general introductory text-books in this field, Dr. Morton Prince's *The Unconscious*. In a course which I give, with *The Unconscious* as the chief text, I illustrate many of the points made by Dr. Prince by means of experiments not only in hypnosis but also in automatic writing and crystal gazing with profit, I am sure, to the class. Books intended for classroom use in certain fields of applied psychology also, sometimes make use of data regarding hypnosis. President Scott's *Influencing Men in Business* is a good example of this, and to a less degree, his *Psychology of Advertising*. The importance of suggestion in advertising, salesmanship, public speaking, and indeed in all fields in which the aim is to influence in any way whatsoever behavior and opinion, can be taught in no better way than through reference to hypnosis, in which suggestion operates in its most extreme degree. It is not often, however, so far as my own observation has extended, that actual experiments in hypnosis are performed in courses other than those in abnormal psychology.

"There would seem to be many obvious advantages that might be gained through an extension of the practice of hypnosis by instructors not only in courses in applied psychology, but even in introductory courses in general psychology. First among these advantages would be that of the increased interest which would be aroused among the students in the class. . . .

"A second advantage to be gained through including experiments in hypnosis in introductory courses in psychology would be the aid thereby given in proper instruction against spiritism and occultism in its various forms. . . . To produce contractures and anæsthesia in a subject by suggestion, and then to teach the subject to produce the same contractures and anæsthesia by autosuggestion, is an excellent way of disabusing the popular mind or a class of students of the superstition that hypnosis involves in some way the direct domination of one will by another. Moreover, in terms of certain processes which hypnosis may be used to illus-

In *The Unconscious,* also, Dr. Prince treats of many phenomena of the more generally dissociated conditions. An important type of such conditions is described in the following selection from Professor Jastrow:

---

trate, an explanation of some aspects of the work of mediums can be made without any need of reference to occult explanations.

"More important, however, than the above two general uses of hypnosis for educational purposes is a third and more specific use, namely, that of teaching more adequately and illustrating more clearly many common psychological facts. For example, the meaning of hallucinations can be illustrated quickly and forcibly by hypnosis. . . . Specific use may be made of deep hypnosis in the general psychology class as an aid to instruction regarding sleep and the dream consciousness. The denial of dreamless sleep in those cases where there is no memory for dreams upon awakening may be shown to be possible in view of the complete amnesia that may follow a hypnotic trance crammed with vivid experiences. The solving of problems during sleep may be illustrated by hypnosis. Instructional use of hypnosis may be made in the discussion of one very important aspect of human motivation, namely, subconscious motivation, which can be illustrated briefly and strikingly through post-hypnotic suggestion. Post-hypnotic suggestion more than anything else, perhaps, except automatic writing, illustrates the nature of dissociation and of subconscious processes. . . .

"If some of these subjects are now outside the field of general psychology as usually taught, this fact alone might suggest one reason why courses in general psychology are often unsatisfactory and unattractive to students. Such topics are among the most fundamental in the understanding of normal human behavior and consciousness. Especially in courses in general psychology that run through the whole college year there could easily be found a place for these subjects, and for the illustration of them through hypnosis. A present-day trend in the direction of broadening the scope of courses in general psychology is illustrated by a text-book recently published, Dr. C. R. Griffith's *General Introduction to Psychology* (published by Macmillan, 1923). This book contains one chapter on 'Hypnosis and the Subconscious,' and another on 'Psychology and Medicine,' which includes a further discussion of hypnosis. And Dr. B. C. Ewer's *Applied Psychology* (published by Macmillan, 1923) illustrates a tendency to include in applied psychology more material of the sort which may be illustrated by hypnosis. In this book of less than 500 pages, practically 50 pages are devoted to the two chapters on 'Subconsciousness' and 'Suggestion,' and five chapters (more than 100 pages) deal with 'Mind and Health.'"—WESLEY RAYMOND WELLS, "Hypnosis in the Service of the Instructor," *Psychol. Rev.,* 31: 88-91, 1924. [See also Professor Wells' discussion of "Experiments in Waking Hypnosis," included in the present volume, p. 531*ff., infra.*]

Phenomena of Somnambulism

JOSEPH JASTROW, *The Subconscious*, 267-271 (Houghton Mifflin, 1906);
used by permission of and by special arrangement with the publishers

As a modification or accident of sleep, somnambulism presents
an altered disposition of brain-functioning, whereby a part of the
mental machinery is set into action without arousing the rest.
The mental condition of the somnambulist is an interesting one,
and not so much for what it leads him to do, as for his attitude
and sensibilities while thus occupied. He is manifestly not wholly
awake; his senses respond to a peculiarly circumscribed range of
stimuli, and his actions make no report to that phase of consciousness upon which his waking memory depends.   Unmistakable cir-
cumstantial proof falls short of completely convincing him that it
was he who performed in sleep the versatile achievements that the
normal memory so completely repudiates, for the very reason that
the sleep-acting self is not the self—not the complete self—that con-
ducts the introspective inquiry.

The objective evidence is fortunately quite definite. There is
in the older literature the record of a sleep-walker whose inquiring
friends tested his powers while engaged in his nocturnal excursions.
With a restricted type of awareness, he saw and felt and recognized
familiar objects, and behaved toward them in routine, partly intelligent fashion. If a pipe were placed in his hands, the somnambulist
handled it correctly, but could not light it; if it were lighted for
him, the pipe went out because he did not inhale properly. He
could be induced to sit at a table and to go through the actual
movements of writing. If given a book, he turned its pages, resting
his gaze on each page, but without reading; and he continued in
this automatic mimicry if the light were withdrawn. When forcibly aroused, he was shocked to find himself out of bed and in the
presence of his friends. Had he awakened of his own accord, he
might, with equal suddenness, have come to himself and without
memory of his immediate occupation.

Dr. Hammond found similar opportunity to observe a confirmed
somnambulist,—a young woman,—who arose, dressed, walked slowly
and deliberately, with eyes open in a fixed stare, found her way from
her bedroom to the parlor below, and there scratched a match
(which she had brought with her) against the under side of the
mantel-shelf. waited until it caught fire, turned on and lighted the
gas, and flung herself into a chair, gazing with rapt absorption at

a portrait of her mother that hung above the mantel. Her eyes did not wink when threatened, not even when the cornea was touched. When a book was placed between them and the portrait, she took no notice of the obstacle. A burning sulphur match held under her nose aroused no response; and a bit of bread saturated with quinine, that was forced into her mouth (and which presently she chewed and swallowed), failed equally to arouse any reaction. Upon her own initiative she arose and paced the room, sobbing and weeping violently. While thus excited she was led back to her chair, to which procedure she offered no resistance, and again became composed. Banging two books together, pulling her hair, pinching her face, tickling the sole of her foot,—the last followed by laughter and a withdrawal of the foot,—failed to awaken her. When at length awakened by violent shaking, she was startled to realize her situation, and had no recollection either of her actions or of any dream that may have aroused them.

Observations of this general import have been sufficiently verified to establish that the somnambulist is suggestible; that to some extent an appeal to his senses arouses appropriate response; that he, in part, appreciates the felt and seen positions and nature of things; and that his reactions, though automatic, reflect a simply intelligent yet limited adaptation to routine situations. They show further that spontaneously he takes cognizance only of that particular area of sensations and movements that fits in with his self-imposed quest. The somnambulist, bent upon finding a lost object, avoids obstacles, manipulates latches and locks and keys and doors and drawers, finds the proper material in the kitchen for washing dishes or baking a pie, but is insensitive to the happenings about him, does not hear or see the person who, with lighted candle, is approaching to awaken him, and is likely to stumble against any unfamiliar object, and unintelligently to fumble about the knob of the door that, without his knowledge, has been locked to prevent his escape. Thus thwarted in his purpose, he may wander back to bed without awakening; yet a sufficiently violent stimulus breaks through the narrow circle of his contracted perceptions, and brings him to normal wakefulness. Many a somnambulist who is aware of his failing, and who has found it unavailing to lock the door and to hide the key (the nocturnal consciousness being quite equal both to securing the key and to opening the door), has resorted to the expedient of dropping the key into a basin of cold water, relying upon the shock, when the sleeper's hands were plunged into the water, to awaken him. This group of possibilities and limitations of mental behavior sufficiently establishes the close affiliation of natural somnambulism to other conditions, and especially to hypnosis, and indicates that what they have distinctively in common is the general type of mental disintegration that permits the spontaneous or suggested episode to be enacted without sanction or knowledge of the normally directing stage-manager. . . .

There may be cited the adventure of a lady who had walked in her sleep upon the roof of a church. Her husband found that when in a natural sleep, she would, without awakening, answer queries whispered in her ear; and by this means he obtained from the sleeper some account of the nocturnal excursion, including the confession that in her wanderings she had injured her foot by stepping on a nail. Upon awakening she was again questioned in regard to her foot, acknowledged that it pained her, but could not account for the injury. There are also authoritative records in accord with the common belief that somnambulists, who in sleep have hidden objects of value and who were quite unable in their waking condition to find them, have, in a succeeding night-walking, gone directly to the place of concealment. By a distinctive type of registry the night-staff of the brain thus keeps account of its own doings, though without reporting to the consciousness in charge of its daylight operations.

It was these familiar characteristics of natural somnambulism that a century ago suggested the name of "artificial somnambulism" for an analogous condition induced by a trance-like lapse from the normal waking state. This condition and its subordinate varieties we now know under the term hypnotism, or the state of hypnosis.

Phenomena of Multiple Personality

MORTON PRINCE, "Miss Beauchamp—The Theory of the Psychogenesis of Multiple Personality," *Jour. Abn. Psychol.*, 15: 130-133 (1920)

The phenomena of hypnotism, as already suggested, cast a great deal of light on the various types of dissociated behavior. These hypnotic phenomena will receive special treatment in the chapter on Hypnotic Conditions. Another and most important source of understanding of many of these processes is provided by Dr. Prince's work, *The Dissociation of a Personality*, in which he shows clearly the variety of occurrences that result from conflict between large systems organized as personalities. It is especially illuminating to note there the many phenomena thrown into the dominant consciousness without this consciousness understanding these phenomena. As Dr. Prince says:

In the pages of the study of Miss Beauchamp already published [1] will be found numerous examples of subconscious conflicts of this kind. The resulting phenomena by which they have been revealed have been aboulia, hallucinations, inhibitions, and abolition of consciousness, emotion, mistakes and falsifications of speech, writing, visual perceptions and hearing, amnesia, motor acts, etc.

When the subconscious elements become constellated into a personal self, possessing a self-consciousness, and the faculties of willing, wishing and expressing itself in muscular acts, as is sometimes the case in dissociated personalities (e. g., Miss Beauchamp, C. N., M. R., and B. C. A.), the subconscious factors become more complex and the phenomena of resistance and conflict become multiform and take on a more volitional, purposive, and intellectual character. The principle, however, is the same. There is a conflict between the personal consciousness and a subconscious complex. The fact that the subconscious complex belongs to a highly constellated subconscious system, capable of independent thinking, willing, and action, and of intending the consequences of a conflict with the principal consciousness, gives a more purposive and often more elaborate character to the resulting phenomena. For this reason they often have a dramatic aspect which withdraws attention from the psychological mechanism underlying them. In principle these phenomena produced by a constellated subconscious self, do not differ from those produced by simpler subconscious complexes in less complicated pathological conditions and everyday life. Cases of multiple personality are often, therefore, peculiarly fitted for experimental investigation of the influence of subconscious complexes upon the personal consciousness, as we are able in these cases by technical procedures to discover and identify the precise subconscious processes (motives, volitions, etc.) which have determined the disturbances of the personal self. I will recall here, as a few instances, the following observations in the case of Miss Beauchamp:

First, the occasions when in consequence of a suggestion to the hypnotized personality meeting resistance from the subconscious self there resulted an inhibition or blocking of thought.[2]

Second, the occasions when a similar resistance resulted in false

---

[1] *The Dissociation of a Personality.*
[2] Prince, *op. cit.*, 275, 306, 457.

hearing, *e. g.,* the words "badly" and "B I" being heard as "beautifully" and "B IV" respectively;[3] or in word deafness.[4]

Third, the occasions when the hypnotized personality became dumb under similar conditions.[5]

Fourth, the occasions when the subconscious personality spoke automatically[6] in opposition to a suggested idea are examples of the same kind of resistance and reaction to a suggested idea, although the expression of the reaction in the form of volitional speech involves more complicated processes.

Fifth, falsifications of writing were frequently observed in Miss Beauchamp's letters, produced by purposive interference by the subconscious self. One of the more elaborate of these was a letter in which the letters of every word were misplaced.[7] The fact that this letter is a product of intelligent subconscious thought does not in any way controvert the principle.

Sixth, negative and positive hallucinations and auditory hallucinations were very common.[8] One of the most elaborate of these was an hallucinatory letter which the subject read on a blank sheet of paper.[9]

Seventh, aboulia,[10] falsification of vision[11] and purposive motor acts.[12]

Eighth, displacement and substitution were common phenomena.

Many of these, and other phenomena, could be shown to be due to the volitional action of an integrated subconscious self upon the personal consciousness. The former was constantly in conflict with the latter and expressed this conflict in such purposive phenomena. On the other hand some of the most marked examples of these conflicts were seen in the resistance to suggestions which were met with, not from a subconscious self (Sally), but from ideas which had belonged to the consciousness of the personality B IV, and conserved as dispositions in the unconscious. These resistances offered some of the greatest obstacles to the reconstruction of the dissociated personality and the cure of the case. Thus, even when B IV desired to be hypnotized for therapeutic purposes, the previous auto-suggestion which she had given herself, to the effect that no suggestions should affect her, came at once into conflict with my therapeutic suggestions and counteracted them. Owing to this antagonism at

---

[3] *Ibid.*, 321, 416, 497.
[4] *Ibid.*, 457.
[5] *Ibid.*, 275, 537.
[6] *Ibid.*, 157, 275, 459, 501.
[7] *Ibid.*, 205.
[8] *Ibid.*, 190, 440, 483, 484, 486, 507, 210, 538, 539, 561.
[9] *Ibid.*, index and 283-5.
[10] *Ibid.*, 120, 469.
[11] *Ibid.*, 432-3.
[12] *Ibid.*, 157.

these times it was almost impossible to hypnotize her, i. e., to change the mental synthesis, and every suggestion was counteracted and inhibited.[13]

Although I have cited examples from only one case they are not unique for I have observed a large number of identical phenomena in other cases, notably B. C. A., C. N., and M. R.

The displacement in mass of a system of innate and acquired dispositions by another system by the force of its antagonistic emotional impulses, and the substitution in consciousness of the latter. A hypnotic consciousness may by such forces be replaced by the waking personal consciousness or by another hypnotic one, and vice versa; one psychopathic state may be replaced by another; the personal consciousness may be replaced by a psychopathic or disintegrated one. In such displacements and substitutions there may be and often is *amnesia* in one state for all the experiences belonging to the displaced state, as when, to take a simple illustration, one hypnotic state is replaced by another or the waking state. In more complex conditions there may be a disintegration of the normal personality of such a kind that one or more emotional instincts and sentiments and other acquired dispositions, even that of the conception of self, may be displaced and suppressed, with the substitution of their antagonists. There thus results a splitting and reintegration of the elements of personality—alteration of character. In all such instances some antagonistic but dormant sentiment is "struck" by the stimulus and awakened, and the awakening brings into being the whole system with which it is integrated. From one point of view such reactions are often, not always, defense reactions,[14] but this is not an explanation of the How, but only of the Why.

By the technique of so-called "tapping" the subconscious, (automatic writing, speech, etc.), in favorable subjects, the precise antagonistic and resisting sentiment that has been struck can be

---

[13] *Ibid.*, 447, 450.

[14] Many writers seem to be satisfied that they have reached a complete solution of a phenomenon by calling it a "defense" reaction. This may explain the motive but in no way the mechanism. Pretty nearly everything that involves resistance may, from one point of view, be called a defense against something, but the mechanisms of the behavior in defense may be widely different. From another point of view they are not defenses but the awakening of stronger impulses (desires?) for the gratification of something else. The awakening of subconscious Sally's impulses to play may be called a defense against the boredom of Miss Beauchamp's religious sentiments, but it was also the awakening of the urge of joyous emotions for their own gratifications.

reached and identified.   The whole process can then be brought to light and the Why disclosed.   Thus in such cases we are not limited to *inferring* that the phenomenon is due to the resistance of subconscious conflicting ideas, but, by this tapping of the subconscious, we can actually obtain direct evidence of and identify the specific subconscious ideas and impulses which did the resisting and caused the phenomena.

Cases of Multiple Personality

Félida X., and Léonie B.

WILLIAM JAMES, *Psychology*, 210-212 (Holt, 1892)

The phenomenon of *alternating personality* in its simplest phases seems based on lapses of memory.[1]   Any man becomes, as we say, *inconsistent* with himself if he forgets his engagements, pledges, knowledges, and habits; and it is merely a question of degree at what point we shall say that his personality is changed.   But in the pathological cases known as those of double or alternate personality the loss of memory is abrupt, and is usually preceded by a period of unconsciousness or syncope lasting a variable length of time.   In the hypnotic trance we can easily produce an alteration of the personality, either by telling the subject to forget all that has happened to him since such or such a date, in which case he becomes (it may be) a child again, or by telling him he is another altogether imaginary personage, in which case all facts about himself seem for the time being to lapse from out his mind, and he throws himself into the new character with a vivacity proportionate to the amount of histrionic imagination which he possesses.   But in the pathological cases the transformation is spontaneous.   The most famous case, perhaps, on record is that of Félida X., reported by Dr. Azam of Bordeaux.   At the age of fourteen this woman began to pass into a 'secondary' state characterized by a change in her general disposition and character, as if certain 'inhibitions,' previously existing, were suddenly removed.   During the secondary state she remembered the first state, but on emerging from it into the first state she remembered nothing of the second.   At the age of forty-four the duration of the secondary state (which was on the whole superior in quality to the original state) had gained upon the latter so much as to occupy most of her time.   During it she remem-

---

[1] [*Cf*. the instances of hysterical fugues, from Janet, *supra*, pp. 69 and 349*ff*.]

bers the events belonging to the original state, but her complete oblivion of the secondary state when the original state recurs is often very distressing to her, as, for example, when the transition takes place in a carriage on her way to a funeral, and she has no idea which one of her friends may be dead. She actually became pregnant during one of her early secondary states, and during her first state had no knowledge of how it had come to pass. Her distress at these blanks of memory is sometimes intense and once drove her to attempt suicide.

M. Pierre Janet describes a still more remarkable case as follows: "Léonie B., whose life sounds more like an improbable romance than a genuine history, has had attacks of natural somnambulism since the age of three years. She has been hypnotized constantly by all sorts of persons from the age of sixteen upwards, and she is now forty-five. Whilst her normal life developed in one way in the midst of her poor country surroundings, her second life was passed in drawing-rooms and doctors' offices, and naturally took an entirely different direction. To-day, when in her normal state, this poor peasant woman is a serious and rather sad person, calm and slow, very mild with every one, and extremely timid: to look at her one would never suspect the personage which she contains. But hardly is she put to sleep hypnotically when a metamorphosis occurs. Her face is no longer the same. She keeps her eyes closed, it is true, but the acuteness of her other senses supplies their place. She is gay, noisy, restless, sometimes insupportably so. She remains good-natured, but has acquired a singular tendency to irony and sharp jesting. Nothing is more curious than to hear her after a sitting when she has received a visit from strangers who wished to see her sleep. She gives a word-portrait of them, apes their manners, claims to know their little ridiculous aspects and passions, and for each invents a romance. To this character must be added the possession of an enormous number of recollections, whose existence she does not even suspect when awake, for her amnesia is then complete. . . . She refuses the name of Léonie and takes that of Léontine (Léonie 2) to which her first magnetizers had accustomed her. 'That good woman is not myself,' she says, 'she is too stupid!' To herself, Léontine, or Léonie 2, she attributes all the sensations and all the actions, in a word all the conscious experiences, which she has undergone *in somnambulism,* and knits them together to make the history of her already long life. To Léonie 1 [as M. Janet calls the waking woman], on the other hand, she exclusively ascribes the events lived through in waking hours. I was at first struck by an important exception to the rule, and was disposed to think that there might be something arbitrary in this partition of her recollections. In the normal state Léonie has a husband and children; but Léonie 2, the somnambulist, whilst acknowledging the children as her own, attributes the husband to 'the other.' This choice was perhaps explicable, but it followed no rule. It was not till later that I learned that her magnetizers in early days, as audacious as certain hypnotizers of recent date, had somnambulized her for her first *accouchements,* and that she had lapsed into that state spontaneously in the later ones. Léonie 2 was thus quite right in ascribing to herself the children—it was she who had had them, and the rule that her first trance-state forms a different personality was not broken. But it is the same with her second or deepest state of trance. When after the renewed passes, syncope, etc., she reaches the condition which I have called Léonie 3, she is another person still. Serious and grave, instead of being a restless child, she speaks slowly and moves but little. Again she separates herself from the waking Léonie 1. 'A good but rather stupid woman,' she says, 'and not me.' And she also separates herself from Léonie 2: 'How can you see anything of me in that crazy creature?' she says. 'Fortunately I am nothing for her.' "

Mr. Hanna

JOSEPH JASTROW, *The Subconscious,* 394-403 (Houghton Mifflin, 1906); used by permission of and by special arrangement with the publishers

The subject of the case is the Rev. Mr. Hanna.[1] The sudden change of his mental condition came upon him in full health, as the result of an accident while driving on the evening of April 15,

[1] The record will be found in the volume by Dr. Sidis and Dr. Goodhart, cited below. It is notable not only by reason of the careful investigation that was expended upon it, but as well for the success with which the pursuit of the psychological method of diagnosis and treatment led to a reintegration of the personality. The record gains in value through the coöperation of the patient, whose mental training enabled him to add an introspective account, written after complete recovery, recording his own analysis of his mental states during the disintegrated period. Abridged accounts of the several cases cited may be found as follows: in Binet: *Alterations of Personality,* the case of Felida X. (6-20); of Louis V. (25-32); of Emil X. (32-36); and of Mesnet's soldier (42-64). In Sidis and Goodhart: *Multiple Personality,* the case of Mr. Hanna (83-229); of Mesnet's soldier (310-315); the case of Mr. S. (368-373); of the tinsmith (365-368); and of Louis V. (427-434). In James's *Psychology,* the case of Mary Reynolds (1: 381-384); and of Ansel Bourne (391-393). Additional cases and original sources may be found in these references.

1887. After a period of unconsciousness during which he was carried indoors and put to bed, he opened his eyes with a dazed, inquiring expression. Owing to a misunderstanding of his condition, the attendants bound Mr. Hanna, to which proceeding he made vigorous objection. In this struggle under an exciting emotion he made good use of his strength and gave evidence of a considerable measure of motor control. As soon as a careful investigation of his condition was possible, it was determined that he had apparently lost the complete range of his knowledge and acquisitions, not only of his acquaintance with the simplest objects, but even with the meaning of the elementary organic sensations of his own body. His condition was described as akin to that of a new-born infant; and the stages of his relearning offered close analogies to the progress of early infancy. Though suffering from hunger, he was unable to interpret the sensation or to appreciate the method whereby to satisfy it. Food had to be forced into his mouth, and only when reflexly swallowed, did he appreciate its purpose. His eyes had to learn the quality of size, and distance, and color. His ears were affected by sounds which he referred to the vocal apparatus of the speaker, and which he proceeded to imitate, but of the existence of speech, or of its meaning, he was entirely ignorant. He seemed equally to have to discover the power which he exercised over his own muscles, so as to distinguish between his own movements and those of other persons. Naturally, his interpretations were crude and often erroneous. The difference between men and women and children, between his family and strangers, had all to be learned anew. His surroundings were utilized in the manner of the simplest object lessons, to teach him the rudimentary nature and uses of what a one-year-old child has already acquired in considerable measure. Thus, when looking at a distant tree through a window, he attempted to grasp the tree and knew nothing of the nature of the object that attracted him. He mistook a piece of soap for food and tried to eat it. Upon his first sight of a man riding a bicycle, he regarded the combined object as a new variety of man. With the first learning of words, his mind acquired the material necessary to its elaboration, and developed with such remarkable rapidity as to bring complete conviction that the reacquisition was proceeding upon the basis of the benumbed but not destroyed facilities of his normal self. He rarely forgot anything thus reacquired; and in a few weeks was able to read and write, though slowly and with effort, and to use a considerable vocabulary, though with occasional gaps and circumlocutions to eke out his enfeebled phraseology. . . .

The method pursued to restore Mr. Hanna to his original condition was to overwhelm him with a great mass of impressions, presumably familiar to his early life, to bombard his senses with experiences that might arouse the latent vestiges of his buried self, and thus gradually to bring back by vigorous subconscious stimulation what his conscious effort could not command. It may be anticipated that the stages by which this result was accomplished proved to be, first, a spontaneous but brief recurrence of the original condition, followed by a lapse back to the impaired state; then more frequent and longer maintained reversions to the normal; finally, conflict between the two states and their fusion. For a time the two conditions remained independent, neither knowing aught of the other, and with the subject at the mercy of wholly unexpected alternations. By special effort and with the assistance of certain promptings, the two states were then brought in a measure face to face, so that it became proper to speak of this newer, more complete condition as a period of contest, in which the individual was called upon either to choose between the two, or, if that might be, to accept both as portions of a single life, to fit them together with such measure of gap as was inevitable, and thus reconciled, to continue the normal life.

The first step in this consummation was taken in early June, when Mr. Hanna went with his brother and his physicians to New York city. His first evening there (June 8) was spent at a popular restaurant, amid bright surroundings and cheerful talk, all of which bewildered the new Mr. Hanna, who naturally had met with no experiences of this nature. Awakening from a few hours of sleep, not easily procured after so exciting an evening, Mr. Hanna called his brother at three in the morning, wanted to know where he was, and upon being told that he was in New York, persisted in knowing why he was there. His brother returned question with question, and so ascertained that Mr. Hanna was awakening from the period of the drive of April 15. He related what he did on that evening up to the point of the accident; he even recalled a humorous ode that one of the family had written on that day. He remembered his college life, but became impatient of all this questioning, and persisted in knowing why he was in New York. His brother, wishing to light the gas, asked him where he had put the matches; but as these had been bestowed by the other Mr. Hanna, the present Mr. Hanna did not know. The doctors, who at this stage entered the room, were naturally strangers to him; and he refused to believe that he had known them for weeks, thinking the whole affair a joke perpetrated by his brother. He evidently knew nothing of the intervening weeks, looked about the room in the manner of one just entering, and examined objects as though encountering them for the first time. In the midst of the conversation he suddenly exclaimed, "What a funny taste in my mouth; you have been feeding me on tobacco." (He had been induced to smoke a cigarette the evening before, a custom that the original Mr. Hanna had entirely given up.) He said that he felt hazy like Rip Van Winkle, and as if recovering from the fall of "last Thursday." The state lasted for about three quarters of an hour, whereupon Mr. Hanna fell asleep, and awoke at nine in the morning, presenting again, to the surprise of his physicians, the Mr. Hanna of the reacquired state. He knew nothing of the night's adventure after his reading at night and his placing the matches on the mantel. When the name of Rip Van Winkle was used, he did not know what it meant, but thought it might be the name of a hotel.

As already indicated, the lapses back to the primary condition occurred with greater frequency, and their occurrence was continually stimulated by the deluge of experiences from the life that was presumably familiar to the older self. He had to be told sufficient of his doings in the one condition to enable him to orientate himself with his surroundings; and the two personalities began thus to be more and more aware of their own alternation. A new condition, which was called the "complete" state, at times came on spontaneously, and seemed more like a state of arrest in which all functions were in abeyance, and in which Mr. Hanna, according to his later confessions, was busy with the puzzling perplexities of his inner life. The conflict of the two gave rise to a painful sense of loss and confusion, underlying which was the intense attempt to choose between the two personalities, or by effort of the will to combine them into one. It was six months after the original attack that Mr. Hanna's personal stability had been sufficiently restored to enable him to write his autobiography, by which the essential features of the account were verified. . . .

In conformity with our previous analyses, it will be well to give evidence of the submerged presence during the period of recovery, of the subconscious registry of the primary self. In the case of Mr. Hanna, the evidence is particularly convincing, because it appears, at least partly, in the spontaneity of dream-life. During the weeks of his reëducation, Mr. Hanna was able to describe two kinds of dreams; the one weak, difficult to recall, while the other, the "clear picture-dreams," as he called them, are vivid and detailed with unusual precision. These vivid dreams were really recollections of the forgotten life, though Mr. Hanna naturally did not recognize them as such. In one of these he described the scene as placed at a railway station. A man stood there, who, by some peculiar knowledge, he knew was named Bustler. He was tall, not stout, and had on a black coat rounded in front. The man said to Mr. Hanna, "I thank you for helping me yesterday,"—a remark interpreted to refer to his assistance at the church service. Then the man Bustler disappeared, and the dreamer saw a square house with the letters N-E-W-B-O-S-T-O-N-J-U-N-C on it. These letters, Mr. Hanna, in telling the dream, did not pronounce as words, and could attach no meaning to them. He also described in his dream a scene in which he saw a horse with long ears and a tail like a cow (a mule), and, in the background, peculiar buildings, and black mounds,—all of which were scenes from his early life in the coal district in Pennsylvania. There were still other types of intrusions from the lost experiences that presented themselves at times of deep absorption, and occasionally by chance association, all of which gave evidence that Mr. Hanna occasionally lapsed into an intermediate condition, in which some measure of intercourse of each condition with the other was momentarily, yet confusedly, possible. Such fragmentary enlightenment was in marked contrast with the sudden and complete recall of his normal experiences that occurred with the first reappearance of the old self during the night of June 8. The standard relations, both of alternation, of possible fusion, of conflict, and of casual intercourse, that have been emphasized as significant for comprehension of altered personality are peculiarly well exhibited in this instructive case; while the value thereof is enhanced by the normality and unpreparedness of the subject for any such transformation.

Patience Worth

CHARLES E. CORY, "Patience Worth," *Psychol. Rev.*, 26: 397-406 (1919); published also in Edward Stevens Robinson and Florence Richardson-Robinson, *Readings in General Psychology*, 555-563 (Univ. of Chicago Press, 1923)

In describing the case it will make for clearness if the reader will understand that Patience Worth, the writer, is a subconscious personality of Mrs. John Curran, of St. Louis. About five years ago Mrs. Curran began to write, automatically, literature of an unusual character. Since that time novels, plays, and poems have appeared. Over fifteen hundred poems have been written. Two of the novels, "The Sorry Tale" and "Hope Trueblood," have been published by Henry Holt & Co. Four additional novels are in various stages of completion. Most of this literature is conceded by critics to be of a very high order. No two of the larger works are written in the same English. They range from a very old English to one that is in nearly all respects modern. *The New York Sun* said of "Hope Trueblood": "It is a story that George Eliot might not have been ashamed to own up to." On the "Sorry Tale," *The New York Times* in reviewing it, said: "The long intimate tale is constructed with the precision and accuracy of a master hand. It is a wonderful, a beautiful, and a noble book." And from the *Boston Transcript's* review of the same book I quote: "The thoughtful reader will marvel at its beauty, its poetry, its power. The impression is that it is the work of a literary artist." Mr. Reedy, the editor of *The Mirror,* and a distinguished critic, says of it: "This is the most remarkable piece of literature I have ever read. I have no hesitation in saying that this production (I ignore any religious claim for it, and I discount that adventitious interest in the manner of its appearance) is a world literary marvel."

Mrs. Curran is a woman thirty-five years of age. Her education did not extend beyond the grammar school. Her general reading has been meager and desultory. She has not been abroad, and has traveled but little in America. She has no experience or practice in writing, and never entertained any aspiration to authorship. The one ambition of her life has been to sing. She has a good voice, and until Patience Worth "arrived," her entire energy was given to its cultivation. No one could be more surprised and mystified by what has taken place than Mrs. Curran. It should not be inferred that Mrs. Curran is an unintelligent woman. On the contrary, she is very intelligent. Her quick intuitive understanding is recognized by all who know her well. A conversation with her, however, though based upon an extended acquaintance, does not give the impression that one is in the presence of the mind that wrote "The Sorry Tale." And so foreign to her entire life do Patience Worth and her writings seem, that both she and Mr. Curran have, from the beginning, looked upon her as a disembodied spirit. Toward her they hold an attitude of awe and reverence.

Before writing, Mrs. Curran appears to have no intimation of what is coming. She shares with those present complete ignorance on this point. It may be one of several novels, poetry, or general discourse. Without delay the writing proceeds, and with a speed that frequently outstrips that of the most expert longhand writer. In the most difficult part of a novel she has written as high as five thousand words in an evening. The composition is final. A complete record has been kept of all that has been written. These records, running back to the first manifestations, afford a good outer history of the case. Aside from the literary output, the discussions and conversations fill many volumes.

A thing that gives special interest to this literature is that most of it reflects the life and manners of other times, and this it does with an intimacy that astonished the reader. They presuppose upon the part of the author, a wealth of information, a richness of contact that is normally secured only through a prolonged study. "The Sorry Tale" is a large and intricately woven novel dealing with Jewish and Roman life at the beginning of our era, involving an enormous mass of knowledge of the life and customs of that time. It is a powerful drama, full of subtle humor and seasoned wisdom. "Telka," an unpublished poem of seventy thousand words, has an English background. The language used is unlike that of her other works. It is in archaic English of different periods, and various localities. It is difficult to understand how it could be used as a medium of poetry by a modern writer. And the source of this language is a part of the general problem. "Hope Trueblood" has an English setting of the early mid-nineteenth century. "The Merry Tale" goes back to the days of the cross-bow. It is a humorous tale of rough tavern life. The language is not modern, and the general reader would find it difficult. Only a reading of the million and a half words that have been written can give an adequate idea of the great reservoir of knowledge that is accessible to this secondary personality. A careful survey of Mrs. Curran's reading from childhood leaves the problem of its source largely unsolved. What she may have heard, or rather, what may have been said in her presence, is another matter, and, obviously, a far more difficult thing to determine. But a knowledge of the interests that have dominated her life forces the conclusion that most of this material did not pass into her mind through the channel of her conscious attention. What her total environment has been, and just how that environment has been appropriated, is the question. And the problem is complicated by the fact that there have been two selves, that is, two centers of apperception drawing upon that environment. Hence no history of Mrs. Curran in terms of an ordinary biography could hope to solve the problem. Not one, but two histories must be traced. So far only one has been followed. And its value, in view of the probability that the dissociation is of long standing, is, and could be, only indirect. It only defines the problem, marking off the residue to be explained by processes which did not enter her consciousness. And there is in the material thus left, much that is significant for the study of subconscious perception and memory.

But even more significant, it seems to me, is the bearing which the case has upon the problem of subconscious reflection processes, or those that are commonly so called. It offers a new answer to the question that is of growing interest, namely: What degree of rationality may the processes of a subconscious center attain? Here there is a product showing a mentality of a very high order. It is original, creative, possessing a delicate sense of beauty, a hardy rationality, and, above all, and perhaps most surprising, a moral and spiritual elevation. Patience Worth easily meets most tests that are applied to the normal personal consciousness. In conversation she displays a quickness of insight, a readiness of repartee that enables her to hold her own in the company of the learned. Mrs. Curran is an intelligent woman, but her mind is much inferior to that of Patience Worth. In short, here is a subconscious self far outstripping in power and range the primary consciousness. This is an indisputable fact, and it is a significant one for psychology. In some way the dissociation has resulted in the formation of a self with greatly increased caliber. It has not only given it access to a much wider range of material, but it has given it a facile creative power amounting to genius. It is hard to give an adequate impression of the versatility of this mind. Intricate composition proceeds with astonishing ease. During an evening she may write alternately upon several novels, passing from one to the other without a moment's pause. And this work is accomplished without the aid of manuscripts. While writing Mrs. Curran does not have before her the finished portions of these works. A novel untouched for weeks or months will be resumed at just the point where it was broken off.

When writing, Mrs. Curran goes into no trance. In other words, the primary self is not displaced, or it would be more accurate to say that the modification that occurs does not amount to an alternation of personality. To the casual observer no change is noted. There is, however, some abstraction. This is more pronounced than it was formerly. When the writing began, it was read from the board; a *ouija* is used, in the usual manner. But years of practice have made it possible to write with only an occasional reference to the printed letters. A general movement of the hand is now sufficient to throw the letters into the consciousness of Mrs. Curran, and these are rapidly spoken as they appear. Not only do the letters appear but the entire panorama of the story seems to move before her, like pictures on a screen. Within the field of the primary consciousness there is a smaller field, and within this field the characters of the novels act their rôles and are seen as vividly as on a stage. Apparently the only effort required on the part of Mrs. Curran is that involved in passivity. With the proper abstraction she receives from the secondary self the letters and imagery. The meaning of what is written is, naturally enough, frequently not understood by her. Neither its form nor its substance is determined by her consciousness. They are apparently the creation of a self whose existence she is, for the most part, completely unaware of. And this self is no mere by-product of a more fully developed mind. Patience Worth is a personality of tremendous creative energy. And unlike most dissociated personalities she is morally sound.

Is there not here, then, material for a new answer as to what a subconscious mind is capable of doing? But one may ask, is this mind really submerged when it does this creative work? In other words, may it not all be done at the time of writing when Mrs. Curran's abstraction permits a slight emergence above the threshold? And is not this approach to the surface a condition of lucidity? A brief study of the case will eliminate that possibility. It is true that some of the poems are thought out as they are written, that is, they are improvised at the time of writing. And the actual composition of the larger works probably receives at that time its final form. But it is inconceivable that these elaborate and intricately wrought novels should not have been planned before they are so hastily written. And that they are the work of previous thought is confirmed by Patience Worth's own statement. This means that while Mrs. Curran goes about the cares of the household, the other self, unknown to her, may be deep in an English novel. The selves, to repeat, are not alternating but co-existent or co-conscious. Such coconscious phenomena are now familiar enough to psychology. That which is peculiar to this case is the quality of the mentality of the secondary self. The passage from the primary to the secondary self is not one into a twilight zone or semi-darkness. On the contrary, there is met a mind of a higher order, a mind of decidedly greater power. And of the activity of this self, aside from the slight contact while writing, Mrs. Curran has no knowledge. There is evidence, however, that the secondary consciousness includes much, or possibly all, of the field of the primary consciousness. That is, while Mrs. Curran has no knowledge of Patience Worth, the latter is probably aware, in a way, of all that the former experiences, or may at any time become so.

It is evident that the term subconscious is misleading when used to describe the source of this literature. As generally used it would imply that these works are the product of marginal or submarginal tendencies. This they are, only with reference to the other field. With reference to the self that created them, they are distinctly within the conscious. The term coconscious, as used by Prince to describe somewhat similar cases, is helpful here. At all events, and this is the significant thing, these delicate and finely rational processes, these highly elaborate compositions, are performed apparently without the aid or knowledge of Mrs. Curran. Just how these works are composed, and just what the sources for much of the material are, this report has little that is definite to give. It is chiefly interested in attesting to the above facts.

Some reflections, however, have occurred to me in reviewing the case. I accept the judgment that Patience Worth is a genius of no mean order. And, perhaps, there is in the genius of this writer a concrete illustration of what freedom a mind may achieve when released from the inhibitions that clog and check the normal consciousness. She is a dissociated self, and this dissociation has taken place in such a way as to free her from the burdens and concerns of life, from all the claims that split the will and bind the fancy. And perhaps in this fact, and all that it implies, lies the condition of her genius. The division of the self has resulted in a division of labor. To Mrs. Curran falls the care of the needs of the body, and the interests of the social life. Their reactions and distractions are hers. From all this Patience Worth is free. Between her and the entire active phase of life stands the buffer consciousness of Mrs. Curran. In aloofness and abstraction she dwells. She is beyond the reach of perturbation and confusion, and therein lies her strength. Her mind seems to possess the effortless activity, and facility of a dream, a dream without chaos. The normal consciousness is forced constantly to divide its attention between the world of idea and the world of action. The imminence of action is never far removed. Consequently its moments of abstraction or thought are brief and fitful, sustained with effort against the solicitation and lure of sense. The organism requires constant orientation. This holds the attention and divides the energy. It is well that the imagination, in normal life, is weighted and somewhat inert. Action and its world have their claims, and these are, as they should be, strong. But unless they are to some degree inhibited they tend to absorb consciousness. Fancy is crowded out or sustained with effort. Irrelevant it perishes.

But turn to this dissociated mind and the conditions have changed. The work of adjusting the organism to the environment being left to the other self, the inhibitions which perception places upon the imagination are removed. This sets free and unfettered the mind of Patience Worth. In the realm of the idea she lives, and there she sustains herself without effort. She acknowledges no tie or bond that might take her out of her dream. She is a dreamer that never awakens. And the conditions of this spell are, in a way, the condition of her genius. With her, our moments of abstraction, moments that life affords us the luxury of thought and imagination, are prolonged indefinitely. They are, in fact, a fixed condition. In other words, she lives only in a world of thought. And so far she has shown no desire to displace the other self, and alternate with her in the rôle of action. To do so would result in essential modification of her consciousness, and put her under inhibitions from which she is now free.

It is clear that we are here dealing with a mind so constructed as to open up most interesting possibilities. Structurally, the type is so novel that it is hard to imagine either its range or its limitations. Its actual behavior is instructive from every angle, whether it be from that of memory, feeling or thought. In regard to all of these, interesting modifications of normal experience are observable. It is difficult to give an adequate impression of her composition, its ease and rapidity, and no less impressive are her feats of memory, such as reproducing immediately, upon request, an early chapter of "The Sorry Tale" which had been mislaid, months having elapsed since the time of its writing.

A reference has been made to dreams. While surely very unlike dreams in most respects, there are, I believe, some points of resemblance. Some things are done that would suggest that in a mind of this type the processes have a tempo not normal, probably much accelerated. And since, as in dreams, this mind is not correlated with action its tempo may resemble more that of dreams than that of normal life. Something like this I know to be definitely affirmed in a case of alternating personalities, that is, one of the selves insists that upon taking control or possession of the body she experiences a noticeable restriction and loss of freedom in her thought. The structural changes involved in such forms of dissociation would provide the explanation for these accounts, should they prove to be statements of fact.

The point in question is one upon which all available data should be brought to bear. The idea would admit significant alterations of normal experience. Processes of mediation, normally requiring considerable time, might approximate immediacy, as seems to be the case in certain dreams, when a highly complex experience presents within itself directly its meaning. Some of the performances of Patience Worth would suggest that she may have some advantage over the normal consciousness in this regard. Such a supposition would also throw some light on her power of orientation, as illustrated in her shifting without pause from one novel to another. In doing this she changes periods of history, and passes at once into another world of feeling and action, and clothes it in a different style and language. As in dreams the appropriate mood and background follows quickly any idea, unchecked by the stability of outward circumstances. Within the mind itself, however, all seems under a nice control.

I have spoken of the rationality and sanity of this strange author. This is the impression of hundreds that have talked to her. And I believe there are few writers that get nearer to the heart of human life. But one need not concede that she is a great genius in order to see the problems involved, and their interest to psychology. I have briefly sketched what they appear to me to be. At another time I hope to make more detailed statement of the case.

One more thing should be mentioned. The assertion was just made that Patience Worth was highly rational, sane. Upon one subject, however, this mind is under an illusion. It is well known that she insists that she is the discarnate spirit of an English woman who lived in an age now long since passed. She not only insists upon it but she argues her claim at length, and with cleverness. And, to my mind, it is doubtful whether the S. P. R. has on hand better "evidence." That she is honest in this belief there is no reason to doubt. The full history of this illusion, this idea that she is a returned spirit, can be secured only by psycho-analysis. But it is worth noting that Patience Worth made her appearance after Mrs. Curran had spent many evenings with a friend, a confirmed spiritualist, with a view of getting a message from the spirit world. In the atmosphere of expectancy, of hope that a voice from the dead might be heard, she may be said to have been born, and it is more than possible that the idea became, at that time, a vital part of the dissociate self then developing. Thus in this self is found just that idea that would sever it most completely from the dominant personality of Mrs. Curran. This idea, although having, I believe, nothing to do with the real cause of the disintegration, has helped shape and mould her character. What is more she has lived in the atmosphere of the idea ever since the day of her appearance, those about her acting their part in sustaining the illusion. This chapter of the story is too large for this context, but it is an interesting one.[1]

---

[1] [Mrs. Curran's own interpretation and description of her automatic writing is given in her article, "A Nut for Psychologists" (Bibliog.). A valuable criticism of that account, with excellent examples, though per-

Miss Beauchamp

MORTON PRINCE, "Miss Beauchamp—The Theory of the Psychogenesis of Multiple Personality," *Jour. Abn. Psychol.*, 15: 67-69, 79, 82, 87 (1920). *Cf.* further *The Unconscious*, 545 *ff.*, and xiii n., for the interesting B. C. A. case

For those who have not read *The Dissociation* and to refresh the memories of those who have, a brief résumé of the chief characteristics of the different personalities (B I, B IV, and "Sally") will be necessary for an understanding of this study.[1]

Miss Beauchamp manifested three secondary personalities, B I, B IV, and "Sally." B I, known as the *"Saint,"* was characterized by extreme piety, religious scruples, and moral traits that are commonly regarded as the attributes of saintliness—meek and dependent, never feeling anger or resentment or jealousy, bearing her hard lot with almost inconceivable patience, never rude or uncharitable, never self-assertive, she might well be taken as typifying the ideals of Christian morality.

B IV was the *"woman"*: strong, resolute, self-reliant, "sudden and quick in quarrel," easily provoked to anger and pugnacity, resenting interference and obstruction to her own will, determined to have her own way in all things at all costs, intolerant of the attributes of saintliness, the antithesis of B I, she belonged to womankind and to the world. She may be called the Realist.

Sally, the *child* in character, thought, and deed—a mischievous delightful child, loving the out-door breezy life, free from all ideas of responsibility and care, and deprived of the education and acquisitions of the others—belonged to childhood to which she was in large measure a reversion.

Here are three personalities sharply differentiated in traits, health, educational acquisitions, tastes, feelings, etc., yet all derived from one and the same person and alternating with one another. . . .

One of them, however, "Sally," besides alternating with the others, had a coconscious existence, in that she persisted as a self, *i. e.,* a separate mental system possessing a differentiated self-consciousness, while each of the others was present. Thus there were two selves existing at one and the same moment, one coconscious to the other. . . .

---

haps with some questionable interpretation of "the Unconscious," is supplied by another individual who writes automatically (upon occasion), Mary Austin, in "Automatism in Writing."]

[1] [*Cf.* also the present volume, pp. 87*ff.*, *supra.*]

Coconscious activity of this kind is most frequently observed under conditions where alternations of personality are not observed. As a phenomenon it is quite common by itself. It is in cases like those of "Lucie" and Mme. B, made classical by M. Janet, and that of Mlle. Hélène Smith, an unprofessional medium, so beautifully studied by M. Flournoy, that coconscious activity can be observed in its most highly developed form. Indeed the phenomena manifested by mediums, who claim through automatic writing and speech to give expression to the thoughts of spirits and send messages from the spirit world, often present the best examples of autonomous coconscious life. . . .

In view of the large part emotional dispositions, as elements of instincts and sentiments, and the other innate dispositions play in the determination of personality it may be instructive to tabulate the emotions as present or absent in the three personalities for purposes of comparison. With this purpose in mind it will be convenient to follow, chiefly, McDougall's classification of the primary and compounded emotions and of the innate dispositions.[1] In doing so it is not necessary to commit ourselves to an entire acceptance of its correctness or of the soundness of the analyses upon which it is based. For the purpose I have in mind it makes no difference whether an affective state is primary or composite. It is not easy or always possible, of course, to determine the retention, and still more difficult the total absence, of affective dispositions in an individual. The disposition may exist but its emotional reaction may be excited only by some special situation in which the person may be placed. If a person flies into a rage in a given situation, as B IV did on numberless occasions, we know he possesses the anger reaction (and instinct), but if he does not exhibit this emotion it may be that the situation is not one that will excite the disposition in him, but it might be that another situation would do so. Still such simple everyday emotions as anger, fear, tender feeling, subjection, etc., are easily determined under prolonged observation. The difficulty is with the more complex and rarer affective states (sentiments) like awe and gratitude. Special situations peculiar to each individual are necessary to elicit these states,

---

[1] There is considerable difference of opinion as to what emotions should be regarded as primary and what affective states as compounds of these or others. The analysis of an affective state is no easy matter. It is largely one of interpretation, of the correctness of which we have no absolute test—no test by which it can be determined that all the elements have been differentiated, or even that the true elements have been discovered.

and particularly to build them up as sentiments. When, however, a person has been under continued and close observation in all sorts of situations during six years, with every opportunity to examine the content of consciousness, it is possible to determine with certainty the presence and absence of many affective states, though we may not be able to satisfy ourselves regarding others. In the following table [p. 462] when there has been any doubt as to the fact recorded a question mark has been added. When the evidence has been insufficient to form any opinion the fact has been recorded alone by a query. It should be further said that the personalities were not absolutely fixed in respect to their emotions; they had their moods as well as normal people. And, although these moods were mainly characterized by feelings of pleasantness or unpleasantness and of exaltation and depression, nevertheless in one mood an emotional reaction might be excited by a given situation while it would not be in another by the same situation. This is also true of normal people. There was, however, always, I believe some situation, as with all people, which would induce the reaction peculiar to the personality. Whatever the amiability at a given moment of B IV, for instance, she could not be trusted too far, for there was always some irritant that would arouse anger; on the other hand, in no mood could B I be excited to anger, which must be rare in normal people. Sally was the least changeable and rarely showed differences of moods.

INTELLECTUAL DEFECTS AND CHARACTERISTICS

Of the *intellectual stigmata* the dissociation of many of the educational acquisitions of Miss Beauchamp is noteworthy. In a general way it may be said that Sally had lost Miss Beauchamp's culture—the knowledge of foreign languages, shorthand, mathematics and general higher culture. This means that she did not have access to the unconscious storehouse of these conserved dispositions. Their complexes could not be switched on to those constellations which constituted her personality. It is interesting to note that when attempts were made by her—in experiments to test her intellectual faculties—to make use of this culture, for example, to make different calculations, with the synthesis of the lost knowledge she changed to Miss Beauchamp (B I). That is to say the B I constellation replaced in mass the Sally constellation. For this reason the latter objected to the experiments. The same phenomena often happened when she was forced to recall certain intense

Instincts

	Sally	B I	B IV
Primary Emotions			
Anger	Present	Absent	Present
Wonder	"	Absent ?	"
Elation (Self-assertion)	Present	"	Present
Fear	Absent	Present	"
Disgust	"	"	?
Subjection	"	"	Absent
Tender Emotion	Present	"	?

Sentiments

	Sally	B I	B IV
Compound Emotions and other affects			
Love	Present ?	Present	Present ?
Hate	Present	Absent	Present
Admiration	?	Present	?
Awe	?	?	?
Reverence	?	Present	Absent ?
Gratitude	Absent	"	Absent
Scorn	?	Absent	?
Contempt	?	"	?
Loathing	?	"	?
Fascination	?	?	?
Envy	Present	Absent	?
Reproach (self)	?	Present	?
Anxiety	Absent	Present	Present
Jealousy	Present	Absent	?
Vengeful	"	"	?
Resentment	"	"	Present
Shame	Absent	Present	Absent
Bashfulness	"	?	"
Joy	Present	Absent [1]	Present
Sorrow	"	Present	Absent ?
Pity	Absent ?	?	?
Happiness	Present	Absent ?	Present
Surprise	"	?	?

Other Innate Instincts and Tendencies

	Sally	B I	B IV
Play	Present	Absent	?
Sexual	Absent	"	Absent ?
Acquisition	Present	"	?
Sympathy	"	Present	Absent
Suggestibility	"	"	Present

---

[1] Excepting when in a special condition of ecstasy (Prince, *op. cit.*, chap. XXI). Joy and sorrow are not accepted by McDougall as true emotions.

emotional experiences.[1] The impulsive force of these emotions, which were dissociated from Sally, when thus awakened, determined the awakening of the whole B I (or B IV) constellation. . . .

I have frequently been asked what was the final outcome of this case. Did Miss Beauchamp remain well, a complete, united, normal personality? I am happy to be able to answer that question in the affirmative. In my account of the case I cautiously left the question in doubt, not knowing whether her reintegration would prove stable and withstand the stress and strain of life. But it proved durable, and Miss Beauchamp not only has remained well, but, like the traditional princess in the fairy story, soon married and "lived happily ever afterward."

Etiology of Multiple Personality

A

MORTON PRINCE, "Miss Beauchamp—The Theory of the Psychogenesis of Multiple Personality," *Jour. Abn. Psychol.*, 15: 82-85, 87-91, 96-98, 102-104, 135 (1920)

[In the Beauchamp case,] the ideas which took a dominating part in Sally's personality and stamped individuality upon her character were, as we shall see later, derived from conserved complexes which had been formed by the experiences of childhood and youth. Invested with emotions of joy and happiness and feelings of pleasure and excitement, they were the centres of sentiments. They were also to a large extent organized with the innate disposition or instinct of play. The mental systems into which they entered, and which may be summed up as play complexes, formed the settings or context which determined her point of view and perceptions. Other ideas of course belonged to her memories for, with the exception of book learning and general culture of which I have already spoken, she possessed all the memories of Miss Beauchamp and B I [2] and was aware of all their experiences. But, as has been stated, these ideas were devoid of the emotions with which they were invested as sentiments in the other personalities. In the Sally phase ideas of outdoor pastimes, sports, games, riding, hunting, skating, boating, and sailing; ideas of these and similar pleasures appealed to her imagination, and invested with complex emotions—

---

[1] *The Dissociation*, etc., 221.

[2] Excepting, also, of course, certain sensory memories.

joy, happiness, play, curiosity, interest, etc.—aroused feelings of pleasure and excitement; and tales of adventure and hair-breadth escapes; of hunting and fishing and outdoor sports, and all that excites the spirit of youth—the spirit that bubbled over within her —awakened an intense interest and emotional excitement.

It was these sorts of ideas which, invested with emotions, formed the main sentiments and, therefore, determined the character of the personality; it is also to be noted that the sentiments were those which are generally characteristic of childhood and youth, and there is evidence that they were the persistence and *recrudescence* of sentiments formed during those early years, but long since dissociated, or repressed, from the consciousness of the self-cultivated personality—Miss Beauchamp—and dormant.

It should be further noted that these ideas are those which normally are associated with the play "instinct," particularly in immature years, and in Sally this was the dominant instinct. One might almost say that everything naturally connected with this instinct awakened a response and expressed itself in impulsive tendencies. Even her fondness for and habit of teasing and mischief, much to the discomfiture of her other selves, was merely the expression of this instinct; for teasing was only a game which she, like a child, loved to play.

We may further say, from what we have been able to learn of Miss Beauchamp's early history and our knowledge of child life, that the Sally complexes were once, far back in childhood, a side to her character, just as they reappeared as a side to the character of the restored resurrected Real Self. With the restoration of the normal self, in situations which would naturally awaken the play instincts in a healthy normal person, Sally's sentiments and feelings and instincts bloomed again in Miss Beauchamp. In other words, to a large extent Sally was a *reversion* to a stage of childhood—to the complexes and reactions of that period.

But the Sally complexes we shall see reason to believe, when studying the psychogenesis of this phase, were the result of something more than a simple reversion to and reawakening of conserved dispositions deposited by the experiences of youth. There undoubtedly had been going on for years a subconscious incubation of these dispositions which had been continuously gathering into themselves new experiences, conscious and subconscious. The youthful dispositions had thus been receiving fresh accretions of formative material until they had flowered into a personality. To this we shall presently return.

It remains to mention one other class of processes which entered into the constellation that formed this phase. As I have said, Sally was a coconsciousness as well as an alternating personality. As a coconsciousness she had perceptions of her environment which never entered the awareness of the principal consciousness. In this state she saw, heard, and was generally cognizant of much that neither B I nor B IV consciously recognized. She often perceived correctly external relations which were incorrectly perceived by them. When Sally became an alternating personality this unusual and accessory knowledge was retained by her. Consequently her experiences, and her knowledge of the environment differed to a certain degree from those of the others and contributed to this extent in differentiating the personalities. Likewise a large mass of evidence goes to show that as a coconsciousness there were trains of thought and feelings that did not enter the conscious stream of the principal consciousness. This large coconscious mental life tended further, by coconscious elaboration, to build up complexes which later appeared in consciousness as memory when she was an alternating personality, and thus to further characterize and differentiate this phase. . . .

By way of summary, then, we may say that primarily Sally was made up of split-off fragments of personality repressed from the main consciousness during childhood. Secondly; she was a reversion to a stage of childhood. Thirdly; in her mental composition there was a recrudescence of sentiments of early life, long ago repressed. Fourthly; there were incorporated complexes which were the result of the subconscious incubation of dispositions deposited by the experiences of youth. Fifthly; her mental composition included independent coconscious perceptions and thoughts elaborated into complexes and systems of memory distinct from those of the other personalities.

If this be a correct summary of the facts it remains to determine, on the basis of the given data, by what genetic influences this personality was created. . . .

In pathological cases the beginning of such a system is apt to be some strongly emotional experience (memory) which had been dissociated by some psychological trauma (shock), or mental conflict, or voluntary repression. The memory of this experience is conserved in the unconscious, and from time to time, excited by some stimulus, takes on coconscious activity. In other cases, as with the development of mediums, the beginning may be some idea which has been awakened from its dormant condition in the storehouse of unconscious experiences by experimental or environmental stimuli. Whatever the origin may be, beginning in a small way as a few dissociated ideas, they may undergo a sort of subconscious incubation, rob the personal consciousness of some of its functions and possessions, and by the synthesizing effect of repeated experiences (hysterical attacks, experimentation, so-called séances, etc.) develop into a large egoistic system capable of thought, feeling, and volition.

Such a subconscious system commonly gives expression to its ideas through automatic writing (or mechanical contrivances like the Ouija Board) and speech, or, particularly in hystericals, through other forms of automatic motor phenomena of one kind or another. The system is then entirely coconscious. But it may be made experimentally to replace the primary consciousness which then temporarily becomes extinguished and dormant. When this happens the previously coconscious system becomes an alternating consciousness or self. The method by which this is accomplished is that of external suggestion (hypnotism) or, what in principle is the same thing, that of the subject going voluntarily into the trance state (autosuggestion) as with mediums. In either case the personal consciousness becomes dormant and the coconscious system comes into being and replaces it. The subject will now be found to be in either one or two states: either in the trance state, which is a lethargic condition in which the previously coconscious system continues to express itself by writing or speech, having only control of the hand or tongue, the remainder of the body being in a paralytic condition, corresponding to the dormant personal consciousness, or in the somnambulic state.

In the former state the consciousness present seems to casual observation to be still coconscious because it still makes use of the same methods of expressing itself as it did before the personal consciousness became dormant. As a matter of fact, however, it will be found that the personal consciousness has become dissociated and that there is only one consciousness in existence, namely, that which was previously coconscious. This has, therefore, become an alternating consciousness.

In the somnambulic state, the previously coconscious system becomes enlarged, taking on some of the functions, which it had not previously possessed, of the personal consciousness (e. g. general and complete muscular control of the body). The somnambulist is then capable of an independent mental and physical life comparable in every way to that of the personal self. This state is commonly spoken of as a secondary self or personality. In other words through the induction of dissociation a previously existing coconscious system [1] replaces the personal consciousness and becomes an

---

[1] Of course other dissociated states may be induced in the same individual.

alternating system. After the alternating phase has become once established and has built up independent experiences of its own, the change from the normal to the secondary phase is readily evoked. There are, of course, other ways by which alternating systems are developed (e. g. B I and B IV) ; [1] I am only describing the way in which a coconscious system may become alternating. It was in this way, as I interpret the evidence, that Sally became an alternating somnambulistic personality.

But how did the coconscious system originate, and how did it come to develop? This is the problem with which we are concerned.

We have already seen that as an alternating personality this phase was a secondary system of mental processes, the centre of the system being certain complexes, instincts, and innate tendencies which once had belonged to the principal system but which at some early time had been dissociated and conserved as dispositions. The recrudescence of these dispositions formed the nucleus of a secondary system which at first, as we shall see, was solely coconscious. It remains to discover the forces which determined the primitive dissociation and to trace the growth of the subconscious system. We shall find, I believe, according to the evidence at hand, that as the result of conflicts within the consciousness of the child, ideas at an early date in childhood were split off and segregated as coconscious ideas. Later they received constant increments from the same source from which they derived their own origin. Thus subconscious complexes began to be formed which later became organized into a system. This subconscious secondary system then began to have experiences of its own, in the form of thoughts and perceptions, distinct from those of the primary system, and thus became in time enlarged into a self. The final and accidental emergence in hypnosis of the complete secondary personality was only the awakening by the force of conflict of an already preformed submerged conscious system under favoring conditions. These were a personal consciousness dissociated first by trauma and then further artificially by hypnosis and made dormant. Substantially the same sort of series of psychological events and the same sort of history I have obtained in another case, that of Maria.[2]

The source from which we are obliged to draw for information

---

[1] An alternating system originating by dissociation of the personal consciousness may later become coconscious, as was the fact with B (B. C. A.).

[2] This case has been interestingly studied and reported by Mr. C. E. Cory ("A Divided Self," *Jour. Abn. Psychol.*, Vol. XIV, No. 5), through whose kindness I have been able also to study it from the point of view of this problem.

bearing on the origin and development of a subconscious personality are necessarily subconscious memories. Fortunately we have a fairly full account of these in "the autobiography of a subconscious self" by Sally.[1]

According to the memory of the coconscious personality the beginning of doubling of consciousness dates back to the time when the child was learning to walk. "Learning to walk," she writes, "was the first experience of separate thoughts. I remember before this there wasn't anything but myself, only one person." "It was at this time, too, that I was conscious, not exactly of being a different person, but of being stronger in purpose, more direct and unswerving than I appeared, and of being in a certain sense *opposed* to myself. This feeling was much stronger at times than at others. Why, I do not know. Then first began my *impatience* with C., who instead of attending to whatever she might be doing would suffer herself to be distracted by a thousand and one things. For instance in walking, just as I would get interested and eager to go on, down she would flop in a heap to study her shoes, to gaze at the people in the room, or to play with some treasure she had discovered on the floor [curiosity instinct]. *Then* I was conscious both of the child on the surface, so easily affected and diverted, and of the other child who was years and years older (I insists I was older) and stronger."

Sally, when cross-examined about these statements regarding the date of the beginning of double consciousness, and asked for specific instances, made the following additional statement:

"She was just a very little girl just learning to walk, and kept taking hold of chairs and wanting to go ahead. She didn't go ahead, but was all shaking in her feet [fear instinct]. I remember her thoughts distinctly as separate from mine. Now they are long thoughts that go round and round, but then they were little dashes.

---

[1] *The Dissociation*, Chap. XXIII. At first disposed to accept with considerable reserve these subconscious memories, the wider my experience with such phenomena, and the more intensive my studies in other cases, the more credence I am disposed to give to them. To-day I am satisfied that this subconscious account is substantially correct in essentials, so far as it goes. The hypermnesia exhibited by subconscious processes is truly remarkable and if evoked under stringent conditions which will exclude artifacts is reliable, as has often been demonstrated. This hypermnesia must of course be distinguished from fantasies and fabrications. It is noteworthy that some of Sally's statements of the forces at work in producing dissociation accord with present day conceptions although she could not possibly have foreseen and therefore have had even an inkling of these psychological theories.

Our thoughts then went along the same lines because we had the same experiences. Now they are different; our interests are different. Then she was interested in walking, and I was too, only I was very much more interested, more excited, wildly enthusiastic. [Instincts of play and self-assertion with emotions of joy and elation.] I remember thinking distinctly differently from her; that is, when she tried to walk she would be distracted by a chair or a person or a picture or anything, but I wanted only to walk. This happened lots of times." . . .

As the child grew older and became occupied with the moral problems of her unhappy life—serious problems for a neurotic, sensitive, visionary child brought up in an unsympathetic atmosphere —she withdrew more and more within herself and gave herself up to introspection, self-criticism, and day-dreaming. Now two consequences followed. The one was the formation of a fixed idea—complex building—which ruled her life and appeared later as the dominating idea in B I; the other was the widening and deepening of the rift between conscious systems of thought to which different and antagonistic instincts were linked. By this rifting the coconscious system became still further developed and separated from the personal consciousness.

The fixed idea was the "saintly complex"; visionary that she was, "she believed that God wanted her to save her mother from some dreadful fate, and that in order to do this she must, before the day should come, have attained a certain ideal state mentally, morally, and spiritually. Everything that came up was tested in its relation to this; she was always fretting about it, always dissatisfied with herself, and fancying that she fell short (as she did)." This impossible ideal haunted her day and night—there was no escaping it. She fancied her mother's illness (the autobiography goes on to state) "had all come because of her; that she had fallen short of God's requirements. She tormented herself, and *me* [1] too, night and day with going over, and over, and over, everything that had happened since she was born, thinking this, that, and the other,— that she had not been earnest enough, that she had not loved mamma as deeply as she should, that she had been dreaming away her life instead of acting. It was all rubbish. She had never done anything then." In other words she sought spiritual perfection, not as an end but as a means of obtaining something else. This means the *repression* of all other sides to her character, the human sides with their instincts of anger and self-assertion, as well as the play in-

---

[1] Note the conflict.

stincts with the joy of youthful pleasures. One effect of this repression was to produce the B I and B IV systems. This is another problem which will be considered in the study of those systems.

Another effect of repression was to push into the coconscious certain ideas which were unacceptable and incompatible with the saintly complex, but which were compatible with the already existing coconscious complex. Some of these ideas consequently became synthesized with this complex which thus became still further enlarged. "Ruled by one idea" the personal consciousness continued "steadfast and unswerving," striving for one end and seeing and interpreting the world about her through this idea. All other points of view and interpretations were disregarded. Persons, scenes, incidents were perceived and interpreted through this idea; "seeing things," as the autobiography says, "always rather through her own thought than clearly and truly." Things *were* seen, however, clearly and truly, but coconsciously, just as things not perceived in hysterical anæsthesia may be perceived coconsciously. This expansion and autonomous activity of the coconscious probably would not have happened if another and more effective factor had not been at work to cause a splitting of consciousness; this was her habit of putting herself into abstraction, extreme absentmindedness, or dreamy states. "She used to go mooning about, not knowing half the time what she was doing." In these absentminded states she would be day-dreaming of fairy stories (at an earlier period) or of her fancied sins. One incident indicates the depth of this condition of abstraction; it was the occasion of the death of the baby. "C. had been very restless and nervous during the day, had been scolded and sent to bed several times that evening, but had finally managed to steal unnoticed into the room where the baby was kept to prevent its disturbing mamma, for it cried incessantly. She took it in her arms . . . to soothe it, and after a time it grew quieter; then still more quiet, until finally it gave a curious little gasp and stopped breathing altogether. But C. had not noticed it, for she had entirely forgotten the child in going over and over for the ten thousandth time her sins. She sàt there gazing into space until morning, until the nurse came, and for a wonder the nurse wasn't cross. . . . C. did not know until late that afternoon, when she heard the nurse telling some one, that the baby had died in her arms, although I knew immediately that it must be dead."

Abstraction means not only repression, but, it may be, a dissociation, or splitting of the elements of the content of consciousness. Indeed Janet went so far as to explain the peculiar dissociation of hysterical anæsthesia with the formation of coconscious perceptual ideas as chronic absentmindedness. Here was a powerful factor making for the splitting of personality and the developing of a coconscious system. In the frequently repeated "dreaminess" the stream of perceptions of the environment, neglected by the one-ideaed and absentminded personality, to say nothing of the constant normal stream from the fringe of the conscious field, helped to swell the subconscious reservoir, to form a large coconscious system, independently apperceiving the environment and retaining memories thereof until it became organized into a self with memories and feelings and impulses of its own, and possessing a self-consciousness. At what period this system acquired a self-consciousness it is impossible to say, but it must have been at an early period in youth, about the time the saintly complex began to be formed, and its growth was probably gradual. . . .

By way of summary then we may say that the psychogenesis of Sally was due to several cooperative and successively active factors:

1. Primitive early conflicts between opposing impulses—those of the play dispositions and joy versus those of curiosity and possibly fear, leading to the dissociation of the former.

2. Formation later of studious interest and of a fixed idea—the saintly complex—in antagonism with the joyous play instinct and frivolous sentiments, etc. By the force of the former the desire for youthful pleasure, such as "outdoor things, climbing, running, etc.," of which "she was awfully fond," were further and repeatedly repressed into the coconscious system.

3. Dissociation of consciousness through the force of self-cultivated habits of abstraction (absent-mindedness, day-dreaming).

4. General habit of repressing all expression of inner conflicts and innate tendencies of youth.

5. Autonomous subconscious functioning.

6. Subconscious incubation.

7. General synthesization of the coconscious systems thus formed with the experiences of the alternating phase.

There remains the question. . . .

How came this system to erupt as a personality after so long being held in quiescence? The explanation is to be found in the principle of conflict acting during an unstable condition. This condition was that of an enormously increased state of dissociation of consciousness. It will be remembered that Miss Beauchamp, although supposed at the time to be an ordinary neurasthenic, was in reality a secondary dissociated personality, B I. The discovery was only made at a later period, but such was the fact. This dissociated personality was again still further dissociated by being

hypnotized. The state of hypnosis is, as is well known, characterized by increased suggestibility and diminished resistance to subconscious influences. This is not only a generalization but was
particularly true in this case as was evidenced time and again by
objective manifestations. In the hypnotic state as well as in dissociated hysterical states to which Miss Beauchamp was subject,
the coconscious system easily influenced the personal consciousness
and produced automatic phenomena.[1] The state of a secondary
personality in hypnosis was then a particularly favorable condition
for the impulses of the coconscious system to repress the personal
consciousness and emerge as an autonomous system. That the
impulses of the pleasure loving, childish, coconscious self were antagonistic to and in conflict with those of the morbid saintly personal self almost goes without saying. They had always been in
conflict and they continued in conflict during the six years while
the case was under observation. Any stimulus which awakened the
desires and impulses of this coconscious self was liable thereby to
repress the personal consciousness, push its constellated system into
the oblivion of the unconscious, there to remain for the time being
quiescent, while itself emerged as the dominant consciousness.
When, therefore, in hypnosis, coconscious Sally came to life, the
conditions of the experiment gave not only the opportunity but the
stimulus which awoke the desires and impulses which won the
victory. . . .

In the alliance of the psychological dispositions, the conception
of a primitive unconscious sexual or other desire, sitting apart and
underneath, as an "anima" or an "animus" (as Tristram Shandy's
father would have said) "taking up her residence, and sitting
dabbling, like a tadpole, all day long, both summer and winter,"
in an unconscious puddle, or like Descartes' soul in the pineal gland,
pulling the wires and directing the dynamic forces of organized
systems constituting personality, both "shocks the imagination"
and is, to my mind, untenable. The present-day tendency to find a
quasi-philosophic single principle to explain the complex psychological phenomena of personality, a sort of psychological monism,
is not only fallacious but is bound to remove psychology from the
field of science. Psychology deals with concrete phenomena which
are the resultants of a complexity of forces driving in different
directions. The law of the final drive is more comparable to the
physical law of the "resultant of forces."

---

[1] For example compare *The Dissociation*, Index (automatic phenomena,
automatisms, etc.).

B

CHARLES E. CORY, "The Problem of the Individual," *Jour. Abn. Psychol.*, 16: 378 (1922)

[In] the study of the causes of dissociation . . . . always there is found some deep seated emotional conflict. Tendencies that are apparently irreconcilable press their claims. In this conflict each elicits all the associations that are congenial to it. If the nervous system has a high degree of stability the strain may be borne. As with the British political life strong conflicts occur but they do not disrupt it. A common tradition weathers the shock. But if an instability exists the strain, in time, undermines the integrative forces. The way out is the way that life, in its evolution, so often takes when incompatible tendencies appear together. A bifurcation, or division takes place. This reduces the tension, as when two occupants of a room finding themselves hopelessly incompatible agree to occupy it alternately.

Note: Judging by the frequently acknowledged rôle of traumata (severe frights, etc.) in the formation of multiple personality, it would appear that such traumata should themselves be regarded as special instances of Prof. Cory's principle, conflict: a great fright, even if not the recoil from a *moral fear* (as occurred in the genesis of B I in Miss Beauchamp[1]), represents a conflict between the tendency to remember the painful experience and the tendency to live in contented ignorance of that experience.

---

[1] *Cf.* Morton Prince, "Miss Beauchamp—The Theory of the Psychogenesis of Multiple Personality," 114-117.

CHAPTER XVII

THE SUBCONSCIOUS

On the basis principally of what has gone before, the selections which comprise this chapter attempt clarification of a topic frequently mentioned.

Phenomena That Have Suggested Conceptions of the Subconscious

MORTON PRINCE, "Awareness, Consciousness, Coconsciousness and Animal Intelligence from the Point of View of the Data of Abnormal Psychology," *Pedag. Sem.*, 32: 177-181 (1925)

I cannot do better than begin with the old and classical phenomena of *hysterical anæsthesia.* These have long been known to students of abnormal psychology. I prefer to begin with them, because they are as important as they are old and have not been as yet adequately analyzed. . . .

Hysterical anesthesia is a loss of sensation by the personal consciousness due to dissociation from functional causes. It may involve only some of the senses, or all of the senses, and only part of the body, or the whole of the body.

Now, given an hysteric of a certain type with absolute anesthesia of the skin, no tactile stimulus is felt, much less perceived, *no matter how intensely the attention is concentrated* on the stimulated area. The lack of awareness of the tactile stimulus is not due, therefore, to lack of focusing the attention; *i. e.,* to the unfelt sensation—a prick of a pin, or the touch of a hand, or the burning of a hot iron, or whatever it may have been—having been in the fringe of awareness. There was simply and plainly absence of awareness.

Now put that hysteric into another state of mind, or personality, that is to say hypnosis, and he recalls, first, that there did actually occur the sensation of a "prick" or "touch"; and, second, that when it occurred he was unaware of it. He further insists that it was a veritable sensation-in-being. More than this he recalls and insists that there was a coconscious perception of which he was at the previous moment unaware, and in evidence thereof, when put to the crucial test, he describes accurately what the experimenter did—that he pricked the hand five times, drew a figure on the skin, put a pair of scissors, a knife, a key in the hand, bent the third and fifth fingers, and so on. These he now claims to remember were true coconscious perceptions of which the hysteric was unaware in spite of concentration of attention.

Again modify the experiment. Instead of hypnotizing the hysteric try tapping the so-called unconscious dispositions by automatic writing at the moment of the tactile stimulus. The writing now describes accurately the tests and insists there are at the very moment coconscious sensations and perceptions experienced synchronously with the tactile stimulus by that which writes, while at the same instant the subject testifies he is not aware of the stimulus. More specifically, that which writes feels and perceives while the subject is unaware. . . .

In *absentminded acts* there is commonly dim sub-awareness by the subject of the act, but there is a type in which no such awareness of it, or of the conscious process which determines it, can be detected. But this process can afterwards, in hypnosis, be recalled to memory as having been a coconscious one, often rich in visual imagery. It may be quite complex and determine complicated purposive behavior, such as we all know absentminded acts may be, sometimes to our mortification. . . .

Of the various conditions in which dissociated coconscious processes are found, the one in which they are, perhaps, most beautifully studied by experimental methods is that of artificially *suggested post-hypnotic acts*. These, as you all probably know, are acts performed by a favorable subject in a waking state as a result of a suggestion given while he was hypnotized. The subject, for example, is told in hypnosis that after waking, at a given signal, he will arise from his chair, walk across the room, take down a certain book from the bookcase, carry it to some part of the room and place it in a given place, and so on. If the subject is a good one the act will be performed as suggested in a sort of absentminded way without even, it may be, his being aware of what he is doing. Indeed such acts are in principle absentminded acts.

Now, in experiments of this kind I have found that there is a conscious process of which the subject is unaware which determines the act. In the example I have cited there is at each step in the act a coconscious visual image of and preceding the next step to be performed. Thus there develops the image of the subject walking across the room—whereupon he arises and absentmindedly walks across the room; an image of the bookcase—he arrives at the bookcase; an image of a hand reaching for the designated book—he reaches for and takes down the book, and so on.

These coconscious images of which the subject is not aware are found in a good many conditions besides absentminded and suggested post-hypnotic acts. They occur in frankly repressed thoughts, in the subconscious perseveration of dreams after waking (e. g., automatic kleptomania), in artificially induced hallucinations, in automatic writing, in concentrated attention as when we are in a "brown study," and various other conditions. In some conditions they come and go repeatedly, or may remain more or less stabile, or they may behave like cinema pictures and symbolically represent elaborate thoughts or ideas. Sometimes they erupt into the personal consciousness and then the individual becomes aware of them as hallucinations or visions. Indeed this is the psychological mechanism of the visions of saints and sinners; but saints and sinners are aside from the subject in hand.

What I want to call attention to now is that further investigation has shown, as I believe, that, first, these images are elements in a conscious process of which the personal consciousness is unaware—a coconsciousness—and which may be very simple in composition, or of greater or less complexity; and, secondly, this process may determine intelligent purposive behavior of various types varying from kleptomanic attacks to subconscious writing; and, thirdly, it has all the characteristics of intelligence and cognition. . . .

When we come to study *coconscious perceptions* in normal everyday life, we have a mass of observations showing perceptions of the environment and of the body of which the personal consciousness is not aware—auditory, visual, tactile, kinesthetic, coenesthetic, etc. These are of sounds in the street, voices, visual images of the environment, sensations of warmth, cold, and discomfort, of positions of the body, tension, and coenesthesis, generally, streaming in from the body, none of which enters the content of the personal consciousness at all. They are all comparable in principle to the perceptual phenomena I have already described of hysterical anesthesia.

As to behavior, the coconscious bodily sensations may cause shifting of the position of the subject, or general restlessness, and sometimes discontinuance and change of occupation, or location without the subject realizing the reason therefor. . . .

The phenomena I have cited are sufficient, I think, for my purpose without detaining you with a further recital of actual examples of the performances of coconscious processes in other normal and abnormal conditions I have referred to, such as automatic writing, mathematical calculations, subconscious perseveration of dreams after waking, phobias, tics, and other states.

Then, in addition to the *activities* of subconscious character, as described by Dr. Prince in the foregoing paragraphs, mention should be made of the apparently *non-active storings,* both of ordinary memories, and of the systems of memories that constitute complexes, alternating personalities, etc. These storings have seemed to many students to require for their explanation something that does the storing, the conserving; and that something has frequently been assumed to be an "unconscious mind" or "the subconscious."

Some Unnecessary Conceptions of the Subconscious

W. S. TAYLOR; revised from " 'Modern Theories of the Unconscious' (Northridge): A Review with a Discussion of 'Repression,' 'Catharsis,' and 'The Unconscious,'" *Jour. Abn. Psychol.*, 20: 87-88 (1925). In the work referred to, Dr. W. L. Northridge's volume, *Modern Theories of the Unconscious* (Dutton, 1924), interesting historical anticipations of the Freudian conception of the unconscious may be found

Sometimes the question is raised as to whether those processes beyond the field of immediate awareness are conscious or not. But to the present writer this seems to be a question which is, as yet at least, one of the *innocuously* theoretical sort. That is, it appears that the question is incapable of any logical or experimental proof either way: it is purely a matter of the metaphysical and epistemological assumptions one brings to bear upon the problem. Also, no difference would result for practice, apparently. The subconscious processes may be unconscious or coconscious, or even "rapid oscillations of different dissociated systems of consciousness, each for the moment becoming the personal consciousness, but with amnesia for the preceding moment," [1] for all we really know. But we do know, through abundant demonstration, that subconscious processes, as processes, are often of a highly complex character, and occur in varying degrees of independence of that most complex system of processes that we call "the main personality."

---

[1] Morton Prince, "The Actuality and Nature of Subconscious Processes," p. 130.

Whether this requires the employment of "physical" or "psychical" conceptions exclusively, again, is perhaps a most important problem; or perhaps it is only a question of descriptive terminology. Possibly, indeed, it is not really out of order for us to employ both sorts of language interchangeably: possibly it is only some unexamined allegiance to Cartesian conceptions which would seem to require "ontological consistency" for our nomenclature. But however that may be, whatever the color of the metaphysical spectacles one sees through, or whatever the ontological stuff in which the problem arises, the structure or type of organization of "the unconscious," and the principles which describe the operations of subconscious processes, are worthy of presuppositionless observation.

And what are those principles, and the type of organization? Here opinions differ. But to many students [2] the evidence is clearly against the assumption of (to sketch roughly in composite) (1) an entity, (2) which mechanically echoes its supposed past (archaic symbols, etc.), and (3) speaks a cut-and-dried language now (orthodox dream symbols, etc.), (4) wishfully antithetical to civilized life, or else (5) mystically overflowing with ambition and spirituality, and (6) peculiarly close to a living soul of the race; all (7) compressed somewhat effectively by a well-meaning censor or two. The evidence rather is in favor of, as was said above, a mass of hereditary and acquired processes which may be organized in all sorts of ways; processes which have indeed a history, but a history which requires scientific tracing in each individual case; some of whose associations may appear variously as symbols; whose elements, in so far as they become to any serious degree distinct from the individual's daily scope of attention, are become so distinct in many cases because of a conflict with the waking elements, hence may well comprise rebellious elements, but elements normally capable of integration into any scheme of real civilization; an integration in which conflict,—which is truly of many sorts and complications, including the types called "censorship"—instead of being followed by evil "repression," resolves into normal inhibition of those impulses that threaten the organism's major interests.

This means a concrete and relativistic, rather than an abstract and absolutistic, theory of "the unconscious." True, the latter is easier to grasp, with the imagination at least, and so gives quicker comfort to the unquestioning in times of perplexity. But as statistical and experimental tests multiply, that theory must win which is explicatively applicable to more cases and more phenomena.

---

[2] Agreeing in a number of points with Dr. Northridge.

A Descriptive Conception of the Subconscious

HOWARD C. WARREN, "The Subconscious," *Scientia*, August, 1923, pp. 91-
97; reprinted from *Scientia*, International Review of Scientific Synthesis,
edited by Eugenio Rignano, Milan; published by
Williams & Wilkins Co., Baltimore

The investigations of the psychoanalytic school have drawn general attention to the substrata of mental life. The evidence which these writers have gathered points to the conclusion that many intelligent actions are brought about independently of conscious guidance. As a result, the traditional view, which considered all automatic actions unconscious, is giving place more and more to the notion of the *subconscious*.

But while full credit should be given to the psychoanalysts for establishing this intermediate stage between conscious and non-conscious phenomena, many psychologists are disposed to challenge their conception of the subconscious in several important particulars. For one thing, their descriptions seem altogether too anthropomorphic. The notion of a "censor," who guards the portals of the conscious and prevents unwelcome thoughts from entering that domain, is too naïve to fit into the scientific conception of mental organization. Even though the censor be regarded as a mere figure of speech, the very term itself implies a degree of subconscious organization which the facts scarcely warrant. The following interpretation of subconscious phenomena is suggested as being more in accord with known neural conditions.

The province of psychology, we shall assume at the outset, is to investigate all the phenomena which occur in the course of neural activity from stimulus to response. Within this series of events belong the phenomena of conscious experience. Their relation to the rest of the series is not clear and has been variously interpreted. In attempting to picture the entire process from stimulus to response, the present writer finds the Double-Aspect hypothesis more helpful than either the Interaction or the Parallelistic view. This hypothesis regards subjective experiences and central nervous activity as merely two different ways of apprehending the same series of events. A certain set of activities occur in your brain. Observed by another person, the occurrences consist of a series of physical and chemical changes in the nerve substance; you, the man whose brain is concerned, observe the events directly, as part of yourself, as your own experience.[1]

It will readily be seen that this unification of mind-body phenomena has an important bearing on the relation between consciousness, subconsciousness, and unconsciousness. If consciousness is merely the subjective apprehension of central nervous activity, there is no reason for regarding the activity of the lower centers as devoid of a similar subjective experience. In other words, we should not speak of *unconscious* behavior; all behavior that is not conscious is *subconscious*. It is not usual to consider the simple reflexes, such as the eye-wink or the knee-jerk, as possessing any conscious character at all. Yet these actions involve definite nervous arcs with definite centers. The cortical processes are regarded as experiences of the integrated person. May not the neural activities at any reflex center be regarded as experiences of that specific center?

In short, one result of the double-aspect view is to make the distinction between consciousness and subconsciousness a mere matter of position and relationship. If a given center is connected up with the general system of cortical activity, then its activity is conscious; if not, its activity does not form part of the individual's conscious personality, and the experience is subconscious. This simplifies the interpretation of split-off states and multiple personality.

Before proceeding further, attention must be called to two different meanings of the term subconscious. Their interchangeable use has caused confusion at times. The prefix *sub-* is used sometimes to denote *lack of intensity or vividness,* at other times to denote *subordination.*

In psychophysics a stimulus which is subliminal has often a real effect. This is demonstrated, for instance, by Fechner's Method of Right and Wrong Cases. If a subliminal difference between two stimuli tends to produce a preponderance of right judgments, it is proper to call the influence subconscious. But this does not mean that the effect has been worked out in any subordinate center. Subconsciousness, in this sense, means a minimal or subliminal degree of consciousness. We shall not have occasion to use the term subconscious in this sense in the present discussion. It is mentioned to prevent confusion. In Psychical Research literature the two meanings are sometimes used interchangeably, and unjustified conclusions are drawn in consequence.

---

[1] See: "The Mental and the Physical," *Psychol. Rev.,* Vol. 21 (1914); "Psychology and the Central Nervous System," *ibid.,* Vol. 28 (1921).

The more common (and probably more satisfactory) use of the term subconscious is to denote nervous activity and experiences in nerve centers which are not functionally united with the general system of *cortical* activity and *personal* experience. The term is used in this sense in the present paper.

Another source of confusion lies in the failure to distinguish between the active processes physiological or subjective) which take place in the lower centers, and the underlying structural conditions of conscious experience. Take the case of memory. Sensations and perceptions leave a *trace* of some sort in the nerve structure. On occasion this trace serves as a basis for the revival of corresponding experiences which are not actual perceptions, but memories. Here the basis of the new conscious experience is certain underlying structural conditions. It would not be correct to say that the rise of this specific underlying experience is due to a continuing subconsciousness. There is no evidence that throughout the long interval between the original experience and the memory experience activity is continually going on in these centers.

On the other hand, when we determine to do something at a certain future time, then dismiss the matter from thought, and recollect it when the proper time comes, it would seem that some activity goes on during the interval—at least just before the conscious revival. In such cases an active process appears to be involved in addition to the permanent structural basis, and this process may be regarded as subconscious.

The Freudian school does not distinguish between nervous activity and structural modification of the centers. Everything that underlies consciousness is called subconscious and is pictured as activity and as constituting an intelligent personality. The picture of a subconscious thought *striving to force itself* through some celestial gateway leading to consciousness, and of the "censor" —a sublimated Saint Peter—forbidding entrance to the unredeemed, strikes the ordinary psychologist as belonging to the prescientific type of explanation. Undoubtedly the facts reported by the psychoanalysts are genuine occurrences—just as sunrise and sunset are occurrences, despite the fact that the sun neither rises nor sets. It is not the facts but the anthropomorphic implications of the terminology that are open to challenge. Repression, censorship, sublimation, symbolism, surely have a neurological meaning. Something happens in the nerve centers. What is the neural basis of these phenomena?

Suppose a road so worn by traffic that at one place its surface consists of a series of ridges or humps. Then every automobile passing over this section will be subjected to the same succession of jolts. It is not necessary to assume that a special local car is continually going back and forth over these humps. The permanent fact is the worn condition of the roadway, not the jolting of some car. Just so, a large portion of our mental substratum is probably not a continuous flow of subconscious activity but a permanent disposition of the nerve structure.

This permanent modification of nerve structure would account for our various attitudes. A cheerful attitude is built up gradually out of repeated emotions of joy; a cautious attitude grows out of emotions of timidity. When an individual possesses a cheerful or a cautious nature it does not mean that joyous or timid experiences are happening to him at every instant, either consciously or subconsciously. What persists is the *disposition* toward the given emotion; and this disposition or attitude is a structural, not a functional phenomenon. In the dark a red book cover is not actively red. But its surface is permanently set for red, so that whenever mixed light rays strike this surface, the reflected light is red. There is a permanent structural disposition toward the red in the book cover.

Many of the characteristic phenomena reported by the psychoanalysts may be explained by means of this structural concept. In early childhood the nervous system is exceedingly plastic and impressible. A great fear may leave a deep and lasting impression in the nerve substance. Suppose this fear was originally part of an experience concerned with a furry animal. Then later in life any fur stimulus is likely to be associated with fear. These fears, the psychoanalysts tell us, tend to be repressed. But this notion of repression seems to be rather a figure of speech. The normal person, when he begins to have one of these experiences, by the very nature of things passes quickly to something else. Nothing is repressed or suppressed; the stream of conscious experiences merely flows off in some other direction.

In pathological cases there may be something additional. There is a tendency to dissociation in certain types of mental disorder. The man's personality is split up into partial personalities. Insistent ideas absorb the attention; the stream of thought plays around them continually. It may well be that when the stream of conscious thought passes quickly over certain unpleasant associations, a repercussion of these experiences will be active for a time in some dissociated portion of the personality. The dissociated, subconscious self may hark back constantly to these deep-rooted fears or fear-arousing experiences. But in normal cases the permanent basis of the fear seems to be merely a structural disposition—there is no evidence of a subconscious "censor."

Janet and Prince have given us admirable studies of multiple personality. Their investigations show beyond doubt that our organized unitary personality can be split up into two or more well-organized partial systems. Personalities A and B may be quite cut off from each other; or there may be a one-way connection, so that A takes on the experiences of B as memories, while B is quite unacquainted with the experiences of A. In either case there is a picture of two organized personalities which operate within the same organism at different times. The phenomena of automatic writing show two coördinate personalities working through different motor channels at the same time. The organization in this case is less complete.

How far is this picture applicable to normal personality? Is the human individual normally split up into a number of fairly well-organized selves? The abnormal and normal are not altogether distinct. They are closely enough related to throw light on one another. But in this instance the attempt to explain the normal by means of the abnormal appears to be wrongly directed; it picks out certain essentially abnormal features and carries them over to the normal, instead of eliminating these and carrying over only what is typical of the species.

In the normal individual the organization of acts is largely a structural disposition. Suppose I have acquired a fixed habit of walking on certain days along a given route to my laboratory and up the stairs. Then when I start out in the morning the conscious part of the program is limited to getting myself under way. Once started I think of all sorts of problems—never once of the walk. The proper turns at the street corners are made without hesitation, and I reach my destination according to schedule. Usually there is no recollection of the process afterwards. It appears, then, that after the initial decision the activity is entirely subconscious. This does not mean that the subconscious part of my being gets at any time a thought-picture of the entire process. There is probably no subconscious planning out of each successive step, in the way that my conscious personality might plan out and visualize the trip beforehand. The subconscious process is piecemeal; each movement leads to the next because the habit has become ingrained in the structure of my lower brain centers. Nothing is pictured out of its proper turn. Each subconscious experience leads directly to the next phase of motor activity.

The Freudians interpret the subconscious after the pattern of the conscious. They do not conceive it as merely controlling stereotyped actions, but as "thinking ahead" in a truly cortical manner. Indeed, they make its organization more cortical than the cortex itself. For while cortical thought takes but one direction at a time, the subconscious activity of the Freudians is almost omniscient. The fallacy of the assumption lies in their failure to realize that the splitting up of the unitary cortical personality into partial personalities is a pathological phenomenon. The Freudians would make the cortical dissociation typical of the normal mind. In normal individuals subconsciousness is not a single, systematically organized personality. Each habit, small or great, is separately organized. There are many organized systems of connections in the nerve structure. But there is no general unitary subconscious personality in the normal man.

The Subconscious and the Various Orders of Cerebration

HAROLD E. PRESSEY. [Prepared for this volume, largely on the basis of studies by Prince, Freud, Rivers, Northridge, and others. The writer is indebted also to Professors H. M. Halverson and W. S. Taylor, of the University of Maine, for valuable suggestions]

NOMENCLATURE

Investigations in the field of abnormal psychology have resulted in a varied nomenclature. Thus one school speaks of the subconscious, where another speaks of the unconscious, in referring to the same phenomena of mental life. The result to the student is a confusing mass of data which must be pigeon-holed correctly before a grasp of the subject can be obtained. It is the aim of this paper to examine briefly the conception of the subconscious, to illustrate schematically, and especially, to define the various orders of cerebration discussed in this volume.

Normal Orders of Cerebration. From the results of the introspective school of psychology, it appears that there are various degrees of consciousness or awareness, of which attention is but one form. According to the reports, at least three divisions of *the field of consciousness* can be made out.[1] First of all there is attention, or focal awareness. At the other extreme of awareness is the zone of marginal or peripheral consciousness composed of very faint sensations, images and perceptions. This peripheral zone is often

---

[1] There may be differences between individuals in this respect. *Cf.* W. B. Pillsbury, *The Fundamentals of Psychology*, 267 *ff.*

called subconscious, and is usually unavailable except to a trained introspectionist, or through artificial methods such as hypnosis. Between this outermost zone of consciousness and the focal area, first mentioned, there is an intermediate region, made up of elements which are not directly focal at the moment, yet are fairly clear.

Focal consciousness or attention has as its correlate in the nervous system, functioning neurograms [2] which are the most central to the integration of the moment. The intermediate region of consciousness has as its neural basis, neurograms also active but somewhat subordinate to the preceding. The neural correlate of the peripheral zone is composed of active neurograms still less central to the moment's integration.

Passing on from the field of awareness, we find evidence for a variety of cortical activities which are not correlated directly with that field. It is proposed here to comprehend all such activities under the caption, *the subconscious,* and to divide this group into as many categories as seem necessary. In examining the evidence presented, it appears that even in normal persons the subconscious consists of functioning elements and non-functioning elements. In these normal persons, the functioning subconscious elements are those which are not within the field of consciousness at the moment but which nevertheless integrate with it. These are the *normal subconscious processes* which form with the field of consciousness the mental "set" of the moment, or which may be working out problems without occupying the field of awareness ("unconscious cerebration"—Carpenter; "incubation"—James, Prince [3]). The elements which are not functioning at the moment comprise *the normal unconscious.*

From a neurological point of view the normal unconscious is composed of non-functioning neurograms on the one hand, and untried synapses, or possibilities for the making of neurograms, on the other. Of these, the actual but non-functioning neurograms fall into two groups: first, those neurograms which are readily available or easily revivable; and second, those neurograms which are not available through ordinary means, having faded beyond ordinary recall. The easily revivable neurograms are the physical

---

[2] Neurograms are described by Dr. Prince as brain records. In similar fashion, we may define a neurogram as a synaptic connection which has been traversed at least once by an impulse, the impulse leaving a temporary or permanent configuration to the connection.

[3] *Cf. The Unconscious,* 227, *circa.*

correlates of memories, sentiments, systems, which are ordinarily available to the individual.

In the case of the untried synapses, there are again two classes. At the outset, there are what we may call *pro-neurograms:* connections which have not yet been traversed, but which are peculiarly liable to use. These are whatever instincts there may be. In addition, there are the possible synaptic connections which instead of being so predisposed to particular patterns are open to all the possibilities of learning.

We find, then, within the subconscious of the normal individual, integratively functioning elements (normal subconscious processes), and those elements which are inactive for the moment at least (the normal unconscious); and of these inactive elements there are both neurograms and what may become neurograms, the latter including pro-neurograms and the other untried synapses.

Abnormal Orders of Cerebration. Thus far nothing has been said concerning pathological or abnormal kinds of cerebral activity. Abnormal individuals in addition to having normal orders of cerebration (which would naturally be more or less incomplete), have dissociated cortical groups, dissociated mental elements. These neural groups too may be functioning or non-functioning at any one moment; and they may be merely small systems called complexes, or systems as inclusive as personalities. Because of their dissociatedness, their disparateness from the normal personality, all such split-off processes belong properly to a special category which we may designate by a special caption, *the disconscious.*[4]

Any disconscious processes which are not functioning at the moment are, of course, unconscious. Any disconscious processes, on the other hand, which are active at the moment, we shall call *coconscious processes;*—with apologies to Dr. Morton Prince. The usage proposed here differs from Dr. Prince's development of this essential concept, "coconscious," in the distinction between "coconscious" and "fringe." In the present exposition, "the fringe" is the periphery of normal consciousness, whereas "coconscious" is limited as a term for disconscious (abnormal) activities only; admitting, however, intermediate cases. Also, the present writer's criterion for "coconscious," as already remarked, is disparate *activity,* regardless of the question as to whether or not such activity is accompanied by consciousness.

In short, we may comprehend all dissociated functions of the

---

[4] For this label the writer is indebted to Professor Taylor.

cortex under the term disconscious: a term which covers both inactive (unconscious) and active (coconscious) complexes and separate personalities.

The Schema on pages 488-9, following, represents neural bases for these various kinds of cortical activity. The large dots represent cell bodies. The lines indicate connections between cell bodies. The differences in fullness of lines denote differences in synaptic resistance: the heavier the line the less the resistance. Dotted lines indicate non-functioning synapses. Of these the most faint lines represent untried synapses, and those neurograms which have faded through disuse; while the heavier dotted lines represent neurograms more ready to function. Heavy continuous lines denote functioning neurograms.

In the first of the diagrams a portion of an infant cortex is shown schematically. Here are (let us say) only untried synapses: proneurograms and the other synaptic possibilities. The child (2) shows a later stage of development; while there are many untried synapses, there are also functioning and non-functioning neurograms. In the normal adult (3) there are many more neurograms, of various clearnesses. Naturally, the activities of these neurograms change from moment to moment, as is suggested in (4). The neurograms which functioned in (3), however, are shown in (4) as among the less resistant of the now non-functioning neurograms, while some non-functioning neurograms in (3) have become the functioning neurograms in (4). In (5), an adult is represented in the hypothetical state of dreamless sleep. Yet there are neurograms ready to function at the least stimulation. These neurograms are functioning in (6): the individual is dreaming.

An adult with an unconscious complex (7) is the first of the pathological cases shown. The complex (uc), which is not functioning, is dissociated from the rest of the personality, as shown by the fine dotted lines. There is one connection, however, to the main personality, which allows for the functioning of the complex with the personality at times, especially during dreams, and which serves as the means for getting at the complex through psychoanalysis. The functioning complex in some dreams is illustrated in (8), where the dream is composed of some of the elements which were conscious during the day together with some of the elements which comprise this complex. Incidentally, these two diagrams, (7) and

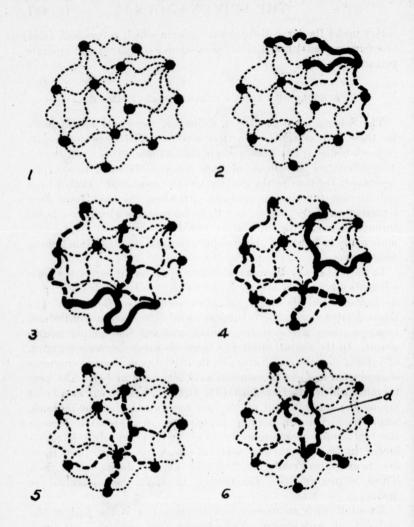

SCHEMA OF NORMAL ORDERS OF CEREBRATION

1. Infant
2. Child
3. Normal adult
4. Same as 3, a moment later
5. Same as 4, but sleeping dreamlessly (if ever)
6. Same as 5, but dreaming (d), or hypnotized

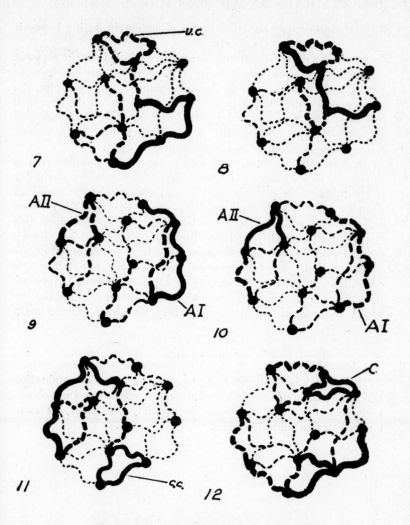

SCHEMA OF ABNORMAL ORDERS OF CEREBRATION

7. Adult with unconscious complex (u. c.)
8. Same as 7, but asleep and dreaming, or being hypnoanalyzed
9. Adult with an alternating personality (AII)
10. Same as 9, but alternated (AII now conscious)
11. Adult with a coconscious complex (c. c.)
12. Adult with a coconscious personality (c.)

(8), seem to represent the conditions which obtain during hypnosis and hypnoanalysis, respectively.

An adult with an alternating personality which is at the moment unconscious, is shown in diagram (9). The unconscious personality (A II) is dissociated in the same manner as the complex, the traversable connection serving in this case as the means by which one personality may be "switched off" and the other "switched on." Figure (10) shows Personality A I as "switched off," now unconscious, with Personality A II functioning instead.

An example of an individual with a coconscious complex (cc) is illustrated in diagram (11). This coconscious complex is similar to the unconscious complex (uc) in (7) except that the conscious complex is by definition functioning now. Diagram (12) shows an individual with a coconscious personality (C). Although this coconscious personality includes functioning and non-functioning elements, it is similar in disparateness to the other abnormal orders of cerebration. In this instance, however, the one traversable connection, in addition to serving as a possible means of psychotherapeutic synthesis, might function as a one-way connection by which the coconscious personality may be aware of the main personality.

CONCLUSION

Thus it has been shown that the different types of cerebration may be listed under two main captions, consciousness and subconsciousness, of which there are important subdivisions, as summarized in the following table:

GENERAL GROUPINGS	SPECIAL GROUPINGS OF ELEMENTS WHICH ARE NOT FUNCTIONING AT THE MOMENT	SPECIAL GROUPINGS OF ELEMENTS WHICH ARE FUNCTIONING
	Normal	
THE FIELD OF CONSCIOUSNESS		The focus of consciousness; attention. (Neurograms most central to the integration of the moment.)
		The intermediate region of consciousness. (Neurograms somewhat subordinate to the preceding.)
		The margin or periphery of the field of consciousness. (Neurograms still less central to the moment's integration.)
THE SUBCONSCIOUS	The Normal Unconscious	Normal subconscious processes.
	Readily available elements. (Neurograms easily revivable.)	(Cortical activities outside the field of consciousness at the moment, but which integrate with it.)
	Faded elements. (Neurograms which have faded beyond ordinary recall.)	
	Untried synapses. (Pro-neurograms and the other synaptic possibilities.)	
	Abnormal	
THE DISCONSCIOUS	Complexes, Unconscious (Small disparate patterns which are inactive.)	Complexes, Coconscious. (Small disparate patterns which are active.)
	Unconscious Personalities (Large disparate systems of inactive neurograms.)	Coconscious Personalities. (Large disparate systems consisting of active—and some inactive—neurograms.)

CHAPTER XVIII

THE NATURE OF SUGGESTION

"TRANSFERENCE"

[MAURICE NICOLL; J. A. HADFIELD]

In recent psychoanalytic discussions of psychotherapy, the nature of hypnosis, etc., the term "transfer," or "transference," often occurs. According to Dr. Maurice Nicoll, "broadly speaking, transference is the sum total of the feelings, conscious and unconscious, that the patient has in relation to his physician. When these feelings are of interest, liking, respect, admiration, hopefulness, friendliness, etc., the transference is positive. When these feelings are of dislike, fear, boredom, hate, anger, vexation, disappointment, etc., the transference is negative." [1] Dr. J. A. Hadfield remarks that "the term 'transference' is often used in a much stricter and limited sense to refer to the transference of the libido (or sexual emotion) of the patient to the physician and then from the physician to some worthier object. But that is only one of innumerable forms of transference." [2] "Transference," as thus conceived, is regarded frequently as of great importance in working with a patient; the cure, it is often supposed, cannot be effected without first establishing a good "transference" as the condition of harmonious dependence of the patient upon the tutelage of the physician.

For such thinkers "suggestion," and the "rapport" of the hypnotists, are only forms of "transference of the libido." The less metaphysical psychologists, however, would prefer to see all these conceptions reduced to understandable mechanisms. In this spirit the following selections are presented.

---

[1] "Psycho-Analysis," in *Functional Nerve Disease* (H. Crichton Miller, ed.), 137 (Oxford, 1920).

[2] *Psychology and Morals*, 101 (Methuen & Co. and Robert M. McBride, 1923).

IMITATION

The intimacy of relation of imitation to the other topics of this chapter becomes apparent through their community of mechanism, as described in the following passage:

The Conditioned-Reflex Basis of Imitation

STEVENSON SMITH and EDWIN R. GUTHRIE, *General Psychology*, 132
(Appleton, 1921)

The dependence of imitation on learning is well illustrated by language acquisition. The baby is at first moved to make a great variety of vowel and consonant sounds by such stimuli as he receives from a moderately full stomach, a soft bed, and a warm, well-lighted room. The sounds he makes accompany the movements that produce them and, because the vowels are sustained and the consonants either sustained or repeated, these sounds also precede the movements that continue or reiterate them. They thus become the conditioning stimuli for their own production, so that when uttered by others they are imitated by the baby. A period of practice, during which the baby plays with these sounds, is necessary before imitation is possible and by this practice the baby is prepared to imitate the particular sounds of any language.

Imitation is seldom an exact replica of the act that is imitated. The imitator's response is that habitual act of his that most nearly resembles the act which he observes.[1]

This "conditioned reflex" principle, as described by Professors Smith and Guthrie, is obviously that which explains "imitation" of any sort: If a chick pecks food more frequently when tapping is occurring behind a screen than when no tapping is occurring, in proportion we must assume that the tapping sound, as a stimulus which the chick always received when it pecked alone previously, now serves as a "conditioning auditory stimulus" to touch off the chick's pecking response; if a non-religious person, at the edge of a group of revivalists who are clapping their hands vigorously, is moved to clap his hands

---

[1] [Compare, for explication of this understanding of imitation, with diagrams, Floyd Henry Allport, *Social Psychology*, 181-189.]

vigorously too but without any religious conviction in the matter, we must assume that he has *seen* and *heard* (perhaps only his) hands clapping before, when his own were clapping, so that his response of clapping follows these conditioned stimuli [2]; if a hypnotized subject, when his attention is caught sharply, is observed to mimic every motion of his hypnotist, we assume that in some lines of work and play he has seen at least the elementary components of those movements when he himself was performing them, hence follows those old pathways now while in a very uninhibited state; and if a morbid person, when placed in a social environment of heartily objective minds, takes on their attitude, in explanation we should allow for such factors as diversion of attention, it is true, but also for the associations established in his past when he felt well at the same times his companions did, associating their pleasant expressions with his own good feelings, and in this new environment is accordingly predisposed to feel well upon being stimulated by cheerful countenances and actions.

Thus a discussion of Imitation leads directly into the topic of Suggestion, which according to the late Dr. E. E. Southard is, in its true nature, "the big problem of psychopathology and psychology." [3]

SUGGESTION

The Normality of Suggestion

HUGO MÜNSTERBERG; adapted from *Psychotherapy*, 85-88 (Moffat, Yard, 1909)

Let us be clear from the start that suggestion is certainly nothing abnormal and exceptional, nothing which leads us away from our ordinary life, nothing which brings us nearer to the great riddles of the universe. There are teachers whose authority gives to every word such an impressiveness and dignity that every opposite thought disappears, while others throw out words which are forgotten. On the other hand, the readiness to accept suggestions is evidently also

[2] For excellent descriptions of important "stampedes" and "mental epidemics," *cf.* Boris Sidis, *The Psychology of Suggestion*, 314-364.
[3] "General Psychopathology," *Psychol. Bull.*, 16: 197 (1919).

quite different with different individuals. A suggestion is an idea which in itself is not different from other ideas, but the way in which it takes possession of the mind reduces the chances of any opposite ideas; it inhibits them. Emotions reënforce our readiness to accept suggestions. Fatigue and intoxicants increase suggestibility very strongly. To look out on a wider perspective, we may add at once that an artificial increase of suggestibility is all which constitutes the state of hypnotism.[1]

Suggestion as Related to Attention

A

Hugo Münsterberg; adapted from *Psychotherapy*, 94-95, 100, 103 (Moffat, Yard, 1909)

Yet the problem of suggestion in the field of ideas stands after all not isolated. Instead of connecting it with the weird reports of mystic influence from man to man, let us rather link it with the simple experience of attention. It shares with attention, the power to reënforce and to inhibit. But if we examine what is involved in the suggestion of an idea, we find surely more than a mere turning of the attention towards one idea and turning the attention away from another idea. That which characterizes and constitutes suggestion is a belief in the idea, an acceptance of the idea as real and the dismissal of the opposite idea as unreal. The difference between suggestion and attention lies only in this: the motor response in attention aims towards a fuller clearness of the idea, for instance, by fixating, listening, observing, searching; while the motor response in suggestion aims towards the practical action in which the object of the idea is accepted as real. In attention, we change the object in making it clearer; in suggestion, we change ourselves in adapting ourselves to the new situation in which we believe.

B

Edmund Parish, *Hallucinations and Illusions*, The Contemporary Science Series, 153-154 (Walter Scott, 1898)

In psychical concentration . . . the tension in certain selected element-groups is heightened and their irritability increased. But

---

[1] [On abnormal suggestibility in relation to delinquency, *cf.* William Healy, *The Individual Delinquent*, 694-708; and on "Personal Differences in Suggestibility," *cf.* W. D. Scott (Bibliography).]

this takes place at the expense of the non-selected elements whose irrritability may be thereby reduced to a minimum, causing a state of dissociation or splitting off to ensue—a state which we may regard with Wundt [1] as arising out of neurodynamic and vasomotor processes, "according to the general principle which holds good for any system of elements where a struggle for equilibrium is going on, that whenever an expenditure of energy occurs at one point there will be an increased flow to that point from all the neighboring parts having a higher tension." That is to say, the consumption of energy caused by fixed attention compels an inflow to counterbalance the waste, and this is expressed in a lowered irritability of the elements yielding the supply.

Suggestion as Related to Dissociation

ROBERT H. GAULT; adapted from *Social Psychology*, 124-127 (Holt, 1923)

An adequate treatment of suggestion and suggestibility must recognize the former as in the nature of a stimulus and the latter as relating to a degree of sensitiveness or of readiness to react on the part of the more or less stable dispositions or tendencies of human nature. The two are functionally related. Suggestibility is the usual or normal, not the unusual or abnormal state of the human organism. Suggestibility is sharpened temporarily by fleeting expectation and by emotional disturbances, but it is not traceable wholly to a temporary emotional condition.

When an individual is receiving suggestion, he appears to be acting on his own initiative because there are no conflicting tendencies. Those that in other situations would conflict have become "dissociated" or thrown out of connection. He is, so far as his *suggested* behavior is concerned, in a state analogous to that of children and other immature persons whose sum of experience is small by reason of their having a paucity of contacts with many angles of life. They have, therefore, not yet developed a host of dispositions or tendencies toward reaction of many sorts which together insure a capacity for inhibition. In normal waking life suggestion operates to reduce restraint; remove inhibitions; in other words, to produce the state of at least partial dissociation. By this we do not mean to imply that the dissociated state we are considering is one of passivity. Obviously it is quite the contrary. But there is a shifting of activity from one department of the organism,

---

[1] Wilhelm Wundt, *Hypnotismus und Suggestion*, 58.

so to speak, to another. Suggestibility is understood, therefore, as that condition of the organism in which one or another determining tendency or disposition may express itself with relative freedom. In extreme suggestibility this freedom of expression is most marked. It is untrammeled by the inhibitions that normally control.[1]

---

[1] [It is interesting to note, as an extreme instance of such narrowing of consciousness, that the phenomena of catatonia were regarded by Tschisch as due essentially to "inability of attention"; by Freusberg as "associated with a condition of reduction of consciousness which causes a loss of control over . . . [the] . . . psychical processes"; and by Sommer as "a diminution of attention." Similarly, "catalepsy according to Sommer is another phenomenon closely related to optical fixation [which again is regarded as involving attention defect] and which he considers 'in all cases as a phenomenon of thoroughly psychic origin.' "—C. G. Jung, *Psychology of Dementia Præcox*, 1, 2 (Nervous & Mental Diseases Publishing Co., 1909).

"During the European War a great spontaneous natural experiment was carried out through the agency of the actual conditions of fighting. Soldiers suffered by the hundred from crude mental dissociation, showing itself by amnesia or loss of memory for definite terrifying events and experiences, together with loss of psycho-physical functions, such as the power of speaking, of hearing, of walking, the power of controlling tremors, etc. Investigation of these patients immediately after their injury showed that they were readily hypnotisable. Moreover, that the ease with which they could be hypnotised was in direct proportion to the degree of their mental dissociation. In other words, one discovered a definite correlation between degree of dissociation and ease of hypnotisability. Such a finding harmonises with the Salpêtrière definition of hypnosis, as an artificial dissociation. On the other hand, in these cases it was found that the suggestibility, though certainly increased in milder degrees of dissociation, was often conspicuous by its absence in more pronounced degrees of dissociation.

"It is clear that we must here call to mind a fundamental distinction in the matter of suggestion. If we define suggestion, as, e.g., McDougall does, as the acceptance of an idea or proposition independently of logically adequate grounds for such acceptance, the further question arises—Whence comes this idea that is accepted? If it is elicited by the patient's outer environment, the people around him, the general physical and mental situation, the process may be called that of hetero-suggestion. If, on the other hand, the idea arises spontaneously in the patient's own mind or is deliberately presented to him by himself, the process may be called that of auto-suggestion. In cases of deep hypnosis, such as we have just referred to, where a patient's suggestibility seems sometimes to be diminished rather than increased, it may well be that it is merely a diminution of hetero-suggestibility—auto-suggestibility may be intensified. . . .

"One might provisionally harmonise the suggestion theory of causation and cure of symptoms and the analytic theory as follows: mental conflict and repression may produce hysterical symptoms as compromise forma-

The Conditioned-Reflex Nature of Suggestion and Conditions Favorable to Suggestion

FLOYD HENRY ALLPORT, *Social Psychology*, 243-245, 249-252 (Houghton Mifflin, 1924) ; used by permission of and by special arrangement with the publishers

Perfectly normal individuals . . . show at times an immediate and undeliberated response to commands. These effects are based upon deeply fixed habits of association between word sounds and the bodily movements which they signify. . . . The motor set thus built up by suggestion we may call an *attitude*. In everyday life attitudes are built up in similar fashion. . . .

Suggestion is concerned with the control of bodily attitudes in three possible ways. First, it serves to build up or prepare the setting for a definite response when the releasing signal is given [1] . . .

tions which simultaneously satisfy repressed desires in the unconscious, and desires of another nature in the conscious mind, but the nature of the symptoms themselves is also partly determined by auto-suggestions arising as the result of diminished unity of the self—chance thoughts, they may be, which otherwise would have no influence over the patient's mental state, and to which he would not succumb. He is in a state of mind divided against itself; he is afraid for himself, afraid of ill-health, afraid that he may fall sick, and yet may desire sickness, for reasons that can be discovered by deeper analysis (*e.g.*, as a self-punishment, or to tyrannise over relatives, etc.). So the idea gains a hold upon him. In this way the dissociation we have previously emphasised does favour the acceptance of auto-suggestion. On the other hand, what particular auto-suggestions, from among all the different possible suggestions, are accepted, is determined by the wishes, desires, etc., of the patient's mind. In order, therefore, to understand fully the realisation of suggestion, we must analyse the patient's mind and learn as much as we can about these mental factors."—William Brown, "Suggestion and Personality," in *Problems of Personality* (C. Macfie Campbell, and others, eds.), 305-306, 308 (Harcourt, Brace, 1925).]

[1] ["The varieties of manifestation in *rapport* which Moll has pointed out in his monograph on the subject (Moll, *Der Rapport*, etc., 51-66) are most simply explained as dependent on self-suggestion. When a certain action is suggested to a group of hypnotised subjects in a manner which leaves some scope for individual modifications in carrying out the command, all manner of individual differences will be displayed. Suppose, for example, the hypnotist says, 'You are limping with the left leg, my poor fellow; just walk up and down the room for a minute and let me see what is wrong.' The first subject will bend his leg inwards, a second will carry out the command with his foot at an abnormal angle, a third will develop a stiff knee, a fourth will drag a broken leg. Each works out the idea independently. In a series of experiments instituted for another purpose

Secondly, it may serve as the signal (social stimulus) which releases the attitude already established. And thirdly, suggestion may augment the released response as it is being carried out. . . .

The main conditions favoring suggestion, like those for sympathy, represent the 'openness' of the organism to the stimulating suggestion, and are based, in particular, upon an attitude of submissiveness toward the suggester. . . . Sex is sometimes a determinant of a suggestible attitude, females usually standing in the submissive rôle toward males, and hence susceptible to suggestions from them. Difference of age is also a strong factor in responsiveness to suggestion. Since most of the child's knowledge comes from his elders, and also because he feels his physical weakness before them, he has formed the attitude of accepting all their suggestions without question. Where, as in childish ignorance, conviction is based entirely upon the authority of the speaker, suggestion shades imperceptibly into simple belief. Poverty of ideas and extreme submissiveness are thus the causes of the notorious suggestibility of childhood.[2]

A situation which speedily places one in an attitude of submissive suggestibility is the presence of a group, or indeed the mere allusion to large numbers. We bow before the will of the majority. . . .

To complete our account we may mention a number of devices and special conditions for rendering suggestions effective. 1. It is useful closely to concentrate the subject's attention by instruction or artifice so that the suggested proposal alone is received. 2. Monotony and rhythm, as in the chants of the medicine man or the passes of the hypnotist, relax and soothe the subject, and place him in a drowsy state of non-resistance. 3. Indirect suggestion takes the recipient off guard by avoiding the direct issue at first

---

I regularly introduced this experiment, and usually obtained varied representations like those just described. I was the more astonished when, on one occasion, among a group of village lads, the same type recurred over and over again. Only one subject showed a distinct divergence from the common type. Further inquiry revealed the fact that in the village to which all these lads belonged there lived a man with a misshapen foot who limped in the way which all the subjects had imitated; all, that is, with the exception of a lad who had broken his leg in childhood, and was no doubt reproducing an experience of his own."—Edmund Parish, *Hallucinations and Illusions*, 208-209 (Walter Scott, 1898).

Examples of all three of these phases of suggestion are provided by Prof. Allport, in *op. cit.*, 245-248. *Cf.* also Robert W. West, *Purposive Speaking*, Ch. XII.]

[2] The same considerations apply to the unusual suggestibility of ignorant adults, and to the widespread belief in the Middle Ages in miraculous events backed by the authority of the clergy.

until a suitable attitude can be prepared for its acceptance. . . .
4. A similar distraction of attention is produced by the interesting
motions made by the conjurer with his right hand while his left
unobtrusively performs the trick. 5. Fatigue and intoxicants sometimes increase suggestibility. 6. It is important, finally, to word
a suggestion in a positive rather than a negative manner. . . .

*Suggestion is a process involving elementary behavior mechanisms
in response to a social stimulus; the nature of the process being that
the one who gives the stimulus controls the behavior and consciousness of the recipient in an immediate manner, relatively uninfluenced by thought, and through the method of building up motor
attitudes, releasing them, or augmenting the released response as
it is being carried out.*

*'A suggestion' is a social stimulus producing the effect just
described.*

Contrary Suggestion and Negativism

A

ROBERT MacDOUGALL, "Contrary Suggestion," *Jour. Abn. Psychol.*, 6: 372·
380, 387-388, 391 (1911-1912)

Several forms of associative integration closely allied to one
another may be grouped under the single term "contrary suggestion," since in each case the direct tendency of the stimulus to
provoke an imitative response is suspended, and a reaction of an
opposed type takes its place. The first of these forms is the inhibitive reaction proper, having its typical embodiment in the response
to a situation previously accompanied by pain. The primary
tendency, in such a case, is characteristically replaced by a condition of hesitation—if the pain were slight—in which the opposing
solicitations alternate, and the tendency is now to do the act and
then to refrain from it; or by immediate suppression of the reaction
if the pain have been sufficiently intense or the association repeatedly experienced. Discomfort, dislike, humiliation, disadvantage,—
any adversely or disagreeably toned aspect associated with a given
situation may thereafter act as an inhibitive suggestion when the
stimulus recurs. It is not the remembrance of the past suffering
and the suppression of an act as the result of weighing alternatives
which is here referred to, but a tendency to react immediately and
uncritically, though negatively, to the suggestion which has been
made. An idea, the circumstances of whose original occurrence,

together with the character of its associations, has wholly lapsed from consciousness may thus set up the old inhibitive reaction when it recurs in such psychical isolation. This is most strikingly illustrated in the case of hysteria, in which the original moral shock which gave rise to the taboo or fear or dislike has been wholly forgotten. In normal life the same type of occurrence is by no means rare. It happens to most of us to have contracted at some time in our lives a dislike for certain things,—foods, odors, colors, or even persons—for which no reason can be given, but for which a cause exists in some earlier experience of mental or physical discomfort, with which the object or person in question has been connected.

Negative reactions of this type arise, finally, as the result of many processes of training in self-control. The thing to be avoided or prevented or anticipated is at first done in spite of the will and can only be lamented after it has happened; later it is accompanied by an acute, and in a sense anticipative, consciousness, but one which is only imperfectly effective; one is painfully embarrassed by the occurrence of the reaction, but its successful inhibition takes place only occasionally and uncertainly. Then, finally, the process is customarily anticipated from its incipient stages and suppressed without conscious hesitation or deliberation. When the latter condition has been established the stimulus may be said to bring about directly the inhibitive reaction.

The conception of contrary suggestion might usefully be extended to include what is commonly called suggestion by contrast. This form of suggestion comprises all those cases in which the idea or impression calls up its natural or conventional correlative. In this class of cases—perhaps in all—the opposites are, from a logical point of view, most closely allied. . . . What is more intimately connected with father than son, with subject than object, with cause than effect, with long than short; or, to take a class of cases less specifically defined, what is white more likely to suggest than black, day than night, woman than man? The two are members of a single logical pair, each of which, by virtue of the term applied to it, is singled out from a host of others for the most constant and intimate association with its fellow.

The same general features appear in the class of contrary suggestions at large. To name any specific act or relation carries the mind by an almost inevitable movement toward the thought of its opposite, if once the path of individual experience and its memories be left. In the way of associated ideas what can "go out" so readily suggest as "come in," "stand up" as "sit down," "obey" as "rebel," and so forth? To form such associations is part of the general discipline of life, which is already far on its way when the child first comes to self-consciousness. Association by contrast thus appears as a special case of the more general fact of contrary suggestion.

Gould's cases of incoherent action, due to the insistence upon training the right hand when the subject is naturally and strongly left handed, are probably to be classed here. These incoherences consist in making the reciprocal of an intended movement, of speaking a word of opposite significance to that which should be used, of putting into the waste-paper basket a paper which should have been kept, while the scraps to be thrown away are carefully filed, and the like. In these cases, while specific suggestion is lacking and no verbal formulation or purpose has taken place, the adaptive reaction proper to the situation is replaced by one of an opposite type as the result of a more profound and permanent disturbance of the normal relations between action and its ideal antecedents.

In its narrowest application, the term "contrary suggestion" [or negativism] is restricted to those forms of reaction in which an idea definitely formulated and constituting a proposal for the adoption of a specific course of conduct or logical attitude provokes a response of opposite character on the part of the one to whom it is made. Baldwin (Ment. Devel., pp. 137, 138) thus describes and illustrates the phenomenon: "By this is meant a tendency of a very singular kind observable in many children, no less than in many adults, to do the contrary when any course is suggested. The very word 'contrary' is used in popular talk to describe an individual who shows this type of conduct. Such a child or man is rebellious whenever rebellion is possible; he seems to kick constitutionally against the pricks. My child E. showed it in her second year in a very marked way. When told that a new taste was good,— a suggestion readily taken in its positive sense by her sister at that age—she would turn away with a show of distaste even when she had liked the same taste earlier. When asked to give her hand into mine, —a case of direct imitative suggestion—she thrust it behind her back. The sight of hat and cloak was a signal for a tempest, although she enjoyed outdoor excursions. . . . The tendency yielded to the all-conquering onset of imitation late in her second year."

Within the field of contrary suggestion in this narrow sense of the term, two subtypes must still be discriminated, a more elementary and a more complex form. The psychologically simpler, and apparently earlier, phase appears in a form of reaction which is probably as direct and uncomplicated in character as that in which the suggestion is sympathetically met and embodied in an unreflective imitative response, but which takes a direction opposite to that which the stimulus is designed to evoke. The psychological situation involved is elementary; the mind of the reactor is not the theater of an inner debate, as it becomes in the more complex form. There is no strife of motives to be discerned, no balancing of thesis against thesis. The response, though existing in an exceptional complex of relations, is both direct and naïve, as if one had said, "Let us not go farther," and the hearer had failed to catch the negative.

This type has its analogue in adult life, but in the latter case the contrary suggestion does not habitually lead to a practical reaction which opposes that implied in the stimulus from which it arose. It appears characteristically in moments of detached consciousness when the words to which we listen, or on which the eye rests by chance, arouse the idea of their opposite in the unoccupied mind, where they hang idly for a moment before disappearing. In some individual cases this logical preoccupation amounts almost to an obsession. The failure of the representative movement to follow upon the arousal of its ideal antecedent, in such cases, is a secondary feature of the phenomenon, due to the habit which the developed mind had acquired of treating ideas in isolation from the reactions in which they find embodiment. This detachment is the essential feature of the imaginative life and the incessant ideal reconstruction of situations and problems which constitutes reflection, results at last in an isolation of the mental system which has probably little representation at the second year of life, when contrary suggestion makes its appearance in the child.

In the more complex of the two types of negative reaction the result of the suggestion is neither to inhibit the action of the stimulus as such, though it is commonly rendered void, nor is it to substitute a type of response opposed to that of sympathetic imitation, but equally simple and direct; on the contrary, its effect is to complicate the situation by a new range of suggestions. The mental content is enriched rather than depleted; for there is raised in mind the consciousness of an alternative course of conduct, an action reflectively contrasted as well as contrasted in nature with that primarily suggested. The proposal to go out arouses the intention to stay indoors; to turn to the right, that of turning to the left; to return home, that of going farther, and so on.

It is of interest to consider the possible significance of this phase of individual development, and the function it may perform in the enrichment and organization of experience. When a contrary suggestion of this kind arises it does not involve the disappearance from consciousness of the original suggestion. Both alternatives develop before the mind, and, if the child be sufficiently advanced, commonly find expression in speech as well as act. "I don't want to go out; I won't go out," the child says, at the same time that it pushes hat and cloak away. "Be good, and do such and such a thing," results, in this mood, in the conscious resolution, "I won't be good; I hate this thing and will not do it," as well as in the disobedient act itself.

Consciousness is thus complicated by a strife of inner motives, the opposition to the primary suggestion arousing an activity which is at the same time critical and synthetic. The situation develops on both sides; for, since contrary suggestion occurs typically in connection with stimuli to action having a personal origin, the opposition to such a suggestion commonly provokes its repetition and reinforcement by additional stimuli, arguments, threats, entreaties, rewards. If the opposition persists, these positions must be met critically and the reasons for the alternative course of action developed in the reacting mind.

The significance of this phase of development lies in the mental processes thus aroused, and its importance is beyond question. However bizarre its various manifestations and however perverse the attitude it reveals, contrary suggestion represents the method by which the child naturally passes from an uncritical acceptance of suggestions and their immediate embodiment in action, to a reflective consideration of the respective values of two alternative courses when offered for selection, and finally to deliberate action and reasoned reflection in all their forms.

The period at which this form of response appears in the development of the child is significant. Baldwin, in the paragraph quoted, notes it in the second year; and Miss Shinn (*Devel. of Child,* p. 27), speaking of the ninety-first week, says: "Contrary actions became more common. They increased in frequency up to the beginning of the twenty-fourth month. At the close of the twenty-fourth month they became less frequent; the child, understanding language better, became more amenable to verbal suggestion"; and again, a little later (p. 31), she says: "In the later half of the second year it became possible for a purely mental stimulus to arouse an inclination towards action. Then the strange period of perverseness through which so many children pass, developed. At the time of the appearance of this phase, the child acted almost entirely from suggestion through association. Hence, when a certain course of action was proposed, the representation of the opposite course was at once called up and appealed to him with some force, since the ability to perceive the consequences of either act was as yet undeveloped. The child never expressed (in contrary mood) the mere negation or refusal; he proposed an alternative. Frequently, though not always, the representation did not prompt to action, and fell away upon the repetition of the suggestion. If, however, one agreed with him, saying, 'Well, we shall do as you wish,' he often burst into tears, demanding that the original plan be carried out, and thus showed the side on which the preponderance of desire hung."

At this age the child has made some progress in walking and is beginning to acquire speech. His recently achieved control over his limbs carries him away from his mother's side, and his eagerness to handle things brings him into contact with a multitude of novel objects. He is no longer protected, as he was during the first year of life, by his own helplessness and the more continuous attentions of his mother, but is exposed to new dangers and compelled to face problems and solve them through his own ingenuity. This advance, together with his growing understanding of language and alertness of observation, increases the range of his objects of attention and of his ideas, and thus furnishes him with the materials for a more complicated mental life.

At the same time the situations into which he is plunged with increasing frequency as his movements are made with more and more freedom and the range of his activities is extended, are such as to call for caution and preliminary examination to a degree never demanded when nothing was allowed to reach him until it had passed the mother's inspection. This period of his existence is consequently marked by incessant minor tragedies, by mental shocks and physical suffering; and the child's conduct begins to reflect the uncertainties of the world in which he finds himself.

Along with these phenomena appears another form of change which probably coöperates in preparing the child's mind to be the theater of the contrary suggestion. With the mastery of the art of walking comes a disposition toward roving and adventure. The child wanders away from the mother's side and incessantly ventures into strange places and seeks to escape beyond bounds. At the same time, and doubtless as a significant correlative of this change, the old indifference to the presence of strangers and to novel objects is replaced by a trepidation at their appearance, a shyness in the presence of unfamiliar persons, and a dread of unusual phenomena of all kinds. Thus there appear the spirit of venturesomeness, which affords the instinctive basis for the development of self-direction and self-reliance; and the sense of fear and shyness, from which, later, caution and the measures necessary to self-preservation in part take their rise. These two attitudes are now at war with one another,—as indeed they continue to stand related throughout life—and give rise to a form of reaction which is characteristic of the period, namely the rapid oscillation between confidence and timidity, approach and flight, in the presence of persons and objects of all kinds.

It is a transitional stage between lower and higher forms of conduct, and presents elements of discoördination characteristic of all changes of direction in development. The phenomenon of contrary suggestion may be said to sum up and represent the essential features of this phase in the individual's history. The child is now breaking up an old habit and a new reaction is under process of establishment. His response to the stimulus is no longer directly receptive and imitative, nor is it yet, in the proper sense, reflective and rational. The alternative is provoked in consciousness, as it must be if any proposed course of conduct is to be weighed and rationally decided; but it is not critically compared with the original suggestion, as again it must be if the course of conduct which emerges is to constitute the highest attainable adaptation to the situation. The contrary suggestion is thus not to be viewed as rebellion against discipline, or the rude assertion of the self against the oppression of a foreign will, and nothing more; it represents rather that stage in the normal process of self-development in which the crude materials of rational action have been given, but in which successful coördination has not yet become possible. In it one of the two elements of deliberate action has appeared, but the second and peculiar feature is still lacking; there is present to the consciousness of the reactor the idea of an alternative course of conduct aroused by that which has been suggested, but not the weighing of considerations for and against each course as a preliminary to the final adoption of one of them.

The type of reaction which contrary suggestion represents thus falls far short of the ideal of rational conduct. To have become the characteristic form of reaction in an adult is an indication of arrested development. It is essentially a transitional stage, to be transcended by the utilization of the content of the contrary suggestion to develop the various motives for action involved in the case on either side, and thus step by step to establish that habit of reflecting upon the reasons for and against any suggested course of conduct which we call deliberative or rational procedure. . . .

Within the bounds of strictly normal experience, however, this form of elementary reaction is commonly neither general nor persistent. It appears either as a transitory mood or as a characteristic reaction to some specific point of view or individual will. In the first of these two cases the normally consistent mind has suffered momentary disintegration, and instead of responding with either an acceptance or a rational objection, it meets each advance with an obstinate and elementary opposition. In moments of irritation and on occasions of intellectual defeat the normal subject is likely to fall back upon this primitive mode of reaction, and to indulge in petty carping and futile, because inconsistent, faultfinding. The attitude becomes more pronounced as the demand upon physical and mental energies increases; with some persons it is one of the most characteristic accompaniments of nervous fatigue. In the disturbances and exhaustion of disease the type presents still more striking features, as in the fretfulness and unreasonable perversity of the dyspeptic; but here one passes the limits of normal experience and enters a field where its manifestations are as varied as they are extreme.

In the second of the cases referred to the individual responds normally to the general range of stimuli, but in relation to some particular class the rational reaction fails and is replaced by a persistent and meaningless opposition to all suggestion. This reaction appears most commonly in connection with the attitude of personal hostility to some individual human will, but it arises also as a characteristic response to some particular point of view or order of concepts. For most of us, perhaps, some individual exists the very sight of whom sets our teeth on edge. We dislike his looks or his manners; he annoys us by the way he walks and talks; we resent his opinions, and if we hear him express approval of a point of view we have ourselves adopted in the past, it is enough to turn us against it. His errors are regarded as deliberate sins, and under the most casual attitude we spy some hidden perversity. Nothing he does escapes our condemnation, and he has only to assume a point of view or express an opinion to arouse our opposition. This attitude most commonly appears when some form of intense personal rivalry is involved, as in the jealousies of a lover; but it extends also to all classes of opponents, social, political, religious. One person can see nothing good in Impressionism in art; another in political Socialism, or in Protection or Free Silver in economics; another in Realism or Empiricism, in Hegelianism or Hedonism in philosophy. For one everything that Bismarck did, or Thiers, or Gladstone, or Jefferson, is distrusted; no motive is above suspicion and every attitude is a political ruse or a personal pose. Every one of us acknowledges such irrational prejudices when they appear as momentary whims, but few can see that their lives show systematic misconstructions of this kind issuing in permanent antipathies which render the individual incapable of any full and impartial apprehension of the facts in question. In these forms of prejudice lie the beginnings of those dread perversions in the pathological subject which we call delusions of persecution. . . .

The sane consciousness is that which is grounded in habit and organic memory, but which also expresses itself through the free utilization of past experience as plastic materials for the realization of ideal purposes. So, also, the rational social institution is that which is based upon tradition and reflects the substance of a people's history, but which, at the same time, is continuously modified to meet the changing needs of those who live under it. And one who is curious may trace in the more permanent and complex features of institutional life a series of individual modifications and specific defects which form the analogue, not only of the normal variations in suggestibility which have here been described, but also of its aberrations in the pathological subject.

B

C. G. JUNG, *The Psychology of Dementia Praecox,* 14-15 (Nervous & Mental Diseases Publishing Co., 1909)

The most general standpoint on the question of negativism is taken by Bleuler in his work on negative suggestibility.[1] He shows that negative suggestibility, that is, the impulse toward contrast associations, is not only a constituent part of the normal psyche, but also a frequent mechanism of pathological symptoms in hysteria, impulsive phenomena, and dementia praecox. The contrast mechanism is an independent function entirely rooted in "affectivity." It therefore manifests itself mainly in presentations of strong feeling as in decisions and similar things. "This mechanism protects against a rash act and forces the consideration of, for and against." The contrast mechanism is a counterpart of suggestibility. Suggestibility is the faculty of the reception and realization of strong feeling-toned ideas, while the contrast mechanism guards the opposite. It is for this reason that Bleuler appropriately calls it negative suggestibility. The fact that these two functions are so closely related readily explains why they are met with together clinically. In hysteria we have suggestibility near insuperable con-

---

[1] Bleuler, "Die negative Suggestibilität ein psychologisches Prototyp des Negativismus, der conträren Autosuggestion und gewisser Zwangsideen," *Psych.-Neurol. Wochenschr.,* 1904.

trary autosuggestion; and negativism, automatism and echopraxy in dementia praecox, etc.

The importance of negative suggestibility in everyday psychical occurrences explains why contrast associations are everywhere enormously frequent. They are in the closest relationship.[1]

In language, too, we see something similar. The words which express the usual contrasts are very closely associated and therefore mostly belong to the intimate associations of language, as, white, black, etc. In primitive languages one occasionally finds only one word for contrasting ideas. According to Bleuler a relatively mild emotional disturbance will suffice to produce negativistic phenomena. Janet (*Les Obsessions*, 1 : 60) shows that in persons suffering from impulsive ideas, the *"abaissement du niveau mental"* suffices to liberate a play of contrasts. What, therefore, can we expect from the "apperceptive dementia" in dementia praecox! Indeed, here we really find the apparently irregular play of positive and negative which is very often nicely reflected in the associations as expressed in speech.[2] Hence in the problem of negativism we have sufficient evidence that this symptom too, is in close relationship with "apperceptive dementia." The central control of the psyche is so weakened that it can neither further the positive nor inhibit the negative acts, or the reverse may be true.[3]

The Significance of Negativism and Suggestibility in Children

LEE EDWARD TRAVIS, "Suggestibility and Negativism as Measured by Auditory Threshold During Reverie," *Jour. Abn. Psychol.*, 18 : 364-365 (1924)

When a mother says "don't", and the child does the thing nevertheless, being rewarded by the act itself or by the indulgence on the part of the parent, the pleasure the child receives is interpreted as

---

[1] The following express themselves in a similar manner: Paulhan, *L'activité mentale et les elements de l'esprit*, 1889.—Svenson, "Om Katatonie," *Hygiea*, 1902.—Janet, *Les Obsessions*, 1903.—Pick, "On Contrary Actions," *Jour. Nerv. & Ment. Dis.*, Jan., 1904.—An instructive case is given by Josiah Royce, "The Case of John Bunyan," *Psychol. Rev.*, 1894, 143. [Jelliffe, "Pre Dementia Praecox," *Am. Jour. Med. Sc.*, 1907. Ed.]

[2] Compare the analyses of Pelletier, *L'Association des idées dans la manie aigue et dans la débilité mentale* (Thèse de Paris), 1903; as well as the experimental examinations of Stransky, *Über Sprachverwirrtheit*.

[3] Further works on negativism have already been criticised by Bleuler, *loc. cit*

a direct result of the disobedience. In this manner a child can be taught that reward follows disobedience and the way to receive pleasure is to disobey. Furthermore if one parent in correcting a child is not supported by the other parent, the child is accordingly taught to disobey the former in order to receive the reward of the latter.

Another way that negativism can be developed is by teasing and nagging. It is a well known fact that dogs and ponies can be taught to be resistive, spiteful, contrary, stubborn, balky, and mean by this method. People familiar with horses immediately refer the cause of balkiness to bad training.

Just as a quiet and docile animal can be turned into a disturbing and vicious one by teasing and maltreatment, so also a gentle and good-natured child can be transformed into a stubborn and negativistic one by torment and nagging.

In these ways the characteristic of stubbornness or negativism is begun and as time goes on, is strengthened. Whether or not a child possesses by original nature the trait of negativism, is not determined; but that this trait, howsoever it may arise, can be modified by environmental influences is demonstrable.

To what negativism may lead if possessed to an extreme degree is well brought out in abnormal cases. The dementia præcox patient has developed the responses of his life so far that any stimulation from outside environment is an unbearable interruption. In order more efficiently to resist the influences from without, he entirely withdraws all interests from his surroundings and becomes the recluse *par excellence,* becoming dead so far as the things of this world are concerned. Even satisfying the most demanding and necessary physiological needs becomes an intolerable burden.

If the characteristics of this type of abnormality are learned or even exaggerated through training, then their presence in a normal individual means the potentiality for developing into such a mental disorder under undue stress. It is imperative that the trait be determined and measured early so that the proper training can be given which will modify the personality and avoid a possible psychosis.

It also can be shown that suggestibility is learned just as negativism is learned. It is taught by rewards being given only when the child accepts suggestions from the environment or by punishments being dealt only when the child fails to receive suggestions from his surroundings. Suggestibility really means dependence, as is illustrated by the individual who always relies upon another person for his decisions, modes of behavior or stimulation to endeavor.

Often in the case of twins, or of two children about the same age, one comes to depend upon the other and fails to develop a will of his own, being amenable eventually not only to the suggestions from his brother or sister, but from anyone.

A child begins by being permitted to lean too heavily on the mother or father, resting his future on their wisdom. The responses of incredulity, scepticism, and want of faith are not learned or exercised so that the individual comes to be susceptible to every environmental factor, good or bad, adequate or inadequate.

Suggestibility by no means indicates a lack of intelligence. It is not indicative of either the absence or presence of intelligence, as is amply proven by the intelligence quotients of highly suggestible individuals.

To what suggestibility, if possessed in an extreme degree, may lead, has been pointed out in various places in this study. The mental disorder characterized chiefly by suggestibility is hysteria. The hysteric has learned to take suggestions so unreservedly and whole-heartedly that he mirrors every slight play of environmental forces. He can be made to forget part of his life, and the use of part of his body by mere suggestion. He is ill or well, happy or sad, loving or hating, just according to the stimulation of external circumstances. Thus amnesias, paralyses, hallucinations, fantasies, and dream states are produced or removed by word of command.

In order to avoid the overdevelopment of a trait to the extent that it may lead the individual to make all sorts of maladjustments to the realities of life, it must be detected early in its formation and development so that it can be modified and guided.

It has been shown that the presence of these traits can be detected by raised and lowered thresholds.[1]

---

[1] [*Cf.* Dr. Travis' article, "A Test for Distinguishing Between Schizophrenoses and Psychoneuroses."]

CHAPTER XIX

HYPNOTIC CONDITIONS

In Prof. Charles Hubbard Judd's discussion of Dissociation, above, we find hypnosis regarded as a condition of partial dissociation of the higher centers which can be induced through holding the attention by various methods of soothing, gazing at bright objects, and the like. The hypnotic condition is considered possible for normal persons, whether such persons are taken alone or in groups; and habits of being hypnotized are easily formed. The person hypnotized frequently shows abeyance of some functions, and heightening of others, within normal limits. His extreme suggestibility is manifested in the lack of criticism of ideas urged upon him while in the hypnotic state.

That hypnosis is not an absolute condition, but is rather a name applied to a group of conditions which shade insensibly into other mental states, is illustrated by the following conception of Sidis:

The Hypnoidal State as Contrasted with the Hypnagogic State

BORIS SIDIS, *Symptomatology, Psychognosis and Diagnosis of Psychopathic Diseases*, 33, 34, 36-37 (Badger, 1914)

By the method of hypnoidization we produce a peculiar state which, for the lack of a better term, I designate as "hypnoidal," twilight state. What is the hypnoidal state? The hypnoidal state is essentially a borderland state. The subject is apparently awake and seems to be in full possession of all his powers, and still he is more closely in touch with the dissociated experiences than he is otherwise in the full waking state. Perhaps the *sub-waking* state would . . . be an apt term for the hypnoidal condition. The subject seems to hover between the conscious and the subconscious, somewhat in the same way as in the half-drowsy condition we hover between wakefulness and sleep.

The hypnoidal state is not a stable condition, it keeps on fluctuating from moment to moment; not falling more deeply into a
subconscious condition in which outlived experiences are easily
aroused, or again rising to the level of waking states. In such conditions the patient often tells you "something has come . . . but
it is gone." The hypnoidal state has changed, it has become lighter,
and the dissociated moments have become again submerged. There
is a constant struggle going on in the hunting out of the stray dissociated systems. . . .

The hypnoidal state may either lead to sleep or to hypnosis. . . .

A somewhat related state has been long known in psychological
literature as the hypnagogic state which precedes the oncome of
sleep and is rich in hallucinations known under the term of hypnagogic hallucinations. In coming out of sleep, a closely related state
may be observed, a state which I have termed *hypnapagogic*. In
both states, hypnagogic and hypnapagogic, dream-hallucinations
hold sway. . . .

Typical Hypnotic Phenomena

ALBERT MOLL, *Hypnotism*, 4th ed., The Contemporary Science Series, 35,
    31-35, 47-48, 55-57, 107-108, 110-112, 119-120, 123-128, 131-133,
        138, 142-144, 154-162, 175-179 (Walter Scott, 1897)

I mean by *hypnosis* the state into which the subjects were thrown
during the experiments described. . . .

Hypnotism is not the name of the state itself, but of the whole
science which deals with the phenomena of this state. . . .

In order to give the reader an idea of the phenomena of hypnotism it will be best, first of all, to describe a few experiments. The
phenomena will in this way be made more comprehensible than by
means of any number of definitions.

I begin the experiments with a young man of twenty. I request
him to seat himself on a chair, and give him a button to hold, telling him to look at it fixedly. After three minutes his eyelids fall;
he tries in vain to open his eyes, which are fast closed; his hand,
which until now has grasped the button, drops upon his knee. I
assure him that it is impossible for him to open his eyes. (He
makes vain efforts to open them.) I now say to him, "Your hands
are stuck fast to your knee; you cannot possibly raise them." (He
raises his hands, however.) I continue to converse with him; I
find that he is perfectly conscious, and I can discover no essential
change in him whatever. I raise one of his arms; directly I let go,

he drops it as he pleases. Upon which I blow upon his eyes, which open at once, and he is in the same state as before the experiment. The young man remembers all that I have said to him. The only striking thing is, therefore, that he could not open his eyes, and that he feels a certain degree of fatigue. . . .

Mr. X., forty-one years old, seats himself on a chair. I tell him that he must try to sleep. "Think of nothing but that you are to go to sleep." After some seconds I continue: "Now your eyelids are beginning to close; your eyes are growing more and more fatigued; the lids quiver more and more. You feel tired all over; your arms go to sleep; your legs grow tired; a feeling of heaviness and the desire for sleep takes possession of your whole body. Your eyes close; your head feels duller; your thoughts grow more and more confused. Now you can no longer resist; now your eyelids are closed. Sleep!" After the eyelids have closed I ask him if he can open them. (He tries to do so, but they are too heavy.) I raise his left arm high in the air. (It remains in the air, and cannot be brought down in spite of all his efforts.) I ask him if he is asleep. "Yes." "Fast asleep?" "Yes." "Do you hear the canary singing?" "Yes." "Now you hear the concert?" "Certainly." Upon this I take a black cloth and put it into his hand. "You feel this dog quite plainly?" "Quite plainly." "Now you can open your eyes. You will see the dog clearly. Then you will go to sleep again, and not wake till I tell you." (He opens his eyes, looks at the imaginary dog and strokes it.) I take the cloth out of his hand, and lay it on the floor. (He stands up and reaches out for it.) Although he is in my room, when I tell him that he is in the Zoological Gardens he believes it and sees trees, and so on.

In this case X. is thrown into the hypnotic state by my arousing in his mind an image of the sleep. This manner of hypnotizing is used by the Nancy investigators, and may be called the method of Nancy. The subject is completely without a will of his own. It is not only possible in his case to prevent the most various movements by a mere prohibition, but I can also control his sense perceptions. On my assurance, he thinks he hears a canary, or hears music. He takes a black cloth for a dog, and believes himself to be in the Zoological Gardens when he is in my room. But the following phenomenon is still more striking. X. hears all that I say to him, and allows himself to be influenced by me in every way. Yet two other men, A. and B., who are present, appear not to be observed by the hypnotic at all. A. lifts up the arm of the subject; the arm falls loosely down, and when A. desires the arm to remain in the air the subject takes no notice. He obeys my orders only, and is *en rapport* with me only. In order to wake him I now call to him: "Wake up!" He wakes at once, but only remembers going to sleep; of what happened during the sleep he knows nothing.

I interrupt here for a time the description of the experiments; I shall describe others in the course of this work, and shall occasionally return to those already depicted. I will merely remark that in all these experiments, however different they might be, the voluntary movements were always inhibited, that in one case hallucinations of the senses could be induced, and that it was possible for me in all cases to converse with the subject, and we could understand each other. . . .

If the awakening is not brought about by artificial means, persons in a light hypnotic state, such as is described in the first two experiments, habitually wake of their own accord after a few minutes or even seconds; this especially happens when the continuance of the state has not been expressly ordered. Some people wake at the exact moment when the experimenter leaves them, as they then no longer think themselves under his influence. Others awake of their own accord out of deep hypnosis if they hear an unexpected and loud noise, or have exciting dreams. Thus, I once saw a grownup person wake herself by screaming, because in the hypnotic state she had believed herself to be a little child, and in that character had begun to cry. The awakening which comes about without any apparent cause is remarkable and unexplained (*mouvement psychique*.) The same thing is sometimes observed in natural sleep, especially at its beginning; O. Rosenbach traces it to increase of the reflexes. Generally, however, the deep hypnoses continue for some time when they are not artificially terminated. Sometimes many hours pass before the subject wakes.

The old mesmerists (Du Potet, Lafontaine) describe as a rare occurrence in hypnotic experiments a state of lethargy, in which artificial awakening was impossible. After some time there was a spontaneous awakening, and no evil consequences were to be observed. Guermonprez described lately how a person had remained three days in hypnosis, nobody being able to wake him. It appears that these incidents occur more often when sense stimulations are used—for example, the fixed gaze or the mesmeric passes. And again, this state has only been observed among hysterical subjects, so far as I am aware. Therefore I believe that this lethargy must be distinguished from hypnosis, the chief symptoms of which are wanting. . . .

The question whether hypnosis can be induced against the wish of the subject is by no means unimportant. We must distinguish here whether the subject complies with the prescribed conditions or whether he does not. If he does; if, for example, he sufficiently concentrates his attention; if he gazes at some object with the necessary attention, then hypnosis may be produced at the first attempt, even against the wish of the person experimented on. However, it must be remembered that a person who does not intend to allow himself to be hypnotized will hardly place himself in the necessary mental state. He will not generally fulfil the conditions; he will fix his eyes, but will allow his attention to wander. However, I think I may assert that certain persons accustomed to obedience can be hypnotized at the first attempt even against their will, and without the ordinary necessary straining of the attention, if only they are told that hypnosis will occur. Notwithstanding, these cases appear to be rare. It is not to be doubted that many people who have been frequently hypnotized can be re-hypnotized against their will and without their intentional compliance with the ordinary conditions. The experiments of Heidenhain show that people can be hypnotized against their wish. He hypnotized soldiers in the presence of their officers, who had strictly forbidden them to sleep. Such a command would have as much effect on a soldier as the personal wish not to sleep. Post-hypnotic suggestion, of which I shall speak later, is also a means of sending persons to sleep against their wish. There is a third possibility, namely, that no wish should exist in either direction. The conditions necessary for hypnosis may occur occasionally by chance, without the subject being conscious of them (Max Dessoir). For example, some one over his work is obliged to look fixedly at a certain point; this suffices to induce hypnosis (sometimes after earlier unfit experiments), without the person thinking of it. In this case the will is neither interested for it nor against it. The statement of Preyer, that persons being photographed sometimes remain sitting rigidly still after the taking of the photograph is finished, may be referred to a hitherto unsuspected hypnotic state, brought on by the fixed stare necessary to the process. It is known that some of the inmates of the Salpêtrière in Paris fall suddenly into catalepsy in consequence of some loud unexpected noise. There is an interesting case of a girl who had often been hypnotized by loud noises, and who went to a drawer to appropriate some photographs out of it. The casual beating of a gong threw her into a cataleptic state, so that she stood motionless in the act of carrying out her theft, and was discovered. Hack Tuke remarks that it is a pity all thieves cannot be taken as easily.

As Bertrand related, with certain persons natural sleep can be transformed into magnetic sleep. Many attempts have been made to do this in later times. Baillif, Gscheidlen, Berger, Bernheim, and Forel have even made these experiments on persons who had been refractory to hypnotism. I myself have been able to make some observations of this kind. One person concerned was a gentleman whom I had already frequently hypnotized, and whom I often threw into the hypnotic state while he was taking his afternoon sleep, without waking him. In another case I succeeded in producing various movements, as raising of the arms, through slight suggestions to a gentleman who was in his afternoon sleep. I was obliged to speak in a whisper to avoid waking him. It is doubtful whether such experiments would succeed with persons who had never heard of hypnotism. Schrenck-Notzing reports a case in which hypnosis was produced from post-epileptic coma. Cases in which conditions of hysterical sleep have been led on into hypnosis have been described by Löwenfeld and others. I may refer here to the question already raised, whether hypnotic states can be produced by chemical substances, such as chloroform.

In any case, however, previous consent is not absolutely necessary to the production of hypnosis, and, on the other hand, there are people who are refractory in spite of a decided wish to be hypnotized (Preyer, Forel). In general, however, the intentional resistance of the subject hinders hypnosis, simply because a person who is willing to be hypnotized complies more easily with the necessary conditions than another. Consequently it is not astonishing that patients who come to a doctor on purpose to be hypnotized, particularly when they come with full confidence, are more easy to hypnotize than others. These others often allow an attempt to be made with them, with the silent resolution to show that "they are not to be caught," or they submit themselves, as Nonne says, "only for fun," and yet many believe that susceptibility to hypnosis is a sign of defective will or intelligence! . . .

We observe numerous hallucinations and illusions in hypnosis. We have seen . . . that it suffices to assert that a dog is present, and a dog will apparently be seen. A handkerchief was in this case taken for a dog, consequently this was an illusion. An illusion is more easily induced than a hallucination; in the absence of an external object, such as the handkerchief, the suggestion very often fails. When I do not offer some such object the hypnotic often finds it for himself. Hallucinations of sight are more easily caused when the eyes are closed; the subjects then see objects and persons with their eyes shut, as in dreams. They think, at the same time, that their eyes are open, just as we are unaware in dreams that our eyes are shut. If we wish to cause a delusion of the sense of sight at the moment of opening the eyes, it is necessary to make the suggestion quickly, lest the act of opening the eyes should awaken the subject. I advise the use of fixed attention while the suggestion is being made . .. so that the subject may not awaken himself by looking about. The other organs of sense may also be deluded. I knock on the table and give the idea that cannon are being fired, I blow with the bellows and make the suggestion that an engine is steaming up. A hallucination of hearing something, e. g., the piano, is induced without the aid of any external stimulus. In the same way smell, taste, and touch may be the senses deceived. It is well known that hypnotics will drink water or even ink for wine, will eat onions for pears, will smell ammonia for Eau de Cologne, etc. In these cases the expression of face induced by the suggested perception corresponds so perfectly to it that a better effect would scarcely be produced if the real article were used. Tell the subject he has taken snuff, he sneezes. All varieties of the senses of touch, of pressure, of temperature, of pain, can be influenced. I tell a person that he is standing on ice. He feels cold at once. He trembles, his teeth chatter, he wraps himself in his coat. "Goose-skin" can be produced by the suggestion of a cold bath (Krafft-Ebing). In like manner itching and so forth can be induced. I say to a gentleman, "Tomorrow at three o'clock your forehead will itch." The post-hypnotic suggestion proves true; the forehead itches so much that the subject rubs it continually. It appears to me that the senses of touch and taste are the most easily and frequently influenced. For example, the suggestion of a bitter taste takes effect much sooner than the suggestion of a delusion of sight or hearing. It is true that the subjects often account to themselves for the delusion; they taste the bitterness, but say at the same time that it must be a subjective sensation, since they have nothing bitter in their mouths.

Sense delusions can be suggested in any way. We can tell the subject that he sees a bird. We can suggest the same thing by gesture—for example, by pretending to hold a bird in the hand—particularly after the subject has received some hypnotic training. The chief point is that the subject should understand what is intended by the gesture.

Naturally, several organs of sense can be influenced by suggestion at the same time. I tell some one, "Here is a rose"; he not only sees, but smells and feels the rose. I pretend to give another subject a dozen oysters; he eats them at once, without further suggestion. The suggestion here affects sight, feeling, and taste at the same time. . . .

In contrast with the delusions of sense hitherto described, which are sometimes called positive, there are also negative hallucinations, or negative delusions of sense. The older mesmerists (Deleuze, Bertrand, Charpignon) published many observations of them. This kind of suggestion, which at first seemed more incredible than the positive, nevertheless has analogies in the normal state, like all the hypnotic phenomena. Consider the juggler, who knows how to use the most important psychological laws for practical purposes. Let us watch him carefully, and we shall see how he hides things, how he makes a change, how he substitutes one card for another under the very eyes of the spectators. But he knows how to draw off their attention by clever talk, so that even those who have watched him are unable to give an account to themselves of his proceedings. For example, the cards are changed in the spectator's field of view; the sense stimulation takes place, but does not penetrate to the consciousness. We find analogous occurrences in ordinary life. It has happened to everybody to look for something which is before his eyes. In this case also the thing is not perceived, although it is in the seeker's field of view and he is actually thinking about it. It is no longer incredible, then, that we should find analogous processes in hypnosis. If we can make the hypnotic see what does not exist, after the above explanation it is no longer surprising that we can prevent his seeing what does exist. . . .

Forel has lately pointed out that the insane often have these negative hallucinations. He has also pointed out that hypnotics complete the hallucination at their pleasure. Thus I say to X., while A. is sitting on a chair, "A. has gone away; there is nobody on that chair." X. examines the chair, and as he feels something there he imagines that a plaid is lying on it. We see here how a suggested negative hallucination passes into an illusion through the auto-suggestion of the hypnotic; this is very common. To be exact, we can regard every illusion as the sum of a positive and a negative hallucination, as in each illusion something present is not perceived and something not present is perceived. . . .

I say to a subject who complains of want of appetite, "The loss of appetite has disappeared; you are hungry." I can cause another to feel thirst. Feelings of pleasure can likewise be excited. Debove, on the other hand, has induced loss of appetite by suggestion to such an extent and for so long a time that the person concerned took no regular meal for fourteen days. Further, it is possible up to a certain point to satisfy the hunger and thirst of subjects in deep hypnosis by merely suggested food and drink, as Fillassier informs us. It is a pity, however, that this result can only be obtained with a few persons, and in a certain measure; for otherwise our politicians would no longer need to puzzle their heads over social questions and the feeding of the masses. ⌐ Sexual feeling can also be produced by suggestion. Leopold Casper tells of a case in which Tissié hypnotized a patient, and suggested to him that the right ring-finger should indicate sexual desire and the left abstinence. When the patient awoke, contact with the right ring-finger caused sexual excitement, contact with the left subdued it. Once Tissié forgot to remove the suggestion, and the consequence was that for twenty-four hours the patient was unable to refrain from coitus and masturbation, as well as spontaneous emissions.

I shall here particularly discuss the feelings of pain. What effect has hypnosis upon them, with and without suggestion? Apart from some particular hypnotic states, in which Berger finds increased sensitiveness to pain, we occasionally find analgesia in hypnosis. Sometimes this exists to such a degree that the severest surgical operations can be performed during the state. It is also known that needles may be run into some persons during hypnosis without their feeling pain, though they feel the touch. And yet a complete analgesia is extremely rare in hypnosis, although authors, copying from one another, assert that it is common. There is an immense difference between pricking the subject with a needle and using the faradic brush. The pain caused by the use of the latter is so great, especially when a considerable electric force is employed, that very few persons in hypnosis can endure it, even when they show no pain on being pricked with a needle. In some cases, where analgesia does not appear spontaneously, it can be produced by suggestion. But suggestion more easily produces a certain decrease of sensitiveness to pain. Complete analgesia is seldom attained. Many cases described as completely analgesic—for example, those of Tamburini and Seppilli—proved on a closer examination not to be so, as a strong faradic current finally produced pain. I will just remark that all kinds of pain can be induced by suggestion; the pain caused by a needle as well as that caused by a knife or a burn. The face of the subject expresses pain in such a manner, that an impartial person can hardly decide whether the pain is real or suggested. . . .

Let us now ask, To what extent can the involuntary muscular system be influenced by suggestion? The peristaltic motion is relatively easy to affect. I have had several experiences of the facility with which the bowels of some hypnotics are affected by suggestion. I say to one of them, "In half an hour after awakening your bowels will act." This is certain to happen. "To-morrow morning at eight your bowels will act." The effect follows. "To-

morrow between eight and nine your bowels will act three times."
Exactly the same result, though the subject remembers nothing of
the suggestion on awaking. It is interesting to note that the action
of aperients can be checked by suggestion, though this does not
often happen. A patient takes a dose of castor-oil which is sufficient to procure copious action of the bowels. He is told in hypnosis
that the medicine will only take effect in forty-eight hours. The
suggestion is effectual, although with this person the dose habitually
acts quickly and abundantly (*v.* Krafft-Ebing). Or let a few drops
of water be given to the hypnotic with the assertion that it is a
strong purge; motion of the bowels follows. Suggested emetics act
in the same way. This is not very surprising, as we know that these
and other functions, even though they are independent of our will,
are yet under the influence of the mind. Vomiting at the sight of
disgusting things, and the celebrated *mica panis* pills administered
as aperients prove this well enough.

In some persons the vessels and the heart can be influenced in the
same way, as several experiments have proved. Dumontpallier has
made some, which should here be mentioned. He induced by suggestion a local increase of temperature of as much as 3° C. Forel,
Beaunis, and F. Myers have also observed local reddening by suggestion. Even this phenomenon should not surprise us too much,
since we observe the same sort of vasomotor disturbance to result
from mental condition. I have spoken above [*op. cit.,* p. 69] of
the blushing which occurs when any one is confused. I will here
mention the contrary of this—the paleness which often follows
fright. And as a curiosity I will mention the local reddening of
the skin which has often been observed in spirit mediums (Carpenter, Carl du Prel), and which has been explained as a supernatural phenomenon. As these mediums are often at these times
in a state of trance—that is, in a state resembling hypnosis, and
perhaps identical with it—this phenomenon admits of a perfectly
natural explanation.

Some observations have also been made upon the influence of suggestion on the action of the heart. I myself have often been able
to produce a slowing of a normal or rapid pulse. However, we
should be cautious how we draw the conclusion that the suggestion
has affected the nerves of the heart directly; the effect is an indirect one, rather. For, independent of the fact that the action of
the heart is to a certain degree dependent on the respiration, it is
likewise under the influence of ideas, which affect the emotions.
Such ideas have the power of quickening or slowing the heart's
action; it is possible that the suggestion which retards a quick

pulse only produces this result indirectly by a removal of the mental exciting cause, or, *vice versa,* quickens the pulse by excitement. My observations of the quickening and slowing of the heart's action by suggestion lead me to take this view rather than that of a direct influence of suggestion on the nerves and nerve centres of the heart. In any case it would be difficult to exclude this indirect action, especially as its effects are rapid. However, the method is of no consequence. Beaunis has seen a momentary effect of suggestion in several people without change of respiration from suggestion. He has seen the pulse fall in consequence of suggestion from 98 beats to 92, and then rise to 115 beats. He infers a direct action of suggestion upon the inhibitory centre of the heart, and thinks himself also obliged to exclude ideas which affect the mental state, such as are mentioned above, since the effect of the suggestion was always momentary. But his reasoning on this point is not conclusive. . . .

The secretion of milk is also under the influence of suggestion. A case, which only shows, however, the indirect influence of suggestion, has been reported by Hassenstein. In a wet nurse in whom the secretion had ceased, it again flowed copiously by suggestion. It had ceased, however, owing to excitement over the child's condition, and was renewed by suggesting away the excitement. Grossmann reports a case in which the secretion of milk was produced by direct suggestion.

Heidenhain induced discharge of urine by tickling the perineum. I do not think this phenomenon should be regarded as a physical reflex ; I believe that the patient emptied the bladder because he believed that he was intended to do so. Preyer mentions this as an example of secretion; I hold a different opinion; I believe that the patient did not *secrete* the urine in consequence of the external stimulus or command, but merely passed it. This is, then, a motor suggestion. I have often been able to produce the same effect: "After waking you must make water five times." The patient is surprised after the hypnosis that he wishes to make water so often, but obeys. Few investigations have been made as to whether the kidney secretions can be influenced by suggestion. However, Wetterstrand mentions results produced in diseases of the kidneys which almost justify the conclusion that in certain persons it is possible to influence the kidney secretions by suggestion. This is not so strange when we reflect that many diseases in which there is increased secretion of urine are of nervous origin, and that anxiety and fear also appear to influence it.

Krafft-Ebing draws conclusions as to the increase of intestinal secretions from one experiment. He suggested to his subject a profuse watery evacuation of the bowels, which followed. As the bladder had been emptied shortly before, and only a small quantity of urates had been found in the urine, Krafft-Ebing thinks himself obliged to consider the fluid as an increase of the intestinal secretions. . . .

Among the experiments in this direction I will first of all mention the cases in which menorrhagia is induced or arrested by suggestion. It is not to be doubted that this is practicable in the case of certain persons. Forel has made a whole series of experiments on this point, and has also partly confirmed the accuracy and the effect of suggestion by personal investigation. Many other experimenters have also been able to confirm the effect of suggestion on menstruation (Sperling, A. Voisin, Gascard, Briand). Liébeault's statement that he was never able to cause abortion by suggestion is curious. The influence of suggestion in menorrhagia seems less wonderful and striking when we reflect how very much psychical influences otherwise affect it. It is known, for example, that the periods often become irregular in women who are about to undergo a surgical operation.

I have mentioned the influence of suggestion in this place in spite of the fact that these experiments do not, properly speaking, demonstrate an organic influence. We may be concerned here with a vasomotor disturbance, which secondarily induces the organic changes. This appears to me probable.

Jendrássik and Krafft-Ebing obtained marks like burns on their subjects by means of suggestion. If some object, such as a matchbox, a pair of scissors, a snuff-box, a linen-stamp, etc., was pressed upon the skin, and the subject was at the same time told that the skin was being burned, a blister in the form of the object resulted. The marks remained a long time visible. If the object was pressed upon the left side of a hysterical patient anæsthetic on the right, the burn appeared symmetrically on the right as it would if reflected in a glass, as could be especially seen when letters were used. Jendrássik maintains that deception was absolutely excluded in these cases of suggested burns. Besides this, a dermatologist, Lipp, at one of the experiments, declared that it would be impossible to cause the suggested lesion mechanically or chemically. Burns caused by suggestion have often been observed in the Salpêtrière. The same may be said of the experiments of Bourru, Burot, and Berjon, who induced bleeding by suggestion in the same subject as Mabille, Ramadier, and Jules Voisin. Puységur had witnessed the same thing. Bleeding of the nose appeared at command in the abovementioned subject, and later on bleeding from the skin at a time decided on beforehand. When the skin had been rubbed with a blunt instrument in order to give point to the suggestion, bleeding of the skin is said to have appeared at command, the traces of which were visible three months later. It is interesting that in the case of this person, who was hemiplegic and anæsthetic on the right side, the suggestion would not take effect on that side. Mabille's observations of this subject are particularly interesting, because they show that a person in hypnosis can cause these bleedings by auto-suggestion. Unfortunately the accounts we possess of such cases do not enable us to draw a definite conclusion as to whether contact will induce bleeding under other circumstances (F. Myers). Meanwhile we must remember that the bleeding did not follow closely on the contact, which would have been the case if the effect were mechanical. Berjon reminds us, also, that precautionary measures were taken to prevent the subject from touching his own arm, and thereby causing a wound. Artigalas and Rémond have published the case of a woman of twenty-two in whom tears of blood appeared. By suggestion it was also possible to call out bloody sweat on her hand. In the abbreviated report, which alone I have seen, it is not stated whether the sweat was subjected to a microscopical and chemical analysis. . . .

It is to be understood that great caution is necessary in dealing with experiments in which anatomical injury is caused by suggestion. This is all the more necessary because by certain spiritualists these experiments are regarded as proving that the soul is an organising as well as a thinking power. Apart from this, as already mentioned, it sometimes happens that no sufficient precautions against deception are adopted, so that many experiments lose in significance. This is unfortunately the case with Hebold's successful removal of a wart by suggestion in a hysterical subject. . . .

It has often been observed that memory after awakening can be produced by a special effort of the hypnotist (Bleuler, Pierre Janet). Some persons remember all the hypnotic proceedings during their nightly sleep; it is not rare for the hypnotic dream to be repeated in natural sleep.

However, in some cases, chiefly in the deepest hypnoses, memory cannot be recalled by any of the above named expedients, though some think that a carefully directed conversation will always reconstitute it through the association of ideas. In such cases there is complete loss of memory in the waking state. Such a person does not even generally know how long he was in the hypnotic state. On the other hand the subject remembers in hypnosis all that has happened in previous hypnoses. Things that happened in hypnoses dating many years back, even as many as ten, may be recalled, although they are completely forgotten in the waking state. Wolfart relates the case of a woman who remembered in the "magnetic sleep" all that had taken place in a "magnetic sleep" thirteen years before, although in the meantime she had never recollected it.

Events of the normal life can also be remembered in hypnosis, even when they have apparently been long forgotten. This increased power of memory is called hypermnesia. Benedikt relates a case of it. An English officer in Africa was hypnotized by Hansen, and suddenly began to speak a strange language. This turned out to be Welsh, which he had learnt as a child, but had forgotten. Breuer and Freud point out that many cases of hysteria are called forth by some psychic moment that the patient cannot recall in the waking condition, though hypnosis may again bring it back to memory.

Such cases as these recall others which are mentioned in the literature of hypnotism; for example, the famous one of the servant who suddenly spoke Hebrew. She also, in an abnormal state of consciousness, spoke a language which she did not know, but which she had often heard when young in the house of a clergyman. We hear of like cases of hypermnesia in dreams. Maury, whose investigations on the subject of dreams are classic, relates a number of things which returned to his memory in dreams, although when awake he knew nothing about them. . . .

Dreams, also, which have occurred in natural sleep are sometimes reproduced in hypnosis, although they may have been forgotten on waking. It is naturally very difficult to judge of the accuracy with which dreams are reported. But as dreams sometimes lead to talking in sleep, it is then possible to make observations. I know of a case in which a person betrayed his dreams by talking in his sleep; the loss of memory which followed on waking disappeared in hypnosis, and the dream was remembered. A bed-fellow was able to confirm the accuracy of the recollection. . . .

I will here remark that all the above-mentioned suggestions influencing the memory can also be made post-hypnotic, and in all hypnoses it is only necessary to tell the subjects before awakening them that they will remember everything, and they will do so. Also, in some of the hypnotic states, memory may be prevented by command. We can also cause loss of memory of particular events or things; for example, we can prevent the recollection of certain letters, as we have seen before. Retroactive hallucinations can be transferred to waking life in the same way. I say to a subject in my house, "You know that we drank two bottles of wine just now, and that we had roast goose for supper." When he answers, "Yes," I further tell him that after he wakes he will remember all about it. He wakes and relates it all; he declares he has eaten too much, and that the wine has made his head heavy; he even thinks himself slightly intoxicated. This is a purely imaginary intoxication produced by suggestion. Hytten relates an even more interesting case; he says he has cured real intoxication by suggestion.

These delusions of memory may last for weeks and months. However, I have seen them disappear a short time after waking. A man, who directly after waking believed he had seen his mother at my house before the hypnosis, forgot all about it after a few minutes. We had spoken of other things in the meantime, and this probably caused the rapid oblivion. Bernheim has lately shown that in some cases the subject forgets not only what has taken place during the hypnosis, but also what immediately preceded it, and this without any kind of suggestion having been made. . . .

I have said above that hypnotic subjects remember the events of earlier hypnoses in later ones. But this statement needs some limitation, apart from what has just been said. In the first place, we see that when there is a change of personality, there is generally loss of memory also; a subject as Napoleon does not remember what he did as Frederick the Great. I further mention some little unconscious actions, which cannot be recalled to the subject's memory; I say, for example, "In five minutes you will say, 'Ha!' three times." The subject obeys, but remembers nothing about it later. In the same way certain post-hypnotic suggestions may be obeyed in a new hypnosis, and the subject may be unconscious that they were suggested in an earlier one. . . .

Any suggestion that takes effect in hypnosis will also take effect post-hypnotically; movements and delusions of the senses, itching, pain, action of the bowels, hunger, thirst, &c., can be induced. Dreams can be influenced. "To-day you will dream that you are at Swinemünde; you will go on the Ostsee in a boat with six people; the boat will be upset, and you will fall into the water and wake." The subject dreams this in detail. Dreamless sleep can be induced in the same way; or at least the subjects do not remember if they have dreamt.

It is possible to carry on suggestions from hypnosis into waking life; they are then called continuative suggestions. I suggest that my photograph is on a visiting card, and say that the subject will continue to see it after awakening. The subject is firmly convinced that the photograph is there. According to Londe an illusion of this kind has lasted for two years. This carrying on of the suggestion into normal life happens sometimes by chance, when the suggestion has not been cancelled before the awakening. One of my subjects drinks what has been suggested to her as peppermint water; I awake her, and she says for an hour after that she has a taste of peppermint in her mouth. The following often-repeated experiment belongs to the continuative suggestions: I say to the subject, "Count up to ten, and wake when you get to three." He counts up to ten, but is awake while counting from four to six.

In other cases the suggestion only takes effect after waking. I say to the subject, "You will not be able to move your right arm after you wake." He wakes, and is unable to move it, though otherwise in a normal state. Exactly the same effects may be produced after an interval of hours, days, weeks, and months. I say to a subject, "When you come to see me in a week you will not be able to speak when you come into the room." He comes to see me in a week, and is fully awake when he enters the room; I ask him his name, but he is unable to say it, or anything else. Here we have an example of fulfilment of suggestion after an interval, or *suggestion à échéance,* deferred suggestion. . . .

The moment for the fulfilment of the suggestion can be decided in several ways. To one subject I say, "An hour after you wake you will hear a polka played; you will believe you are at a ball, and will begin to dance." To another, whom I wake at eight o'clock, I say, "When the clock strikes nine you will take the water-bottle from the table, and walk up and down the room three times with it." The moment of fulfilment is decided differently in these two cases. In the second case the moment is decided by a concrete external sign, in the other an abstract term, an hour, is fixed.

The suggestion in this second example, where the moment of action is decided by some external sign, nearly always takes effect, especially after a little hypnotic training. The first more rarely succeeds. There are some subjects, however, with whom such suggestions take effect punctually. But the greater number are not only unpunctual, but often do not execute the suggestion at all, if some external impetus is not given; others carry out the suggestion, but inexactly—in forty-five minutes instead of one hour, &c.

I will point out a frequent source of error in these time experiments: this is the behavior of the spectators. They look at the clock at the appointed time, or make some other unconscious signal that the right moment has arrived. This has sometimes happened in my own experiments.

There is a third way of appointing the moment for the execution of a post-hypnotic suggestion, which has been carefully experimented upon by Gurney and Pierre Janet. In many respects it is like the first method. I say to a subject (X.), "When I rub my foot along the floor for the tenth time after you awake, you will laugh." The subject wakes, and does not remember my order. I talk to him, and rub several times without his paying any attention; at the tenth shuffle he laughs. Consequently the suggestion has taken effect. I make the experiment again, but at the fourth shuffle I ask X. if he has not heard the noise. He says, "No." Nevertheless at the tenth shuffle he laughs, though he is quietly talking to me. In most experiments the result was less exact. The suggestion succeeded, but not at the right moment.

Many deferred suggestions resemble these suggestions in which the moment of fulfilment is fixed by counting. Post-hypnotic deferred suggestions can be made in two ways; for example, on the 3rd of May I say to a person who sees me every day, "On the 6th of June, when you come into the room, you will see me with a black face, and you will laugh at me." The suggestion succeeds. But here a fixed date is named which helps the subject to carry out the suggestion. . . . It would have been another matter if I had made the suggestion thus: "On the 35th day, reckoning from to-day, you will come into my room and see me with a black face," &c. According to Gurney's observations, suggestions of this kind succeed, and a few of my own experiments confirm him. An example may make this sort of suggestion clearer. I suggested once to X., "You will come to my house on the sixteenth Tuesday, reckoning from last Tuesday, and will abuse all the people present," &c. This suggestion succeeded completely, although no fixed time was named. . . .

I have as yet only discussed the manner of determining the point of time for the carrying out of the post-hypnotic suggestion. The question now is, What is the condition of the subject while carrying out the post-hypnotic suggestion? . . .

A man (X.), thirty years old, is in the hypnotic state. I say to him, "When you wake, directly I cross my knees you will take the inkstand from the table and put it on the chair." He wakes at my order, and I talk to him. After a time I cross my knees; he begins to stare at the inkstand and hardly answers me. He goes to the table, takes the inkstand and puts it on a chair; upon which I suggest to him that he sees his brother, that he is eating his luncheon, &c., all of which suggestions he accepts. I am obliged to reawaken him to put an end to this new state of suggestibility. After waking he remembers absolutely nothing. This case is characterized by loss of memory of all that happened during the state, and further by susceptibility to suggestion. I do not know how this state is to be distinguished psychologically from a true hypnosis, and to my mind Delbœuf is right when he says that to make a post-hypnotic suggestion is really to order a new hypnosis at a fixed moment, and the carrying out of the suggestion in this new hypnosis. There are other very different cases. I say to a hypnotized subject, "When you awake, directly I rub my hands together, you will forget your name. When I separate my hands you will remember it again." The order is obeyed; we talk to one another, but when I bring my hands together the subject forgets his own name. He is, however, completely awake, and incapable of accepting any further suggestion. When I separate my hands he knows his own name, and knows also that he had forgotten it a moment ago. Directly I bring my hands together he forgets it again. He goes away, and in a few days we meet again; but now he remembers his name, however I hold my hands. But he remembers perfectly that the other day he was several times unable to say his own name. He maintains that he was awake all the time.

We are not justified in calling this case one of hypnosis. There was no mental symptom of hypnosis, no loss of memory, no suggestibility, no fatigue; the subject did not think he had been asleep; nothing remains but to consider the state a perfectly normal one, except on one point. Whether such a state may be regarded as normal, generally speaking, is another matter. . . .

It is difficult to say to what length of time the carrying out of a post-hypnotic suggestion may be deferred, since this depends upon the patient's character and the method employed. The longest post-hypnotic suggestion I have seen was executed at the end of four months; no hint had been given to the subject in the meantime. The longest which has ever been described, as far as I know, was in a subject under Liégeois and Liébeault; in this case exactly a year elapsed before the suggestion was carried out. The case of the photograph, mentioned on p. 140 [op. cit.], in which the photograph remained visible for two years, is rather different, as it appears that the suggestion was often recalled to the subject's memory in the meantime. The case mentioned by Dal Pozzo is, perhaps, of the same kind: a person who was afraid of thunderstorms was cured of the fear by suggestion; the effect is said to have lasted twenty-six years (Belfiore). . . .

I have hitherto only discussed those post-hypnotic suggestions in which there is loss of memory after waking from the hypnosis. This loss of memory greatly favours the carrying out of the suggestion. But loss of memory is not absolutely necessary; post-hypnotic suggestion succeeds also in light hypnoses, where there is complete recollection after waking. These cases, though more rare, are highly interesting, because the compulsion can be better observed in them. The subject may be able to say to himself, "The suggestion was made to me in hypnosis; I remember it perfectly, but I cannot help obeying it." . . .

We have now studied the memory and the post-hypnotic suggestions dependent upon it. We have seen that the faculty of memory is an important one in hypnosis; it is also a chief condition for the continuance of mental activity. This is certainly much circumscribed by suggestion in the deep hypnoses.

But a certain adherence to rule in the chain of ideas, conditioned by the laws of association, exists in many deep hypnoses. When, without hypnoses, we form in our own minds a mental image—of a fir tree, let us say—a number of other images are formed in connection with it: we think of Christmas Day, presents, &c. An analogous process takes place generally in hypnosis. A suggested idea does not remain isolated; on the contrary, it at once awakens new ideas dependent upon it.

I suggest to A., "Here is a pack of cards." A. believes it. The mental picture of the cards arouses the idea that he is playing a game, and also another idea—that he is at a restaurant with his friends B. and C. The single suggestion of the cards has sufficed to call up a whole scene before A., by association of ideas. A new suggestion suffices to destroy this association at once. I tell A., while he still thinks he is holding the cards, that he is in the train, and the chain of ideas connecting the cards and the restaurant is at once put an end to. However, in many hypnotic subjects a certain rational coherence of ideas persists, so that a suggested idea calls up others in one way or another connected with it. A large number of the phenomena of hypnosis depend upon this principle. Many mentally induced paralyses, of which I spoke on p. 63 [*op. cit.*], also depend upon it; the idea of a motor paralysis produces anæsthesia, vaso-motor disturbances, &c. I would emphatically say that the fact of their independence of the will has nothing to do with their being an indirect result of suggestion.

This mechanical associative process shows no real mental activity. The mental activity only appears when we destroy the natural associations, and see how the subject exerts himself to create a new sequence of ideas. In the example quoted above I told the subject as I gave him the cards that he was in a train. In order to bring these ideas into some logical connection, the subject A. now explained that he had bought the cards for a birthday present for the friend he was travelling to meet.

The fact that the subject sometimes allows himself to be persuaded to do something, if a reason is given to him for it, shows even more plainly that the thinking process is not always arrested in hypnosis. It is often necessary to suggest a false premiss to the subject before he will do what is wanted. X. cannot be induced to spill a glass of water in my room, but when I tell him that the room is on fire he does it at once.

On the other hand it should be said that even delusions of the senses are sometimes corrected purely by a reasoning process. A subject declines to believe that he sees a wolf in my room; or, rather, he explains that he sees an image of a wolf plainly enough, and could point out the exact spot. But he knows quite well that it must be a delusion, as I should certainly not allow a wolf to come into my sitting room. Macnish says that people can guard themselves against bad dreams and control them in sleep by a process of thought. [*Cf.* Mary Arnold-Forster, in the present volume, p. 596.]

Phenomena of Waking Hypnosis

WESLEY RAYMOND WELLS, "Experiments in Waking Hypnosis for Instructional Purposes," *Jour. Abn. Psychol.*, 18: 389, 392-404 (1924)

The general trend of opinion has been, and still is, to regard hypnosis as a state allied to natural sleep. This seems strange, however, especially in view of the *complete* history of the term and of *all* the observed facts from the time of Braid to the present. For, ever since the time of Braid, phenomena commonly called hypnotic have been repeatedly produced in the completely waking state.

In 1847 Braid attempted to suppress the term "hypnotism," having discovered that sleep is not essential to all the phenomena which he had previously called hypnotic.[1] He attempted to substitute the term "monoideism." If the term "hypnotism" were still to be used, Braid said, it should be restricted to those cases of artificial sleep which are followed by amnesia. In 1883 Bernheim reported to the Congress for the Advancement of Science, at Rouen, France, the production in the waking state of apparently all the phenomena usually called hypnotic except amnesia.[2] At

---

[1] See Bramwell, *Hypnotism*, 3d ed., 283; Bernheim, *Suggestive Therapeutics*, 86.

[2] *Op. cit.*, 85.

that time Bernheim was unaware of Braid's observations of the production of hypnotic phenomena in the waking state, but shortly afterwards Bernheim came upon writings by Braid which showed that Braid had discovered the production in the waking state of paralysis, contractures, illusions, and hallucinations. Bernheim seems to have been the first to add analgesia and anæsthesia to the list.[3] In 1892 a Committee of the British Medical Association reported that "sleep . . . is not necessarily present" in what is called hypnosis.[4] Since Bernheim's rediscovery of hypnotic phenomena in the waking state, numerous observers have confirmed and restated this fact, e.g., Lloyd Tuckey, Moll, and Forel. Some have supposed that hypnotic phenomena in the waking state could be produced only in "trained subjects," previously hypnotized by the sleeping method. James, e.g., expressed this opinion.[5] But Bernheim, Lloyd Tuckey, Moll, Forel, and others have observed and reported the production of hypnotic phenomena in the waking state *with subjects never before hypnotized*.[6] And finally, Bernheim has reported that amnesia is no exception to the rule that, as he has expressed it, *all* the phenomena commonly called hypnotic can be produced in the waking state.[7]

If *all* the phenomena commonly called hypnotic, including amnesia, can be produced in the completely waking state, in subjects who have never been hypnotized before, should we follow Bernheim's counsel and "suppress completely the word 'hypnosis' and replace it by 'the state of suggestion' "?[8] Or should we be determined more by practical convenience than by etymology, and say, with Moll,[9] "Hypnosis is not invariably a state of sleep"? The second alternative is clearly to be preferred. "Post-state-of-suggestion," e.g., would be a cumbersome substitute for "post-hypnotic." And furthermore, to speak of "suggestion in the waking state" does not convey the meaning intended if one refers to the production of contractures, anæsthesias, etc., even including amnesia and post-hypnotic phenomena. Sidis recognized the production in the waking state of a *few* hypnotic phenomena with a

---

[3] *Op. cit.*, 86.

[4] Bramwell, *op. cit.*, 36.

[5] *Principles of Psychology*, 2: 615.

[6] Bernheim, *De la Suggestion*, 16, Paris, 1911; Lloyd Tuckey, *Psycho-therapeutics*, 3d ed., 69, note; Moll, *Hypnotism*, 4th ed., translated, 197; Forel, *Hypnotism*, 5th ed., translated, 117.

[7] *De la Suggestion*, 86.

[8] *Hypnotisme et Suggestion*, 3d ed., 77, Paris, 1910.

[9] *Op. cit.*, 47, note.

few subjects but called it rare,[10] and an exception to the general rule that the suggestibility of waking persons is of an opposite type to that of subjects in the hypnotic sleep. The general rule is, according to Sidis, that suggestion to waking subjects in order to be effective must be indirect and veiled; while to subjects in the hypnotic sleep effective suggestions may be direct. Sidis was certainly wrong in failing to observe that *direct* suggestion is effective in producing hypnotic phenomena in the waking state with practically all subjects; and yet, through usage, "suggestion in the waking state" does convey the meaning which Sidis ascribes to it, namely, indirect suggestion, and not the production of the typical hypnotic phenomena.

The long and practically universal recognition given to amnesia (following the state) as a test of hypnosis—usually a test of the deepest stages, is evident to any student of the subject. Thus Braid, as we have seen, after attempting to suppress the term "hypnotism," or, as we would now say, "hypnosis," admitted it in cases where amnesia could be produced. "The earlier classifications such as those of Liébeault and Bernheim . . . made the criterion that they worked on, the loss of memory." [11] Sidis said, "Amnesia is the ripe fruit of hypnosis." [12] Coriat calls "loss of memory" one of the "four most important symptoms of hypnosis." [13] Pierre Janet says, "Hypnosis is just a state that leaves no remembrances with the patient when he awakes." [14] And Moll said, "We must call a state hypnosis . . . if there is a subsequent loss of memory." [15]

Since amnesia has received such long and general recognition as a test either of hypnosis in contrast with a non-hypnotic state, or of the deeper stages of hypnosis in contrast with the lighter stages, there is certainly sufficient justification for calling hypnotic a state in which amnesia can be produced, even though the state is a waking one. Such would be a state of waking hypnosis, the amnesia being produced by direct suggestion, and the waking condition being maintained normally in the absence of any suggestion of sleep. And having admitted the use of the term "waking hypnosis" in cases where amnesia is produced in the waking state, we have made the way clear for an extension of the term to those cases of contractures, anæsthesias, and the like, suggested in the

---

[10] *Psychology of Suggestion,* 27.

[11] H. C. Miller, *Hypnotism and Disease,* 70, Boston, 1912.

[12] *Op. cit.,* 71.   [13] *Abnormal Psychology,* 197.

[14] *Mental States of Hystericals,* 96.   [15] *Op. cit.,* 197.

waking state even without the production of amnesia. However, subjects in whom amnesia cannot be produced in the waking state are not suitable for the experiments which I am going to describe, and consequently insistence upon this last point is not necessary.

Waking hypnosis is in no sense to be construed as a form necessarily of light or slight hypnosis, for in the production of amnesia and some of the other hypnotic and post-hypnotic phenomena it is like the usual deep hypnosis except for the absence of sleep. It is to be defined, not by contrast with deep hypnosis, but merely by contrast with sleeping hypnosis. It is to be called hypnosis for, inasmuch as the *essential* feature of sleeping hypnosis (as Sidis, Prince, McDougall, Coriat, and others, have shown) is dissociation, it would claim to be a more direct application of the principles of dissociation without reference to sleep at all. All sleep is dissociation, but not all dissociation is sleep. Ordinary lapses of memory in everyday life and absent-minded acts occurring during times of concentrated attention are cases of dissociation, but not of sleep. Just as exponents of sleeping hypnosis take their cue from dissociation as illustrated by sleep, exponents of waking hypnosis would take their cue from such examples of dissociation in normal waking life as absent-minded acts or ordinary lapses of memory.

Comparison of waking hypnosis with what Sidis called the hypnoidal state may make the meaning of the former clearer. The two are directly opposite. Waking hypnosis is genuinely hypnotic and genuinely waking, while the hypnoidal state is a sort of sleep state, and is not hypnotic. Sidis said of it: "We must warn . . . against . . . confusion with any hypnosis, light or otherwise. The hypnoidal state . . . is widely different from hypnosis. The hypnoidal state . . . is a sleep state. . . . Sleep developed out of the hypnoidal state." [16]

The relationship between what I call waking hypnosis and the theories and practice of the "new Nancy school" (Coué and his disciple at Geneva, Baudouin) should be pointed out. There seems to be even *less* recognition of real waking hypnosis by Coué and Baudouin than by Bernheim, of the old Nancy school. Coué has largely abandoned sleeping hypnosis,[17] and his simple experiments in contractures for the purpose of teaching autosuggestion "are carried out when the subject is in the waking state." [18] Coué him-

---

[16] *The Causation and Treatment of Psychopathic Diseases*, 363. [Cf. also the selection from Sidis, p. 512, *supra*.]

[17] Baudouin, *Suggestion and Autosuggestion*, 308

[18] *Ibid.*, 262.

self denies that such experiments are hypnotic, apparently quibbling over the etymological significance of the term. Baudouin prefers to say that Coué's "method is now wholly based upon slight hypnosis." [19] But, Baudouin says, these "slighter degrees of hypnosis . . . are not followed by amnesia"; [20] and, in fact, Coué and Baudouin have apparently expressed no interest in the production of the typical phenomena of deep sleeping hypnosis with the subject in the waking state. Baudouin seems not to recognize that amnesia can be produced in the waking state, saying even that it can rarely be produced on the first occasion in sleeping hypnosis.[21] The recognition by Bernheim that amnesia can be produced in the waking state seems to have been overlooked by the new Nancy school. And I might add that I have not found in Bernheim's writings any description of significant experiments involving amnesia in the waking state.

In the development of my technique, however, as I shall point out later, I have been influenced to some extent by the methods employed by Coué as described by Baudouin. These methods are capable of elaboration and extension so as to produce the phenomena associated with deep sleeping hypnosis, such as amnesia and post-hypnotic phenomena, without the production of a sleeping or even a drowsy state.

A description such as I have attempted of waking hypnosis and its contrast with sleeping hypnosis can be given without raising the vexed question of just what constitutes sleep in its physiological and psychological aspects. The objection might be made that my method produces an hypnotic sleep state without such being suggested directly; and in the case of subjects previously put into the deep hypnotic trance this is true enough. For this reason I have confined my experiments in waking hypnosis to [several hundred] subjects never before hypnotized. Anyone who has seen the production of simple contractures such, for example, as those of the Coué type, by direct suggestion to subjects never before hypnotized and without any suggestion of sleep, has noted the entire absence of the characteristics of hypnotic sleep. And there are no more signs of sleep even when one goes further by similar methods and produces amnesia and post-hypnotic phenomena. . . .

---

[19] *Ibid.*, 245.
[20] *Ibid.*, 296.
[21] *Ibid.*, 244.

EXPERIMENTS IN WAKING HYPNOSIS

The method of waking hypnosis possesses the following advantages, in my opinion, over the various methods of sleeping hypnosis, at least for class demonstration and instructional purposes, and in some cases for therapeutic purposes. First, it is less mysterious in appearance, and the total impression is more desirable. The psychologist who uses hypnosis partly for the purpose of teaching against occultism desires to avoid the appearance of an occult procedure. Second, it usually takes less time. With an individual subject or with a group, one usually begins to get results in two or three minutes, if not in five or ten seconds; while sleeping hypnosis, when first used with a subject, usually requires a longer time before results are obtained. Third, it is easier, requiring less effort on the part of the experimenter; and it is easier for the beginner to learn. Fourth, it can be employed on a larger percentage of subjects with success at the start than can the usual methods of sleeping hypnosis. Fifth, if for any reason sleeping hypnosis is desired, one can easily change to the methods of producing the sleeping state with greater chance of success if the first suggestions by the method of waking hypnosis have been successful.

The technique of waking hypnosis which I employ may be described in part by contrasting it with the usual methods of sleeping hypnosis. To hypnotize by the most usual sleeping method one begins by explaining to the subject the psychological conditions of normal sleep. One calls attention to the part played by a lessening of external stimuli, especially light and sound, by the concentration of attention on some one simple situation, as in the classic method of putting oneself to sleep by counting sheep, and by the sleep-producing effect of slight monotonous stimuli. One may speak of the way in which the mother puts her child to sleep, and of the sleepiness that often comes upon a man while in the barber's chair, experiencing the manipulations of the barber. The hypnotizer explains that he is about to employ similar methods to induce in the subject first a drowsy condition and finally a condition of deep sleep, like normal sleep except that the subject will always be conscious of what the operator is saying. Then, in terms of the usual immobility of the body during sleep, contractures may be explained. In terms of normal dreams, illusions and hallucinations occurring in the hypnotic sleep are made clear. Amnesia that may follow the hypnotic sleep is compared to the amnesia for one's dreams that usually follows waking from natural sleep. Somnambulism in the hypnotic sleep is compared with the somnambulism that sometimes occurs in natural sleep. Then the hypnotizer proceeds to suggest drowsiness in various ways. He may have the subject gaze fixedly upon a bright object and at the same time suggest that a feeling of drowsiness will begin to appear. If the eyes soon close so that the subject cannot open them, the operator says this is because of the sleep that is overcoming the subject. Passes may be used, accompanied by suggestions of sleep; and so on, according to old and familiar methods. The subject manifests increasingly the external signs of drowsiness, and actually begins to feel drowsy and sleepy; and finally he may fall into the somnambulistic state, though more frequently stopping short of this.

Now, in all this there have been the following features: first, a preliminary explanation in terms of sleep; second, a continued suggestion of sleep by direct and indirect means; third, an experiencing by the subject of the familiar symptoms of drowsiness and sleep; and fourth, some of the external bodily signs of drowsiness and sleep. Those who, like Münsterberg, Sidis, Coriat, and Prince, as referred to above, explain hypnosis primarily in terms of concentration of the attention and of dissociation, without reference to sleep, would not give a preliminary explanation to the subject such as I have described; but the other three points which I have mentioned would apply in most cases to their practice of hypnotism. In what I call waking hypnosis, however, all four of these features are absent: sleep is not mentioned in the preliminary explanation to the subject; sleep is not suggested, directly or indirectly; the subject experiences neither drowsiness nor sleepiness, if we may trust his introspective account; and there are present none of the objective indications of drowsiness or sleep. . . .

Waking hypnosis may be used either in group or in individual experiments. The group experiment has two main purposes (aside from its therapeutic uses) : first, to teach large numbers easily and quickly, through their own experiences as subjects or through observation of a considerable number of other subjects, the meaning of hypnosis; and second, to select the better subjects for individual experiments. After a preliminary explanation to a group of students regarding the chief principles of dissociation and of suggestion, direct suggestions to the group that their eyes, when closed, cannot be opened, or that their hands, if clasped together tightly, cannot be unclasped, will cause such contractures in a considerable proportion, if not in the majority or even all, of the group, if made properly, as a little experience enables anyone to make them. I recently obtained results with 100 per cent of a group of 12, and a few months ago I obtained results with 24 of a group of 28. In no instance have I failed to get results from some members of the group.

In individual experiments the meaning of dissociation and the fact of the independent functioning of dissociated "neurograms" (to use Prince's term) may be illustrated by suggesting to the subject in the waking state amnesia, for example, for his name, and then by causing, through appropriate suggestions, automatic writing of the name while the amnesia still persists. By proper suggestions to a good subject one can cause automatic writing such that the subject is not aware either of what his hand is writing, or even that his hand is writing anything. To do an experiment like this by waking hypnosis takes only a short time, seems very matter of fact, and can be done with subjects who have never been hypnotized before. If one wishes in this connection to illustrate how the planchette works, a planchette may be substituted for pencil and paper. In elementary classes this is worthwhile. It was Gurney, as James relates,[22] who first conceived the idea of using the planchette to "tap" the subconscious processes involved in post-hypnotic suggestions; but Gurney used sleeping hypnosis for this purpose.

Such an experiment as I have described would illustrate what Prince devotes considerable space to, in *The Unconscious* (pp. 15ff.), namely, the conservation of forgotten experiences. An experiment designed to show the independent functioning of dissociated neurograms in a greater degree is Prince's experiment in subconscious calculation (p. 96). This experiment, however, can be done by means of waking hypnosis, with subjects never before hypnotized. With a subject in whom amnesia can be produced quickly in the waking state, a problem in mental arithmetic may be given, for which amnesia is produced immediately, before there is time for any effort at solution. The suggestion may be made that the answer will be written automatically at the end of five minutes, with complete amnesia for the problem persisting during this time. In the working out of these suggestions we have an illustration of the simultaneous activity of the dissociated cerebral processes involved in solving the arithmetical problem, and of other cerebral processes involved in conscious attention to the class discussion or to some assigned task. Professor Woodworth refers approvingly to one of Prince's experiments of this sort, with a subject, however, who has a double personality; and Professor Woodworth says, "It

[22] *Op. cit.*, 615.

is weird business, however interpreted, and raises the question whether anything of the same sort . . . occurs in ordinary experience". [23] If the experiment is done with a subject never hypnotized before, selected from the class, and in a completely waking state, there is nothing in the least "weird" about it; and it answers the question which Woodworth asks in the last part of the sentence quoted above, being evidence that "separate [cerebral] fractions of the individual" [24] can and do function independently and intelligently at the same time, in strictly normal and healthy subjects. . . .

The step to effective autosuggestion, or autohypnosis, is shorter from waking than from sleeping hypnosis. My usual routine in giving a first lesson in autosuggestion is first to close the eyes of the subject, then to produce contractures of the hands, and then to produce analgesia in one hand or arm—all by direct suggestion in the waking state. Then I ask the subject to produce the same results by his own suggestion to himself. After he has done this, instruction may be given in the effective use of autosuggestion in various practical ways. I recently gave an interesting lesson in autosuggestion to one of my students. When he had produced analgesia in his right hand by autosuggestion alone, he was still unconvinced by the test of pinching with his left hand, and he asked for a needle. I gave him one, properly sterilized. He pricked his right hand repeatedly, so that the blood flowed from each needle wound, before he could fully satisfy himself that he had actually learned to produce analgesia by autosuggestion. As a final illustration of the practical applications of the principles of waking hypnosis, I removed by direct suggestion a headache of which the subject had complained at the beginning of the experiments. A further lesson is apparently needed by this subject, however, before he will be able to use autosuggestion effectively in practical ways; for he reported two days later that he had been able to produce contractures by autosuggestion, but not analgesia, when working alone.

The following description of a series of experiments in waking hypnosis carried out during a single class hour, on the first occasion of reference to hypnosis, shows what can be done in a short time. If more time is at one's disposal, variations and elaborations of such experiments are possible. At the end of one class hour I did a group experiment with the whole class, of fifteen students, in order to select the better subjects. Then, at the beginning of the next class

---

[23] Psychology, 560.   [24] Ibid.

period one of these better subjects volunteered for individual experiments. The subject selected was a man about thirty-five, never before hypnotized (except in the group experiment of the day before), and with a good history of physical and mental health. I first tested him to see if amnesia could be produced in the waking state. I readily produced amnesia for his name, with the suggestion that his hand would write it, while the amnesia still persisted. Pencil and paper were then provided, and his hand was concealed from his view, behind a screen. His hand immediately began to write his name. When the name was about half written the subject spoke up to say that he was sorry that the experiment did not seem to be working. After the name was completely written, and after amnesia for his name disappeared in five minutes as had been suggested, his writing was shown to him. The genuineness of his surprise and interest may be easily imagined. I next tested his normal ability in mental arithmetic, finding it fair. Then I made preliminary suggestions to him of the waking hypnotic type. I explained that I would give him a problem in multiplication, which he would solve subconsciously and the answer of which he would write automatically, with amnesia all the while both for what the problem was, and for the fact that a problem had been given to him. I then said, "Multiply 175 by 25," and I *immediately* thereafter caused amnesia for the figures and for the fact that a problem had been given. Then, testing his normal conscious attention to the class discussion, which I continued, by asking him miscellaneous questions, I allowed time for the subconscious computation of the problem and for the automatic writing of the answer. His hand wrote 4,325. The correct answer to the problem is 4,375. In tests given to the subject in the solution of similar problems before dissociation had been produced in waking hypnosis, similar errors had occasionally been made. I have in general not found subconscious computation either more or less accurate than the conscious solution of similar problems. I next caused by suggestion a sharp burning pain on the back of one hand, which I touched with a pencil. Amnesia for the cause of the pain was produced, and the pain remained constant for a minute, as had been suggested. I had produced analgesia in his right hand as one of the preliminary experiments. I have found it generally more difficult to cause pain by suggestion than to cause analgesia.

As a final experiment, towards the close of the hour, I illustrated subconscious perception.[25] I tested the subject's memory for details

---

[25] *Cf.* Prince, *The Unconscious*, 52 ff.

of the clothing of a man on the back seat of the classroom, a man, however, whom the subject had talked with earlier in the day. Finding him unable to recall any details whatever of the man's clothing, I tried the method of automatic writing without the use of hypnosis, and got an imperfect description. Then, through waking hypnosis I obtained a detailed and accurate description of the man's clothes. He persisted in saying that the man wore a white shirt with a dark stripe in it, in spite of suggestions from me that he would gradually come to recall it more accurately. To me the shirt seemed to be pure white; but after the termination of the experiment I discovered that there had originally been a dark stripe, which had faded out to such an extent that it was not visible to me at a distance of ten feet.

In conclusion I might add that I am interested in the employment of the ordinary type of sleeping hypnosis for some purposes, especially in therapeutic work. I am interested in the sort of psychoanalysis by means of hypnosis which Dr. Hadfield, in England, has called hypnoanalysis; [26] and in attempting to remove phobias, for example, through hypnotic exploration of childhood, or later, amnesias, I have thus far preferred the sleeping type of hypnosis. However, I almost invariably begin the induction of sleeping hypnosis by the method of waking hypnosis described above; and I do not begin to suggest sleep until suggestions of contractures in the waking state have been effective. In this paper I have chosen to limit my discussion to waking hypnosis, and to emphasize its possibilities; for, if its possibilities were generally recognized, as is very obviously not the case, much of the present disinclination among psychologists to the use of hypnosis for experimental purposes would, I believe, entirely disappear.

Comparison of Hypnotic with Waking Abilities

PAUL CAMPBELL YOUNG, "An Experimental Study of Mental and Physical Functions in the Normal and Hypnotic States," *Am. Jour. Psychol.*, 36: 230-231 (1925)

. . . It is clear that some of the popular conceptions in regard to hypnosis which have more or less won their way into scientific psychological thinking are untrue, or need to be restated in a way which casts a different light on the nature of the hypnotic con-

[26] See H. C. Miller (ed.), *Functional Nerve Disease*, Ch. 5, by Dr. Hadfield. Dr. W. S. Taylor has introduced the term "hypnoanalysis" in America through recent articles in this journal [*Jour. Abn. Psychol.*]

sciousness. Despite individual differences in both the waking and the hypnotic states, differences which are very great, the following facts stand out in the results of the experimenter's work.

(1) The hypnotic state seems to vary as much between individuals and, in the same individual, between different times, as does the normal state. As far as abilities are concerned, there is no unitary hypnotic consciousness which is pretty much alike in various persons.

(2) There seems to be about as much variation in the individual, on the whole, from one normal session to another, or from one hypnotic session to another, as there is from a normal session to an hypnotic session, or from an hypnotic session to a normal session.

(3) An exception to the two statements just made lies in the fact that there is in hypnosis (at least in the somnambulistic stage) greater ability to resist fatigue, to resist pain, and to recall long past events (a later article will give the data on long past memories), on account of the tendency in hypnosis to take a certain mental attitude with conviction.

(4) A possible exception to the first two statements is found in the slightly lower ability in hypnosis to do tasks which require continuous responses, on account of the great relaxation amounting at times to inertia.

[Would this be true in the condition of "waking hypnosis," described by Prof. Wesley Raymond Wells in the preceding selection?]

(5) There is in hypnosis a definitely lower ability in the making of muscular movements, on account of the feeling of easiness which influences the judgment, and results in considerably freer, sometimes almost reckless movements. (Cf. intoxication, which lowers inhibitions and manifests itself in largeness of movement.)

(6) On the whole, there is no noticeable difference between the normal and hypnotic states in the ability of normal persons in the fields of sensation, perception, finer discriminations, present memory (learning and retention), or physical work which does not involve fatigue.

(7) Judging from the great individual variations in both hypnotic and control Ss [subjects], the past reports of greatly bettered performances of normal Ss in hypnosis may be explained by one or all of the following considerations: (a) the small number of Ss,

(*b*) the small number of sessions, or (*c*) the lack of strictly comparable methods in the two states.

(8) Instead of Trömmer's twofold division of the various conditions as regards mental abilities (light hypnosis, in which abilities are increased; deep hypnosis, in which abilities are decreased), there seems to be a threefold condition: (*a*) light hypnosis, in which the performance is fully as good as in waking; (*b*) deep hypnosis (exclusive of somnambulism), in which the performance is perhaps slightly lower than in waking; (*c*) somnambulism, the classical form of hypnotism, in which the normal performance is again equaled.

(9) The so-called hypersensitivity, *e. g.*, to a light touch, seems to be really a fact of subjective sensitivity, or better, perhaps, hyperactivity, *i. e.*, of an attitude of mind which makes the bodily reaction out of all proportion to the size of the stimulus actually felt. Instead of being able to react to a lighter stimulus (as would be the case if there were objective hypersensitivity), the S in hypnosis reacts more strongly than in waking to a stimulus which he can, however, feel in waking. That this subjective attitude may continue at the very time that the threshold of sensitivity is raised is probable from the results of Experiment 4. ["Pressure of Two Hairs on the Skin."] The cause, perhaps, is the removal through dissociation of the ordinary inhibitions.

(10) The possibility remains, of course, that the results shown in this research are a function of the methods of hypnotizing or of the class of Ss used. It is thinkable, for example, that results such as S. Alrutz described [1] may be got by using his method or by using his Ss; but until the comparative method as described in this paper is assiduously used in such cases, the results of his experiments (*e. g.*, affecting the sensitivity of the hand by passes which never come in contact with the hand) must be considered as without scientific repetition and verification. . . .

The hypnotic state is thus seen to be but a modified state of normal consciousness, which is differentiated from other normal states, not so much by way of any changes in physical ability, or of peculiar bodily conditions, as by the tendency to take an attitude suggested (within what limits no one has yet determined) in spite of bodily conditions. Since almost all persons can be hypnotized, and yet not all hypnotized persons (perhaps only one in twenty) can attain to the state of somnambulism, in which the increased abilities referred to in (3) above occur, the differences which appear

[1] *Proc. Soc. Psy. Research*, 32, 1921, 151.

in somnambulism are differences in the constitution of the persons involved; and would be better described, perhaps, merely as individual differences in normal persons than as differences between the normal and the hypnotic states as such. This would leave the term "hypnosis" with a fairly definite meaning: a state in which a person *will do,* in a *bona fide* manner, possessed of conviction, what he *will not do* in waking life for lack of such conviction.

Crystal Gazing

Isador H. Coriat, *Abnormal Psychology*, 36-38 (Dodd, Mead, 1910)

In spite of the part played by crystal gazing in necromancy and Eastern mysticism, nothing can be reproduced as a crystal vision which has not already been a part of personal experience, although this experience may have been dissociated. In the production of these visions the subject gazes into a crystal globe and at the same time attempts to keep the mind a blank and free from external stimuli. The state of abstraction thus produced in crystal gazing "taps" the subconscious experiences in the same manner that they are tapped through automatic writing. After a short time isolated or complex pictures appear in the crystal. These are usually very vague at first, but later become more distinct. Like automatic writing, crystal visions may take place in normal individuals, although they are produced with greater ease in those persons who have an abnormal instability or who are victims of a pathological disintegration of the personality. . . .

Mrs. Y. showed four multiple hypnotic states for which she was amnesic in her waking condition. The crystal visions in this patient were revivals of past experiences. Some of these experiences the patient remembered; others could only be recalled in hypnosis. For instance, in one of the hypnotic states for which there was no memory on awakening, the emotional reaction was one of hatred and disgust. When a crystal vision of the same experience was produced, the emotional reaction was the same. It seems that whatever device was used for synthesis, either hypnosis or crystal gazing, the reproduced memories were associated with certain emotions. These emotions had attached themselves to the dissociated experiences, and when these experiences were revived by either of the methods, the associated emotions likewise appear.

Shell Hearing

EDMUND PARISH. *Hallucinations and Illusions,* The Contemporary Science
Series, 70 (Walter Scott, 1898)

Just as visual images may be called up by gazing on a shining
object, so by placing a sea-shell to the ear it is possible to induce
auditory hallucinations. I therefore class such hallucinations with
crystal-visions, which they resemble in their content. This analogy
is borne out by cases like that of the lady who, if she listened to the
shell after a dinner party generally heard repeated, not the conversation of her "lawful interlocutor," to which her attention had
been directed, but the talk of her neighbours on the other side,
which she had not consciously noted at the time.[1]

["The vague, indistinct buzzing coming from the shell affects
the sense-organ and gives rise to a peripheral process that forms the
nucleus round which the subconscious experiences become crystal-
lized and projected in the form of auditory hallucinations. Here,
too, as in the case of crystal gazing, experiences of one sensory
character may be transformed into that of another. Psychic states
originally of a visual character become auditory on being projected
by this reverse movement from the subconscious to the central consciousness."—Boris Sidis and Simon P. Goodhart, *Multiple Personality,* 257-258 (Appleton, 1919).]

---

[1] Myers, "The Subliminal Consciousness," *Proc. of the Soc. f. Psych. Res.,*
8: 493.

CHAPTER XX

ILLUSIONS AND HALLUCINATIONS

Variations of Sensibility

JAMES SULLY, *Illusions*, 64-67 (Appleton, 1897)

We will now pass to a number of illusions which depend on something variable in the condition of our sensibility, of some more or less exceptional organic circumstance. These variations may be momentary and transient or comparatively permanent. The illusion arises in each case from our ignoring the variation, and treating a given sensation under all circumstances as answering to one objective cause.

First of all, the variation of organic state may affect our mental representation of the strength of the stimulus or external cause. Here the fluctuation may be a temporary or a permanent one. The first case is illustrated in the familiar example of taking a room to be brighter than it is when emerging from a dark one. Another striking example is that of our sense of the temperature of objects, which is known to be strictly relative to a previous sensation, or more correctly to the momentary condition of the organ. Yet, though every intelligent person knows this, the deeply rooted habit of making sensation the measure of objective quality asserts its sway, and frequently leads us into illusion. The well-known experiment of first plunging one hand in cold water, the other in hot, and then dipping them both in tepid, is a startling example of this organized tendency. For here we are strongly disposed to accept the palpable contradiction that the same water is at once warm and cool.

Far more important than these temporary fluctuations of sensibility are the permanent alterations. Excessive fatigue, want of proper nutrition, and certain poisons are well known to be causes of such changes. They appear most commonly under two forms, exalted sensibility, or hyperæsthesia, and depressed sensibility, or anæsthesia. In these conditions flagrant errors are made as to the real magnitude of the causes of the sensations. These variations may occur in normal life to some extent. In fairly good health we experience at times strange exaltations of tactual sensibility, so that a very slight stimulus, such as the contact of the bed-clothes, becomes greatly exaggerated.

In diseased states of the nervous system these variations of sensibility become much more striking. The patient who has hyperæsthesia fears to touch a perfectly smooth surface, or he takes a knock at the door to be a clap of thunder. The hypochondriac may, through an increase of organic sensibility, translate organic sensations as the effect of some living creature gnawing at his vitals. Again, states of anæsthesia lead to odd illusions among the insane. The common supposition that the body is dead, or made of wood or of glass, is clearly referable in part to lowered sensibility of the organism.[1]

It is worth adding, perhaps, that these variations in sensibility give rise not only to sensory but also to motor illusions. To take a homely instance, the last miles of a long walk seem much longer than the first, not only because the sense of fatigue leading us to dwell on the transition of time tends to magnify the apparent duration, but because the fatigued muscles and connected nerves yield a new set of sensations which constitute an exaggerated standard of measurement. A number of optical illusions illustrate the same thing. Our visual sense of direction is determined in part by the feelings accompanying the action of the ocular muscles, and so is closely connected with the perception of movement, which has already been touched on. If an ocular muscle is partially paralyzed it takes a much greater "effort" to effect a given extent of movement than when the muscle is sound. Hence any movement performed by the eye seems exaggerated. Hence, too, in this condition objects are seen in a wrong direction; for the patient reasons that they are where they would seem to be if he had executed a wider movement than he really has. This may easily be proved by asking him to try to seize the object with his hand. The effect is exaggerated when complete paralysis sets in, and no actual movement occurs in obedience to the impulse from within.[2]

---

[1] For a fuller account of these pathological disturbances of sensibility, see Griesinger, *Mental Pathology and Therapeutics* (London, 1867); also Dr. A. Mayer, *Die Sinnestäuschungen*.

[2] Helmholtz, *Physiologische Optik*, p. 600, *et seq.* These facts seem to point to the conclusion that at least some of the feelings by which we know that we are expending muscular energy are connected with the initial stage of the outgoing nervous process in the motor centres. In other pathological conditions the sense of weight by the muscles of the arms is similarly confused.

Action of Expectation

JAMES SULLY, *Illusions*, 102-106, 108-110 (Appleton, 1897)

We may not be distinctly anticipating any one kind of object, but are nevertheless in a condition of *subexpectation* with reference to a large number of objects. Accordingly, when an impression occurs which answers only very roughly to one of the associated images, there is a tendency to superimpose the image on the impression. In this way illusion arises. Thus, a man, when strolling in a cathedral, will be apt to take any kind of faint hollow sound for the soft tones of an organ.

The disposition to anticipate fact and reality in this way will be all the stronger if, as usually happens, the mental images thus lying ready for use have an emotional colouring. Emotion is the great disturber of all intellectual operations. It effects marvellous things, as we shall presently see, in the region of illusory belief, and its influence is very marked in the seemingly cooler region of external perception. The effect of any emotional excitement appears to be to give a preternatural vividness and persistence to the ideas answering to it, that is to say, the ideas which are its excitants, or which are otherwise associated with it. Owing to this circumstance, when the mind is under the temporary sway of any feeling, as, for example, fear, there will be a special readiness to interpret objects by help of images congruent with the emotion. Thus, a man under the control of fear will be ready to see any kind of fear-inspiring object whenever there is any resemblance to such in the things actually present to his vision. The state of awe which the surrounding circumstances of a spiritualist *séance* inspires produces a general readiness of mind to perceive what is strange, mysterious, and apparently miraculous.

It is worth noting, perhaps, that those delightful half-illusions which imitative art seeks to produce are greatly favoured by such a temporary attitude of the interpreting imagination. In the theatre, for example, we are prepared for realizing the semblance of life that is to be unfolded before us. We come knowing that what is to be performed aims at representing a real action or actual series of events. We not improbably work ourselves into a slightly excited state in anticipation of such a representation. More than this, as the play progresses, the realization of what has gone before produces a strong disposition to believe in the reality of what is to follow. And this effect is proportionate to the degree of coherence and continuity in the action. In this way, there is a cumulative effect on the mind. If the action is good, the illusion, as every play-goer knows, is most complete towards the end. . . .

So much as to the effect of an indefinite state of subexpectation in misleading our perceptions. Let us now glance at the results of definite preimagination, including what are generally known as expectations.

Such expectations may grow out of some present objective facts, which serve as signs of the expected event; or they may arise by way of verbal suggestion; or, finally, they may be due to internal spontaneous imagination. . . .

An officer who superintended the exhuming of a coffin rendered necessary through a suspicion of crime, declared that he already experienced the odour of decomposition, though it was afterwards found that the coffin was empty.

It is, of course, often difficult to say, in such cases as these, how far elements of actual sensation coöperate in the production of the illusions. Thus, in the case just mentioned, the odour of the earth may have been the starting-point in the illusion. In many cases, however, an imaginative mind appears to be capable of transforming a vivid expectation into a nascent stage of sensation. Thus, a mother thinking of her sick child in an adjoining room, and keenly on the alert for its voice, will now and again fancy she really hears it when others hear nothing at all.

Transition to Hallucination. It is plain that in these cases illusion approaches to hallucination. Imagination, instead of waiting on sensation, usurps its place and imitates its appearance. Such a "subjective" sensation produced by a powerful expectation might, perhaps, by a stretch of language, be regarded as an illusion, in the narrow sense, in so far as it depends on the suggestive force of a complete set of external circumstances; on the other hand, it is clearly an hallucination in so far as it is the production of the semblance of an external impression without any external agency corresponding to this. . . .

In persons of a lively imagination any recent occupation of the mind with a certain kind of mental image may suffice to beget something equivalent to a powerful mode of expectation. For example, we are told by Dr. Tuke that on one occasion a lady, whose imagination had been dwelling on the subject of drinking fountains, "thought she saw in a road a newly erected fountain, and even distinguished an inscription upon it, namely, 'If any man thirst,

let him come unto Me, and drink.' She afterwards found that
what she had actually seen was only a few scattered stones." [1]

The Rôle of Dissociation

EDMUND PARISH, *Hallucinations and Illusions*, The Contemporary Science
Series, 152, 158-161, 73-74 (Walter Scott, 1898)

By dissociation is here understood that state in which the nerve
stimulus no longer flows through the channels determined by habit,
and by the coöperation of simultaneous stimuli, because inhibitions,
or obstructions, whether from pathological or physiological causes,
have been set up in the normal association-paths, or obstructions
which normally exist in other connecting tracts have been weakened
or altogether abolished. . . .

The action of dissociation on the impressions received from the
so-called external world has already been described; it causes excitations which normally produce "correct" or objective sensory perceptions to be misinterpreted. But it also plays a very important part
through its action on the impressions which arise within the physical organism itself. These form so large and so constant a factor
in our experience, and are so closely knit up together, that the elements concerned in them discharge into each other with great ease,
and the resulting state of consciousness is dim and undefined. But
should a particular element from any cause be released from this
compact system, its irradiation becomes impeded, in the same way
that the irradiation of quite new and unfamiliar stimuli is impeded
by the absence of well-worn connecting paths. Either it is completely blocked, or else it is rendered slow and difficult; and our
consciousness of the resulting physiological or pathological irritation becomes proportionately intense—hence singing in the ears,
ocular spectra, and other "elementary sensations." [2] If, on the
other hand, a practicable path can be found the irradiation will
stream through it to new groups, and thus become the cause of
sensory delusions.

In mental alienation, for instance, the coöperation of stimulus
with the predisposing state is expressed in various ways. Thus in
many such cases only subjective phenomena are remarked at first,

---

[1] Mentioned by Dr. Carpenter (*Mental Physiology*, 207), where other
curious examples are to be found.

[2] No doubt hypochondriacal preoccupation with bodily processes often
admits of this simple explanation.

and not until a later stage do apparitions or voices make their appearance.[1] In the same way isolated hallucinations sometimes begin with subjective phenomena and then, as Müller [2] has shown, are presently replaced by the sight of a *phantasma*.[3] But the need for a specific psychical state to prepare the way if a given stimulus is to result in hallucination is best shown when the stimulus has been acting for some time, and only subjective sensations have been present, until after an emotional crisis, or some such disturbance, hallucinations supervene. Graefe [4] gives a case in point where vivid (subjective) fiery spheres seen by a patient with *phthisis bulbi* were transformed into full-fledged visual hallucinations after emotional disturbance. Similarly in the case of a lad, mentally sound, but with a perforation of the left ear, the result of a blow, typhus led to the development of hallucinations.[5] . . .

It is to be remarked further that Köppe found in cases of ear-disease among the insane, and where both conditions were therefore present, that auditory illusions and hallucinations invariably accompanied the subjective sounds, but failed to appear when one of the conditions was wanting. Thus the hallucinations may gradually disappear under purely local treatment of the local ailment, or they may cease when the patient's mental health improves, though the subjective images and sounds still persist. . . .

It is clear that the state of dissociation is not always the same. Rather we find an endless series of gradations from the deepest stages of beclouded consciousness to one which is hardly to be distinguished from the normal; or, to express it differently, from the slightest indications of obstructed association to its almost complete inhibition; or from the profound cleavage of consciousness to the

---

[1] Compare Köppe, "Gehörsstörungen und Psychosen," *Allg. Zeitschr. f. Psych.*, xiv.

[2] J. Müller, *Phantast. Gesichtsersch.*, §§ 34-41. By the word *phantasma* he understands subjective phenomena of sight and hearing—*e.g.*, visions of buildings, plants, etc.—which arise suddenly, and unconnected with specks of light, in the completely dark visual field, in contradistinction to appearances which are gradually elaborated to complicated forms, the original speck of light in the eye remaining all the while to serve as a *point de repère* for the hallucinatory images.

[3] Bottex, *Sur les hallucinations;* Ruf, *Delirien*, p. 7; Morel, *Traité des maladies mentales*, p. 318; Baillarger, *Des hallucinations;* Max Simon, *Lyon médical*, xxxi., p. 439; especially in the abuse of quinine, ringing in the ears and undue sensitiveness to light occur first, and only later auditory delusions, less often visual images.

[4] A. Graefe, *Collected Works*, Vol. VI.

[5] *Neurol. Centralblatt*, 1882; compare *Centralblatt Nervenheilkunde*, etc., N. F. v. p. 57 *ff*.

mere splitting off of single elements, or small groups of elements. The more complete the obstruction of the association paths, and the deeper the disturbance of consciousness, the more numerous are the sensory delusions (as in collapse and fever-delirium, for instance), and the less likely are they to be remembered.   Thus, states of profound disturbance of consciousness, like epilepsy and deep sleep, are subjectively described as dreamless; whilst states of only slightly disturbed consciousness, for instance, the periods of transition between sleeping and waking, are regarded as favourable to the occurrence of sensory delusions (hypnagogic and hypnopompic hallucinations).   It is natural, therefore, that the occurrence of hallucinations should be reported, not only in such transition states between sleeping and waking when in bed at night, or during the afternoon siesta, but also in analogous states otherwise produced.   The performance of automatic movements, for instance, such as the monotonous tramping on a long walk or march, often induces such a condition.

"In the winter of 1814 Herr Prus had left the regiment to which he was attached to visit his family, who lived about two leagues off. He relates his experiences as follows:—'I had hardly walked one league in the extreme cold when I noticed that my condition was no longer normal. I walked mechanically, and my body seemed to me strangely light. I knew well the cause and the danger of this state, and tried to hasten my steps, but in vain. Worse still, my eyes kept closing in spite of all my efforts. Then delightful visions visited me. I seemed to be in a beautiful garden, and saw trees, lawns, and streams,' etc." [1]

Sensory Factors in Hallucinations

C. G. JUNG, *Analytical Psychology*, 61-63 (Baillière; Moffat, Yard, 1916)

The part played by entopic perceptions of light in the origin of hallucinations deserves further consideration. Schüle [1] says: "The swarming of light and colour which stimulates and animates the field of vision although in the dark, supplies the material for phantastic figures in the air before falling asleep. As we know, absolute darkness is never seen; a few particles of the dark field

---

[1] Brierre de Boismont, *Des Hallucinations*, p. 349. He mentions also the visions, sometimes gay, sometimes melancholy, which haunted the soldiers of the Grande Armée on the retreat from Moscow.

[2] Schüle, *Handbuch*, 134.

of vision are always illumined; flecks of light move here and there, and combine into all kinds of figures; it only needs a moderately active imagination to create out of them, as one does out of clouds, certain known figures. The power of reasoning, fading as one falls asleep, leaves phantasy free play to construct very vivid figures. In the place of the light spots, haziness and changing colours of the dark visual field, there arise definite outlines of objects." [1]

In this way hypnagogic hallucinations arise. The chief rôle naturally belongs to the imagination, hence imaginative people in particular are subject to hypnagogic hallucinations.[2] The hypno-pompic hallucinations described by Myers arise in the same way.

It is highly probable that hypnagogic pictures are identical with the dream-pictures of normal sleep—forming their visual foundation. Maury [3] has proved from self-observation that the pictures which hovered around him hypnagogically were also the objects of the dreams that followed. G. Trumbull Ladd [4] has shown this even more convincingly. By practice he succeeded in waking himself suddenly two to five minutes after falling asleep. He then observed that the figures dancing before the retina at times represented the same contours as the pictures just dreamed of. He even states that nearly every visual dream is shaped by the retina's own light figures. In our case the fantastic rendering of these pictures was favoured by the situation. We must not underrate the influence of the over-excited expectation which allowed the dull retina-light to appear with increased intensity.[5] The further formation of the retinal appearances follows in accordance with the predominating presentations. That hallucinations appear in this way has been also

---

[1] J. Müller, quoted *Allg. Zeit. f. Psych.*, Vol. XXV, No. 41.

[2] Spinoza hypnopompically saw a *"nigrum et scabiosum Brasilianum."* —J. Müller, *loc. cit.*
In Goethe's "The Elective Affinities," at times in the half darkness Ottilie saw the figure of Edward in a dimly-lit spot. Compare also Cardanus, "imagines videbam ab imo lecti, quasi e parvulis annulis arcisque constantes, arborum, belluarum, hominum, oppidorum, instructarum acierum, bellicorum et musicorum instrumentorum aliorumque huius generis adscendentes, vicissimque descendentes, aliis atque aliis succedentibus." (Hieronymus Cardanus, *De subtilitate rerum*).

[3] *Le sommeil et les rêves*, 134.

[4] G. Trumbull Ladd, "Contribution to the Psychology of Visual Dreams," *Mind*, April, 1892.

[5] Hecker says of the same condition, "There is a simple elemental vision through over-excitation of mental activity not leading to phantastic imagery even without sense presentation; that is the vision of light free from form, a manifestation of the visual organs stimulated from within" (*Ueber Visionen*, Berlin, 1848).

observed in other visionaries. Jeanne d'Arc [1] first saw a cloud of light, and only after some time there stepped forth St. Michael, St. Catherine and St. Margaret. For a whole hour Swedenborg [2] saw nothing but illuminated spheres and fiery flames. He felt a mighty change in the brain, which seemed to him "release of light." After the space of one hour he suddenly saw red figures which he regarded as angels and spirits. The sun visions of Benvenuto Cellini [3] in Engelsburg are probably of the same nature. A student who frequently saw apparitions, stated: "When these apparitions come, at first I only see single masses of light and at the same time am conscious of a dull noise in the ears. Gradually these contours become clear figures."

Memory Factors in Hallucinations

MORTON PRINCE, *The Dissociation of a Personality*, 548-550 (**Longmans,** 1905)

Miss Beauchamp [the case of dissociated personality] as a child frequently had visions of the Madonna and Christ, and used to believe that she had actually seen them. It was her custom when in trouble, if it was only a matter of her school lessons, or something that she had lost, to resort to prayer. Then she would be apt to have a vision of Christ. The vision never spoke, but sometimes made signs to her, and the expression of his face made her feel that all was well. After the vision passed she felt that her difficulties were removed, and if it was a bothersome lesson which she had been unable to understand, it all became intelligible at once. Or, if it was something that she had lost, she at once went to the spot where it was. On one occasion when she had lost a key, her vision of Christ led her down the street into a field where under a tree she found the key. She constantly used to have the sense of the presence of some one (Christ, or the Madonna, or a Saint) near her, and on the occasion of the visions it seemed simply that this person had become visible.

On the night of the very day when the account of her early visions was given to me by B II and confirmed by the Real Miss

---

[1] Jules Quicherat, *Proces de condamnation et de rehabilitation de Jeanne d'Arc, dite La Pucelle*, etc.

[2] Hagen, "Zur Theorie des Hallucinationen," *Allg. Zeit. f. Psych.*, Vol. XXV, No. 10, p. 57.

[3] Goethe, *Benvenuto Cellini*.

Beauchamp, the latter had a vision of Christ which I was able to investigate. Miss Beauchamp had lost a bank check and was much troubled concerning it. For five days she had made an unsuccessful hunt for it, systematically going through everything in her room. She remembered distinctly placing the check between the leaves of a book, when some one knocked at her door, and this was the last she saw of the check. She had become very much troubled about the matter, and in consequence after going to bed that night she was unable to sleep, and rose several times to make a further hunt. Finally, at 3 o'clock in the morning, she went to bed and fell asleep. At 4 o'clock she awoke with consciousness of a presence in the room. She arose and in a moment saw a vision of Christ, who did not speak, but smiled. She at once felt as she used to, that everything was well, and that the vision foretold that she should find the check. All her anxiety left her at once. The figure retreated toward the bureau, but the thought flashed into her mind that the lost check was in the drawer of her desk. A search, however, showed that it was not there. She then walked automatically to the bureau, opened the top drawer, took out some stuff upon which she had been sewing, unfolded it, and there was the check along with one or two other papers.

Neither Miss Beauchamp nor B II has any memory of any specific thought which directed her to open the drawer and take out her sewing, nor of any conscious idea that the check was there. Rather, she did it, so far as her consciousness goes, automatically, as she used to do automatic writing. B II, however, was able to give facts which make the matter intelligible. Miss Beauchamp remembers distinctly putting the check in a book, but B II says that she did not actually do this. She held the book in one hand and the check in the other with the full *intention* of placing the check in the book, but at this moment a knock came at the door. Thereupon she laid the book and check upon the table. After answering the summons at the door she went to the table and picked up her sewing, and unconsciously, at the same time, gathered up the check and the other papers in the folds of the stuff, and folding the whole together placed it in the bureau drawer. B II remembers distinctly each detail of the act, but Miss Beauchamp cannot recall it even now after being told of it. . . . Miss Beauchamp's real memory ceases with the intention, and the latter afterward became evolved into a delusional memory of having carried out the intended action. A delusion of this kind is quite common in normal people, and I suppose most people have experienced it.

It is pretty clear, then, that the finding of the check in this case was accomplished automatically by a subconscious memory of Miss Beauchamp's act of putting it away, and that the vision of Christ was the resuscitation of an old automatism, under the influence partly of this subconscious memory, and partly of the suggestion derived from our conversation about some visions of her childhood held a few hours previously.

Visions like those of Christ and the Madonna, which express the conscious or the subconscious thought of the individual, are very common in religious history. From the point of view of abnormal psychology they are all to be interpreted as sensory automatisms of which the genetic factor is the person's own consciousness. (See Chapter XXXI.[1]) The part played by the secondary consciousness in solving the problems of her school lessons will be in itself an interesting subject for later study.

Some Hallucinations as Wish Fulfilments

STEWART PATON, *Signs of Sanity*, 142-143, 153-154 (Scribner, 1922)

An excellent example is given by Varendonck[2] of the effect of a directive desire upon visualization of that which one wishes to believe a fact. A distinguished botanist was walking along the streets of Paris engaged in thinking about some problem connected with his work. As he passed a restaurant he was surprised to see upon the entrance door the Latin words, "Verbascum Thapsus." After proceeding a few steps it occurred to him that it was extraordinary to have such words on a restaurant door, and he hastily retraced his steps. He found, not the words "Verbascum Thapsus," but "Bouillon" painted upon the glass door. Immediately he saw that his visualization of the Latin words was due to the fact that "Bouillon," a word naturally associated with a restaurant, was also associated with "Bouillon Blanc," the common name for the plant "Verbascum Thapsus." Because the direction given to desire by hunger was at the moment stronger than the intellectual interest in his work the push of the unsatisfied desire for food had broken the sequence of his thought, making him associate the Latin words not with his intellectual interests, but with the drive of hunger. . . .

Harrington[3] tells of a man whose home surroundings were

---

[1] [Prince, *op. cit. Cf.* also James H. Leuba, *The Psychology of Religious Mysticism.*]

[2] Varendonck, J., *The Psychology of Day Dreams* (Macmillan, 1921). [This example was originally reported by Binet.]

[3] Harrington, M. A., *Jour. Nerv. & Ment. Dis.*, Vol. 54, No. 3, Sept. 1921.

cheerless and unsympathetic, with an alcoholic father who was harsh or cruel. The man had been taken from school at an early age and put to work. He did not mix well with his fellows, developed anti-social tendencies, and was further hampered by deafness. He found relaxation from his lonely life by indulgence in trances, in which he sang, danced, performed absurd antics, and heard imaginary voices and saw visions. In spite of all these mental peculiarities, he was able to run a farm and save money until sixty years of age. The absurd relaxation was evidently nature's effort to supply emotional expression for his wishful thinking. But when neighbors ridiculed him he attributed their remarks to envy of his superior accomplishments.

Some Hallucinations as Defense Reactions

ELIDA EVANS, *The Problem of the Nervous Child*, 124-126 (Dodd, Mead, 1922)

An interesting instance . . . was seen in the case of a fourteen-year-old boy who had gone the rounds of clinics and was shown in the Academy of Medicine as the beginning of a Dementia Praecox. He had no appetite. He was said to have various hallucinations of the sense of sound; he heard voices, or his mother's voice, calling him; he also had hallucinations of taste, where everything tasted salt; and of touch, when every night he had the most terrible sensation of being tickled all over the surface of his skin. It began as soon as he went to bed. He could not sleep and lay with his knees drawn up to his chin. He was declared to lack emotional reaction; he lived in a small apartment with mother and older sister and brother but cared for none of them. Upon investigating the environment, I found the boy was sleeping with his mother. He was as tall as she, five feet, six inches. I ordered a couch prepared for him by the open windows of the dining-room. The mother was reluctant to try it; she thought it unnecessary, but the first night the boy slept instantly, and always afterwards. After a few months of analysis the hallucinations entirely disappeared; he ate heartily and returned to school, when the mother concluded it was not necessary to have her dining-room used as a sleeping room, that what I had told her was all nonsense and as the boy was well he could just as well sleep with her again. She told him not to tell me about changing his room. He did not, but he came to me with the same pale face and thick, glaring-looking eyes. The day for his next visit his mother in great alarm came just ahead of him. The boy had not eaten for two days, she said he could keep nothing on his stomach. After severe questioning as to what had happened to cause a return of the illness she confessed with tears what she had done. As soon as he slept alone he was well again and his mother was convinced.

Some Hallucinations as Justification for Behavior

MANDEL SHERMAN and BERT I. BEVERLY, "Hallucinations in Children," *Jour. Abn. Psychol.*, 19: 165-170 (1924)

In studying young children referred for examination because of behavior problems, a number were found in whom a diagnosis of schizophrenia was made. Many of these patients developed hallucinations immediately before the examination or while under observation. . . .

The content of the hallucinations was determined by the environmental and mental condition of the individual case. In some children the hallucinations were apparently simple projections of the mental difficulty; in others a means of compensation or explanation for the difficulty. The hallucinations often passed through several stages, indefinite to definite, inacceptable to acceptable, and from doubtful to positive.

The sequence of development of the hallucinations is illustrated in the case of a fourteen-year-old boy referred by a Superintendent of Schools for the following reason: "He fights upon the least provocation. During these periods of anger he almost loses the semblance of a human being." These violent emotional outbreaks had been observed in this boy for several years. The family history and physical examination were negative. By the Stanford-Binet intelligence test he was found to have an intelligence quotient of 74. The boy complained chiefly of "nervousness"; he felt something moving in his body and especially in his head. "When my head feels funny I have to get in a fight." After fighting he could give no reason for his action, but stated that his "head felt all right again." His "nervousness" was greatly increased during the two months preceding the examination. He complained of having to argue with himself about being good or bad; and whether or not he should fight. At these periods he avoided other boys. Often one part of his mind seemed to say "be good," another part "be bad." Later he saw a person on each side of him, one saying, "be good," the other saying "be bad." There was at first a marked reaction to the hallucinations, often one of violent anger. Later he paid less attention

to them. This was the only case in the series in which the hallucinations occurred at the time of the emotional outbreaks. The boy
was at first certain that the hallucinations might be imaginative.
Later the hallucinations were absolutely real to him and took on
more definite characteristics. The figures seen were described
as being dressed in white. One had long hair, the other short
hair and a funny face. One was God, the other the devil. The
boy was positive of the reality of these final images as true
perceptions. . . .

It was pointed out above that the hallucinations in most cases
were traceable through several stages in their development. The
boy who saw God on one side and the devil on the other first argued
with himself about being good, then recognized vague images, one
saying "be good," the other "be bad." He finally perfected the
images so that they became God and the devil. After reaching the
final form and meeting all of the patient's requirements the hallucination was fully accepted as an explanation for the difficulties, and
all fear and anxiety concerning it disappeared. . . .

The basis for hallucinations is apparently to be found in imagination. Most psychologists have long recognized the marked vividness of imagery of certain types in children as compared to adults.
Campbell,[1] in fact, prefers to list hallucinatory experiences in
young children under the heading of an exaggeration of imagination, having constitutional and emotional idiosyncrasies as a basis,
and precipitated by different environmental factors. The normal
child constantly uses imagination in building up situations which
are unattainable in his daily life. As pointed out by Bain,[2] "one
finds scope in an imaginary world for the gratification of longings,
that are not answered by anything in the realities of one's lot."
"Each one . . . finds in imagined domains an outlet for the in-
satiable craving." The content of the image is determined normally
by the previous experience, the environmental factors at hand, and
by the mental processes most active at the time. As already pointed
out, the affective disturbance, both past and present, as well as the
resulting maladjustment, plays a prominent part in the patient's
reactions, even to the domination of his thinking. Hence the mental
processes must of necessity be influenced. In the psychotic child
these same factors also markedly influence the nature of the

---

[1] Campbell, C. Macfie, "The Nervous Child," *School and Society*, 18: 391
(1923).

[2] Bain, Alexander, *The Emotions and the Will* (3d. ed.), 427-28. London:
Longmans, Green & Co., 1888.

imagery. The psychotic child attempts to adjust his difficulty in the environment by means of imagery in the same way that the normal child builds up imagery as a means of wish fulfillment. For the psychotic child, however, the imagery is a necessity to explain his difficulties, in contradistinction to the imagery of the normal child in his play. Furthermore, as Robinson [3] has pointed out, in the normal child ". . . the satisfaction which is derived from compensatory behavior depends to some extent upon its being within the limits of the child's own credulity," whereas the psychotic child, under the stress of difficulty, recognizes no boundary between his imaginary world and reality.

It is seen in this series of cases that the hallucinations appeared some time after the recognition by observers of the mental difficulty, and developed through fairly definite stages. These hallucinations offered a means of relief of the situation, either through the justification of the patient's behavior or in the satisfaction of his wishes.

Fatigue Hallucinations

A. Mosso, *Fatigue*, 233-235 (Putnam, 1906)

Some people tell me that when they are greatly fatigued by brain work, they are subject to passing hallucinations, similar to those which are sometimes experienced toward the end of an exhausting walk. To some degree these open-eyed dreams are, I believe, produced in all slightly nervous subjects who have somewhat over-fatigued their brain. More especially in the evening, but sometimes also during the day if we are tired, our mind begins to wander in our reading, and visual images arise. These disappear, leaving only the memory of their passage, as soon as attention reawakens; and then for a little we are allowed to resume work. A fresh distraction supervenes, the same or another image appearing quite clearly; occasionally it is some one we know or a landscape we have seen. And this takes place when we are convinced that we are not asleep. In the morning when we are fresh and fit for work, such images hardly ever appear. [How far is this conscious encouragement, close to dramatics? J. J.]

An able dramatic writer once told me that when he composes he has to shut himself up in his study, because he is obliged to make his characters continually talk aloud. He receives them as if on the

---

[3] Robinson, E. S. "The Compensatory Function of Make-Believe Play," *Psychological Review*, 27: 434-438 (1920).

stage, shakes hands with them, offers them a chair, follows them in every little gesture, laughs or cries with them as occasion demands. When he writes he always hears the voices of his actors, but faintly. If they become loud, he at once stops writing and goes for a walk. Experience has taught him that this is a premonitory symptom of fatigue, and that he must cease working if he does not wish to spend a sleepless night. When he was writing one of his dramas, the composition of which exhausted him greatly, he fell into such a morbid state that he not only heard his actors talk when he summoned them in order to write or revise the scenes, but he found that some of them would not be quiet again. He did not trouble himself much about this phenomenon, being convinced that it was simply the result of fatigue; he went off for a little holiday and the hallucinations completely disappeared.

Hypnagogic Hallucinations

N. S. YAWGER, "Hypnagogic Hallucinations with Cases Illustrating these Sane Manifestations," *Jour. Abn. Psychol.*, 13: 73-76 (1918)

In medical writings it is seldom that more than mention is made of sane hallucinations, though they are not of such uncommon occurrence and occasionally we are consulted as to their significance. From Bible times down there always have been persons who beheld visions, and history records many instances where men of genius have had either a single hallucinatory experience or have been subject to their occasional reappearance.

Hypnagogic phenomena were first studied and so named by the French psychologist, Maury;[1] subsequently, the matter was given consideration by Kraepelin,[2] and in this country it is mentioned by White,[3] but for the most part the subject has been left to psychologists.

These curious experiences are familiarly known as visions, and, though innocent in their nature, might be mistaken as heralding some grave mental disorder. In discussing the subject some writers have included phenomena of the special senses manifested on

---

[1] Maury, L. F. A.: *Le Sommeil et les Rêves*, Libraire Academique et Cie, Libraries-Editeurs, Paris, 1861, p. 41.

[2] Kraepelin, Emil: *Psychiatrie*, Johann Ambrosius Barth, Leipzig, 1: 130, 1903.

[3] White, W. A.: *Outlines of Psychiatry*, 45 (Nervous and Mental Disease Publishing Co., 1918).

wakening; the derivation of the word hypnagogic prohibits this, and, furthermore, while experiences preceding sleep are mostly visual, those occurring on wakening are more likely to be associated with hearing.

MEANING OF THE TERM

By hypnagogic phenomena, hallucinations or visions, we understand those experiences, usually optical, of a few sane persons, observed during the transitional stage from wakening to slumber and in which scenes or objects of various kinds pass rapidly before the sight. While in some individuals such hallucinations are observed with the eyes closed, in others they are seen with them open.

The character of the visions vary; at times they assume architectural forms, they may be of streets or of interior decorations, and in other experiences persons are represented either singly or in groups. These recurring scenes are likely to be more or less of a similar character in each individual.

ILLUSTRATIVE CASES

CASE 1.—A woman, aged 72, was long a sufferer from chronic rheumatic arthritis but her hallucinatory experiences antedate her invalidism. The visions were first manifested at 40 years, since then not oftener than once in two or three years and still less often of recent years. The sights appear only on retiring and always with the eyes closed. They are of no particular type—scenes from nature, different patterns of lace and sometimes human heads with distorted features. Once, this individual recalls seeing a castle with doors standing open. It appeared to her that she entered the structure and walked along a wide corridor and into a number of large vacant rooms.

CASE 2.—This is of a gentlewoman, aged 47, of unusual intelligence and in exceptional health. Her own statement follows. The visions appeared first at about 15 years and have been continuous ever since at longer or shorter intervals. Sometimes they appear for several consecutive nights and then remain away for months at a time.

"So far as I can judge they are not more likely to be with me when I am overtired or disturbed in mind. I exercise no control over them as I have repeatedly endeavored to recall the sights but without success; again, when I least expect them they appear, though never until after having retired. In character they are panoramic, one scene appearing for a few seconds to be followed a moment later by a vision entirely different. I regard their development with great interest and enjoyment. At times when others have been in my rooms I have been pleased to entertain them with descriptions of these visions as they appeared one by one. Though my eyes are closed, I know I am fully awake, else how could I describe the sights accurately at the time and furthermore have the power of recalling them long after?

"My experiences are almost invariably of a pleasant nature and through many years there have been but few instances when I have met with decidedly unpleasant sights. These experiences are not the projected images of things previously seen or read but seem an entirely new creation. To me a singular feature is that the visions are entirely void of life—never a living creature nor the image of one—all is so deserted and still.

"As to the subjects of these visions: They are sceneries from nature of various kinds, streets where I see rows of houses mostly of dark brown sandstone and of stately architecture, handsome rooms with beautiful furnishings and hangings, all of gorgeous hue and wondrous design. When I distinctly see interiors, patterns of tapestries and decorations, they are usually in oriental style. Most all that I see is so beautiful that I long for the power to reproduce it in reality.

"Once, I vividly recall that there suddenly appeared lying on a highly polished round-top table of about 2 feet in diameter and within easy reach of my hand, a jewel, of oval shape and about 4 inches in its greatest length. This jewel was a most beautiful, rich, shining topaz, set in a golden scroll and in the center was a jet-black pulsating star. Soon the whole scene vanished from my sight.

"More frequent but less elaborate experiences are with me as I waken. These are usually associated with hearing and consist for the most part of jabbering, incoherent words or snatches from sentences. A recent instance of this kind was my distinctly catching these words, 'I paid my million dollar debt to E. P. André.' To me these words are always meaningless since I can associate them with nothing in my past life."

In the latter case cited the visions began at 15 years and in the former at 40. This, according to Steen,[4] is unusual. In speaking of such manifestations he says:

---

[4] Steen, R. H.: "Hallucinations in the Sane," *Jour. Ment. Dis.*, July, 1917, p. 328.

These are more marked in youth and as a rule disappear when adult life is reached. He quotes DeQuincy who wrote, "I know not whether my reader is aware that many children have a power as it were of painting on the darkness all sorts of phantoms; in some that power is simply a mechanical affection of the eye; others have a voluntary or semi-voluntary power to dismiss or summon such phantoms; or, as a child once said to me when I questioned him about this matter, 'I can tell them to go and they go, but sometimes they come when I don't tell them to come.'"

These manifestations do not have their origin in peripheral disturbances; they have been perceived in persons blind and deaf. Individuals having such experiences may be physically healthy and entirely sane. The phenomenon is just a state of mind and probably as far removed from disease or disorder as is dreaming.

ETIOLOGIC FACTORS

One finds among psychologists various theories accounting for hypnagogic hallucinations. In some general discussion of analogous states James [5] says:

Whenever the associative processes are reduced and impelled by the approach of unconsciousness, as in falling asleep, or growing faint or in becoming narcotized, we find a concomitant increase in the intensity of whatsoever partial consciousness may remain.

As to theories regarding hypnagogic phenomena: Some have considered them due to shutting off the drainage through association paths, thereby making more intense the activity of those cells that retain any activity, until finally the accumulation is so great that a sensory explosion occurs in the form of a vision.

Another theory lays stress on the approach of drowsiness, at which time the sensations cease, consequently, we have an absence of their reductive power; in other words, the channels of comparison being shut off, there is in operation no toning down process and thus the imaginary sights are permitted to spring into existence unopposed.

---

[5] James, William: *Psychology*, 2: 124 (Holt, 1890).

Hallucinations from Dissociated Systems

A

Boris Sidis and Simon P. Goodhart, *Multiple Personality*, 259, 259-260
(Appleton, 1919)

A subject of mine suffering from alcoholic amnesia falls into a
very deep state of hypnosis. When in this state his hand is made
anæsthetic by post-hypnotic suggestions; it is then suggested to
him that objects put into his anæsthetic hand will be seen by him
on a screen. When he wakes up his hand is anæsthetic even to the
most painful stimuli. The anæsthetic hand is then put behind a
screen and another screen is kept in front of his eyes. When objects
are put into the subject's anæsthetic hand, he has visual hallucinations of them. Thus, if half a dollar is put into his anæsthetic
hand, no matter how lightly, he sees it on the screen first as a circle
on a flat surface, then the visual hallucination is gathering more
solidity and reality, more details are gradually emerging, and
finally it begins to look like a solid half dollar. This rather be-
wilders the subject, as this coin is not like ordinary ones, for it
does not feel like a solid object at all when the hand is passed over
it, and he looks up in surprise, asking for the explanation of this
curious phenomenon. The additional interest here is the extreme
hyperæsthesia which the patient manifests in his apparently anæsthetic hand. . . .

Instead of a visual hallucination of the tactile impressions, the
subject may be made to have auditory hallucinations. When, on
waking up, objects are put into the patient's anæsthetic hand, he
begins to listen intently. He hears voices accusing him of keeping
in his hand money or the particular object placed there by the experimenter. He calls the voices "foolish and lying," as he has no
money about him, nor has he any other of the objects the voices
tell him of. Subconscious tactile impressions become here converted
into auditory experiences.

Similarly, in an extremely interesting case which is at present
under my investigation, the sensibility of the whole right side of the
body presents striking phenomena. The patient feels neither
touches nor pricks on the right side; even pain is completely gone,
but when he looks into a glass of water while the anæsthetic hand
is hidden from his sight by a screen, he has visual hallucinations
of the correct numbers of touches, or of pricks given to the anæs-

thetic side, or of objects put into his anæsthetic hand; he has visual
hallucinations of letters and words lightly written on the insensible
hand. On the whole he manifests extreme subconscious hyperæsthesia, but, strangely enough, in *symbolic* terms of another sense.[1]

B

MORTON PRINCE, *The Dissociation of a Personality*, 539-540 (Longmans,
1905)

[Returning once more to the case of Miss Beauchamp:] Sally
conceived the idea that if she could only read French and know as
much as the other personalities, she would not be looked down upon
as "nothing but a subliminal," but would be held in equal esteem
and be allowed to stay. She had "just as much right to stay as
they had," she often repeated. At any rate, if she couldn't read
French they shouldn't. So much by way of explanation.

I was desirous of testing the Idiot's field of consciousness, and,
in particular, of determining whether a knowledge of French was
still within it, or whether it was only within that of B I. B IV had
said that she could read French, but when offered a French novel
she declared it was nothing but a blank notebook. Her manner
at once changed to offended dignity. It was a practical joke that
was being played upon her, she insisted, and her manner plainly
showed that she considered it a discourtesy. It was in vain that
I disclaimed the discourtesy and insisted that the pages were not
blank, but French text. Finally, after much insistence, I said,
"If you won't believe me, go pick out a French book from the
bookcase." She then saw no bookcase at all and no books, but declared, in spite of every assertion on my part to the contrary, that
it was a blank wall sheathed with wood panels, as was the other side
of the room. Thinking the tactile sense might correct the visual
hallucination, I bade her feel the books with her hand and convince
herself. The bookcase was in a recess between the chimney breast
and the end wall of the room. She placed her hand in mid-air on
an imaginary line running across the recess from the chimney-piece
to the end wall, about twelve inches in front of the books. She
insisted that the wood panels ran across the recess at the site of
her imaginary line. I rapped on the books, thinking that the sound
would enable her to distinguish the books from her hallucinatory
panelling, but she explained the sound in an ingenious way. I then

[1] [*Cf.* Pierre Janet, *The Mental State of Hystericals*, 264-265; and Morton Prince, "An Experimental Study of the Mechanism of Hallucinations."]

made an effort to force her hand against the books and past the imaginary line, but she resisted the force by muscular counter-effort. There was both a positive hallucination and a negative one, the former being the wood panel which was not there.

All this, of course, increased her sense of discourtesy, and I could only insist she was mistaken. There was a twinkle in Sally's eye when she was asked later if she could explain these hallucinations. "No, it is a mystery," she replied. A few days later she confessed her part in the trick, adding, "The Idiot sha'n't do anything that I can't do. She sha'n't read French. She may at home, but she sha'n't here." Sally further claimed—a point of importance—that she caused only the negative hallucination and had nothing to do with the positive hallucination,—that of the wood panel. This latter, then, was the logical expression of B IV's belief that no bookcase was there. . . .

Phenomena similar to the foregoing suggest a number of conclusions: [1]

1. There is a type of visual hallucination in which the imagery has its source in a dissociated mental process of which the subject is not consciously aware. Such a process is by definition a subconscious one.

2. The content of this subconscious process contains images identical with the normal imagery of conscious thought.

3. The hallucination is due to the emergence into consciousness of the previously subconscious images. This emergence necessarily results in a hallucination in that the imagery of the latter is not related to the content of the conscious train of thought but is foreign to the latter. This is a necessary consequence of the imagery being normal elements in a separate dissociated train (mental process).

4. The subconscious process is essentially a coconscious one of thought.

5. There is a type of auditory hallucination which has essentially the same mechanism.

6. As there is a type of hallucination (visual and auditory) occurring in the insanities which is identical in form, structure and behaviour with that produced experimentally in this study, the con-

---

[1] Morton Prince, "An Experimental Study of the Mechanism of Hallucinations," *Brit. Jour. Psychol., Med. Sect.,* Vol. II, Part 3, April, 1922, 207-208.

clusion is justified that such hallucinations of the insane are due to the same mechanism.

7. The implication follows that when hallucinations of this type occur in the pathological psychoses, they are indications of the activity of a dissociated subconscious process as a factor in the psychosis.

8. The hallucinatory phenomenon carries the further implication that the genesis and psychopathology of the psychosis are to be found in the forces which have determined the dissociation and motivated the subconscious process.

9. It is not to be assumed that all hallucinations have the mechanism of the type here studied. It is possible that in those occurring in the intoxication psychoses and in certain forms of organic brain disease, particularly where the hallucination is of a simple unelaborated static structure, the imagery is induced by direct irritation of the cortical or subcortical neurones. It is difficult, however, to exclude the possibility that the intoxicating agent or organic process simply removes inhibition and permits subconscious dissociated processes to function. Nor can we find any analogy with the known effect of irritation of motor and other areas of the brain. Irritation, as observed, produces simple movements and simple sensory phenomena (noises). Still, the possibility of irritating factors becoming the immediate excitants of organized complexes of neurones underlying the hallucinations, cannot be excluded. This theory needs, however, to be proved. Even the irritative theory, as opposed to the psychogenetic theory, permits of the interpretation that the irritation excites a dissociated subconscious process from which images emerge into consciousness.

10. The psychological problem of differentiating between normal imagery and hallucination disappears in that they are identical, the hallucination being only the normal imagery of a dissociated subconscious process.

11. If the evidence given by subconscious introspection be not accepted, a possible interpretation of the hallucinatory imagery is that the images do not themselves occur primarily as subconscious elements, but by the same mechanism appear in awareness as the conscious correlates of a co-active dissociated physiological process. In other words, a subconscious process is neural, not psychical. On the other hand, such an interpretation does not take into account a large mass of collateral evidence for the psychical nature of processes occurring outside the field of awareness.

12. So far from a hallucination being a regression to an infantile

form of thought (Freud), it is an element in highly developed adult thought processes.

13. The mechanism of the imagery of some dreams is the same as that of the hallucinations of the type here studied.[2]

---

[2] [Further material on hallucinations may be found in Nicolas Vaschide, *Les hallucinations télépathiques.*]

CHAPTER XXI

DREAMS

Dreams is a subject lately brought into great prominence in abnormal psychology. As however it is infrequently touched upon in general psychology, and as a very comprehensive treatment is now available,[1] only broad outlines will receive attention here.

The Dreams of the Blind

JOSEPH JASTROW, *Fact and Fable in Psychology*, 341-342, 367-368, 347-350 (Houghton Mifflin, 1900); used by permission of and by special arrangement with the publishers

Beginning with cases of *total* blindness (including under this head those upon whom light has simply a general subjective "heat-effect," enabling them to distinguish between night and day, between shade and sunshine, but inducing little or no tendency to project the cause of the sensation into the external world), I find on my list fifty-eight such cases. Of these, thirty-two became blind before the completion of their fifth year, and not one of this group of thirty-two sees in dreams. Six became blind between the fifth and the seventh year: of these, four have dreams of seeing, but two of them do so seldom and with some vagueness; while two never dream of seeing at all. Of twenty persons who became blind after their seventh year *all* have "dream-vision"—as I shall term the faculty of seeing in dreams. *The period from the fifth to the seventh year is thus indicated as the critical one.* Before this age the visual centre is undergoing its elementary education; its life is closely dependent upon the constant food-supply of sensations; and when these are cut off by blindness, it degenerates and decays. If blindness occurs between the fifth and the seventh years, the preservation of the visualizing power depends on the degree of development of the individual. If the faculty is retained, it is neither

---

[1] Lydiard H. Horton, *The Dream Problem.* Excellent general selections, too, are found in Robinson's *Readings.*

stable nor pronounced. If sight is lost after the seventh year, the sight-centre can, in spite of the loss, maintain its function. . . .

[Hence] many of the dreams present no special differentiation from those of the seeing, but the most carefully recorded ones usually reveal some traces of a defective or peculiar apperception. A blind boy with more than usual imagination dreamed that he was in a battle in which Alexander the Great put the Gauls to flight; he heard the thunder of the cannon, but saw no flash. A young man dreamed that his mother was dead; this he knew by the cold touch of her body. He next heard the chanting of the Mass at her funeral. This young man at times improvises airs in his dreams. A partially-sighted girl dreams repeatedly of a wide river, and is afraid of being dashed across it, while anxious to secure the flowers on the opposite bank, which she dimly sees. A boy dreamed of being picked up by some mysterious agency, and then suddenly allowed to fall from a tremendous height. Here he awoke, and found his head at the foot of the bed. Another dreamed of the Judgment Day, mainly in terms of hearing. He was drawn to heaven by a rope, clinging to a pole used for exercising; he heard the trumpets sounding, and the voices singing, and so on.[1]

---

[1] The dreams of those both blind and deaf are especially instructive. Many of Laura Bridgman's dreams have been recorded; and an unpublished manuscript by Dr. G. Stanley Hall places at my service a valuable account of her sleep and dreams. Sight and hearing were as absent from her dreams as they were from the dark and silent world which alone she knew. The tactual-motor sensations, by which she communicated with her fellow-beings, and through which almost all her intellectual food reached her, also formed her mainstay in dreams. This accounts for the suddenness and fright with which she often waked from her dreams; she is perchance dreaming of an animal, which to us would first make itself seen or heard, but to her is present only when it touches and startles her —for she lacks any anticipatory sense. Language has become so all-important a factor in civilized life, that it naturally is frequently represented in dreams. We not only dream of speaking and being spoken to, but we actually innervate the appropriate muscles and talk in our sleep; this Laura Bridgman also did. "Her sleep seemed almost never undisturbed by dreams. Again and again she would suddenly talk a few words or letters with her fingers, too rapidly and too imperfectly to be intelligible (just as other people utter incoherent words and inarticulate sounds in sleep), but apparently never making a sentence." So, too, all the people who enter into her dreams talk with their fingers. This habit had already presented itself at the age of twelve, four years after her first lesson in the alphabet. "I do not dream to talk with mouth; I dream to talk with fingers." No prettier illustration could be given of the way in which her fancy built upon her real experiences, than the fact recorded by Charles Dickens, that on picking up her doll he found across its eyes a green band

The Problem of Dream Interpretation

A

HAVELOCK ELLIS, *The World of Dreams*, 172-174 (Houghton Mifflin, 1911) ; used by permission of and by special arrangement with the publishers

There is a symptom of mental disorder called *extrospection,* in which the patient fastens his attention so minutely on events that he comes to interpret the most trifling signs and incidents as full of hidden significance, and may so build up a systematised delusion.[1] The investigator of dreams must always bear in mind the risk of falling into morbid extrospection. . . .

It must also be said that even when we admit that a strong emotion may symbolically construct an elaborate dream edifice which needs analysis to be interpreted, we narrow the process unduly if we assert that the emotion is necessarily a wish. Desire is certainly very fundamental in life and very primitive. But there is another equally fundamental and primitive emotion—fear.[2] We may very well expect to find this emotion, as well as desire, subjacent to dream phenomena.[3]

---

such as she herself wore. The organic sensations originating in the viscera, though often prominently represented in dreams of normal persons, seemed especially prominent in her dreams. She tells of feeling her blood rush about, and of her heart beating fast when suddenly waking, much frightened, from a distressing dream. One such dream she describes as "hard, heavy, and thick"; terms which, though to us glaringly inappropriate in reference to so fairy-like a structure as a dream, form an accurate description in the language of her own realistic senses. In short, her dreams are accurately modeled upon the experiences of her waking life, reproducing in detail all the peculiarities of thought and action which a very special education had impressed upon her curious mind.—*Ibid.,* 347-350.

[What light do such dreams as these cast on the doctrines of Freud and of Jung with regard to "symbols"?]

[1] Extrospection has been specially studied by Vaschide and Vurpas in *La Logique Morbide.*

[2] On the psychic importance of fears, see G. Stanley Hall, "A Study of Fears," *American Journal of Psychology,* 1897, p. 183. Metchnikoff (*Essais Optimistes,* pp. 247 *et. seq.*) insists on the mingled fear and strength of the anthropoid apes.

[3] Foucault has pointed this out, and Morton Prince, and Giessler (who admits that the wish-dream is common in children), and Flournoy (who remarks that not only a fear but any emotion can be equally effective),

The infantile form of the wish-dream, alike in adults and children, is thus, there can be little doubt, extremely common, and even in its symbolic forms, it is a real and not rare phenomenon. But it is impossible to follow Freud when he declares that all dreams fall into the group of wish-dreams. The world of psychic life during sleep is, like the waking world, rich and varied; it cannot be covered by a single formula.[4]

B

Lydiard H. Horton; adapted from "How 'Stimulus and Reaction' Explains Levitation Dreams," *Jour. Abn. Psychol.*, 15: 15 (1920); "Scientific Method in the Interpretation of Dreams," *ibid.*, 10: 379-382 (1916); "What Drives the Dream Mechanism?" *ibid.*, 15: 226, 227, 229, 236 (1920); "How 'Stimulus and Reaction' Explains Levitation Dreams,"
ibid., 15: 13-14 (1920)

The Interpreter should not let his free play of fancy rival that of a dreamy or drowsy subject. In gathering information about trances and those phenomena of the Unutterable Revelation (to which Professor Leuba has recently called attention) I had met with the "Will to Interpret"; for the subjects under trance conditions, gave to their scant impressions and slight corporeal disturbances most extraordinary meanings. Such changes as "blood-vessel sensations," however slight they may be, furnish the basis for extraordinary fancies of power, locomotion, levitation.

---

as well as Claparède. The last remarks that Freud might regard a fear as a suppressed desire, but it may equally be said that a desire involves, on its reverse side, a fear. Freud has indeed himself pointed out (*e. g. Jahrbuch für Psychoanalytische Forschungen*, Bd. 1, 1909, p. 362) that fears may be instinctively combined with wishes; he regards the association with a wish of an opposing fear as one of the components of some morbid psychic states. But he holds that the wish is the positive and fundamental element: "The unconscious can only wish" ("Das Unbewusste kann nichts als wünschen"), a statement that seems somewhat too metaphysical for the psychologist.

[4] ["There is, however, one class of dream, in which no wish seems to be operative; there is rather a tendency of the mind to revert in sleep to some significant past experience, generally of a painful character. The battle-dreams so common among soldiers during the war are good examples of this kind of dream. Here the dream seems merely to repeat some terrible experience, and it is doubtful if there is any hidden wish behind it. Freud thinks that the *function* of dream formation may be abrogated by shock and that the tendency of the mind to revert to significant experience is perhaps more primordial than the pleasure-principle."—T. W. Mitchell, *The Psychology of Medicine*, 107-108 (Methuen, 1921); reprinted by permission.]

Let me illustrate these points by the analysis of a sample dream; speaking first as the dreamer giving the simple narrative; next as Freud applying the reductive method; then as Jung employing the constructive method; and finally explaining the dream, as I would myself prefer, by the use of what I may call the reconstitutive method. The dream itself, for reasons that will be obvious, I call the "Scratch-Reflex Dream."

"I was looking down upon a microscope from the right side of the lens-tube, and could see, laid upon the stage, a glass slide. Under the cover-glass, in place of an ordinary specimen, there was supposed to be a new reflex,—one of those discovered by my friend the neurologist, Dr. X., whose scrawly handwriting I recognized on the label. I was anxiously trying to decipher what he had written, and was having the same trouble with it that I had experienced in real life with the record of some of his dreams, which I had interpreted successfully. The handwriting on the label, as I gazed, appeared less and less like script and more like disconnected, scratchy lines or hachures, owing to the formation of lacunae in the inky traces. It became scratchier and scratchier as I wakened. On coming to my senses . . ."

"That is enough," we hear Dr. Freud saying; "it is obvious what kind of reflex-action you have in mind! The word 'slide' is of a punning nature, and in conjunction with the easy moveability of the microscope-barrel suggests a meaning akin to that of dreams of skating and sliding, which are usually sexual. From the standpoint of symbolics, the geometric forms and relative positions of cover-glass and microscope suggest allusions to the generative powers of nature—like the phallicism of the ancient Egyptian religion, whose sacred emblems of sexual objects still confront the explorer and the tourist. Here, the 'stage' of the microscope refers obviously to the theatre, so often the scene of exhibitionistic activities. Your dream represents the male and the female principles in such a manner that it must mean a survival of infantile curiosity related to the mystery of parenthood. Sir, this proves your Libido to have been fixated at the 'voyeur' level." [1]

"Not so fast," says Dr. Jung, while the dreamer remains non-plussed at the foregoing example of the reductive method. "It is not good for the health to overvalue the past, as my colleague does. Nous avons changé tout cela, in Zurich. Your curiosity, according to the constructive method, is a demand for satisfaction in new and

---

[1] Freud, "Drei Abhandlungen . . .," trans.: "Three Contributions to the Sexual Theory," Monograph, (Nerv. & Ment. Dis. Pub'g. Co., 1909).

better ways than those of infancy. I will prove this to be so, by an investigation of the dream material. This Dr. X., what of him and his handwriting?"

The dreamer then explains that Dr. X. had consented to have his dreams analyzed, and that the outcome had been the uncovering of his secret intention to be married; the dreamer also states that Dr. X. had written some very original papers on periosteal reflexes.

"Ah," says Dr. Jung, as it were, making quotations from his own writings, (as indicated in italics) *"one has only to hear this dream material in order to understand at once that the dream is not so much the fulfilment of infantile desires as it is the expression of biological duties hitherto neglected because of . . . infantilism.*[2] To be sure these are sexual objects that you are looking at in the dream, as Freud would have it. But your interest in them is not so primitive as it would seem. For do you not, symbolically speaking, 'look down upon' them in your fancy. And moreover, since you are looking at these emblems of parental union 'from the right side,' does it not therefore mean that you are contemplating something legitimate; namely, marriage on your own account—not exhibitionism on the part of others. One infers you wish to put away childish sex-curiosity and fulfil your destiny as a parent. *In this case symbolical value, not concrete value must be attached to the sexual phantasy."*

At this point, the dreamer makes free to admit that he is a bachelor, and that he would not be averse to marriage if he could manage to take a wife and at the same time keep up his research work.

"Precisely," Dr. Jung might say, rapidly turning these clues to account, "your interest in future advancement is clearly reflected in your anxiety to decipher the handwriting of Dr. X., with whom you have identified yourself. You desire to emulate his scientific achievements; his published work on reflexes excites your ambition. The handwriting on the label, which perplexes you is an allusion not only to his authorship but to the difficulties in the way of your own contribution to the science of dream interpretation. By imitating Dr. X.'s triumph you wish to make your marriage possible. Your *Hormé* or *élan vital* is pushing you to evolve new and higher forms of the Libido. You are sublimating!"[3]

"No, gentlemen," the dreamer replies at last, "your reductions

---

[2] Jung, C. G., "Psychoanalysis," an address before the Psycho-Medical Society of London, 1913, August; *Transactions of the Society.*

[3] Jones, Ernest, *Papers on Psycho-Analysis*, Chapter XX (Wood, 1913).

and your constructions are too easy-going, too conjectural, too much dominated by prepossessions and the 'will to interpret.' The alleged sources or determinants for this dream may or may not have played the parts you assign to them; the mystery of the matter must remain inscrutable. But what your methods, so plausible in effect, certainly do show is how easy it may be to confabulate an explanation that goes no deeper than a phrenological reading of cranial bumps or than a séance in the cabinet of a palmist. Let us turn away from all this and consider what really happened, as by the grace of luck I can bear witness. Permit me to reconstitute the dream as an actual event, by the employment of certain clues which I was about to give when the ready-made symbolism of Dr. Freud was interposed."

Inasmuch as the dream is one of my own, I may be permitted to testify that it was unmistakably connected with a scratching sensation at my ear, as I distinctly perceived on awaking. This stimulation proceeded obviously from a mouse, which I had time to observe in close proximity, as it remained perched on the bedclothes, until my own startled movements put it to flight. Tracing the stimulation from this external source, I shall try to maintain the following interpretation:—

First, that the dream is an associative reaction to the sensation of scratching, in the form of evocations of imagery related in experience to this sensory element; and that the dream-process was a part of the perception, or recognition or apperception of the stimulus.

Second, that this reaction—let us name it apperception of the stimulus—took place slowly and imperfectly, owing to the state of sleep, so that the reaction was, to begin with, only remotely relevant to the stimulus, but improved in relevancy with successive evocations, until the mental representation closely approximated the character of the stimulus.

Third, that in and among the secondary images [4] so evoked, incidental processes of thought, tertiary compoundings of these images, were immediately set up; the selection and re-arrangement of these secondary and tertiary features, constituting the revelation of a significant state of mind which had preceded the dream.

Specifically, in addition to the mental response to the external stimulus, there was a phantasy representing an imaginary wish-fulfilment: namely, the desire to forsake the study of histology, with the eye-straining search through the microscope, in favor of the study of reflex-action or reflexology.

---

[4] Prince, *The Unconscious;* doctrine of secondary images.

My contention is that this blended response [5] to a physical and to a psychic cue arose very naturally and simply out of a single context, prepared by events of the night before; and I would show that by comparing the phantasy with this context, it is possible to reconstitute the dream in a way that amounts to a refutation of the two other interpretations, which I have essayed in accordance with the methods of Freud and of Jung, respectively.[6]

---

[5] Galton, Francis, *Inquiries into Human Faculty* (Macmillan, 1883); see essays on association, doctrine of blends.

[6] [For a "forced gastronomic interpretation," contrasted with the inventorial reconstitution again, *cf.* Lydiard H. Horton, "How 'Stimulus and Reaction' Explains Levitation Dreams," 12, 17, 19.

Dr. J. A. Hadfield has described the situation as follows: "I am quite aware that each authority claims to interpret the dreams solely from the associations given by the patient. But (1), in the first place, the *interpretation* is something more than the associations given. As you may give half a dozen matches to several men, and each will make an entirely different pattern, so the interpretation of your dream depends less on the association given than on the meaning which the analyst provides. However, it does not matter much which method of interpretation you adopt, it will always do the patient good, because it will make him examine himself!

"(2) In the second place, the associations themselves are usually suggested, perhaps unconsciously, by the analyst, from whom the patient gets to know what is expected of him. If I go to a Freudian, I cannot but be influenced by what I know is expected of me; sex symbols would undoubtedly be the first to suggest themselves to my mind. If to a Jungian, my associations would be mythical and primordial images. It is no wonder that the adherents of each school are firmly convinced of the truth of their own interpretation, for in the nature of things they receive the associations they expect. When I myself, as analyst, changed my theory of dream interpretation, I found that my patients followed suit with their associations.

"The absurdity grows still greater when the analyst carries about in his mind a little pocket-book of symbols with the meaning in the opposite column. In these days one has only to be armed with a tabloid equipment of this kind to call oneself a psychologist, and to feel extraordinarily wise when a lady at a dinner-party says that she dreamed of poking the fire.

"That dreams are extraordinarily valuable for obtaining an insight into the patient's inner life I do not deny. Nor do I wish to cast discredit on the valuable work that has been done in their psychological investigation. But to use them as the main instrument of interpretation of the patient's mind, when they themselves are as yet so arbitrarily interpreted, is unjustified as a scientific procedure. Just as Freud got tired of hearing the patients whom he was trying to hypnotize say, 'But, doctor, I am not asleep,' so I have become tired of my patients saying, or more often thinking, of the interpretation of a dream, 'Very ingenious, doctor, but rather far-fetched, don't you think?' Obviously I had not obtained the

The slow progress being made in reaching a satisfactory explanation of dreams is due to a deficiency in the "drives" that move the interest of observers: (1) The dreamer himself is not always scientifically minded and is influenced by egocentric drives. (2) The drive of scientific curiosity falls short of the goal for lack of sufficiently laborious study of other people's dreams at first hand. (3) The reputed absurdity of dreams and the tediousness of dream narratives make serious investigation precarious.

The psychoanalytic formulation of dream processes remains unsatisfactory because it over-simplifies the data of dynamic and social psychology and disregards the large part played by purely physiological and sensory factors in driving the dream, let alone wishes, desires and other motives.

Many specific cases of seemingly absurd dream imagery can be explained as the concurrent effects or confluence of separate drives. Among dream-drives one is logically compelled to include ordinary sensory cues. They should be distinguished and classified as external drives. These are apt to require—in the case of dreams—a process of "resolution" as complex as that demanded by the other sort of motive power or motives, namely, the drives that seem to originate internally to the nervous system.

The process of dreaming is essentially the finding of the resultant of these forces and the projection into consciousness of the images that are experientially coupled with particular nerve-patterns mobilized in this "resolution." [An example is found in the (waking) response of the Japanese poetess, who when asked to "combine in one word-picture the ideas of a triangle, of a square, and of a circle," replied: "Detaching one corner of the mosquito netting, lo, I behold the moon." [7]]

In fine, as I have stated earlier, the true pursuit of dream-study should be to trace the wave of nervous excitation from its origin in a particular set of nerve stimuli and to show how the several images in the dream-panorama were produced under the influence of the group of stimuli, acting in couple with the pre-existing state of mental preparation ("facilitation" or "Bahnung"). All these ele-

---

patient's 'transference!' If I had had it, I should have been encouraged to continue with this method of treatment—he swallowing, while I administered, the pill."—*Psychology and Morals*, 121-122 (Methuen & Co. and Robert M. McBride, 1923); reprinted by permission.]

[7] Lydiard H. Horton, "Scientific Method in the Interpretation of Dreams, with a Theory to Explain the Dream Process as Apperceptive Trial and Error," *Jour. Abn. Psychol.*, 10: 389 (1916).

ments can usually be found and accounted for, if one prepares an adequate inventory of the items of the dream.[8]

---

[8] ["When a neurogram is strongly activated, we have the consciousness that belongs to that particular grouping of neurones, while all those patterns that are inactive represent the ideas or experiences of which we are unconscious. In deep sleep all neurones are quiet. In a fully waking condition, every stimulus tends to arouse a pattern to activity and thus to produce consciousness. There is reason to believe that between these two extremes we have all gradations. From which it is easy to see that toward the sleep end of the scale we may conceive the brain as being in a condition that we, perhaps, for want of a better term, may call 'dormant.' Ordinary stimuli do not arouse any neurone patterns to activity. An excessive stimulus will arouse a small pattern which in turn may arouse a few cells that have been intimately connected with it, and these may arouse another group, and so on. The two situations may perhaps be likened to a surface covered with gunpowder. When the powder is dry, a spark applied to any one grain explodes the whole mass. If, however, the powder has been wet, the spark will have no effect. But, if it has partly dried out and is drier in some spots than in others, there will be a slow burning, following irregular lines, the flame creeping along from particle to particle, until, perhaps, it reaches a little mass that is drier than the rest. There will be a flash, followed again by a slow creeping along of the combustion. This represents the dream. Now, our problem is, what determines the course of events. In our illustration, the determinant is the more or less completely dried-out part of areas or lines. In the dream, it is the groups of neurones scattered here and there through the cortex which, for some reason, are in a condition to be activated, either because the stimuli at these points are excessively strong, or because these patterns are all ready to explode, possibly because they have recently been active. The recency is shown in the accepted fact that a part of the dream at least relates to the events of the previous day, what Freud calls 'the dream day,' and it is quite possible that the dream in its entirety relates to the thought of the dream day—not necessarily the thoughts that have been at any time in the focus of consciousness, but perhaps largely thoughts that have been in the margin. And there may be neurone patterns whose activity did not even produce any awareness, because, as we have already explained, some other group of neurones was more violently active, and so monopolised the field of consciousness, so to speak. Moreover, it seems equally possible that the activity of cells that have been concerned with consciousness in the 'dream day' may activate nerve patterns that have not been active for many days or perhaps for years. Thus we dream of things that we have not thought of for a long period, or that we cannot remember ever having thought of."—Henry Herbert Goddard, "The Unconscious in Psychoanalysis," in *Problems of Personality*, C. Macfie Campbell and others, eds., 326-327 (Harcourt, Brace, 1925).]

C

Morton Prince, "Foreword" to Mary Arnold-Forster's volume, *Studies in Dreams*, xi (London: George Allen & Unwin, Ltd.; Macmillan, 1922)

What is still needed, as the author has pointed out, is systematic and accurate recording of their dreams by many persons, and the correlation of the phenomena with identical phenomena occurring in certain other states of the waking mental life. If this were done, we should be surprised to find what a great variety of forms and structure dreams have, how greatly they differ in type, and in the mental processes involved. We thus should have the material from which we could safely construct theories of mechanisms that would satisfy the different types. After the collection of this varied material, we could then begin, with greater safety, to analyse and interpret. In some we should find symbolism, in others none; in some repressed wishes, in others unrepressed wishes, or fears, doubts, and scruples; in some sex urgings, in others the urgings of one or more of the other various innate instincts which are the prime movers of human behaviour; in some the solution of problems which have baffled our waking consciousness, in others the mere illogical fantasies of a weak, dissociated extract of our mental selves; in some the reproduction of memories, and living over again in realistic form previous actual experiences, in others imaginary episodes or apparent super-knowledge constructed out of previous information; in some incongruous, grotesque phantasmagoria in cinema-like scenes, in others romances or well-constructed fantasies requiring for their invention a large system of thought and an intelligence and imagination comparable to the waking self-consciousness. And in some we should find that the dream, as in waking life, is only the manifested expression of deeper-lying subconscious processes; and in some, probably in most, that it is just what it appears to be—nothing more.

Use of Dream Analysis in Psychotherapy

A

GEORGE H. GREEN, *Psychoanalysis in the Class Room*, 156-159 (1922; U. S. A. and Canadian rights, G. P. Putnam's Sons; other rights, University of London Press, Ltd.; reprinted by permission)

A woman of about thirty years of age had a morbid horror of cats, somewhat like that of the late Lord Roberts. She could hardly bear to remain in the same room or even the same house as a cat.

She narrated the following dream: "I was standing with something in my hand, which I was holding very tightly. I looked down and to my horror saw that I was holding a kitten, which I had squeezed to death. I was very distressed, because, although I detest cats, I would not willingly hurt one for anything."

The circumstances of her life about the time of the dream were these. She had applied for a post that was higher than the one she was holding. She held a certificate granted by an examining body, which we will call X. She was chosen for an interview, but discovered that the members of the board before whom she appeared were interested in another examining body (which we will call Y) and refused to consider the certificates issued by X.

She applied for a second post, and was again selected for an interview. She discovered, however, that the members of this second board were interested in Y, and refused to recognise the certificates of X. Consequently she declined the interview.

She applied for a third post, and at the same time wrote to the secretary of X, stating her experiences, and saying that X should take measures to see that the holders of its certificates were treated fairly. It was now that she dreamed the dream recorded above.

In reply to a question, she stated that the first thought that came into her mind when she thought of a cat was deceit. Deceit made her think of a girl who had been sent into a room to dust, but who began to read instead of working so soon as she found herself alone. This she admitted was a personal experience. The person who used to send her to dust was her elder sister.

The elder sister dominated her a great deal. She did not resent this very much. What she could not forgive in the elder sister was her favouritism for a younger sister. The latter was very pretty, whereas the subject was considered plain. As a small child she had crooked legs, straight hair, and a cast in one eye. She has grown out of these defects, and now realises their unimportance. But they used to result in a good deal of praise for the younger sister, whilst she herself was ignored. The younger sister was taken out a good deal more, "shown off," and dressed in a prettier way. She states that the mother and elder sister always used to say that the two girls were dressed and treated alike, but that she was convinced that the younger sister was favoured.

She says that the preference for the younger sister used to make her very miserable. She used to weep about it, and used to feel jealous.

At this point she was asked, "What is the name of your younger sister?"

"Katherine," she replied.

"Used you to call her Katherine?"

"Oh, no, never," said she. "We used always to call her Kitty. . . . *But I never wanted to kill my sister.*"

It is interesting to notice, in this case, that without any suggestion on the part of her interlocutor, the subject suddenly realises that the cat she consciously hates is the sister of whom she used to be so jealous. The vindictive thoughts that were felt in early childhood are repressed so soon as she is able to realise that they are "wicked," and are directed towards a harmless substitute, a cat. The hatred still lives. Only its expression has been repressed.

The occasion of the dream is one that repeats in outward form the circumstances of her early childhood. The candidates who hold the certificates of Y are unfairly preferred to her. Hence these stand in relation to herself as "Kitty" used to stand to her. Her action in writing to X is designed to enable her to defeat her rivals, as her once-cherished plans against "Kitty" would have enabled her to defeat her sister. Her wish is to be successful against rivals. Hence the dream shows her as crushing a "kitty" to death. . . . The questioning brings into consciousness the repressed attitude towards her sister, whom she has now learned to love. Hence there are in consciousness two opposed judgments, viz. :—

(a) I want to kill my sister.

(b) I do not want to kill my sister.

Since no normal human being is able to entertain as true at the same time two judgments, one of which is the contradiction of the other, one of the two must be destroyed. In the case in question (a) is destroyed, because (b) is regarded as true. . . . As a result the fear of cats has completely gone.

B

W. H. R. RIVERS, *Instinct and the Unconscious*, 170-181 (Cambridge, 1922)

The case I am about to record is that of a medical man, aged thirty-one, who from childhood has suffered from a dread of being in an enclosed space, and especially of being under conditions which would interfere with his speedy escape into the open.

When I saw him first his earliest memory of this dread went back to the time when at the age of six he slept with his elder brother in what is known in Scotland as a box-bed. The bed stood in a recess with doors which could be closed so as to give the appearance of a sitting-room. The child slept on the inner side of the bed next to the wall, and he still vividly remembers his fear and the desire to get out of bed, which he did not satisfy for fear of waking his brother. He would lie in a state of terror, wondering if he would be able to get out if the need arose.

His next memory bearing on his phobia is of being taken to see some men descending the shaft of a coal-pit. There came to him at once the fear that were he going down something might happen to prevent his getting out. He remembers that whenever in childhood he was taken for a journey by train he dreaded the tunnels, and if by chance the train stopped in a tunnel he feared that there might be an accident and that he would not be able to get out. This fear of tunnels became worse as he grew older. He would not travel by the tube-railway, and remembers his horror when on one occasion he had to do so. When he began to go to the theatre or other crowded building he was always troubled unless he was near the door, and he was never happy unless he could see a clear and speedy mode of exit. As long as he can remember he has felt an intense sympathy whenever he has read of prisoners being confined in a narrow cell, and he has always been greatly disturbed by tales of burial alive.

He was always nervous and excitable as a child and suffered from night-terrors. He has been liable, as long as he can remember, to worry without knowing why. When about twelve years old he began to stammer, ascribing its onset to the imitation of a school-fellow. It soon passed off, but ever since he has been liable to stammer when out of health.

During boyhood he had occasional attacks of sleeplessness, loss of appetite, and inability to work. When about twenty-two years of age he decided to go in for medicine, and while reading for the

Preliminary had an attack of this kind more severe than usual, which prevented his working for some time. A similar attack during the second year of his medical studies made him fear that he would have to give up medicine, but the leisure of a vacation restored him, and he completed his medical course. While serving as house-surgeon he again broke down in health, but managed to finish his period of office, and then did very light work for nine months.

About six years ago, while a medical student, he heard of a German, whom I will call A., who received patients into his house in order to cure them of stammering and other nervous ailments. He stayed with him for two weeks, the treatment consisting mainly of a variety of suggestion in which the patients were told to relax their muscles and concentrate their minds on the qualities they desired to attain. A. had recently become acquainted with the work of Freud, and had visited Vienna in order to learn something of his methods. Some time later the patient again put himself under the care of A. in order to undergo a course of psycho-analysis. The analyst in this case does not appear to have been acquainted with the method of free association, and after an unsuccessful attempt to carry out a series of word-associations the process of psycho-analysis resolved itself into an inquiry into dreams. In company with others the patient was instructed about Freud and his views. He was told that the cause of his trouble certainly lay in some forgotten experience of childhood of a sexual nature. When he related his dreams they were invariably interpreted by means of symbolism of a sexual character. Thus, if he had dreamed of water, he was told that this indicated a wish for sexual intercourse. It is a striking feature of the process of examination and treatment to which the patient was subjected that it failed to discover the special dread of closed spaces from which he suffered. At this time he had not realised that his dread was exceptional or was capable of treatment. He had supposed that everyone objected to conditions which were so trying to himself, and it was only on account of his stammering and his general nervousness that he had sought treatment. Consequently he told A. nothing about his dread and the process of "analysis" failed to detect it. Not only did the treatment lead the mind of the patient exclusively in a sexual direction, but it also failed to discover or remedy the claustrophobia.

This process of so-called psycho-analysis had no result which satisfied the patient. On the contrary, after two months of it his sleep became so disturbed and his general condition so much the worse that he gave up the treatment and returned home. Nevertheless, he was left with the firm conviction, which he retained till he came under my care, that the root of his troubles lay in some forgotten sexual experience. This belief was so strong that he continued to search out for himself some forgotten experience of this kind, but without success, and shortly before the outbreak of the war he was thinking of going to Vienna to consult Freud and find whether the master himself might not succeed in discovering the lost memory.

The outbreak of the war interfered with this plan. At that time the patient was still suffering from the effects of his breakdown when a house-surgeon, but as soon as he had recovered sufficiently he joined the R.A.M.C. and went to France. When he reached the front he had to live and work in dug-outs and was at once troubled by the dread of the limited space, and especially by the fear that he might not be able to get out if anything happened. His dread was greatly stimulated on his first day in a dug-out when, on asking the use of a spade and shovel, he was told that they were to be used in case he was buried. It was only when he found others living and working in comfort in dug-outs that for the first time he realised the exceptional nature of his dread, and recognised that he was the subject of an abnormal condition. After two attacks of trench-fever his dread was greatly accentuated and increased to such an extent as to make his life almost unendurable. He slept so badly that he had recourse to hypnotics and often spent a large part of the night walking about the trenches rather than remain in his dug-out. His health became so impaired that he was advised by his commanding-officer to consult the A.D.M.S., who sent him into hospital. He was there treated by rest and was given paraldehyde every night. He was told to keep his thoughts from war-experience and to dwell exclusively on pleasant topics such as beautiful scenery.

After three weeks in hospital in France he was sent to London where he was again treated by rest and hypnotics. When he came under my care he had been sleeping very badly in spite of the hypnotics. He had been having terrifying dreams of warfare from which he would awake sweating profusely and think that he was dying. These dreams had become less frequent but still occurred. He stammered very badly and was often depressed and restless. He found it difficult to read anything which required a mental effort and complained that his memory was defective, especially for recent occurrences. He had occasional frontal headache and suffered from pain and discomfort after food, which he ascribed to the paraldehyde he had taken, and he was liable to alternating constipation and diarrhea. His deep reflexes were somewhat exaggerated.

In obtaining his history I learnt about his interest in Freud, and about the previous attempts to remedy his condition by means of psycho-analysis. It was only when I explained to him my views concerning the exaggerated interest in sex shown by Freud and his disciples that he learnt for the first time that forgotten experience of other than a sexual kind might take a part in the production of nervous states. It was agreed that "psycho-analysis" should be given a fresh trial from this point of view.

The next interview was devoted to a full inquiry into his previous experience in analysis, the results of which have already been given. As a preliminary to the following sitting I asked him to remember as fully as possible any dreams he might have in the interval, and to record any memories which came into his mind while thinking over the dreams. He was instructed to come to me at once if he had any dreams of interest. A few days later he dreamed of being in France, and of being chased by someone into a deep hole in which his pursuer killed a rabbit in place of himself, and threw it into a pond covered with scum. The rabbit came to life again, and was swimming in the pond when a girl tried to kill it with a poleaxe, but only succeeded in making a gash in its back with the sharper end. The patient told her to kill it with the blunt limb and awoke. In the dream the rabbit was regarded as a ferocious animal which the patient feared would get away, and this fear continued for some time after he awoke.

While thinking over the dream in bed immediately after awaking, there came into the patient's mind an incident which had occurred soon after he had gone to live in the house with the box-bed. At this time his brother kept pet rabbits, and in order to annoy his brother after a quarrel the patient had struck one of the rabbits on the head and it had become unconscious. The brother became angry and was proceeding to "hammer" the patient when the rabbit came to life again. The incident had made a great impression at the time, but so far as the patient knew he had not thought of it since he was a boy. While telling me the dream on the following day another incident from the same period came into his mind. Near the house was a pond, and shortly after the incident with the rabbit the patient saw three boys trying to drown a dog. They threw it into the water with a brick tied round its neck, but as the animal was still able to swim the boys threw stones at it, injuring its eyes and mouth till it sank. Here again the patient had not thought of the incident for years, though he remembered that he could not visit the pond later without fear. This recollection was followed by another which occurred a year or two later. He and two other boys tried to drown a cat in a bucket at the house of one of the boys, but the animal was so strong that they could hardly keep it in. The patient remembered that he experienced definite fear at the thought that the animal would escape.

In the light of the incident which came to mind later the prominence of animals in these recollections of childhood may have been significant, and all the incidents are more or less connected with the emotion of fear, but they did not seem at the time to have any relation to the phobia. It is especially noteworthy that they were not thought by the patient himself to be significant as was the case with the recollection which occurred later. They were, however, very useful in convincing the patient of the possibility of recalling forgotten incidents of childhood, and showing him that incidents other than those of a sexual nature might be recalled. They suggested that the method he was following might, if persevered in, lead to memories more obviously related to his symptoms.

Three nights later he had another dream. As he lay in bed thinking over the dream, there came into his mind an incident dating back to three or four years of age which had so greatly affected him at the time that it now seemed to the patient almost incredible that it could ever have gone out of his mind, and yet it had so completely gone from his manifest memory that attempts prolonged over years had failed to resuscitate it. The incident was of a kind which convinced him at once that the long-sought memory had been found. Unfortunately his interest in the regained memory was so great that the dream which had suggested it was completely forgotten and all attempts to recall it were unavailing.

The incident which he remembered was a visit to an old rag-and-bone merchant who lived near the house which his parents then occupied. This old man was in the habit of giving boys a halfpenny when they took to him anything of value. The child had found something and had taken it alone to the house of the old man. He had been admitted through a dark narrow passage from which he entered the house by a turning about half-way along the passage. At the end of the passage was a brown spaniel. Having received his reward, the child came out alone to find the door shut. He was too small to open the door, and the dog at the other end of the passage began to growl. The child was terrified. His state of terror came back to him vividly as the incident returned to his mind after all the years of oblivion in which it had lain. The influence which the incident made on his mind is shown by his recollection that ever afterwards he was afraid to pass the house of the old man, and if forced to do so, always kept to the opposite side of the street.

Ten days later the patient dreamed that he visited Edinburgh for the purpose of taking the Diploma in Psychological Medicine. As he lay in bed thinking over his dream and its possible antecedents, he found that he was saying to himself over and over again the name "McCann." He could not at first remember that he knew anyone so called, but it suddenly flashed on his mind that it was the name of the old rag-and-bone merchant in whose house he had been terrified.

One thing was needed to make the story complete. It seemed possible that these thoughts, recalled in consequence of thinking over dreams, might be purely fictitious. It might be that in his intense desire to find some experience of childhood which would explain his dread, the patient might have dreamed, or thought of, purely imaginary incidents which had been mistaken for real memories. Luckily the patient's parents are still alive, and on inquiry from them it was learnt that an old rag-and-bone merchant had lived in the neighbourhood in such a house as the patient remembered and that his name was McCann. Until they were told some twenty-seven years later they had no idea that their child knew anything of the old man or had ever entered his house.

I propose first to consider this case in so far as it affords evidence concerning the forgetting of unpleasant experience and the possibility of recalling such experience to manifest memory. It is well to distinguish this problem from the quite separate problems how far such forgotten experience acts as the basis of morbid states and how far the recalling of the forgotten experience to manifest consciousness is of value therapeutically.

The main facts of the case from the first of these three points of view is that by following a certain procedure there came back to the patient a memory from early childhood which had, so far as he knew, been completely absent from his manifest consciousness for about twenty-seven years. It had been so completely forgotten that even six years devoted to research into his infantile memories had failed to recall it. If it had not been for the independent confirmation of his parents the whole memory might have been dismissed as fictitious, but their evidence makes it clear that we have to do with the revival of a genuine memory.

It will be well here to consider the conditions which led to the recovery of this long-forgotten incident. The facts that it should have eluded observation although diligently sought for six years, and that it should have come so readily to light at a later time, suggest that there was something faulty in the process by which the search had been conducted before the patient came under my care. We may inquire why his previous attempts to discover the memory had failed when they succeeded so rapidly as soon as the subject was approached by a different method.

One cause of failure is undoubtedly to be found in the previous turning of the patient's thoughts exclusively in the direction of sex. He had been assured that the memory to be revived would be concerned with sexual experience. All his endeavours had been devoted to the end of finding such an experience. We could hardly have a better example of the obstruction placed in the path of knowledge by the exclusive preoccupation of the Freudian school with the problem of sex. In dealing with this subject on another occasion [1] I have dwelt on the part taken by the exaggerated, if not morbid, interest in sex in producing the widespread prejudice against Freud's psychology which undoubtedly exists. The case I now record shows that the evil goes much deeper, and that the exclusive interest in sex may actually obstruct the discovery of an infantile experience which furnishes as good an example as could be desired of unconscious experience and of the possibility of recalling it to manifest memory.

A second, and perhaps more important, cause of failure is that until the patient came under my care his attention had not been especially directed to his claustrophobia. It was only when he recognised that his fear of being in a dug-out in France was not shared by others that he realised the specific character of his dread. It was only when he came under my care that for the first time the process of analysis started from and centred round the dread of closed spaces. Throughout all our conversations the attention of the patient was turned in this direction, thus leading the dream-thoughts to occupy themselves with this topic until they reached and brought to the surface the memory which had lain dormant for twenty-seven years. The case well shows that the process of analysis by which forgotten experience is laid bare is not a loose method of examination which may start anywhere and be carried on anyhow, but, if it is to be successful, must be based on definite principles. It must start from some special symptom or other experience, and must be conducted with a definite relation to the experience it is desired to reach.

The previous failure of the patient to recover his infantile experience is to be explained, partly by the exclusively sexual direction

---

[1] See p. 163. [Rivers, op. cit.]

of his interest, partly by the process of examination and inquiry having failed to start from the dread of closed spaces to which the infantile experience has so obvious a relation. A problem which remains for consideration is whether the later success was merely due to these two faults having been remedied, or whether there was any positive virtue in the special method which was then employed. This method is essentially that of free association as understood by Freud—the method of "abstraction" of Morton Prince—but starting from the incidents of a dream and carried out during the time immediately following the dream. In my own experience I have found this time especially favourable for the recovery of memories, the state of half-wakefulness seeming to be especially favourable to the freedom of association. The employment of free association under these conditions must, except under very special circumstances, be conducted in the main by the patient himself. The physician helps in the process by leading the waking thoughts of the patient in a direction calculated to arouse the desired experience, and he may also, as in the present case, help to elicit memories other than those which are recalled immediately after the dream, but the method is only suited to intelligent and well-instructed patients.[2]

---

[2] Another problem for consideration is how far his case supports Freud's special theory of "repression" ("suppression" according to the terminology of this book) and active forgetting. What is needed here is some definite explanation of the process by which the acute and fully conscious terror of the child became converted into forgotten experience which was only restored to manifest consciousness after many years. . . . It seemed possible that it was the result of an illness in which the forgetting was assisted by some condition which produced an obvious modification of consciousness. I therefore asked my patient to make inquiries into the history of his early illnesses. He found that when between two and three years of age he had an attack of scarlet fever, so severe that the doctor despaired of his recovery. Between five and six he had enteric fever, which does not seem to have been especially severe. When about six or seven years old he had an abscess in the shoulder which lasted some months. Later he had pleurisy and was delirious, and there was again for a time little hope of his recovery. This was followed by an abscess in the foot which took some months to heal. The patient thus had a succession of severe illnesses both before and after the incident which seemed to have determined his claustrophobia. The scarlet fever may have so weakened his health as to make him susceptible to suppression or to enhance an innate susceptibility in this direction, while one of the later illnesses may have provided an opportunity for conditions which would assist the process of suppression itself.

After-Effects of Dreams in Some Instances

The way in which *moods,* touched off in dreams, tend to persist during the day, has often been observed. It was Thomas Hobbes, I think, who remarked that passions, aroused by thoughts, are liable to persevere after the thoughts have turned elsewhere; just as the waves of the sea continue their motion for some time after the winds have vanished.

False Recollection

JAMES SULLY, *Illusions*, 274-275 (Appleton, 1897)

It is highly probable that our dreams are, to a large extent, answerable for the sense of familiarity that we sometimes experience in visiting a new locality or in seeing a new face. If, as we have found some of the best authorities saying, we are, when asleep, always dreaming more or less distinctly, and if, as we know, dreaming is a continual process of transformation of our waking impressions in new combinations, it is not surprising that our dreams should sometimes take the form of forecasts of our waking life, and that consequently objects and scenes of this life never before seen should now and again wear a familiar look.

That some instances of this puzzling sense of familiarity can be explained in this way is proved. Thus, Paul Radestock, in the work *Schlaf und Traum,* . . . tells us: "When I have been taking a walk, with my thoughts quite unfettered, the idea has often occurred to me that I had seen, heard, or thought of this or that thing once before, without being able to recall when, where, and in what circumstances. This happened at the time when, with a view to the publication of the present work, I was in the habit of keeping an exact record of my dreams. Consequently, I was able to turn to this after these impressions, and on doing so I generally found the conjecture confirmed that I had previously dreamt something like it."

Hysterical Paralysis and Contractures Following Dreams

ISADORE H. CORIAT, *Abnormal Psychology*, 125-126 (Dodd, Mead, 1910)

Hysterical paralysis and contractures sometimes follow a dream. Under these conditions, the subject dreams of the identical paralysis or contracture which comes on after awakening. Whether the dissociated state of a purely imaginary dream is projected into the waking life or whether an emotional shock occurs during the awakening, is dissociated in sleep and reproduced as a dream, is a question that cannot be answered with certainty until we have more data on these curious phenomena. In a case reported by Janet, the patient developed a contracture of the hands following a vivid dream of piano playing. In another the subject dreamed that he was falling and awoke to find a beginning paralysis of the right arm and leg. That his paralysis was purely functional in nature was demonstrated by further investigation. In a case of hysterical paralysis which came under personal observation, the following curious condition was present. While walking, the patient would suddenly experience a sense of severe weakness in the legs, then there would follow a sensation "as if I had no legs," and she would fall. These episodes would occur a number of times during the day but only when the patient was walking. On further analysis, it appeared that there was no history of an emotional shock, but during the week previous to her first attack, she dreamed that she was walking down a hill, then suddenly fell down and landed full length on her face. This sensation of falling did not awaken the patient at once, but when she did awaken, she felt perfectly normal. The dream was not repeated, but a week elapsed before the weakness of the legs developed. Here we have a condition almost identical with the cases reported by Janet.[1]

Conduct Disorders Connected with Dreams

MORTON PRINCE and G. A. WATERMAN; reported by Dr. G. A. Waterman to Dr. Morton Prince, and described by the latter in "Coconscious Images," *Jour. Abn. Psychol.*, Dec., 1917

A woman of thirty applied to me for treatment of her condition which she termed kleptomania. Her trouble consisted in the habit of taking jewelry whenever she came across it on the counters in stores. She never had taken any of the jewelry home but would find herself with it gathered in her hands; at this juncture she always became frightened at the realization of what she was doing and would put it back on the counter and hurry from the store. A careful analysis of her mental state at such times revealed

_____

[1] [An after-effect of a dream of somewhat different sort, is the case of hysterical blindness described by Dr. Morton Prince in *The Unconscious*, '02.]

no evidence of any impulse to take the jewelry nor did she have any desire for it, being the wife of a man in affluent circumstances.

After trying during several visits to discover the mechanism that was giving rise to her troublesome condition, I resorted to hypnosis. A state of complete hypnosis was readily obtained, the patient becoming relaxed and anaesthetic. On being asked in this state what was the cause of her trouble she at once replied that it was a dream that she had had a year and a half previously of which she had never been conscious in her waking state. The memory of the dream, however, was still as vivid to her in hypnosis as it was the day after she dreamed it.

The patient dreamed that she was standing before a counter on which was displayed a pile of glittering jewels. A burglar stood before her and in a threatening manner commanded her to steal the jewels for him. She pleaded to be allowed to go, but he exclaimed, "If you do not steal them I will have your mother murdered." It seemed at the time that her mother was in an adjacent room, separated from her only by a partition, and she could hear her groaning. Overcome with anxiety for her mother she seized a handful of jewels, but on looking down at them she realized what she was doing and looked up weeping at the burglar to ask him to let her go. At this point she awoke sobbing. Her husband beside her, who had been awakened by her distress, asked why she was crying and she answered "I do not know, I must have had a bad dream." For she had no conscious memory of her dream. It was shortly after this that she found herself taking jewelry in the stores.

(It happens that two of the elements of this dream were associated with distressing circumstances of the patient's life:—First: the burglar as he appeared in the dream was the same one who had featured in a terrifying experience in the patient's early life; for at the age of twenty she had been held up by this man at the point of a revolver and at the time really had a narrow escape. Second:— About the time the patient had the dream her mother had been taken ill and was told that she had hardening of the arteries and could not live very long. This had caused the patient great anxiety. It is therefore natural that both of these factors in her dream were associated with strong emotions.)

While the patient was still hypnotized she was asked in what way this dream acted on her mind at the time she took jewelry in the stores. She said that whenever she saw jewelry on a counter that this dream recurred to her. It did not come to her consciously but *the pictures of the dream were coconscious and were going on independently of the train of thought in her conscious mind.*

In order to illustrate the mechanism of her dream and its relation to her trouble I placed a key in a leather case and put the case
on a couch across the room, and while the patient was still under
hypnosis told her that when she awakened, at the moment I raised
the shade next my desk, that she would walk across the room, pick
up the case, open it and take out the key. A short time after this
the patient was awakened and while she was arranging her hat
at a mirror across the room I raised the shade. At once she walked
slowly across the room conversing with me about certain social
things that she had been doing the day before and, passing behind
me, picked up the case on the couch. At this juncture I turned and
saw her standing with the key in her hand and looking at it with a
puzzled expression. The following conversation ensued:—

Q. "What are you doing?"

A. "I do not know."

Q. "Why have you that key?"

A. "I don't know."

Q. "Don't you know that it is a key of my private box?"

A. "No."

Q. "Don't you think that some explanation is needed when you,
behind my back, open a case and take the key to my private box?"

Patient flushing and looking embarrassed: "I don't know what
to say. I am sure I am very sorry."

Q. "What was in your mind, what were you thinking of when
you did it?"

A. "I really was only thinking of what I was talking to you
about, about going to the theatre, etc."

"Surely," I said, "there must have been some cause. Perhaps it
was not in your conscious mind, let us see if we cannot find it."

The patient was hypnotized again and asked what made her open
the case and take out the key. She at once replied, *"Why, pictures
of myself doing it;"* and, on being further questioned, described *the
flow of coconscious pictures of herself performing the act. She said
that at the time these pictures were acting in her mind she herself
was correspondingly performing the act.*

After explaining the relationship of the subconscious with the
act performed, and making her see the connection between the
experiment in the office and her actions in real life the patient was
awakened. She was, of course, amnesic to all that had taken place
in hypnosis, but the same explanation was made to her in the
waking state with the result that she was no longer troubled by her
so-called kleptomania.

Dream Prophecy

H. Tasman Lovell, *Dreams*, 72-73 (Australasian Ass'n. Psychol. & Philos., 1923)

Freud, as is well known, denies that he has found any evidence for the prophetic quality in dreams. We have also learned that Jung and Maeder, although they insist upon a prospective or forward-looking character in dreams, yet do not mean by that what is commonly meant by dream prophecy. They simply mean that what one thinks in one's dreams is not without influence upon the solution of one's problems after one awakes. . . . There is here no outside agency, making the dreamer the vehicle of some message.

When, too, Professor Griffith Taylor says: "It is a queer fact that both Atkinson and myself dreamed that the Cape Crozier party were returning on the night before they arrived," [1] the dream is merely the outcome of their anxiety concerning this party, an anxiety which is actually recorded in the following words a few pages before: "We had very strong winds about this time, and were *very anxious to* know how the Cape Crozier party were progressing. They were *due back,* and had had awful weather, judging by our experience." The only difficulty here is that of dreaming the dream on the night before the party arrived. This, however, is explained by the fact that the dreamers knew that the party was "due back." The same explanation may be offered for many of those cases in which the dream presages a death that actually takes place. In those cases in which the dreamer knew of the illness of the person who dies, we have in that fact of knowledge, a sufficient explanation, especially if there can be added a certain interest in the person. But where there is no knowledge of illness or other reason why the person should die, the difficulty of explanation begins to appear. However, it is often difficult to show that there is no knowledge of illness or other reason for death. There are all sorts of fragments of information which are overlooked, and which the dreamer had forgotten; and until we are able exhaustively to examine the half-forgotten and wholly unconscious information which bears upon the probable death of a person, we cannot say that the occasion of such a dream is not wholly given in the dreamer himself.

A case for explanation by the foregoing method was reported to the compiler recently by the dreamer herself. She dreamed,

---

[1] Griffith Taylor, *With Scott, The Silver Lining*, 287.

the night before a college examination, of finding before her in the examination room a set of questions, some of which she could not answer. Upon waking from this dream, she was so impressed that she looked up the answers to those unanswered questions. Great was her surprise, upon entering the real examination room, to find that all of the questions she had looked up were asked on the real examination paper.

Striking evidence for the type of explanation suggested by Professor Lovell, is found in the following case: At breakfast one morning, a minister's wife told her family that she had dreamed that at breakfast she received a telephone call that she had overdrawn her bank account by eighteen dollars. She wondered why she should have dreamed this, since she was always very careful in such matters. Hardly had she spoken when she was called to the telephone and received a message from the bank that she had overdrawn her account by eighteen dollars.

Duly mystified, also certain that there must have been some mistake, it was only upon discovering that a deposit she had sent to the bank had not been credited, that she remembered that her sister, who had offered to make the deposit, had called out as our subject was hurrying away to an engagement that she would be unable after all to do the errand at the bank.

Dream Control

MARY ARNOLD-FORSTER; adapted from *Studies in Dreams*, 23-25, 26, 27-28, 31. (London: George Allen & Unwin, Ltd.; Macmillan, 1921.)

A long personal experience teaches me that the dream mind is far less independent of our will than is supposed, and that, to a degree that is not generally thought possible, the waking mind can and does direct the activities of the mind in sleep. I believe, in short, that we can at will stop the recurrence of "bad" dreams, or of dreams that we dislike or dread, and that we can, to a considerable extent, alter the very nature of our dreams by using in our sleep the same faculty of rational selection and rejection that we use with regard to our thoughts and to our wandering fancies by day. We shall find when the habit is learned, that we can make desired dreams recur more or less at will, and that we can develop in them certain qualities and powers. In this way the habit of dream control will gradually become ours. The problem is how to acquire this controlling power, how, in short, we are to set up in the dream mind such a habit of response and obedience to the command of the waking mind as to make voluntary dreaming possible.

Our first practical need when we begin to acquire any control over our dreams is to get rid of "bad dreams" of all sorts; for whether they take the form of dreams of grief, dreams of evil, or dreams of fear, "bad dreams" are the occasion of real misery to very many people. Children and grown-up persons often confess that if they had their choice they would rather never dream at all than face the chance of a bad dream or the recurrence of some particular night-fear which they have learned to dread.

Charles Lamb has described the anguish of his own sensitive childhood from this cause. "I was dreadfully alive to nervous terrors. The night-time, solitude, and the dark, were my hell. The sufferings I endured in this nature would justify the expression. I never laid my head on my pillow, I suppose, from the fourth to the seventh or eighth year of my life, without an assurance, which realised its own prophecy, of seeing some frightful spectre."

A suggestion that greatly helped me to cure such dreams came from an experience that is common to almost every one. Probably we have all at some time or another realised that our dream was "only a dream" and not a waking reality. The idea contained in this very general experience made the point from which I succeeded in starting a successful experiment in dream control. On various occasions long ago, when a dream of grief or terror was becoming intolerably acute, the thought flashed into my sleeping mind, "This is only a dream; if you wake, it will be over, and all will be well again." If only we could ensure the realisation of this fact directly bad dreams appeared, they would cease to have any terrors for us, for a way to escape would always be open. Therefore I tried repeating this formula to myself from time to time, during the day and on going to bed, always in the same words—"Remember this is a dream. You are to dream no longer"—until, I suppose, the suggestion that I wanted to imprint upon the dream mind became more definite and more powerful than the impression of any dream; so that when a dream of distress begins to trouble me, the oft-repeated formula is automatically suggested, and I say at once: "You know this is a dream; you shall dream no longer—you are to wake." For a time after this secret had been fully learned, this would always awaken me at once; nowadays, the formula having been said, I do not have to wake, though I may do so, but the original fear dream always ceases. It is simply "switched off," and a continuation of the dream, but without the disturbing element, takes its place and goes forward without a break.

A child's silence about his bad dreams adds to the power that they have to make him suffer. He may be willing to speak of his good dreams, but he is often ashamed to say anything about the night-terror that oppresses him. He is checked by the mere possibility that the fears that are so real to him, but that he can hardly put into words, will be met with a smile; and so he does not venture to speak of things that by day he knows will seem absurd, but which nevertheless have power to torture him inexpressibly when night falls. Now if a child is to be helped at all in this matter there must first of all be deeply rooted in his heart an absolute confidence that he will not be laughed at.

In the pages which follow the foregoing passages, Mrs. Arnold-Forster describes the conscious induction of pleasant dreams: night-phantasy, it would seem.

CHAPTER XXII

HIGHER PROCESSES IN THE LIGHT OF ABNORMAL PSYCHOLOGY

Imaginary Satisfaction

ALEXANDER BAIN, *The Emotions and the Will*, 4th ed., 428-429, 431-432 (Longmans, Green & Co., 1899), reprinted by permission; included also in Robinson and Robinson, *Readings in General Psychology*, 347-350 (Univ. of Chicago Press, 1923)

A feeling persisting after the fact, or recovered by mere association, without the presence of the proper stimulus, can sometimes approach the fulness of the real experience; so much so, that we are content in many instances with this bare conception, or ideal resuscitation. The recollection of a time of gaiety and excitement, of some interesting conversation or discourse, or of a book that we have read, may give such an amount of the feeling of actual experience that we rest satisfied with that, and wish nothing further. On a matter, therefore, where we have a power of restoring mentally the full-toned delight of a real experience it is easy to convert memory into imagination, and to construct future gratifications of the same sort, with or without a basis of reality. We speak occasionally of such and such a one having a strong imagination, when we mean that he can so body forth an ideal pleasure, as to derive from it an entire satisfaction of the want of the moment. In the physical cravings, this is an impossibility. Something may be done to stave off for a little the insupportable agony of thirst, hunger, drowsiness, or cold, or to lull the acute pinch of a neuralgic pain; but the actual in these cases is too strong for the most highly stimulated counter-ideal. We have thus two opposite extremes among our multitudinous sensibilities; one where actuality alone can fill up the aching void, the other where the mere idea amounts to the full demands of the system; and between those extremes lies the whole range of imaginary volition, put in motion at the instance of pains or pleasures, such as we cannot work for in the regular compass of our voluntary exertion. . . .

The ardent Greek, remembering the excitement of an Olympic gathering, has a certain elated feeling stirred up by the mere remembrance; but at the same time he recognizes the great difference between his present tone of enjoyment and that full tide of hilarious glee that belonged to the days of the great celebration; and it is upon this sense of difference that he is moved to be present at another festival, or failing that, to visit it in imagination. The pleasurable part of the state urges the will for an additional draught; the sense of the shortcoming of the recollection is of the nature of a pain, and operates for its own removal. If that amount of excitement stirred up by the memory of some happy day gone by, could exist in the mind without any comparative reference, we might probably feel gladdened, without any spur of desire; it is the idea of still greater delights that mars the peace of the mind.[1]

The Basis of Magic

NELSON ANTRIM CRAWFORD, "Literature and the Psychopathic," *Psychoan. Rev.*, 10: 441 (1923)

The fundamental basis of all magic, as Doctor Freud [2] points out and as most students of anthropology agree, lies in the mistaking of an ideal connection for a real one. As Goldenweiser says, "This is how a doll can be made to impersonate a distant enemy whose sickness or death may be brought about by maltreating the doll. A similar psychology underlies the process of so-called fertilizing magic, where various physical manipulations are believed to bring about rain. The similarity between the desired result and the performed act evokes, through the ideational reproduction of the former, the belief that the result has been attained. The moving principle in magic is man's desires which are realized by being psychically lived through and objectified. The disregard of the limitations of time and space so characteristic of magical idiosyncrasy is nothing but a projection into objective reality of a similar disregard so characteristic of thought. The whole animistic world, the realm of supernaturalism, is permeated by the 'omnipotence of thought.' " [3]

---

[1] [*Cf.* Hobbes on Phantasy, as quoted by F. C. Prescott, *The Poetic Mind*, 36.]

[2] See *Totem and Taboo* for a detailed statement of the theory. Compare Wundt's *Elements of Folk Psychology* and Simmel's *Die Religion*.

[3] *Early Civilization*, 390 (Knopf, 1921).

The human race (and in particular, according to students of the subject, the female members of the race, who are at present the most extensive readers of fiction) still clings strongly to magic explanations. Its superstitions, its interpretation of various relations as cause and effect, and many other everyday phenomena, exemplify the continuance of the primitive belief in magic. The scientific use of objective facts, as a basis for intellectual conclusions, dates back but a few centuries even in science itself, and this method has scarcely touched the consciousness of the average individual.

Imaginary Playmates

[NATHAN A. HARVEY]; abstracted by Alberta G. Pierce for the purposes of this volume, following largely the language of Nathan A. Harvey, *Imaginary Playmates and Other Mental Phenomena of Children*, 7-24 (State Normal College, Ypsilanti, Mich., 1918); *cf.* also Hugh Walpole's stories which appear under the title, *The Golden Scarecrow*

Some children have playmates that are imaginary, but which are as real as living children to them. Yet they are not hallucinations, for the child recognizes the fact that they are different from real playmates. These imaginary playmates have some general characteristics which hold true for at least half of the cases reported, though there is great variation.

First of all, they are real playmates and are characterized by vividness. They are usually described as a living child would be, and are often called by names like other children. They appear at a very early age and disappear gradually and without attracting any especial notice, somewhere between the ages of about eight to twelve. The reason for their disappearance is rarely recognized. It may sometimes result from a scolding, or from punishment, or from reasoning with the child.

Most frequently there is no questioning on the part of the child as to where the imaginary playmates come from or where they live, though sometimes they may have a definite location. They are almost always children of about the same age as the child himself, but they may be animals, dwarfs, or in fact almost anything at all. For example:

Miss Marguerite H. lived in a town only two blocks from a railroad. Her house had a front door that was seldom used, and a side door which was the usual means of entrance. Whenever she was going from the front around to the side door, she would "see" a train of cars moving along at her side. Whenever she was walking downtown, the train would accompany her, moving along at her side until it came to the railroad track, when it would jump on to the rails and continue its journey. She was not in the least afraid of the train, and even designated it familiarly by the name of John. When her family removed from that town, the train never reappeared.[1]

Perhaps the most important feature, however, of the imaginary playmates and the one that does the most injury to the child is the repression of the experience. Parents and teachers seldom understand this phenomenon. They assume that it is an indication of mental unsoundness, or something which they consider as equally disgraceful. Thus that which should naturally be a helpful and pleasant association often becomes a thing of which the child is ashamed and which he tries to conceal.

The conditions of children who are "only" children or who are forced to play alone a great deal of the time are favorable to the development of imaginary playmates. Yet loneliness is not absolutely necessary to the production of such playmates. It is probable that we have in the phenomenon of imaginary playmates an explanation of all the materializing phenomena of spiritualism that are not deliberately fraudulent. The spiritualistic and mystical explanation collapses at once when we trace the development of many cases of imaginary playmates out of make-believe and arrange a large number of cases in a series that proceed by infinitesimal gradations from those that are scarcely to be classed as genuine cases of imaginary playmates to those that furnish spiritualists with their stock arguments.

An imaginary playmate is an idea that becomes as vivid as a visual or auditory perception would be. The principal distinction between the idea which is projected as the imaginary playmate, and other ideas, is found in the unusual strength of the centrally initiated impulse which accounts for the development of these playmates. Children generate a great amount of nervous energy, and this large amount of nervous energy and the strong centrally initiated impulse, is one condition for mental capacity. Hence it is that we

---

[1] [There is the case of a boy of seven who, instead of imaginary playmates, has an imaginary Utopia, with organizations, rules, celebrations, escapades, etc., pictured in detail. Other similar cases have been observed. In these instances, the construction has the same function as of imaginary playmates, namely, "self-aggrandisement and fondness for the imaginary, as a means of overcoming (and adding interest to) the limitations of reality; but without confusion with reality or intrusion from phantasy into the real world."]

find nearly all cases of imaginary playmates manifested in children who are distinctly above the average capacity for children of their own age. No stupid child ever had an imaginary playmate. Instead of the experience indicating mental derangement, it is rather an indication of unusual mental capacity.

Not all children have imaginary playmates. Investigation has shown that about six out of one hundred experience the phenomenon though it is possible that the number may be somewhat larger due to forgotten experiences.

Daydreams in School Children

GEORGE H. GREEN, *Psychoanalysis in the Classroom*, 42-45, 76-77 (1922; U. S. A. and Canadian rights, G. P. Putnam's Sons; other rights, University of London Press, Ltd.; reprinted by permission)

It would be easy to quote at length some hundreds of daydreams, collected from children attending the higher standards of elementary schools, or from pupils in secondary schools. But no useful purpose would be served. These fantasies differ in material details, but the majority are concerned with the theme of successful display by the dreamer before an applauding audience. For convenience they may be grouped in the following categories:—

(1) The Fantasy of Display. The dreamer, in some capacity which is usually at variance with the facts of real life, performs a feat which wins applause for him.

(2) The Saving Fantasy. The dreamer performs some act, of which he is in reality incapable, by which he saves life, gaining at once the devotion of the rescued person (usually of the opposite sex), the gratitude of her parents, and the applause of bystanders. It is noteworthy that a great many boys who indulge in saving fantasies specify that the person saved is of higher social standing than her rescuer, though this fact makes no difference to her attitude towards him. Further, a number of daydreams with "display" characteristics, such as shooting the winning goals for a football team, may be regarded as "saving fantasies," inasmuch as a great deal of stress is laid on the fact that these goals "saved the side."

(3) The Fantasy of Grandeur. The dreamer occupies an exalted rôle in the daydream, generally that of a royal person or a deity. A fairy queen, the chief of a band of robbers, "somebody known all over the world," the champion boxer of the world, etc., are examples taken from the daydreams of school children.

(4) The Fantasy of Homage. Here the dreamer by doing a

service to some admired person, usually a superior, gains the love of the person in question. Sometimes the person is of the opposite sex to the dreamer, but more often, apparently, in school children, of the same sex. It is particularly common, as might be expected, in girls who are given to "raves" over women teachers.

The simple fantasy of the imaginary companion, with which this study was at first concerned, has disappeared when the child is at school. It expressed, as we have seen, the cravings of a baffled ["] Instinct of Gregariousness, ["] and serves well to illustrate the comments of McDougall on this instinct: "Its operation in its simplest form implies none of the higher qualities of mind, neither sympathy nor capacity for mutual aid." The instinct is apparently gratified when the child goes to school, and real companions make imaginary ones unnecessary.

The fantasies enumerated above express a wish for admiration, for elation, the emotion which McDougall regards as appropriate to the Instinct of Self-Assertion. It is important to notice that though the end of the assertion is the same, the mode of assertion that is conceived as best adapted to attain the end differs. We have evidence in the daydream of an attitude towards the world.

The fantasy of homage reveals an attitude essentially different from that which is to be found in the fantasy of display or of grandeur. The one gains its end by subservience, by homage, by insinuating conduct; the other by means of a forcing upon the attention of onlookers. Adler regards these attitudes as "protests" against the real life, and names them respectively the "feminine" and "masculine" protests: unfortunate terms, since the "masculine" protest is by no means characteristic of males, nor the "feminine" protest of females. He conceives the attitude which the protest expressed as having been formed as a result of perceived inferiority in childhood; and believes that a process of judgment has decided for the child what place he occupies in his environment, and the mode he is to adopt in order to attain to his wishes. It is certain that children fall sharply into the categories of "naughty" or "good," "noisy" or "quiet," "disobedient" or "obedient," "thoughtful" or "thoughtless"; and that they exhibit these characteristics from very early years. Further, that these attitudes persist through life.

It cannot be insisted too strongly, however, that all fantasies are egoistic in character. There is displayed in them a complete absence of any lofty moral purpose, even though the modes of action they depict may appear blameless. The central figure is invariably the dreamer, and the end that is striven for is invariably a personal and selfish end. I have omitted, for the present, abnormal daydreams of an apparently unpleasant character; but hope to show later that these are not to be regarded as exceptions. The feeling that is experienced is a happy or pleasant one: children say their daydreams "make me very happy," "make me feel pleased with myself," or "are much more pleasant than real life." . . .

Is there no way of putting an end to the daydream? The question seems of importance, for if this could be achieved, the teacher would immediately benefit, inasmuch as his most serious rival for the pupil's attention would disappear. . . .

Since, however, the daydreaming activity is concerned with the wishes that are unfulfilled, it would seem as if the solution lay in fulfilling them all. This is impossible. We have already seen the socially valueless and egoistic nature of these wishes. Their fulfilment would make human society of any sort impossible. There is no savage community where the unrestricted play of all instinctive wishes is permitted. Contrary to the general opinion on the subject, the life of the savage is hedged about with a great number of restraints, so that it is doubtful if the number of his unfulfilled wishes is less than that of the civilised man of European civilisation. Freedom, in this particular sense of the word, is unknown where any organisation exists, and seems to be impossible. It is certainly incompatible with any high human development.

There is a third course, and one which is possible. This is, to direct the instinctive tendencies to fulfilments that are of social value. So far as material results are concerned, daydreaming is an apparently futile process. It leads, however, to the formulation and expression of the wishes that may, if opportunity arises, motivate actions of great value to society. If the daydream of display expresses the individual's desire for distinction over his fellows, so also does the public activity of our greatest men. These things are obviously not equal, but they have a common source.

The Transition from Phantasy to Fabrication

EDWARD S. ROBINSON, "The Compensatory Function of Make-Believe Play," *Psychol. Rev.*, 27: 434-38 (1920); cited also in Edward Stevens Robinson and Florence Richardson-Robinson, *Readings in General Psychology*, 353 (Univ. of Chicago Press, 1923)

Just as overt play often passes over into private fantasy owing to a struggle against the limitations of the actual social and physical world, so private fantasy often passes over into overt play in the interests of greater credibility. As a child I was full of baseball fantasies. Although I played baseball a great deal, these games did not satisfy certain standards set up by reading athletic stories and watching older and more skillful players. But the fantasies, too, often became unsatisfactory on account of their intangibility. As a result I formed the habit of laying out a diamond upon the lawn and there, without ball or playmates, carrying out the overt movements of an heroic baseball performance. Many a time, I pitched nine long innings to baffled athletes who swung immaterial bats at my imaginary curves. Here was fantasy improved and made realistic by the actuality of its muscular accompaniments.

The topics of private fantasy are perhaps even more apt to find increased tangibility by being brought into contact with a real social world. The child knows that his daydreams are unreal, but the insistence of that fact becomes less troublesome if only he can get someone else to believe or act as though he believes in the reality of those imagined events. Many of the lies of children arise out of such circumstances. A boy longs for a pony and a box of tools. He fancies these things in his possession, and before a great while he somehow feels driven to tell his friends either that he already has the things he desires or that he has been promised them. An acquaintance of mine spent her earliest years on a farm which was more or less out of touch with the livelier affairs of the world. Now it so happened that an older sister in this household was sent to town to finish her education. Upon her return she had much to say of her experiences. These tales thrilled the younger sister and stimulated her to daydreaming. Soon after this the little girl began her own education at a neighboring country school. As she tells of it now, almost her first intercourse with her schoolmates was marked by her own spectacular reports of what *she* had seen and heard while sojourning in the town which really she had never been near.

Fabrication; Children's Lies

EUGENIE ANDRUSS LEONARD, "A Parent's Study of Children's Lies," *Pedag. Sem.*, 27: 123-124 (1920)

The habitual liar may be a child who has not learned to distinguish clearly between memory and imagination, or he may recognise the difference but substitute the one for the other to obtain his own ends until they have become so confused that he can no longer distinguish clearly between what is true and false. The continuance of any cause such as indistinct memory, fear of punishment, lack of appreciation or too great restraint in play will eventuate in habitual lying. It could scarcely be otherwise. Each success in lying makes the next easier, the skill greater and the temptation keener; and although most children do in a measure outgrow the habit, the frequency with which we find lying among adults indicates that the habit once established is difficult to overcome. One college student wrote that while she had outgrown the tendency to fabricate imaginary tales the tendency still remained to exaggerate to create a sensation and lie cleverly from fear of social discomfiture.

Occasionally the habit develops a pathological case. It would not be of interest here to go into any lengthy discussion of pathological lying yet a brief statement of what is known of exaggerated lying may be of profit if only because in such abnormalities we find the normal "writ large." William Healy [1] has defined pathological lying as "falsification entirely disproportionate to any discernible end in view engaged in by a person who, at the time of observation, cannot definitely be declared insane, feeble-minded or epileptic." He found it to be a trait rather than an episode in the life of the child and shown throughout life. It is, however, never the sole misconduct but always follows other delinquencies. The mental processes are similar to that of authors only the pathological liar wants to both create his story and act the leading rôle. He confuses real life with his story and becomes so fascinated in the delightful pastime of living the assumed rôle that he ceases to pay the proper attention to other details of living. His moral judgment becomes vague and indecisive. He grows poetic and drifts about in free imaginative play. He resents being disturbed by real facts or jostled by real experience. In the "aussage tests" he uniformly invents additional objects and accepts many of the suggestions offered by the questions, indicating how vague the distinction in his mind is between real and imagined objects. All but two of Judge Healy's printed cases had inherited an unstable moral make-up and several had had mental conflicts due to unfortunate early sex knowledge and experience which had given rise to the habit. He found that any period of mental or physical stress and especially adolescence tends to unbalance the mental abilities and befog the power of clear judgment. All of his cases developed during pubescence or adolescence and it is chiefly for this reason he feels that most such cases can be cured by sympathetic and intelligent

---

[1] William Healy, *Pathological Lying* (Little, Brown & Co., 1915). [Mrs. Leonard gives a Bibliography on lying, *loc. cit.*, 135-136.]

care. When the period of physical and mental stress is over the child if carefully guided through the storm may recover poise and complete mental balance. The cure lies in following such simple rules as checking up at once, each lie, taking care in developing accuracy of memory and, where there is special ability in constructive imagination, an opportunity to use that ability in some literary pursuit. Such advice is sound for all parents and needs only to be emphasized where habitual lying has been allowed to develop.

Mythomania

Tom A. Williams, "Malingering and Simulation of Disease in Warfare," *Am. Jour. of Insanity*, 77: 572-575 (April, 1921)

. . . The statement of a cured mythomaniac, illustrating the condition in childhood:

I entered school when I was five years old. Shortly before that, and for perhaps a year and a half after, my aunt and mother tried to inculcate in me a respect for truth which they felt I lacked. I was repeatedly corrected for misstating things, the misstatement being purely unconscious on my part. I did not distinguish clearly between what I imagined and what actually happened. To illustrate:

One icy morning I saw the Governor of Vermont going past our home carrying an axe in his hand. I immediately pictured him in my mind as falling on the axe. The image was so clear that not long after I told my mother that the Governor had fallen on the axe and hurt himself. My mother inquired of his family concerning the accident. When reprimanded I still felt that he had fallen on the axe, but that for some reason he did not wish to have it known.

I frequently believed people had said what I felt they thought. I startled my mother by quoting to her what friends of hers had said. She knew that they had not said the things in question, but was equally confident that they had thought them. The only illustration which I remember is this:

I was playing alone and began to cry. My mother asked me what the matter was and I said that two little friends of mine had said that I could not sing and therefore could not take part in a cantata which local talent was to give. . . . Mother spoke to the girls about it and they denied saying it. My cousin asked them if they had not thought so, and one of them admitted that she had thought so.

This patient when aged nine, realizing her fault, set about reforming herself, and succeeded in doing so after years of struggle. She now occupies a situation of trust, and although of seclusive temperament, is not mythomaniac at all.

According to Dupré, pathological mythomania often leads to vicious tendencies, or to instinctive perversions. It is a particular form of intellectual activity guided by pathological sentiments. It is no longer a game, but a particularly dangerous weapon, so much the more so if the psychopath is intelligent.

Normal mythomania appears to have a cause, a motive, and is proportioned to it; whereas abnormal mythomania seems insufficiently or not motivated at all, its duration is persistent, and its intensity is out of proportion to its cause.[1]

There are different degrees of mythomania, from simple alterations of truth to simulation, fantastic fabulation.

In abnormal children as well as in grown-up psychopaths three kinds of mythomania are to be differentiated, *vain, malicious,* and *perverse.*

1. *Mythomania Caused by Vanity.*—All weak beings are more or less vain, a morbid desire for glory; and instinctive need of being spoken of, of acting a part, of being "somebody" drives them to lies and fabulation.

All children are vain, and weak children are particularly so. Most interesting is the case of the 12-year-old girl who came into school one day and said her mother was ill; every day she gave fresh details on the illness and its progress. She said at last, her mother was dead. She stayed away one or two days, and came back crying and dressed in black and gave details on the mother's burial. Some

---

[1] ["The execution of an idea in the form of acting, of a pretense, of a falsehood, is only a start at execution and in the tendencies that thus develop there is only a feeble degree of tension. This is the reason, as we know, that neurotics of feeble psychic tension delight in falsehood, pretense, and acting.

"But it would be very wrong to conclude from this that in other conditions and in certain subjects, criminal and dangerous acts could not be brought about by the mechanism of suggestion."—Pierre Janet, *Psychotherapy*, 140-141 (copyright, 1924, by The Macmillan Company); reprinted by permission.

Professor Jastrow communicates the following:

"I was told of one case in which a small girl was so impressed (whether by her own projections or through fairy tales, etc., is uncertain) with the world to be discovered at the bottom of a well, that she jumped and was rescued with difficulty. She proved in later life to be unstable nervously."]

time after she explained her father had married again and gave new details on the wedding ceremony. It appeared unexpectedly that the child's mother was living, had been ill and lived with her husband. Inquiry proved that the child had only wanted to be noticed, and wished to wear a black dress that had been promised her for her birthday.

Very striking is the case of a young man who said he had killed his sister by filling her room with carbonic oxide gas he had himself prepared in a neighboring room; he was exceedingly proud of the fact and gave long explanations on the way he had prepared the gas. Nobody believed him for his sister was known to have died after a long illness. He at last acknowledged that all he had said was false.

Mythomania caused by vanity will drive certain individuals to automutilations. Such a young girl . . . said she had been assailed in a train compartment, and proved what she said to be true by showing a small wound on her chest. Inquiry proved that nothing was true and that she herself had bought, a month before, the knife she had been wounded with.

Varieties of mythomania caused by vanity manifest themselves by simulation of crime, of disease, of exterior lesions and of organic perturbations.

X. was most surprised and disturbed one night when coming home on finding his wife apparently senseless in a chair, and her throat strangled with a string.

Everything in the room had been disturbed. He called for help and the victim on coming to said she had been assailed by two masked men who had taken her keys from her and had left her after having stolen two thousand francs and valuable jewels in her desk. Inquiry proved everything to be false and some days later Mme. X. owned she had simulated a crime for reasons she could not account for.

Simulation of disease may cause serious errors: A man pretends he suffered from tuberculous peritonitis and shows signs of great pain till at last a surgeon is induced to operate. Two more surgeons are afterwards induced to do the same, till at last he is found to be a simulator who only wants to be an interesting case.

N. has himself carried to a hospital and says he has been run over by a carriage, goes into the smallest details concerning the accident, says he has vomited blood, etc.; he undergoes an operation and apparently recovers health.

No accident had befallen him and all was fabulation, as the inquiry proved.

2. *Malicious Mythomania.*—Is associated with the various forms of destructive instinct from simple malice to the most atrocious ferocity, to all kinds of mystifications, to slanderous hetero-accusations, such as the case of a 19-year-old weak-minded hysteric girl who told the magistrate about three persons who had drowned a man. These three persons were condemned to imprisonment but soon had to be released, for nothing proved to be true. The girl then said her own father had drowned the man. The drama ended by a convulsive hysteric attack.

The well-known case of Lieutenant R. who was charged by Mlle. M. for having attempted rape and was condemned to 10 years' imprisonment which he effectually underwent, is a most demonstrated instance.

Attempts at rape with serious violence are as a rule the theme of these hetero-accusations.

3. *Perverse Mythomania.*—Psychopaths are led to perverse mythomania for the sake of satisfying their vicious tendencies. Often in these cases, the three kinds of mythomania are combined (vain, malicious, and perverse).

The case of Thérèse Humbert is most interesting and shows what an intelligent and clever mythomaniac can realize by fabulation. In this extraordinary case, the highest and cleverest classes of society were completely imposed upon by the effects of an extensive but really absurd suggestion emanating from weak-minded Thérèse, who was gifted with the particular qualities of an active mythomaniac and with remarkable creative power. Of a similar nature was the case which victimized Mr. Carnegie and other financiers.

It is necessary to remember that fabulation may have its foundation in what is or what appears to be true. There is often a groundwork of fact. Also the mythomaniac's appearance of truthfulness and of conviction and . . . surprising logical conformity between his words and his acts and a minute account of details win the confidence of onlookers and the most sceptical are forced into belief. An atmosphere of suggestion is created emanating from the psychopath himself. He, himself, by a phenomenon of auto-suggestion, believes everything he has invented. . . .

Mythopathic activity is often unconscious and involuntary, but often also works with the help of conscience and will, specially at the beginning of the fabulation.

These factors disappear progressively without there being any change in the evolution and consequences of the morbid processes. Suggestion must not be neglected in this study, as it plays a most active part with children and psychopaths. . . .

It is hardly necessary after what has been stated to draw attention to the importance of mythomania from a legal and medico-legal point of view. . . .

Phantasy and Delusion

BERNARD HART; adapted from *The Psychology of Insanity*, 146-151 (Cambridge, 1919)

Most of us at one time or another console ourselves for the failure of our ambitions in the real world by the creation of pleasant fancies.[1] But a path opens here which leads us easily across the bridge into the regions of insanity, and the processes just considered provide a key to the interpretation of many of the symptoms which we observe in the asylum.

In the normal cases the individual is aware that he is daydreaming, and does not altogether lose touch with the real world. His friends observe that he is "absent-minded" and absorbed in his own ideas, and that he takes no notice of what goes on around him. But he is able if necessary to drag himself back into relation with the actual environment, although to do so often requires an appreciable effort. In other words, he is dissociated to some extent from the realities of everyday life, but this dissociation is only partial, incomplete, and temporary. If, however, the process assumes proportions which are definitely morbid, this dissociation becomes more pronounced and permanent. The patient, as he may now be called, separates himself altogether from the real world and devotes all his mental energy to daydreaming. He lives permanently in a self-made world where all the desires and ambitions belonging to the complex are luxuriantly fulfilled. This mechanism is responsible for the symptoms observed in two types of insanity which, although closely allied to one another, may be roughly separated for descriptive purposes.

The first type, which may be regarded as an exaggeration of normal daydreaming, comprises a number of those cases grouped under the heading of "emotional dementia." The patient has apparently lost all interest in life; he expresses no desires or ambitions, makes no effort to employ himself in any way, and sits from day to day in

---

[1] [Instances of the production of pleasant phantasies in the form of night dreams are recorded. *Cf.* Malcolm W. Willey and Stuart A. Rice, "The Psychic Utility of Sleep," cited in the present volume, pp. 299 *ff.;* and Mary Arnold-Forster, *Studies in Dreams.* 37-51.]

the same corner of the ward, inert and lethargic. His face is vacant and expressionless, and he seems oblivious of everything which takes place around him. If he is addressed he will perhaps vouchsafe a monosyllabic reply, but it is impossible to rouse him from his apathy, and he will receive the news of his parents' death with the same untroubled equanimity with which he eats his dinner. To the casual observer such a patient appears to have lost all mental activity, but, if we examine his mind more closely and look below its congealed surface, we find that activity still exists, although it is diverted into channels which lead to no external manifestations or practical result. All the available mental energy is absorbed in the construction of pleasant phantasies of the kind we have described. The patient has retired altogether into a world of daydreams, and for him the facts of real life have lost all significance and interest.

In the second type the patient has immersed himself in his imaginary world even more completely and efficiently. The phantasy created by his own mind acquires the tang of actual reality; he believes that he *is* the conquering hero or the multi-millionaire, and that the pleasant pictures he once imagined have become the facts of life. He has crossed the barrier which separates in the normal man daydreams from the dreams that accompany sleep, and the creations of an idle fancy have become the delusions of the lunatic. A further degree of dissociation has been attained, and the complexes achieve a luxuriant expression undisturbed by the flagrant contradictions which experience everywhere presents to them.

This mechanism, which has been termed "wish fulfilment," furnishes a psychological interpretation for a vast number of the manifestations of insanity. One of the simplest examples of its action is seen in the so-called "betrothal-delirium," occasionally to be observed in women who have been jilted. All the desires and ambitions which hitherto formed the kernel of the patient's life have suddenly become incompatible with reality. Out of the intense emotional stress engendered by this conflict an attack of insanity develops, characterised by a dream-like delirium in which the frustrated complexes attain an imaginary fulfilment. In this delirium the patient believes that she has been reconciled to her lover, preparations for the wedding are in progress, the bridegroom arrives, the marriage ceremony takes place, and the dream-state is prolonged indefinitely in pictures of a subsequent wedded life, each of which is lived through with all the intensity of reality.

In other cases the symptoms are less dramatic in character, but essentially similar in their mode of origin. A system of morbid mental processes develops in which the complexes that have been denied expression in the world of reality obtain a delusional fulfilment. The patient believes that the defaulting lover has returned to his allegiance, or perhaps that she has actually become his wife. The obvious inconsistency of such beliefs with the real facts of life is glossed over by the production of suitable rationalisations, and the development of secondary delusions.

A similar mechanism accounts for those complicated and fantastic delusional systems which characterise a large percentage of the cases met with in the chronic wards of the asylum. Thus one of my patients announces that she is descended from Queen Elizabeth, and is herself the rightful Queen of England. She has been given the title of "Rule Britannia," has several armies under her control, and is at the moment engaged in issuing orders to her generals to make a combined attack upon all the nations of Europe. She complains bitterly, however, that her movements are hampered by a conspiracy directed by "Mr. Guelph," who has succeeded in obtaining her incarceration in an asylum, and who strives to rob her of all the privileges which belong to her rank.

This patient, prior to the outbreak of her insanity, was a hard-working woman of the servant class, whose life had contained little but a constant succession of hardships. In the grandiose delusions which she exhibits the daydreams of the class that thrives on cheap romantic literature may easily be recognised, now elevated by a process of dissociation to the rank of an actual belief, and pursuing their course in a logic-tight compartment secure from the contradiction of facts. Protected in this way from the controlling influence of real experience, the self-assertion complexes strive to achieve a luxuriant expression by the production of constantly elaborated phantasies of grandeur. The persecutory ideas concerning the conspiracy, on the other hand, are to be regarded as the secondary delusions which generally arise in such cases as processes of rationalisation.

In all these cases the final outbreak of insanity occurs as the solution of a conflict. The patient is unable to achieve his ambitions, either because the environment opposes insurmountable obstacles or because his capacities are not equal to his desires—in other words, there is a conflict between the complex and reality. This conflict is avoided by allowing the complex to obtain a partial expression by the construction of phantasy, while the incompatibility of the real world is masked by the production of the requisite degree of dissociation. Under such circumstances it might be said that reality is repressed, while the complex plays unchecked upon the surface of consciousness.[2]

The foregoing, of course, does not mean that all delusions have their sources simply in phantasy. Dr. E. E. Southard wrote a paper, "On the Somatic Sources of Somatic Delusions"; and in another paper, he discussed the question, "How Far is Environment Responsible for Delusions?" (See references in Bibliography.)

More similar to the kind of sources just described by Dr. Hart, is Dr. Thomas H. Haines' study, "The Genesis of a Paranoic State, Delusions of Persecution Based Upon a Character Defect in Volitional Equipment." This example of delusion as a (wish-fulfilling) defense-mechanism suggests, too, the closeness of Delusion, as a topic, to the mechanism of Projection.

Projection

BERNARD HART, *The Psychology of Insanity*, 118-122 (Cambridge, 1919)

"Projection" may be defined as a peculiar reaction of the mind to the presence of a repressed complex, in which the complex or its effect is regarded by the personality as belonging no longer to itself, but as the production of some other real or imaginary individual. The meaning of this definition will be made clear by the consideration of some simple examples. People who possess some fault or deficiency of which they are ashamed are notoriously intolerant of that same fault or deficiency in others. Thus the parvenu who is secretly conscious of his own social deficiencies talks much of the "bounders" and "outsiders" whom he observes around him, while the one thing which the muddle-headed man cannot tolerate is a lack of clear thinking in other people. In general it may be said that whenever one encounters an intense prejudice one may with some probability suspect that the individual himself exhibits the fault in question or some closely similar fault. An excellent illustration of this mechanism is to be found in "Hamlet," in the excessive aversion with which the Player-Queen regards the possibility

---

[2] [On the rôle of phantasy in the etiology of neuroses, *cf.* C. G. Jung, *The Theory of Psychoanalysis*, 86-89, 94-95.]

of a second marriage, although a secret desire for such a marriage is already present in her mind.

> "The instances that second marriage move
> Are base respects of thrift, but none of love . . .
> Nor earth to me give food, nor heaven light.
> Sport and repose lock from me day and night,
> To desperation turn my trust and hope,
> An anchor's cheer in prison be my scope,
> Each opposite that blanks the face of joy
> Meet what I would have well, and it destroy,
> Both here and hence pursue me lasting strife,
> If, once a widow, ever I be wife."

Shakespeare's acquaintance with the psychological mechanism we are considering is evidenced by the comment of the real Queen :—

"The lady doth protest too much, methinks."

We may express the psychological processes seen in these cases as follows: the fault constitutes a complex which is repugnant to the personality as a whole, and its presence would therefore naturally lead to that particular form of conflict which is known as self-reproach. The personality avoids this conflict, however, by "projecting" the offending complex on to some other person, where it can be efficiently rebuked without that painful emotion which inevitably accompanies the recognition of deficiencies in ourselves. That is to say, the personality reacts to the repugnant complex by exaggeratedly reproaching the same facts in other people, thereby concealing the skeleton in its own cupboard. The more comfortable expedient of rebuking one's neighbour is substituted for the unpleasant experience of self-reproach. The biological function served by projection is, therefore, the same as in all other varieties of repression, the avoidance of conflict and the attainment of a superficial peace of mind.

In the sphere of insanity the mechanism of projection plays a prominent part, and a great variety of symptoms may be ascribed to its action. Alcoholism, described in the last chapter as one of humanity's refuges from the stress of conflict, provides many excellent examples. The chronic alcoholic develops with great frequency delusions concerning the conduct of his wife or other relatives. Thus one of my patients complained bitterly that his wife was dissolute, a drunkard, and a spendthrift, that she neglected both himself and the children, and that she allowed the home to go to rack and ruin. Investigation showed, however, that all these ideas were purely delusional, and without foundation in fact. The patient himself was the real culprit, and each statement that he made was true of himself but not of his wife. The psychological explanation of his delusions is to be found in the mechanism of projection. . . .

Many so-called "delusions of persecution" may be similarly explained by the mechanism of projection. The patient has some secret desire which is repugnant to the personality, perhaps because it is incompatible with the individual's general principles or trends of thought. The mind therefore refuses to treat the desire as part of itself, and projects it into some other real or fictitious person, who then becomes an enemy striving to achieve the patient's downfall. In its minor degrees this mechanism is to be seen in the excuses with which we frequently endeavour to mitigate our moral lapses. We will not acknowledge to ourselves that it was our own ambitions and desires which led to the commission of the fault, but seek to shift the blame to the shoulders of our neighbour. Through all ages "the woman tempted me" has been a stock excuse of erring man. This type of projection attains a much greater development, however, in certain varieties of insanity. In "Old Maids' Insanity," for example, an unmarried lady of considerable age, and of blameless reputation, begins to complain of the undesirable attentions to which she is subjected by some male acquaintance. She explains that the man is obviously anxious to marry her, and persistently follows her about. Finally certain trifling incidents lead her to believe that he is scheming to abduct her by force, and on the strength of this she perhaps writes him an indignant letter, or lodges a complaint with the police. Investigation follows, and it is found that the man is not only entirely innocent of the charges levelled against him, but that he has never expressed the least interest in the lady, and is probably hardly aware of her existence. The lady is certified to be suffering from "delusions of persecution," and is removed to an asylum.[1]

Easily confused with "projection," as that process has just been described by Dr. Hart, and often found associated with true projection, is the mechanism of simple "goat making" or selecting a victim. This is noticeable whenever an individ-

[1] [An amusing instance of projection from one personality into another, in a case of multiple personality, is Sally's list of epithets applied to Miss Beauchamp, in Morton Prince's *The Dissociation of a Personality*, 128-129.]

ual, or a group, having all ready a great amount of emotion, such as anger, pressing for release, works it off on some convenient object. An example is the man who, while a certain youth was calling on his daughter, would regularly go out and cut wood vigorously until the young man had gotten out of the way again.[2]

Projection as Related to the Psychology of Rumor

PAUL RICHER; appearing in translation in Frederic Lyman Wells' article, "Mental Regression: Its Conception and Types," *Psychiat. Bull.*, Oct., 1916; cited from Leopold Loewenfeld, *Sexuelle Konstitution*, 215, 230-1 (J. F. Bergmann—Verlagsbuchhandlung), quoted from Paul Richer, *Études cliniques sur la grande hystérie*, 816 (1885)

The signs of the [demon] possession appeared in the Ursuline cloister of London (1632-1639). The nuns accused a good-looking priest of the town, Urbain Grandier, of having bewitched them. The principal rôle in the epidemic is played by Madame de B., the Superior. She was a proud woman, of lively intellect, and marked hysterical temperament. The hallucinations began with her: during the night a phantom appeared to her, in whom she recognised her deceased Father Confessor. The phantom explained to her that he had simply come to console her, and to instruct her about various matters which he had not had time for during his life. On the following night the phantom again appeared. But this time a change took place in it. She perceived suddenly a strange alteration in the person, and he spoke to her. He was no longer the person of her Father Confessor, but the visage and body of Urbain Grandier; who changing his intentions with his countenance, spoke to her amorously, and assailed her with enforced and shameless tendernesses. The sexual hallucinations of the Superior were repeated not only every night, but also infectiously. "And the majority of the nuns, as well as other girls annoyed by evil spirits, hallucinated, that they received nightly visits from Urbain Grandier, and had carnal commerce with him. Their senses were deceived in such measure, that the accusations which they brought against the innocent priest had the appearance of absolute truth, and were well calculated to convince unprejudiced judges." After

---

[2] [For further examples, *cf.* Roy Franklin Richardson, *The Psychology and Pedagogy of Anger.*]

being put to the most extreme tortures, Urbain Grandier was burned to death.[1]

Other than projection factors in the psychology of rumor are of course the action of expectation or preparation through early teachings, dissociation through the emotion of fear or other agents, some appearance of basis for the rumor, and suggestion from other persons. Excellent examples of the operation of these mechanisms occurred in rumors during the war.[2] Professor Robert H. Gault has shown how it is the same mechanisms again, which produce group hallucinations, such as the angels the soldiers saw at Mons.[3] In Dr. E. W. Taylor's study of witchcraft a further factor in the production of rumor is shown, namely, the more or less conscious creation of rumor in self-defense to divert the attention of the group to other persons.[4]

Obsessions of Normal Minds

CHARLES SCOTT BERRY, "Obsessions of Normal Minds," *Jour. Abn. Psychol.*, 11: 19-22 (1916)

Without going into the mechanisms of obsessions at this point, closely related as they are to other phenomena, and without recounting the variety of types, other than to observe that obsessions may be either conscious or subconscious,[5] we note the occurrence of obsessions in everyday life:

The following study is necessarily fragmentary as it is merely a

---

[1] [References of interest in connection with the psychology of rumor include C. G. Jung, *Analytical Psychology*, 176*ff.*; and E. W. Taylor's study of Witchcraft in *Problems of Personality* (C. Macfie Campbell and others, ed.) especially 174-188.]

[2] *Cf.* Robert H. Gault, *Social Psychology*, 142-151.

[3] Gault, *op. cit.*, 153.

[4] E. W. Taylor, in *Problems of Personality* (C. Macfie Campbell and others, eds.) 174-188.

[5] *Cf.* Pierre Janet, *The Mental State of Hystericals*, 278*ff.* Very interesting in this connection are the phenomena of Double Thinking and Double Hearing, as discussed by Boris Sidis, *Symptomatology, Psychognosis and Diagnosis of Psychopathic Diseases*, 204, 211-214. Along with this selection from Sidis perhaps James Burt Miner's discussion of primitive doubling of visual images should be read: "A Case of Vision Acquired in Adult Life"; cited also in Edward Stevens Robinson, and Florence Richardson-Robinson, *Readings in General Psychology*, 266-268.

part of a larger investigation which has not yet been completed. But possibly the facts that are here presented may be of some value in throwing light on the character and extent of obsessions in normal individuals.

About two hundred students in educational psychology, almost all of whom were seniors, were asked a series of questions which they were to answer in writing. The answers to these questions were handed to the instructor at the next meeting of the sections two days later. The two questions asked that bear directly upon the subject of this paper were as follows :—

1. "Do you have or have you had any fixed ideas ?"

2. "Do you have any ideas which involuntarily come to you when fatigued ?"

The writer explained that he meant by a fixed idea any idea which came unsolicited and remained even when the subject tried to get rid of it. The term obsession was not used as it was feared that this term would carry with it the idea of a pathological condition, and consequently stand in the way of an honest confession on the part of the student. The student was not required to describe his fixed ideas, but he was requested to do so if he were willing. Of the two hundred or more students who were asked these questions, about twenty-five per cent said that they either had or did have fixed ideas. Many of them did not attempt to describe their ideas but a large percentage did and from these we gain an idea of the character and extent of the obsessions common to such a large percentage of normal individuals. The following are some of the answers given to these questions :—

"I used to have a fixed idea of a monstrous stone so high that I couldn't see its top, and the stone would begin to roll toward me menacingly. I haven't had it, however, since I was a little youngster. So now it is very vague. Only the fearful sensation remains."

"When I am fatigued I always get the idea that I must solve some weighty problem that is awaiting me. I don't know what sort of problem it is to be solved, but whatever it is, it makes me worry because I realize it is my duty to unravel it, and the power to do so is just beyond my reach. I have another real problem which I try to solve when I am fatigued. I can see a table with objects upon it. This table moves upward through the air until it touches the ceiling. The objects go on through the ceiling, then I turn the table upside down and all of the objects stay on it. I try to get the table to touch the floor and have the objects go right through the floor as they did through the ceiling. The distressing thing about this is that I can never get the table clear down to the floor. It seems as if it were always an inch above it. If I try to think of it a half inch from the floor it usually ascends about three inches higher."

"I have had and still have a fixed idea that causes me any amount of discomfort. I don't remember ever being seriously injured with a knife wherefore I should feel great fear toward one. I can't imagine where I ever developed such a feeling of perfect terror for that object. The thought of it comes at most inopportune times when there is no occasion at all for its appearance. I can be talking on an apparently interesting topic of conversation when all at once without any warning, whatever, I shudder as I feel the blade of a knife hurting me. I know it is ridiculous to imagine that I am being cut, but I cannot help being frightened. The knife seems to wound me in various places at different times. Sometimes I can feel the sharp blade in my mouth and I am perfectly certain that in real life it never was there. I haven't told anyone of the queer sensation for I do not wish to be considered abnormal. I was discouraged from telling by my mother, who, noticing me shudder on one occasion, said I had either a very vivid imagination, or that I should apply for a place in the psychopathic ward. I prefer to be at large" . . .

"For three years whenever I allowed myself to be idle I was obsessed by the idea that I saw a large roll of carpet which rolled or unrolled itself eternally. As for recurrent words, I have a habit while dreaming of different things of breaking in on my reflections with the words, 'and then' or 'and after that.' The idea of the coolness of the grass is the one which comes to me most often when fatigued."

"When I was about eight years of age I had a fixed idea. I thought I was going to cut my throat from ear to ear with a certain large butcher-knife in my grandmother's kitchen. I couldn't throw off the idea. I was afraid to go near the knife. This persisted for about two weeks, then gradually wore off. When fatigued certain combinations of words or letters recur again and again. Often I am wholly unaware of their origin. For instance the words 'sy,' 'cip' have come to me over and over the last few days, and I am absolutely ignorant of where or when I heard or saw them. Often at night when very tired just before I fall asleep I read page after page of a large magazine in which there is absolutely no meaning— just a jumble of words. Yet I feel no irritation and my mind is absolutely satisfied with the jumble. I read down the columns, turn the pages and am aware of a half-tone illustration in the middle of the page but never see it distinctly."

"Whether it is to the point or not I do not know—but for the past ten years I have repeatedly found myself when thoughtlessly scribbling, writing the name 'Claudius.' I have no idea why this is, but it certainly has stuck."

"When fatigued I always picture vast horizons with a single occupant—as for instance, a single ship upon a large sea, or a vast desert in the middle of which is a single tent—outside, a camel and then a lonely Arab on his knees toward Mecca." . . .

In studying these obsessions in normal individuals one is struck by two things: First, that without external assistance the obsession in so many cases seems to run its course and disappears, or at least loses its emotional force; second, that in a large percentage of these cases the beginning of the obsession goes back to childhood.

A careful study of the mechanisms of the obsessions of normal minds by means of the psychological methods of investigation which have proved so successful in the study of pathological obsessions would doubtless be of value not only in adding to our knowledge of the obsessions of normal minds, but also in showing their relation to pathological obsessions.[1]

A Case of Poor Spelling Caused by Mental Conflicts

LEE EDWARD TRAVIS, "Mental Conflicts as the Cause of Bad Spelling and Poor Writing," *Psychoan. Rev.*, 11: 175-179 (1924)

The following study reports the case of a boy who was able to do fourth grade work in all subjects except spelling and writing. In regard to the former he was about a second grade pupil, while in regard to the latter, not much better than a first grade one. . . .

To a great many observant workers it is becoming clear that the "law of exercise" or the "law of use and disuse," which is forwarded as the most fundamental law of learning by the majority of psychologists, will either have to be extended, modified, or entirely set aside in order to account for *certain kinds* of learning and particular types of forgetting. In this case it will be seen that the patient was able to spell words, after certain inhibitory factors were removed, which had been to all intents and purposes forgotten. The return of the ability to spell these words was not due to any practice of

---

[1] [The following reference will illustrate the wealth of material on obsessions of *abnormal* minds: Pierre Janet, "Memories that are too Real," in *Problems of Personality*, (C. Macfie Campbell and others, eds.), 141-150.]

the bonds involved for the patient was not told how to spell the words which he had apparently forgotten. The return of the ability was rather due to the withdrawal of certain forces operating that caused the words, which were related to the various conflicts, to be continually misspelled. Even Thorndike's addition, the "law of effect," is too confining, at least the way he advances it. . . .

History. This case is that of a lad of ten with a negative family history. His personal history will be greatly abbreviated as only a minor part of it bears on the facts to be noted.

The social service record states that the patient started to school at five and finished the fourth grade at ten. No grades were repeated. His school work has been average or better except in penmanship and spelling. In the latter his skill is about second grade in regard to certain words and about fourth grade if a great many other words are considered. In writing he hardly excels the first grade standard. He had been passed from grade to grade with the hope that his spelling and writing would improve. When he had completed the fourth grade and hadn't improved in these two subjects, the teachers were unwilling to let him go farther. From all reports the teachers were of the first rank, doing all in their power to help the boy. When other means failed he was turned over to a special teacher who had no better success with his apparent inability to spell and write than did the regular teachers.

This lad has always been a very sensitive and emotional character; presenting a picture of activity, energy, and vitality.

Examination. His physical condition was negative except for a slight undernourishment. According to the Stanford Revision of the Binet-Simon Test he had an intelligence quotient of 110. . . .

As the teachers and mother had said, the boy's inability to spell certain comparatively simple words and his lack of coördination in handwriting were his outstanding abnormalities. Coupled with his poor handwriting was a peculiar phenomenon consisting of spelling a word one way orally and writing it another way. For instance he could spell "boy" orally but when he came to write the word he spelled it "boye" or "wboy." On one particular occasion when he was doing this the teacher had him spell each letter as he wrote it and while he spelled "boy" orally, he wrote at the same time, "dog."

Analysis. At the first session the patient was given the following list of words: afraid, girl, boy, rough, fruit, heard, autumn, learn, dead, teacher, mamma, woman, father, daddy, before, whip, because, finger, cap, run, supper, man, come, dog, nose, spell, dream, peanut, leg, hip, rest, horse, some, big, wind, and start. He was required to write them as well as spell them orally. In all instances the oral agreed with the written spelling. Following are the words misspelled: afraid, girl, rough, fruit, heard, autumn, learn, dead, teacher, mamma, woman, whip, because, and finger. Just a glance at the misspelled words will indicate a preponderance of reference either directly or indirectly to sex with a large percentage referring to muliebrity. The patient was asked to spell "girl" every way that he considered might be correct and he gave these: "garl," "girle," "gerl," "gerle," "gearle," "gearl," "gairle," and "dirl." Almost as many ways were given for "mamma" and "teacher." "Finger" was spelled "funger." It was soon discovered that he disliked girls in general and especially his two and a half year old sister and his teachers.

Further analysis revealed an incest fixation, a sexual curiosity in the form of a strong desire to see the female genitalia, and a masturbation conflict, all of which were deeply suppressed and released only after several weeks of intensive work. When these conflicts were being dissolved some very beautiful abreactions were displayed, the explicitness of which one cannot appreciate without having observed them or similar ones. The incest fixation was very strongly repressed, making itself felt in roundabout ways and finding indirect expression in the symptomatic acts of misspelling certain words such as mamma, sister, girl, etc. In other words, one of his symptoms was misspelling.

His sexual curiosity was, however, the most potent factor in the production of his symptoms. When about five years of age he was told by some older boys concerning the difference between the female and male genitals. This acquired information he shared with his mother who told him to immediately forget it, not to talk or think further of it. His curiosity to find out for himself was not thus easily set aside and for about a year he gave in to his desire to see by hanging around the girls, observing them when they sat or squatted. Soon a conflict began to be waged between his feeling of guilt on the one hand and his libidinous desires and wishes on the other, with the result that he ceased to recognize any craving for sex knowledge. Directly he discovered that he was beginning to dislike the girls and the teacher without knowing exactly why, being suspicious, however, that they were in league against the boys and that the teacher was showing favoritism in behalf of the girls. This conflict continued for about three years with a compromise in the form of misspelling certain words agreed upon by the two opposing forces. One day during the course of analysis after his incest fixation and his sexual curiosity had been brought to the surface and thoroughly dissolved, he spontaneously spelled girl, mamma, and teacher. He took a paper and pencil, which were lying on the desk and wrote the three words down to see if they looked familiar. The lad was very joyous over the fact that he could now spell the words and that they appeared known and "friendly." It was established that he had been able once to spell these words and that his ability to spell them now was not due to relearning. Thus the only conclusion to draw is that they were simply released from the hold of his conflicts and allowed to appear as words in their usual relationships and not as standing for a thing with which he was in tremendous conflict. Now when asked to spell afraid and fruit he could do so correctly. At this point it might be mentioned that it is futile to maintain that all the words the patient was supposed to learn to spell and didn't should be released spontaneously and correctly spelled due to the dissolving of conflicts. Conflicts not only operate to misspell a word which at one time could have been spelled correctly but they also operate to keep from learning how to spell a word in the first place. Thus which misspelled words are due to distortion subsequent to learning and which ones are the result of factors operating to keep them from ever being learned is another problem. If time and interest warranted it, there is no doubt that it could be worked out. . . .

Just before the patient was discharged he was given several hard words to learn to spell. He had no difficulty at all in learning to spell them. In addition he passed successfully the fourth grade in spelling as given by Lippincott's Horn-Ashbaugh Speller.

Rationalization

W. S. TAYLOR; revised from "Rationalization and Its Social Significance," *Jour. Abn. Psychol.*, 17: 410-418 (1923)

RATIONALIZATION, GIVING OF REASONS, AND REASONING

Rationalization, in the new sense of the word, is a term applied first by Dr. Ernest Jones [1] to important phenomena studied by Freud especially.

Partly bcause of the currency of older meanings, Dr. Jones' careful descriptions of "rationalization" have not prevented considerable misunderstanding; misunderstanding not only with regard to

---

[1] "Rationalization in Every-Day Life," *Jour. Abn. Psychol.*, 3: 161-169 (1908); published also in the same author's volume, *Papers on Psychoanalysis.*

the meaning of the term itself, but also confusion relative to the rôle of rationalization in life in general.

For in our usual thinking, the adjective *rational* has meant, broadly speaking, display of the faculty of intellectual consideration, as contrasted with prejudicial emotion. A synonym for the same state is the phrase, to be *reasonable*. But this latter phrase has been used also in another sense, namely, to do things moderately or the way they "ought" to be done, living the way reasonable people live. Rationalization itself has usually meant consideration from a rational point of view; or the translation of impulsive, esthetic, or mystical phenomena, into the language of reason, for clear understanding and test by reason.

But now we have before us processes which belong under none of the definitions just given. Rationalization, in the new sense of the term, means *unconsciously fictitious justification for behavior:* fictitious because the justification is not fair to the facts, as we shall see; and unconscious, because otherwise it would be not "rationalization" but lying. Thus so far from representing scientific rationality, this sort of rationalization (hereinafter called simply rationalization) means only the appearance of rational goodness, unconsciously put on to appease social expectations. For rationalization consists in giving an acceptable "reason" for an action, when the action really springs from an unacceptable cause. The cause, that is to say, may be too primitive and uncivilized to be admitted to society; yet, the action being desired by the individual and permitted by his fellows, merely offering it under an acceptable "reason" masks the cause and allows it to pass. Thus rationalization is a form of hypocrisy, supposedly necessary to keep the peace between our aboriginal natures and the artificial make-up of society.

And this is what makes rationalization so disturbing a phenomenon to the student of the nature and rôle of thinking. Rationalization is recognizable in so many fields of thought that it becomes liable to confusion with true *giving of reasons* (to be defined shortly), even with the process of *reasoning*. Perhaps, indeed, human nature has been deluding itself: perhaps any sort of rationality which is better than this rationalization, is but a figment of scholastic imagination, and without any existence in real life. We know that humanity has a tremendous wish to regard itself as rational; and where there is a wish, there may arise a compensatory delusion. Hence man's belief that he can and does show rationality by giving real *reasons,* is perhaps itself an intellectual compensation, to defend against painful admission that we are compelled by universal and irrational forces. However, a moment's reflection shows that the same should be said of the arguments we could give for holding such a theory. This puts us in a dialectical circle which leads nowhere; and from which we can escape only by assuming that there are some reasonings available, by which we can test other processes. Somewhere within the maze of reasons, must be the better ones which are fitted to stand at the top. Among these are the ones which seek to evaluate the respective places of reasoning, rationalization, and giving of (true) reasons, in human life.

Properly, "a *true* reason" for any action is a motivating cause of the action. In the case of purposive behavior, the general predisposition of the organism, the "determining tendency," [2] would be a motivating cause, as would be also each factor which determined the mode of release of the tendency. Where an action is performed without conscious purpose, say from habit merely, and is justified later upon request, the complete justification should include factors whose presence conditioned even unconsciously the performance of the action.

Obviously, then, a complete exposition of the true reasons for any action would amount to a detailed inventory of the determining antecedents of the action. But human motives being as multiple as they are, such inventories are impracticable if not impossible. It is but natural that society should have formed the habit of accepting only the high points of the causal description, where actions are questioned at all.

And it is this habit of which the rationalizer takes advantage. While his professed "reasons" come only from the field of—to his mind—*possible* causes, the rationalizer may have suppressed a number of important causes altogether. Or, since a partial list of his springs of action is all that will be required, he may (unconsciously) shift the emphasis, so as to make unimportant motives seem important, hiding the forces which really move him. The rationalizer may even offer reasons which are not at all connected with the action in his case, but which might have been connected with it, and which therefore serve to shield him from the light of knowledge. Thus he takes advantage of society's lack of discrimination, a lack which is occasioned partly by inability and partly by unwillingness to examine motives closely. Society itself includes individuals who have motives which ostensibly require rationalizing.

---

[2] *Cf.* Prof. R. B. Perry's "Behavioristic View of Purpose," *Jour. Philos.*, 18: 85-105 (1921).

RATIONALIZATION MECHANISTICALLY VIEWED [3]

How is rationalization to be explained? Must it be given an animistic description, as suggested by the more metaphysical aspects of Freudianism, or can we find a place for it in the world of descriptive science?

I believe that the mechanistic hypothesis is the way of truth. Certainly science is ever discovering causes for what had previously been ascribed to free spirits. Such experience suggests that the mechanistic interpretation of behavior is the interpretation which must often be corrected in detail, but which has no need to fear that its most precious assumptions are subject to discard by science. And a mechanistic account of behavior, it would seem, should offer better support both for psychotherapy and for an understanding of different types of thought processes in human behavior.

Now it appears that rationalizing is a form of "compartment mind" believing. The rationalizer's advertised "reasons" are, for him, beliefs; while other ideas are "repressed," i.e., inhibited or dissociated, as the case may be. Inhibition and (localized) dissociation are alike in one important respect, namely, that in both, a large portion of the personality gains ascendancy, in such manner as to shut off conscious action of all other response systems of the organism. The important difference between inhibition and dissociation lies in the fact that inhibition is normal, and necessary to life in a complex environment; while dissociation is pathological, and results from the organism's inability to maintain integration before stress. And when a course of action, or an idea, is only inhibited, it may be "switched on" again at will, for it is still in connection with the principal cortical centers. Until such occasion for functioning arises, an inhibited idea remains "successfully suppressed," as the Freudians say. A dissociated idea, on the other hand, has been torn loose from the centers of consciousness; so that as long as the ascendant consciousness persists, the dissociated idea can function only through lapses of speech, automatic writing, and other discrete channels.[4] Hence a dissociated system cannot be called upon at will, until reattached to the waking consciousness, when integration is regained.

In rationalization, such integration is lacking. There are lines of division, which separate the motivating causes from the professed

---

[3] This treatment agrees essentially with the position maintained throughout Professor Holt's *Freudian Wish.*

[4] As described in Dr. Morton Prince's work, *The Unconscious.*

"reasons." In some cases these lines of division are reinforced by hyperactivity on the part of the dominant system. This occurs particularly where the thwarted responses still tend to function, as they do when dissociated. The danger of rivalry is communicated to the conscious portion in some way, perhaps through the excitement of receptors which are unable to touch off adequate responses, and which therefore stir up the fear reaction, with flow of adrenin. But however it is brought about, the fact remains that an excess of activity in the ascendant portion is frequently observable. This portion, which is called the "higher self," the "will," the "conscience," and the like, according to circumstances, is that which "is deceived," remaining blind to what goes on in the disparate portions of the "self."

Having attempted an explanation of self-conflict in this way, the paradoxical language of everyday psychology, which it is hardly worth attempting to avoid in all cases, should not cause confusion. Let us turn now to a little survey of the principal varieties of rationalization.

TYPES OF RATIONALIZATION

There is first a form of behavior which in mechanism is the same as rationalization, but which concerns chiefly the individual himself. Jones suggests that it might well be called "evasion." It consists in the exclusion of painful systems of ideas from consciousness, or in the establishment of pleasant systems, so that the organism's hedonic tone is improved. The most familiar examples of such behavior are the various forms of compensatory belief, from the ones which come easily during moments of phantasy, to those established more through effort, as in "faith." For the only essential difference between phantasy and faith, is that in phantasy there is that type of easy abstraction which allows everything to fade out of consciousness except the pleasant system; while in faith, the rival responses are not entirely quieted, so they call forth an excess of conscious activity to preserve the favored system. In either case satisfactory thoughts are indulged in while more immediately painful ideas are carefully overlooked.

In phantasy and faith, then, the individual may find escape from unpleasant aspects of his environment. But in those preoccupations, too, he may find escape from the unpleasant aspects of himself. If he has pain, like Kant with the gout, he may concentrate upon Cicero; or if he is homely, or has some humiliating weakness, he may dwell fondly upon himself as idealized, or upon beauty in the abstract, or physical power in general (*e.g.,* Nietzsche). Evidently, it is but a step from such phantasies to the delusions of the insane, or to the rationalizations of the ordinary mind. For rationalization, as "compartment mind" belief, is really a defensive overdevelopment of ideas.

Such overdevelopment can take one of two general forms: The rationalization may either protect a tendency which the individual is willing to accept, or work against a tendency which the individual is unwilling to accept.

The latter type is illustrated in a mild fashion by the unsuccessful business man who banishes the feeling of failure by securing a position as teacher of business methods. But this form of rationalization stands out more clearly where there are motives which seem to be incompatible with "conscience." Thus the sadist who is unable to direct his tendency into some channel of social value, may develop a violent defense belief in the cruelty of vivisection. The young woman who falls in love against her will, is liable to assert that she thoroughly hates her object, and perhaps all men who have some of the same characteristics. There have been cases of women converted to Christian Science, because of defense hatred for medical men. In its extreme form, apparently, this type of defense becomes paranoia, where the patient is convinced that the object of his subconscious liking is for infinite reasons anything but likable. Similarly, secret hatred is often covered up by excessive devotion. Mercenary interests, likewise, may be covered up by professions of love. One young man, whose fiancée's parents suddenly lost their money, announced his intention to marry her at once, "to provide for her." Analysis showed that this was really a defense against popular suspicion that his real devotion was to her money—which it was.[5]

The other type of rationalization, namely, that which instead of defending against unwelcome urges serves as protection for acceptable impulses, is exemplified in the common observation that anything that comes into consciousness from oneself, tends to call out some kind of reinforcement. Thus Pascal, when suffering protracted pain, found comfort in the belief that since the crucifixion of Christ, "suffering has become a link of resemblance, a link of union, between man and God. Moreover, it is the only link between them in the life that now is." Thus the coward finds "insuperable difficulties" in the way of the dangerous task he ought to perform. Dr. Frink analyzes the attitudes of two of his cases toward former

---

[5] H. W. Frink, *Morbid Fears and Compulsions,* 178.

President Wilson's peace policy. One was a coward, who found great satisfaction in defending the administration. The other was a quarrelsome fellow who had hoped, by holding out against his family, to obtain certain things from them. He discovered, however, that through his unwillingness to arbitrate, he had not only failed to get what he wanted, but had lost much more besides. His chagrin was great; yet he would not allow himself to think that his method had been mistaken. Naturally, for him the policy of peace was an irritant, and he attacked it bitterly.[6]

Again, the staunch defender of the established order *may* have high principles, or he may have objective interests at stake; but it is quite possible for his defense to spring from custom, or from prejudices established in youth. For that matter, a habit of any kind may find ready support in rationalization. The drunkard takes his "last" not admittedly because he likes it, but because he feels he needs it to steady his nerve for obtaining the work which will help him keep straight. In another class of cases, in which emotion arises without conscious intent, and seems to require justification, a single feature of the object is often represented as cause for the emotion. This feature, however, when removed, tends to be replaced by another. Thus a neurotic wife dislikes her husband's mustache; but when he has cut it off, she dislikes something else about him.

This habit of providing reasons for what springs from subconscious forces, is beautifully demonstrated in cases of hypnotic suggestion. When the hypnotized subject is told that he will be unable to recall what went on during the period of hypnosis, but that ten minutes after waking he will open a certain window, he carries out the order exactly. Then when asked why he opened the window, he is quite surprised at the question, but gives a reason, according to his intelligence. The lowest type of response will be that he "just wanted to open it." From this intuitive variety, there will be all degrees of apology, up to philosophical justification of the act. Indeed, through the pressure of life in a social environment, the rationalization habit may become so fixed that it becomes a necessity before action is possible. This is particularly evident in cases of highly developed "conscience," where through training in accountability to parents, to sovereign, or to God, the individual has become scrupulous in his habit of testing every act by reference to standards of truth or goodness. The passion for consistency, built up in this way, reveals itself with especial clearness when through

---

[6] H. W. Frink, *op. cit.*, 179-180.

repression of some real or imagined fault, the individual becomes distressingly consistent in all the other departments of his life.

Evidently intelligence is not always a protection against rationalization. Indeed, intelligence is what makes rationalization possible. Intelligence is required to recognize the unsatisfactoriness of reasons, and to supply the means of supplementing them. It is also, fortunately, the means of correcting them; though too often it fails to find its use in this respect. But it follows that great thinkers have not been free from the charge that their philosophies were rationalizations. "Our systems, perhaps," said Amiel, "are nothing more than an unconscious apology for our faults—a gigantic scaffolding whose object is to hide from us our favorite sin." Certainly many systems of thought serve to protect our conscious wishes and our submerged prejudices; while still others defend us from doubting these protective systems.

Phenomena of the types described above are observable also in international conflicts. The anger of a people is justified by appeals to the atrocities and unholy ambitions of the enemy, while all selfish motives are banished from consideration. Where selfish motives are really pressing, as in times of overpopulation, or where racial pride of conquest has been built up to a high point, the search for reasons may discover anything, from strategic necessity to a great need for civilization on the part of opponents.

ETHICAL STATUS OF RATIONALIZATION

Throughout all the varieties of rationalization, a common factor appears. In every case, the individual has made some effort to present a unified front to his environment. Where there is a permissible but unpopular impulse, all allies among the socially approved motives are encouraged to the maximum, so that the common may be surrounded by the more worthy. Where the impulse is socially impossible, the "better side" of the individual's nature exerts itself to the utmost, so that he may still secure the approval of his fellows. The constant motive underlying rationalization is thus a desire for that unity which spells success in meeting the problems of life; an expression of the will to survive in a social world.

And to this end, a part of the insistence on the better "reasons" springs from a more or less conscious appreciation of the power of autosuggestion. That this attitude is somewhat justified, is a commonplace of experience. Our voluntary faiths may become our customary beliefs, as phantasies sometimes become beliefs. It would seem that nature has made it possible for us to suppress doubts for the moment, and act according to reasons that we desire, with the result that success reinforces the reason for next time, while driving doubts and unworthy motives into oblivion. This must be through inhibition of as many unsuitable responses as possible, and dissociation of the rest; supplemented by a tendency to reintegrate, in retrospect, for the sake of future adjustments of the same kind. In a social environment there is added incentive to this process, because our advertised reasons become precedents, to which our fellows expect us to remain fairly loyal.

But there is a limit to this type of autosuggestion. Complexes too far removed from consciousness can only with the greatest difficulty be worn down by such crude countersuggestion, if they can be reached by it at all. And society puts a real hindrance upon this type of effort, through its failure to trust the process. A great show of reasons is itself often cause for suspicion. Society prefers individuals whose behavior is more transparent; and where the motives are at odds with one another, intelligent men would rather see the individual set out to look his motives squarely in the face, to readjust his behavior and his beliefs, not from the outside, but from within, at the roots.

Evidently there are urges both individual and social which would drive rationalization into something better. Fortunately, with the knowledge now at hand, an individual blessed with sufficient intelligence to be a good rationalizer, has in the same intelligence a means of analyzing his motives, so as to direct them into more useful channels, according to a wiser program of life. When this is done, his list of reasons for any act, when required, can amount to a wholesome self-analysis. Then the propositions he states as a little inventory of his motives, are not "compartment mind" beliefs; they are real reasons, actual causes, which stand in his conscious life as integrated beliefs. In other words, instead of his believing propositions which fail to describe what is going on within his complicated make-up, this subject's speech apparatus is associated with all of the central (cortical) portions of his stimulus-response arcs, so that he is able to tell us what his interests really are. His beliefs represent his behavior; and his behavior expresses his beliefs.

Perhaps the notion of the complete irrationality of all human behavior may occur again, in connection with the question of the *origin* of belief-behavior. It is true that a great number of instances of belief-behavior are mere results of suggestion from the social environment: the beliefs are suggested and result simply in behavior, or the behavior is suggested and corresponding but natu' rally effectual beliefs follow simply. But while many instances of integration between belief and action are only such results of sub-rational suggestion, it is also true that highly important instances of belief-behavior are the outcome of individual reasoning (incipient trial-and-error adjustment to a new situation). Indeed, the process of discovering the real causes, the true reasons, for an act, may begin as a process of reasoning; for it may be a problem to give a true inventory.

In further connection with the "higher side" of the individual's nature, we should note that among those true reasons for an act, there may well be, in a thoroughly normal manner, recognition by the individual that certain lines of action are *moral*. *I.e.*, the individual may carry out some action primarily because it is, in his opinion, right, the better act, quite regardless of what the common herd may think. The facts that this sort of behavior may be unusual, and that many cases resembling it are motivated by inferiority complexes, and the like, should not prevent our escaping metaphysical entities like "the herd instinct" sufficiently to appreciate the natural way in which ethical responses are built up in a person.

Of course, even if there were complete self-analysis among the people generally, suspicion that "reasons" are still only shams might arise from the fact that different persons give different reasons for the same behavior. This, however, is inevitable, considering the complexity of human interests.

With the general acceptance of a fairer view of human nature and its possibilities for living, and with the growth of applied psychology, it would seem that we may hope for reduction in the quantity of rationalization. This should result in gain, both for individual happiness and for the social welfare.

Adult Revery

A. G. TANSLEY, *The New Psychology*, 147-153 (Dodd, Mead, 1924)

When we are engaged in any occupation to which we are attending with full mental control, the objects of cognition involved successively come into the focus of consciousness in the order we desire —in other words, our "conscious stream" is directed entirely with reference to the occupation. But we are all familiar with the condition in which this desirable state of things is not maintained throughout the occupation, in which the mind "wanders" from the subject on which it is engaged. . . .

When the mind is unoccupied by definite purposeful attention, it is given over to this kind of wandering, directed sometimes by sense impressions, sometimes by complexes. This is the state commonly known as a "reverie" or "brown study," and depends on what Bleuler [1] called "autistic" thinking, which we may oppose to "realistic" thinking, which is directed by purposes rooted in reality. "Autistic" thinking, which may also be called "affective" thinking, though neither term is quite satisfactory, is of the same type that we became acquainted with in the last chapter as characteristic of the dreaming mind. It is also a necessary part of the mental activity of the artist, and is carried to a length in which the mind becomes quite divorced from reality in types of insanity such as paranoia and dementia praecox, where affective complexes from the unconscious continuously dominate the mind. In the normal waking mind it finds its completest expression in daydreaming, the subject of the daydream being often remote from reality, though elements of reality may be interwoven with it, and the mind, unlike that of the paranoiac or dement, is always able to distinguish clearly between thought related to reality and purely fantastic thought. . . .

In the second half of his book Dr. Varendonck [2] calls attention to the advantages and disadvantages of freely wandering as opposed to consciously directed thinking. Its first great advantage is that it works without the friction and strain involved in conscious attention, and thus the whole available psychic energy can be employed— none of it is used up in inhibitions. Further, in the absence of these inhibitions, it has much fuller access to memory than has consciously directed thinking. Its disadvantage, on the other hand, is that it is entirely uncritical, it cannot pause in its course to correct errors: it lacks the power, which consciously directed thinking gives us, to adhere closely to the requirements of reality. If it is to serve conscious purpose, its results must be subjected to conscious criticism in the waking state.

This is what actually happens in constructive scientific thinking. The new idea is arrived at by allowing the mind to wander freely round the points of the problem to be solved. Success in arriving at the new idea is signalized by the emergence of an affect of jubilation which stops the wandering process and brings the mind back to the fully conscious state. The idea thus brought into the search-

---

[1] Bleuler, "Das autistische Denken," *Jahrb. f. psychoanalyt. u. psychopath., Forschungen,* 1912.

[2] J. Varendonck, *The Psychology of Day-Dreams* (London, George Allen & Unwin, Ltd., 1921).

light of consciousness must then be consciously criticized, related to all the relevant knowledge available to consciousness. After all, it may have to be rejected as out of harmony with established relevant knowledge. But sometimes it represents an actual valid new discovery. This is the mechanism of all "inspiration," and it is seen, of course, not only in scientific thought, but, very conspicuously, in all artistic creation. Very often the mind is not consciously set to wander in search of inspiration, but wanders of its own accord round the points of the problem to be solved—the explanation of freshly revealed phenomena, the right means of expression of a freshly conceived æsthetic idea. And this voyage of discovery may be pursued in the daytime, unconsciously during sleep, or in the semiconscious condition preceding or following sleep. It is in this last condition that a successful result of the search very commonly rises to the surface and emerges into the arena of consciousness— in other words, "bright ideas" often occur in bed in the morning.

CHAPTER XXIII

PROBLEMS OF PERSONALITY AND CHARACTER

Constitutional Predisposition to Neuroses

FREDERICK W. MOTT, *War Neuroses and Shell Shock*, 109-113, 223-224, (Oxford, 1919); *cf.* also Southard, in *Psychol. Bull.*, 16: 193 (1919); and the selections on Heredity in the present volume, *supra*, pp. 102 *ff.*

At my suggestion and under my direction Captain J. M. Wolfsohn of the American Army Medical Service investigated the personal history and the leading nervous state of 100 of my cases of soldiers suffering with shell shock or war psycho-neuroses (neurasthenia and hysteria), and compared the same with 100 surgical cases suffering with wounds under the care of Captain Turner at the 4th London General Hospital.

The three following tables of the results [p. 638] are quoted from his paper in *The Lancet,* February 3rd, 1918.

. . . Burton-Fanning found that the majority of cases of hysteria and neurasthenia owe their condition to an inborn temperamental neurotic disposition, which accords entirely with my own experience of recruits and of soldiers suffering from these nervous affections. Indeed, the inborn factor dominates ,as a rule, in proportion to the failure to discover adequate cause of stress arising from military service. These conscripts, as Burton-Fanning says, disagree with the doctor's "Fit for Service." "They resent being found fit and bring certificates of their unfitness for which they are willing to pay considerable sums." Such cases give a typical prof of Dejerine's dictum of the essential condition of neurasthenia being a continued emotivity and mental preoccupation which in the recruit's case concerns their unfitness or unwillingness for military service. . . .

Allowing for possibilities of error, I should say that at least 60 per cent. of the 147 cases of war neurosis admitted to the Maudsley Hospital were total abstainers, which is a percentage double of that of the 62 cases admitted to Ruskin Park suffering with wounds or diseases other than functional nervous conditions.

TABLE I—*Family History*

Percentages of characteristics named in (A) Neurosis, (B) Wounded

	(A)	(B)		(A)	(B)
Nervousness	64	15	Tuberculosis — immediate family	12	4
Alcoholism (parents and grandparents)	50	24	Tuberculosis—relatives	6	4
Teetotaller (parents and grandparents)	30	16	Stigmata	10	0
Irritability of temper	36	12	Positive history for one of several of above	74	38
Insanity	34	0			
Epilepsy	30	0			

TABLE II—*Personal History*

Percentages of characteristics named in (A) Neurosis, (B) Wounded

	(A)	(B)		(A)	(B)
Stigmata	34	4	Enuresis	12	4
Previous Nervousness	66	12	Frights in childhood	4	0
Fears	50	8	Excessive religion	6	0
Head injury	38	12	Positive personal history	76	12
Epilepsy	8	0	Positive family and personal history	70	6
Tobacco—excessive	8	4	Recurrences and relapses	14	0
Alcohol—excessive	6	16	Acquired neurosis	12	3
Alcohol—teetotaller	48	20			
Married	42	28			
Moody	55	8			
Previous breakdown	2	0			

TABLE III—*Present Illness*

Percentage of conditions named in (A) Neurosis, (B) Wounded

	(A)	(B)		(A)	(B)
Unconsciousness	55	24	Insomnia	86	0
Dazed	84	24	Fears	76	0
Tremor	84	12	Dreams	88	50
Poor memory	88	4	Fatigue	94	40
Poor concentration	88	4	Headache	88	36
			Moody	92	0
			Vertigo	74	8
			Fits	10	0

The high percentage of total abstainers among cases of war neurosis and shell shock was associated with fear of the consequences of drink, or a dislike of the taste of drink, consequently refusal to take the rum ration. Fear of the consequences, in a great number of instances, was due to the results in the home of paternal drunkenness, and in fewer instances of maternal drunkenness, or drunkenness in both parents.

Characteristics of the Neurotically Predisposed

A

[H. L. HOLLINGWORTH; BORIS SIDIS; WILLIAM HEALY; J. A. HADFIELD]

Prof. H. L. Hollingworth has attempted to prove statistically that the psychoneurotics of the war averaged lower in intelligence than the soldiers who maintained nervous stability.[1] According to Sidis,

on the contrary, it is quite possible, and in many patients we actually find it to be so, that the psychopathic individual may be even of a superior organization. *It is the sensitivity and the delicacy of nervous organization that make the system susceptible to injurious stimulations,* to which a lower form of organization could be subjected with impunity. An ordinary clock can be handled roughly without disturbance of its internal workings, but the delicate and complicated mechanism of a chronometer requires careful handling and special, favorable conditions for its normal functioning. Unfavorable conditions are more apt to affect a highly complex mechanism than a roughly made instrument. It is quite probable that it is the superior minds and more highly complex mental and nervous organizations that are subject to psychopathic states or to states of dissociation. Of course, unstable minds are also subject to dissociative states, but we must never forget the fact that highly organized brains on account of their very complexity, are apt to become unstable under unfavorable conditions. A predisposition to dissociation may occur either in degenerative minds or in minds superior to the average.[2]

With regard to those individuals who develop mental conflicts which lead to delinquencies, Dr. William Healy concludes after a series of intelligence and ability tests:

---

[1] H. L. Hollingworth, *The Psychology of Functional Neuroses*, 80-99. For a similar comparison of civilian neurotics with normal soldiers, *cf. ibid.*, 190-191. Note, however, Dr. William Healy's different conclusion in *Mental Conflicts and Misconduct*, 316-317, *circa*.

[2] Boris Sidis, *The Causation and Treatment of Psychopathic Diseases*, iii-iv (Badger, 1916).—Elida Evans, in *The Problem of the Nervous Child*, 243-244, presents a most flattering estimate of the endowment of the neurotic.

Summary of the tests. . . . shows our cases to possess good mental abilities,[1] but we find no one test or a group of tests of diagnostic worth either for discovering the general fact of conflict or indicating the type of personality that is particularly prone to conflicts.

We confess to being unable to satisfy even our own inquiry about the complete *normality or abnormality in reaction type* to those who develop mental conflicts. It boots little to say that this or that individual or kind of individual would not have reacted thus, because it would be very rare to find identical circumstances obtaining. I must bring to the front once more, however, the fact that the experiences which start the complexes under consideration have had peculiar settings, with ominous secrecy and the like, and have come from socially abnormal sources. Besides this, they often have certainly arisen at moments and ages of special psychological import and, as I have frequently emphasized, always when there has been no normal opportunity for confiding the experiences to sympathetic elders.

The possibility of the existence of general predisposing causes of conflicts many readers will feel has not been exhausted by the above statement. With regard to correlation of conflicts with *physiological malfunctioning,* it may be said that, while perhaps outbursts of reactive tendencies may in some occur more readily in periods of special stress, such as menstruation (*Vide* p. 265),[2] on the whole there is no sign of there being any such relationship.

Environmental circumstances in our cases are most diverse. The histories show misdoers coming from all classes and conditions of society. There is one common feature, however, that belongs to what may be termed the physical environment. These misdoers with mental conflicts never have had any one near to them, particularly in family life, who supplied opportunities for sympathetic confidences. Repression has gone on very largely as the result of this need.[3]

Dr. J. A. Hadfield maintains that

in itself, a nervous temperament is not a disease; *everything depends on what we make of it.* Thus in a nervous family the father

---

[1] [That a considerable number of such cases possess *superior* intelligence, is evidenced by John Christian Tjaden's monograph, "The Causes of Delinquency in Boys of Superior Intelligence."]

[2] [*Op. cit.*]

[3] *Mental Conflicts and Misconduct*, 320, 321 (copyright, 1921, by Little, Brown & Co.).

and mother are both highly strung; of the children, one becomes an artist, one a neurotic, another a poet who commits suicide, another an alcoholic, and another a great preacher. The man of nervous temperament may be over-sensitive to the hurts of life, but he is also more sensitive to the beauties and exquisite delights of nature, which the more phlegmatic can only behold with cow-like stolidity. If nervous people are the "crocks" of the earth, they are also the salt of the earth. A neurotic is often a potential genius.[1]

But what is the nature, or what are the kinds, of these "nervous temperaments," for which Dr. Hadfield uses "neurotic" in one sense, as a synonym?

B

AUSTEN FOX RIGGS, "The Psychoneuroses: Their Nature and Treatment," *Am. Jour. Psychiat.*, O. S. 80: 94, 100-102, 95, 103-106, 109 (1923)

The conclusions of one observer of many neurotic individuals are as follows:

In the first place, the typical psychoneurotic was evidently an individual possessing a physical apparatus well above the average in resistance to disease and intrinsically sound. Histories peculiarly free from serious previous illnesses and thorough physical examinations made this clear. Secondly, no typical environmental cause for his difficulty, common to all or even a majority of cases could be found. Last, most important, and most helpful of all, it became increasingly clear that all psychoneurotics in sharp contrast to their physical and mental *adequacy* (which distinguishes them from the so-called organic cases, such as the major psychoses), were markedly and typically *inefficient*. The outstanding characteristic or manifestation of this personal inefficiency, was *imperfect adjustment to environment*.

In short, the conception which further years of experience have confirmed and clarified, is that the problem of the psychoneuroses is the problem of the maladaptation of intrinsically normal individuals to what in the vast majority of cases, proves to be an environment also well within normal range.[2] . . .

[1] *Psychology and Morals*, 12 (Methuen & Co. and Robert M. McBride, 1923); reprinted by permission.

[2] Of course the social environment may be too easy or too hard. In being too easy, *i. e.*, arranged to adapt itself to the individual demands, it

There is at least very suggestive evidence that the psychoneurotic tendency is most often an acquired one, in the fact that given the knowledge, the requisite insight, the vast majority of these cases

---

"spoils" the individual, and a grown spoiled child results. It may be too hard, especially too hard, too early, demanding an adaptability that the individual has not attained, thus forcing him to regard the adaptation as impossible, the world as his enemy and throwing him back into an unsocial self-protective (instinctive) attitude.

However, environment rarely if ever furnishes in itself the causative factor in the therapeutic problem of the psychoneuroses, except from the point of view of early influence, training, education and suggestion. But this aspect of the problem has to do only with prevention—not with cure and, therefore, belongs to the realm of mental hygiene, a subject far too wide for the scope of this paper. . . .

Let us examine the following statistics for evidence of the truth of this theory:

In 800 cases only 26.3 per cent gave a history of drastic changes in social environment preceding the attack, while only 31 per cent had operations or physical illnesses of any severity. As some of these cases had both of these mental and physical elements in their histories, and consequently appear twice in these statistics, it is safe to say that not one-half of the total number gave any evidence in their histories of environmental changes important enough to be considered casual. Furthermore, I wager that at least as high a percentage of illnesses and disappointments would appear in the histories of the vast majority of non-neurotic individuals.

Irrespective of type, *all* cases show an inability to adapt themselves to the common changes (social) of environmental conditions. This inability, however, manifests itself in different ways according to the individuality of the patient, and is an inability which is based not on inadequacy but on inefficiency, due largely to mis-interpretation and lack of the knowledge called "know how."

The source of this inability in some cases lies chiefly in that part of the individuality called temperament; in others an instinct of exaggerated strength; in still others in the elements of character. In short, it is to be found in the influence of reason upon the reaction of personality to its environment. In one case temperamental sensitiveness is the predisposing cause which unfavorably affects this influence; in another it may be an overstrong instinct. The environmental influence plays at most the part of the immediate exciting cause.

["With qualitative and quantitative differences in the inherent ability of individuals to adapt themselves to a complex community life, with differing educational and environmental influences at play upon these inherent differences, there result, as we may expect, varying degrees of success in adjustment, from complete failure—those with psychoses—through partial success—the neuroses—to more or less complete success. On this scale appear those who suffer from fear and anxiety representing a degree of successful compromise. This compromise is born in conflict, conscious or unconscious, and the anxiety and fear represent the degree of failure or success and stand as the symptoms of the underlying difficulty. Whether benign or malignant, anxiety and fear mean conflict, and relief

are able to adjust themselves most satisfactorily and permanently, even in those rarer cases where the environment is manifestly and grossly a very difficult and trying one. It is not probable that an organic and, therefore, deeply rooted abnormality could so readily be overcome.

The old classification of the specific varieties of psychoneuroses is still of use for "psychasthenia" and "neurasthenia" are descriptive labels even though they describe only symptoms. The psychasthenic is a psychoneurotic whose symptoms refer to the mental side of life, while the neurasthenic's symptoms refer to his bodily functions. "Hysteria" on the other hand, though it is also descriptive of symptoms only, will outlast the other two labels, for the symptoms it describes arise from a fundamental hyper-suggestibility and a tendency to dissociation, which is in itself a distinct and specific predisposition of certain individuals. One should bear in mind, however, the fact that this old classification is based purely on the superficial basis of difference in the symptoms manifested and that this difference is due to the difference in indi-

---

will be found only in meeting frankly the issues of the conflict. In most cases the cause of the conflict is apparent and can be dealt with. In many cases the apparent cause is not the real cause, which is more likely to be unconscious than conscious, and not until the source of the difficulty is revealed can relief be brought. But benign or malignant, conscious or unconscious, the mechanism and the general method of its handling are the same."—Frankwood E. Williams, "Anxiety and Fear," *Mental Hygiene*, 4: 81 (1920).]

Largely independent of gross environment, the familiar varieties of the psychoneuroses develop, the form in each case being determined almost entirely by the individuality of the patient. One can see evidence in the family history of these cases that the personal qualities responsible for these maladies are, in the majority of cases at least, certainly not of the distinctly inherited *native* sort, for only a comparatively few show histories of similar difficulties in parents or grandparents, whereas not a few prove to have been under the environmental influence of high-strung nervous companions. In case, however, that the contention be brought forward that organic diseases of other types may be responsible for psychoneurotic tendencies in descendants, I wish to point out that in the histories of my cases, the incidents of such diseases in parents and grandparents are certainly no greater than, nor different from, those one finds recorded in the histories of any other clinical group.

Per cent
A history of a nervous breakdown in one or more antecedents...... 12
A history of high-strung or nervous antecedents without breakdown 33
A family history of insanity (including drugs and alcohol)........ 14
A family history of organic diseases (rheumatism, gout, etc.)..... 36
(Statistics strikingly common to general medical groups.)

viduality as outlined above. What then are these differences in individuality which incidentally produce different symptoms, complexes, different forms of maladaptation? . . .

As the mathematicians deliberately and coolly say, let "A" equal such and such, so let us say let *individuality* equal the sum total of the native and acquired predispositions of the individual, and let it include also temperament and character. . . .

The specifically characteristic tendencies of the psychoneurotic individuality are roughly as follows:

1. *Over-sensitiveness to emotions and sensations* the primary basis being a temperamental predisposition to over-respond to the pleasurable and painful; the secondary basis being poor training and discipline, allowing the predisposition to become habitual in action.

2. *Relative unbalance of instincts,* for instance, and most commonly, the basis is a relatively over-active instinct of self-preservation with a consequent prominence of fear and anger; the secondary element being misapprehension of the significance of these emotions and a consequent exaggeration of both the affective and physical elements of emotion. In short it is this instinctive unbalance which makes the general temperamental sensitiveness specific, to fear or anger for example.

3. *Suggestibility* combined with an inherent, probably inherited, tendency to dissociation of function, secondarily accentuated by wrong training, resulting in maladaptation of hysterical type.

4. *Character faults* usually a lack of training and discipline with a consequently imperfect connection between ideals and performance, resulting in an egotistic type of maladaptation.

5. *Lastly, the environmental* conditions may be so terrifically hard both socially and physically as to defy the normal power of adaptation.

In general the psychoneurotic adaptation shows a more or less extreme tendency to "short circuit" on the lower instinctive level. The individuality does not respond as a whole, but reacts only in part, showing a break in the integration of character in its response to life.

It is to be noted that all of these characteristics are found in the perfectly normal individuality; it is only when they become exaggerated or relatively unbalanced that they constitute psychoneurotic tendencies.

1. To illustrate these generalities more specifically, let me attempt a tentative etiological classification somewhat less general.

(a) Individuals being temperamentally over-sensitive to painful sensations and emotions react to the ordinary ills that flesh is heir to and tend to develop a hypo-chondriacal variety of the neurasthenic syndrome.

(b) The same type of individual will also react to the ordinary emotional conflicts of life by exaggerating their importance, and will habitually mismanage them on the conception that feelings rather than actions should be controlled. The maladaptation which usually results is a *psychasthenic* syndrome with emotionalisms.

Etiologically it is obvious that a and b are fundamentally the same though the symptomatology is very different.

2. Individuals usually hypersensitive but also with unbalanced personalities, for instance those possessing relatively over-strong instincts of self-preservation, tend to react to the ordinary difficulties of life whether they be emotional or physical by yielding to these instincts and thus developing a psychasthenic syndrome of the phobic or irritable type as the case may be. The environmental cause, in other words, is in each sub-variety merely the exciting cause, but does not determine the variety of the disorder.

3. If the psychoneurotic individual be also hypersuggestible his adaptation to life takes on the hysterical character exhibiting protean somatic disturbances such as motor paralyses, disturbed organic functions and pain habits.

4. Character faults (weaknesses) if they occur in individuals possessing any or all of the psychoneurotic elements described in 1, 2, 3, result in maladaptation characterized according to the individuality by automatisms of escape, avoidances, protective illusions of self, and indecision, in some cases accompanied by marked emotionalism.

5. Lastly, there are those rare cases where environmental conditions both mental and physical may be so extraordinarily abnormal and difficult and prolonged as to defeat the power of adaptation, and break the integrity of the most stable individuality. (In my experience this is the rarest type, the simplest, and I have never seen a case in which some form of physical hardship was not present.)

In general, a tendency to over-mobilization of energy, a dead level of intensity of effort, irrespective of need, is the commonest form of inefficiency exhibited by all types.

I must add that most often cases do not fit definitely into any one class, but seem to belong to several.[1] This is to be expected

---

[1] ["The nervous infant, restless, wriggling, and constantly crying! The nervous child, unstable, suggestible, passionate, and full of nameless fears! The nervous schoolboy or schoolgirl prone to self-analysis, subject-conscious,

when one realizes that individuality more than any other element determines the type of syndrome, and of what complex and variable factors individuality is composed. . . .

When it comes to treatment, all types are amenable to re-education, obviously their greatest need. The character fault type is perhaps the hardest to reach; the emotional type more difficult than the sensitive, even though the latter may have gastro-intestinal and other secondary disorders to a marked degree. In general the simplest is, of course, the easiest, as for instance the war neurosis. Difficulty or ease of treatment, rapidity or slowness of progress, depends more on the individuality of the patient, especially his intelligence, than on anything else. . . .

In conclusion I wish to point out that the tentative classification submitted is merely tentative, that the hypothesis it is based upon has developed from experience and lastly that the technique of treatment as outlined is in accord with this hypothesis, and that it seems by practical test to be a sound beginning, pointing the way hopefully to greater success.

C

W. S. TAYLOR; adapted from "Characteristics of the Neurotically Predisposed," *Jour. Abn. Psychol.*, Vol. 20 (Jan., 1926)

Differentia of Dissociability. Dr. Riggs' classification of psychoneurotic tendencies suggests a number of points:

In the light of "the over-sensitiveness to emotions and sensations," "a . . . predisposition to over-respond to the pleasurable and painful," it does not seem strange that some sons of families that have endured the world only through the consolations of religion should, upon losing their religion, flee to the Greek classics, to pure science, or to wine, women and song. In Dr. Hadfield's apparently typical sketch of a "neurotic" family, above, we seem

---

and easily exhausted! And how many and how various are the manifestations of this temperament! Refusal of food, refusal of sleep, negativism, irritability, and violent fits of temper, vomiting, diarrhœa, prompt and exaggerated reactions to toxins of all sorts, morbid flushing and blushing, habit spasms, phobias—all controlled not by reproof or by medicine, but by good management and a clear understanding of their nature.

"The hygiene of the child's mind is as important as the hygiene of his body, and both are studies proper for the doctor. Neuropathy and an unsound, nervous organization are often enough legacies from the nervous disorders of childhood."—Adapted from Hector Charles Cameron, *The Nervous Child*, 219, 170, 220 (Oxford, 1924).]

to note in each of the children a certain shunning of, or at least failure to meet, the difficulties of ordinary life.

Yet we must take into account the possibility that, in the example given, the preacher, as well as the artist, *may* be hewing out needed goods; and in any case, both artist and preacher are, in the achievement of their callings, overcoming technical difficulties from which the average citizen would flee most neurotically. The average citizen would so flee, because he has not the *capacity to adapt to that province of "reality."* Just as a feeling of inferiority, even based upon some real defect, may account for the development of many a genius, it also accounts for the development of many a tramp. Endowments differ.

And in how many instances the sensitiveness itself is owing to the ability of these individuals to *represent* to themselves the unhappy consequences of too ordinary or foolishly directed living, in other words, is owing to a variety of intelligence, is a question too important to be disregarded. Carlyle's dyspeptic theory that "man's unhappiness comes from his greatness" is truly applicable to some circumstances. The intelligence testers inform us that our common schools have slighted the superior child very much more than the dullard; and the psychiatrist is familiar with the little thinker who develops immense "wonderments" about important but tabu topics, and who is able to appreciate keenly any "perils" of existence, and the magnitudes of sundry "sins." Such a child must develop keen conflicts, conflicts altogether beyond the one whose intellectual life is limited practically to the sensation of the moment. An example, more common than appreciated, is the acutely wasteful conflict in the intelligent mind over masturbation, while thoughtless fellows, no more righteous with regard to the same tabu (whatever its element of worth), but less appreciative of the horrors alleged to ensue, are sleeping and eating well.

Of course parents, who have read books and have been to high school, know more than ignorant urchins; and naturally the preacher, who has been to college where ordinary teachers go to learn, knows best as to what is worth while in this world! Natural enough are "repressions" in such a mind, in such a society. Naturally, for Giordano Bruno, there must be something essential in the religious forms he saw about him, forms to which so many souls were pinning their best faiths. But the findings of science were telling a different story. Must we regard Bruno as a born neurotic, *merely* because appreciating that conflict, he set about to *understand* that world *in toto, i.e.,* to have a truer philosophy with regard to it? Society, it is true, expressed its appreciation of his appreciation, by burning him at the stake; and according to society, the will of society is the will of God.

That a morbid hypochondriacal twist can enter to account for such differences, is obvious in many cases; and we must admit, too, that the ability to see through elders' and society's misplaced emphases is a sign of good health. But the truly intellectual type of conflict, sensitiveness to contradiction, remains to be distinguished; and the minds harboring such conflicts cannot therefore be called born neurotics. They are blessed with brains; and a pity it is to see these brains consumed in avoidable turmoils, instead of functioning understandingly in positive ways.[1]

But the recognition of intelligent conflicts is not to reduce all neurotic sensitiveness to native intelligence. We need to take account of plenty of other factors. On the credit side, *e.g.,* the degree of sensitiveness of the receiving apparatus needs to be ascertained and its rôle evaluated. Obviously a color-blind person cannot be disturbed by colorful incongruities. Yet this sensory acuity may be a manifestation of central defect, as evidenced by the way in which the nervous system sometimes compensates by hyper-acuity for the action of certain drugs, and as evidenced further by the phenomena of functional hyperæsthesias. Where sensory acuity is of this pathological sort, it represents ordinarily of course not an asset but a liability.

More noticeable as an aspect or variety of sensitiveness in those who often develop neuroses, is their great emotionality. The thresholds for overflow from the cerebro-spinal into the autonomic nervous system seem relatively easily crossed. Such emotionality is as we know a characteristic of inadequate inhibition, inadequate integration, ineffective adjustment through the higher system's use of the long muscles.[2]

In speaking of emotionality, however, we should not over-simplify that "trait." For example, as Hume observed, "lively passions commonly attend a lively imagination. In this respect, as well as others, the force of the passion depends as much on the temper of the person, as on the nature or situation of the object." [3] Here we see again the operation of capacity to *represent.* Yet we cannot say that "a good imagination" is a proof of superiority. For interesting

---

[1] For convincing proof of such unnecessary conflict, we are indebted to the late G. Stanley Hall: *The Life and Confessions of a Psychologist,* 132-133, 177-185.

[2] May it in some instances be the result of overflow of impulses which come over unusually "open" receptors?

[3] *Treatise,* 427.

is the possibility that this *imaginative* capacity may in some instances at least depend upon a native *dissociability:* the individual has the capacity to a high degree of shunting off immediate sensory impingements while living his inner life keenly.[1] Imagination of *this* sort, again, we should expect to find associated with emotionality, judging by the inhibitory rôle of the later nerve structures in neurological organization as suggested by Rivers:[2] a dissociated cortex cannot inhibit crude emotional responses well.

An outstanding manifestation of the sensitiveness of the potential neurotic is the great impressionability, observed by various writers. This impressionability frequently shows itself in the unadaptive persistence of wrong attitudes absorbed in childhood, such as prudery. Here (in some sub-species of the phenomenon, at least) those injunctions which might be more or less effective in keeping the ordinary person moral, have resulted in complete inhibition or even negative reaction. But the question arises again, How many of these cases of impressionability reduce to sheer human educability, of the sort that animals and morons cannot possess; and how many cases depend, on the other hand, upon dissociability, dissociability such that impressions received, instead of being linked up in perspective with many other impressions, are linked closely with only a few elements, so that stereotyped responses of a segmental, undiscriminative, character result? How many cases, in short, of this category of "impressionability" are really superior human material, and how many are inferior in nervous organization (either constantly or during only a particular phase of development)? This is an essential point not yet determined. And in any event, in the individual case, the possibility of unusually impress*ive* environmental influences, such as too *limited* a life, will always have to be taken into account.

Not surprising, in view of these types of impressionability, is the "narrowness of interests" said to be common to the neurotic. We should distinguish here however between depth of interest, which represents a wide range of organized associations, and true narrowness, which approaches more the character of an obsession. But given whatever is *taken* to be narrowness, we have a feeling of

---

[1] With regard to "preoccupation," as Professor Max Meyer calls it, we should note again two sorts: The "autistic" or "pleasure-pain" sort, characteristic of the obsessive day-dreamer, *e. g.*, and the "reality" type observable in the scientist, who works concentratedly in his laboratory, deaf to the irrelevant world about him.

[2] *Supra*, pp. 138 *ff.*

inferiority in social contacts, a feeling which often motivates compensatory egotism.

The dissociation type of impressionability, mentioned above, would seem identical with the category of "suggestibility combined with . . . tendency to dissociation of function," as Dr. Riggs has expressed this "specifically characteristic tendency of the psychoneurotic individuality." For as we have seen in connection with the topic of suggestion,[1] suggestibility depends upon freedom from inhibitions relative to what is suggested. But we note in passing that dissociability is an essential, not only of suggestibility, but also of the morbid types of sensory acuity, emotionality, and impressionability. In short, (permanent or temporary) dissociability appears as the common basis of all *morbid* sensitiveness, or pathological oversensitiveness, and of all abnormal suggestibility.[2]

Unbalanced urges. Evidently favorable to any tendency to dissociation, because highly productive of conflicts in a society of expectations and conventions, is the situation designated by Dr. Riggs as a "relative unbalance of instincts." Such unbalance is in his experience illustrated most commonly by an overactive urge to "self-preservation with a consequent prominence of fear and anger." But it may also be illustrated by an excess of sex desire, whether conscious or unconscious (and whether or not itself motivated by a "self-preservation" craving for proof of vigor, or for feeling very much alive). Again, the unbalance referred to can at least manifest itself in an over-development of acquisitive propensities, or any urge, native or acquired, that results in conflict. For that matter, our attention may well be called to the fact that the *under*-development of any tendency or trait, or of energy in general, relative at least to the expectations of the individual concerned,

---

[1] *Supra.* pp. 496 *ff.*

[2] In any attempt to *rate* the neurotically inclined individual, we should consider the possibility that while his defective integration may make him not easily mobilized, unified for action, except when stimulated by adrenin, *e. g.*, he may nevertheless (if highly endowed) attain to mobilization when given time, and effectively so, within certain limits of further adaptability. In this respect he may be like a country whose citizens are not easily organized into a foreign cause, but who, intelligent and wealthy, when they do get organized through a period of education, accomplish things. . . .

Upon reading the foregoing, Dr. Riggs added the following note to the manuscript: "I consider the hypersensitiveness of the neurotic as great an *asset* when trained, as it is a liability when untrained. A highly valuable risk, in short."

frequently results in the development of sundry defense mechanisms and Adlerian compensations.

But in every such case of "unbalance," the psychological question is, whether in the first place the unbalance is a true one; and whether, in the second place, the unbalance is a native or acquired asymmetry. If native, we should want to know whether, *e.g.,* an excessive *fearfulness* traces really to an easily-jangled sensorium. Where acquired, or at least secondary, we should expect to find acquired egocentricity, especially, or any variety of preoccupation with self-survival, resulting from the natural focussing of attention upon real or imagined defects of organization. Thus just as unbalance of urges encourages dissociation, dissociation or any maladjustment predisposes to manifestation of unbalance of fundamental urges, especially of the general "ego" urge.

The Vicious Circle. In this field of the constantly relative, the vicious circle plays a fundamental rôle. Given a small personality defect, whether native or acquired, and whether actual or imagined; this defect exaggerated by autosuggestion, developing self-consciousness, and producing defense-mechanisms, perhaps resulting in over-driving the individual so that his stability is weakened; if any dissociation occurs, the remainder is still more easily dissociated, because less able to meet complex situations; in any case, the individual becomes more or less "different," and is thereby somewhat automatically retired from the society of his fellows, thus losing a principal means of getting normalized through suggestion, talking things over, etc.; this makes him still less able to participate in the common world, he becomes still more self-conscious, develops further peculiarities, etc.;—unless he catches himself very successfully or is stayed at some stage of the process. (We should not overlook, too, the fact that the same difference–isolation–difference vicious circle may operate upon the child who, because brighter than the average, finds no playmates who will keep company to his interests.)

Neuroses as Heirlooms. When a neurosis has resulted either through the "difference" just discussed, or by any other means, the individual, if he (or she) marries, is very likely to marry neurotically. *I.e.,* he is likely to be attracted in a "short circuited" fashion to an individual who, instead of satisfying the majority of his personality, satisfies only an unintegratively active portion, such as his narrowly sexual urge, some phantastic ideal of childhood, or a regressive desire for a nurse. Such fractional mating usually means discontentment later. Then if there are children, they sense the disharmony, perhaps taking sides, at any rate becoming warped by the unhealthy emotional environment, and develop untoward attitudes in their turn. Thus neurotic conditions tend to perpetuate themselves.

Specific neuroses, too, are naturally contagious, though perhaps more often as a nervous habit than as a subconscious phenomena. A peculiar shake of the head, for instance, or a fear of cats, may be and often is handed down (through suggestion) from generation to generation.[1]

Traits of Neurotics

PIERRE JANET, *The Mental State of Hystericals*, 208-209 (Putnam, 1901)

Linked with the foregoing discussions are the following passages:

[Extreme] hystericals, above all, lose quickly social sentiments, altruistic emotions, perhaps because they are the most complex of all. Bertha, who for some time retained some affection for her brother, at last lost all interest in him. She herself complains of not being any longer able to love anyone seriously. Marcelle, at the outset of her disease, avoided everybody. It was very soon seen that Isabella wished to be alone. All, in fact, very soon fall into a state of unsociability, of misanthropy, which they try in vain to disguise. They wish, they say, to think all alone; and, in fact, their tendency toward revery has something to do with this partiality for isolation. But, really, they do not like society; they lose gradually their friendships and their affections. During their illness, they are generally incapable of acquiring serious sentiments of gratitude and sympathy.

In the pages of his work which follow the above lines, Professor Janet describes the great egocentricity,[2] selfishness,

---

[1] *Cf., e. g.,* Morton Prince, "Hay Fever, Due to Nervous Influences, Occurring in Five Members of the Same Family."

[2] Sidis, also, is very emphatic about the extreme selfishness of psychopathic patients in general. "This does not mean that every egotist is necessarily psychopathic, but *every psychopathic case is essentially egotistic,*" he says (*Nervous Ills*, 115, Badger, 1922). "Even in the best of patients one can find glimpses into the depths of the psychopathic soul which is nothing but the immense egotism of the beast, worsted in the struggle for existence, tortured by the agonizing pangs of the fear instinct" (*ibid.*, 116). "One of my patients used to be anxious about my going and coming. Was it love or devotion? I found out that he was afraid that I might be killed. This fear was developed in him by an actual accident in which his brother had died, but the same fear associated with me was

jealousy, laziness, depression, and childish instability of these patients. The sex instinct, too, he shows to become defective. As Sidis remarks on this point, "in many neurotic cases of the severe type even the sexual instinct becomes gradually atrophied. The patient's life is narrowed down to the impulse which is absolutely requisite for individual life existence, namely the impulse of self-preservation with its concomitant fear instinct." [1] According to Sidis, also, the life of the neurotic "is characterized by automatism and routine. This tendency to recurrence is characteristic of all forms of primitive life as well as of mental activities which are on the decline,— it is the easiest way to get along." [2]

Space does not permit inclusion of discussions of "the epileptic temperament," "the dementia præcox type of personality" or "autistic personality," "the paranoic disposition," "cyclothymic personality," etc. These are discussed in works on psychiatry. We may note, however, that in E. Kretschmer's volume, *Physique and Character*,[3] the manic-depressive disposition is found to be associated with the "pyknic" or soft rounding type of body, while dementia præcox appears rather in the "athletic" and elongated ("asthenic") physical types.

The Problem of Personality

MORTON PRINCE, "The Problem of Personality," *Pedag. Sem.*, 32: 269-274, 289 (1925)

That abnormal psychology furnishes insights which are important in the general problem of personality, is brought out in the following:

---

due to the fact that the patient was sure that my treatment was requisite for his health and welfare. He was in fear lest I might be killed, he would be unable to get his treatments, and thus lose time in getting back his health" (*ibid.*, 129). But as suggested by Sidis, this is an understandable reaction for an individual whose dealings with the world have been regularly unsuccessful, and unsuccessful because of his own psychological unhealth; it is natural that his attention should be turned back toward himself, and that it should form the habit of being focussed there, especially as relatives and friends get sympathetically interested. As someone has remarked, "Men and women are alike egotists when they are in emotional conflict."

[1] *Nervous Ills*, 132 (Badger, 1922).　　　　　[2] *Ibid.*, 358.
[3] Harcourt, Brace. 1925.

A fact to be noted and which must be taken into consideration by any theory of personality, is that of the various and many organized dispositions, or neurograms, comprehended potentially in the whole personality and when functioning providing the traits, all are not assembled under all conditions and at all times into a functioning whole. The individual reacts at one moment with one set of traits and at another with another, perhaps of an opposite character. Indeed he may possess, as I have said, traits that are antagonistic to one another, such as sentiments of hatred and love, or interest and disinterest, for the same object; or he may manifest both charitableness and uncharitableness; intelligence and stupidity; etc. Obviously such opposing traits cannot be manifested at one and the same moment. But let the conditions of the organism be altered, such as occurs in fatigue, or illness, or intoxication, or states of dissociation, or moods; or let the conditions of the environment be altered and one or the other of these opposing traits comes in functional activity. The dispositions underlying its opposite then may be said to be dissociated from the functioning systems of the personality, or be suppressed, or switched off. In other words, that which is the functioning part of the personality undergoes alterations from time to time, one set of traits being predominant at one time and another at another. There occurs a dissociation, or switching out, of some dispositions and re-synthesis, or switching in, of others. . . .

An acquaintance of mine, for example, is a practical business man, a steel manufacturer. In the management of his business he displays the characteristics of a capable executive and money maker. His character, expressing his interests and ideals and impulses at such times, is only that of a business man bent on industrial and financial success.

But from time to time he shuts himself up in his room, bars out the world and his friends and even the enticements of every social pleasure, and alone with his violin as a companion loses himself in the land of dreams—of music and emotion and sentiment until the wee sma' hours of the morning. At these times the business self disappears, and a dream self of emotion and sentiment, oblivious to all else, takes its place.

So also will a person appear as a shrewd, hard, selfish, ruthless egotist in his dealings with business competitors, when one side is uppermost; and to the public, when it is the other side, as a compassionate, generous, philanthropic altruist, interested in bettering the welfare of his fellow beings by the use of his millions.

Or again, may I take the personality of Abraham Lincoln which has been such a puzzle to his biographers, and is now puzzling a distinguished biographer, so he tells me, who is writing a new life. There were at least two sides to Lincoln's personality. There was the uncouth, coarse-minded, hilarious Lincoln, constantly repeating the unprintable jests and language of the youths of the rough pioneer life that was the lot of the early settlers and of the sordid vulgar civilization of the primeval forest. And there was the sad Lincoln, the idealist whose thought was not only the manifestation of a sublime character, but embracing the loftiest concepts of human nature, was expressed in language that recalls in purity and beauty the most inspiring ethical and poetic imagination. No wonder his biographer . . . is puzzled. . . .

In woman, as every woman knows—but few men,—one or more sides of the character are by the necessity of social customs camouflaged. From childhood she is taught by the conventions of society, by the social tabu, to restrain and repress, often even from herself, many impulses and cravings which are born within her, as well as many thoughts and sentiments which she has acquired by experience, by contact with the world and therefore by riper knowledge. The repression under the social codes of these, the natural expressions of a part of her personality has belied her nature which has been confined for centuries in a cage hung with opaque curtains, like unto the spiritualist's dark cabinets. But within her social cabinet, all sorts of urges of human nature have been seething. . . .

But to go back: in each of the examples, real and imaginary, above cited—and I might draw in different individuals from life, dozens of contrasting and contradictory pictures—it would appear that in the different relations of life the personality presents contradictory traits and conduct, and, in popular language, we might say different "selves" alternating with one another from moment to moment. But these "selves" are plainly only different sides or phases of the same personality. . . .

If there had been an irreconcilable conflict, and if it had been strong enough and could not be otherwise compromised, any of the characters I have described . . . might have been dissociated into two or more independent personalities. The first, the music-loving business-man might have split into a money-making steel manufacturer robbed of his musical talent and into an idealistic unpractical dreaming musician. The second into a hard, selfish miser and into an idealistic philanthropist . . . and so on. But—there were no conflicts, no consciences to be shocked, etc.; and so they only manifested moods, or alternating traits.

"Introverts" and "Extroverts"

MAX FREYD, "Introverts and Extroverts," *Psychol. Rev.*, 31: 74-75, 78-79, 84-87 (1924)

These two terms as applied to complementary types of personality have their origin with Jung, although he probably drew upon preceding writers in his formulations. He first presented the concepts in his *Psychology of the Unconscious* and later elaborated his views in his *Analytical Psychology*. Recently he has expanded his opinions on these types of personality to the scope of a volume (which will not be reported upon here). Since Jung's original contribution these concepts have been showered with attention, especially by writers of the psychoanalytic schools. Among those who have discussed the concepts at length, or who mention them in their writings, are Nicoll, Tansley, Hinkle, Kempf, White, Wells, Downey, McDougall, and Allport. The terms are increasing in vogue among laymen, and may often be encountered in non-technical articles. It becomes necessary, therefore, to examine closely the sense in which the terms are used, and to decide whether or not they are to be received into the fold of legitimate psychological categories.

Definitions of the Terms. None of the writers seems to have attempted a concise definition of the two terms, each contenting himself with descriptions and explanations. The introvert, according to practically all of the writers, is characterized by a withdrawal from reality and a great emphasis on the thought processes, whereas in the extrovert we have the tendency to face reality and the ready issuance of thought processes into overt action. The reality which these writers infer, or to which they refer, is social reality or the social environment. The following definitions are probably fair composites of the various opinions.

Introvert: An individual in whom exists an exaggeration of the thought processes in relation to directly observable social behavior, with an accompanying tendency to withdraw from social contacts.

Extrovert: An individual in whom exists a diminution of the thought processes in relation to directly observable social behavior, with an accompanying tendency to make social contacts.[1] . . .

---

[1] The writer has collected at times from several psychologists of standing and from graduate students in psychology, lists of what they considered the traits of the introvert and the extrovert. There is considerable agreement among the various contributors, which would point to a popular recognition and identification of the types were it not for the fact that

The writer (4) made a comparison of men who chose an occupation which brought them into contact with others and which demanded considerable social ability, with men who chose for their

these men had learned of the types from the same literary sources. This list is interesting in itself and is given below in condensed form. Only the traits of the introvert are given, since those of the extrovert would be merely the opposites of these. The descriptive terms apply to tendencies shown by introverts.

1. Blushes frequently; is self-conscious.

2. Avoids all occasions for talking before crowds; finds it difficult to express himself in public.

3. Prefers to work alone rather than with people; prefers to work at tasks that do not bring him into contact with people.

4. Dislikes and avoids any process of selling or persuading anyone to adopt a certain point of view (except in the religious field).

5. Takes up work which requires painstaking and delicate manipulation.

6. Hesitates in making decisions on ordinary questions that arise in the course of the day.

7. Introspects; turns his attention inward.

8. Depreciates his own abilities, but assumes an outward air of conceit.

9. Is critical of others.

10. Is extremely careful about the friends he makes; must know a person pretty thoroughly before he calls him a friend.

11. Limits his acquaintance to a select few. (This may be beyond his control.)

12. Has ups and downs in mood without apparent cause.

13. Has ups and downs in mood with apparent cause.

14. Works by fits and starts.

15. Worries over possible misfortunes.

16. Feels hurt readily; apparently sensitive about remarks or actions which have reference to himself.

17. Is outspoken; says what he considers the truth regardless of how others may take it.

18. Keeps in the background on social occasions; avoids leadership at social affairs and entertainments.

19. Is absent-minded.

20. Is reticent and retiring; does not talk spontaneously.

21. Shrinks when facing a crisis.

22. Prefers to work things out on his own hook; hesitates to accept or give aid.

23. Is meticulous; is extremely conservative about his dress and painstaking about his personal property.

24. Prefers participation in competitive intellectual amusements to athletic games.

25. Is a poor loser; considerably upset and indisposed after the loss of a competitive game.

26. Makes mistakes in judging the character and ability of others.

27. If he unburdens at all, he does so only to close personal friends and relatives.

life work an occupation which demanded mechanical skill almost entirely. The differences between these two groups brought out by a long series of tests and questionnaires and a rating scale indicated that the group that we shall call the socially inclined excelled the mechanically inclined in excitability, self-confidence, open-heartedness, present-mindedness, good-nature, adaptability, talkativeness, neatness in dress, and quickness to make friends. The mechanically inclined were somewhat more self-conscious, conceited, and careful of details in their work, and were capable of making finer coördinations. The conclusions reached in this study were not that the two represented types, but rather that they represented the extremes of a normal distribution curve of mechanical-social inclination, most people showing very slight inclination in one direction or the other. More will be said of this concept of extremes

---

28. Indulges in self-pity when things go wrong.
29. Day-dreams.
30. Limits his acquaintances to members of his own sex.
31. Is persistent in his beliefs and attitudes.
32. Shrinks from actions which demand initiative and "nerve."
33. Gets rattled easily; loses his head in excitement or moments of stress.
34. Expresses himself better in writing than in speech.
35. Is governed by reason rather than impulse or emotion. Is a good rationalizer.
36. Derives enjoyment from writing about himself.
37. Is thrifty and careful about making loans.
38. Is conscientious.
39. Resists discipline and orders.
40. Admires perfection of form in literature.
41. Is sentimental.
42. Rewrites his social letters before mailing them.
43. Pays serious attention to rumors.
44. Believes in "mind" cures; accepts an idealistic philosophy.
45. Talks to himself.
46. Keeps a diary.
47. Is strongly motivated by praise.
48. Is selfish.
49. Is slow in movement.
50. Prefers to read of a thing rather than experience it.
51. Is suspicious of the motives of others.
52. Is effeminate (if a man).
53. Is a radical; wants to change the world instead of adjusting himself to it.
54. Is creative of new and sometimes eccentric ideas and things. . . .
Few of the writers on the subject mention the causes of introversion and extroversion or the psychological theories which underlie the states.

later. The socially inclined group seems to be related to the extrovert and the mechanically inclined to the introvert.

Do Introverts and Extroverts Belong to Types? In spite of the strong criticism which the term "types" has received at the hands of statisticians and psychologists, there is nothing to indicate that it will go out of use. It recurs frequently in psychological literature and is a common word in conversation. If the existence of types could be proved it would be a great advance in psychology. The psychologist may certainly be envious when he compares his few ill-defined classifications of human beings with the more objective and complex classifications used by the zoologist. The difficulty, of course, lies in the fact that psychology is a subdivision of zoology and its data are more limited in range and therefore more difficult to classify. Its data are furthermore less tangible and stable than the data of sciences which are concerned with structure rather than behavior.

If we assume that types are characterized by having a certain amount of any one ability or combination of abilities, then we should expect each type to be differentiated from other types on the distribution curve of the ability or abilities in the general population. Each type would be represented by a mode in the distribution curve. Thorndike (*14*, Vol. 3, ch. 15 and 16) in a statistical discussion of types, shows that the distributions of single abilities or combinations of abilities are almost invariably unimodal, arguing for the existence of but one type—mediocrity. He says, furthermore: "It is very, very hard to find any case of a negative correlation between desirable mental functions. Divergence toward what we vaguely call better adaptation to the world in any respect seems to be positively related to better adaptation in all or nearly all respects" (*14*, Vol. 3, p. 362). The most probable condition in any individual is one of mediocrity in most traits, with slight variations toward extremes in the remainder of the traits.

There is a sense in which the concept of types may be retained while still accepting the normal distribution of abilities, although the word "extremes" should be substituted for "types." We may conceive of the distribution curve as attenuated by two opposing forces, and as a person is subject to one or the other of these influences he will score to one or the other side of the central tendency. If the forces do not act upon him or if they neutralize each other, he will score near the measure of central tendency. The two opposing forces may be called tendencies. The extreme individuals whom people tend to resemble may be described as those two persons whose scores in the ability or combination of abilities lie at the two remote extremes of the distribution curve of the general population. Or they may be conceived as hypothetical individuals who do not exist, or who lie at points on the distribution curve beyond the most remote point at which an individual has been known to score.

With some modification, this is the manner in which Weininger (16) views the absolute male and the absolute female and the intermediate manifestations in all human beings. All human beings tend to resemble the absolute male or the absolute female, but these are creations which have no actual existence. The tendency is determined by the relative strength of resemblance to the absolute male or female. Most people will show a slight tendency in one direction or another, and as the strength of the tendency becomes greater the frequency becomes less.

In some such sense as this lies the hope of harmonizing the concept of introvert and extrovert types with statistical facts. But there are other important theoretical matters which must be cleared up before the concepts can lay claim to a place in a scientific psychology. The writers must come to an agreement on the ability or constellation of abilities by which the extrovert-introvert opposition is identified. They must satisfy themselves that there are no other oppositions of personality extremes involving other combinations of traits, which may be fully as important as extrovert-introvert. Since the number of such oppositions is practically limitless, the thing may easily be reduced to absurdity. These matters of theory should be resolved in clear-cut terms and not in the verbiage of the psychoanalyst.

Following upon this is the problem of measuring the extent of the two tendencies in any individual. This reduces itself to the question: How may one differentiate between the extrovert and the intervert behavioristically? Apparent absorption in thought is not necessarily a criterion of introversion, unless the effects on overt behavior are studied. Certainly we should find difficulty in learning anything accurate about this attitude of thinking from the individual himself, for other psychoanalytic mechanisms such as rationalization interfere to color any report which he may make. The distinction between the two types or extremes must rest basically upon readily identified abilities or traits.

The theory of introversion and extroversion has opened up an interesting field of speculation, but as yet it has failed almost wholly to attract the experimenter. To find a place in the body of psychological knowledge the theory must be expressed with less inconsistency and with more attention to experimental evidence. The field seems a promising one for the psychological investigator.[2]

REFERENCES

1. Allport, F. H., and Allport, G. W. "Personality Traits: Their Classification and Measurement, *Jour. Abn. Psychol.*, 16:6-40 (1921).
2. Baldwin, J. M., *The Story of the Mind* (New York, 1902).
3. Downey, J. E., *The Will Profile*, 2d ed., (Univ. of Wyoming, Dept. of Psychol., Bull. No. 3, 1919).
4. Freyd, M., *The Personalities of the Socially and the Mechanically Inclined.* (To be published in the Psychol. Monog.)
5. Hinkle, B. M., "A Study of Psychological Types," *Psychanal. Rev.*, 9:107-197 (1922).
6. James, Wm., *Pragmatism* (New York, 1907).
7. James, Wm., *Psychology*, 2 Vols. (New York, 1890).
8. Jung, C. G., *Analytic Psychology*, Trans. by C. E. Long (London, 1916).
9. Kempf, E. J., *The Autonomic Functions and the Personality* (New York, 1921).
10. McDougall, Wm., *Is America Safe for Democracy?* (New York, 1921).
11. Nicoll, M., *Dream Psychology* (London, 1921).
12. Ostwald, W., *Grosse Männer* (Leipzig, 1910).
13. Tansley, A. G., *The New Psychology* (London, 1920).
14. Thorndike, E. L., *Educational Psychology*, 3 vols. (New York, 1914).
15. Watson, J. B., *Psychology from the Standpoint of a Behaviorist* (Philadelphia, 1919).
16. Weininger, O., *Sex and Personality* (London, 1916).
17. Wells, F. L., *Mental Adjustments* (New York, 1917).
18. White, Wm. A., *Mechanisms of Character Formation* (New York, 1916).
[19. Laird, Donald A., as per Bibliog.]

---

[2] [For further material on Personality, *cf.* the text and references in Floyd Henry Allport, *Social Psychology*, 99-143; Abraham A. Roback's interesting monograph relative to decision types, "The Interference of Will-Impulses"; the same writer's chapter, "Character and Inhibition," with its marshalling of many points of view, in *Problems of Personality* (C. M. Campbell, etc., eds.), 79-138; the portions not already included here of Max Freyd's article, "Introverts and Extroverts"; Aaron J. Rosanoff, "A Theory of Personality Based Mainly on Psychiatric Experience"; Pierre Janet's observations on decision types and orders of "depression" or of what we might call "letting down" of mental activities, in *The Major Symptoms of Hysteria*, xvii-xxiii; and Alfred Adler on the possible influences of bodily defects upon the development of the personality, especially in *Individual Psychology*, 318-320.]

Note on Character

W. S. Taylor; adapted from "Character and Abnormal Psychology,"
Jour. Abn. Psychol., 1926

The attitude in the field of abnormal psychology toward such
ethical concepts as "character" has within recent years been thrown
into a certain dubiety, probably because of the somewhat unorthodox
statements by Freudians, the effective disintegration of scholastic
conceptions of personality by Dr. Morton Prince and others, and
the relatively unorganized condition of much of the field of abnormal psychology, particularly in relation to ethics. It is the writer's
intention here to state a conception of character which agrees in
some essentials with definitions by a number of ethicists,[1] and which
seems to express the fundamental interest of all students of abnormal psychology.

For students of abnormal psychology *are* interested in the mechanisms that produce and support moral character, and they are
concerned with the standards by which it is evaluated. On the
latter point, probably the majority of abnormal psychologists incline
definitely to the modern conception of ethics. This modern conception has been formulated by one writer as "the science of values
in their relation to the conduct of life as a whole"; [2] meaning by
life, this life, with its biological heritage and human developments.
Accordingly, probably the majority of abnormal psychologists
would agree with such critical discussions as, for example, Professor
Everett's "Non-ethical, Ethical, and Anti-ethical Elements of
Religion," [3] or the same author's treatment of "The World-denying
and the World-affirming Spirit." [4] But many abnormal psychologists have been so conscious of the truly anti-ethical elements in
popular evaluations of character, and so aware of the evolutionary
nature of *mores* in general, that they have failed to make explicit
their essential agreement with the modern ethicist's understanding
of the relation between "Moral Law and Natural Law," to illustrate
once more from this one of the current texts.[5]

This is not the place for any attempt to define the standards by

---

[1] De Laguna, Drake, Everett, Perry, Sharp, and others; also, from the
psychological side, Holt, McDougall, Warren, and Woodworth.

[2] Walter Goodnow Everett, *Moral Values*, 7 (Holt, 1918).

[3] *Ibid.*, 396-405.

[4] *Ibid.*, 425-428.

[5] *Ibid.*, 312-318.

which character should be evaluated and to which character should seek to conform. Such questions are discussed in the texts on ethics. From the psychological point of view, however, what character is, in terms of mechanisms, is important. From this point of view, the following broad definition is submitted:

We may define character in terms of degree of ethically effective organization of all the forces of an individual. In other words, the more ethically approvable the integration of an individual, the "better" his character. A suggestible hysterical may have such a fluid personality that he does not possess any very effective organization. Organization involves some degree of inhibition.[6] On the other hand, a paranoic, or an obsessed person, may have very definite organization of his inner forces; he may accomplish great things. Yet such organization may not be ethically effective; it may be directed at unworthy objects, or may be incapable of adapting to improved methods, or of recognizing that new conditions require new virtues. To be ethically worthy, an individual's integration must be good for the life of individuals in a community.

The chief function of this definition is psychologically to distinguish character from temperament, mood, intelligence, and other aspects of personality. And it is clear that this general conception of character points directly to many of the specific conceptions of abnormal psychology, as well as of general psychology, as mechanisms of explanation and control.

---

[6] *Cf.*, A. A. Roback, "Character and Inhibition," in the Prince commemorative volume, *Problems of Personality* (C. Macfie Campbell, etc., eds.), 79-138, for a discussion of the psychological rôle of inhibition in character in general, regardless of ethical evaluation.

CHAPTER XXIV

GENERAL CONCEPTIONS OF FUNCTIONAL DISORDERS

Basic Relation between Types of Functional Disorders

A

J. A. HADFIELD; adapted from *Psychology and Morals*, 27-29, 32-33, 124-125 (Methuen & Co. and Robert M. McBride, 1923);
reprinted by permission

In origin the [true] Psychoneuroses are due to repressed complexes: they differ from one another in *the disposal of the complex.* In *neurasthenia* the complex is deeply and effectively repressed, so deeply that there is no expression in consciousness of the repressed fear, sexual desire or ambition; indeed, these neurasthenic patients may be callous, indifferent, and devoid of feeling or passion. The neurasthenic is tired because he spends all his energy in keeping down or repressing the instinctive forces within him. He succeeds in his effort, but in doing so saps his vitality to such an extent that no energy is available for the ordinary purposes of life, and he becomes exhausted by the most trifling effort. Such a man frequently suffers not only from physical fatigue, but from mental depression.

In the moral sphere the type is exemplified in the man whose "morality" is preserved by the effective repression of all his passions: he succeeds in being moral but suffers from lifelessness and moral "neurasthenia." He has no temptations, and denies ever falling into sin; all these years has he served without breaking any commandment. Such paragons of virtue would be unable, even if presented with a calf, to make merry like the rest with music and dancing. . . . They are good but not happy, they have lost the capacity for cheerfulness. They are tired, neurasthenic, joyless. They end by being thoroughly weary with well-doing.

In *anxiety neurosis* the complex is not so deeply repressed, the fight between the "self" and the complex being, as it were, *at close quarters;* the self is in imminent danger, and becomes anxious. When two opposing forces come into close antagonism there results a condition of tremor and strain. To take a physiological analogy;

if I contract the flexor muscles of my arm, and at the same time the opposite extensor muscles, so as to make my forearm stiff, the whole arm is put into a condition of tremor. So when two emotional forces fight at close quarters [the conflict] is often accompanied by physical symptoms of anxiety, such as sweating, trembling, starting, palpitation, and general excitability.

There is, however, a distinction between "anxiety" and "anxiety neuroses": anxiety may result from an actual *recognized* conflict of instincts, such as we have illustrated. Anxiety neurosis, on the other hand, as distinct from mere anxiety, is occasioned by the fact that our fear is of something unknown, of which we get terrifying glimpses only in our nightmares, and which haunt our days with a pursuing horror. The patient is afraid not of any danger outside, but of an unrecognized impulse within which threatens to overthrow his dominant sentiments.

Perhaps the most interesting cases of neuroses are those which manifest themselves in a definite physical symptom, such as blindness, pain in the back, sickness. They are well called *"substitution"* or *"conversion" hysterias,* because a definite physical symptom is substituted for the mental and moral conflict.

The purpose of every neurosis is to deliver us from a mental conflict. A gunner has spotted and is sighting a German submarine. Torn between fear and his sense of duty, he suddenly finds himself getting blind, but his blindness is purely psychic, there is nothing wrong with his *eyes.* Now, of course, he *must* go below, for what is the use of his remaining to sight his gun when he is blind? The neurosis is a compromise to deliver him from his mental conflict: his instinct of self-preservation and his sense of duty are both satisfied. Denied normal expression his fear satisfies its impulses by a back door. . . . Even the business man's breakdown, commonly due to the conflict between a phantasy of power and a fear of failure, delivers him from this conflict, for he can still say, "I *should* have succeeded, if it had not been for this physical illness." He is excused for failing, and yet retains his phantasy of the great things he *might* have done. In the Neurasthenic [War Neuroses] Hospital it is very interesting to observe that patients may be divided at a glance into those who suffer from mental anxiety and distress, but without any localized physical ailment, and those who have such symptoms as blindness and paralysis, but are extraordinarily free from all mental distress. These latter, indeed, are often the life and soul of the party, getting up entertainments, and hobbling about the football field in perfect happiness. They have found a way out of their mental conflict.

In Neurasthenia, then, the complex is *completely* repressed; in Anxiety neurosis it is only partially repressed, and fights at close quarters with the self; in Conversion hysterias, obsessions, and moral diseases, the complex emerges by some back door in the form of a definite symptom, physical, mental or moral.

One case will illustrate these points. A barrister suffers from severe pain in the leg, and from moods of depression and bad temper, the one a functional nervous disease, the other a moral disease. The pain in the leg was suggested by an incident in boyhood, when on the way to school he witnessed a severe accident, in which a man's leg was smashed. Consequently, he did his work badly at school, yet the horror of the incident prevented him from explaining. This incident was not only associated in his mind with horror, but what affected him more particularly was that he, a clever and "bright" boy, was blamed for inattention. The symptom was thus associated with a complex of humiliation. By this means we discover not only the historical origin, which in itself is unimportant, but the repressed emotion, in this case, *the over-sensitiveness to blame,* which not only then, but now, unknown to himself, plays an important part in his psychology and in the determination of his character. The recovery of the original experience was sufficient to cure the pain symptom; but it did not cure the depression, nor, of course, did it cure the sensitiveness to blame, which was the fundamental disease. The analysis, therefore, had to proceed, and revealed the fact that for five years he was the only child, petted and admired by fond parents, who loved to show him off. His instinct of self-display was exaggerated; he was, in fact, "perfect." Then, in succession, came five other children, and this oldest boy was shelved, and retired to brood over his miseries in sullen rage, and became morbidly sensitive to blame. The endo-psychic conflict between self-importance and insignificance thus gave rise to all his symptoms, both nervous and moral. It originated his morbid depression and bad temper, and later by association was the cause of the pain in the leg.

The next phase in the analysis is then to bring the psychological conflict up to date and demonstrate it in the present psychology. This is done by analysing not the original but the most recent occurrence of the symptom. In this case it was found that whenever the symptom recurred, it was always associated with some incident in which humiliation and over-sensitiveness to blame played a part; for instance, when he lost a case owing to slackness, which he was unwilling to admit, and when he arrived a few minutes late for a consultation. This bringing up to date of the analysis is most important.

B

MORTON PRINCE, *The Unconscious*, 523-527, 372-374, 527-528 (copyright, 1921, by The Macmillan Company); reprinted by permission

It is evident, that, theoretically, if antecedent conditions have prepared the emotional soil, and if an emotional complex, an intense sentiment, or instinct should be aroused by some stimulus, any one of a number of different possible psychopathic states might ensue, largely through the mechanism of conflict, according, on the one hand, to the degree and extent of the dissociation, inhibition, etc., established, and on the other to the character and systematization of the emotional complex or instinct. As with the physiological manifestations of emotion, we can construct various theoretical schemata to represent the psychological structure of these different states. Practically both types—the physiological and psychological —must necessarily almost always be combined.

1. The impulsive force of the emotion might repress all other ideas than the one in question from the field of consciousness, which would then be contracted to that of the limited emotional complex awakened; all opposing ideas and instincts would then be dissociated or inhibited—a state substantially of mono-ideism. Let us imagine the dominating emotional complex to be a mother's belief that her child had been killed, this idea being awakened by the sudden announcement of the news. The parental sentiment with child as its object would become organized into a complex with the emotions of fear, sorrow, painful depressed feelings, etc., which the news excited. This complex, being deprived—as a result of the ensuing dissociation—of the inhibiting and modifying influence of all counteracting ideas, would be free to expend its conative force along paths leading to motor, visceral, and other physiological disturbances. An emotional complex of ideas would be then formed which after the restoration of the normal alert state would remain dormant, but conserved in the unconscious. Later, when the emotional complex is again awakened by some stimulus (associative thoughts), dissociation would again take place and the complex again become the whole of the personal consciousness for the time being. This theoretical schema corresponds accurately with *one type of hysterical attack*.

2. If again the awakened complex should be one which is con-

stellated with a large system of dormant ideas and motives deposited in the unconscious by the experiences of life, the new field of consciousness would not be contracted to a mono-ideism. We should have to do with a phase of personality, one which was formed by a rearrangement of life's experiences. In this case the usual everyday settings (or systems) of ideas being in conflict with the sentiments of the resurrected system would be dissociated and become dormant. The ideas, with their affects, which would come to the surface and dominate, would be those of previously dormant emotional complexes, and their constellated system. The prevailing instincts and other innate dispositions would be, respectively, those corresponding to the two phases, the antagonistic dispositions being in each case inhibited. This schema would accurately correspond to a so-called "mood." If the demarcation of systems were sharply defined and absolute so that amnesia of one for the other resulted, the new state would be recognized as one of *dissociated or secondary personality*. A "mood" and secondary personality would shade into one another.

3. Still another theoretical schema could be constructed if, following the hysterical dissociated state represented by schema 1, there were not a complete return to normality, *i.e.*, complete synthesis of personality. The dissociation effected by the impulsive force of the evoked emotional complex and the repressed personal self-conscious-system might be so intense that, on the restoration of the latter, the former would remain dissociated in turn. The emotional complex would then, in accordance with what we know of the genesis of subconscious ideas, become split off from the personal consciousness and unable to enter the focus of awareness. Amnesia for the emotional experience would ensue. Such a split-off idea might, through the impulsive force of its emotion and that of its setting, take on independent activity and function coconsciously and produce various automatic phenomena; that is, phenomena which are termed automatic because not determined by the personal consciousness. The dissociation might include various sensory, motor and other functions, thereby robbing the personal consciousness of these functions (anæsthesia, paralysis, etc.). Such a schema corresponds to the *hysterical subconscious fixed idea* (Janet).

In such a schema also, in accordance with what we know of the behavior of emotion, though the ideas of the complex remained subconscious, the emotion linked with them might erupt into the consciousness of the personal self. The person would then become aware of it without knowing its source. The emotion might be accompanied by its various physiological manifestations such as we have studied. If the emotion were one of fear the subject might be in an *anxious state* without knowing why he is afraid—an indefinable fear, as it is often called by the subjects of it.

4. If, owing to one or more emotional experiences, an intense sentiment were created in which is organized about its object one or more of the emotions of fear, anger, disgust, self-subjection, etc., with their physiological manifestations (tremor, palpitation, vasomotor disturbances, nausea, exhaustion, etc.) and their psychological disturbances (contraction of the field of consciousness, dissociation, etc.) ; and if the whole were welded into a complex, we would have the structure of an obsession. Such an organized complex would be excited from time to time by any associated stimulus and develop in the form of attacks: hence termed a recurrent psychopathic state as well as *obsession*. (As we have seen, the psychogenesis of the sentiment is to be found in antecedent experiences organized with its object giving meaning and persistence to the obsession.) [1]

---

[1] This question of the functioning of unconscious complexes as subconscious processes is of fundamental importance for psychology, whether normal or abnormal, and if well established gives an entirely new aspect to its problems. We cannot therefore be too exacting in demanding proof for the postulation of subconscious processes as part of the mechanisms we are considering, or, at least, requiring sufficient evidence to justify them as a *reasonable theory*. If assumed as an hypothesis many otherwise obscure phenomena become intelligible by one or other theory making use of them.

Let us examine for a moment the obsessions as one of the most important problems with which abnormal psychology has to deal, and which offer themselves as exaggerated examples of ideas with insistent meanings. The phenomena are psychological and physical. They occur in a sporadic form, as well as in a recurring obsessional form. Let us consider them simply as phenomena irrespective of recurrence. They may be arranged by gradations in types in which they appear:

A, as purely physical disturbances;

B, as physical disturbances plus conscious emotion;

C, as physical disturbances plus conscious emotion plus a specific idea of the object of the emotion, but *without* logical meaning;

D, as physical disturbances plus emotion plus idea plus meaning.

In the first type the physical phenomena (such as commonly attend emotion) can be traced to a functioning subconscious emotional complex of which the phenomena are physical manifestations; in the second to a functioning subconscious complex ejecting its emotion into consciousness. In the third we find by analysis an associated unconscious complex (setting), which logically would account for the emotion of the obsessing idea, and infer, by analogy with A and B, that it is a dynamic factor in the psychosis. In the fourth we find a similar complex, which logically

Finally (to add one more schema out of many that might be constructed), if a number of physiological disturbances (pain, secretory, gastric, cardiac, etc.), such as occur as the symptoms of a disease, were through repeated experiences associated and thereby organized with the idea of the disease, they would recur as an associative process whenever the idea was presented to consciousness. Here we have the structure of an *"association or habit-neurosis,"* a disease mimicry. Numerous examples of the type of cardiac, gastric, pulmonary, laryngeal, joint, and other diseases might be given. The physical symptoms in such neuroses are obtrusive, while the physical elements (including emotion) which, of course, are always factors, conscious or subconscious, remain in the background.

The study of the individual psychoneuroses belongs to special pathology, and need not concern us here. We are only occupied with the general principles involved in their structure and psychogenesis.

Perspective in Understanding the Functional Disorders

TOM A. WILLIAMS, "Some Neglected Psychopathic Factors," *Jour. Am. Med. Ass'n.*, 79: 1514-1517 (1922)

. . . I venture to present anew some further reflections upon neglected factors which play a part in the induction and management of psychoneurotic situations. They illustrate again the old principle that all things are not always what they seem, and that very often the presenting symptom is not that of the highest importance.

REPORT OF CASES

Case 1.—*Phobias from discordances in childhood.* A woman having multiple phobias, which rendered her life and occupation very difficult, was referred to me recently because she had previously been under a psychoanalyst for a year and had after a while relapsed into as distressing a state as before. Her chief fear was that she would poison some one by accident.

Out of a highly discordant environment in childhood the psycho-

---

would account for all the physical and conscious phenomena.—Prince, *op. cit.*, 372-374. [These types are clearly illustrated in pp. 374-422 of that work.]

analyst had projected several erotic experiences on the pathogenic nature of which he had insisted. A more judicial study of the situation of her childhood, however, led me to believe that the sexual factors were relatively insignificant, and that great importance should be attached to prejudices aroused by family quarrels, which had centered her interest on herself because affection for either parent caused friction on the part of the other. This led to a watchfulness for blame which created a sense of guilt; but, being a character of sthenic and active tendencies and of high suggestibility, she was in constant flux, finding no stability in her discordant home. Against these conditions a resentment occurred, of which she scarcely knew the meaning, which she exhibited apropos of what seemed trifles, and which made her afraid lest she should do violence in her rage against some one for a transgression of slight degree. Because of the frequent scoldings she received, the fear of doing the wrong thing became obsessive; and this led to her trying to avoid the expression of her impulses. This, of course, added further to her resentfulness.

Naturally of a joyous and expansive disposition, she became attuned pejoratively, and hence attracted every vibration of calamitous import which came within her range. Naturally, among her calamities, the sexual transgression took its place, which in her case was a comparatively small one until the suggestiveness of the Freudian procedure exalted it. The man of straw, having been set up by the psychoanalyst, was in the course of a year knocked down by him; and the suggestion of well-being from the elaborate procedure relieved the patient for a time, and she felt that she had no grounds for her fears, as the "sexism" supposed to be responsible for them had been dealt with so learnedly. But the suggestion was not proof against the further assault of circumstance; and the patient, not having been truly reëducated, relapsed.

Better adjustment and greatly improved physical health occurred when a truer perspective was acquired by the patient through the learning of the great importance of her feeling of resentment, more especially during the inception of her disadaptation in childhood, and after constructive activities were fomented.

Case 2.—*Impotence from diffidence grounded in misinformation.* In the case of a man sent by a genito-urinary specialist because of an impotence in view of which he was afraid to marry, an undue emphasis on the physical sexual had caused him to lose perspective, and rendered him almost hypochondriac, as is often the case. When a new setting of his mind was given by a dispassionate presentation of the whole sexual relation, his difficulties were enormously mitigated in only a few days; for the efficient factor in his disability proved to be diffidence, which is not sexual at all.

Case 3.—*Craving of security and for fulfilment.* In another patient the overemphasis on the sexual factor almost paralyzed the efforts of some of those who had been dealing with her in fear of what is termed by some "the transference." As a matter of fact, an affection which seemed inordinate, and wore a carnal mask, was in reality a craving for protection, safety and trust.

Vacuity played a part in this also. The patient, in an institution thoroughly discordant, had been left to her resources, which became more and more circumscribed. She fell into ruminations concerning her hard lot and how to escape from it. When she was set at liberty, comparatively speaking, and when incentives toward accomplishment were furnished, she became interested in the art she had formerly professed, which was one of the principal motivations of her former life.

Even the frank expression of wish for sex gratification proved to be rather the yearning for upliftment from a state of depression due to prolonged anxiety, with ensuing doubt and suspicion and ultimate bewilderment.

Few psychopathologists seem to realize the great importance of this mechanism when sex stimulation is concerned, even though there have been many studies concerning attempts to compensate for feelings of inadequacy by the patient's emphasizing qualities that will utilize them. (Little persons, big esteem; weakly persons, prowess in sport; dull persons, working hard and becoming wealthy and distinguished; physically unattractive persons, cultivating charm.)

One would have thought that the exhilaration from depression sought in alcohol and other drugs would have afforded a parallel sufficiently striking to permit of its application in the sphere of libidinous craving.

Case 4.—*Awkwardness and shame, paralyzing initiative in work and society, due to environmental repression.* A woman, aged 26, was referred by a physician who had unsuccessfully treated her several months. She was very reticent, disclosing her complete story with much difficulty and trepidation. She was eating her heart out in routine work in which she was neither using her college education nor satisfying her craving for contact with other human beings. Nor did her leisure afford her the kind of companionship she longed for. She did not know how to reach away from the safe monotony of a sheltered life into the adventurous variety of the constructive idealism which she worshipped. She was immensely handicapped by a lack of ease of manner and charm, which she envied in others: she was ashamed of her awkwardness.

This situation might only too readily have been attributed to the humiliation she felt at the intense and facile stimulability of her physical sexuality, and a prolonged analytic search might have proved too strong a temptation to those psychopathologists who can think only conventionally.

But as insistent as were the physical discomforts of the patient, I considered that the psychosocial problem was even more important, and that to solve this, a change of environment was imperative. It should not need to be said that explanations as to the significance of reproductive physiology were given, and that these were of great comfort to the patient. Although they scarcely affected the phenomena themselves, they altered many of the psychologic consequences. The patient was assisted to take steps to prepare for an occupation which would favor human contact in constructive work, in which she is now, a year and a half later, happily engaged without supervision.

In each of these four patients the superficial aspect of the case is highly sexual, and in one of them physical ebullitions are perhaps the most painful of the discordant elements of a scarcely tolerable situation. But even in this case they are not the main factor of the maladjustment at all; for the adjustment was effected without any success in mitigating these difficulties. The real issue was a psychosocial one, and affective satisfaction was gained by the provision of opportunity for the kind of intellectual activity craved.

HEDONIC FACTORS

There are some who smile at the assertion that the hedonic factors of the psychoneuroses have been much neglected; nevertheless, many of them have been entirely ignored because of the overemphasis placed on one of them. So great has been the desire of some to drag everything into one net that efforts have been made to interpret the pleasure derived from stroking, and the sensation of tickling, as having to do with sex stimulation.

One of the arguments adduced in facor of this is that occasionally stroking elsewhere will stimulate the erectile tissue of the genitals. The argument ignores the fact that any kind of stimulus anywhere may at times induce genital erethism. Furthermore, the opinion is disregardful of the fact that cutaneous stimulation elsewhere may stimulate the nasal erectile tissue also, and that such stimulations influence the blood pressure, pulse rate and respirations, sometimes quite strongly, and often interfere with both peristalsis and secretion in the digestive tube; while another reflex almost invariably consists of a series of motor contractions and relaxations often calculated to escape excessive stimulation.

The argument that because some of these purely hedonic sensations are sometimes utilized to reinforce sexual pleasure they are therefore sexual might be applied to cold, warmth, certain special foods and drinks, music, painting, literature, philosophy, ethics and religion, or any other human activity, as all are sometimes used to reinforce sexual impulse. And yet all of them have primary uses of their own entirely apart from the pleasure contingent on reproduction.

That stroking and caressing are primary pleasures apart from sex is easily seen in the watching of a group of geldings on a hot day stroking one another's necks, and the nestling of reptiles and swine in heaps for mutual comfort. Among human beings the slap on the back of cronies, the linking of arms of boy and girl companions, and such rapprochements, although hedonistic in purport, are surely primitive, even though at times some of them are manifested previous to and during the approaches of courtship. For this is equally true of all animal gests; any may be carried over into the dearer relationship, even though originating otherwise. But the busy bees were too firmly wedded to the phallic flower to see aught else, sipping the only honey they love.

FRUSTRATION OF CONSTRUCTIVE IMPULSES; POWER

The impulse toward self-assertion, dominance of one's surroundings, usually accompanied by a feeling of self-esteem, has until recently received surprisingly little attention from psychopathologists. This is all the more astonishing when one remembers the emphasis already laid on these tendencies by certain philosophers, more particularly Hobbes, by whom what he called "sudden glory" is made into a most important nucleus round which to constellate his concepts of human psychology.

In this respect he anticipates the better known philosophy of Nietzsche, whose writings are perhaps responsible for belated recognition of the "will to power," which was, however, already foreshadowed in the philosophy of Schopenhauer.

Not only have these three philosophers strongly emphasized the rôle of the will to power in human motivation, but the inevitability of its frustration has been used as the basis for the consolations afforded by two religions, one of which still pervades the earth more widely than any other hitherto has. The declaration, "Blessed are the meek, for they shall inherit the earth," is a prophylactic against countless disadaptations.

Buddhism preaches a mental hygiene very similar, in which gentleness and love for one's fellows replace force and ferocity as ideals.

The mitigation of the assertion of power having been a prime essential of life in community, devices have been elaborated from the cradle up calculated to curb it; hence the opportunities of adjustment in this sphere are afforded to most individuals, but, unfortunately, in a haphazard fashion, and they often stultify development through unwise restraints of the conventional type. The psychologic reactions against frustration of ambition are conspicuous enough in the biographies of such men as Napoleon, Julius Cæsar and Byron. But even when not conspicuous they exist in the lives of every one, and when looked for can be detected as important factors in the disadaptations of many of our patients.

Still greater stultification of the individual ensues, however, when immoderate play is permitted to the craving for power without corresponding intellectual and moral cultivation. Many of the sons and daughters of the newly rich afford a glaring example in our day. Even though ludicrous, this has its dangers in the fomenting of unwise revolutionary impulses of the kind that appeal less to reason than to passion. We smile, to, at such pretensions as were exercised by the Stuart dynasty with the mystical justification of their power known as the divine right.

We have reached a degree of political cultivation in which the scandalous tyranny of the Roman emperors would not be tolerated. But there are still large bodies of men whose intelligence has not yet developed to a point at which they cease to tolerate the assumption of power by authority which speaks in the name of religion, and who rest still benighted in darkness where superstitions impede each grouping for a healthier adaptation, condemned to lifelong inadequacy, and enthralled without possibility of egress into a better day.

That the exercise of untrammeled power is psychologically unhealthy for those who exercise it is clearly shown in the history of dynasties and of all institutions which have oppressed. But it is unhealthy also for those who are oppressed, as it arouses resentment and hate, when it does not paralyze personal initiative in the development of the intelligence and the truly moral qualities. . . .

ACQUISITIVE TENDENCIES

The disjunctions caused by the frustration or interruption of acquisitive tendencies are very striking in some persons. . . .

VACUITY AND MALADJUSTMENT

Action.—Former somewhat empiric neurologists laid great emphasis on ennui as a prime cause of neurotic disturbances, so much so that what was then called neurasthenia was considered to be a disease solely of the leisured rich. While we have learned better than this, there is no justification for modern psychopathologists to ignore completely the state of boredom as a potent and not infrequent prime factor in the development of psychoneurotic states. Much of the alleged feminine restlessness of today expresses an implicit craving to escape the ennui to which artificial life subject women, more especially when childless, having command of modern domestic conveniences and devoid of cultural interests. From the stagnation of their psychic life, they seek to escape through meretricious amusements; but when they are not shallow-minded enough to be satisfied by these, when they find no interest within their narrow walls, and when external solicitations make no appeal, the monotony of their existence, even if not an active explicit discontent like that of a caged animal, or expressing itself as domestic nagging, fretfulness and quarreling, may cause them to adopt the attitude of resignation so very prone to turn into obsessive thinking, the fabrication of fears, the product of inturned imagination with its magnification of trifles. . . .

Creation.—The frustration of the creative impulse is a factor of the poor psychic adjustment of some persons which has been almost entirely neglected by psychopathologists, if one is to judge by the literature. These are individuals in whom desire for a particular intellectual activity is the dominant passion. This usually has quite a specific direction, whether into a manual art, into a fine art, or into invention of science. Not every one has the strength of character and special advantages of young Shelley, who succeeded in overcoming colossal impediments toward the growth of his passion for human welfare and beauty; nor is every one gifted with the tenacity of Charles Darwin, who quietly developed his natural bent even in an English public school. There must be countless mute, inglorious Miltons whom not environmental inertia, but the actual antagonism of others has frustrated into psychoneurotic misfits unable to channel into another direction the urgings of their spirit, and who eat out their hearts in introverted desolation.

ANGER AGAINST FRUSTRATION

Of the passion of rage and its correlates resentment and hatred, and perhaps jealousy in some of its features, as a primary factor, I need say nothing, as Stanley Hall in a masterly fashion has drawn attention to its neglect before this very association.[1]

I have encountered numerous cases in which maladjustments and character deviations have been the product of the need for frustration of the impulse of rage against irrefragable impediments imposed by the authority of parents and guardians of the young, and of managers and supervisors of adults.

A considerable number of situations have been presented to me in which the fundamental element of discordance has been the resentment of the patient concerning situations into which he has fallen. In some of these cases the feeling reaches an abhorrence for the particular person or persons who have initiated the discordance. The torticollis in a treasury employee which I reported some years ago in my study of occupational dyskinesias is a striking example in point. . . .[2]

MORTIFICATION

Many of the situations which have been invoked in support of the sexual origin of the psychoneuroses are in reality issues depending on mortification. But the inhibitions of personality produced by mortifying experiences or the dream of them occur even perhaps more frequently regarding social intromission of kinds other than sexual. The conventions of fashion are a particularly frequent source of these. In young persons the ethics of sport furnish occasions. Relationships in business are another source in which motivation by fear of mortification plays a strong part. This is particularly true with hierarchal organized services, such as the army. It is most true of all, perhaps, in that form of activity among women which, under the misappellation of society, has become an occupation to which great devotion is paid.

---

[1] Williams, T. A., *Jour. Abn. Psychol.*, 1915.

[2] Williams, T. A., ". . . Genesis of Writers' Cramp, etc." [*Cf.* the present volume, p. 731.]

THE FEAR FACTOR

Dread, anxiety and fears are in my experience the commonest efficient factors in maladjustments with which we psychopathologists have to deal. These factors, however, have been adequately realized and dealt with by only a few since Hobbes. However, I shall have to refrain from the discussion in this short paper, having already dealt with them casuistically,[3] and being about to issue a book devoted to dreads and obsessions.[4] I cannot forbear, however, referring to the dread so prevalent among the gregarious which drives them to seek the safety of dogma, and causes them to smother the germinations of truth, which would otherwise produce a conflict from which they cower in terror of the disapproval of those with whom they herd. For though the day of inquisitions is passing, that of anathema is still with us in full force. In the absence of the motive of personal animosity, which is the usual man behind the gun in apostates, the avenue of escape from conformity is a thorny one. The path is passable only by one who is armed with truth, a weapon quite exceptional, unfortunately; for the average education is far from calculated to foster a search for a way to verity through the thorns of error, which so often bear the sensual berries of acquiescence, companionship, wealth, and preferment. The spirit of martyrs, which inspired men even to die for the right as they saw it, and which made the political institutions of Great Britain and the United States, is being corroded into a self-satisfied and narrow partisanship voiced in such expressions as "my country, right or wrong."

Pusillanimity which refuses to look at right lest it may threaten one's prejudice sidesteps a conflict of readjustment at the price of the otiose self-contentment which is only the prelude to decay.

The limitation of time forbids a discussion of two other very important occasional psychopathogens, namely, disgust and grief. Envy and jealousy, too, should enter into consideration in a small proportion of cases. The latter, in my experience, has been rapidly dispelled in every case.

["Some may have too many 'resistances,' some too few; some may fret against the delay due to the toilsome sifting of data of little

---

[3] Williams, T. A., "Differentia Regarding Obsessions and Phobias with Reference to Their Pathogenesis and Treatment," 180; "Removal of Morbid Fear."

[4] Williams, T. A., *Dreads and Besetting Fears.*

emotional appeal, and may indulge in imaginative constructions of shadowy outline and vague formulation, while others may be too little responsive to what is suggestive in these products of intuition and imagination, and remain somewhat fettered by their insistence on particulars and their demand for scientific proof.

"What is sometimes forgotten is the wider audience, both medical and lay, and the social problems which form the wider setting of those strictly medical. If we remain sensitive to these wider issues we shall cultivate a sobriety of thought and presentation, involving to some uncomfortable self-restraint, but which holds out a promise of much wider usefulness. The neglect of these considerations may delay the recognition by medicine of the place due to psychopathology; inspired by them the psychopathologist will have the better claim to be good physician and good citizen."—C. Macfie Campbell, "The Psychopathologist and His Responsibility," *Jour. Abn. Psychol.*, 14: 53] [5]

---

[5] [*Cf.* also George Humphrey, *Jour. Abn. Psychol.*, 15: 350-402; Irving R. Kaiser, *Pedag. Sem.*, 28: 344-346; R. S. Woodworth, "Some Criticisms of the Freudian Psychology," 174-194; A. Wohlgemuth, *A Critical Examination of Psychoanalysis;* and J. Laumonier, *Le Freudism Exposé et Critiqué.*]

CHAPTER XXV

PSYCHOTHERAPY

Psychotherapy, or treatment by mental means, is of course applicable only to "purely mental," *i.e.,* functional, disorders. It is because many types of insanity have some organic basis, it appears, that psychotherapy is not depended upon to empty the institutions for the insane. Even troubles which seem at first to be largely functional are sometimes found to have an organic nucleus which remains after the functional penumbra has been dissipated. This is true, apparently, in certain cases of stammering.[1] Yet even in organic diseases, those physical conditions which are subject to "mental" influences, come within the field of psychotherapy, thereby making psychotherapy a constant resource of every physician. The cancer patient, for example, who loses "spirit" and hence fails to assimilate food well, has a functional disorder of morale, so to say, and needs "non-physical" treatment accordingly. In short, in all processes which are susceptible of re-education, whether the processes in question be central or peripheral to a given disorder, psychotherapy is the suitable instrument.

A number of aspects of psychotherapy have been brought out incidentally in connection with previous topics. Further aspects of this fascinating subject follow.

General Methods of Psychotherapy

Hugo Münsterberg, *Psychotherapy*, 186-192, 194-200, 203-210 (Moffat, Yard, 1909)

The variety of the psychotherapeutic methods is great and only some types are to be characterized here. But one rule is common to all of them: never use psychotherapeutic methods in a schematic way like a rigid pattern. Schematic treatment is a poor treatment

---

[1] *Cf.* Hugo Münsterberg, *Psychotherapy*, 275-276.

in every department of medicine, but in psychotherapeutics it is disastrous. There are no two cases alike and not only the easily recognizable differences of sex and age, and occupation and education, and financial means, and temperament and capacity are decisive, but all the subtle variations of prejudices and beliefs, preferences and dislikes, family life and social surroundings, ambitions and prospects, memories and fancies, diet and habits must carefully be considered. Every element of a man's life history, impressions of early childhood, his love and his successes, his diseases and his distresses, his acquaintances and his reading, his talent, his character, his sincerity, his energy, his intelligence—everything—ought to determine the choice of the psychotherapeutic steps. . . .

The first method to bring back the psychophysical equilibrium is of course the one which is also demanded by common-sense, namely, to remove the external sources of the disturbance. External indicates there not only the outer world but also the own body outside the conscious parts of the brain. If we take it in the widest meaning, this would include every possible medical task from filling a painful tooth to operating on a painful appendix, as in every case where pain results the mental equilibrium is disturbed by it and the normal mental life of the patient reduced in its efficiency. But in the narrower sense of the word, we shall rather think of those sources of trouble in the organism itself which interfere directly with the mental functions. The examination of any public school quickly leads to the discovery that much which is taken for impaired mental activity, for lack of attention, for stupidity, or laziness may be the result of defective hearing or sight or abnormal growth of the adenoids. Growths in the nose may be operated upon, the astigmatic or the short-sighted eye may be corrected by glasses, the child who is hard of hearing may at least be seated near the teacher; and the backward children quickly reach the average level. No doubt in the life of the adult as well, often almost insignificant and from a strictly physical point of view unimportant abnormities in the bodily system, especially in the digestive and sexual spheres, are sources of irritation which slowly influence the whole personality. To be sure, the brain disturbance may have reached a point where the mere removal of the original affliction is not sufficient to reinstate the normal balance of mental energies, but wherever such a bodily irritation goes on, it is never too late to abolish it in the interests of psychotherapy.

The less evident and yet even more important source of the painful intrusions may lie outside of the organism in the social surroundings and conditions of life. Most of that has to be ac-

cepted. The physician cannot bring back the friend who died or
the fortune which was lost in speculation or the man who married
another girl. He will even avoid suggesting far-reaching social
changes in the private life of the patient, changes like divorce in
an unhappy marriage or the breaking of the home ties, however
often he may get the impression that such a liberation would stop
the source of the mental trouble. He will be the more careful not
to overstep his medical rights as he seldom has the possibility to
judge fairly on the basis of the one-sided complaint, and the probability is great that the character and temperament of the com-
plainant may be a more essential factor of the ailment than the
personalities which surround him. Yet even the conservative
physician will find abundant opportunities for advice which will
remove disturbing energies from the social surroundings of the
sufferer. Even a short release from the burdening duties, a short
vacation from the incessant needs of the nursery, a break in the
monotony of the office, may often do wonders with a neurasthenic.
Often within a surprisingly short time the brain gathers the energies
to overcome the frictions with unavoidable surroundings. . . .

[Or] our neurasthenic may complain about the life which he
has to live and yet after all he is frequently so completely adjusted
to it that it may not be in his interest to remove him far away
from the conditions which cannot ultimately be changed but to
which he has to return. The instinct of the physician has to find
the middle way between a temporary removal of irritation which
really allows a development of new energies and a mere interruption
which simply damages the acquired relative adjustment. Every
cause of friction which can be permanently annihilated for the
patient certainly should be removed.

This negative remedy demands its positive supplement. The
patient must be brought under conditions and influences which give
fair chances for the recuperation of his energies. Too often from
the standpoint of the psychologist, the prescription is simply rest.
As far as rest involves sleep, it is certainly the ideal prescription.
There is no other influence which builds up the injured central
nervous system as safely as sound natural sleep, and loss of sleep
is certainly one of the most pernicious conditions for the brain.
Again rest is a great factor in those systematic rest cures which
for a long while were almost the fashion with the neurologist.
Experience has shown that their stereotyped use is often unsuccessful, and moreover that the advantage gained by those months
spent in bed completely isolated and overfed is perhaps due to the
separation and changed nutrition more than to the overlong absolute

rest. Yet used with discrimination, the physiological and the psychical effect of lying in bed for a few weeks has certainly often been a marked improvement, especially with young women. But more often the idea of rest in bed during daytime is not meant at all when the nerve specialist recommends rest to his over-strained patient. It is simply meant that he give up his fatiguing daily work, even if that work is made up of a round of entertainments and calls and social engagements. . . .

Above all, the intensity of mental stimuli is always relative. . . . The rush of stimuli which might mean a source of nervous disturbance for the villager whose quiet country life has brought about an adjustment to faint impressions may cause very slight stimulation for the metropolitan accustomed for a lifetime to the rhythm of the surroundings. Yet that quiet countryman may react in his narrow system not less when the modest changes in his surroundings provoke him. The gossip of his neighbor may undermine his nervous system just as much as a political fight or the struggles of the exchange that of the city man. . . .

Rest ought to have the character of vacation; that means interruptions without the usual activity ought to be short periods spent with the distinct feeling that they are interruptions of that which must last and that they are not themselves to become lasting states. Thus the inner adjustment to the work ought to be kept up and ought not to be substituted by a new adjustment to a less exacting life. In this way the episode of the vacation rest ought to be in a way included in the strenuous life almost as a part of its programme. Strenuosity must not mean an external rush with the gestures of overbusy excitement, but certainly the doctrine of the lazy life is wretched psychotherapy, as long as no serious illness is in question. By far the best alteration is, therefore, even in the periods of interruption, not simply rest but new engagements which awaken new interests and stimulate neglected mental factors, disburdening the overstrained elements of mental life. The most effective agency for this task is contact with beauty, beauty in nature and life, beauty in art and literature and music. To enjoy a landscape ought to be not merely a negative rest for the man of the office building, and good literature or music absorbs the mental energies and harmonizes them. In the second place come games and sport, which may enter into their right if fatigue can be avoided. Harmonious joyful company, as different as possible from the depressing company of the sanitariums, will add its pleasantness.

While the advice of the physician ought thus to emphasize the positive elements which work, not towards rest, but towards a harmonious mental activity, we must not forget some essential negative prescriptions. Everything is to be avoided which interferes with the night's sleep. Furthermore, in the first place, alcohol must be avoided. There cannot be any doubt that alcoholic intemperance is one of the chief sources of brain disturbances and that the fight against intemperance, which in this country is essentially the fight against the disgusting saloon, is a duty of everyone who wants to prevent nervous disaster. . . . In the same way all passionate excitements are to be eliminated and sexual life to be wisely regulated. An especial warning signal is to be posted before all strong emotions, and if the patient cannot be asked to leave his worry at home, he can at least be asked to avoid situations which will necessarily lead to excitement and quarrel and possible disappointment. . . .

Yet this general treatment may take and very often ought to take the opposite direction, not towards rest but towards work, not towards light distraction but towards serious effort, not towards reduction of engagements but towards energetic regulation. . . . Married women without children, without household responsibilities, and without interests of their own and without strong nervous constitution will soon lose the power of effort and their brain will succumb. A dreary monotony is dangerous even for the worker; for the nonworker it may be ruinous.

Yet mere flippant excitement and superficial entertainment is nothing but a cheap counterfeit of what is needed. Voluntary effort is needed, and this is the field where the psychotherapist must put in his most intelligent effort. There is no one for whom there is not a chance for work in our social fabric. The prescription of work has not only to be adjusted to the abilities, the knowledge, and social condition, but has to be chosen in such a way that it is full of associations and ultimately of joyful emotions. Useless work can never confer the greatest benefits; mere physical exercises are therefore psychophysically not as valuable as real sport, while physically, of course, the regulated exercises may be far superior to the haphazard work in sport. To solve picture puzzles, even if they absorb the attention for a week, can never have the same effect as a real interest in a human puzzle. There is a chance for social work for every woman and every man, work which can well be chosen in full adjustment to the personal preference and likings. Not everybody is fitted for charity work, and those who are may be entirely unfitted for work in the interest of the beautification of the town. Only it has to be work; mere automobiling to charity places or talking in meetings on problems which have not been studied will, of course, be merely another form of the disorganizing superficiality. The hysterical lady on Fifth Avenue and the psychasthenic old maid in the New England country town both simply have to learn to do useful work with a concentrated effort and a high purpose. From a long experience I have to confess that I have seen that this unsentimental remedy is the safest and most important prescription in the prescription book of the psychotherapist.

There is one more feature of general treatment which seems almost a matter of course, and yet which is perhaps the most difficult to apply because it cannot simply be prescribed: the sympathy of the psychotherapist. The feelings with which an operation is performed or drugs given do not determine success, but when we build up a mental life, the feelings are a decisive factor. . . . Without some power of awakening this feeling of personal relation, almost of intimacy, the wisest psychotherapeutic treatment may remain ineffective. That reaches its extreme in those frequent cases in which social conditions have brought about an emotional isolation of the patient and have filled him with an instinctive longing to break his mental loneliness, or in the still more frequent cases where the patient's psychical sufferings are misunderstood or ridiculed as mere fancies or misjudged as merely imaginary evils. Again everything depends upon the experience and tact of the physician. His sympathy may easily overdo the intention and further reënforce the patient's feeling of misery or make him an hypochondriac. It ought to be sympathy with authority and sympathy which always at the same time shows the way to discipline. Under special conditions it is even advisable to group patients with similar diseases together and to give them strength through the natural mutual sympathy; yet this too can be in question only where this community becomes a starting point for common action and common effort, not for mere common depression. . . .

From sympathy it is only one step to encouragement, which indeed is effective only where sympathy or at least belief in sympathy exists. He who builds up a new confidence in a happy future most easily brings to the patient also that self-control and energy which is the greatest of helping agencies. The physical and mental efforts of the physician are alike deprived of their best efficiency if they are checked by worry and fear that the developments of the disease will be disastrous. As soon as new faith in life is given, and given even where a sincere prognosis must be a sad one, a great and not seldom unexpected improvement is secured. There is no doubt that the routine physician is doing by far too little in these respects. . . . The nervous patient often needs a larger hold upon life, while the routine prescriptions may too easily reduce that hold by fixing the attention on the symptoms.

Here then is the right place for the moral appeal and the religious stimulation. . . . We should not underestimate the manifold good which can come from the causal effect of religious and ethical ideas. Those faith curists who bring mutual help by impressing each other with the beauty and goodness of the world really bring new strength to the wavering mind; and the most natural channel for religious help remains, of course, the word of the minister and the own prayer. Religion may work there causally in a double way. The own personality is submerging into a larger all-embracing hold and thus inhibits the small cares and troubles of merely personal origin. The consciousness sinks into God, a mental process which reaches its maximum in mysticism. The haphazard pains of the personality disappear and are suppressed by the joy and glory of the whole. This submission of will under a higher will and its inhibitory effect for suppression of disturbing symptoms must be wonderfully reënforced by the attitude of prayer. Even the physiological conditions of it, the clasping of the hands, the kneeling, and monotonous sounds reënforce this inhibition of the insignificant dissatisfactions. . . . Neglected functions of the brain become released and give to the mind an energy and discipline and self-control and mastery of difficulties which restitutes the whole equilibrium, and with the equilibrium comes a new calmness and serenity which may react almost miraculously on the entire nervous system and through it on the whole organism and its metabolism.

Seen from a causal point of view, however, there is no miracle in it at all. On the contrary, it is a natural psychophysical process which demands careful supervision not to become dangerous. It is not the value of the religion which determines the improvement, and it is not God who makes the cure; or to speak less irreligiously, the physician ought to say that if it is God who cures through the prayer, it is not less God who cures in other cases through bromide and morphine, and on the other side, just as God often refuses to cure through the prescribed drugs of the drug store, God not less often refuses to cure through prayer and church influence. But the real standpoint of the physician will be to consider both the drugs and the religious ideas merely as causal agencies and to try to understand the conditions of their efficiency and the limits which are set for them. From such a point of view, he will certainly acknowledge that submission to a greater power is a splendid effect of inhibition and at the same time a powerful effect for the stimulation of unused energies; but he will recognize also that the use of those silent energies is not without dangers.

Certainly nature has supplied us with a reservoir of normally unused psychophysical strength, to which we may resort just as the tissues of our body may nourish us for a few days when we are deprived of food, but such supply, which in exceptional cases may become the last refuge, cannot be used without a serious intrusion and interference with the normal household of mind and body. To extract these lowest layers of energies may mean for the psychophysical system a most exhausting effort which may soon bring a reaction of physical and nervous weakness. The chances are great that such a religious excitement, if it is really to have a deep effect, may go over into a mystic fascination which leads to hysteria or into an exhausting eruption of energies which ends in neurasthenic after-effects. The immediate successes of the strong religious influence on the weakened nervous system, especially on the nervous system of a weak inherited constitution, are too often stage effects which do not last. . . . [From one] point of view, they may be complete successes. They may have turned the immoral man into a moral man, the skeptic into a believer, but the physician cannot overlook that the result may be a moral man with a crippled nervous system, a believer with psychasthenic symptoms. From the point of view of the church, there cannot be too much religion; from a therapeutic point of view, religion works there like any other nervous remedy of which five grains may help and fifty grains may be ruinous.

Moreover this power of inhibiting the little troubles of the body and of bringing to work and effectiveness the deepest powers of the mind belongs not less to any other important idea and overpowering purpose. The soldier in battle does not feel the pain of his wound, and in an emergency everybody develops powers of which he was not aware. The same effect which religion produces may thus be secured by any other deep interest: service for a great human cause, enthusiasm for a gigantic plan, even the prospect of a great personal success.[1]

---

[1] [Some further references on general methods: on considering the individuality of the patient, E. E. Southard and Mary C. Jarrett, *The Kingdom of Evils*, 328-331; on simplifying the environment, the reference just given, and Pierre Janet, *Psychotherapy*, 177-206; on isolation, Janet, *op. cit.*, 47-51; on rest, *idem.*, 85-91; on hobbies and general occupation of mind, including thoughtfulness for others, J. Walsh, *Psychotherapy*, 218-229; on reducing the egocentricity of the psychoneurotic, Boris Sidis, *The Causation and Treatment of Psychopathic Diseases*, 347-348; on general

Special Methods of Psychotherapy

W. S. TAYLOR.   A few portions of this survey appeared in a discussion in
Jour. Abn. Psychol., 20: 82-88 (1925), under the title, " 'Modern Theories
of the Unconscious' (Northridge) : A Review with a Discussion
of 'Repression,' 'Catharsis,' and 'The Unconscious' "

An effective method in a number of the lighter cases, though
not a technical method at all, consists in merely getting the patient
to *confess* his obsessions, to a friend, priest, or physician.[1]   Here it
would seem that the individual's *real* appreciation of his listener's
understanding the unworthiness of the process confessed, is a far
more effective inhibitor of that process than an *imagined* confession
could be.

But a step beyond mere confession is frank discussion followed
by *explanation* by a competent advisor.[2]   Sometimes such explana-

---

personality reëducation, Paul Du Bois, *The Education of Self;* on character
reconstruction through the aid of social service channels, Drucker and
Hexter, *Children Astray;* on therapeusis by extra load or responsibility,
in the case of stutterers, William H. Burnham, *The Normal Mind*, 441; and
in general, Janet, *op. cit.*, 225-226, also Sidis *op. cit.*, 358-362, also in
the general physicians' regimen (of food, dress, sleep, work, recreation) in
Walsh, *op. cit.*, 163-185, also in Southard and Jarrett, *op. cit.*, 335-337d;
on conscious coördination of muscles, Hugo Münsterberg, *Psychotherapy*,
217, also the article by Tom A. Williams on the cramp of writers, etc.,
cited in the present volume, p. 731, *infra*, also the interesting volume by S.
Mathias Alexander, *Man's Supreme Inheritance;* on active and passive
exercises of muscles, Janet, *op. cit.*, 51*ff*, and Shepherd Ivory Franz,
Nervous and Mental Reëducation.   Belonging rather to the category of
special methods of psychotherapy, would be terrorism and infliction of
pain mentioned by Southard and Jarrett, *op. cit.*, 481, and illustrated in
L. R. Yealland's *Hysterical Disorders of Warfare*.]

[1] An interesting case of this came to my attention recently.   A young
doctor of philosophy found his attention being taken up by "hero" phantasies of a particular "small boy" type: he would imagine himself saving
the people of his town from hungry animals which, according to his daydream, had escaped from a passing circus.   This recurrent phantasy obsessed him for several weeks until, by a great effort, he forced himself to
tell it to a friend.   Disgusted at himself as he told it, it never bothered
him again.   A somewhat similar case is described by William H. Burnham, *The Normal Mind*, 410-411.

[2] An excellent exposition of this method intimately related as it is to
the other methods mentioned, is provided in Hugo Münsterberg's *Psychotherapy*, 212-215.   Interesting examples of the method, eschewing unnecessary assumptions, are given by Tom A. Williams, in *Dreads and Besetting
Fears*, 15-20, 97-100, and by E. W. Taylor, in *Jour. Abn. Psychol.*, 6: 449*ff*,
(1912), also in Vol. 5 (1911), and in *Psychotherapeutics*.

tion is made more effective by bringing in the humorous side of the situation.[3] But in any case the explanation must be *realized* by the patient to a degree which is often overlooked.[4] A little more vigorous than explanation, again, is the method of persuasion.[5] This is naturally followed by *practice*.[6] And confession, explanation, persuasion, and practice all involve the effective basis of suggestion, namely, the formation of new associations, reconditioning of reflexes, the basis of that reëducation, whether conscious or subconscious, of which psychotherapy consists. This becomes clear in Münsterberg's case of the psychasthenic physician whom he cured of the feeling that his wrists were cut by having him look hard at his perfectly normal wrists "for ten minutes three times a day after waking, after luncheon, and before going to bed."[7] On the therapeutic uses of *waking suggestion* in general, there is an abundant literature.[8]

But not all therapeutic suggestion is of the waking type. *Hypna-*

---

[3] *Cf.* Tom A. Williams, *op. cit.*, 176-179.

[4] This point is well made by J. A. Hadfield, *Psychology and Morals*, 126-127, and by Tom A. Williams, *op. cit.*, 200-206.

[5] H. E. Wingfield, *An Introduction to the Study of Hypnotism*, 57-58; Williams, *op. cit.*, 176 *ff.*; and J. A. Hadfield, in *Functional Nerve Disease* (H. Crichton Miller, ed.), 82-87.

[6] Williams, *op. cit.*, 190-194; and article on the cramp of writers, etc., in the present volume, p. 731, *infra*.

[7] *Psychotherapy*, 246-249.

[8] One of the clearest accounts is still Hugo Münsterberg's *Psychotherapy*, 215-225. The principle underlying all therapy by suggestion is well brought out in J. A. Hadfield's volume, *Psychology and Morals*, 148-150. Further discussions with examples are the following: Arthur F. Hurst, *The Psychology of the Special Senses and their Functional Disorders;* Hector Charles Cameron, *The Nervous Child*, 113-120, describing a case of enuresis in a child; Morton Prince and Isador H. Coriat, describing the cure by suggestion of a case resembling Jacksonian epilepsy, in *Jour. Abn. Psychol.*, 2: 168-169; special methods, H. E. Wingfield, *An Introduction to the Study of Hypnotism*, 58-59, 153; general methods, J. A. Hadfield, "Treatment by Suggestion and Persuasion," in H. Crichton Miller's volume, *Functional Nerve Disease*, 61 *ff.*; David W. Wells, *Psychology Applied to Medicine;* Alfred Binet, *La Suggestibilité*, with its discussion of the suggestibility of children; Bernheim, *Suggestive Therapeutics;* J. J. Walsh, *Psychotherapy*, 162 (waking suggestion effective as compared with hypnotic), 86 (effects of a popular superstition regarding "amputation stump aches"), and 186-188, 194-198, 242 *ff.* (general); E. R. Micklem, *Miracles and the New Psychology*, 11-14; and, on all types of suggestion, including hypnotic suggestion, Clara Harrison Town, "Suggestion," which provides many valuable references.

gogic suggestion is an important instrument,[9] as is also *hypnotic suggestion,* in its various degrees.[10]   Autosuggestion, finally, now popularized by Coué and Baudouin, is within certain limits a valuable method.[11]

A method claiming greater insight and effect than any variety of suggestion, has been that of *"catharsis."*   Here the patient is induced to revive (in the etymological sense) any "repressed" emotion so as to give that old emotion expression (in the sense of outlet).   This has been taken to mean "emotional catharsis of dammed up libido."   It is only fair to Dr. Freud, whose name has been the most important one associated with this doctrine, to say that in later writings he has emphasized rather the "bringing of submerged memories to the light of consciousness," [12] which, however frequently associated with the method of "catharsis" in practise, is essentially a distinct method.   And that there is *something,* and something important, in the notion of catharsis as such, appears to be true: vesicular or equivalent pressure, unused adrenin, etc., may well result in restlessness until released through some direct or indirect channel.   But if *that* is what catharsis means, then catharsis is not the therapeutic factor often supposed.

It might be supposed to be a mental hygiene factor; and such it has been believed to be, by an enthusiastic group of persons.   These persons see in uncensored "movies," plays, novels, etc., a blessed safety valve for our too-repressed society; a safety valve which will perhaps keep some of us going until the dawn of a Utopia (?) in

---

[9] *Cf.* Münsterberg, *op. cit.,* 225-227.   Haydn Brown (though he says nothing about sleep to his patient), in *Advanced Suggestion,* gives examples of the effects of such suggestion upon hay fever, arthritis, etc., in certain instances.

[10] On the question of the use of hypnosis, *cf.* Albert Moll's *Hypnotism;* and H. E. Wingfield, *An Introduction to the Study of Hypnotism,* 152-154, 184-191.

Excellent examples of the successful employment of hypnotic suggestion may be found in Münsterberg, *op. cit.,* 227-231, 241-246, 256-258, 263-267 (describing mailing his pencil) ; Boris Sidis, *The Causation and Treatment of Psychopathic Diseases,* 376-395, and *Symptomatology, etc.,* 70-72; J. Milne Bramwell, *Hypnotism, Its History, Practise, and Theory,* 154-183; Henry Yellowlees, *A Manual of Psychotherapy, etc.,* 238-239; and John J. B. Morgan, "Hypnosis with Direct Psychoanalytic Statement and Suggestion in the Treatment of a Psychoneurotic of Low Intelligence."

[11] Münsterberg, *op. cit.,* 219, 277-278; Hadfield, *Psychology and Morals,* 150 *ff.;* and Charles Baudouin, *Suggestion and Autosuggestion* (Allen & U., 1921; also published by Dodd, Mead).

[12] Sigmund Freud, *A General Introduction to Psychoanalysis,* 375-376 (Boni & Liveright, 1920).

which inhibitions will be few. True, the "ideal" just described is extreme, and contrary to some of the express statements of the founders of psychoanalysis. But these particular "followers" of Freud may perhaps be pardoned for their excessive inferences, since it seems that Aristotle himself anticipated Freud's notion of "katharsis." What is overlooked, however, is the fact that it was Aristotle, the student of esthetic, whose view agrees with that of Freud; Aristotle as moralist preaches a different and convincing doctrine.

Unfortunately for the view that ready "release" of every emotion means true mental hygiene, there is good reason to regard the failure to learn to inhibit, within reasonable limits, as a failure to develop a well-knit personality: within the limits set by *a real ethics* (as contrasted with any unbiological and unintelligent prejudice), discriminative inhibition appears as a *sine qua non* of integration, just as fatigue (within measure) is necessary in order that development can take place. Hence catharsis in this "mental hygiene" sense cannot serve to guarantee nerve stability for all. Moreover, catharsis in the psychotherapeutic sense of draining off "old pent-up emotion" cannot *of itself* effect any cure at all, as the Freudians early observed, and as will be shown presently.

To turn to the method of "bringing to the light of day," or *recall to consciousness,* as a method of psychotherapy, we find highly interesting cases where such recall has been followed by recovery. Especially important, it would seem, are those instances in which the cure followed a recall which was spontaneous or accidental, without the ministrations of a physician. An example would be an individual who fears open places until, upon going back to his boyhood home, he is reminded of what it was that originally frightened him there; and after recollecting this, fears no more.[13] The surprising recoveries that occur when amnesias are repaired with the help of a psychotherapist, likewise seem highly convincing.[14] Before attempting to interpret or evaluate this method, however, we should note that the recall referred to may be effected in a number of ways

---

[13] *Cf.* English Bagby, "The Etiology of Phobias," and J. A. Hadfield, *Psychology and Morals,* 130.

[14] *Cf.* e. g., H. E. Wingfield, *An Introduction to the Study of Hypnotism,* 128-152; Isador H. Coriat, *Abnormal Psychology,* 173 *circa;* W. H. R. Rivers, *Instinct and the Unconscious,* 185-204; and especially William McDougall, in *Functional Nerve Disease* (H. Crichton Miller, Ed.), 191-192, 194-196, and the general theory of psychotherapeutic recall, 192-193.

which, because they are to some degree distinguishable, may perhaps involve different factors: Recall may be effected, amnesia may be repaired, through (1) ordinary reminiscence, (2) sensible reminders (photographs, letters, visits to old scenes, etc.), (3) analytic inference by the subject himself (*e.g.*, an inference as to where a building must have been, may remind one of the building itself), (4) word association tests directed by the psychotherapist, (5) free association tests ("letting the mind play" about some central point) as directed by the therapist, (6) unexpected recall in moments of spontaneous waking abstraction, (7) lone crystal gazing (*i.e.*, without the ministrations of any helping person), (8) crystal gazing in the presence of the therapist, (9) spontaneous hypnagogic hallucinations in solitude [perhaps very closely related to (6)], (10) autohypnosis (patient solitary but making direct attack upon the amnesia, (11) hypnosis by the psychotherapist with recall as an objective, (12) dreams remembered for the sake of recall, and (13) automatic writing.[15]

Not surprising, in view of the successes that have followed upon recall of dissociated or "repressed" memories, is a general misconception that has grown up about the therapeutic value of recall-as-such. Too many have supposed that recall is *of itself* a curative and prophylactic process; just as the misleading character of the Freudian terminology has led some to think that emotional-

---

[15] The foregoing list was worked out in collaboration with Dr. Elmer Culler of the University of Illinois. A few illustrative references to the literature follow: On (4), C. G. Jung, *Studies in Word Association;* Tait, "A Short Study in Dislike"; Hugo Münsterberg, *Psychotherapy*, 233-235; Justin R. Kaiser, in *Pedag. Sem.*, 28: 358-364; Clark L. Hull and L. S. Lugoff, "Complex Signs in Diagnostic Free Association"; and Morton Prince and James J. Putnam, *Jour. Abn. Psychol.*, 7: 259 *ff.*, 277 *ff.* On (5), Münsterberg, *op. cit.*, 236. On (11), Boris Sidis, *Symptomatology*, etc., 28-32; Münsterberg, *op. cit.*, 231-233, 236; H. E. Wingfield, *An Introduction to the Study of Hypnotism*, 126-152; and the three cases and references by W. S. Taylor in the present volume, pp. 697 *ff.* On (12), H. Tasman Lovell, *Dreams*, 31 *ff.;* and Meyer Solomon, "Analysis of a Single Dream as a Means of Unearthing the Genesis of Psychopathic Affections." On (13), *cf.* the selections from Anita M. Mühl in the present volume, pp. 406 *ff.*

It is interesting too to note that "analysis," often confused with but properly to be distinguished from recall, may proceed through study of phantasies (Jung, *Theory of Psychoanalysis*, 96 *ff.*, and George H. Green, *Psychoanalysis in the Classroom*). "Mental Analysis," also, is advocated by Meyer Solomon ("On the Use of the Term Psychoanalysis and Its Substitute") and by William Healy (*Mental Conflicts*, 19-20, 55-57). Finally, throughout all, the physiological indicators of complexes are watched for, as mentioned for example by Hugo Münsterberg, in *Psychotherapy*, 235-236.

expression-as-such will relieve all the tensions of the soul. The way in which these notions mislead, though supposedly stated on the basis of clinical proof, may be indicated by this query from a student of economics: "I would like to ask," he writes, "what the psychologists would have us do to cure our prejudices. I have heard some say that the correct thing to do is to trot them out and think about them, and perhaps exercise them consciously. That seems to me to be a dangerous proceeding, as likely to start a habit. Of course, merely recognizing a prejudice will not start a habit, but what good would mere recognition of a conflict or prejudice do in solving the conflict or removing the cause of the prejudice?"

The answer which both popular and scientific psychology would give is, of course, that the principle of habit formation has not been superseded as yet, and is not likely to be superseded. And in fact there is excellent experimental evidence to prove that *mere* "bringing up to full consciousness," like *mere* "emotional catharsis," never cures any prejudice or any neurosis. The cures that do result when these practices are professedly engaged in, result from the fortunate incidental fact that in the process, in the confusion of burning down the house to roast the pig, the beast's organization gets changed: in recovering the "submerged affects" of the patient, interesting him in the problems of his dreams, etc., he is led to, or hits upon, new linkages with, new attitudes toward, his old memories; he gains new associations, reconditioned reflexes, re-education.

For example: A woman of about forty years of age is seized with fear and anguish whenever she sees a church steeple or tower of any kind. The patient cannot remember the origin of the fear, when it had originated, nor understand why she is afraid. It is all a mystery. "Free-association" by psychoanalysis reveals nothing either in the waking state or hypnosis. Finally, Dr. Prince, by means of automatic writing in hypnosis, recovers for her a memory of a girlhood experience which was the origin of the fear. This experience related to the circumstances of her mother's illness, subsequent operation and death, during which time the girl went to church daily to pray for her mother's recovery, and cried constantly. At the same time the church bells were ringing and got on her nerves and she "hated them." During the automatic writing, though she is totally unaware of its contents, she exhibits intense mental and physical anguish, and tears roll down her cheeks. After waking, on being shown the writing, she remembers all the incidents referred to, and further narrates in detail an earlier act of disobedience as a child and the way it led to her mother's death, of which, as she believes in consequence, she was the cause. But she now realizes, what she did not know before, that the real object of the fear is the ringing of bells in steeples and towers and that this fear dates from the episode described by the automatic writing. She blames herself for her mother's death which occurred, as she believes, as a logical consequence of her disobedience when a child.

No argument or reasoning on Dr. Prince's part has the slightest effect in changing this false belief or relieving the phobia, nor does bringing the facts to the full light of consciousness alter them.

But when the patient is led to recall and connect a lot of other facts (not forgotten) in her mother's life that give *an entirely different point of view*, she suddenly and dramatically sees for herself that her disobedience had nothing to do with her mother's death. This new viewpoint is at once accepted. She no longer blames herself and she is as suddenly cured.[16]

The same principle is beautifully demonstrated by recalling the shocking memories to the mind of a patient who is under hypnosis, and then recalling the reinterpreting memories and establishing a sounder point of view, giving a new meaning to the buried experiences, all while the patient is hypnotized, and without having those memories brought into the waking consciousness at all. The cure results just the same.[17]

Again, the same principle appears to explain those cases in which a patient is made worse by psychoanalytic efforts. In such instances, the Freudians speak of "incomplete analysis"; or as Dr. Hadfield puts it: "The most real danger in amateur analysis is that it may raise questions and arouse emotional forces which it cannot control. It is essential that, when an analysis is commenced, it be carried through to the end. If we simply probe into a shrapnel wound without extracting all the shrapnel, we make the patient worse: when it is completely extracted the pain ceases and the wound heals. So it is with the mind." [18]   (This author's interpretation of the true rôle of "catharsis" is however essentially the same as the view maintained here.) [19]   But would it not seem most reasonable to

---

[16] Morton Prince, an abstract from *The Unconscious*, 389-410. *Cf.* also 401 n, and 420, *circa*, of that work.

[17] The relative values-in-practice of these two methods (resetting what become waking memories, and resetting memories which are allowed to remain subconscious), is a different problem. Questions like keeping the patient's confidence would seem to enter here.

[18] J. A. Hadfield, *Psychology and Morals,* 131 n.

[19] *Op. cit.,* 128-131.

regard those exacerbations as the natural result of *practicing* the emotional tones of bad memories in the process of recognizing them?

For in this connection it should be acknowledged that to encourage emotional expression during analysis seems to help the recall of memories, if only because such emotion is associated with the memories in the mind of the patient; the recall of memories being effected, as already remarked, to find out on what points the patient needs reëducation.

This is indeed to admit that there are many elements of truth in the *procedure,* though not necessarily in the supposedly corresponding *theory* of the orthodox psychoanalysts. But restatement should free those elements of truth from the utterly misleading implications of the current doctrines.[20]

Whatever be the therapeutic theory and practice followed in any case, however, the final aim must always be, as Dr. Jung has stated it, *"the personal freedom and moral independence of the patient."* [21]

When Recall Is Necessary

MORTON PRINCE, *The Unconscious*, 416-417 (copyright, 1921, by The Macmillan Company); reprinted by permission

All psychotherapy, it seems, requires observation of the *relativeness* of pathological conditions. This is well brought out in the following statement with regard to obsessions, *e.g.:*

---

[20] The above reduction of all psychotherapy to reëducation is not a new idea. *Cf.*, especially, Morton Prince, *The Unconscious*, 5, a view definitely anticipated in his papers, "The Educational Treatment of Neurasthenia and Certain Hysterical States," (1898), "Hay Fever, Due to Nervous Influences, Occurring in Five Members of the Same Family" (1895), and "Association Neuroses" (1891) (*cf.* also his paper, "Traumatic Neuroses," 1889); Tom A. Williams, "Suicide and Civilization"; and the clear exposition by John E. Donley, "Psychotherapy and Education," especially 1-5.

[21] C. G. Jung, *The Theory of Psychoanalysis*, 109.
Of some interest in connection with the general problem of psychotherapy are: Münsterberg's discussion of the application of psychotherapy, especially hypnotism, to those who are not definitely pathological (*op. cit.*, 383-388); and the question of the application of psychotherapy by religious institutions, as discussed by Dr. Richard C. Cabot, in "Whose Business is Psychotherapy?," written at the time of the controversy concerning the Emanuel Movement. This is also discussed by Münsterberg, *op. cit.*, 381-383. Dr. William Healy, in *Mental Conflicts and Misconduct*, 11, suggests that, with regard to those disorders of motivation that result in delinquency, at least, great opportunity for usefulness is open to properly qualified pastors.

There are theoretically two ways in which an obsession might be corrected.

1. A new setting with strong affects may be artificially created [directly, without any deep analysis] so that the [conscious] perception acquires another equally strong meaning and interest.

2. The second way theoretically would be to bring into consciousness the setting and the past experiences of which the setting is a *sifted* residuum, and reform it by introducing new elements, including new emotions and feelings. In this way the old setting and point of view would become transformed and a new point of view substituted which would give a new meaning to the perception.

Now in practice both these theoretical methods of destroying an obsession are found to work, although both are not always equally efficacious in the same case. In less intense obsessions where the complex composing the setting is only partially and inconsequently submerged, and to a slight degree differentiated from the mass of conscious experiences, the first and simpler method practically is amply sufficient. We might say that the greater the degree to which the setting is conscious and the less the degree to which it has acquired, as an unconscious process, independent autonomous activity the more readily it may be transformed by this method.

On the other hand, in the more intense obsessions, where a greater part of the setting is unconscious, has wide ramifications and has become differentiated as an independent autonomous process, the more difficult it is to suppress it and prevent its springing into activity whenever excited by some stimulus (such as an associated idea). In such instances the second method is more efficacious.

CHAPTER XXVI

SOME GENERAL ILLUSTRATIONS

Three Cases Illustrating Mechanisms and Interpretations of Neuroses

W. S. TAYLOR; revised from "A Hypnoanalytic Study of Two Cases of War Neurosis," *Jour. Abn. Psychol.*, 16: 344-355 (1921-1922); and "Behavior under Hypnoanalysis, and the Mechanism of the Neurosis," *loc. cit.*, 18: 107-124 (1923)

THE METHOD EMPLOYED IN THESE CASES

In the following account, the term "hypnoanalysis" is used as Dr. Hadfield and Professor McDougall, respectively, use it.[1] I believe my method is essentially the same as the one they have employed with success in shell shock cases,[2] except that I always give the "explanation" while the subject is still under hypnosis. At that time he seems to be in such an objective, dispassionate frame of mind, that he can check up or revise any hypothetical explanation which is submitted to him, provided he is requested to do so.[3] Then, after its test in this fashion, I feel that the explanation, when positively stated and followed by forcible suggestions, takes hold better than if given when the subject is wide awake. Finally, in the interest of maximal integration, or to obviate any possibility of a forgotten hypnotic incident itself becoming a little dissociated system, the subject is told to remember the entire

---

[1] *Cf. Functional Nerve Disease*, edited by H. Crichton Miller. *Cf.* also H. E. Wingfield, *Introduction to Hypnotism*, 122 *ff.*

[2] As described in pages 67-73 and in Prof. McDougall's chapter in that work.

[3] This experience is quite contrary to Judd's statement that "the hypnotized subject is quite incapable of subjecting any ideas to critical comparison" (*Psychology*, 291). It is a fact that he is relatively incapable of resisting ideas which are urged upon him. But this is why he must criticize ideas, to the limit of his capacity, if he is urged to do so. With the rest of Judd's account of hypnosis, and of its relation to sleep and to the neuroses (aside from his opposition to the use of hypnosis), I can heartily agree.

hypnotic experience upon waking. To make sure such remembering occurs, full notes are kept by a third person.

All three studies were carried out in the summer of 1921.

A CASE OF "SOLDIER'S HEART"

The Neurosis and Treatment. HT, as we may call him from his symptom, is a promising college graduate, aged twenty-five years. His ancestry, which is Scandinavian and British, is vigorous. His father, however, has a quick temper, is unreasonable and threatening toward his relatives, and has deserted the wife and mother. The first home of the family was in a lonely district, where HT grew up very shy and self-conscious in regard to outsiders. "Always of a rather timid disposition," he had a number of severe scares in childhood. He seems to remember these shocks fairly well, however, although he had not thought of the one mentioned below for many years.

At the time of the hypnoanalysis, he complained particularly of a rapid pulse (often reaching 120), which would appear "without cause," as when he was merely reading or talking; and which would always come up upon the slightest physical exertion, failing to go down to normal again for perhaps hours. Strictly speaking, the pulse never went down to normal. For while his lowest ordinary pulse at this period was 92, at the time of his enlistment it had been 72. In addition to the heart trouble, there were intense headaches, nervousness, poor sleep, complete lack of appetite for breakfasts, and general inability to work and recreate. Several medical examinations having revealed no organic defects, HT was hypnotized, and during the hour the following story was obtained:

He is an eldest son. He resembles his mother, and has always gotten along perfectly with her. For his father, on the other hand, he has no affection. His father and mother have disagreed constantly; and shortly after HT's enlistment for oversea's service, his father disappeared without making provision for the wants of the large family.

This desertion on the part of the father left HT much depressed. As he expressed it, he wanted to be up at the front "with the boys," but he feared that in the event of his death his mother would lose her home, and his younger brothers and sisters would have to go to work. For he was now their only support; after his enlistment as "without dependents," he had had to make out allotment papers. He soon came to the conclusion that under such circumstances he was worth more to Uncle Sam alive and well, than through death at the front. In order that his mother might entertain the same hope, he wrote frequent letters telling her that he was in no danger of bodily injury, and that he would probably be kept behind the lines until the war was over.

One day an officer told HT that shell shock involves a rapid heart and general nervousness.[4] Within twenty-four hours from the time of this conversation, as it happened, a shell exploded near our subject. He was seized with a violent trembling, ran some distance, and was shelled again. (At this point in the narrative HT was asked, "Did you ever have a childhood scare in connection with a 'bang' of any kind?" He remembered that when seven years old he had bitten a small powder-cap, with the result that it exploded in his mouth. This had frightened him to the point of violent trembling. His fear had been intensified by his mother's excitement and anxiety about tetanus. The incident had been followed by a headache which lasted for some days.[5]) The night following the shock from the shell, HT lay awake until towards morning. Then after a short sleep he awoke with a severe headache, a rapid, paining heart, general nervousness, and complete lack of appetite. These, it will be noted, are the symptoms which have recurred since the time of shock.

These incidents having been recalled, HT was asked whether, regardless of his conscious intentions, his neurosis had not served as a resolution of the conflict between devotion to country and devotion to mother; whether, that is to say, the neurosis had not made it possible for him to be at once a soldier in France and a living eldest son. He saw at once that this was the case, and assented to the idea heartily.

He was then put much deeper into hypnosis. The operator placed his hand over the subject's heart, and said, "Now, you feel the nervous energy coming back into your heart.[6] This means

---

[4] This item, which came at the beginning of the original course of events, was not obtained from the hypnotic subject until late in his narrative, and then only after close questioning.

[5] On this point of previous formation of pattern through experience and suggestion, cf. E. E. Southard, "General Psychopathology," 193-194; and Frankwood F. Williams, "Anxiety and Fear," 77.

[6] Although I hold to the stimulus-response type of deterministic psychology, I do not regard this suggestion to the patient as a mere metaphor. Rather, his report upon waking that he "felt as though electric needles were going through his heart" (sensations which came purely from suggestion, of course), denoted a real breaking-down of synaptic resistances, a redistribution of nervous energy. One is reminded of Münsterberg's remark, regarding the production of blisters, nose-bleeds, and pulse and temperature

that you will be bothered no longer by any defective innervation causing rapid pulse. From this moment on, your heart will work as it should. Nor will you be bothered by the other symptoms. Your cure will be complete, partly because I tell you so now; but principally because you have recalled the determinants of your troubles, so that you no longer need to behave as though you were still back in that original war situation. And you now *understand, how* you were predisposed to allow that shell shock type of behavior to 'set,' and *why* it is absolutely unnecessary for the reaction to continue. In short, you are cured.

"Now you will remember all these things upon waking, so that you can tell me about them. You will feel fit, able to meet all the ordinary eventualities of life. Tonight, you will sleep well. You will be hungry for your breakfasts, your headaches will disappear; and your heart will be normal. Hereafter, no one will be able to put you into this condition without your deliberate, express, consent. Now as I count ten, you will wake up, cured, and able to tell me all that has been said during this hypnosis."

When awake, the recall, the explanation, and the suggestions were repeated, and HT felt convinced that further trouble was unnecessary. The whole time taken, including that required for the preliminary explanation to the patient, for the hypnosis, and for the waking recall, was approximately two hours.

Outcome of the Treatment. One month after the hypnoanalysis, HT reported verbally that from the day of hypnosis he had had no further trouble from the heart; he was enjoying hearty breakfasts every morning; regularly he was experiencing sound and refreshing sleep; the headaches were recurring with about their usual intensity, but only after severe excitement; and he felt generally stronger and more sure of himself. (The recurrence of the headaches would suggest either a psychically irreducible organic weakness, or an earlier, as yet uncovered functional predisposition toward this trouble.)

About a week after the foregoing report, it developed that HT was operated on for a deviated nasal septum. The operation revealed considerable nasal catarrh and inflammation which had been affecting the eyes and possibly the ears. Correction of the trouble made his head feel lighter and clearer, and enabled him to breathe through his nose instead of through his mouth.

---

changes under hypnosis, that "our understanding of these indubitable facts indeed does not go further than the acknowledgment that the paths for such central connections exist." (*Psychotherapy*, 302). *Cf.* also H. L. Hollingworth, *The Psychology of Functional Neuroses*, 34.

Two months from the time of the hypnosis, he wrote: "I know you are expecting a word from me, and I certainly owe you a debt of gratitude. When you last saw me I was weak—but I have had a fine vacation since and now weigh nearly as much as I ever did. I feel better—surer of myself in every way—thanks to you and Dr. Walton [whose book, *Why Worry*, I had lent HT in order to insure a good mental attitude], I don't feel the morbid curiosities I used to. If you were the discoverer of 'Tanlac' I could write a wonderful newspaper testimonial and tell the world about it—but as it is, all I can do is to tell you of my sincerest gratitude for your interest and help.'

Three months after the hypnoanalysis, HT wrote as follows: "I have continued gaining weight, and now weigh within a pound of what I weighed when enlisted. The Veteran Bureau nurse . . . took my pulse and was surprised to find it 75, standing. . . . I get a great deal of exercise regularly, and the heart is normal. . . . Dr. Walton taught me how to go to sleep, and I sleep soundly. My general efficiency is greatly improved—greater than it ever was before, it seems to me. I have no more of those sharp, splitting headaches which were so troublesome. My morbid curiosities were due to introspection.—'Was I subnormal in bravery?' 'Inferior to others?' 'Were others more intelligent than I?' 'Why didn't I have special gifts like others for music, baseball, or some specialized activity?' I constantly pictured myself inferior to others by comparing myself to them. This may be due to poor teaching early in life. I am getting over this attitude once and for all. I have a career motive now that does away with all this."

Four years later, HT remains well.

Of course it is impossible to say how much of the improvement in HT's condition resulted from the hypnotic treatment, and how much from the surgical operation. But I believe that each removed a great part of the burden upon his system.

Suggested Implications of this Case. HT's neurosis is clearly a result of conflict. But there is nothing "teleological," or "purposive," about it, in any other sense than that all behavior is purposive, from one point of view. The neurosis was a resultant of forces, these forces being response systems, set at various pressures, awaiting opportunity for release. At first, there was prepared, through education, the system for responding to a call to the Front. HT's behavior followed that system, and he went to France. Then all reflexes naturally antagonistic to that course of action were re-enforced by his father's desertion, and were organized into a "wish"[7] to remain alive. The antagonism between these two systems of approach and withdrawal, respectively, was intense. He must inhibit one of them; he must develop a new and peace-making response system; or he must be broken between the urges.

At this juncture, there appeared a third action-possibility in the form of the officer's suggestion as to the nature of shell shock. The suggestion fell upon ground prepared somewhat by heredity, perhaps, but certainly by a childhood experience (the cap explosion) and doubtless by occasional general phantasies about shell shock.[8] This new, implicit sensory-motor "set" was soon touched off as an explicit system, and became the final common path for the opposed major systems. In other words, the new system emerged in the form of a neurosis; that is to say, in the form of a functionally abnormal pattern, a pattern which was *not* adaptive for new situations in ordinary life.

This resulted from several conditions. In the first place, the new system was "stamped in," or fixated, in a moment of great fear; and fear may be, like hypnosis, a time of general dissociation,[9] in which the then unrestrained mental elements can easily be bound into complexes. In the second place, the ideational factors of this system were painful. Hence as their integration would be difficult, they continued their life in the realm of amnesia; *i.e.*, as a system whose cortical portion was dissociated from the rest of the subject's cortical life.[10] Indeed, when the painful system had thus become dissociated, the fear threshold was thereby lowered, making the memories still more painful, still harder to recall (a vicious circle). Again, this separation was perpetuated through a struggle for its own integrity on the part of the system of higher social responses (often called "conscience," "ethical self," or "Censor"). For obviously, these higher responses, as then organized, could not function at the same time that the self-protection (the withdrawing) system was functioning; at least not through the same central apparatus. Hence the higher system found it most difficult to come to terms with one component of the neurosis, and did not effect an intelligent correction of that response pattern. And finally, there was no immediate environmental demand, no great ambition, which compelled an alignment of all the forces of the personality, were

---

[7] As behavioristically interpreted by Holt in *The Freudian Wish.*

[8] *Cf. supra*, p. 699.

[9] *Cf.* Morton Prince, *The Dissociation of a Personality*, 456-459.

[10] Prof. McDougall's theoretical picture of this state of affairs, in terms of nervous organization, appears in his discussion of "The Revival of Emotional Memories and its Therapeutic Value," 26-27.

such an organization possible. The net result was the neurosis: an action pattern, protected by high synaptic resistances from inhibition by the rest of the brain; an automatism, a subcortical redintegration, which, being dissociated, must function mechanically, like a spinal reflex. The individual had suffered a division of his response forces, a division which persisted until he found the desire and the means to attain to re-integration.

Now for the Freudian, this conflict would be a clear case of the "œdipus complex": The son was in love with his mother. It happens, however, that this man was genuinely in love with some one else, and that there seems to have been no "dammed up libido" awaiting "conversion" into somatic symptoms.[11] It would seem preferable to regard the "œdipus" aspect as an infantile fixation of mutual-understanding-and-protection responses, which had grown up through the principle of the conditioned reflex; and which would not have loomed so large in the young man's life had he ever been provided with a wider horizon for his behavior.[12] In this sense it is true that his close home life had not fitted him for meeting the world of facts.

AN EXAMPLE OF WAR NIGHTMARES

DR is a veteran of twenty-two. He is intelligent, well-balanced, and virile. His ancestry, home adjustments, and personal history have been eminently normal.[13]

Upon learning from a friend that I had been working in this field, he came asking to be hypnotized purely for the sake of the experience, not knowing that hypnosis could be put to a practical use. When asked whether he had any morbid fears, or mental bothers of any kind, he remarked that since his return from France he had been generally "on edge," and unable to concentrate well; that he could not sleep more than six hours at a stretch; and that about four nights a week he had a certain nightmare, as a result of which he frequently awoke in the act of choking his bed-fellow, or

---

[11] This statement is proffered with recognition that some Freudians insist such "damming up" must not be interpreted in any crude sense. Cf. Dr. H. W. Frink's Morbid Fears and Compulsions, 268. I think, however, that the "cathartic" aspect of that theory finds adequate answer in Prof. McDougall's article, cited in the preceding footnote; and that the more strictly ontological (libido) aspect receives sufficient treatment in, for example, Dr. George Humphrey's "Education and Freudianism," 384.

[12] Cf. Watson's discussion of the readjustment of outworn habit systems, in his Psychology from the Standpoint of a Behaviorist, 435-440.

[13] Cf. James V. May, Mental Diseases, 194, for evidence that fully normal persons can become neurotic under extreme stress.

found himself on the floor in all sorts of queer postures. The dream which inspired this behavior was about a time in France when he was "cornered up." Of the dream, however, he could remember only the beginning, just as in his waking state he was unable to recall the climax of the actual incident.

Under hypnosis, by the aid of much urging DR recalled the events of a thirty-seven hour gap in his memory. At 2.00 A.M. on a summer's day the sentry had deserted, and his dugout was surprised by Germans. All but four of his party were killed by hand grenades; and of the four, two were captured. The remaining two, the Captain and the subject of this study, escaped into a ravine. Although the place was full of gas, they removed their masks in order to see the way. In spite of this precaution, however, DR became separated from his Captain and never saw him again. DR went on until a piece of shrapnel struck his hand, wounding it and knocking his revolver out in the darkness. At the same time he received sensations of warmth and wetness, which never came into consciousness, however, until this hypnosis, explaining the origin of a wound on his buttock. He tried to press on, but found himself bleeding from the lungs and unable to rise from a creeping position.

After a time DR felt a kick in his side, and looked up to see two Germans standing over him. He tried furiously to get his trench knife, but found that his wounded hand could not be made to grip it. In the struggle, one of the Germans, called Hans, hit him over the temple with the butt of a Mauser revolver. Hans was for leaving DR, but the other German's suggestion that they might be able to get information out of the American resulted in his being carried back to a dugout. Although at least partially unconscious at that time, under deep hypnosis DR was able to recall the appearance of Hans, the stretcher made of two guns and a gray coat, and the bleeding from his buttock upon the coat.

At the dugout, a German Lieutenant and his orderly tried to force DR to drink a lot of black coffee, in order to make him talk. DR explained at this point that when he got back to the hospital, the doctor said that hot drinks were very bad for those whose lungs were full of chlorine. "For some reason" this remark made a great impression upon him, in spite of his amnesia for his own hot drink.[14] The Germans' effort to get information was not successful, however, as he "did not wake up."

---

[14] This is evidence for the essential similarity of a traumatic amnesia to one hypnotically induced. A number of such instances of connection between "the conscious" and "the subconscious" are given by Jastrow in *The Subconscious*, 291 *circa*.

In a short time a heavy barrage started. This was followed by the appearance of a party of Americans who took possession of the dugout. One of the Americans, a Sergeant of DR's own Company, was bayonetted gruesomely. A big Prussian was bayonetted to the doorway and was left standing there, dead. The remaining Germans were marched off as prisoners by American marines. Finally DR was picked up by rescuing hospital corpsmen (one of whose number had been killed on the way to the place) and was put in an ambulance with several wounded German and American soldiers. The roads were very rough, and he experienced such difficulty in breathing that one of the ambulance men gave him a dose of morphine. At the same time the fellow stole DR's spy glasses, remarking: "If this keeps up much longer, it'll be said that the hospital corpsmen won the war, because they'll have all the souvenirs." After the morphine, according to DR, "there were no more rough roads." He woke up in a hospital some hours later, when a nurse was sponging him; and he remembered nothing of all the events that had occurred since he was struck by shrapnel in the ravine.

As this story seemed to cover "every bit of space," DR was told to remember it all upon waking. He was then given the usual positive suggestions, and was aroused gradually.

When awake, DR was most reluctant to repeat the story, because he feared it would give the impression that he was fabricating. Evidently he was so surprised by the outcome of the hypnosis, that he completely forgot the explanation which had been given at the start. His waking narrative was punctuated by such remarks as these:

"Why, a member of my Company just the other day told me that Sergeant K— was wounded, but he did not know how. . . . This must be everything that happened during those thirty-seven hours. . . . Is *that* how I got the scar on my temple? The nurse asked me but I never knew before. . . . So the doctor was right about the buttock wound. He said that it was probable that I got it at the same time that my hand was hit, only I felt no pain from it because I was thinking of my hand. . . . Did that fellow take my spy-glasses? Gee, I'm sorry to remember this, for I know him. If I should meet that guy again . . ," [15] etc.

Thus DR retold his story. At its conclusion, he felt that he

---

[15] Thus far we have been unable to locate the spy-glass man for corroboration of this tale.

understood the situation so well that he would have no more night-mares of the war experience.

As in the preceding case, the total time required was not more than two hours.

(Note: It is not to be assumed that all neurotic cases yield to treatment as quickly and easily as did these. The war neuroses are often among the simplest of functional disorders; and the cases before us were young persons, whose conditions were not compli-cated by present environmental stresses, misleading theories of the origin of their troubles, etc.)

Outcome of the Treatment. One month after the hypnosis, DR reported verbally that he had had only one bad dream, and that he remembered that one upon waking. Otherwise his sleep had been fully up to normal. He felt a new fitness, and a balance, which made his work a pleasure.

Three months from the time of treatment, he wrote: "Since last interview, I had *one* of the old dreams; that night I had eaten welsh rarebit; perhaps this accounts for the dream.[16] From time of experiment to present date, have gained ten pounds and my general condition is improving all the time."

Suggested Implications of this Case. Especially interesting is DR's gain in strength after re-integration. Sometimes this phe-nomenon can be observed through physical measurement. One of Professor McDougall's cases had the strength of his grip increased 200 per cent (from 30 to 90 kilograms) through sudden recovery from a large amnesia.[17] And this would seem to be the natural result. For when antagonistic action systems are in competition for the effector apparatus, only the free margin of the victorious forces can be expected to move that machinery. Or if the compe-tition is such that one third of the cortical apparatus, in repressing

---

[16] Perhaps the welsh rarebit only occasioned the release of a small unre-called portion of the original amnesia. True, he had stated, near the end of his hypnosis, that the history was complete; but I did not urge him to be "absolutely certain" that such was the case, because he had already recalled so many distressing experiences, and because by that time he had been under hypnosis for nearly an hour and a half. But upon waking, he hesitated a great deal when describing the happenings in the German dug-out, and said he felt "there was something more." As he had repeated all that was told during the hypnosis, however, I urged him to recall the rest when awake, or to come back for another, short, exploration of that portion of his memories. This was never done.

[17] *Functional Nerve Disease*, 192. It is gain of this sort, I would add, which explains such sayings of psychoanalysts as "The patient has attained to a soul."

another third, is in a state of deadlock with it, the free third which remains is naturally overworked.

In DR, apparently, we find a robust constitution which was simply broken by excessive environmental demands. The break occurred when DR's powers of resistance were at their lowest ebb; that is to say, in this instance, when his dissociability was greatest. For he was exhausted by severe fighting; he was depressed by the casualties in the ranks of his fellows; he was deprived of the moral support of comrades, even of the strength that comes from fresh air, during his effort to escape; then he was shelled, wounded, unexpectedly struck on the head by his enemies, and was subjected to further mental torture. Much of all this occurred while he was in a partially unconscious condition; and the distance from his waking life was increased by a morphine sleep.[18]

But while the only important conflict in this personality seems to have been that between a pleasant system and a painful system, the methods of repair were essentially the same as those employed in the preceding case: Preliminary explanation, hypnotic recovery of the dissociated system, and re-integration through (hypnotically suggested) waking recall.

A CASE OF CHOKING AND PHOBIA

The Subject and Method of Study. The subject of this study is an American, twenty-five years of age, with a brilliant scholastic record. While there seems to be nothing unusual about his parents, he reports some nervous instability in near relatives. He himself has experienced hallucinations of persons on three occasions, but thinks he may have been dozing during two of them. He believes that he requires an unusual amount of sleep, yet has always been capable of a lot of mental and physical work. Certainly he is an unusually good subject for hypnosis. His complaint was of violent spasms of the throat from which he suffered when drinking cold water or when bathing. These manifestations were accompanied, as he says, by a "feeling of inexplicable fear—horror—an icy hand clutching at my throat—a cold wave sweeping over me." From one aspect of his neurosis, dysphagia, we may call him DY for short.

At the outset, the assumption was made that the neurosis must have resulted from traumata, or from habits, as the case might be,

---

[18] *Cf.* Isador H. Coriat, "The Experimental Synthesis of the Dissociated Memories in Alcoholic Amnesia."

which could be brought out clearly and quickly by getting the sufferer into the most plastic condition possible. Accordingly (though not a universally applicable rule), DY was put into deep hypnosis, and by the aid of persistent questioning with suggestion that he would remember easily, he recounted incidents which had built up the complex. Those tender points in his memories were manifest, during the analysis, through display of emotion and what seemed to be the original motor accompaniments of the experiences. Each such manifestation, instead of being suggested away by the examiner, was deliberately kept in DY's consciousness as an aid to recall. Thus each emotional display served as the basis of questioning which persisted until the subject seemed to have settled that particular score entirely, coming to emotional equilibrium with regard to it.

The Recital and Behavior During the Analysis. The recital was essentially as follows:

When very little, but old enough to wear trousers, DY was "all scared up" by an uncle's stories one winter evening. In particular, he was told that there was something up a tree in the yard, which might come down at him "like that" (clawing with both hands). At the conclusion of these tales, the boy was very thirsty, and wanted to go out to the pantry to get a drink. He was afraid, but went anyway because ashamed of cowardice before his family. The uncle (by marriage) called, "There's a light out there," but the child misunderstood the words to mean that "It" was coming, so was frightened further until his mother explained what had been said. Then he went to the sink, pumped it full of water (he made all the motions here), pumped a tumblerful for himself, and started to drink. He choked on the first swallow,—here, in telling his story, he was seized with terror, and almost awoke from the hypnosis.

Upon further putting asleep, he went on: He did not know why he choked. The window,—(more terror); the door,—; the dog Brownie—. Finally, after much urging, he remembered that a nail was sticking out of his heel ("not a heel like these," pointing to his present shoes), and that the nail caught in the rug by the sink, as though he were going to be held fast. As he hastily pulled free of the rug, he noticed that in the sink, which was very black, the wash basin was going "round and round and round" on the water; and that "there was a funny noise" as bubbles of air came up from the pipe, "just like choking." He was afraid "The Thing" was under the sink, like a frog he had seen in a pond; and that "It" might pull him down in, so the water would choke him by getting up to his mouth, as he had choked when given a bath. Then he was afraid "It" might be under his grandmother's bed, and would come clawing at him through the half-open door on the other side of the pantry.

And as for the window,—there was a storm-window outside, so that the lamp (which "stood *here*," pointing to an imaginary support), and seven tumblers, and a china cup, and some milk-pails, were reflected doubly. (Here he described the various patterns on the seven tumblers.) It was snowing outdoors,—no, he had merely thought it was snowing, but it wasn't really; it was only the flickering lamp, which made the reflections from the tumblers and things dance on the window panes as though it were——raining? Oh! It was this way: There was a lot of snow on the ground, so it could not have been raining. But one time before, when it *was* raining, he had looked up at the window just in time to see a cat trying to get in. That time he was not scared at all; but on this occasion,— "The Thing" must be a *great, big* cat, which was coming through the window to claw him! Why must it be a big *cat?* he was asked. (Extreme emotional resistance, before he was brought around to examining his own memories.) Well, what had happened was that the drain-pipe from the roof was blown around against the window, striking the glass a little below the two reflections of the lamp flame, so forming the crude design of a face. Hence he had thought "The Thing" had indeed come down from the tree.

Thus the shock was built upon earlier experiences. The original cat incident was of no emotional significance at the time it occurred; the sight of the original frog seems to have startled him only a little; but the choking, which he connected so easily with the gurgling of the sink-pipe, was based upon some memories of intrinsic importance. It developed that his mother had told him that if he went down near the river, a big old man would come out clawing after him, to pull him under the water; he had seen "Brownie" swim out, and feared the dog would choke; one time "Brownie," wet from the river, had jumped into DY's crib and given him a momentary fright; as a small child, he called water "do-ut," because of the noise it made in the sink-pipe; for "a long, long time" he had a terror of being bathed, and would scream as his grandmother put him in the little tin tub, often getting water in his mouth so that he choked ("the dish with yellow soap in it stood *here*, . . ." etc.); and his fear of baths went back to a time when, as a baby, he had pulled a quart of water over upon himself, with both choking and spanking as a reward. "That's the first time I was really scared," he said, as this incident was recalled, almost at the close of the two-hour period. The air of relieved finality with which he added, "That's everything that's important," was interesting, to say the least.

This self-criticism appeared throughout the whole narrative, however, as a few more illustrations will suggest. "Was that the door which opened into your grandmother's room?" he was asked at one place. "No, no, no, that was the door to the kitchen." And, in passing, he described the funny oak graining on the door. "Wait a minute," he would say. "Something is wrong here. I was in dresses when this happened, and yet the water pitcher which my mother was carrying, was one we got after I was five years old. It was a yellow pitcher, with red roses on it. . . . Oh, I am mixing up two different times." Again, "Now I see a baby, lying on a bed,—this does not seem real. Am I that baby? No, I must be imagining it, because I've heard my mother tell of it. She said I pulled some water over on myself. Before I could walk. —*I* can't remember doing any such thing, though; I can't remember it at all.—Oh! Yes! That's right! I *was* the baby! I was lying on the bed in the large room, with the pillow *here*" (gesture), "to keep me from rolling off; and the little table *here;* and on the table was a quart measure full of water, *here.* I was on the floor all afternoon, and I would creep, creep, creep" (making the motions with enthusiasm), "and I got dirty *all* over the front of my dress. And my grandmother washed me, and dressed me up clean, to go to a party at X's, and laid me on the bed. And then I pulled the quart measure over, and the water went all over me, in my mouth, and in my ears, and all over my clean dress. And my mother was mad, and spanked me."

At the conclusion of his story, it was explained to DY, while still under hypnosis, that these things were the causes of his throat spasms, and that since he would *remember* and understand all this upon waking, he would appreciate the difference between the early water situations and those of the present, so that he would have no further trouble. He remembered so well, indeed, that when awake he was able to make a sketch showing where each of the important experiences occurred. He was told to keep his drawing as a memorandum; and to recall the details and practise auto-suggestion when going to sleep at night, and again upon awakening in the morning, should the trouble ever come back. This has not happened, however, as he went swimming the next day, and during the two years which have elapsed since the evening of the hypnoanalysis he has had no recurrence of the spasms. Also, he felt an increase of energy, with seeming greater power to withstand the stresses and strains of daily life; just what we should expect from a release from conflict.

The Validity of the Memories. Before being aided by hypnosis, DY had been able to remember scarcely anything of what he described so fully in the two hours. He says, however, that he had often been observed to cry out and make motions in his sleep, very similar to those which occurred during the hypnosis. This suggests that he must have had dreams which, if studied by Dr. Horton's methods,[19] would have made possible a similar recovery of dissociated experiences.

As for the historicity of DY's account, the data are, unfortunately, very inadequate. According to his family, he was being washed upon one occasion in a little wooden tub, not tin as the hypnotic account gave it, when his leg got wedged in so they had great difficulty in getting him out. Granting for the moment that the memories of his family are more reliable, after twenty years, than his own hypnotic report, perhaps the question would be: How accurate, as to details like the material of the tub, must the recall be in any case, in order to fix adjustment with regard to that point? In other words, if a "repressed" memory is to be recovered, is it always essential that it be brought back into consciousness with any more vividness than belongs to the other memories of the same period? Such items as the designs on the seven tumblers, too, we would check up if we could.[20] But in this instance we shall have to content ourselves with the description of the analysis.

However, we should grant the possibility of the truth of Dr. Jung's contention that "the earlier in childhood an impression is said to have arisen, the more suspicious is its reality"; its reality, that is, as a historical event, though not as an etiologically real factor. It may well have been a positive factor in the formation of the neurosis-pattern, through the child's having practised that pattern through phantasy; phantasy which may have been projected back into the past, with ultimate conviction by DY of historical truth, but on the basis of the fears later instilled, plus a few remembered minor incidents.[21] And there is evidence that some very early incidents are remembered even when normally awake.[22]

---

[19] *Cf.* Lydiard H. Horton, "Resolution of a Skin Phobia with Nightmare." *Cf.* also Pierre Janet, *The Mental State of Hystericals*, 95. Similar, also, in the mechanism of the neurosis, is the War Nightmares case, just described.

[20] Some verifications of the truth of subconscious memories of this sort have been made. *Cf.*, *e. g.*, Dr. Morton Prince, *The Unconscious*, 18.

[21] *Cf.* C. G. Jung, *The Theory of Psychoanalysis*, 92.

[22] *Cf.* Guy Hamilton Crook, "A Memory of Infantile Life."

Some Recent Explanations of the Neurosis. In spite of the aqueous nature of this man's troubles, there seems to be nothing sexual about them, unless we are under compulsion to read sexuality into the boy's attitude of listening to his uncle, or of cringing before the chimerical cat at the pantry window.

Nor do we have to hold "the libido" responsible,—though I believe there is a sense in which "the libido" may serve as a most useful term, not for a metaphysical entity, but for a certain *grouping* of affective and emotional behavior-processes.

A more down-to-earth hypothesis for such cases has been proposed by Professor Max Meyer. Professor Meyer insists at the outset that we must distinguish two functions of the neuron: (1) increase of conductivity due to "change in the permanent chemical properties of the neuron"; [23] and (2) "some imaginable kind of increased permeability *between* neurons . . . by contact improvement . . . —this is a conceptual peg on which to hang innumerable facts—a *temporary* stretching of the dendrites as always resulting from the passage of a current through them. *The important thing here is that we avoid thinking of a permanent change in the whole neuron.*" [24] What is thought of is a temporary functional change [25]—contact improvement—which is due to such continued functioning of some nerve-paths through the higher centers [26] that nervous currents in other pathways are diverted into those involved in the occupation of the moment, or more precisely, in the "preoccupation." [27] And it is this conception of "preoccupation" by which Professor Meyer intends to explain close attention, absentmindedness,[28] hypnosis,[29] and the neuroses; the neuroses being only very persistent preoccupations.[30]

Indeed, neurotics as well as neuroses are explained in the same way, for Professor Meyer. For "if we hold the contact improvement in the synapses of any higher centers responsible for any symptoms of preoccupation, it follows that these neuron terminals must have in these abnormal cases an inherited tendency to 'stick' after having extended in consequence of a nervous flux passing through them. Normally they would recede within a few seconds or minutes after the cessation of the nervous currents. These neurons in the case of this neurosis seem to have lost this ability to recede again. The consequence is that, whatever nervous current passes through the

---

[23] *The Psychology of the Other-One*, 125.

[24] *Ibid.*, 93. [25] *Ibid.*, 130.

[26] *Ibid.*, 202, 95. [27] *Ibid.*, 95.

[28] *Ibid.*, 94. [29] *Ibid.*, 393.

[30] *Ibid.*, 383.

nervous system, finds through these synapses a path more conducive than it ought to be." [31]

Certainly it would seem natural that the synapses of some individuals might have a trick of surrendering completely to powerful nerve-impulses, so that they would never be able to "come back" for new adjustments as required. And this would seem to explain perfectly some of the mild types of emotional fixation like those in certain "œdipus" cases and some fetichisms, a number of neurotic cases,[32] even some varieties of dementia præcox, possibly, as far as "mental" mechanisms are concerned. Also, such impressionability as Professor Meyer describes would explain many "over-determinations" in intellectual and motor spheres, including certain individuals' lack of ability to outgrow early prejudices and personal attitudes generally.

But clearly Professor Meyer's theory of "contact improvement" implies relative contact *un*improvement occurring simultaneously in other parts of the nervous system; for otherwise the diversion of nervous current, so characteristic of "preoccupation," would not take place. However, before deciding whether "contact improvement" is sufficient explanation for *all* functional neuroses, we may consider another recent effort to provide neurological description for neurotic phenomena. This other theory is Professor H. L. Hollingsworth's conception of "redintegration."

According to this view, "Redintegration is to be conceived as that type of process in which a part of a complex stimulus provokes the complete reaction that was previously made to the complex stimulus as a whole." [33] Such behavior is neurotic whenever a response so released fails to take account (through the individual's "sagacity") of essential *differences* between the present environment and the original situation; in other words, when the response is to a detail of the original situation which is irrelevant to the present case. In fact, "the more irrelevant the detail responded to the more lacking in sagacity, and hence the more psychoneurotic is the individual to be considered." [34] This single principle [35] of redinte-

---

[31] *Ibid.*, 383-384.   [32] *Ibid.*, 384-387.

[33] H. L. Hollingworth, *The Psychology of Functional Neuroses*, 19.   Prof. Hollingworth mentions Hamilton as having used the term "redintegration." The mechanism Prof. Hollingworth describes by it has also been pointed out by Dr. Prince as follows: "It is possible that, through chemical changes of some kind left in the system of neurons corresponding to an experience, the neurons may become sensitized so as to react again as a whole to a second stimulus applied to one element." (*The Unconscious*, 122).

[34] *Ibid.*, 21.   [35] *Ibid.*, 15, 18.

gration Professor Hollingworth aims to substitute for the variegated and more or less metaphorical descriptive concepts which have been proposed to explain neurotic phenomena in recent years.

Thus while Professor Hollingsworth's view does not allow for particularly temporary reduction of neuron resistance, his theory is nevertheless similar to Professor Meyer's in that it reduces to *linkage*-property of neurons.[36] For Professor Hollingworth, as for Professor Meyer, neuroses are cases where elements of experience got stuck together so hard that they were not able to break up again as new occasions demanded. And hence "redintegration" would similarly explain, for example, the fixation of aversion to ice-cream through finding a hair in it under embarrassing circumstances on a consciously remembered occasion.[37]

But it becomes evident, as one reads further in Professor Hollingworth's exposition, that the single principle of redintegration is not able to support all of the explanatory burden. To begin with, he points out that the redintegrative mechanism easily becomes conspicuous "in ordinary conditions of exhaustion, fatigue, drowsiness and delirium," [38] though what factor accounts for the production, or the revelation, whichever it is, of the mechanism at these times he does not make explicit. When he comes to explain, however, the predisposition of certain individuals to neuroses, he says: "The normal nervous system is so organized and integrated that activity in any arc or on any level is definitely under the influence of determining tendencies and action patterns operating in the system as a whole, and in its various parts. The response to one detail of a situation is thus conditioned by the relevance of this item to the context, to the total experience . . ." In the nervous system of the psycho-neurotic, on the other hand, there is a marked tendency for the system of *"relatively* successful organization of complex arcs and levels . . . to respond always by total reaction patterns, to prepotent but often irrelevant details of a new situation.

---

[36] This idea has also been stated in the language of conditioned reflexes, especially by John B. Watson, in "Behavior and the Concept of Mental Disease." In view of what follows in the present discussion, however, we may note that Dr. Watson recognizes naturally the occasional abeyance of "the normal associative mechanisms upon which the individual depends for inhibitory or counter-suggestions." (*Psychology from the Standpoint of a Behaviorist*, 335).

[37] An example cited by Prof. Hollingworth, *op. cit.*, 46. Even in this case, however, we ought perhaps to inquire whether the aversion was not based partly upon older associations, in the manner explained by Dr. Prince, *The Unconscious*, 395-410.

[38] *Ibid.*, 29. *Cf.* also, 53, *circa.*

. . . Faulty sagacity, rather than faulty learning, to use James's terms, is at the bottom of the difficulty. A marked tendency to dissociative activity or a pronounced insufficiency of 'nervous energy,' both of them old concepts in this field, and given special importance by Janet, are not without suggestive value here." [39]

General Mechanism of the Neuroses. Clearly the *establishment* of nervous connections can be but half the ultimate explanation of the neuroses. For while for convenience in description, emphasis upon such establishment of connections may often be sufficient, as already suggested there is necessarily the complementary factor of relative reduction of nervous connections in other parts of the nervous system. And for many neurotic phenomena, as I shall attempt to show, the mere establishment of nervous connections is not even convenient explanation; in some neurotic phenomena it is the disjunction of neuron connections, *dissociation* (though *perhaps never complete*), which deserves the emphasis.[40]

True, some have objected to the idea of dissociation, on the ground that it is not *dynamic* enough, or something of the sort.

---

[39] *Ibid.*, 63-64. Italics mine.

[40] I take the term dissociation in a physiological sense primarily, though not thereby excluding its application to "mental" states as well (as explained in the "Conclusion," below). To quote from Dr. F. L. Wells' *Mental Adjustments*, 154: "In so far as the organic functions proceed independently of one another, they are dissociated. In so far as they modify one another, they are integrated." Dr. I. H. Coriat, in his *Abnormal Psychology*, 7, puts it in more mental terms. "A mental dissociation is . . . directly opposite to a mental synthesis. By the former, we mean that experiences are detached or split off—by the latter, that these split off experiences are made whole again." Prof. Charles H. Judd, in his *Psychology*, Ch. XIV (cited in the present Vol., pp. 189 *ff.*, *supra*), applies the idea of dissociation to hypnosis (as does Prof. McDougall in his article "Hypnotism") and to sleep and dreams. Here he agrees with Prof. Knight Dunlap's position on sleep and dreams; for while Prof. Dunlap does not use the term dissociation, he speaks of "high" integration as contrasted with that "low" or "reduced" integration which occurs "when the integration of the nervous system falls to pieces, as it manifestly does during sleep" (*Jour. Abn. Psychol.*, 204). This point of view is for Prof. Dunlap a corollary of his description of the functional dependence of consciousness upon "the systematic activity or coöperation of large groups of cells, . . . *integration* of the nervous system" (Knight Dunlap, *Elements of Scientific Psychology*, 206-207). The same conceptions, again, are employed by Prof. Warren, in his *Human Psychology*, 346-349, *circa;* while Donald E. Core, M.D., suggests neurological basis for dissociation, in his *Functional Nervous Disorders*, Ch. VIII. It seems clear that, granted the economical principles of neurones (at least functionally) coming together and going apart, we are able to explain a host of mental complexities.

Thus Dr. T. W. Mitchell thinks "dissociation" involves too great emphasis upon "the purely cognitive aspect of consciousness," to the neglect of the real efficacy of "the emotions and the will." [41] But if science is largely a history of escapes from animistic ways of thinking, and if entifying conceptions of "the will" have shown themselves to be much worse than useless in psychological theorizings, may we not forget our love for finding our own pre-Humian images even in human nature, and adopt instead the economical type of description which is characteristic of science?

Again, Dr. Mitchell is unable to see how the dissociation point of view can tell where dissociations (amnesias) *are* remembered, and how sensations from anæsthetic areas *are* somehow felt, when we consider [his conviction that] "we have no knowledge of any thoughts or feelings that are not the thoughts or feelings of some personal self." [42] In reply to these objections, it seems to me that we need only ask whether by all the wrestlings of the metaphysicians a "personal self" can explain *any* memories, to say nothing of dissociated memories; and whether such a personality can explain *any* feeling, let alone the sensations from anæsthetic areas which are indeed registered somewhere in the nervous system. It is by correlating such processes with physical phenomena that we can most comfortably think and communicate our ideas of them.

Even Professor Hollingworth objects to dissociation as an explanatory conception, partly on the ground that dissociation, and similar concepts, lack "entirely the dynamic descriptive value which a given concrete case merits and fail to account for the personal and individual direction clearly present in the reaction of individual neurotics." [43] Incidentally, Dr. Mitchell raises the same objection when he says the dissociation theory fails "to account for the localization and nature of the defect in any particular case." [44] This argument seems answerable simply by pointing out that dissociation may take as many forms as do the bits of china that were once a dish, or as do the fragments of organized mental life displayed in dementia præcox cases.[45] (We avoid raising here the question as to just what "dynamic" means.)

Dissociation is thus not limited to the mere fading out of what-

---

[41] *The Psychology of Medicine*, 40.
[42] *Op. cit.*, 33.
[43] *The Psychology of Functional Neuroses*, 17.
[44] *The Psychology of Medicine*, 39.
[45] *Cf.* Dr. F. L. Wells' *Mental Adjustments*, Ch. V, "Types of Dissociation."

ever nervous activities the organism happens not to be preoccupied with. On the contrary the breaks often occur *between* preoccupation systems, *between* redintegrations even, so that action patterns are left to pull against one another in certain situations. This is most obvious, of course, in studies like Dr. Morton Prince's *Dissociation of a Personality,* but the same mechanism is often observable in, for example, the war neuroses.[46]

For while scholastic simplicity is our heritage in psychological theory, and while such phrases as "the integrative action of the nervous system" tend to confirm too simple habits of thinking, we know that action patterns do not always coöperate ideally. The ass between the two bales of hay is paralleled, more or less, by the man who gazes blankly at his newspaper when spoken to, but without comprehending either the print or the question for a moment;[47] by the individual who is having difficulty making a momentous decision; by the spinal dog whose left scratch reflex is inhibited by a stimulus to the right foot;[48] and by the neurotic with unresolved conflicts,—conflicts, *i. e.,* between uncoördinated response systems.[49] In every similar case, it would seem, there is no complete "inhibition by drainage" until the connection for such drainage is established at as high a level in the nervous system as may be necessary; and until such connection is established, the organism must function very crudely, inefficiently, at odds with itself, perhaps in merely *emotional* response.

For the theory that strong emotion [often] originates in conflict between action patterns[50] certainly explains a host of facts. We

---

[46] The writer attempted to show this in the preceding two cases.

[47] Stevenson Smith and Edwin R. Guthrie, *General Psychology,* 46.

[48] Charles S. Sherrington, *The Integrative Action of the Nervous System,* 135-136.

[49] As Dr. Prince has expressed it: "Psychology deals with concrete phenomena which are the resultants of a complexity of forces driving in different directions. The law of the final drive is more comparable to the physical law of the 'resultant of forces.'" (*Jour. Abn. Psychol.,* 15: 135.) For further description of human personality as a composite structure functionally related to the environment, *cf. The Unconscious,* 530; also Chs. XV and XVI, which describe the mechanisms of conflicts.

[50] As developed by Angell (after Dewey): "The emotion itself is in essence our *consciousness* of the *conflict* between the several reactions which the stimulus tends to call forth." Thus our emotion at the sight of an advancing bull is strong as our curiosity and our flight impulses conflict; and the conflict does not subside until the several groups of coördinations "are in some way unified and brought into a larger and more inclusive coördination." For example, with reference to the bull, "if we succeed in *really* putting our *whole* minds into the running, the emotion of fear is

should note, however, that conflict frequently (at least) results in *regression, or regressive dissociation,* as the higher levels give up functioning first. And apparently the basic mechanism of such regression resembles that of the confusion studied by Dr. Roback, where the subject was met by more stimuli than he could respond to adequately in the time allowed, with the result that his behavior degenerated through inferior coördinations to random reactions and blankness of mind.[51] Thus it was that our subject DY, for example, was frightened, intellectually confused, by the excessively weighted stimuli that came to him on the evening of his big scare.

A most important further fact in this connection seems to be that such a situation favors the stereotyping of certain response patterns; if not because of greater synaptic impressionability at that time, then certainly because, as in hypnosis, the ground is relatively clear—the mind is relatively free from the usual competing ideas, inhibitions. Neurotic impressionability, like suggestibility, certainly increases as competing ideas fall away.[52] Perhaps this should be explained partly through the "preoccupation" which Professor Meyer elucidates; only we would add that it is at a time of general dissociation that any afferent impulse finds no central mechanism of overflow ready, and hence must all press on through whatever efferent outlet does get into operation.

One further aspect of the general situation deserves our attention, before passing on to concrete application to the case in hand: Though DY's ideational systems were dissociated as above, and unadaptive response patterns were impressed, there was throughout

---

practically at an end." (J. R. Angell, *Psychology*, 328, 329, Holt, 1904. The last italics the compiler's, in view of the contextual assertion by Dr. Angell that although there may under the conditions supposed be no *emotion* of fear, there may be very vivid consciousness of another kind.) So, also, Breese writes: "In emotions there is a sudden stoppage of all the avenues of mental activity. Especially is there a blocking of the higher cognitive activities. We are seized, as it were, by emotions. The neural excitement caused by an emotional object or event fails to be adequately drained off through the usual channels of adjustment. As a consequence the nervous energy aroused is turned back into the organism and diffused throughout the organic and motor pathways, thereby causing a condition of conflicting bodily impulses." (B. B. Breese, *Psychology*, 374-375, Scribner, 1921. *Cf.*, also, 391*ff.*) All this reminds us of Spinoza's explanation that an "emotion, which is called a passivity of the soul, is a confused idea . . ." (Ethics, Part III, last section) ; and "an emotion, which is a passion, ceases to be a passion, as soon as we form a clear and distinct idea thereof." (Ethics, Part V, Prop. III.)

[51] *Cf.* A. A. Roback, "The Interference of Will-Impulses," 50, 93.
[52] *Cf.* Prof. McDougall's article, "Suggestion."

all a singular unity of emotion, for while he did not know what memories were (subconsciously) functioning when he had his choking spells, he always knew what emotion (fear) was going on. (He also felt the tugs of the fright-system's muscular operations, without being normally aware of the stimuli for those responses.) Thus he resembled the victims of phobias, infatuations, etc., who do not know where their bothersome emotions come from;[53] just as a person who dreams may have his ideation colored by some fundamental emotion;[54] the mechanism being apparently identical with that which operates in the automatic writer who, while answering whispered queries to which his main personality is deaf, may not suspect that those "foreign" emotions which surge into his main consciousness from time to time during the writing are only the emotions which the operator is touching off at will by words directed to the secondary conscious system, the automatically writing system. Although intellectually dissociated, emotional unity remains.

Explanation of this Case. In DY we have, then, not an animistic enigma, not a hierarchy of spooks, but a system of reflexes[55] whose elements were not pulling together properly.[56]

It may be that DY was easily disorganizable, dissociable, by original nature; or perhaps he was made fragile by some very early shock which broke some off, leaving the remainder less able to meet emotional stresses, as seems to be the situation in an unrepaired war neurotic. At any rate, according to the story, as a child and at a time when his integrative resistance was perhaps weakest, DY had been worked up to a great emotional pitch by the suggestions coming from a high authority, his uncle. This had amounted to such a disintegration of his higher centers that he was at that

---

[53] As explained by Dr. Prince, *The Unconscious*, 3; *The Dissociation*, 133; and in many other places; also by Dr. Frederick W. Mott, *War Neurosis and Shell Shock*, 121.

[54] *Cf.* Lydiard H. Horton, *Jour. Abn. Psychol.* 15: 12; and in others of his articles. *Cf.*, too, his volume, *The Dream Problem.*

[55] Reflexes, *i.e.*, in the broad sense in which the term is used in Dr. John B. Watson's *Behavior*, 184.

[56] This is not intended as confession of faith in Hume's theory of mental atomism. On the contrary, I believe every person can obtain ready proof for James' thesis that consciousness is characterized by continuity—*as consciousness*, we should, add; since unity of this type appears to obtain in each system of higher reflexes (main consciousness, secondary consciousness, etc.) there may be. But it is more convenient to use objective language here; as explained in the "Conclusion" of this paper.

moment susceptible to the formation of some rigid new patterns of conditioned reflexes.

The pattern so formed was a painful one, one associated with intense fear, and therefore one which he would naturally allow to rest in peace, as far as possible; he would tend, that is, not to do that, apparently as an animal tends to avoid some painful course of action. Thus the fright-pattern was not given a place in that system of reflexes which was his regular waking consciousness, and which included his speech apparatus.[57] Had the fright-pattern *been* linked on to the "higher" system, as for example by talking the whole thing out with his mother until he became negatively adapted to the incident, he would have known what he was about thereafter when drinking cold water; the fright-pattern being inhibited into relative insignificance, by other responses which were developed with regard to the same stimulus.[58] As it was, however,

---

[57] This is not an effort to maintain that consciousness and (at least implicit) speech-behavior are metaphysically one and inseparable. It would seem far more reasonable to expect to find "consciousness" wherever we find integration involving the higher centers. Then there could be a consciousness associated with the speech apparatus, and different consciousness associated with the right hand, etc.; exactly in line with Dr. Prince's findings regarding the life of coconscious personalities (*The Dissociation*, *etc.*).

[58] This brings out the fundamental distinction between inhibition and dissociation. It is true that there are *resemblances* between dissociation and normal inhibition, as the late Dr. W. H. R. Rivers suggested. When, *e.g.*, a dominant system of ideas is not functioning, a suppressed one, perhaps a neurosis pattern, may readily manifest itself, reminding us of the way protopathic sensibility appears when epicritic sensibility has been put out of the way (W. H. R. Rivers, *Instinct and the Unconscious*, 25). And again, just as normal inhibition is primarily an aid to survival, so the immediately self-protective character of cortical dissociation is apparent in that the dissociated elements are frequently those which when recalled would be painful and therefore prejudicial to the best immediate health of the organism (*ibid.*, 35). It is on such grounds that Dr. Rivers proposes that "the suppression by which experience becomes unconscious is only a special variety of the process of inhibition, common to every phase of animal activity." "In all cases we have to do with the means by which behavior, whether of human being or animal, is adjusted to the needs with which man or animal is confronted" (31).

Dr. Rivers admits, however, that such dissociation (called suppression by him) "is a process of reaction to the pleasures and pains which are immediately present, and takes no account of the more extended experience with which it is the function of intelligence to deal" (21); whereas regular inhibition is essentially discriminatory and adjustmental for complicated conditions (30-31). When we consider, too, the great decrease in the amount of overt mechanical work which can be done by a dissociated, conflictful organism, as contrasted with that efficiency which is characteris-

if the fright-pattern was not actually torn away from the other
nerve centers by some disruptive effects of emotion, that pattern
at least failed to have the pathways *much* worn [59] between it and
the other patterns which composed our man DY; the result was a
dissociated system.

As such a system, however, the fright-pattern maintained at
least occasional communication with the outside world, responding
overtly, though on the side (*i. e.,* unconsciously, as far as "DY" [60]
was concerned), to at least one stimulus, cold water. This stimulus
necessarily operated upon the fright-system through some channels
of sense, possibly, *e.g.,* through cold-spots on certain areas which
were dissociated into this fright-system.[61] But to the fright-system,
the stimulus was not, as to us, "cold water, useful to life," it was
something distinctly opposed to all the best interests of life. The
(redintegrative) responses naturally given then were in the form
of choking, trembling, etc., and *fearing.* (All of these responses
were "defensive," but quite mechanically so; the "teleological"

---

tic of normal integration, it seems clear that while cortical dissociation
may be phylogenetically related to adjustmental inhibition, pathological
dissociation is such a degenerate branch from that stock as to deserve a
different name.

(Dr. Rivers uses the term dissociation, but in a special sense, as contrasted with "suppression" [which I have been calling dissociation]. Dr.
Rivers prefers to limit the use of "dissociation" to suppressions which have
an independent and conscious activity of their own [*op. cit.,* 73, 76]. "Alternate consciousness" and phobias, he thinks, do not have such consciousness [75, 78]; something, I think, we are not at all sure of. Dr. Rivers then
goes on to suggest that there are different degrees of dissociation, degrees
which resemble epicritic and protopathic behavior [82], and which answer
in some sense to biological need. But he acknowledges that the "furtherance of the growth of intelligence would follow even more naturally from
the substitution of a process of integration for an earlier phase in which
experiences which did not readily harmonize were kept in the separate
compartments provided by the process of dissociation" [81].)

[59] I say *"much* worn," because all psychoanalysis by free association, for
example, suggests that the law of "association by contiguity," conditioning
reflexes elsewhere in the nervous system, holds universally; the only variation being as to how far above or below the threshold of consciousness the
learning has gone. Though the wearing of pathways be very small, and
totally unconscious, it is very important when it comes to getting the
connections fixed up again, through recovery of the memories that constitute the complex. *Cf.* Prince, *The Unconscious,* 421-422, 483.

[60] I use the quotation marks from this point on to distinguish "DY," the
main consciousness, from DY, the entire organism with its several stages
of integration.

[61] Clear instances of this mechanism are given in Dr. Prince's *The Unconscious,* 29, 35, 56-59, 105, and 357.

character of the whole being accounted for simply in terms of the stamping in of defensive reflexes at the time of original shock.)

But the stimulus so aggravating to the fright-system was also responded to by the other system of reflexes which we are calling "DY"; and this response was very different. For "DY" the cold wet stimulus *was* "cold water, very useful to life." Thus the same stimulus had tremendously different meanings,[62] different values, for the two systems. And it was when the two systems began to function at the same time, literally competing about the same stimulus, that the trouble began. For they got in each other's way. "DY," wishing to drink, found his throat muscles behaving in a way that he did not will, and at the same time felt an emotion which he did not desire. "DY," that is to say, responded to the stimulus by those movements which are preparatory to drinking, while at the same moment the fright-system initiated responses (at a lower level) which go with avoiding the stimulus. "DY" felt these contrary muscular activities just as Dr. Prince's "Saint" felt the muscular maneuvers of "Sally," [63] and tried to control them but could not because the paths for normal inhibition were interrupted. "DY" also felt the inrush of an emotion—fear—which he did not want, and which he had often tried to control but could not without understanding its source.

Hypnosis, however, broke down barriers between the parts of his cortical life, apparently through destroying the identity of those parts by breaking them up into their elements, except for those elements which were kept active by the suggestions which came from the operator. Then, all mental pathways being more equally permeable, the hypnotizer was able to prowl about in DY's field of memories with relative ease, to find out what was going on in the hitherto inaccessible areas. This was possible seemingly because the fright-system, at that time free from effective inhibition by its old rival "DY," was able to link up with the speech machinery. (Its tendency always had been to link with everything in DY. It had been kept from doing this by the fact that the emotion of fear which it always started to effulgerate had invariably spurred "DY" into putting the speech apparatus, etc., to some other work.) As the fright-pattern came to the surface, it was possible to put DY together again. This was done through further questioning, urging closer examination of the memories, etc., so forming direct linkages

---

[62] As accounted for in terms of associations, often unconscious, by Dr. Prince, *op. cit.*, 311-386.

[63] *The Dissociation*, 122, etc.

between the elements of the fright-system and whatever other ideational elements in DY's total stock seemed requisite to the settle-
ment of each tender point. Such direct linkages, new bridges for
old gaps, were the result, in other words, of concentrating the hypnotic subject's attention upon the faint associations between the
fright-system and other elements, and making him practise those
associations, perform those conditioned reflexes, until they were as
good as the rest. Thus the elements that were the fright-system
became part of a successful adjustment to what was after all an
ordinary situation. This reintegration was made secure by telling
the hypnotic subject that upon waking he would remember everything that went on during the period of sleep. That he did remember, was ascertained by the aid of notes taken during the hypnosis;
and that this meant real integration, freedom from conflict on this
point, is clear from his normal attitude toward cold water ever
since.

Conclusion. That the foregoing account is a demonstrated (or
completely original) [64] theory, is by no means the contention of the
writer. We do not seem likely for some time at least to have real
demonstration for the neurological bases of these phenomena. But
it is certainly unnecessary for us, in our thinking in this vital field,
to regress from the use of scientific language.

True, it may seem that the writer has lapsed seriously from
scientific language in several places where he mentioned introspective things. It is his conviction, however (suggested by Ernst Mach
and others), that while the language of extreme behaviorism is the
best for many purposes, because of its eminently communicable and
constant character, extreme devotion to that language represents a
subservience to metaphysics (in this case, materialism) which is
unworthy of the scientist. It is the business of the psychologist to
describe, not to refuse to report, the experienced data of mental
life; and where there are "mental" data for which "physical" correlates have not yet been worked out, these "mental" (introspective)
data may be necessary to the picture. And often, where the
"physical" correlates have been worked out, the introspective
language is as yet more convenient.

---

[64] Thus, while much of the above account puts the descriptive emphasis
upon reflexes and action patterns, I do not see how it differs essentially in
biological character from Dr. Morton Prince's employment of "neurograms"
(*The Unconscious*, 131, etc.) as descriptive terms. An action pattern includes receptors, central nerve paths or neurograms, and effectors; and the
organization of the neurograms is the heart of the organization of the
action patterns.

It may seem, however, that strictly "scientific language" must give way in any event: for, it is sometimes urged, "science" is always mechanistic; whereas *teleology,* as contrasted with mechanism, is characteristic of mental processes in general, and of the *neuroses* in particular.

To this the reply may be made that some students have never been able to conceive of "teleology" or "purpose" in any other than a mechanistic sense: "a purpose" represents a naturally acquired neuro-muscular attitude from which certain behavior processes follow; and "teleological striving," *e.g.,* means that there is some external or internal stimulus at work upon the organism so that a special restlessness persists. In human beings, admittedly, these varieties of behavior loom larger than in the lower animals. But to trace such behavior to its causal (deterministic) roots, seems to these mechanistic students to represent a more modern and certainly a more useful means of understanding human behavior.[65]

To this, the neuroses are no exception. When 2100 of 2500 war neurotics recover automatically within a couple of days after the armistice,[66] the student of mechanisms observes that one at least of the *causes* of those neuroses has disappeared. And for the remaining 400 cases, he infers that causes are still operative; some of these causes, probably a very large percentage, being wishes (special "sets" of the organism). But it does not follow that all who remain ill therefore prefer not to get well. Some are broken to their own hurt, and remain so until helped. In the civilian sphere, DY was just such a case. Neuroses, like dreams, are responses to stimuli, some of which may be stimuli from within in the form of wishes. All wishes are causes, but not all causes are wishes.

Throughout all, then, the causal series—determinism—which seems fundamental to science, appears able to support an indefinite increase of knowledge of human personality organization.[67]

---

[65] *Cf.* Walter Goodnow Everett, "The Natural History of Indeterminism," *Moral Values,* 339-343.

[66] James V. May, *Mental Diseases,* 200-201.

[67] Interesting further cases, somewhat resembling the foregoing, are described by the following: Tom A. Williams, in *Jour. Abn. Psychol.,* 9: 80-85; Meyer Solomon, *loc. cit.,* 11: 309-324; and Margaret J. Hamilton, *ibid.,* 13: 324-350.

The Traumatic Neurosis

TOM A. WILLIAMS, "The Traumatic Neurosis," *Jour. Am. Inst. of Criminal Law and Criminology*, 7: 689-701 (Northwestern Univ. Press, 1917).

Psychological Fundamentals. . . . An injury in itself cannot cause a "neurosis," meaning [what the writer of this paper would prefer to call] a psychosis. This condition occurs only when the patient broods over the injury, and imagines that he is a very sick person. To represent to oneself feelingly a disease, is to make oneself feel very sick, even although the disease one conceives may not itself be manifested with verisimilitude. The patient then, having the idea that he is sick, acts so and feels so; so that after a while he actually is sick.

This is on account of the fact that the very idea of pain is capable of arousing the concomitants of pain, *viz.*, depression of vegetative functions. This occurs because of the emotional reactions inseparable from the concepts which experience has associated with them. The situation is merely that of the dog in which Pavlow, during his experiments, suppressed the flow of gastric juice by merely showing a whip. It is a "conditioning" of a reflex, and is feasible with any dog.

This fact makes manifest how erroneous is the common opinion that the "conditioning" of affective reactions in a morbid fashion requires previous morbidity for its accomplishment. This is usually stated in the formula that traumatic neurosis occurs only in the predisposed. The real factor in its induction is the momentum of the conditioning stimulus. A homely illustration is that used by the penetrating dramatist August Thomas, in "The Harvest Moon," where he makes a hard-headed lawyer, against his will, the rapid victim of the suggestion that he is dangerously ill.

Of course, it should be obvious that the patient, although a victim of imagination, may become really ill physically; just as it is obvious that Pavlow's dog, a mere victim of imagination, is ill therewith to the extent of an incapacity to secrete gastric juice, which means very ill indeed. Indeed psychogenetic physical illness of this kind may reach such a degree as to cause death; as has been experimentally shown by Crile and others.

Furthermore, if the reactions have gone too far, the removal of the cause will not save the life of the animal. Short of death, secondary organic changes may occur, so that recovery will be incomplete.

But even when the stimuli are insufficient to produce organic changes, the cure of the subject demands more than a mere material removal of them; for the stimuli live in memory, where they have become associated with many elements of the environment; so that the cause is not *really* removed until a complete reconditioning is effected of all the associational reactions which have gathered around the initial dread-bringing circumstance.

For instance, a tachycardia produced by fear, if long continued, should not be less injurious to the heart and blood vessels than is excessive athletics; an outpouring of an excess of substances from the adrenals should just as likely produce vessel sclerosis or exhaust the gland when it is the result of chronic anxiety, as when it is due to a physiological stimulus of more direct kind; a dyspepsia or chronic constipation is just as likely to lead to malnutrition and toxemia when it is the result of mental depression as when it is due to sluggish habits or disease.

The mechanism by which the modification of reaction occurs is usually that of suggestion. The dog which secretes gastric juice when it hears a bell does so because of the suggestion that meat will be presented him forthwith. It does not know why a bell brings meat; it mistakes it for a reaction of cause and effect, like that of a wetting when it enters the water. The process is not one of genuine reasoning. The person who is hypochondriacal after an accident has as little reason in calling accident cause, and neurosis effect, as has the dog in believing bell cause and meat effect. It is belief without proper ratiocination, received blindly, credulously, from someone else without criticism, that is, by suggestion. This is, unfortunately, the commonest method by which opinions are acquired by human beings. Indeed the vast majority acquire their beliefs in no other way; and only a few superior minds have eliminated this manner of appraising the facts they encounter. It is small wonder then that the conditioning of reactions becomes morbid so easily; for we find morbidity all around. It is often dramatically impressive and frequently comes home to us by associations with the deepest affections. Hysteria, then, which is merely the "effects of suggestions when these cause disease," is necessarily very widespread, and the circumstances that give rise to it and the forms that it takes are proportional to their impressiveness, which means suggestive power, and in accordance with fashion and the *zeitgeist* of the country and time.

The mechanism is always the same and the victim is not aware of the systems of ideas and associated affects which constitute his psychosis.

*The Induction of Suggestion Psychoses. The Emotional Conse-
quences. Cases and Discussions.* In the gross these are most clearly
manifest in what our attitude of detachment easily enables us to
label the superstitions of alien peoples. Thus the sufferings induced
by the "gnawing fox" of the Japanese are made possible only by a
deeply rooted belief in its existence. For example, a woman after
labor declared she felt the "fox coming"; this was her interpretation of the after-pains she felt. The great parade by the neighbors
in attempting to prevent the fox's attack only reinforced the patient's apprehension and soon a horrible convulsion signalized her
seizure by the fox. Terror and convulsions held her until the
exorciser was called. He declared that the fox would leave her at
four o'clock the next day provided certain offerings were placed on
a certain tomb for it to eat. This simple suggestion caused her to
dismiss her terror suddenly at the hour designated. The crudeness
of the mechanism in the case of this ignorant peasant need not
make us smile, for our Western case is very little better, as the
following illustration shows:

It is the familiar case of an incapacitated railroad employee to
whom we were called to determine whether or not there was organic
disease of the nervous system. The fact that there was not is shown
elsewhere in the full report of the case.[1] The psychogenesis of the
man's condition was evident in his fixed idea, due to the common
belief of railroad employees, that serious nervous disease may slowly
ensue upon an accident. This common belief was strengthened by
the injudicious sympathy and inquiries of his friends and the
doubtful prognosis of some medical men he had consulted. He
"answered a thousand questions a day," he "did not know what to
think about his health," and worried about his condition and circumstances; he was "too much preoccupied with his health even
to miss his wife"; he had lost weight and appetite, had a sort throat,
and wept much, and finally his attitude was strengthened by the
lawyers who sought redress for him. He was cured within a month
as a result of one interview, during which he was instructed in the
rôle of ideas over bodily activity and the effects of worry and anxiety
upon nutrition. In the certificate it was stated "there is and has
been no disease of the spinal cord or peripheral nerves at play in
the induction of any of the symptoms which I find. The erroneous
belief that there has been such an injury powerfully contributes to
the anxiety which maintains his present state."

---

[1] *Medical Record*, N. Y., May, 1909; also *Trans. Internat. Cong. Industrial Accidents, Rome*, 1909.

The rôle of the idea of "shock" in perturbing this man's emotional life is strictly comparable with that of the gnawing fox of the Japanese folklore. In both cases, too, there was the period of reflection and incubation of the morbid notion, a familiar feature of such cases which has been insisted upon by Souques. It is rare that the symptoms ensue until after a time of meditation, during which the complex is systematized.

The cure was not so simple as that of the Japanese exorcist. But it was a definite one, for the railroad brakeman was taught to understand the mechanism of his affection and thus to overcome any future harm from the credulity in which he had grown up.[2] The Japanese woman, on the other hand, remained liable to another attack, as her belief in the fox was only reinforced by the manner of its removal.

A contrasting case where therapeutics failed will further push the lesson home. A government employee was injured by a falling case and remained barely able to walk even after his bruises of head and shoulder had healed. Called in consultation, we explained the mechanism of his present incapacity and directed how to remove it. His family physician's acquiescence to our directions was only formal, as his bent was not psychological enough to grasp the principles at work. The fearful solicitude of the man's wife too constantly reinforced his timidity, so that in spite of a considerable temporary improvement he did not progress to full recovery, but remained lachrymose, depressed, and relatively incapable on account of the persistence of his false belief about his health and powers.

. . . [In many cases re-adaptation might be accomplished but for the pernicious influence of the struggle for indemnification.] Instances of this kind are numerous. Isolated examples spring to the mind of every railroad surgeon; but an extensive comparison between cases equal in value to a deliberate experiment is best afforded by the observation of a train wreck in which 200 passengers were injured, about half of them severely. Only about 20 of the passengers developed traumatic neurosis. Some of these received heavy damages, upon which their health was immediately restored. In one case, however, a cure was effected by Dr. Bevan,[3] the observer, without recourse to a lawsuit; but even this was done against the active protestations of the patient and only by extraordinary perseverance and determination on the part of the physican, whose method of persuasion was so insistent as to make the patient weep.

---

[2] Five years later the man continued at work, well.
[3] *Jour. Am. Med. Ass'n.*, 1901.

Compensation Not Curative. But it is not always that the indemnity effects the cure. There is a case well known in Washington where $17,000 was allowed by the court to a man in whom a street car accident induced the belief that he was incapable of locomotion. This lasted for seven years, during which the patient went about in a wheel-chair administered to by a solicitous wife. His wife's belief that he could not walk was rudely disturbed after the plaster had fallen from the roof while they were asleep in bed one night, when she found her husband seated in the corner of the room twelve feet from the head of the bed. She argued that if he could walk while asleep at night he could walk while awake by day. This he did in trembling fear after insistent persuasion by her, and eventually recovered a few days subsequent to my seeing him.

The Psychological Criteria of Simulation and Hysteria in Relation to Indemnity. It would be idle to pretend that these are deliberate simulators for gain. They were honest pretenders, just so much as is any genuine hysterical the victim of a suggestion that he is incapacitated. These cases must be carefully differentiated from those who intentionally imitate symptoms in the hope of gain, even although the gain be merely the sympathy, attention, or notoriety from other people. . . .

These genuine psychoneurotics are entirely curable, quite apart from any question of indemnity in itself; but the struggle for indemnity cannot be given up without loss of self-respect in the implied confession of dishonesty or at least of the gross error of psychological interpretation concerning the rôle of the accident itself as the provoker of the illness; so that there is a preoccupying search by the patient for facts to ratify his belief that the accident had damaged him. This inevitably leads to imaginations, exaggerations and falsifications inevitable for a mind not scientifically trained. It is only when the patient has a glimmering of his mistake that he begins in desperation to defend it by conscious self-deception in order to bolster up a psychosocial attitude the negation of which would, he believes, be derogatory.

The construction of this state of mind is thus described in my article before the 1913 International Congress of Medicine:[4]

"Especially prone to this damaging sequence are persons whose imagination has been made rampant by the cultivation of the credulous fears of childhood: their fear-reaction to that which they do not understand is a dominant one, and they are easily beset by an idea linked with fear. The commonest of the fears which result from

---

4 *Transactions of Neurological Sect.;* also in *Cleveland Med. Jour.,* 1914

accident or injury is that of bodily harm. It is difficult for a person of this type, when ignorant of his own structure and functions, to shake off the foreboding created by an impressive catastrophe: and it must not be forgotten that what others regard as trifling the victim may look upon as catastrophic, judged by its possible effect on him. Prepossession by the idea of one's own disability is an inevitable consequence. This leads to abstraction from and inattention to the affairs of ordinary life, which, if not trifling by comparison in the patient's mind at least cannot claim the attention properly needed. Hence ensues the well-known diminution of the capacity to think, work, or take part in social life. This incapacity, when the patient becomes aware of it, leads him to still further accentuate the result of his injury and thus to augment his alarm about his health. Thus is constituted the vicious circle of hypochondria. Even a nosophobia may ensue, such as the fear of lost manhood, insanity, paralysis. Alarm at this impending disaster must, of course, be distinguished from the primary alarm due to the accident itself."

Forensic Presentability. This mechanism is so simple that it can clearly be grasped by any intelligent person even without medical training; it has been very convincingly popularized by Mr. Addington Bruce in the "Outlook," of May, 1914. . . .[5]

---

[5] For additional discussion of this matter see the following by the same author, more especially number 4.

(1) "Traumatic Neuroses and Babinski's Conception of Hysteria," *Transactions of Congress of Industrial Accidents, Rome,* and *Medical Record,* 1909.

(2) "Successful Psychotherapy of Traumatic Neurosis," *Amer. Jour. Surg.,* 1909.

(3) "Idea and Affect in Traumatic Neurosis," *Jour. Abn. Psychol.,* 1910 also *Charlotte Med. Jour.*

(4) "Psychic Effects of Accidents," *Transactions of Southern Railway Surgeons,* 1912, and *Monthly Cyclopedia,* and *N. Y. Med. Jour.* 1913, where many cases are related not due to trauma.

(5) "Occupation Neurosis," *International Congress of Hygiene,* 1912; *Medical Record,* 1913; *Transactions of International Congress of Medicine,* 1913; *Cleveland Med. Jour.,* 1914.

(6) "Treatment of Hysteria," *Jour. Amer. Med. Assoc.,* November, 1912.

(7) "Hysteria and Pseudohysteria," *Amer. Jour. Med. Sci.,* September, 1910. "The Traumatic Neurosis," *ibid.,* 1915.

(8) "Mental Healing," *British Med. Jour.,* Vol. II, 1913, and *Ill. Med. Jour.,* October, 1914.

(9) "Treatment of Psychoneurotic Patients," *Cleve. Med. Jour.,* 1914.

The Cramp of Writers and Telegraphers

Tom A. Williams; adapted from "Studies of the Genesis of the Cramp of Writers and Telegraphers: the Relation of the Disorder to Other 'Neuroses': their Pathogenesis Compared with that of Tics and Habit Spasms," *Journal für Psychologie und Neurologie*, Bd. 19, Heft. 2/3, 1912.

The mechanism of professional cramp is always psychological. Accordingly the treatment must address itself to the psyche. It must be clearly understood that the disorder of the apparatus is not structural but regulative. It is not an incapacity of muscle and nerves to perform their function; for this is intact except for performing the particular professional acts which fail. A want of harmony in the controlling of the mechanism is the fault. We have not even to deal with the kind of want of harmony which occurs upon the destruction or toxic inhibition of a cortical centre, such as happens in aphasia. Professional cramp is a strictly psychodynamic inhibition or disorder in the habitual series of coördinated associations gained by education in some art.

It has been placed in a class apart from the tics, on account of certain peculiarities which have been regarded as essential. But from this study it will appear that the differences are less essential than adventitious, and that none of them conflicts with the definition of true tic. Hence both as regards genesis and treatment occupation-cramp-neurosis should be regarded as a form of tic.

The chief source of error of former writers is to look upon the mechanism of occupation cramp as an immediate deprivation of function. A deeper analysis shews that a particular function is impossible only because another act, *viz*. the derived movement or cramp, tremor or atonia, has preempted the muscles so that they cannot at the same time perform the desired act. It is this superfluous, though coordinate, purposive and once voluntary set of contractions, which by definition constitutes a tic. Only because of the occurrence of this other motor phenomenon is the patient unable to make the habitual movements of his art. This interpretation has been hidden by the fact that the tic usually begins and preponderates in or near the very muscles used in the occupation; and this has in the past obscured its analysis.

In order to furnish the basis for and make concrete the argument for this thesis, the cases upon which it has been developed are now introduced. Their careful study is needed for an estimation of the evidence and the validity of its sequences.

Case of Torticollis Causing Grapho-spasm.

Single woman, E. L., aged thirty-one, expert counter in a **Treasury.**

Complaint. Cannot use right arm; for each motion causes the head to turn to the right; "and I am compelled to look right backwards with a most powerful force, over which I have no control." It began three months before with a pain behind the right shoulder running round to the right side. She now has pain all the time. She consulted a physician, who called it neuritis, and advised massage. The nurse who was called feared to massage her; so electricity (sic) was tried; and did good at first to both the pain and the movements.

She had fallen on this shoulder in August; but it did not trouble her after the first few days.

The movements and pain had been bearable until a month before she saw me; and she had left her work from time to time, on one occasion for three weeks.

Present State. Appetite good, no indigestion or pain; and the general physical examination shewed nothing abnormal except loss of weight, hypotonia and exaggerated reflexes.

Psychic Examination. No marked defect of memory, attention, judgment in general matters, nor emotional reactions; but she is much worried about her condition, which she *believes to be a physical malady.* As will appear from the psycho-analysis, there are other worries which she did not at first reveal.

Onset. She had no unusual worry at the time, she declares; but on account of straightened finances and the delicacy of her mother, she has been anxious for some years. As a result of psychoanalysis, it was ascertained that three months before the tic, there had occurred a serious unpleasantness with a comrade in the office, whom she stigmatised as an ignorant, conscienceless woman. The emotional bitterness displayed in the patient's account was an immediate index of the serious pathological significance of this episode. Her attempts at harmony caused no satisfaction; so she declares that she ceased worrying. "I had tried to adjust it, but failed; for she is a married woman older than and above me in the office. She is angered because I do not associate with her. But as she had spoken disparagingly of my mother, I taxed her, only to meet with denial."

She brooded deeply over this episode; and as her work in counting can be performed quite automatically, her thoughts were free all day long to dwell upon the constant unpleasantness of being in the same room as the other woman, who *sits behind her on the right.*

Some three years before, she had renounced marriage for the sake of her mother, on account of a love affair which had turned out unfortunately. Her mother too had had an unfortunate marital experience, the knowledge of which has tended to strongly depress the patient's mind. But in spite of all this she declares that her home is happy with her mother and sister, for whom she has a strong affection and admiration, and terms "a practical Christian." She has always been most anxious to do her duty and to "make good" at her work; but she confesses that since the quarrel with her fellow worker, her thoughts have been preoccupied by the unpleasantness it has caused, in which, however, she believes herself to have the sympathy of many of the other girls. But at work she cannot help thinking of the other woman.

Examination of the Origin of the Tic. It is evident that the girl's thoughts about her enemy cause her head unconsciously to veer and turn towards where she knows her to be. This is the less easy to resist because her attention is partly occupied by the counting of the money which is her duty. As she is anxious to do this as rapidly and well as possible, mistakes or insufficient work not being condoned, she is less able to resist the motor response to her underlying thought, which is essentially a desire for an understanding with the other woman and a reconstitution of her own desire to be in harmony with her surroundings.

By now, however, by a process of psychological substitution, the need of turning the head has come to accompany *every* use of the right hand; so that she is unable to use her knife at the table without a turning of the head and an ensuing rigidity of the arm and head in the effort to arrest the torticollis and to accomplish the act she wishes. In writing, it is the same thing; and the case affords an example of writer's cramp mechanically produced by torticollis of mental origin, which by a psychological association has in turn become producible by *any* use of the hand or arm.

The cause of pain is the action of the muscles antagonistic to the turning movement, which she consciously seeks to prevent. Between the automatic desire to turn the head and the conscious effort not to do so, the muscles of the shoulder, neck and upper part of the chest are maintained more or less constantly in a state of powerful contraction; and the severe drag upon their attachments, combined with a state of fatigue, provokes the pain of which the patient complains.

Even at rest, the patient now holds the head somewhat to the right, and keeps contracted the neck and shoulder muscles on that side. The attempt to turn the head straight or to the left is not accompanied by *angoisse* strictly speaking, but causes a distress referable to the muscles at the right side and to the consciousness of her incapacity to freely perform the desired movement. She feels an actuating force stronger than herself. It is from such feelings in the credulous and superstitious that may arise the notion of possession by an external being, *a dæmon.* If the woman's tic is not cured, I have no doubt that in course of time anguish will accompany efforts to suppress the movements; but at present the syndrome is not complete.

There are somatic factors in the case; for the tic is always much worse during the catamenia, when she has much pain, nausea and sinking feelings of the heart with flushes, chills and headache, and often has to take to bed. These symptoms are said to be due to uterine malposition.

She has also a marked exophoria, and had to abandon on account of dizziness her original work of spreading bills.

But the psychological factor is the main one, as will appear; for the torticollis is proportional to the insistence of the thought of her painful relationship with her fellow worker; and when she succeeds in dismissing this from her mind, the tic rarely occurs. This, however, has been difficult, because she had no confidence, not being willing to trouble her tired sister as had been her habit, and a clergyman to whom she was much attached having left the city. Hence, there was no relief from brooding over her grievance.

Treatment and Progress. I explained the genesis of her affection and gave a good prognosis. My first prescription was to take ten days of joy in the country and to try to be less hyperconscientious during that time, paying no attention to her troubles or to the torticollis. Six days later she returned not having followed the prescription, with pain in the head and the tic worse than ever. I gave her exercises in psychomotor discipline, consisting of dealing a pack of cards into two heaps while her head was turned away from the affected side, and cutting along lines ruled on a piece of paper. In a few days she greatly improved in performing these tasks, the tic greatly diminished and the pain in the shoulder disappeared.

But the fact that this improvement became less rapid, as was to be expected, so discouraged her that she relaxed her efforts during the exercises, and substituted therefor a constant tension of the muscles in an attempt to rectify the abnormal posture of her head and neck. This created pain at the angle of the scapula, where the latissimus dorsi is attached, and she lost courage. She was advised to go out and relax, and to abstain from work for at least another month. This she declared herself unable to do, and persisted in returning to work against advice. In consequence the torticollis was greatly aggravated, and she gave up attending. I have learnt recently that she had to remain away from work for two months, during which she took chiropractic treatment, which improved her torticollis, but not the professional cramp; and she does her work entirely with the left hand, and her bitter mental attitude is worse than before.

A Case of Partial Tremulous Scrivener's Palsy: the psychogenesis of which was discovered in one interview, which led to recovery within a month, through the patient's own efforts.

A paymaster, aged 32, single, was referred to me early in 1908 by a physician; because when he returned to work after the drainage of a large perityphlitic abscess which discharged for a month, he found that his signature was no longer uniform. Instead of improving, he became worse with practice; and although his other writing was not so seriously impaired, he had ceased writing entirely and conducted his correspondence by dictation and signatures. [But] this signature is exceedingly shaky; and as it was made with ever increasing difficulty as the day progressed and became almost illegible in the afternoon, he feared that he would lose his position. As may be imagined, the ever-recurrent anxiety of this tended to make his writing still more difficult and tremulous.

Previous Illness and History. The patient had a good recovery from typhoid fever in 1890. In 1900, he had inflammatory rheumatism, which however left no cardiac weakness or other after effect. As a child, he had pertussis, scarlatina, mumps, measles and pneumonia. He is still subject to tonsilitis, which is sometimes febrile and makes him feel out of sorts. Nine years ago, he had gonorrhœa. He is positive there has been no chancre. He used to have malaria, but has had none since 1900 or so.

Present Illness. His trouble is comprised in the statement that he is "unable to write as his work requires." He admits that he is nervous in making a signature before me; and says that he can make it better than this. He had not fully recovered his strength on returning to work after his operation, and used to tire. But he had not noticed any particular change in his writing until his attention was drawn to a lack of uniformity in his signature of the cheques he signed, by the declaration of a bank official who refused one of them. He had not worried about his writing at all before this; but afterwards became apprehensive about it all the time. The doctor whom he consulted merely gave him bromides, which of course did him no good as regards the power to write. The physician believed he had toxemia and post-operative shock.

Examination. The deep reflexes were exceedingly active. The cutaneous reflexes were feeble. But the toes flexed upon stroking the sole. The pupils reacted to light and accommodation.

The cardiac rhythm was not perfectly regular. But there was no enlargement, thrill nor bruit. There was no sclerosis of the arteries, and the pulse was soft, moderate in frequency and without abnormal characters, although the right impact seemed feebler than the left.

There was slight emphysema of the lung. The examination was otherwise negative.

This condition of the reflexes is consistent with a toxicosis interfering with the full function of the cerebral neurones which inhibit the activity of the deep reflexes and, it is believed, subserve that of the cutaneous reflexes.

But as the state of the reflexes of this patient threw no light upon the genesis of his condition, it was necessary to ascertain this otherwise. The question which arose was whether the patient's incapacity at present arose directly from an intoxication of his neurones, or whether both his incapacity and the toxicosis were psychogenic.[1] Analysis of his psychological history might elucidate this problem. So it was undertaken.

Psychological History. The patient never had a "nervous breakdown," but has sometimes been depressed after very hard work. He has applied himself very closely to his duties, the responsible nature of which he fully realizes. He is unusually young for the position he fills. In consequence, he has neglected physical exercise since the age of sixteen, and saves himself from becoming too stout by going without lunch. He works nine and a half hours a day, and likes it.

As a boy, he was very conscientious, and was always annoyed if things were not correctly done promptly. This was shewn by his behaviour with regard to the chicken-house in which he kept chickens for amusement and pocket money as a boy. This extreme orderliness was not a family trait, although his father also had it. He had no over-scrupulous ways, and was not over-particular in his studies, although he worked hard. He had no morbid fears and no religious crises, as he was not particularly devout and had no set views. He thinks that as a boy he was sexually passionate. He has not masturbated since twelve; and has had no sexual difficulties, being able to abstain or indulge as the occasion arises. He does not care for society, and prefers men to girls; and though he has some intimates, he has no deep attachments.

These characteristics have persisted into adult life; so that if things do not go right, the passion for order impels him to rectify them himself rather than take the trouble to make others do it. He has never suffered from tics, not even having made facial grimaces, which are so common in boys. I tested his suggestibility by pushing him by the shoulder. He moved only a short distance, and quickly checked himself by bending his knees. There was no rigidity of movements

---

[1] In purely toxic states, often labelled neurasthenic, while the reflexes are sometimes enfeebled, in some cases they are exaggerated. It perhaps depends upon the nature of the poison producing the syndrome. In *psychogenetic* states of anxiety, the deep reflexes are always exaggerated.

other than those used in writing. In his writing there was no rigidity of the extreme kind seen in the so-called spasmodic form of writer's cramp. His disability would conform to the type called tremulous by Benedict. It was rather a hesitancy than a cramp.

Pathogenesis. From these facts it can be induced that the patient's attempt to resume work necessitating long-continued writing, before he was in a proper state to do so, led to a tremulousness of the hand and arm similar to that which ensues upon excessive consumption of coffee or tobacco or upon the toxine of some infectious or fatigue condition. The condition would probably have been recovered from spontaneously as he regained strength had not another element been added by the dread of permanent incapacity led to by the refusal of his cheque at the bank. This was the really efficient cause of his present disability. Hence, it was to this that therapeusis was exclusively addressed.

Treatment. The rôle of mental prepossession in inhibiting the due coördination of muscular movements was explained to him, and illustrated by means of the strokes used in lawn tennis, more especially that known as the drive. It was shewn that fear of making an improper stroke is very likely to lead to lack of freedom and cramping of the muscles, which are the very positions to be avoided. Still greater anxiety will create an uncertain, wobbling stroke, the incoördination of which is comparable to his writing.

A further illustration used was that of Jastrow's investigation of the relative efficiency of the employees who first used the enumerating machine in the census of 1900, as against those who were brought in later on account of the disappointing output of the others. The special preparation of the first set of clerks, so far from giving greater speed, only produced the feeling of the difficulty of the task, which they never transcended, being quickly surpassed in amount of work by the clerks who received no special preparation whatever.

The relation of these facts to the episode of the refused cheque was discussed with him at length. When he had clearly realized the psychological mechanism of his condition, he was directed to entirely cease writing with purpose, and to begin exercises by making free arm movements with chalk on a black-board, paying no attention to the forms he drew, but concentrating himself upon the attainment of freedom in action. When this was insured, he might pass to a slate, and later to pencil and paper, and then gradually reduce the size of the writing. He was asked to send me specimens of his efforts; but this he did not do; and he did not reply to an inquiry addressed to him one month later. But over two years later, he sent me an excellent specimen, and informed me that he had almost entirely recovered, after one month of the exercises prescribed.

It should be added that this patient's disability was entirely confined to writing; for even in drawing and letter printing there was hardly a tremor of the hand.

[Another patient] said, "Why do my hands tremble when I seem so well to-day?" So I made her hold them out; and a rapid oscillation of the right hand was shewn. I made her count twenty while looking at me; it ceased. I made her look at my hand spread steadily before her: her trembling again ceased. Then I explained its mental nature; and that a tremor of organic origin could not be stopped like this. She at last was convinced.

A Case of Occupational Incapacity Due Merely to Physical Weakness.

A. S. A., telegrapher, aged 63, complained of a weakness of the wrist muscles without paralysis. He "cannot send his writing over the wire unless he raises his elbow off the desk, and that tires him."

Personal and Family History. He has been an operator for over 40 years, has never been a drinking man, but smokes about four cigars and chews about four ounces of tobacco per week. He has always stammered in speech.

Physical Examination. The deep reflexes are a little exaggerated, but there is no sclerosis of the blood vessels or other sensile disturbance. However, there is a distinct diminution in the thickness of the right upper extremity. While the thickest part of the left fore arm measures nine inches, the circumference of the right is only eight and seven eighths inches. In the upper arms, the circumference is $9\frac{1}{2}$ inches of the left and $9\frac{1}{4}$ inches of the right. On the other hand, the right wrist is slightly larger than the left. The muscles of the right arm, besides being diminished in volume, are in a condition of hypotonia.

Psychic Symptoms are absent, there being no anxiety or phobia; and the man indeed, who has felt his weakness for eight or ten years, continues his work efficiently enough to maintain his position, though fully conscious of his diminished capacity.

Interpretation. The contrast with the other cases is striking. Although in this old man the atrophy which proceeds from over use has reached a degree where it can be measured, yet his relative occupational disability has provoked no morbid psychological reaction. Neither cramp nor tremor has appeared; and work is continued as far as capacity allowed. . . .

Criticism of Orthodox Interpretations of Occupational Cramp-Neurosis and the Term Neurosis.

Physical symptoms in E. L., etc., are not the cause of cramp in themselves, but may furnish the initial motive from which comes the notion of incapacity or of perverted movements.

Such physical disabilities are frequently perpetuated into psychical ones; *e.g.:*

Hysterical prurigo. A girl aged nine came to the dispensary on account of itching of the right face. Her frequent scratching had kept up pityriasis. This had begun two years after her father had for some weeks suffered much from furuncle, when he had itched all over, scratched much, and spoken of it a great deal. He still does so when he eats pork, thinking that it makes him itch. The little girl had only one boil on the right heel; and this she feared to scratch. It does not appear that the child's face had really been diseased; but I believed that the eruption was kept up by a morbid impulsion; so I prescribed sulphur ointment with the object of inculcating belief, pressed upon mother and child the need of never touching the face, and assured them that the itching would totally disappear in two weeks, which prediction was verified by the result.

It is the reacquisition of an impaired or lost efficiency, not due to a fault of the machine, but to an error in the order in which its parts are put in action. It is the directing force which needs to be scientifically applied, and not the physical mechanism which requires repair.

Interpretation of "Professional-Cramp-Neurosis" as a Tic.

The psychological mechanism of the muscular cramps produced during the attempt to perform the acts of a very ordinary occupation is so complex that its consideration has been passed over both by *Janet (2)* and *Meige (1)*, each of whom, however, has pointed out the resemblance of occupation-cramp-neuroses to true tic.[2] To

---

[2] This is not the place to enter into a discussion of the various dyskineses or myoclonias. A few words, however, must be said of habitual gestures and attitudes and of the true tics. The former occur in perfectly normal individuals as well as in the insane, in whom they are called stereotypies. Examples in the normal are stroking of the moustache, wrinkling of the brow, whistling, playing with the watch-chain, grimacing of the face, waving of the hand or sawing the air while speaking. So long as these are unconscious automatisms, and so long as they could be prevented without suffering by a little care on the part of the performer, they do not merit the name of habit spasm, nor can they be classed with the tics. The latter are convulsive, and intemperate in character, are accom-

these authors, they differ, however, from the tics in being a disorder of a *different* normal act, whereas a tic is more in the nature of a *new,* acquired act, irrespective of a previously acquired automatism. The tic is, in the first place, deliberate and volitional from beginning to end. The occupation-cramp is only a modification of an act, once deliberate and volitional, which has become automatic, as far as any action under constant control of the neopallium can be so considered. But both tic and occupation-cramp may be summed up as acquired functional automatism of pathological nature.

Physical treatment does not cure the cramp; but it makes easier the patient's effort, by putting him into the most favourable state of physical vigour for the mental exertion needed in giving the close attention required to wean himself from a bad habit and reëducate his special psychomotor activities into a good habit. That is, *a sequence of energic discharges of a psychomotor area, which have by association acquired an order not desirable, is changed by*

---

panied by a consciousness of the act, are preceded by a desire, sometimes amounting to a passion, to perform the act, and are followed by a feeling of relief after performance of the movement. At all events the victims of tics feel compelled to make the movements comprising the tic. The movements always represent, however incompletely, some voluntary act, *e. g.* turning the head, shrugging the shoulders, biting the cheek, winking the eye, sniffing, etc. The end to which the movement was first directed has, however, often passed from the recollection of the patient; and the act itself has often degenerated into a caricature of what it originally was. A simple example is a winking of the eyes which has continued for years in spite of the fact that the irritation of the foreign body which first excited it has long subsided. It often originates in an idea which, however, ultimately becomes ignored or forgotten by the patient, such as in the case of E. L.

Nor is this the place to discuss the forms of tic; suffice it to say, that in hypersuggestible individuals, tics are easily induced sometimes, make little impression upon the patient, and are very simply removed by reëducation and persuasion or even by suggestion. These we call hysterical.

The tic, on the other hand, which is preceded by an imperative longing, the struggle against which causes intense suffering, occurs in over-scrupulous individuals of little suggestibility, whom *Janet* has called psychasthenics, and who shew numerous stigmata of their constitution in addition to the tic for which they may seek advice. E. L. is of this type to some extent.

The principles of treatment of the tics as laid down by *Brissaud* and developed by *Meige* are entirely similar to those which have proved successful in the cases of professional cramp here presented.

A tic must be distinguished from a true spasm, which is due to direct physical [causes] beyond voluntary or emotional control; and hence insusceptible of psychotherapeusis.

intelligent practice into a sequence which conforms to the order desired. . . .

A Preliminary to Treatment. The greatest difficulty in the treatment of these cases is the patient's firm belief that the part incriminated is itself diseased. So long as this is believed, rational cure is impossible; but the belief is very difficult to dislodge; for so many medical men have acted in conformity therewith; and the true explanation involves a line of thought so unfamiliar that it requires time for assimilation. This subjects it to the danger of interference by meddling friends or other advice. Thus it is essential that the patient should attend the doctor frequently at the beginning of the treatment; and if possible the more intelligent friends should be interviewed and their coöperation invoked.

The Principles of the Psychorthopædics. The treatment consists of a reconstruction of the impaired function under psychological conditions unfavourable to the tic which impairs it. The chief means is graduated exercises of the function. In order not to excite the cramp tic, these must be performed with great care, but without anxiety, very slowly and with attention to minutiæ. The sittings should be frequent, but short, ceasing as soon as attention flags.

It is not the exercises themselves which are curative; for unless the patient's mental attitude is reformed the exercises are useless. Automatic performances are actually hurtful. . . .

Hence, often the first task of the therapeutist is to convince the patient of the pathogenesis of his affection in order that he may be persuaded to undertake a treatment which will be neither short nor easy.

The keynote to this treatment is that the patient clearly understand the mechanism of his affection. Upon the basis of this understanding, physician and patient then develop procedures for the reeducation of the perverted psychomotor succession which determines the abnormal movements.

The Psychomotor Discipline; Its Technique. These difficulties having been faced, and treatment resolved upon, a psychomotor discipline is instituted. It begins with the movements of the larger joints, which are phylogenetically better established, and within their limits easier to control.

The end aimed at is largeness and smoothness of movement; all sudden jerking must be avoided; and the binding of muscles must be unlimbered. Gentle swinging movements, followed by Indian club exercises are a convenient introduction. Success is usually rapid, and then the second stage can be begun. This consists of directing the same principles to the use of the joints around which the cramp has occurred. Slow, smooth movements in different directions are at first practiced, and at least, until complete control is attained.

Then some tool or instrument is grasped in the hand and wide sweeping movements made with this. Until this can be done with complete freedom, no use of the tool should be permitted; but when cramping ceases to occur the patient is directed to use his pencil or other instrument in a professional act. When this is begun, there is a great tendency for the patient's mind to concentrate upon the product of his act *viz.,* the writing or other work, and to wander from the act itself. This is the great difficulty at this stage of the treatment. To avoid this, the patient must be induced not to think of the form he is drawing, but to concentrate upon the movements he is making. . . .

When large writing can be performed automatically without tendency to cramp, a gradual reduction of amplitude of movement is attempted; and when a reasonable size of writing is attained, the patient may be gradually permitted to resume writing in which the end is not the manner but the matter. The cure is then only a matter of continued attention and further practice. Relapses, which are frequent, are due to the relaxation of earnest attention by the patient; and it is sometimes a hard task for the physician to prevent the natural tendency to a relapse into easy-going automatism before perfect freedom of movement has been attained.[1]

---

[1] REFERENCES. *Brissaud* describes in his clinical lectures (1894) the psychomotor discipline he devised for the cure of the tics.

(1) *Henry Meige* and *E. Fiendel* published in 1902 a monograph on the tics and their treatment, which systematized and amplified the teachings of *Brissaud*. It has been translated into English recently by S. A. K. Wilson of London. (2) *Janet,* in his book with *Raymond* on the Obsessions and Psychasthenia in 1903, shewed the pathogenetic relationships of the tics, and included them in the syndrome of psychasthenia with a completeness which systematized previous vague attempts to relate them to the mental degenerations. Of the German writers, only *Friedrich* had even approached this conception. And it was not until *Patrick* of Chicago analysed the works of *Meige* and *Fiendel* in 1904 that the ideas of *Brissaud* penetrated to an appreciable extent beyond French-speaking countries.

Hitherto, no application of the psychopathological conception of the tics had been made to the occupational parakineses. This study is an attempt to fill this gap in neuro-pathology and treatment.

CHAPTER XXVII

MENTAL HYGIENE

W. S. Taylor

As the name implies, the ideal of mental hygiene is the development of the best mental condition in everyone; meaning by mental, not merely the intellectual powers, but all the processes, affective, emotional, volitional, which in popular speech are comprehended under the term "mental."

Realization of this ideal of mental hygiene must depend mainly upon several forms of prevention. These forms are essentially the following: A eugenic policy which would prevent the birth of the mentally useless; physical welfare, including fresh air, sunshine, and such other factors as make for bodily health; adequate economic conditions which would eliminate under-nourishment and overwork; the social situation, involving, for example, elimination of avoidable ostracism, and supplying instead wholesome personal associations; and finally, what might be called educational methods—the inculcation of sound habits, ideas, and attitudes in general. These educational means are of great hygienic importance, especially for the more intelligent minds, and are accordingly of great interest. It is to these means that we shall limit our present discussion.

EDUCATIONAL MEANS OF MENTAL HYGIENE

Elementary Habits and Attitudes. From the beginning, a child needs to have the right habits and attitudes towards food. This topic may not seem to be very "mental"; but we should not be surprised to find that if the child gets finicky about his meals, insisting upon having particular foods or none, he is liable to become unreasonable about other things, to say nothing of ill health resulting. When the child is encouraged to have a good appetite and to like wholesome foods, he is indirectly being encouraged towards finding good things in life; which is a healthy attitude.

He needs to have a sound attitude regarding sleep and dreams. The benefits of regular habits of sleep are obvious enough. As for his dreams, the child ought to feel free to talk them over with some one who can say, in the case of a nightmare, "That is only a dream. Dreams do not amount to anything." Or, even better, where the nightmare suggests its source, "What frightened you recently?" "And why should that have disturbed you so much?"

The child should not learn wrong attitudes towards play. Some children acquire such a fear of idleness that they are unable to enjoy play for itself. Obsessed always with the idea of working towards perfection, they become very imperfectly adapted to life, unable to profit either from the benefits or the pleasures of pure recreation.

The child should learn to cope with material obstacles. If he does not achieve some degree of mastery of this world of snow-storms, wood-piles, and competitive sports, he can hardly enjoy most really the world of intellect. The world of *touch* is, after all. the realm in which all our castles must be built.

Fear and frights are topics upon which the child is exceedingly liable to develop very wrong attitudes. So many frights occur in the course of nature, as it were; and so many unthinking elders talk of "the bogy-man who is going to get you if you aren't good"; that fears of the cellar, of the dark, or what not, are readily developed, and may persist indefinitely unless properly corrected by experience, or by reasoning with some sensible person. Too often. instead, the child is only made fun of for his apprehensions; or he is forbidden to mention them at all. In such cases he is of course liable to keep all fears to himself, with unfortunate results. Very different are the results of the policy of learning what not to fear, and what to avoid; and why.

Similarly, a right attitude towards anger should be developed. There are parents who regard anger as a noble emotion which if present proves stamina. But this attitude lacks discrimination. Manifestations of temper instead of being "cute," or manly, ought to be regarded as proofs of inability to handle situations precisely.

There are likewise correct attitudes towards disgust. Some children adopt the notion that to be disgusted at many things shows a very fine organization. But it does not. It suggests a sickly organization; and the child should realize this.

Likes and dislikes generally are worthy of careful consideration. Violent dislikes, unreasonable aversions, for particular persons, for example, instead of being proof of artistic genius or other worthy temperament, should be regarded as crude reactions, primitive types of response, which show defect in perspective, if they do not show incipient neuroses.

A topic upon which the child is likely to get a wrong attitude is that of his (or her) own physical and mental traits. A girl may think that because she has flaming red hair or some other sort of hair that she is unfortunately marked for life. She ought to get over that idea, of course. Hair color is nothing but a matter of a little pigment, as the early Stoics might have remarked; and there are more important things than color of hair. If a boy is disproportionately short or tall, or happens to be soft and weak, he should realize that in due season he will mature. And if his head is peculiarly shaped, or he has a curious nose, he should realize that he is not responsible for these items. There are other things that he is responsible for, which it would profit him more to think about. These other things include habits, attitudes, interesting activities, and considerateness of others.

One professor I knew of had three children. The oldest was a girl who was very bright. The second was a very bright boy. The third was a boy of average ability; but the father was openly convinced that he was actually dull. The result was that this son came to believe he was dull. He thus became liable to never put forth the proper effort to show what was in him; or, he may try to compensate and work harder than he ought, trying to be greater than he can. In the latter event, he will be in the same case with all whose strength is really insufficient for their tasks; who need to learn, from Walt Mason, that "we humble skates in our low estates, who fuss with our garden sass, should view the woes of the man who rose above and beyond the mass, and be glad today that we go our way 'mid quiet and peaceful scenes; should thankfully take the hoe and rake, and wrestle with spuds and greens." [1]

On the other hand, the child who is exceptionally good in, let us say, arithmetic, should not get the notion that he is superior to all his fellows. Too many children are practically ruined by elders' admiration, at least for a time, until corrected in the school of experience. Everyone should learn to prefer a reasonable, fair attitude towards his own physical and mental traits, neither expecting himself to be perfect, nor underestimating his own abilities. Indeed, as he finds how hard it is to estimate at all, he will concern himself rather with experimental achievement, doing the best he can, and realizing always that virtue is proportionate, not to innate capacity, but to wise use of one's powers.

[1] Copyright, George Matthew Adams.

Sometimes a child's environmental or economic situation causes him pain. Because he cannot have new shoes as often as the other children he may come to think that he comes from inferior folk. Yet his people may be superior in abilities, physically, mentally, and morally. He should consider the circumstances, fairly.

Some children are brought up with absurd attitudes towards mankind in general. It is easy for children to become suspicious of our race; and perhaps all children are naturally uncooperative during at least one stage of their development. But some individuals get very much out of touch with humanity, and so never learn the satisfactions of cooperativeness. Such persons have lost a significant portion of life, including a number of factors which are most conducive to mental poise. It follows that every one should learn to understand his fellows, to understand why they have their prejudices and how these can be allowed for, if not mollified. Here as elsewhere in the life of a developing individual, emotional control, and habits of courtesy, need to be cultivated.

Sound Development Relative to Sex and Marriage. Every individual should have a right attitude developed in him or her towards the opposite sex. Girls who are taught that all men are absolutely untrustworthy, and boys who grow up with the idea that girls do not amount to much, are developing untoward attitudes, if for no other reason than that approximately half of the world is composed of the opposite sex.

Also, there should be a reasonable attitude towards sex itself. This statement applies to every individual, whether or not he marries; since sex is a fact in the world at large. It has lately become a commonplace, fortunately, that the subject of sex should not be disguised in fearsomeness or disgust; but it has not always been made clear that sex also must not be romanticized. As Dr. Abraham Myerson has well said, "romanticism, which extols sex as the prime and only thing of life, prudery which closes its eyes to it and makes sour faces, need special places in Dante's Inferno." [2] The individual should realize that there is no human impulse which is bad in itself. Desire for food is nothing to be ashamed of: but the hungry individual becomes unworthy when he steals food; it is the setting, thievery, that contaminates the impulse. Sex is not unworthy in itself. It is purely a matter of setting.

Towards marriage a child should have the right attitude developed, again whether or not he marries, but especially in view of

[2] Abraham Myerson, *The Nervous Housewife*, 142 (copyright, 1920, by Little, Brown & Co.).

the possibility; since the happiness and welfare, not only of his mate, but of his children as well, depend very much upon the attitudes brought into the marriage relation by the parents. In this connection, a few special points are worth consideration.

To begin with, we observe that soon after the child has become aware of being either a little boy or a little girl, phantasying begins as to what it would be like to have the position of eminence now held by the father or mother. The natural little egotist may even wish, as Freud has pointed out, that he had his opposite parent all to himself: for in that case, the boy would receive all his mother's attention and affection, while possessing all his father's dignity and power; the little girl would be entirely her father's favorite, and would herself be mistress of the household. And naturally, as Freud has further suggested, this phantasy situation tends to become a more or less reciprocal one; the parent, predisposed to encourage the child's little games, finds also in the play a certain satisfaction of correspondingly romantic desires. Thus it develops, in many cases, that at least during an important period of its life the child becomes attached especially to the parent of the opposite sex.

Perhaps such attachment, within limits, is useful orientation for later life. But when the attachment becomes very close, as it may where the parent of the same sex is much away from, or dislikes, this child; or where the parents are themselves fundamentally incompatible, and the child happens to side with the parent of the opposite sex—the attachment resulting may resemble any of perhaps three types.

In extreme instances it seems to follow the pattern of lovers. This is the type which Freud has urged especially, and which is most contrary to conventional expectations. Yet in pathological cases, and in very inferior families, this species of attachment between child and parent sometimes occurs, just as it does among the animals. It would seem that the tendency is there, in some temperaments at least. And we certainly do see a tendency, frequently manifested in young persons, to idealize the parent of the opposite sex, and to look forward definitely to the event of marrying a person who is of precisely that type. If not outgrown, this expectation may be unfortunate, as a person of that type may not appear.

In very puritanical families, such idealization of the parent may take a second form, one entirely antagonistic to the sex element. For example, if the mother, whether explicitly or tacitly, holds sex interest to be distinctly sub-human, the son who idealizes her may read sexuality out of her kind altogether. Then when he comes of age, he may find that instead of being fully attracted to a girl of his mother's type, he can respect, like, and even have a tender emotion for her; but no more. On the other hand, he may find himself being passionately drawn toward a totally different sort, for whom he has not this same respect. Thus he finds exceedingly difficult the ideal unification of his emotional life.

In a third group of cases, it appears that the growing individual may develop an attachment in which the element of simple dependence upon the parent is the most prominent symptom. As a result, a young woman may prefer a very mature man who will stand, for her, *in loco parentis;* or a young man, correspondingly brought up, may find most satisfaction in the presence of a mature and motherly woman. Or, in the absence of a spouse, the individual may find some organization, or belief, to lean upon:—provided, of course, the young individual does not hit upon means of outgrowing his limitation; an important qualification which applies to all these cases.

Continuing with the topic of a right attitude towards marriage, we may observe that some fundamental factors are not always properly emphasized. Important as well as normal is the presence of genuine sex attraction; although this element in its simplicity is not necessarily fully conscious in the young woman at first. In addition there should be, as a factor of harmony in at least the emotional undercurrent of married life, requisite harmony in the sex relation itself. Satisfactory adjustment here is more rare than it ought to be in our civilization. It would seem self-evident that every person who is about to marry should be required by the state to possess not only physical health, but also an understanding of the nuclear emotion of married life.

Certainly there should be, as well, real affection between husband and wife; tender emotion, which partakes normally of a parental character on the part of each for the other. Incidentally, it seems only miseducation that ever prevents such tender emotion, and the sex attraction already referred to, from mutually reinforcing each other. And the same might be said of admiration, pride of possession, and the other components of human mating. The further goods of some degree of similarity in tastes, interests, and ideals, we need not discuss here; except to observe that our whole educational system appears productive of an unnecessary disparity of refinement between man and woman. Finally, education for mutual understanding, respect, and courtesy, and the grounding of these qualities in adequate *character,* are worthy of more than ordinary care in training for life.

A Sound Attitude towards Morals. It might seem to be a far cry from mental hygiene to morality. But actually, in a social world, the individual who regards morals as inevitably alien to his nature, must live much less richly than does the person who understands morals as racial achievements in living, and who therefore is interested in their continued growth.

Sound Thinking. Upon the fundamental topic, thinking, it is likewise possible to develop healthful as contrasted with undesirable attitudes. Individuals who fear to think, lest they think differently from the way they have thought before, or from the way the average citizen thinks, are persons who do not have a most healthy, well-ventilated mind. As Dr. F. L. Wells observes, "one may truly respect a boy of six, who, when asked by his grandmother whether he was not sorry that she had hurt her foot, replied that he had tried to be, but couldn't." [3] Perhaps this boy will be more able than some other persons, later on, to acknowledge a fault of his own; especially, to appreciate any dishonesty in his own thinking. For sincerity in thinking is essential to mental hygiene. It is by real thinking that our most complex adjustments must be made; along with, let us add, that quality of "sweet reasonableness" which needs development for every sphere of thought and action.

Conclusion. Detailed methods of achieving the foregoing goals of education are beyond the scope of the present discussion. However, in closing, we may remark the value to the child of a wholesome social environment; an environment which provides desirable patterns for imitation, and which includes sufficient understanding of the child's interests, without an excessively close emotional atmosphere. And always, explanation to the child, understanding on his part, and practice, naturally encourage the development of such habits and attitudes as conserve living.

References

General References on Mental Hygiene

The Journal of Mental Hygiene (quarterly), *Mental Hygiene Bulletin,* and the special publications of the Nat. Com. Ment. Hyg.

Publications of Mass. Soc. Ment. Hyg., and of other state societies.
The Journal of Abnormal and Social Psychology.

William H. Burnham, *The Normal Mind,* xi, 3, 8, 18, 19, etc.

E. Stanley Abbot, "What is Mental Hygiene?"

Tom A. Williams, in *Psychotherapy* (by Morton Prince, and others), 159-181.

---

[3] Frederic Lyman Wells, *Mental Adjustments,* 25 (Appleton, 1917).

Stewart Paton, *Signs of Sanity.*

George K. Pratt, *Your Mind and You,* 7-12.

George Van Ness Dearborn, *Nerve-Waste.*

Frankwood E. Williams, and others, *Social Aspects of Mental Hygiene.*

Donald A. Laird, "The Duty of the Psychopathologist to the Man on the Street."

—— "Does There Exist a Need for a Program of Education in Mental Hygiene?"

James V. May, *Mental Diseases,* 121-137.

Importance of the Early Years

Douglas A. Thom, "Habit Clinics for Children of the Pre-School Age."

Charles Macfie Campbell, "Psychology of the Pre-School Period."

—— "The Experiences of the Child."

J. A. Hadfield, *Psychology and Morals,* 17-19.

Austen Fox Riggs, *Just Nerves.*

John J. B. Morgan, *The Psychology of the Unadjusted School Child.*

Frank Watts, *Abnormal Psychology and Education.*

M. V. O'Shea, *Faults of Childhood and Youth.*

Eugenic Policy

Edward Huntington Williams and Ernest Bryant Hoag, *Our Fear Complexes,* 288-299.

Physical Benefits

Publications of the U. S. Dept. of Labor, Children's Bureau, Washington, D. C.

Mother and Child (published monthly).

Economic Factors

Charles Macfie Campbell, "Mental Factors in Industrial Hygiene."

—— "The Relation of Social and Economic Factors to Mental Hygiene."

Sociological Factors

Abraham Myerson, *The Nervous Housewife.*

Elmer E. Southard and Mary C. Jarrett, *The Kingdom of Evils.*

Douglas A. Thom, "Results and Future Opportunities in the Field of Clinics, Social Service, and Parole."

William Healy's works (Bibliog.).

Food Habits

James L. Mursell, "Contributions to the Psychology of Nutrition."
Josephine A. Jackson and Helen M. Salisbury, *Outwitting Our Nerves*, 250-277.
Charles Macfie Campbell, "Psychology of the Pre-School Period."

Sleep Habits

Josephine A. Jackson and Helen M. Salisbury, *Outwitting Our Nerves*, 322-332.

Mental Hygiene and Dreams

Mary Arnold-Forster, *Studies in Dreams* (partly as included in the present volume (pp. 596 *ff.*, *supra*).

The Sense of Humor in Relation to Mental Hygiene

William H. Burnham, *The Normal Mind*, 399-401, 408-409.

The Mental Hygiene of Play

G. W. T. Patrick, *The Psychology of Relaxation*.
William James, *The Gospel of Relaxation*.

Physical and Other Tasks as Related to Mental Hygiene

Pierre Janet, *Principles of Psychotherapy*, 56.
William H. Burnham, *The Normal Mind*.
George Walton, *Peg Along*.

Hygienic Attitudes Towards Fear and Frights

Boris Sidis, *The Causation, etc.*, 199-220.
Frankwood E. Williams, "Anxiety and Fear."
George L. Walton, *Why Worry?*

Anger in Relation to Mental Hygiene

Roy Franklin Richardson, *The Psychology and Pedagogy of Anger*.
George Malcolm Stratton, *Anger: Its Religious and Moral Significance*, 260-262.

Avoiding the Inferiority Reaction

English Bagby, "The Inferiority Reaction."
Tom A. Williams, *Dreads and Besetting Fears,* 21-25, 132-136.
——— "Psychasthenia and Inebriety."
William A. White, *The Mental Hygiene of Childhood,* 129-151, 189-190.

Development of Coöperativeness.

Hector Charles Cameron, *The Nervous Child,* 32, 63, 59-62.
Lee Edward Travis, on the significance of negativism in children, in the present volume, pp. 509 *ff., supra.*

Emotional Control

T. S. Henry, *Jour. Ed. Psychol.,* 8: 409-415 (1917).
Tom A. Williams, "The Treatment of the Emotions in Young People."
L. E. Emerson, *Nervousness.*
Douglas A. Thom, "The Preservation of Mental Health in Children."
H. Addington Bruce, *Nerve Control.*
Josephine A. Jackson and Helen M. Salisbury, *Outwitting Our Nerves,* 359-378.
Abraham Myerson, *The Nervous Housewife.*

Wholesomeness of Emotional Environment

Hector Charles Cameron, *The Nervous Child,* 6-13, 39-40.
Abraham Myerson, *The Nervous Housewife,* 19, *circa.*
——— "Eupathics."
George Van Ness Dearborn, *The Influence of Joy.*
Helen Williston Brown, "The Deforming Influences of the Home."
L. E. Emerson, "The Psychopathology of the Family."
Wm. A. White, *The Mental Hygiene of Childhood,* 64-76.
J. C. Flügel, *The Psychoanalytic Study of the Family.*
Elida Evans, *The Problem of the Nervous Child,* 13-14, 79-80, 118-120, 139-146, 168-170.
C. G. Jung, *The Theory of Psychoanalysis,* 45-53.
Alfred Adler, *Individual Psychology,* 321-323.
Charles Macfie Campbell, "Co-education of Children and Parents."

Sound Development Relative to Sex and Marriage

See references under preceding topic.
Oskar Pfister, *Psychoanalysis,* 160-161.
William A. White, *The Mental Hygiene of Childhood,* 116-122, 187-188.

Elida Evans, *The Problem of the Nervous Child*, 67-73*ff.*, 159, 180.

Smiley Blanton, "The Nervous Child," 4-5.

Tom A. Williams, *Jour. Abn. Psychol.*, 7: 411-413 (1913).

Helen Williston Brown, *Jour. Abn. Psychol.*, 14: 292-296 (1919).

Abraham Myerson, *The Nervous Housewife*, 128-140, 156, 142, 239-240, 158, 241-243, 230.

Wholesome Social Suggestion

Stewart Paton, *Signs of Sanity*, 211-215.

C. G. Jung, in Elida Evans' *The Problem of the Nervous Child*, vi-vii; and Evans, in the same book, 244.

Hector Charles Cameron, *The Nervous Child*, 26-32, 208-209.

Tom A. Williams, *Dreads and Besetting Fears*, 55-60.

Moral Education

Frank Chapman Sharp, *Education for Character*.

Paul Dubois, *The Education of Self*, 34-36.

J. A. Hadfield, *Psychology and Morals*, 43-45, 48-52, 136-147, 169-181.

Cyril Burt, *The Young Delinquent*, 501, *circa*.

Education through Understanding instead of Fearing

Hector Charles Cameron, *The Nervous Child*, 40-42.

Boris Sidis, *The Causation, etc.*, 223-238.

——, *Symptomatology, etc.*, 373.

Tom A. Williams, *Dreads, etc.*, 94-97.

Edward Huntington Williams and Ernest Bryant Hoag, *Our Fear Complexes:* "Introduction," and 189-211, 263-267, 300-306.

Stewart Paton, *Signs of Sanity*, 220-223.

Elida Evans, *The Problem of the Nervous Child*, 98-101, 167-168, 171-173, 177-178, 233, 237-238, 249.

William Healy's works (Bibliog.).

Edwin B. Holt, *The Freudian Wish*.

Mentally Hygienic Thinking

Eugenie Andruss Leonard, "A Parent's Study of Children's Lies," 129-135.

Paul Dubois, *The Education of Self*, 14-20.

George K. Pratt, *Your Mind and You*, 32*ff.*

Problems of Belief, in Relation to Mental Hygiene

Eugenie Andruss Leonard, "A Parent's Study of Children's Lies," 130-131.
Kimball Young, "The Integration of the Personality," 275-284.
Boris Sidis, *The Causation, etc.*, 286.
Poul Bjerre, *History and Practise of Psychoanalysis.*

Ritual in Relation to Mental Hygiene

Poul Bjerre, *History and Practise of Psychoanalysis.*
Hugo Münsterberg, *Psychotherapy,* 207-210, 224-225, 381-382.

Mental Hygiene Work in Connection with Schools and Colleges

Charles Macfie Campbell, "The Responsibilities of the Universities in Promoting Mental Hygiene."
Angus W. Morrison, "Mental Hygiene and Our Universities."
Donald A. Laird, "Should Young People Study Themselves?"
—— "The Reaction of College Students to Mental Hygiene."
—— "Detecting Abnormal Behavior."
"Report of the Committee on Mental Hygiene of the Vocational Guidance Conference," *Jour. Abn. Psychol.*, 19: 127-129 (1924).
Irving J. Sands and Phyllis Blanchard, *Abnormal Behavior,* 464-466.

BIBLIOGRAPHY

A list of books and articles of which direct mention has been made. The numerous other authors and publications referred to within selections will be found through the Index. Abbreviations, also, and publishers' addresses, are explicated in the Index.

ABBOT, E. Stanley, "Preventable Forms of Mental Disease and How to Prevent Them," *Boston Med. & Surg. Jour.*, 174: 555-563 (1916).
—— "The Principles of Diagnosis in Psychiatry," *Am. Jour. Insan.*, 74: 369-379 (1918).
—— "What Is Mental Hygiene?" *Am. Jour. Psychiat.*, 4: 261-284 (1924).
ADLER, Alfred, *Individual Psychology* (Harcourt, Brace, 1924).
—— *The Neurotic Constitution* (Moffat, Yard, 1917).
—— *A Study of Organ Inferiority and Its Psychical Compensation* (Nerv. & Ment. Dis. Pub'g Co., 1917).
AIKINS, Herbert Austin, "Casting Out a 'Stuttering Devil,'" *Jour. Abn. Psychol.*, 18: 137-152 (1923).
ALEXANDER, T. Matthias, *Man's Supreme Inheritance* (Methuen, 1919).
ALLPORT, Floyd Henry, Social Psychology (Houghton, 1924).
—— *Cf.* also Editors of the *Jour. Abn. Psychol.*
ARNOLD-FORSTER, Mary, *Studies in Dreams* (Allen & U., 1922; Macmillan, 1921).
AUSTIN, Mary, in *The Unpartizan Rev.*, 14: 336-347 (1920).
BAGBY, English, "The Etiology of Phobias," *Jour. Abn. Psychol.*, 17: 16-18 (1922).
—— "The Inferiority Reaction," *Jour. Abn. Psychol.*, 18: 269-273 (1923).
BAIN, Alexander, *The Emotions and the Will,* 4th ed., 428-432 (Longmans, 1899).
BAUDOUIN, Charles, *Suggestion and Autosuggestion* (Allen & U., 1921; Dodd).
BENTLEY, Madison, *The Field of Psychology* (Appleton, 1924).
BERNHEIM, H., *Suggestive Therapeutics* (Putnam, 1889).
BERRY, Charles Scott, "Obsessions of Normal Minds," *Jour. Abn. Psychol.*, 11: 19, *circa* (1916).
BIANCHI, Leonardo, *The Mechanism of the Brain and the Function of the Frontal Lobes* (Wood, 1922).

BIANCHI, Leonardo, *Text-book of Psychiatry for Physicians and Students* (Wood, 1906).

BINET, Alfred, *La Suggestibilité* (1900).

BJERRE, Poul, *The History and Practise of Psychoanalysis* (Badger, 1916).

BLANTON, Margaret Gray, and BLANTON, Smiley, "What is the Problem of Stuttering?" *Jour. Abn. Psychol.*, 13: 305-313 (1919).

BLANTON, Smiley, "The Medical Significance of the Disorders of Speech," *Jour. Am. Med. Ass'n.*, 77: 375ff. (1921).

—— "The Nervous Child," *Wis. Med. Jour.*, Vol. 17, No. 71 (1920).

—— "Speech Disorder as a Psychiatric Problem," *Jour. of Oralism & Auralism*, 1-3 (1921).

BRAMWELL, J. Milne, *Hypnotism, Its History, Practice, and Theory* (Lippincott, 3d ed., 1907).

BREESE, B. B., *Psychology* (Scribner, 1921).

BRIDGES, James Winfred, *An Outline of Abnormal Psychology* (Adams, 1925).

—— "Psychoanalysis, a Contribution to the New Psychology," *Public Health Jour.*, June, 1923, 1-7.

—— "A Reconciliation of Current Theories of Emotion," *Jour. Abn. Psychol.*, 19: 339-340 (1925).

BRONNER, Augusta F., "Effect of Adolescent Instability on Conduct," *Psychol. Clinic*, 8: 249-265 (1915).

BROWN, Haydn, *Advanced Suggestion* (Wood, 1922).

BROWN, Helen Williston, "The Deforming Influences of the Home," *Jour. Abn. Psychol.*, 12: 49-57 (1917).

BROWN, Mabel Webster, *Neuropsychiatry and the War*, Supplement 1, 9 (War Work Com., Nat. Com. Ment. Hyg., 1918).

BROWN, Sanger, II, "The Herd Instinct," *Jour. Abn. Psychol.*, 16: 232-237 (1921).

BROWN, William, "Suggestion and Personality," in *Problems of Personality* (C. Macfie Campbell, etc., Eds.), 305-310 (Harcourt, Brace, 1925).

BRUCE, H. Addington, *Nerve Control* (Funk & Wagnalls).

—— *Psychology and Parenthood* (Dodd, 1919).

BURNHAM, William H., *The Normal Mind: An Introduction to Mental Hygiene and the Hygiene of School Instruction* (Appleton, 1924).

BURR, C. B., *Practical Psychology and Psychiatry, For Use in Training-Schools for Attendants and Nurses and in Medical Classes, and as a Ready Reference for the Practitioner* (Davis, 1921).

BURROW, Trigant, an account of Jung's doctrine, *Jour. Abn. Psychol.*, 12: 161ff. (1917).

BURT, Cyril, *The Young Delinquent* (Appleton, 1925).

CABOT, Richard C., "Whose Business is Psychotherapy?", *Psychotherapy*, Vol. III, No. 4.

CAMERON, Hector Charles, *The Nervous Child* (Oxford, 1924).

CAMPBELL, Charles Macfie, "Co-Education of Children and Parents," *The Family*, Vol. I, No. 9, pp. 1-3 (1921).

—— "The Experiences of the Child: How They Affect Character and Behavior," *Mental Hygiene*, 4: 312-319 (1920).

—— "Mental Factors in Industrial Hygiene," *Jour. of Industrial Hygiene*, 5: 130-137.

—— "On the Mechanism of Some Cases of Manic-Depressive Excitement," *Rev. Neurol. & Psychiat.*, 12: 175-198 (1914).

—— *A Present-Day Conception of Mental Disorders* (Harvard, 1924).

—— "Psychology of the Pre-School Period," *Mother and Child*, Vol. 3, No. 3 (March, 1922).

—— "The Psychopathologist and His Responsibility," *Jour. Abn. Psychol.*, 14: 53, *circa* (1919).

—— "The Relation of Social and Economic Factors to Mental Hygiene," *Am. Jour. Public Health*, 6: 1278-1282.

—— "The Responsibilities of the Universities in Promoting Mental Hygiene," *Mental Hygiene*, April, 1919.

—— "The Sex Instinct," *Jour. Abn. Psychol.*, 16: 243-248 (1921).

——, and others, *Problems of Personality: Studies Presented to Dr. Morton Prince, Pioneer in American Psychopathology* (Harcourt, Brace, 1925).

CANNON, Walter B., *Bodily Changes in Pain, Hunger, Fear and Rage* (Appleton, 1915).

CARR, Harvey A., *Psychology* (Longmans, 1925).

CARVER, Alfred, an abstract of W. S. Inman's article, "Emotion and Eye Symptoms," in *Jour. Neurol. & Psychopath.*, 2: 386-387 (1922).

CHURCH, A., and PETERSON, F., *Nervous & Mental Diseases* (Saunders, 1908).

CONKLIN, Edmund S., "Definition of Introversion, Extroversion, and Allied Concepts," *Jour. Abn. Psychol.*, 17: 367-382 (1923).

CORE, Donald F., *Functional Nervous Disorders* (Wood, 1922).

CORIAT, Isador H., *Abnormal Psychology* (Kegan Paul, 1910).

—— "The Experimental Synthesis of the Dissociated Memories in Alcoholic Amnesia," *Jour. Abn. Psychol.*, Aug., 1906.

—— Case of cure by suggestion, *Jour. Abn. Psychol.*, 2: 168-169 1907).

CORY, E., "Patience Worth," *Psychol. Rev.*, 26: 397-406 (1919); published also in Edward Stevens Robinson and Florence Richardson-Robinson, *Readings in General Psychology*, 555-563 (Univ. of Chicago Press, 1923).

—— "The Problem of the Individual," *Jour. Abn. Psychol.*, 16: 374-383 (1922).

CRAWFORD, Nelson Antrim, "Literature and the Psychopathic," *Psychoan. Rev.*, 10: 440-446 (1923).

CROOK, Guy Hamilton, "A Memory of Infantile Life," *Jour. Abn. Psychol.*, 20: 90-91 (1925).

CURRAN, Pearl Lenore, "A Nut for Psychologists," *The Unpartizan Review*, 13: 357-372 (1920).

CUTTEN, George Barton, *Three Thousand Years of Mental Healing* (Scribner, 1911).

DEARBORN, George Van Ness, *The Influence of Joy* (Little, Brown, 1916).

—— *Nerve-Waste* (Health Ed. League).

DODGE, Raymond, "The Problem of Inhibition," *Psychol. Rev.*, 33: 1-12 (1926).

DONLEY, John E., "Psychotherapy and Education," *Jour. Abn. Psychol.*, 6: 1-10 (1910).

DRUCKER, Saul, and HEXTER, M. B., *Children Astray* (Harvard, 1923).

DU BOIS, Paul, *The Education of Self* (Funk & Wagnalls, 1911).

DUNLAP, Knight, *Elements of Scientific Psychology* (Mosby, 1922).

—— "Sleep and Dreams," *Jour. Abn. Psychol.*, 16: 197-209 (June-Sept., 1921).

EDITORS of the *Jour. Abn. Psychol.*, "Editorial Announcement," 16: 1-4 (1921).

ELLIS, Havelock, *The World of Dreams* (Houghton, 1911).

EMERSON, L. E., "The Psychopathology of the Family," *Jour. Abn. Psychol.*, 9: 333-340 (1914).

—— *Nervousness* (Little, Brown, 1918).

Encyclopædia Britannica (Cambridge Press).

EVANS, Elida, *The Problem of the Nervous Child* (Dodd, 1922).

EVERETT, Walter Goodnow, *Moral Values* (Holt, 1918).

EWER, Bernard C., *Applied Psychology* (Macmillan, 1923).

FLÜGEL, J. C., *The Psycho-Analytic Study of the Family* (Internat. Psychoan. Press, 1921).

FORD, James, *Social Problems and Social Policy* (Ginn, 1923).

FOX, Charles Daniel, *The Psychopathology of Hysteria* (Badger, 1913).

FRANZ, Shepherd Ivory, "Experimental Psychopathology," *Psychol. Bull.*, 9: 145-154 (1912).

—— *Nervous and Mental Re-Education* (Macmillan, 1923).

FREUD, Sigmund, *A General Introduction to Psychoanalysis* (Boni, 1920).

—— *Introductory Lectures on Psycho-Analysis* (Allen & U., 1922).

—— "The Origin and Development of Psychoanalysis," *Am. Jour. Psychol.*, 21: 181ff. (1910).

FREYD, Max, "Introverts and Extroverts," *Psychol. Rev.*, 31: 74-87 (1924).

FRINK, H. W., *Morbid Fears and Compulsions* (Dodd, 1921).

FULLER, Justin Keyser, *The Psychology and Physiology of Mirror-Writing* (Univ. of Calif. Publ. in Psychol., 1916).

GAULT, Robert H., *Social Psychology: The Bases of Behavior Called Social* (Holt, 1923).

GILLESPIE, Robert D., "Folie á Deux: Dual Organ Inferiority, Religious Conversion, and Evangelism: Conflict, Psychosis, and Adjustment," *Jour. Neur. & Psychopath.*, 3: 269-273 (1922-23).

GIVLER, Robert Chenault, *The Ethics of Hercules, A Study of Man's Body as the Sole Determinant of Ethical Values* (Knopf, 1924).

GLUECK, Bernard, "The Ego Instinct," *Jour. Abn. Psychol.*, 16: 226-231 (1921).

GODDARD, Henry H., *Psychology of the Normal and Subnormal* (Dodd, Mead, 1919).

—— "The Sub-Normal Mind Versus the Abnormal," *Jour. Abn. Psychol.*, 16: 47-54 (1921).

—— "The Unconscious in Psychoanalysis," in *Problems of Personality*, C. Macfie Campbell, etc., Eds., 313-329 (Harcourt, Brace, 1925).

GOLDENWEISER, Alexander A., *Early Civilization: An Introduction to Anthropology* (Knopf, 1921).

GREEN, George H., *Psychoanalysis in the Classroom* (Putnam, 1922).

GRIFFITH, Coleman R., *General Introduction to Psychology* (Macmillan, 1923).

HADFIELD, J. A., *Psychology and Morals: An Analysis of Character* (McBride, 1923).

—— "Treatment by Suggestion and Persuasion," in H. Crichton Miller's Volume, *Functional Nerve Disease*, 61-87 (Oxford, 1920).

HAINES, Thomas H., "The Genesis of a Paranoic State, Delusions of Persecution based upon a Character Defect in Volitional Equipment," *Jour. Abn. Psychol.*, 11: 368-395.

HALL, G. Stanley, *Adolescence*, 2 vols. (Appleton, 1905).

—— *The Life and Confessions of a Psychologist* (Appleton, 1924).

HAMILTON, G. V., *Objective Psychopathology* (Mosby, 1925).

HAMILTON, Margaret J., a study of psychopathic cases, *Jour. Abn. Psychol.*, 13: 324-350 (1919).

HART, Bernard, *The Psychology of Insanity* (Cambridge Press, 1919).

HARTMAN, D. A., "The Psychological Point of View in History: Some Phases of the Slavery Struggle," *Jour. Abn. Psychol.*, 17: 262-264, *circa* (1922).

HARVEY, Nathan A., *Imaginary Playmates and Other Mental Phenomena of Children* (State Normal College, Ypsilanti, Mich., 1918).

HEALY, William, *The Individual Delinquent: A Text-Book of Diagnosis and Prognosis for all Concerned in Understanding Offenders* (Little, Brown, 1920).

—— *Mental Conflicts and Misconduct* (Little, Brown, 1917).

HINGLEY, R. H., *Psycho-Analysis* (Dodd, 1922).

HOLLINGWORTH, H. L., *The Psychology of Functional Neuroses* (Appleton, 1920).

HOLT, Edwin B., *The Freudian Wish and Its Place in Ethics* (Holt, 1915).

HORTON, Lydiard H., *The Dream Problem* (Cartesian Research Soc., 1926).

—— "How 'Stimulus and Reaction' Explains Levitation Dreams," *Jour. Abn. Psychol.*, 15 : 11-35 (1920).

—— "Mechanistic Features in the Dream Process," *Jour. Abn. Psychol.*, 14 : 168-196 (1920).

—— "Resolution of a Skin Phobia with Nightmare," *Jour. Abn. Psychol.*, 15 : 157-186 (1920).

—— "Scientific Method in the Interpretation of Dreams, With a Theory to Explain the Dream-Process as Apperceptive Trial-and-Error," *Jour. Abn. Psychol.*, 10 : 369-399 (1916).

—— "What Drives the Dream Mechanism?," *Jour. Abn. Psychol.*, 15 : 224-258 (1920).

HULL, Clark L., and LUGOFF, L. S., "Complex Signs in Diagnostic Free Association," *Jour. Exper. Psychol.*, 4 : 111-136 (1921).

HUMPHREY, George, "The Conditioned Reflex and the Freudian Wish," *Jour. Abn. Psychol.*, 14 : 392, *circa* (1920).

—— "Education and Freudianism," *Jour. Abn. Psychol.*, 15 : 372-384 (1920-1921). *Cf.* also 402.

HUNTER, Walter S., *General Psychology* (Univ. of Chicago Press, 1923).

HURST, Arthur F., *The Psychology of the Special Senses and their Functional Disorders* (The Croonian Lectures) (Oxford, 1920).

INMAN, W. S., "Emotion and Eye Symptoms," *Brit. Jour. Psychol., Med. Sect.*, 2 : 47ff. (1921).

JACKSON, Josephine A., and SALISBURY, Helen M., *Outwitting Our Nerves: A Primer of Psychotherapy* (Century Co., 1922).

JACKSON, Theresa M., "Some Current Views with Regard to the Field of Abnormal Psychology and Mental Hygiene," *Jour. Abn. Psychol.* (1926).

JAMES, William, *Psychology* (Holt, 1892).

JANET, Pierre, *The Major Symptoms of Hysteria* (Macmillan, 1920).

—— "Memories that are too Real," in *Problems of Personality* (C. Macfie Campbell, etc., Eds.), 141-150 (Harcourt, 1925).

—— *The Mental State of Hystericals: A Study of Mental Stigmata and Mental Accidents* (Putnam, 1901).

—— "On the Pathogenesis of Some Impulsions," *Jour. Abn. Psychol.*, 1 : 12-17 (1905).

—— *Principles of Psychotherapy* (Macmillan, 1924).

JASTROW, Joseph, *Fact and Fable in Psychology* (Houghton, 1900).

—— *The Subconscious* (Houghton, 1906).

JONES, Ernest, "Freud's Theory of Dreams," *Am. Jour. Psychol.,* Vol. 21, 1910.

—— *Papers on Psycho-Analysis* (Toronto, 1918).

JUDD, Charles Hubbard, *Psychology: General Introduction* (Ginn, 1917).

JUNG, Carl G., *Collected Papers* (Baillière; Moffat, Yard, 1916); now published under the title *Analytical Psychology* (Dodd, Mead).

—— *The Psychology of Dementia Precox* (Nerv. & Ment. Dis. Pub'g. Co., 1909).

—— *The Theory of Psychoanalysis* (Nerv. & Ment. Dis. Pub'g. Co., 1915).

KAISER, Irving R., on conception of perspective, *Pedag. Sem.,* 28 : 344, *circa* (1921).

——, on word association, *Pedag. Sem.,* 28 : 358-364 (1921).

KEMPF, Edward J., *The Autonomic Functions and the Personality* (Nerv. & Ment. Dis. Pub'g. Co., 1921).

—— *Psychopathology* (Mosby, 1920).

KRETSCHMER, E., *Physique and Character* (Harcourt, Brace, 1925).

LAIRD, Donald A., "Detecting Abnormal Behavior," *Jour. Abn. Psychol.,* 20 : 128-141 (1925).

—— "Does There Exist a Need for a Program of Education in Mental Hygiene ?," *Mental Hygiene,* 4 : 293-403 (1920).

—— "The Duty of the Psychopathologist to the Man on the Street," *Jour. Abn. Psychol.,* 14 : 406-410 (1920).

—— "A Mental Hygiene and Vocational Guidance Test," *Jour. Educ. Psychol.,* 16 : 419-422 (1925).

—— "The Reaction of College Students to Mental Hygiene," *Mental Hygiene,* 7 : 271-276 (1923).

—— "Sex Differences in Emotional Outlets," *Science,* 62 : 292*ff.* (1925).

—— "Should Young People Study Themselves ?," *The Survey,* 53 : 405-407 (1925).

LANGFELD, Herbert Sidney, "Conflict and Adjustment in Art," *Problems of Personality,* Studies in Honor of Dr. Morton Prince, (C. Macfie Campbell, and others, Eds.), 373-383 (Harcourt, Brace, 1925).

LAUMONIER, J., *Le Freudism Exposé et Critiqué* (Félix Alcan, Paris, 1925).

LEONARD, Eugenie Andruss, "A Parent's Study of Children's Lies," *Pedag. Sem.,* 27 : 123, *circa* (1920).

LEUBA, James H., *The Psychology of Religious Mysticism* (Harcourt, Brace, 1925).

LOEWENFELD, Leopold, *Sexuelle Konstitution* (J. F. Bergmann—— Verlagsbuchhandlung, Munich).

LORENZ, W. F., LOEVENHART, A. S., BLECKWENN, W. J., and HODGES, F. J., article on tryparsamide, *Jour. Am. Med. Assn.*, 80:1497 (1923).

LOVELL, H. Tasman, *Dreams,* Mono. No. II (Aust. Ass'n Psychol. & Philos., Univ. of Sydney, Australia, 1923).

MACDOUGALL, Robert, "Contrary Suggestion," *Jour. Abn. Psychol.,* 6: 368-391 (1911-1912).

MCDOUGALL, William, "Four Cases of 'Regression' in Soldiers," *Jour. Abn. Psychol.,* 15: 136-156 (1920).

—— "Hypnotism," *Ency. Brit.,* 11th ed.

—— *Outline of Psychology* (Scribner, 1923).

—— "The Revival of Emotional Memories and its Therapeutic Value," *Brit. Jour. Psychol., Med. Sect.,* Vol. I, Part 1, 26, *circa* (Oct., 1920).

—— "Suggestion," *Ency. Brit.,* 11th ed.

—— "Summary," in H. Crichton Miller's *Functional Nerve Disease,* 181-198 (Oxford, 1920).

MARTIN, Everett Dean, *The Behavior of Crowds: A Psychological Study* (Harper, 1920).

MATEER, Florence, *The Unstable Child: An Interpretation of Psychopathy as a Source of Unbalanced Behavior in Abnormal and Troublesome Children* (Appleton, 1924).

MAY, James V., *Mental Diseases, A Public Health Problem* (Badger, 1922).

—— and others, *Statistical Manual for the Use of Hospitals for Mental Diseases,* Com. on Stat., Am. Psychiat. Assn., 3d ed. (1918).

MEYER, Max, *The Psychology of the Other-One* (Missouri Book Co., 1921).

MICKLEM, E. R., *Miracles and the New Psychology* (Oxford, 1922).

MILLER, H. Crichton, *Functional Nerve Disease: An Epitome of War Experience for the Practitioner* (Oxford, 1920).

MINER, James Burt, "A Case of Vision Acquired in Adult Life," *Psychol. Rev.,* 11: 103-113 (1904); also in Edward Stevens Robinson and Florence Richardson-Robinson, *Readings in General Psychology,* 266-268 (Univ. of Chicago Press, 1923).

MITCHELL, T. W., *The Psychology of Medicine* (Methuen, 1921).

MOLL, Albert, *Hypnotism* (Walter Scott, 1897).

MORGAN, John J. B., "Hypnosis with Direct Psychoanalytic Statement and Suggestion in the Treatment of a Psychoneurotic of Low Intelligence," *Jour. Abn. Psychol.,* 19: 160-164 (1924).

—— *The Psychology of the Unadjusted School Child* (Macmillan, 1924).

MORRISON, Angus W., "Mental Hygiene and Our Universities," *Mental Hygiene,* 7: 258-270 (1923).

MOSSO, Angelo, *Fatigue* (Putnam, 1906).

MOTT, Fredk. W., *War Neuroses and Shell Shock* (Oxford, 1919).

MÜHL, Anita M., "Automatic Writing as an Indicator of the Fundamental Factors Underlying the Personality," *Jour. Abn. Psychol.*, 17: 162-183 (1922).

—— "Automatic Writing Combined with Crystal Gazing as a Means of Recalling Forgotten Incidents," *Jour. Abn. Psychol.*, 19: 264-273 (1924).

—— "Use of Automatic Writing in Determining Conflicts and Early Childhood Impressions," *Jour. Abn. Psychol.*, 18: 1-32 (1923).

MÜNSTERBERG, Hugo, *Psychotherapy* (Moffat, Yard, 1909).

MURSELL, James L., "Contributions to the Psychology of Nutrition," "I. Hunger and Appetite," *Psychol. Rev.*, 32: 317-333 (1925).

—— "II. The Sucking Reaction as a Determiner of Food and Drug Habits," *Psychol. Rev.*, 1926.

MYERSON, Abraham, "Eupathics," *Jour. Abn. Psychol.*, 12: 343-347 (1918).

—— *The Inheritance of Mental Diseases* (Williams & Wilkins, 1925).

—— *The Nervous Housewife* (Little, Brown, 1920).

—— *When Life Loses Its Zest* (Little, Brown, 1925).

NICOLL, Maurice, "Psycho-Analysis," in *Functional Nerve Disease*, (H. Crichton Miller, Ed.), 129-152 (Oxford, 1920).

NORTHRIDGE, W. L., *Modern Theories of the Unconscious* (Dutton, 1924).

O'SHEA, M. V., *Faults of Childhood and Youth* (Drake, 1920).

PARISH, Edmund, *Hallucinations and Illusions, A Study of the Fallacies of Perception* (Scribner, 1898).

PARSONS, Robert Percival, "Tryparsamide and Sulpharsphenamine in the Treatment of Neurosyphilis," *U. S. N. Med. Bull.*, Vol. 22, No. 5.

—— and TAYLOR, W. S., "A Case of Obsessive Phantasying." Prepared for this volume.

—— "Psychoses with Psychopathic Personality." Prepared for this volume.

PATON, Stewart, *Signs of Sanity, and The Principles of Mental Hygiene* (Scribner, 1922).

PATRICK, G. T. W., *Psychology of Relaxation* (Houghton, 1916).

PEAR, T. H., *Remembering and Forgetting* (Methuen, 1922).

PERRY, Ralph Barton, "Behavioristic View of Purpose," *Jour. Philos.*, 18: 85-105 (1921).

PFISTER, Oskar, *Psycho-Analysis in the Service of Education: Being an Introduction to Psycho-Analysis* (Kimpton, 1922).

PIERCE, Frederick, *Our Unconscious Mind, and How to Use It* (Dutton, 1922).

PILLSBURY, W. B., *The Fundamentals of Psychology*, Rev. ed., (Macmillan, 1922).

PRATT, George K., *Your Mind and You: Mental Health* (Funk & Wagnalls, 1924).

PRESCOTT, F. C., *The Poetic Mind* (Macmillan).

PRESSEY, Harold E., "The Subconscious and the Various Orders of Cerebration (With Schema)." Prepared for this volume.

PRINCE, Morton, "The Actuality and Nature of Subconscious Processes," *Jour. Abn. Psychol.*, 19 : 129-131 (1924).

—— "Association Neuroses," *Jour. Nerv. & Ment. Dis.*, May, 1891.

—— "Awareness, Consciousness, Co-consciousness and Animal Intelligence from the Point of View of the Data of Normal Psychology," in *Pedag. Sem.*, 32 : 166-188 (1925).

—— "Coconscious Images," *Jour. Abn. Psychol.*, Dec., 1917.

—— *The Dissociation of a Personality: A Biographical Study in Abnormal Psychology* (Longmans, 1910).

—— "The Educational Treatment of Neurasthenia and Certain Hysterical States," *Boston Med. & Surg. Jour.*, Oct., 1898.

—— "An Experimental Study of the Mechanism of Hallucinations," in *Brit. Jour. Psychol.*, Med. Sect., Vol. II, Part 3, 165-208 (April, 1922).

—— "Hay Fever, Due to Nervous Influences, Occurring in Five Members of the Same Family," *Annals of Gyn.*, 1895.

—— "Miss Beauchamp—The Theory of the Psychogenesis of Multiple Personality," *Jour. Abn. Psychol.*, 15 : 67-135 (1925).

—— "The Problem of Personality," *Pedag. Sem.*, 32 : 266-292 (1925).

—— "Traumatic Neuroses," *Boston Med. & Surg. Jour.* (1889).

—— *The Unconscious: The Fundamentals of Human Personality, Normal and Abnormal* (Macmillan, 1921).

—— a case of cure by suggestion, *Jour. Abn. Psychol.*, 2 : 168, *circa* (1907).

—— *Cf.* also Editors of the *Jour. Abn. Psychol.*

—— and PUTNAM, James J., "A Clinical Study of a Case of Phobia—Symposium," *Jour. Abn. Psychol.*, 7 : 259-292 (1912).

—— and others, *Psychotherapeutics* (Badger, 1909).

REED, Ralph, "A Manic-Depressive Attack Presenting a Reversion to Infantilism," *Jour. Abn. Psychol.*, 11 : 359-367 (1917).

RICHARDSON, Roy Franklin, *The Psychology and Pedagogy of Anger* (Warwick, 1918).

RICHER, Paul, *Études cliniques sur la grande hystérie* (1885).

RIGGS, Austen Fox, *Just Nerves* (Houghton, 1922).

—— "The Psychoneuroses: Their Nature and Treatment," *Am. Jour. Psychiat.*, 91-110 (1923).

RIVERS, W. H. R., *Instinct and the Unconscious: A Contribution to a Biological Theory of the Psycho-Neuroses* (Cambridge, 1922).

ROBACK, A. A., "Character and Inhibition," in *Problems of Personality* (C. Macfie Campbell, etc., Eds.), 79-138 (Harcourt, Brace, 1925).

—— "The Freudian Doctrine of Lapses and Its Failings," *Am. Jour. Psychol.*, 30 : 274-290 (1919).

Roback, A. A., "The Interference of Will-Impulses: With Applications to Pedagogy, Ethics and Practical Efficiency," *Psychol. Mono.*, Vol. XXV, No. 5 (1918).

Robinson, Edward S., "A Concept of Compensation and Its Psychological Setting," *Jour. Abn. Psychol.*, 17: 383-394 (1923).

—— and Richardson-Robinson, Florence, *Readings in General Psychology* (Univ. of Chicago Press, 1923).

Rosanoff, Aaron J., *Manual of Psychiatry* (Wiley, 1920).

—— "A Theory of Personality Based Mainly on Psychiatric Experience," *Psychol. Bull.*, 17: 281-299 (1920).

—— and Orr, Florence I., "A Study of Heredity in Insanity in the Light of the Mendelian Theory," *Bull. No. 5,* Eugenics Record Office, Cold Spring Harbor, N. Y., Oct., 1911.

Sands, Irving J., and Blanchard, Phyllis, *Abnormal Behavior: Pitfalls of our Minds: An Introduction to the Study of Abnormal and Anti-Social Behavior* (Moffat, Yard, 1923).

Scott, W. D., "Personal Differences in Suggestibility," *Psychol. Rev.*, 17: 147-154 (1910).

Sharp, Frank Chapman, *Education for Character: Moral Training in the School and Home* (Bobbs-Merrill, 1917).

Sherman, Mandel, and Beverly, Bert I., "Hallucinations in Children," *Jour. Abn. Psychol.*, 19: 165-170 (1924).

Sherrington, Charles, *The Integrative Action of the Nervous System* (Yale, 1906).

Sidis, Boris, *The Causation and Treatment of Psychopathic Diseases* (Badger, 1916).

—— *The Foundations of Normal and Abnormal Psychology* (Badger, 1914).

—— *Nervous Ills: Their Cause and Cure* (Badger, 1922).

—— *The Psychology of Suggestion: A Research into the Subconscious Nature of Man and Society* (Appleton, 1898).

—— *Symptomatology, Psychognosis and Diagnosis of Psychopathic Diseases* (Badger, 1914).

—— and Goodhart, Simon P., *Multiple Personality: An Experimental Investigation into the Nature of Human Individuality* (Appleton, 1919).

Smith, Stevenson, and Guthrie, Edwin R., "Exhibitionism," *Jour. Abn. Psychol.*, 17: 206-209 (1922).

—— *General Psychology in Terms of Behavior* (Appleton, 1923).

Solomon, Meyer, "Analysis of a Single Dream as a Means of Unearthing the Genesis of Psychopathic Affections," *Jour. Abn. Psychol.*, 10: 19-31 (1915).

—— "On the Use of the Term Psychoanalysis and Its Substitute," *Med. Record,* Sept. 18, 1915.

—— "Psychopathology of Every-day Life: A Critical Review of Dr. Sigmund Freud's Theories," *Jour. Abn. Psychol.*, 11: 23-47 (1916).

SOLOMON, Meyer, on case study, *Jour. Abn. Psychol.,* 11: 309-324 (1917).

SOUTHARD, Elmer E., "General Psychopathology," *Psychol. Bull.,* 16: 197, *circa* (1919).

—— "How Far is Environment Responsible for Delusions?," *Jour. Abn. Psychol.,* 8: 117ff. (1913).

—— "On the Somatic Sources of Somatic Delusions," *Jour. Abn. Psychol.,* 7: 326ff. (1912).

—— a review of Southard's *Shell-Shock and Other Neuropsychiatric Problems Presented in 589 Cases from the War Literature,* in *Psychol. Bull.,* 16: 187-199 (1919).

—— *Shell-Shock and Other Neuropsychiatric Problems Presented in 589 Cases from the War Literature* (Leonard, 1919).

—— and JARRETT, Mary C., *The Kingdom of Evils: Psychiatric Social Work Presented in One Hundred Case Histories Together with a Classification of Social Divisions of Evil* (Macmillan, 1922).

SPINOZA, Benedict, *Ethics.*

STRATTON, George Malcolm, *Anger: Its Religious and Moral Significance* (Macmillan, 1923).

—— "An Experience During Danger and the Wider Functions of Emotion," *Problems of Personality* (C. Macfie Campbell, etc., Eds.), 47-62 (Harcourt, Brace, 1925).

SULLY, James, *Illusions: A Psychological Study* (Appleton, 1897).

TAIT, W. D., "A Short Study in Dislike," *Jour. Abn. Psychol.,* 7: 1-4 (1912).

TANSLEY, A. G., *The New Psychology and Its Relation to Life* (Dodd, 1924).

TAYLOR, E. W., "Simple Explanation and Re-Education as a Therapeutic Method," in *Psychotherapeutics* (Badger, 1910).

—— "Some Medical Aspects of Witchcraft," in *Problems of Personality* (C. Macfie Campbell, etc., Eds.), 165-188 (Harcourt, Brace, 1925).

—— on psychotherapy, *Jour. Abn. Psychol.,* Vol. 5 (1911).

—— on psychotherapy, *Jour. Abn. Psychol.,* 6: 449ff. (1912).

TAYLOR, Griffith, *With Scott: The Silver Lining,* 287, *circa* (Smith, Elder, 1916).

TAYLOR, W. S., "Behavior under Hypnoanalysis, and the Mechanism of the Neurosis," *Jour. Abn. Psychol.,* 18: 107-124 (1923).

—— "Character and Abnormal Psychology," *Jour. Abn. Psychol.,* 21: 85-86 (1926).

—— "Characteristics of the Neurotically Predisposed," *Jour. Abn. Psychol.,* 20: 377-383 (1926).

—— "A Hypnoanalytic Study of Two Cases of War Neurosis," *Jour. Abn. Psychol.,* 16: 344-355 (1921-1922).

—— "Mental Hygiene." Written for this volume.

—— "'Modern Theories of the Unconscious' (Northridge): A Review with a Discussion of 'Repression,' 'Catharsis,' and 'The Unconscious,'" *Jour. Abn. Psychol.,* 20: 82-88 (1925).

TAYLOR, W. S., "The Nature of the Complex as Compared with the Sentiment," *Psychol. Rev.*, 33: 68-69 (1926).

—— "Rationalization and Its Social Significance," *Jour. Abn. Psychol.*, 17: 410-418 (1923).

THOM, Douglas A., "Habit Clinics for Children of the Pre-School Age, *Mental Hygiene*, 6: 463-470 (1922).

—— "The Preservation of Mental Health in Children," *Bost. Med. & Surg. Jour.*, Vol. 189, No. 1, pp. 12-14, July 5, 1923.

—— "Results and Future Opportunities in the Field of Clinics, Social Service, and Parole," *Mental Hygiene*, 6: 714-728 (1922).

TJADEN, John Christian, "The Causes of Delinquency in Boys of Superior Intelligence" (The Board of Control of State Institutions, Des Moines, Iowa, 1923).

TOWN, Clara Harrison, "Suggestion," *Psychol. Bull.*, 18: 366-375 (1921).

TRAVIS, Lee Edward, "Mental Conflicts as the Cause of Bad Spelling and Poor Writing," *Psychoan. Rev.*, 11: 175, circa (1924).

—— "Suggestibility and Negativism as Measured by Auditory Threshold During Reverie," *Jour. Abn. Psychol.*, 18: 350-368 (1924).

—— "A Test for Distinguishing Between Schizophrenoses and Psychoneuroses," *Jour. Abn. Psychol.*, 283-298 (1924).

TRAVIS, Roland C., "A Study of the Effect of Hypnosis on a Case of Dissociation Precipitated by Migraine," *Am. Jour. Psychol.*, 36: 207-213 (1925).

TROTTER, W., *Instincts of the Herd in Peace and War* (Macmillan, 1916).

van DYKE, Henry, "The Fringe of Words," *Yale Review*, 12: 78, circa (1922).

van RENTERGHEM, A. W., on the historical relation of Breuer, Freud, Jung, etc., to Charcot and others, *Jour. Abn. Psychol.*, 9: 369ff., 10: 46-61 (1914-1915).

VARENDONCK, J., *The Psychology of Day-Dreams* (London: George Allen & Unwin, Ltd., 1921).

VASCHIDE, Nicolas, *Les hallucinations télépathiques* (Bibliothèque de psychologie experiméntale et de métapsychie) (Blond et Cie., Paris, 1908).

von HARTMANN, Eduard, *Philosophy of the Unconscious* (1869).

WALSH, James Joseph, *Cures: The Story of the Cures That Fail* (Appleton, 1913).

—— *Psychotherapy* (Appleton, 1913).

WALTON, George L., *Peg Along* (Lippincott, 1915).

—— *Why Worry?* (Lippincott, 1908).

WARREN, Howard C., *Human Psychology* (Houghton, 1919).

—— "The Subconscious," *Scientia, Août*, 1923, 91ff.

WATSON, John B., "Behavior and the Concept of Mental Disease," *Jour. Philos.*, 13: 589-597 (1916).

WATSON, John B., *Behavior: An Introduction to Comparative Psychology* (Holt, 1914).

—— *Psychology, From the Standpoint of a Behaviorist* (Lippincott, 1924).

—— "Psychology of Wish Fulfilment," *Sc. Monthly,* 3: 479-487 (1916).

WATTS, Frank, *Abnormal Psychology and Education* (Appleton, 1924).

WELLS, David W., *Psychology Applied to Medicine* (Davis, 1907).

WELLS, Frederic Lyman, *Mental Adjustments* (Appleton, 1922).

—— "Mental Regression: Its Conception and Types," *Psychiat. Bull.,* 9: 445-492 (1916).

—— "On Formulation in Psychoanalysis," *Jour. Abn. Psychol.,* Oct.-Nov., 1913.

—— "Symbolism and Synæsthesia," *Am. Jour. Insan.,* 75: 481-488 (1918).

—— a review of Edward J. Kempf's *Psychopathology, Jour. Abn. Psychol.,* 16: 392-400 (1921-1922).

WELLS, Wesley Raymond, "The Anti-Instinct Fallacy," *Psychol. Rev.,* 30: 228-234 (1923).

—— "Experiments in Waking Hypnosis for Instructional Purposes," *Jour. Abn. Psychol.,* 18: 389-404 (1924).

—— "Hypnosis in the Service of the Instructor," *Psychol. Rev.,* 31: 88-91 (1924).

WEST, Robert W., *Purposive Speaking* (Macmillan, 1924).

WHITE, William A., *The Mental Hygiene of Childhood* (Little, Brown, 1919).

—— *Outlines of Psychiatry,* 8th ed. (Nerv. & Ment. Dis. Pub'g Co., 1921).

—— on Adler, *Jour. Abn. Psychol.,* 12: 168, *circa* (1917).

WILLEY, Malcolm M., and RICE, Stuart A., "The Psychic Utility of Sleep," *Jour. Abn. Psychol.,* 19: 174-178 (1924).

WILLIAMS, Edward Huntington, and HOAG, Ernest Bryant, *Our Fear Complexes* (Bobbs-Merrill, 1923).

WILLIAMS, Frankwood E., "Anxiety and Fear," *Mental Hygiene,* 4: 73-81 (1920).

—— and others, *Social Aspects of Mental Hygiene* (Yale, 1925).

WILLIAMS, Harold J., "The Intelligence of the Delinquent Boy," *Jour. Delinquency Mono.,* Jan., 1919.

WILLIAMS, Tom A., "Differentia Regarding Obsessions and Phobias with Reference to Their Pathogenesis and Treatment," *Internat. Clinics,* 4: 180, *circa* (1919).

—— *Dreads and Besetting Fears, Including States of Anxiety: Their Causes and Cure* (Little, Brown, 1923).

—— ". . . Genesis of Writer's Cramp, etc., *Jour. Neur. u. Psychiat.,* 1911.

—— "Malingering and Simulation of Disease in Warfare," *Am. Jour. of Insan.,* 77: 572, *circa* (April, 1921).

WILLIAMS, Tom A., "Mental Causes in Bodily Disease: The Most Frequent Cause of . . . 'Nervous Indigestion,'" *Jour. Abn. Psychol.*, 3 : 386-390 (1908).

—— "Psychasthenia and Inebriety," *Jour. Abn. Psychol.*, 7 : 68, *circa,* (1912).

—— "Removal of Morbid Fear," *Med. Rev. of Rev.,* 1921.

—— "Some Neglected Psychopathic Factors," *Jour. Am. Med. Assn.,* 79 : 1514-1517 (1922).

—— "Studies of the Genesis of Cramp Writers and Telegraphers: the Relation of the Disorder to Other 'Neuroses': Their Pathogenesis Compared with that of Tics and Habit Spasms," *Jour. für Psychol. und Neurol.,* Bd. 19, Heft. 2/3, pp. 88, 1912.

—— "Suicide and Civilization," *Jour. Sociologic Med.,* 19 : 10, *circa* (1918).

—— "The Traumatic Neurosis," *Jour. Am. Inst. of Criminal Law & Criminology,* 7 : 689-701 (Northwestern Univ. Press, 1917).

—— "The Treatment of the Emotions in Young People," *Arch. of Pediatrics,* March, 1922.

—— on case study, *Jour. Am. Psychol.,* 9 : 80-85 (1914).

—— on functional paralyses and contractures, *Jour. Abn. Psychol.,* 7 :99*ff.*, 161*ff.* (1912).

WINGFIELD, H. E., *An Introduction to the Study of Hypnotism, Experimental and Therapeutic* (Baillière, 1920).

WOHLGEMUTH, A., *A Critical Examination of Psycho-Analysis* (Macmillan, 1923).

WOODWORTH, Robert S., *Psychology, A Study of Mental Life* (Holt, 1921).

—— "Some Criticisms of the Freudian Psychology," *Jour. Abn. Psychol.,* 12 : 174-194 (1917).

YAWGER, N. S., "Hypnagogic Hallucinations with Cases Illustrating These Sane Manifestations," *Jour. Abn. Psychol.,* 13 : 73-76 (1918).

YEALLAND, L. R., *Hysterical Disorders of Warfare* (Macmillan, 1918).

YELLOWLEES, Henry, *A Manual of Psychotherapy for Practitioners and Students* (Macmillan, 1923).

YOUNG, Kimball, "The Integration of the Personality," *Pedag. Sem.,* 30 : 264-285 (1923).

YOUNG, Paul Campbell, "An Experimental Study of Mental and Physical Functions in the Normal and Hypnotic States," *Am. Jour. Psychol.,* 36 : 214-232 (1925).

INDEX

Note: References to direct citations and to names of periodicals are in italic; cases are in small capitals.

INDEX

Instinct, as initiatory tendency to adjustment, 144; controversy on, 142; fear, 168; general description of, 146; "herd," 165; in man, 141, 144; loosely or fully organized, 145; meaning of "acquired" and "inherited," as related to, 143; pugnacity, 346; sex, 154

Integration, function of nervous system, 129

Intelligence ratios, fallibility of, 8, 9

Internat. Jour. of Ethics: International Journal of Ethics; Prof. James H. Tufts, ed., Univ. of Chicago

Internat. Psycho-Analytical Press: International Psycho-Analytical Press, N. Y.

"Introverts," traits of, 657

Involution melancholia, 31

IRÈNE, HYSTERIA, 70

Jackson, Hughlings, 318

Jackson, Josephine A., and Salisbury, Helen M., 751, 752, 760

Jackson, Theresa M., 110, 760

James, William, 114, 186, 228, *376*, 422, 431, *445*, 447, 532, 538, *564*, 661, 719, 751, 760

James-Lange theory of emotion, 171

Janet, Pierre, *38, 68, 70, 71*, 86, 112, 114, 134, 201, 203, 272, *350, 367, 376*, 377, 379, *383*, 385, *391*, 394, 422, 429, *446*, 470, 483, *509*, 524, 528, *533*, 566, *609*, 619, *652*, 661, 687, 711, 739, 751, 760

Jaquet, 323

Jarrett, Mary C. *See* Southard, E. E., co-author

Jastrow, Joseph, *3, 110*, 422, 426, *439, 447, 570, 609*, 704, 737, 760

Jekyll and Hyde, 86, 198

Jelliffe, S. E., 509

Jendrassik, Ernst, 523

Jolly, Pierre, 240, 370, 371

Jones, Ernest, 119, 402, 575, 625, 761

Jost, 103

Jour. Abn. Psychol.: originally Journal of Abnormal Psychology, now Journal of Abnormal and So-

cial Psychology, edited by Dr. Morton Prince, Harvard Univ., Cambridge, Mass., pub'd by Boyd

Jour. Am. Inst. of Crim. Law and Crim.: Journal of the American Institute of Criminal Law and Criminology, Northwestern Univ. Press, Chicago

Jour. Am. Med. Ass'n.: Journal of the American Medical Association, 535 North Dearborn St., Chicago

Jour. Appl. Psychol.: Journal of Applied Psychology, Prof. James P. Porter, ed., pub'd by Florence Chandler, Bloomington, Indiana

Jour. Crim. Law and Crim.: Journal of Criminal Law and Criminology, 306, N.W. University Bldg., Chicago

Jour. Ed. Psychol.: Journal of Educational Psychology, Prof. Harold O. Rugg, ed., pub'd by Warwick and York, 10 East Centre St., Baltimore

Jour. Exper. Psychol.: Journal of Experimental Psychology, Psychological Review Co., Princeton, N. J.

Jour. Industrial Hygiene: Journal of Industrial Hygiene, 240 Longwood Av., Boston

Jour. Med. Sciences: The American Journal of the Medical Sciences, pub'd by Lea

Jour. Ment. Hyg.: Journal of Mental Hygiene; *cf.* Nat. Com. Ment. Hyg.

Jour. Nerv. & Ment. Dis.: Journal of Nervous and Mental Disease, pub'd by Dr. Smith Ely Jelliffe, ed., 64 West 56th St., N. Y.

Jour. Neur. and Psychopath.: Journal of Neurology and Psychopathology, pub'd by William Heinemann, Ltd., 20 Bedford St., London, W. C. 2

Jour. Oralism and Auralism: Journal of Oralism and Auralism, Dr. Goldstein, ed., St. Louis (Mo.) School for the Deaf

Jour. Philos.: formerly Journal of Philosophy, Psychology, and Sci-

(7